SPORTS LAW

Sports law has been growing with increasing rapidity over the years since the first edition of this book was published in 1999, regularly making headlines as well as leading to a developing body of law practised by specialist lawyers. This revised work, by leading practitioners in the field, with a foreword by Lord Coe, provides a coherent framework for understanding the principles of sports law in this area, as well as a deep analysis of its key features. The subject is split into various areas of practice: first, regulatory rules, which embrace the constitutional aspect of organised sport, including the disciplinary procedures of the various governing organisations; second, broadcasting and marketing resulting from the commercial exploitation, including sponsorship, of sports clubs, sporting events and players; and third, player's rights and obligations, which embraces a wide range of legal issues including club transfers and player contracts, and issues arising from employment (including discrimination law), personal injury and criminal law. Special attention is paid to the impact of EU and human rights law as well as to the influential jurisprudence of the Court of Arbitration for Sport.

London 2012 provides an appropriate point at which to assess the current state of the law, as well as a look to the future. The target readership extends from solicitors, barristers and legal advisers, to sports organisations and clubs, corporations involved in marketing and sponsorship, media companies, academics teaching sports law, and sports administrators.

Sports Law

Second Edition

Michael Beloff
Tim Kerr
Marie Demetriou
and
Rupert Beloff

·H A R T·
PUBLISHING
OXFORD AND PORTLAND, OREGON
2012

Published in the United Kingdom by Hart Publishing Ltd
16C Worcester Place, Oxford, OX1 2JW
Telephone: +44 (0)1865 517530
Fax: +44 (0)1865 510710
E-mail: mail@hartpub.co.uk
Website: http://www.hartpub.co.uk

Published in North America (US and Canada) by
Hart Publishing
c/o International Specialized Book Services
920 NE 58th Avenue, Suite 300
Portland, OR 97213-3786
USA
Tel: +1 503 287 3093 or toll-free: (1) 800 944 6190
Fax: +1 503 280 8832
E-mail: orders@isbs.com
Website: http://www.isbs.com

British Library Cataloguing in Publication Data
Data Available

ISBN: 978-1-84113-367-6

Typeset by Compuscript Ltd, Shannon
Printed and bound in Great Britain by
TJ International Ltd, Padstow, Cornwall

For Judith
MB

For Nicola
TK

For Neil
MD

For Laura-Jane
RJB

FOREWORD

For those of us involved in the administration of sport, the need for expert legal advice is a reality, even if a regrettable one. It is therefore a cause for celebration that the four authors of this book were inspired by the return of the Olympic Games to London this year to produce a second edition of *Sports Law* no fewer than 13 years after the first. Michael Beloff QC was Ethics Commissioner for the London bid itself and ensured that the bid team which I led avoided the traps set in the complex bidding rules. He is also someone whom I have known for more than 20 years as a dedicated presence at international athletic events; and it is obvious that his co-authors share his genuine interest in sport as well as his acknowledged legal expertise. The book does not simply seek to set out the substance of the law in the areas it covers, although that it certainly does. It seeks to articulate the principles that underlie what they see as a subject in its own right and not just an amalgamation of other legal subjects. I commend it to everyone who has to administer sport as well as to those who have to advise the administrators or argue cases in the field on whatever side. It is a gold medal book.

Lord Coe KBE

FOREWORD FROM THE FIRST EDITION

Though I am not qualified in any way, I feel sure that there is a great need for this book. Since my own sporting days there has been an astonishing and alarming escalation of legal cases. Sport, essentially simple in nature, is increasingly threatened with issues of professionalism, sponsorship, serious injury, illegal drug use, and much more. These problems affect the essential fairness of sport, and without fairness sport is nothing. Anyone interested in sport must welcome the clarification provided by this comprehensive legal analysis. It is my fervent wish that all the legal problems of sport should be speedily settled with a maximum of good sense and justice.

Sir Roger Bannister
Oxford
August 1999

PREFACE

In the 13 years since the first edition of this book was published in 1999, 'sports law' has become a widely used expression uttered without apology, embarrassment or equivocation. It has, if not come of age, at least reached adolescence. Few now dispute the existence of sports law as a discrete branch of the law.

Regulatory instruments, case law and commentary have proliferated to the point where it is no longer practicable or sensible to cite all the relevant materials. Therefore, while in this second edition we have updated the law, we have not departed from our essential mission: to set out the main principles in a way that is intellectually rigorous, conceptually sound, as simple as possible and of practical use to all with an interest or involvement in sport, lawyers and non-lawyers alike.

We have kept the basic structure of the first edition, for we believe it has stood the test of time. However, we have added fresh sections on the influence of the Olympic movement (in chapter one), a legal legacy of London 2012, and child protection (in chapter four), a sad reflection of a growing concern in the sports world.

Except where we have been able to record later developments, the law is stated as at 1 August 2012.

We are deeply indebted to the team at Hart Publishing for their valuable help and support, to the clerks and staff at Blackstone Chambers, Brick Court Chambers, 11 King's Bench Walk Chambers and No5 Chambers and, last but not least, to our long suffering families for their patience and tolerance during the writing of this second edition.

MB
TK
MD
RJB

London, September 2012

CONTENTS

Contents

TABLE OF ABBREVIATIONS

AAD	appeals arbitration division (CAS)
AAF	adverse analytical finding (doping)
ABAE	Amateur Boxing Association of England
ACPO	Association of Chief Police Officers
ADO	anti-doping organisation
ADR	alternative dispute resolution
ATP	Association of Tennis Professionals
BBBC	British Boxing Board of Control
BJA	British Judo Association
BOA	British Olympic Association
CAS	Court of Arbitration for Sport
Cas Bull	Bulletin of the Court of Arbitration for Sport
CFI	Court of First Instance (now General Court of the European Union)
CFO	Comité Français d'Organisation de la Coupe du Monde de Football 1998
CJEU	Court of Justice of the European Communities
CRB	Criminal Records Bureau
DBS	Disclosure and Barring Service
DfES	Department for Education and Skills
DPA	Data Protection Act 1998
DTF	Danish Tennis Federation
EAT	Employment Appeal Tribunal
EBU	European Broadcasting Union
ECHR	European Convention on Human Rights
ECJ	European Court of Justice (see now CJEU)
ECommHR	European Commission of Human Rights
ECRC	enhanced criminal record certificate
EEA	European Economic Area
EU	European Union
FA	Football Association
FAPL	Football Association Premier League
FEI	Fédération Equestre Internationale
FIFA	Fédération Internationale de Football Association
FINA	Fédération Internationale de Natation
HRA	Human Rights Act 1998
IAAF	International Association of Athletics Federations, formerly International Amateur Athletic Federation

ICAS	International Council of Arbitration for Sport
ICC	International Cricket Council
IF	international federation
IOC	International Olympic Committee
IPC	International Paralympic Committee
ISA	Independent Safeguarding Authority
ISL	International Standard for Laboratories (doping)
ISLJ	International Sports Law Journal
ISLR	International Sports Law Review
ISU	International Skating Union
ITC	Independent Television Commission (predecessor of Ofcom)
ITF	International Tennis Federation
LTA	Lawn Tennis Association
MCC	Middlesex Cricket Club
NGB	national governing body
NOC	National Olympic Committee
OAD	ordinary arbitration division (CAS)
OC	Olympic Charter
OCOG	Organising Committee of the Olympic Games (national)
OM	Olympic Movement
PILS	(Swiss) Private International Law Statute of 18 December 1987
PoCA	Protection of Children Act
POVA	Protection of Vulnerable Adults
RFL	Rugby Football League
RFU	Rugby Football Union
SFT	Swiss Federal Tribunal
SGB	sports governing body
SLB	Sports Law Bulletin
SLJ	Sport and the Law Journal
SLR	Sports Law Reports
SRA	Squash Rackets Association, now known as England Squash and Racketball
SVGA	Safeguarding Vulnerable Groups Act 2006
SWD	Staff Working Document (European Commission)
TCCB	Test and County Cricket Board
TFEU	Treaty on the Functioning of the European Union
UEFA	Union des Associations Européennes de Football
USADA	US Anti-Doping Agency
USFA	United States Figure Skating Association
VBS	Vetting and Barring Scheme
WADA	World Anti-Doping Agency
WADC	World Anti-Doping Code
WBC	World Boxing Council
WPBSA	World Professional Billiards and Snooker Association
WRU	Welsh Rugby Union
WSLR	World Sports Law Report

TABLE OF CASES

Tribunals and Arbitration Panels

COURTS AND TRIBUNALS IN NATIONAL JURISDICTIONS

United Kingdom (England and Wales (including Privy Council), Scotland, Northern Ireland)

Australia

EUROPEAN UNION AND EUROPEAN COURT OF HUMAN RIGHTS

Cases in alphabetical order

Cases in number order

Commission decisions

Table of Cases

TABLE OF LEGISLATION AND
INTERNATIONAL INSTRUMENTS

NATIONAL LEGISLATION

United Kingdom

Statutes

Table of Legislation

1

The Nature of Sports Law

An Introduction to the Subject

1.1 In the first edition of this book, published in 1999, we argued that the time had come to recognise 'sports law' as a valid description of a system of law governing the practice of sports. Over a decade later, in a new century and millennium, the law relating to sport is no longer in its infancy and is starting to come of age. Though not yet fully developed, it is now sufficiently developed for the term 'sports law' to command acceptance by the majority of legal practitioners in the field, and of sports governing bodies and administrators.

1.2 In the 1990s, the existence of sports law as a distinct field of legal practice was not yet universally accepted among lawyers. Nor was the term then in common use among practitioners or administrators of sport. But its existence was then already recognised by the availability of pioneering sports law degrees at Manchester Metropolitan University and the Anglia Polytechnic University; the postgraduate Certificate in Sports Law at King's College London; and by the already active British Association for Sport and Law, bringing together lawyers, academics and sports administrators.[1]

1.3 The British Association continues to publish (in association with De Montfort University in Leicester) the *Sport and the Law Journal*, and lists of experts in sports law appear in lawyers' directories such as *Chambers and Partners Directory* and *the Legal 500*. In the first edition of this book we noted that there was then already in existence the National Sports Law Institute at the Marquette University in Milwaukee, as well as its counterparts this side of the Atlantic. The last decade or so has seen such a proliferation of organisations involved in sport and the law that the website of the British Association for Sport and Law lists 19 other 'International Sports Law Bodies' across four continents.[2]

1.4 As the title of this book implies, we continue to maintain that the subject merits recognition as a discrete field of law, and that in consequence it is legitimate to use the term 'sports law'. This is a less controversial thesis now than it was at the end of the twentieth

---

[1] The senior author of this book is the current President of the British Association for Sport and Law.

[2] They include the Sports Law Unit at the European Commission, Brussels; the Asser International Sports Law Centre, The Hague; the Centre International d'Etude du Sport, Neuchâtel; the Instituto Brasileiro de Direito Desportivo (Brazilian Sports Law Association), São Paulo; and the ANZSLA (Australia & New Zealand Sports Law Association), Melbourne.

century when we first advanced it.[3] Indeed in August 1999 (just too late for inclusion in the first edition of this book), the Court of Arbitration for Sport (CAS) stated:

> Sports Law has developed and consolidated along the years, particularly through the arbitral resolution of disputes, a set of unwritten legal principles—a sort of *lex mercatoria* for sports, or, so to speak, a *lex ludica*—to which national and international sport federations must conform, regardless of the presence of such principles within their own statutes and regulations or within any applicable national law, provided they do not conflict with any national 'public policy' (*ordre publique*) provision applicable to a given case.[4]

The *lex ludica* includes, according to the same CAS panel, 'the prohibition of arbitrary or unreasonable rules and measures'.[5] However, sports law, whether emanating from CAS or other sports tribunals, cannot of course override national or indeed international law. The International Olympic Committee sought unavailingly to persuade the Italian government to suspend its domestic law which provided for custodial penalties for use of prohibited substances by a competitor whereas the World Anti-Doping Code provided only for sporting sanctions.[6]

1.5 It is useful to remind ourselves and our readers of the grounds for asserting the existence of sports law.[7] To make good the thesis that sports law exists, it is insufficient merely to show that there is a phenomenon, sport, which exists in our society, and that legal rules impact on its practice. The law intrudes into many aspects of public and private life: yet not every human activity has a body of legal rules to go with it. Some do and some do not. We travel by ship and by air, and we have shipping law and aviation law. We also do cooking and gardening, and there are laws which apply to both activities but one could not usefully speak of culinary law or horticultural law. To justify recognition of sports law, something more must be shown than the existence of laws which affect sport. Some insight into the question how a distinct field of law is identified can be gained by observing a distinction between branches of the law defined by reference to a particular human activity, for example, aviation law; and those which are identified by reference to the nature of legal rules themselves, for example the law of tort and the law of trusts.

1.6 Both of the latter branches of the law describe categories of rules embodying rights and obligations which apply irrespective of the subject matter of a particular case in

---

[3] A full bibliography appears at the end of this book. The most comprehensive treatment of the subject in England is now the 2nd edition of Lewis and Taylor's *Sport: Law and Practice* (Tottel Publishing, 2008). For a historic compendium of sports laws of various nations in three volumes, see Wise and Meyer, *International Sports Law and Business* (Kluwer, 1998). Early works on sport and the law from which we drew inspiration were: Gardiner, Felix, O'Leary, James and Welch, *Sports Law* (Cavendish, 1997); Grayson, *Sport and the Law*, now in its 3rd edn (Butterworths, 2000); Griffith-Jones with Barr-Smith (consulting editor), *Law and the Business of Sport* (Butterworths, 1997); and Moore, *Sports Law and Litigation* (CLT Professional Publishing, 1997 and 2nd edn 2000); in the USA, Weiler and Roberts, *Sports and the Law*, 2nd edn (Gale Cengage, 1998; now in its 3rd edn, 2004). The major journals are Sport and the Law Journal, published by the British Association for Sport and Law (SLJ); and the International Sports Law Review (Sweet & Maxwell) (ISLR), incorporating the Sports Law Reports (SLR).

[4] *AEK Athens and Slavia Prague FC v UEFA*, CAS 98/200, para 156.

[5] Ibid, para 157. The case concerned a challenge to a rule prohibiting multi-ownership of clubs in the same competition. The challenge ultimately failed on the facts but its introduction was delayed by one season by interim order of the CAS because of procedural unfairness.

[6] See *Hoch v FISI*, CAS 2008/A/1513.

[7] See Beloff, *Is there a Lex Sportiva?* [2005] 3 ISLR 49; Nafziger, *Lex Sportiva and CAS* [2004] International Sports Law Journal (ISLJ), p 3; Beloff, *The Specificity of Sport. Rhetoric or Reality?* [2012] 3 ISLR.

which they are relevant. They could therefore be termed, so to speak, horizontal law; whereas the former categories of law defined by reference to a human activity could be termed vertical law. If, as we maintain, sports law exists, it exists principally as a vertically defined, or activity-led branch of the law which must take its content from rule-led branches of the law: tort, contract, restitution, crime and so on.

1.7 The claim of sport to have a system of law of its own arises from its importance in ancient and modern social life. Sport is one of society's most important leisure activities. It is a primary and atavistic form of self-expression. Bill Shankly, the legendary manager of Liverpool Football Club, once said memorably that football is not just a matter of life and death; it is more important than that. (He also said somewhat unkindly on another occasion that there were two teams in Liverpool: Liverpool and Liverpool reserves.)

1.8 Examples of the potency of sport as a force in civil society are legion. In South Africa the effort to end apartheid was driven forward, with considerable success, by the sporting boycott. Rights of full citizenship for all aroused high passions in South Africa, but so did rugby, cricket, athletics and soccer, for access to which white South Africans were prepared to pay a high political price.[8] And when Georgia became an independent state after the dissolution of the Soviet Union, one of the first acts of its inaugural government was to apply to join FIFA, the world governing body of association football. To the Georgian people, this was probably as much a badge of sovereign independence as formal recognition by other states, membership of the United Nations and other conventional indicia of statehood.

1.9 Sport's importance in society also lies in its benign influence. The continuation of rivalry between Croatia and Serbia in the sporting arena after the fighting ended (and in football the superior achievement of Croatia, including finishing third in her World Cup debut in 1998) shows how beneficial is the substitution of goals for guns. Sport's detractors, who cannot understand why a ball entering a net merits our attention, should remember that people's attention may be more harmfully directed to alternative pursuits. Chariot races are better than riots and war and boxing preferable to gladiators in combat.[9] For that reason if no other, justice in sport is a serious matter.

1.10 It cannot, then, seriously be disputed that sport is a vitally important and mainly benign social force. The thesis that sport influences politics (and association football more than any other sport) has been convincingly demonstrated[10] and is widely accepted. Sporting celebrities are respected and may turn this to political advantage, as in the cases of Imran Khan in Pakistan and Roger Milla in Cameroon.

1.11 The central place of sport in civil society makes it important to ensure that it is properly regulated and justly administered. Legal norms have been developed to make

---

[8] In a case which never came to trial, the South African Athletics Federation argued that it had been invalidly expelled from the International Amateur Athletics Federation, alleging failure to follow the correct procedures and invocation of inappropriate grounds; see Beloff, *Pitch, Pool, Rink … Court? Judicial Review in the Sporting World* [1989] Public Law 95, 98 fn 14.

[9] Even global terrorists take time away from their grim work to watch and play football: see MSN News, 'Osama bin Laden and his years as an Arsenal fan', available (at the time of writing) at http://news.uk.msn.com/world/news-articles.aspx?cp-documentid=157274240. The late and unlamented Al-Qaeda supremo was reportedly a regular attender at Highbury in 2001, and bought his eldest son a replica shirt bearing the name 'Ian Wright'.

[10] In particular by the journalist Simon Kuper in his book *Football against the Enemy* (Orion Books, 1994).

this happen. Yet, as already conceded, to show that a system of law governing sport exists, it is not enough to show that sport is influential and that laws affect it. One must go further and propound a definition of sports law, however qualified and approximate such a definition may be. To define sports law one must delineate its scope, however indistinct its outline.

1.12 Lawyers who may be sceptical of the utility of the term 'sports law' as a term of art, may argue that it amounts to no more than a series of examples of cases in which the parties happen to be concerned in sport. Thus a sporting dispute may in truth be one arising in the law of tort, contract or other 'true' fields of law. The traditionally minded, purist lawyer may indeed distrust any activity-led, 'vertical' field of law, preferring the surer, traditional ground of rule-led 'horizontal' law. We have sympathy with that position, and ourselves firmly reject the primacy of 'vertical' legal classifications over 'horizontal' ones. It is true that, traditionally, the bodies which regulate sporting activity have been treated by English lawyers as a species of domestic tribunal, governed by the same principles as apply to clubs (if unincorporated) or private companies (if incorporated). Likewise, sporting activity has, according to the traditions of English law, been treated as a private activity subject to the rules of private law.

1.13 We do not, however, agree with the view still held by some lawyers active in sports related work that 'there is no such thing as sports law'.[11] The answer to the argument that sports law is merely law in which the parties happen to be involved in sport, is that the law is now beginning to treat sporting activity, sporting bodies and the resolution of disputes in sport differently from other activities or bodies. Discrete doctrines are taking shape in the sporting field which are not found elsewhere, not even necessarily in the case of non-sporting domestic tribunals. There are now clear signs that the courts are beginning to treat decisions of sporting bodies as subject to particular principles better known in the field of public than private law, but most accurately described as principles which are *sui generis*.[12]

---

[11] Charles Woodhouse, an eminent sports lawyer, quoted in Gardiner, *Birth of a Legal Area: Sport and the Law or Sports Law?* (1997) 5(2) SLJ 10, at 12. Gardiner also quotes the views of Professor Grayson, author of *Sport and the Law* (n 3) ('No subject exists which jurisprudentially can be called sports law … it has no juridical foundation'); of John Barnes, author of *Sports and the Law in Canada* (3rd edn, Butterworths, 1996) ('Sports law deals with state interests and the resolution of conflicts according to general legal norms'); and of Hayden Opie, author of *Sports Associations and their Legal Environment* ('"Sports law" is … applied law as opposed to pure or theoretical law; … [it] is concerned with how law in general interacts with the activity known as sport') (in McGregor-Lowndes, Fletcher and Sievers (eds), *Legal Issues for Non-Profit Associations* (Law Book Co, 1996)). Gardiner concludes that a legal theory of sports law is now needed, and suggests that either 'the law is providing a functional role in the context of the modern commercial complexity of sport … This fits in with a functionalist perspective on sport and society'; or that 'the law is a form of regulatory power, a form of control. This fits in with a critical perspective on sport and society.' Alan Sullivan QC, a distinguished CAS arbitrator, believes that while 'it is common nowadays to talk of a body of law called "Sports Law", strictly, there is no unique body of law which can be so labelled. Rather, participation in sport is regulated by the same laws as all other human activities and endeavours': Sullivan, *The Role of Contract in Sports Law* (2010) 5(1) Australia and New Zealand Sports Law Journal 3. Cf the intermediate view of Lewis and Taylor (n 3) at A3.5; and Szyszczak, *Is Sport Special?* in Bogusz, Cygan and Szyszczak (eds), *The Regulation of Sport in the European Union* (Edward Elgar, 2007) ch 1, 3–32. For a recent reconsideration of the issue see Boyes, *Sports Law: Its History and Growth and the Development of Key Sources* (2012) 12(2) LIM 86 ('… the sports law literature has matured astonishingly quickly given its relative youth').

[12] See, eg, *McInnes v Onslow-Fane* [1978] 1 WLR 1520, per Megarry J at 1535F–H; *Cowley v Heatley, The Times*, 24 July 1986, per Sir Nicholas Browne-Wilkinson V-C; *Gasser v Stinson*, transcript, 15 June 1988, per Scott J at pp 37–40; and *Stevenage Borough FC Ltd v The Football League Ltd*, transcript, 23 July 1996, per Carnwath J at pp 35–40.

1.14 The cornerstone of what could be called the founding principles of sports law is the definition of the respective territories of the courts and the bodies which govern sport. The courts in England and elsewhere have firmly established a region of autonomy for decision making bodies in sport, a region within which—unless the reasons for doing so are compelling—the courts decline to intervene. Equally firmly they have charted the outer limits of that region and insisted that those limits be observed by the decision makers in sport, on pain of judicial intervention. We regard that relationship of constitutional equilibrium between courts of law and sports decision makers as the foundation of a developing law of sport.

1.15 Few lawyers would now subscribe to the traditionalist notion that the law relating to sport can be regarded simply as part of ordinary private law, that is to say, as part of the corpus of law governing private transactions between citizens in which the state's only interest is to provide courts as a forum of last resort to enable disputes to be resolved. The public's limitless enthusiasm for sport and its importance to our cultural heritage make sports law more than mere private law. As long ago as 1997, that view received direct support from no less a figure than Lord Woolf MR in *Modahl v British Athletic Federation Ltd*.[13] Ms Modahl claimed damages for breach of contract after an appeal body reversed a disciplinary panel's decision that she had committed a doping offence. Her claim was held to be arguable, though ultimately it failed. On appeal against the Federation's partially successful strike out application, counsel for Ms Modahl invited the court to treat the relation between her and the Federation as one of simple contract, to reject the Federation's 'administrative law approach', and to draw a sharp distinction between an action for breach of contract and proceedings for judicial review, treating Ms Modahl's claim for damages as falling into the former not the latter category. Lord Woolf MR's response was that counsel was:

> wrong in suggesting that the approach of the courts in public law on applications for judicial review have no relevance in domestic disciplinary proceedings of this sort … the complaint in both cases would be based on an allegation of unfairness … I can see no reason why there should be any difference as to what constitutes unfairness or why the standard of unfairness required by an implied term should differ from that required of the same tribunal under public law.[14]

Lord Woolf's approach has since found expression in twenty-first century case law in which the High Court in England has directly and consciously applied principles akin to judicial review to the decisions of sports bodies in private law actions.[15]

1.16 There is another feature of sports law which makes it unique. Most fields of law, defined by reference to the specific human activity or subject, are firmly grounded in legislative intervention by governments. Obvious examples are health, education, social security, consumer credit, compulsory purchase, and so forth. They exist as discrete fields of law in England because the legislature has consciously decided to create them by

---

[13] Transcript, 28 July 1997, CA; appealed on a narrower point: HL, transcript, 22 July 1999.
[14] Ibid (HL), 20F–21C.
[15] *Bradley v Jockey Club* [2005] EWCA Civ 1056; *Flaherty v National Greyhound Racing Club Ltd* [2005] EWCA Civ 1117; *R (Mullins) v Jockey Club Appeal Board (No 1)* [2005] EWHC 2197; *Mullins v McFarlane* [2006] EWHC 986 (QB); *Fallon v Horseracing Regulatory Authority* [2006] EWHC 2030 (QB); *McKeown v British Horseracing Authority* [2010] ISLR, SLR 87–151; cf *Chambers v British Olympic Association* [2008] EWHC 2028 (QB) (injunction refused where rule not in unreasonable restraint of trade). See also Beloff, editorial [2006] ISLR 1.

legislative intervention in society. These are the fields of law best suited to the modern form of loose leaf encyclopaedia, well known to English lawyers, based on the core governing statutes and regulations, regularly updated, and commented on in textual annotations. Such books are immensely useful to the specialist practitioner but, without any disrespect to the eminent lawyers involved in their compilation, they are sometimes necessarily light on discussions of principle.

1.17 Sports law, however, differs markedly from such other activity defined or vertical fields of law, in that it is developing under its own impetus, without any legislative underpinning to speak of—at any rate in the United Kingdom.[16] Legislation is, after all, still mainly a national phenomenon, even in the era of the European Union, the European Convention on Human Rights and many other international legal instruments. Sports law, by contrast with other fields of law, is developing under its own steam. A powerful mixture of international competition, commercial interest and public demand is fuelling the development of legal doctrines particular to sport in a manner which marks sports law as inherently international in character. Its normative underpinning derives not from any treaty entered into between sovereign states, but from international agreements between bodies, many of which are constitutionally independent of their national governments—particularly the Olympic Charter and the rules of the various international governing bodies in sport. Thus sports law is not just international; it is non-governmental as well, and this differentiates it from other forms of law.

1.18 We subscribe to the view that:

> international sports law provides a dynamic, although still incomplete process to avoid, manage and resolve disputes among athletes, national sports bodies, international sports organisations and governments.[17]

Such observations serve to confirm the obvious point that sports law is not a hermetically sealed, self-contained body of law. It crosses boundaries. It demands of its students and practitioners familiarity with traditional areas of horizontal law. What do they know of sports law, who only sports law know? To be a good sports lawyer one must also be a good non-sports lawyer (though, mercifully, not a good lawyer sportsman or woman[18]). But sports law now merits treatment as a branch of law in its own right.

1.19 With that preamble, we offer the following definition of sports law: it is a body of rules governing the practice of sport and the resolution of disputes in sport. That body of rules straddles the boundaries between many well-known branches of our law, but has

---

[16] Contrast, for example, Malaysia, which is in a small minority of countries where sport is heavily regulated by statute. See also Lewis and Taylor (n 3) A1.7–10 ('The interventionist model of regulation of the sports sector').

[17] Polvino, *Arbitration as Preventative Medicine for Olympic Ailments: The Olympic Committee Court of Arbitration for Sport and the Future for the Settlement of International Sporting Disputes* [1994] 8 Emory International Law Review 349–52, cited in Nafziger, *International Sports Law as a Process for Resolving Disputes* (1996) 45 International and Comparative Law Quarterly 130 at 131. Dean Kino of Magdalen College, Oxford submitted a doctoral thesis in 1999 on *The Incursion of the Law into the Rules of Governing Sports Bodies: A Commonwealth and EC Comparison.* See Weatherill, *Do Sporting Associations Make 'Law' or are they Merely Subject to It?* [1998] European Business Law Review, July/August, 217.

[18] Examples of lawyer-sportsmen include Lord Alverston CJ (judge), an athletics blue; Harold Abrahams (barrister), Olympic Gold medallist at 100 metres, Douglas Lowe (barrister), double Olympic gold medallist at 800 metres; Johnny Searle (solicitor), Olympic gold medallist oarsman; Brian Moore, litigation solicitor and British Lion; and Iain Higgins, London Broncos rugby league professional turned lawyer, now at the International Cricket Council.

at its centre an unusual form of international constitutional principle prescribing the limited autonomy of non-governmental decision making bodies in sport.

The Aim of this Book

1.20 When we devised the structure for the first edition of this book, we decided that the best way to give shape and cohesion to a then much looser body of rules was to describe the law relating to, first, the pre-competition stage; second, the competition itself; and third, its aftermath of disputes and disciplinary measures, and legal systems to resolve them. We believe that chronological way of looking at the subject remains useful and has stood the test of time, and have decided to retain it in this updated second edition.

1.21 The first, pre-competition stage requires an explanation of the institutions that govern sport, their relations with each other and with participants in sport (from clubs to competitors to coaches to referees) and the means by which they are able to organise sport according to rules intended to protect its integrity and value; and the rules according to which selection for participation in sports competitions is determined. The most fundamental requirement of all is the principle of uncertainty of results. If the outcome of a competition is pre-ordained through cheating or unfairly tilted through doping, the game is changed from a noble contest to a degrading and pointless ritual.

1.22 The second stage is to give an account of the law governing the sporting competition itself. This does not of course refer to the actual 'laws of the game'. These are virtually non-justiciable as explained later; the maxim drummed into schoolchildren that 'the referee is always right even when he is wrong' is part of international sports law. At the second stage, we explain the principles of criminal and tort law which delineate the responsibilities of clubs, players, coaches, referees and spectators to each other during the game itself, and immediately before and after the game. We also look at the law governing the commercial exploitation of sport, which includes the laws that apply in the marketplace for the provision to the public of live and broadcast sport.

1.23 At the third stage we describe the principles governing the imposition of punitive measures against participants in sport alleged to have violated the cardinal principle of fair play, whether by doping, match fixing, use of force beyond what is acceptable in contact sports, or failure to follow the regulatory requirements of the competition intended to ensure fairness between participants. We then turn finally to the legal systems and structures for resolving disputes regarding those matters, at domestic and international level, which have become sophisticated and experienced, and are widely respected despite today being presided over by lawyers more often than used to be the case. The main engine of international dispute resolution in sport, the CAS, has contributed greatly to the evolution of an international legal order in sport. What used to be done by amateurs is now done by professionals.

1.24 In devising the structure of this book, we have rejected conventional horizontal legal classifications, which would divide the subject by considering traditional fields of law (tort, contract, etc) and explaining their application to sport. This is because sports law straddles so many of them. Nor would it meet our objective to present the material by reference to specific sports (rugby, boxing, etc) since our law generally does not treat as *ipso facto* relevant which sport is being practised; legal principles applied to tennis normally also apply to squash. To deal with different sports individually would take the concept of vertically defined law to an absurd extreme.[19]

1.25 Our original legal background in commercial law, constitutional and administrative law, competition law, European Union law, tort and employment law, is as good a grounding as any for a sports law practice. In this book, we attempt to identify where the interface occurs in sports law between those fields, and others such as personal injury in which we are for the main part considerably less well versed.

1.26 To the non-lawyer involved in sport as a player, coach or administrator, it may be unnecessary to think of sports law as anything more than simply the law which he or she encounters at work within the sports industries—irrespective of what label a lawyer would use to describe that law. This book is intended to assist in answering the questions that may confront practitioners of sport and administrators in the course of their work, and we hope it will be useful to non-lawyers as well as to lawyers. Our hope is fortified by the fact that administrators in sport are, not infrequently, qualified lawyers; and indeed a few lawyers are even notable sportsmen themselves. Some members of the CAS panel of arbitrators are Olympians and domestic sports tribunals often feature respected ex-players sitting alongside the lawyer chairman.

1.27 However, we do not intend this book to serve as a reference manual for the sports administrator. Rather, it constitutes our attempt to provide something like a theoretical foundation for sports law. A *lex specialis* is taking shape from a line of decisions, especially of the CAS, some of which we mention in this book. Publication of reports of those cases is now frequent, aided by access to the internet and hampered only by obligations of confidentiality owed to and by participants in the relevant proceedings.

1.28 A hallmark of a developed system of law is that its content can be easily ascertained by lawyers and by the public. This is now close to being achieved. Publications have proliferated in the past 10 years. We refer to some of them in the footnotes of the pages which follow. As for our own professional experience, we have had to restrict ourselves as to the degree of detail that we can condescend to in some cases, because of confidentiality obligations which we owe to our clients and to arbitral tribunals under their rules. Since the first edition of this book was published in 1999, domestic and international sports related case law has burgeoned to the point where it is no longer practicable or useful to cite every case. Sports law has evolved to the extent that there are now more cases that apply settled principles than cases which establish new ones.

1.29 We have already stated that in our view, sports law is by nature international in character. Terms such as 'English sports law' or national sports law are of only limited utility and usually best avoided, since an account of the law relating to sport confined

---

[19] We have assumed throughout that sport is itself a recognisable concept, although lacking precise definition in English law. The law used to be that a trust for the mere promotion of a particular sport was not charitable as being for the promotion of education (*Re Nottage* [1895] 2 Ch 649); whereas a trust to provide sports facilities for students will be: *IRC v McMullen* [1981] AC 1. See also *R v Oxfordshire CC, ex parte Sunningwell Parish Council* [1999] 3 All ER 385, 396–7. Under the Charities Act 2006, the advancement of amateur sport became a charitable purpose in its own right, if it is 'for the public benefit' (s 2(1) and 2(2)(g)). As for the 'public benefit' test in s 3 (as applied to independent schools), see *Independent Schools Council v Charity Commission for England and Wales* [2011] UKUT 421 (TCC). See also the useful account in Lewis and Taylor (n 3) F1.66–83.

to one legal system, such as that of English statute and case law, would necessarily be fragmentary, incomplete and inadequate. One should think of sports law as a body of law which transcends international boundaries, like European Union law and public international law. The Olympic Charter as a *fons et origo* of international jurisdiction is a phenomenon unique to sports law. But every lawyer is conditioned by the jurisdiction in which he or she primarily practises. As English lawyers, albeit ones with a European Union law dimension and international dimension to our work, our account of the subject is necessarily Anglocentric. Accordingly, where we refer below to domestic law, we are referring to the domestic law of England and Wales except where we state otherwise.

1.30 We recognise that our conception of sports law as a coherent body of rules is quite narrow and that this reflects our legal background as advisers, litigators and arbitrators in contentious disputes. We believe the subject tends to lose its cohesion and become amorphous if too broadly viewed. This book is therefore not intended to deal, except in passing, with non-contentious aspects of sports law, such as the practical considerations involved in negotiating a sponsorship or broadcasting contract, or a contract with a player. Specialist lawyers offer expertise in contract negotiation, the requirements for staging a sporting event, how to submit a tender for a contract to construct a stadium, and the like. These subjects are outside the scope of this book and our expertise.[20]

1.31 There are other topics we have chosen not to include in this book, partly because they are not central to our expertise and experience, and partly because they seem to us to occupy territory at or near the edges, or even beyond the outer limits of, the subject. They include taxation of sporting activity;[21] planning and property law relating to sports premises including stadia; and sport in the law of education. Nor do we attempt to give an account of the political, administrative and commercial structures that govern sport in this country and internationally. Many have changed rapidly over the last decade and some may already be familiar to our readers. In any case their nature is not a matter of law, but of commerce and politics.

1.32 We also pay tribute to earlier pioneers in the field, in particular the late Professor Edward Grayson, the 'onlie begetter' of the subject, David Griffith-Jones QC (now His Honour Judge Griffith-Jones QC), and Adrian Barr-Smith.[22] We have directed the reader at various junctures to their work and to that of more recent entrants to the field where we believe it would be advantageous to pursue a particular topic further. Our approach to the subject is different from that of other authors. There are now many players in this particular field but we hope our book still serves the purpose for which the first edition was written: to give a coherent account of sports law which builds on its theoretical foundations, insofar as they are yet in place.

---

[20] A much broader, indeed comprehensive treatment of the relationship between law and sport is provided in Lewis and Taylor's excellent *Sport: Law and Practice* (n 3), to which no fewer than 41 authors (including one of the present authors) from many different legal and sporting backgrounds contributed. See also Jack Anderson's helpful account of how the law influences the operation, administration and playing of modern sports in *Modern Sports Law: A Textbook* (Hart Publishing, 2010).

[21] For an account of tax laws applicable to sports activities of individuals and organisations see Lewis and Taylor (n 3) chs D8 and F3 respectively.

[22] The author and consulting editor of Griffith-Jones and Barr-Smith's *Law and the Business of Sport* (n 3).

1.33 Our approach is to marry theory with practice. We believe the best way of moving towards a coherent account of sports law as a discrete body of rules is to proceed inductively, deriving principle from practical professional experience. As busy practising barristers, we lack the leisure to view the subject through the medium of profound academic scholarship and thorough research. We must leave that to others, and indeed academic research is increasing with useful contributions from academics at institutions such as De Montfort and Salford Universities in this country, Marquette University in Milwaukee, and the Asser International Sports Law Centre in The Hague.

1.34 Any book on sports law carries with it the danger that it will contain little more than information. We have tried to avoid that, even at the risk of not providing enough information. As a field which has yet to be subjected to thorough treatment from a theoretical perspective, sports law lends itself well, in our view, to broad general chapter headings and discussion of principles under those headings untrammelled by detailed and narrow sub-headings, which could lead to the account becoming bogged down in detail, putting information above exposition.

1.35 In a complex regulated society which often wearies the practising lawyer with its vast amount of regulatory detail and information overload, we have found this a refreshing experience, and we hope our readers will share in it.

The Development of Sports Law

1.36 The stakes in the world of sport have never been higher and they seem to go on rising. The psychological pressures on sportsmen and women in the competitive arena grow ever greater, as the gulf between success and failure tends to widen. At the same time, technological and financial sophistication is increasing the complexity of the regulatory machinery in sport. These developments have increased the potential for conflict between those who participate in sport and those who run it. Judges and arbitrators confronted with the task of adjudicating upon such conflicts in national courts have to strike a balance between avoiding, where possible, the courts becoming embroiled in sporting disputes, and the need to do justice where the facts demonstrate that the regulatory or disciplinary machinery in sport has operated unjustly.

1.37 There has undoubtedly been a rise of legalism in the world of sport. It is often deprecated by sports administrators, though it is more often accepted now than 10 years ago. It is customary to deprecate the entrée of lawyers into new fields of law. Lawyers are not always popular with the public, but are often very popular with their clients when they win cases (and correspondingly less popular when they lose them). The rise of legalism in sport has been encouraged by lawyers, without doubt, but lawyers did not invent it. Their clients did. It is a natural function of raised financial stakes produced by increased sophistication, particularly of a technological nature, and by a ready market fuelled by the demands of a public whose craving for sport appears insatiable and undimmed by occasional doping and corruption scandals.

1.38 More lawyers and more law in sport does not necessarily mean more justice in sport, but it may do, and it should do. The growth of legalism in sport is borne of a desire for higher standards of justice, demanded by the sporting community as a consequence of the rise of professionalism and the increase in earnings potential within sport. If one wishes to make a cogent case against increased involvement of lawyers in sport, one must make a corresponding case against the increase in the power of sports administrators to affect the lives and livelihoods of sportsmen and women, and, conversely, the increased power of sportsmen and women to dictate terms to sports administrators. For it is this increase in power within sport, less often criticised within the sporting community than legal intrusion into its sphere of influence, that leads that same community more frequently than in the past to seek advice and representation from lawyers. In short, the more there is at stake, the more astute must be the law to prevent injustice.

1.39 As a consequence of increased legalism in sport, there is now a body of sporting case law from the Commonwealth and other jurisdictions on which English (and Welsh) law-yers can readily draw. Cross-fertilisation from other common law jurisdictions is a feature of our legal system. But more than in other branches of law, international sporting com-petition has helped to break down the barriers between civil law and common law coun-tries. As we have remarked elsewhere,[23] the Commonwealth authorities disclose a litany of complaints, successful and unsuccessful, including bias or a risk of bias on the part of the tribunal; charges laid or convictions brought in under the wrong rule; charges disclosing no disciplinary offence; procedural unfairness; unreasonable restraint of trade; infringe-ment of statutory competition law; unfair prejudice in the running of a company; and even infringement of the 'right to work'. The courts have had to rule on issues as diverse as the validity of a decision to ban a cricketer who played in South Africa; the proper construction of rules against horse doping; the *locus standi* of individuals to challenge decisions of bod-ies of which they are not members; and whether a sporting association qualified for a tax exemption given to public but not private bodies. The expanding Commonwealth sporting jurisprudence now includes authorities arising out of horse racing in South Africa, athletics in Singapore, cricket in Barbados, rugby league in New Zealand, and trotting in Australia.

1.40 There is a further wealth of authority, less familiar to most English lawyers until recently. The establishment of the CAS (still based in Lausanne, Switzerland but no longer at its former magnificent lakeside setting) led to the phenomenon of a tribunal with an English lawyer president applying Swiss law,[24] and being empowered to apply 'general prin-ciples of law and the rules of law'[25]—a broader concept would be difficult to formulate. In *Volkers v Fédération Internationale de Natation*,[26] the CAS, presided over by a distinguished Nairobi attorney with a common law background like ours, 'found it possible and appro-priate to resolve the dispute in accordance with the rules of FINA, and in accordance with general principles of law'.[27] This is law which is truly international.[28]

---

[23] See Beloff and Kerr, *Judicial Control of Sporting Bodies: The Commonwealth Jurisprudence* (1995) 3(1) SLJ 5. For a more up-to-date account mainly of rule based challenges, including useful references to recent case law from Australia and New Zealand, see Sullivan (n 11), and, on a more general plane, Mitten and Opie, *Sports Law Implications for the Development of International, Comparative and National Law and Global Dispute Resolution* (2011) 19(1) SLJ.

[24] See *Cullwick v FINA*, CAS 96/149, February 1997.

[25] See Art 17 of the Ad Hoc Rules and *Andrade v Cape Verde NOC*, CAS Ad Hoc Division, No 002, July 1996 (CAS OG 96/002).

[26] CAS 95/150, September 1996.

[27] Ibid, para 20.

[28] For the reported CAS jurisprudence in print, see *Recueil de Sentences du TAS: Digest of CAS Awards*, three volumes edited by M Reeb 1982–96, 1996–2000, 2000–4 (Stämpfli editions) (hereinafter 'Reeb 1', 'Reeb 2', 'Reeb 3'). Reeb 3 contains a succinct description of the history and operation of the CAS at pp xxii–xxxii. Many of the CAS's decisions since 2004 are now published on its website.

1.41 CAS Ad Hoc Panels at successive Summer Olympics (Atlanta, Sydney, Athens, Beijing and London) Winter Olympics (Nagano and Salt Lake City) and Commonwealth Games (Kuala Lumpur, Manchester, Melbourne and Delhi) reflected the transnational character of the law being applied. The rules directed the Tribunal to complement its application of relevant regulations with the 'general principles of law and the rules of law, the application of which it deems appropriate'.

1.42 The 'applicable regulations' included primarily the rules of the relevant international federations and, depending on the occasion, the regulations of the domestic Commonwealth Games or Olympic bodies. The 'general principles of law and the rules of law, the application of which [the panel] deems appropriate' gave the panels a broad freedom to determine applicable rules. To identify the 'appropriate' 'general principles of law and rules of law', sports law borrows from private and public law, appropriately mixing Latinisms with French phrases, civilian and common law concepts.

1.43 The influence of civil law domestic legal systems is not a mere curiosity for the English sports lawyer. Cases such as *Lehtinen v FINA*[29] and *Puerta v International Tennis Federation*[30] have influenced decisions before English, foreign or international sports law tribunals or national courts, whichever law they may be applying. In *Lehtinen* the CAS entertained, but dismissed, a claim for damages against an international sporting association by applying Articles 41 and 49 of the Swiss Code of Obligations.[31]

1.44 In *Puerta*, a CAS panel including a distinguished English QC, Peter Leaver, declined to give effect to a rule providing for a mandatory eight-year ban for a second doping offence committed without 'significant fault or negligence', reasoning that 'its decision in the present case does not involve the exercise of a discretion, but is a filling of a gap or lacuna in the WADC [World Anti-Doping Code] in circumstances which will rarely arise'.[32] The rules being applied were governed by English law, but subject to a rule which 'requires the Tribunal to interpret the Programme in a manner that is consistent with applicable provisions of the World Anti-Doping Code'. The CAS panel took this to mean that it should construe that Code in a manner consistent with Swiss law, because the World Anti-Doping Agency had its seat in Switzerland and, therefore, the applicable rules, though governed by English law, also had to comply with the Swiss law principle of proportionality, as they applied 'throughout the world' and must be 'capable of a uniform and consistent construction wherever it [the Code] is applied. Any other construction would negate, or, at the very least, seriously weaken, the purpose and objective of the WADA [World Anti-Doping Agency] and its signatories.'[33]

1.45 Thus, domestic sports arbitrators in England and elsewhere now have to apply principles of law derived not exclusively from any one national legal system, but from international sports jurisprudence. The presence in Switzerland of the CAS and several major international governing bodies including FIFA and UEFA has led to Swiss domestic and international law (particularly the Swiss law of associations) occupying a predominant position in international sports jurisprudence.

---

[29] CAS 95/142, February 1996.
[30] CAS 2006/A/1025, 12 July 2006; [2006] ISLR, SLR 149.
[31] CAS 95/142, February 1996, paras 63 ff.
[32] Ibid, para 11.7.29.
[33] Ibid, para 10.8.

1.46 There is nothing unusual about arbitrators from one country, or in one country, applying the law of another country. But in sports related arbitrations one is never very far from Swiss law principles even if adjudicating in London on issues arising from a contract made in England and expressly governed by English law. Even in such cases the CAS tends to regard its internationally recognised sports related principles as applicable, such as the *lex mitior* doctrine, a creature unknown to English law.

1.47 While the CAS rules[34] provide for Swiss law to be applied in the absence of an alternative choice of law by the disputant parties,[35] it is notable that the decisions of the CAS reflect and promote the distinctive sporting principles of fair play and good sportsmanship[36] in applying technical rules;[37] the equality of athletes before the law;[38] the construction of sporting rules so as not to distort their purpose;[39] a respect for sporting decisions; and a flexible and pragmatic approach to entry deadlines.[40] These same principles are also enunciated in the rules of many international sporting bodies.[41]

1.48 The influence of Swiss law extends to the CAS Ad Hoc Panels already mentioned, set up to adjudicate on the spot at the Winter and Summer Olympic and Commonwealth Games. In each instance, the juridical seat of the arbitrations heard by the Ad Hoc Panels (in defiance of geographical reality) was said to be Lausanne, Switzerland, which meant that the panels were able to look to Article 187 of the Swiss Private International Law Act, which provides:

> The arbitral tribunal shall decide the dispute according to the rules of law chosen by the parties or, in the absence of such a choice, according to the rules of law with which the case has the closest connection.[42]

1.49 The term 'rules of law' did not necessarily mean national law only and, within a national law, allows dépéçage. 'General principles of law' were properly interpreted to comprise rules commonly observed in legal systems worldwide, but not those particular to a discrete area, in terms of either subject matter or country (such as Japanese unfair competition law).[43] As a concept, 'general principles of law' were adapted to the context: the principles appropriate in a sports arbitration are different from those that should apply where the context is the law of nations.

---

[34] The current Code of Sports-Related Arbitration or Code de l'Arbitrage en Matière de Sport entered into force on 1 January 2010 and has been amended from 1 July 2011. The French and English texts are equally authentic but the French text prevails in the event of inconsistency.

[35] Rule R.45. The parties may authorise the arbitrators to decide *ex aequo et bono* ('statuer en équité').

[36] Notably in *Cooke v Fédération Equestre Internationale*, CAS 98/184, September 1998.

[37] For example, what is a low blow in boxing; see *Mendy*, CAS OG 96/004 (Atlanta).

[38] *R v IOC*, CAS OG 98/002 (Nagano), para 5.

[39] *Czech Olympic Committee and Swedish Olympic Committee v IAAF*, CAS OG 98/004–005 (Nagano).

[40] *US Swimming v FINA*, CAS OG 96/001 (Atlanta). However, deadline obligations are strictly enforced if non-observance would disrupt a competition: see *Ulker v Euroleague*, CAS 2002/A/388, Reeb 3 516 (refusal of Turkish club to play Israeli club in Israel, relying on security concerns; yet 'the obligation to appear and compete at the dates and in the venue indicated in the calendar is "the most basic obligation in the sporting system"'); see also *Glasgow Rangers FC v UEFA*, CAS 2001/A/341, Reeb 3 559; *Addo v UEFA*, CAS 2001/A/323, Reeb 3 628.

[41] See, eg, Art 168 of the General Regulations of the Fédération Equestre Internationale, 19th edn ('the common principles of behaviour, fairness and accepted standards of sportsmanship'), which was in play in *Cooke v FEI* (n 36).

[42] Cf also Art 21 of the Arbitration and ADR Rules of the International Chamber of Commerce, latest version 12 September 2011, effective from 1 January 2012.

[43] See *Staatsfabriek Viking BV v German Speed Skating Association*, CAS OG 96/003 (Atlanta).

1.50 In the context of sport, general principles of international contract law may be material.[44] The most commonly applied principles are the following:

Freedom of contract: The parties to a contract may reach agreement on any matter they wish within the boundaries of mandatory provisions of domestic or (if applicable) international law. Such freedom of contract extends to choice-of-law clauses, by which the parties select the legal framework, again within the boundaries of mandatory provisions.[45] The principle of freedom of contract means as a corollary that agreements which are not freely entered into are invalid.

Pacta sunt servanda: A party which freely enters into an agreement and assumes obligations under it must perform as agreed unless excused from doing so by reasons beyond its control.[46]

Force majeure: If reasons beyond a party's control prevent it from performing in accordance with the contractual terms, that party may be excused from performance. The party is discharged from liability for non-performance only if it has made its best and reasonable efforts to overcome the outside event and to perform.[47]

Clausula rebus sic stantibus: This doctrine[48] proceeds from the premise that parties enter into a contract with a certain set of circumstances in mind. If the circumstances change in an unforeseeable manner and to a material extent, then the basis of the contract lapses. The principle is not universally accepted in national laws; for example, French law does not recognise it in private law, only in administrative law. However, it is widely recognised in international arbitration whenever the arbitrators apply general principles of law and *lex mercatoria*.

Good faith: This is a universal principle according to which all persons are bound by a duty to act in a loyal, frank and open manner.[49] For example, when one party acts or makes statements knowing that another party will act in reliance on these statements or acts, the former is precluded from reversing its position at the latter's expense (*venire contra factum proprium*).[50] In common law systems this would be characterised as estoppel.

Protection of legitimate expectations: Arbitrators and tribunals should not depart from the clear intent of the parties unless there is a paramount reason for so doing.[51] It must be assumed that the parties to an agreement intended it to be valid and enforceable.

---

[44] For a general and authoritative presentation see Goldman, *La lex mercatoria dans les contrats et l'arbitrage internationaux: réalité et perspectives* (1979) 106 Journal de Droit International 475. In England, the leading works on arbitration are Merkin, *Arbitration Law*, 2 vols (Informa, looseleaf); St John Sutton, Gill and Gearing, *Russell on Arbitration*, 23rd edn (Sweet & Maxwell, 2007); and Mustill and Boyd, *Commercial Arbitration*, 3rd edn (Butterworths, 2008).

[45] Lalive, *Transnational (or Truly International) Public Policy* in *Comparative Arbitration Practice and Public Policy in Arbitration*, ICCA Congress Series No 3 (1987) 257–318, 301–4.

[46] See Dasser, *Internationale Schiedsgerichte und Lex Mercatoria* (Zurich, 1989) 109–10 and references therein.

[47] See ibid, 110–12 and references therein.

[48] Equivalent to frustration of contracts under Anglo-American law, commercial impracticability under US law, Wegfall der Geschäftsgrundlage under German law, and imprévision under French law.

[49] Dasser (n 46) 108–9 and references therein; Lalive (n 45) 306; Mayer, *Le principe de bonne foi devant les arbitres internationaux* in *Etudes de droit international en l'honneur de Pierre Lalive* (Helbing & Lichtenhahn, 1993) 543–56 and extensive references.

[50] Applied by the CAS in *AEK Athens and Slavia Prague v UEFA*, CAS 98/200, Procedural Order of 17 July 1998, p 14 para 56.

[51] Bucher, *L'attente légitime de parties* in *Rechtskollisionen, Festschrift für Anton Heini* (Schulthess Polygraphischer, 1995) 95–102; Lalive (n 45) 305–6.

Furthermore, arbitrators must be careful not to apply rules of a law which the parties obviously did not have in mind.

1.51 International arbitration practice has developed or adopted the following principles of interpretation of contracts:

Necessity of seeking the parties' intent: When interpreting contracts, arbitrators and tribunals must attempt to reach a result which is in accordance with the real or presumed intent of the parties. The starting point for interpretation must be the contract itself.

In dubio contra proferentem: When one party has drafted a contract and the other party has merely adhered to its terms, eg where an athlete agrees to submit a dispute to arbitration, any doubt arising from the contract's wording benefits the adhering party, and is adverse to the proponent. The same principle applies to the rules and regulations of sports bodies. The *contra proferentem* principle is, of course, well established in English law.[52]

Doubt benefits the party assuming a contractual obligation: When a contract (or rule or regulation) is unclear, any doubt benefits the party on whom the contract is said to impose an obligation. In other words, no contractual duties can be held to exist unless clearly set forth in the contract.

The last two principles are to be applied only in cases of ambiguity.[53]

1.52 The main type of dispute submitted to international arbitral bodies in sport is disciplinary. The legal context is therefore often closer to administrative or even criminal law than to contract law. International sports dispute resolution engages the following general principles of public and criminal law:

Nullum crimen, nulla poena sine lege: Sanctions cannot be imposed unless a rule has been violated and unless sanctions are provided for in the rule. This rule is enshrined in Article 7 of the 1950 European Convention on Human Rights.[54] Although this basic principle has its origins in criminal law, it also applies in administrative law; any infringement of personal freedoms by an administrative body must have a statutory basis.[55]

Equal treatment: Equal (or at least very similar) situations must receive equal treatment; conversely, unequal situations must receive different treatment.[56] The general principle requires the tribunal carefully to examine the facts of the relevant cases to detect material similarities or differences and to explain the same.

Proportionality: Although the imposition of a particular sanction is a matter, within the range provided by the rules, for the discretion of the relevant authority, the principle of

---

[52] *Chitty on Contracts*, 30th edn (Sweet & Maxwell, 2011) vol 1, para 14-009; *John Lee & Son (Grantham) Ltd v Railway Executive* [1949] 2 All ER 581. The principle was applied by eg the (BAF) Drug Advisory Committee in the case of Douglas Walker (1999) para 4.4. It only applies where the ambiguity is real; see *Puerta v ITF* (n 30) (unsuccessful invocation of *contra proferentem* principle in an attempt to prevent a second doping offence being treated as such even though the first occurred before the entry into force of the World Anti-Doping Code).

[53] The principle *in dubio pro reo* was applied by the CAS in *B v ITU*, CAS 98/222, 9 August 1999, paras 43 and 52, to defeat a charge of nandrolone in the athlete's body where the concentration was so low as to be consistent with endogenous production.

[54] See, eg, Ashworth, *Principles of Criminal Law*, 2nd edn (Clarendon Press, 1995) 67–71; Pradel, *Droit pénal, Tome 1, Introduction générale, droit pénal général*, 10th edn (Dalloz, 1995) 169–71.

[55] See Erichsen and Ehlers, *Allgemeines Verwaltungsrecht*, 10th edn (de Gruyter, 1995) 106–7; Moor, *Droit administratif, vol I, Les fondements généraux* (Stämpfli, 1988) 45–47.

[56] Moor, ibid, vol I, pp 376–9.

proportionality means that a sanction must be proportionate to the offence and that the sanction must be necessary to achieve the result sought by the body imposing it.[57]

Good faith: In administrative law in civil law jurisdictions, the good faith principle applies when an administrative body gives assurances to an individual that certain future actions by that individual are legal when in truth they may not be. If such assurances are given (and provided that the body in question was empowered to decide such matters), no sanctions can be imposed upon the individual acting illegally in reliance on these assurances.[58] Another application of the good faith principle (which flows from the doctrine *venire contra factum proprium*, 'no one may set himself in contradiction to his own previous conduct') is that a party may not create an ambiguous situation, for example by making conflicting or unclear statements, and then take advantage of the ambiguity which it has itself brought about. Finally, the good faith principle precludes a party from availing itself of a rule in a manner which is contrary to the rationale of the rule (*abus de droit*).

Influence of the Olympic Movement

1.53 The influence of the Olympic Movement on the world of sport is paramount.[59] An Olympic medal is the acme of ambition of any participant in an Olympic sport. Records are transitory; medals are permanent. '[I]t is difficult to imagine an interest more worthy of protection than the interest of an athlete in securing an Olympic medal which she/he considers to have won fairly.'[60] Hence competition for a sports body to become part of the Olympic movement, for a city to host the Olympics, for an international federation to have its sports included in the Olympic programme,[61] of competitors to be selected for their national team,[62] and for which national team they should be selected[63] and, of those selected, to progress as far as possible and ultimately to a podium place, is intense.[64] All such

---

[57] Erichsen (n 55) 109–10; Moor (n 55) 305–53; Woolf, Jowell and Le Sueur, *De Smith's Judicial Review*, 6th edn (Sweet & Maxwell, 2007) 11-075 ff.

[58] Erichsen (n 55) 110; Moor (n 55) 358–65.

[59] See generally Mestre, *The Law of the Olympic Games* (TMC Asser Press, 2009); Nafziger, *International Sports Law* (Transnational Publishing, 2004) 1–9, 18–28; James, *Sports Law* (Palgrave Macmillan, 2010) ch 14; Oliveria, Comment: Sport as a Tool for Development and Peace: The Role of the IOC (2012) WSLR. Indeed the influence extends beyond sport: for a discussion of boycotts, see Mestre, *Ten Reasons against Boycotting the Beijing Olympics*, World Sports Law Report (WSLR) 6/4, p 8. See also Anderson, *Sports Law in an Olympic Year: Citius, Altius, Fortius?* (2012) 12(2) LIM 72; James and Osborn, *The Sources and Interpretation of Olympic Law* (2012) 12(2) LIM 80; Cho, Olympics: A Sports Law Research Guide (2012) (12)2 LIM 92–97.

[60] *Beckie Scott v IOC*, CAS 2002/O/373, para 23.

[61] In the case of *Sagan v Vancouver Organising Committee* [2009] BC 942, female ski-jumpers brought an unsuccessful constitutional challenge in Canada against the Vancouver Olympic Organising Committee for implementing the decision not to include women's show-jumping; McLaren and Douglas, *Women Ski-Jumpers Allege Human Rights Breach*, WLSR 5/5; Lines and Heshka, *Ski Jumping through Olympic Solid Hoops* [2009] ISLR 92; Patel, *Women's Ski Jumping and Olympic Programme Inclusion*, WSLR 8/7, p 11. In *Martin v IOC* two female athletes had earlier failed in an attempt to compel the IOC to add 5,000 and 10,000 metre track races for women to the programme for the Los Angeles Olympic Games; see Nafziger (n 59) 123–5.

[62] See eg *Watt v Australian Cycling Federation*, CAS 96/A/153.

[63] *Puerto Rican Amateur Baseball Federation v USA Baseball*, CAS 94/O/132, deciding that the Olympic Charter allowed an athlete that choice.

[64] This can prompt another form of corruption, ie by judges: see Nafziger (n 59) 113–15 on 'Skategate' at the Salt Lake City Games of 2002.

competitions have a legal dimension. Disputes arising 'on the occasion of, or in connection with the Olympic Games' are for the exclusive jurisdiction of CAS.[65]

1.54 The Olympic Charter (OC) sets out the fundamental principles and constitution of the Olympic Movement.[66] It has undergone continued mutations since the era of Baron de Coubertin, the founder of the modern Olympics.[67] All members of the so-called Olympic family—athletes, team officials, IOC members, international federations (IFs), National Olympic Committees (NOCs) and Organising Committees of the Olympic Games (OCOGs), together with the Olympic Movement (OM), as well as sponsors, official broadcasters, accredited media and broadcasting licensees—are required to abide by its terms set out in 61 rules to which are added 31 bye-laws by way of interpretative aids. It consists of six chapters: The Olympic Movement; The International Olympic Committee; The International Federations; The National Olympic Committees; The Olympic Games; and Measures and Sanctions, Disciplinary Procedures and Dispute Resolution.

1.55 The Olympic Movement's membership is itself capable of alteration.[68] The IOC can recognise new NOCs, sports bodies and NGOs.[69] The condition for recognition of an NOC is that it is an independent state recognised by the international community and has at least five national governing bodies associated with it.

1.56 The IOC is an international non-governmental not-for-profit organisation of unlimited duration in the form of an association with the status of a legal person, recognised by the Swiss Federation Council in accordance with an agreement entered into on 1 November 2000.[70] It has legal personality within Swiss law.[71] It is an organisation with international character but not an international organisation or the subject of public international law.[72] Its mission is 'to promote Olympism throughout the world and to lead the Olympic Movement'.[73]

1.57 Olympism itself is described in the OC Fundamental Principles of Olympism as a 'philosophy of life, exalting and combining in a balanced whole the qualities of the body, will and mind. Blending sport with culture and education, Olympism seeks to create a way

---

[65] OC rule 59. Even the carrying of the national flag into the arena can generate rivalry within a team: see *Andrade v Cape Verde NOC*, CAS 96/002 (Atlanta), para 20 and its sequel, *Andrade v Cape Verde NOC*, CAS 96/005 (Atlanta).

[66] 'The normative foundation of international sports law': Nafziger (n 59) 2; Mestre, *The Legal Basis of the Olympic Charter*, WSLR 5/11, p 6. In *Iverson v ISAF*, CAS 2004/A/557, [2006] SLR 76 it was held that weight limits for sailors did not infringe the eighth fundamental principle of the Olympic Charter that the practice of sport is a human right.

[67] See Lewis and Taylor (n 3) H1.3–H.1.6; Mestre (n 59) Introduction, 9–11.

[68] OC rule 3.

[69] The World Anti-Doping Agency (WADA), the International Academy, the CAS, the International Paralympic Committee, the ephemeral OCOG, the Olympic Congress, the IOC Commission, the International Olympics Truce Foundation, and the International Olympic Truce Centre. Mestre calls these satellite organisations (n 59, pp 52–60).

[70] OC rule 15(1). See Nafziger (n 59) 19–20; Lewis and Taylor (n 3) HI.13–H1.19; Mestre (n 59) 38–42.

[71] Art 56 of the Swiss Federal Constitution; Arts 52, 60 of the Swiss Civil Code.

[72] Its special status has been recognised in decisions in various court actions, including, importantly, the US Supreme Court: Nafziger (n 59) 25–26.

[73] OC rule 2. For a useful compendium of sources see Cho, *Olympics and International Sports Law Research Guide* (2012) 12(2) LIM 92.

of life based on the joy of effort, the educational value of good example and respect for fundamental universal principles.'[74]

1.58 The IOC itself has up to 115 individual members[75] chosen by its Nominations Commission from stakeholder representation groups. It is composed of individuals, not Member States (OC rule 16, bye-law). IOC members represent and promote the interests of the IOC and of the Olympic Movement in their countries and in the organisations of the Olympic Movement in which they serve.[76] Overall responsibility for the IOC's management and administration is vested in an Executive Board.[77] The IOC's supreme governing organ is the Session, which is the general meeting of the members of the IOC.[78]

1.59 The IFs, which are independent autonomous bodies,[79] set the rules for the practice of their sports at a global level, and are responsible for their sports' promotion, development and management.[80] Their members are the national governing bodies (NGBs) of the sport in each Member State. The IFs of Olympic sports set the eligibility criteria for Olympic competition[81] and determine whether the bid city's plan for its own sport satisfies the necessary technical criteria. They also control all technical elements of the sports competition in the Olympic Games.[82]

1.60 The Charter divides the Olympic programme into sports, disciplines and events.[83]

— **Sports** are admitted to the Olympic programme at the IOC session held seven years before the Games in question.[84] The preconditions for inclusion are, first, confirmation from the IF of a desire to participate in such a programme and, second, its adoption of the World Anti-Doping Code (WADC, or WADA Code).[85] There are 25 core sports, and additional sports may be proposed by the IOC board as long as their IF is recognised by the IOC,[86] up to a maximum of 28 sports.[87] There are detailed voting procedures for inclusion of the sport.[88]

— **Disciplines** are branches of an Olympic sport which consists of one or more events, eg swimming and diving within aquatic sports, for which FINA is the IF. It is the Board, not the IOC Session, that decides on the inclusion of disciplines.[89]

— **Events** are competitions within a sport or discipline. The Board decides on events within the Games in question.[90]

---

[74] It is complemented by the IOC Code of Ethics adopted by the Board on 26 April 2007 in Beijing. The fundamental principles were, inter alia, relied upon in *Beckie Scott v IOC*, CAS 2002/O/373 to ensure that an athlete whose competitors had been disqualified for doping offences obtained a medal in lieu (paras 49–51).

[75] OC rule 16(1) (bye-law 1.1).

[76] OC rule 16(1). See Nafziger (n 59) 20; Mestre (n 59) 42–44.

[77] OC rule 19. See Mestre (n 59) 69–70. The President and his powers are dealt with in OC rule 20: see Mestre (n 59) 70.

[78] OC rule 18(1).

[79] OC rule 25.

[80] Mestre (n 59) 50–52; Lewis and Taylor (n 3) H1.19–H1.28.

[81] OC rules 25 and 26.

[82] OC rule 46.

[83] OC rule 45(2).

[84] OC bye-law 1.3 to rule 45.

[85] OC rule 45(3).

[86] OC bye-law 2.1.3 to rule 45.

[87] OC bye-law 2.1.4 to rule 45.

[88] OC bye-laws 2.2.1, 2.13 and 2.22 to rule 45. In *Martin v IOC* the US appellate court said that it was not for domestic laws on equality to alter the rules of an international competition: Lewis and Taylor (n 3) H1.29–H1.38.

[89] OC rule 45(4) and bye-law 1.4 to rule 45.

[90] OC rule 45(2) and 45(4) and bye-law 1.4 to rule 45.

1.61 Deadlines for the inclusion of sports (seven years) and disciplines and events (three years) before the Games in question can be waived by the IOC with the concurrence of the IF and OCOG.[91] Any can be excluded if the IF does not comply with the OC or WADC.[92]

1.62 The NOCs are the representative bodies of the Olympic Movement within the 200-plus Olympic territories (overwhelmingly, but not entirely, composed of states) as a result of recent revisions.[93]

1.63 Rule 34 of the Olympic Charter formerly provided as follows:

Country and Name of National Olympic Committee

(1)   In the Olympic Charter the expression 'country' shall mean any country, state, territory or part of a territory which the IOC in its absolute discretion considers as the area of a recognised National Olympic Committee.
(2)   The name of an NOC must correspond to the borders and tradition of its country and must be approved by the IOC.

1.64 Under rule 34, NOCs for the following non-independent territories were recognised by the IOC: Dutch West Indies, Puerto Rico (1948), Hong Kong (1951), US Virgin Islands (1967), British Virgin Islands (1982), Cook Islands (1986), Aruba (1986), and American Samoa (1987).

1.65 Olympic competition is between athletes, not countries. General principles of law informed the decisions of the English High Court and Court of Appeal in *Reel v Holder*[94] in which the (then) International Amateur Athletic Federation (IAAF) unsuccessfully attempted to exclude Taiwan from its membership. It was held that the word 'country' in the IAAF rules delineated the area over which one governing amateur athletic association exercised authority, rather than a national or sovereign state. A broad purposive construction of the rule was said to be validated by the principles which underlie the Charter, namely that it is the interests of athletes that are paramount, and that an athletics governing body's authority in a 'country' was not the same as the authority of a sovereign or national state. The interpretation of the word 'country' was not to be based on international political concerns. Since the IAAF's decision to admit the Taiwanese body in 1956 had been valid and in accordance with the rules, there was no power in those rules to expel the Taiwanese body or to treat the Chinese body as having jurisdiction over Taiwan. Accordingly, the Taiwanese body was and remained an IAAF member.[95]

1.66 The present OC rule 30 provides:

Country and Name of an NOC

(1)   In the Olympic Charter, the expression 'country' means an independent State recognised by the international community.
(2)   The name of an NOC must reflect the territorial extent and tradition of its country and shall be subject to the approval of the IOC Executive Board.

---

[91]   OC bye-law 1.5 to rule 45.
[92]   OC bye-law 1.7–1.9 to rule 45.
[93]   Mestre (n 59) 44–52.
[94]   [1979] 1 WLR 1252, [1981] 1 WLR 1126.
[95]   See also *Angel Perez v IOC*, CAS OG 00/005 (Sydney), para 2; and *Celtic v UEFA*, CAS 98/201, *Digest of CAS Awards*, Reeb 2, where the word 'country' in the UEFA statutes was deemed 'not to be understood in its common political meaning' but in line with the purpose of the provision (para 31 at p 119) (Annex F).

1.67 The contrast between the old rule and the new rule is clear. The IOC surrendered its previous discretion to give a broad interpretation to the concept of 'country', and was thenceforth restricted to recognising NOCs of countries which were independent states.

1.68 This recent introduction of the criterion of independent statehood would, if applied retrospectively, disqualify some present members (eg Hong Kong) and is thought to have been motivated by the problems caused by Gibraltar's application. A challenge to the refusal to admit the Gibraltar OC (mainly on the ground that the condition was applied retrospectively) is currently before the Swiss Federal Tribunal.[96]

1.69 NOCs promote Olympism in their territory, take Olympic teams to the Games, ensure that their member NGBs implement the WADC, control the use of Olympic intellectual property rights in their territory, and are alone authorised to select an aspirant host city from their territory.[97] Their composition is dealt with in OC rule 28. They must include all IOC members in their country, all national federations affiliated to IFs governing Olympic sports, and all present or, within a time limit, ex-Olympians.[98] Their legal nature depends upon the law of their own country.[99]

1.70 Chapter 5 of the OC deals with the Games themselves. The election of the host city is dealt with in rule 33. In light of the scandals surrounding the Salt Lake City bid to host the 2002 Winter Olympics, new rules were introduced, including a general ban on visits by IOC members to candidate cities during the bid process, restrictive rules on promotion of a city's campaign and a ban on gifts from bid cities, supplemented by the IOC Code of Ethics which entitles members to receive only gifts of nominal value. Where the IOC led, it may be that FIFA will follow. A bid's legal document in its candidature file contains the aspirant host city's promises for the Games and is complemented by guarantees from bodies involved in the delivery of the Games, from transport to accommodation to security. The candidature file is converted into a legally binding host city contract to which the city selected is the counterparty[100] and governs the relationship of the IOC, host city, host NOC and OCOG. The contract is governed by Swiss law, which takes precedence over the OC in the event of a conflict between the two. Any disputes will be resolved by the CAS or, if the CAS decides that it is not competent, by the ordinary courts in Lausanne, Switzerland.

1.71 OCOGs are established by NOCs to organise the quadrennial games.[101] Bye-law 1 to OC rule 35 states that the OCOG 'shall have the status of a legal person its country'. Bye-law 2 to OC rule 35 prescribes the constituent elements of the host country's OCOG. Bye-law 3 to OC rule 35 requires an OCOG to comply with the Olympic Charter, any agreement entered into by the IOC with NOC or host city, and regulations or instructions of the IOC Board. OC rule 36(2) entitles the IOC to withdraw organisation of the Games for breach of the Charter or of obligations entered into by the host city, NOC or OCOG. The same provision imposes all financial responsibility for the Games on those bodies,

---

[96] Case No 5A 2/2011: against the judgment of the Chambre de Recours du Tribunal Cantonal du Canton de Vaud, 25 January 2010: 287/1.
[97] OC rule 27.
[98] Mestre (n 59) 47.
[99] The British Olympic Association is a company registered in England and Wales with offices in London.
[100] OC rule 35. See, for London 2012, Lewis and Taylor (n 3) H1.58–H1.62.
[101] Mestre (n 59) 61–65.

and none on the IOC; the IOC can also seek compensation for any damage caused to it by breach of such obligations.[102]

1.72 IFs determine their own eligibility criteria[103] for participation in the Games, as long as the criteria are compliant with the Charter and are approved by the IOC Board;[104] and the application of such criteria lies with the IFs, their affiliated national federations, and the NOCs in their respective fields of responsibility.[105] A competitor or other participant (ie an official) must be entered by his NOC and comply with the Charter, WADC and the relevant IF rules, as well as the spirit of fair play and non-violence. This would seem to exclude the possibility of the IOC independently permitting athletes to compete in the Games, but it has been argued that the IOC enjoys a residual discretion to that effect. As we shall see in chapter three, major issues over eligibility are in consequence disputed in national courts between the non-selected aspirant participant and his or her NOC, although CAS Ad Hoc Panels at successive Olympics have found eligibility issues on their agenda, if usually of an inter-state rather than intra-state variety. There is no longer a requirement for a participant to be an amateur, itself reflective of the transformation of sport from leisure to business activity.[106]

1.73 A competitor must be a national of the country of the NOC that enters him or her; and it is for the IOC executive board to resolve any dispute as to which country the competitor may represent (OC rule 41). The bye-law to rule 41 provides an elaborate code for dealing with dual and change of nationality. By requiring a presumptive three-year temporal *cordon sanitaire*, ie the passage of a three year period (subject to its diminution or extinction by agreement of the NOCs and IFs concerned) before an athlete can compete for his country of second nationality, the Charter distinguishes between sporting and legal nationality. It has been noted that this discrimination between a sportsman who has obtained dual nationality and has previously represented his original country in an Olympic Games, and one who has the same dual nationality but has not previously participated in an Olympic Games, may violate the principles of international instruments such as the Universal Declaration of Human Rights Article 15(2) and the European Convention on Nationality Article 17(1), and EU competition law.[107] A CAS Ad Hoc Panel has interpreted the rule benignly, equating a change of nationality with becoming de jure or de facto stateless, so enhancing the athlete's right to change his national allegiance.[108] Paragraph 3 of the bye-law to OC rule 41 itself makes provision for athlete choice in cases of new independence, change of border, merger between countries, or changes in recognition of an NOC.

---

[102] For legal protection of 'Olympic Properties', see the Nairobi Treaty on the Protection of the Olympic Symbol, 26 September 1981; Mestre (n 59) 85–91. Legislation is passed by countries in which the host city is located to protect the Olympic symbol, see eg London Olympic Games and Paralympic Games Act 2006; see Michalos, *Five Golden Rings: Development of the Protection of the Olympic Insignia* [2006] ISLR 64; Miller, *London 2012: Meeting the Challenge of Brand Protection* [2008] ISLR 44.

[103] Mestre (n 59) 71–72.

[104] OC rule 40, and bye-law to rule 40, para 1.

[105] Ibid, para 2.

[106] Mestre (n 59) 72–74.

[107] Ibid, 74–77.

[108] *Angel Perez v IOC*, CAS OG 00/005 (Sydney), paras 25, 27, 32.

1.74 OC rule 42 makes any age limit for participation in the Games dependent upon the IFs' competition rules as approved by the IOC Executive Board.[109]

1.75 An IOC regulation adopted pursuant to the former OC rule 45—the so-called Osaka rule—was designed to ensure that a person who had been banned for more than six months for a doping offence, whether as an athlete or in any other role such as that of coach, could not be invited to the next Games. It was successfully challenged by the American runner LaShawn Merritt, in whose case it was held to be a penalty, inconsistent with, because greater than, the penalties prescribed by WADC (by which the IOC was bound), and also violated the principle *ne bis in idem* (double jeopardy).[110]

1.76 The IOC's mission includes acting against any form of discrimination affecting the Olympic movement[111] and the encouragement and support of the promotion of women in sport at all levels 'with a view to implementing the principle of equality of men and women'.[112] Nonetheless, it is axiomatic that within all Olympic sports (equestrian events apart) the competitions for men and women are separate, reflecting 'obvious anatomical and physiological differences between men and women'[113] and reflecting too that it is the IFs which have technical responsibility for their sports at the Olympic Games[114] as well as establishing their own eligibility criteria. Special rules for transsexuals, designed to ensure that, as far as possible, that dividing line is effectively maintained, are under active consideration at the time of writing. The IAAF has already promulgated a new regime.[115] A disabled athlete who satisfies the eligibility criteria set by his or her IF for both able-bodied and disabled athletes is able to compete in the competitions for both able-bodied and disabled athletes.[116]

---

[109] Mestre (n 59) 79–81.

[110] *USADA v Merritt*, AAA (North American Court of Arbitration for Sport) 77 190 00293; see also *USOC v IOC*, CAS 2011/O/2422.

[111] OC rule 2(6).

[112] OC rule 2(7).

[113] Mestre (n 59) 81–83.

[114] Ibid, 83.

[115] On the history of this issue see Mestre (n 59) 4.1.5–4.1.6.

[116] The well-known case of *Oscar Pistorious* and its implications are discussed by Michael Beloff QC in [2011] ISLR 65 (editorial). See too Murphy, *Pistorious Case: Implications of his Successful IAAF Challenge*, WLSR 6/9, p 6.

2

Overview: Framework of the Law Relating to Sport

2.1 In this second chapter our aim is to provide an overview of the manner in which the law impacts on sporting activity. We seek to give an account here of the ways in which the law creates rights and obligations which impact on participants in the sports industries. Our primary purpose here is not to state the detailed content of those rights and obligations, but to identify and explain in brief the legal nature of the bodies that govern sports, and the sources of rights and obligations to which sportsmen and women, and their governing organs, are subject.

The Legal Nature of Sporting Associations

2.2 All who follow sport in the media are familiar with various acronyms or sets of initials denoting the bodies that administer particular sports. We take for granted that 'the FA' means the Football Association, 'the RFU' means the Rugby Football Union, and 'the WRU' the Welsh Rugby Union. Devotees of squash may be aware that the 'SRA' was the Squash Rackets Association, now known as England Squash and Racketball. On the international plane, most sports aficionados probably know that 'the WBC' means the World Boxing Council but, unless they speak French, are unlikely to know what 'UEFA' stands for (Union des Associations Européennes de Football). Many people who work in sport may never need to concern themselves with the differences in the legal nature of these bodies.

2.3 To lawyers and some sports administrators, however, the differences can be critical. If a dispute arises, it may be of legal importance that the Football Association is in fact a limited company, the Football Association Limited, incorporated in England; that the World Boxing Council is a limited liability company incorporated in Puerto Rico; that UEFA is a limited liability company incorporated in Switzerland; that the RFU is a special kind of body corporate registered under the Industrial and Provident Societies Act 1965; that England Squash and Racketball Limited is incorporated as a company limited by guarantee; and that the WRU used to be an unincorporated association of members but is now also incorporated as Welsh Rugby Union Limited, a company limited by guarantee, without share capital, to which the assets of the former association were transferred on its creation.

2.4 The most unusual legal form encountered in top level sport must surely be that of the America's Cup, established by a Deed of Gift dated 24 October 1887, as amended by orders of the Supreme Court of the State of New York made on 17 December 1956 and 5 April 1985. The coveted cup was owned by George L Schuyler and had been won by the yacht *America* in a competition at Cowes in the Isle of Wight, England, on 22 August 1851. By the Deed, Mr Schuyler gifted the Cup to the New Yacht Club 'upon the conditions that it shall be preserved as a perpetual Challenge Cup for friendly competition between foreign countries'. The Deed went on to establish the now well-known 'challenge' procedure.[1]

2.5 It is not just the bodies which administer sport that may differ in their legal nature. The clubs and individuals that win or lose the games may play to the same rules on the field, but off the field they may differ from each other in their legal characteristics. The FA Premier League includes Fulham Football Club Limited and Fulham Football Club (1987) Limited; Tottenham Hotspur Football & Athletic Company Limited, closely associated with Tottenham Hotspur plc; and Chelsea Football Club Limited (to name some of the clubs we have had the privilege of representing). Individual sportsmen and women naturally have the same status in law as any other individual person.

2.6 Most if not all national sporting bodies in this country, particularly in professional sports in England, are now incorporated as companies with limited liability. But there is no requirement in English law that sports clubs or associations take any particular legal form. They may be limited liability companies, companies limited by guarantee, or unincorporated associations. They enjoy the benefits and are subject to the obligations of the particular form that they have selected in the same way as other non-sports bodies. They are not statutory bodies and are not required to be licensed or registered as in some countries, such as Malaysia.

2.7 International sports bodies are also usually limited liability companies registered in whichever jurisdiction they find most convenient; Switzerland being popular with the European bodies and some worldwide bodies such as FIFA and the international Olympic bodies. Governing bodies are treated in most legal systems as private authorities but exercising quasi-public functions, particularly where they exercise monopoly power over a particular sport. They are strongly autonomous and independent, and therefore can perhaps be expected to act in less predictable ways than if they were statutory bodies created by legislation.[2]

2.8 In the world of sport the main distinction is between bodies which are incorporated and those which are not. A corporation has a legal existence independent of the individuals who are members of the corporation, and is therefore said to have legal personality. The shareholders are not liable for the company's debts. An important consequence of corporate identity is that the company can bring and defend legal proceedings in its own

---

[1] The Deed of Gift was considered in New York court and arbitral proceedings in 2007 which featured a remarkable clash of jurisdiction and inconsistent decisions, following the challenge for the 33rd America's Cup by Club Náutico Español de Vela (CNEV), a specially formed Spanish yacht club; leading to long and acrimonious litigation finally won by the rival challenger, Golden Gate Yacht Club (GGYC), which eventually secured a decision of the New York Court of Appeals on 2 April 2009 that CNEV was not the rightful challenger under the Deed of Gift and that GGYC was the rightful challenger. GGYC then won the 33rd America's Cup in February 2010, off the coast of Valencia, Spain.

[2] See, eg, Charles Woodhouse, *Sport and Law in Conflict: Role of Sports Governing Bodies*, conference paper, Stamford Bridge, 25 November 1996: 'There is little or no standardisation in their constitutions.' By 2008 that remained the position: see the helpful account of *Organisational structures for sports entities* in Lewis and Taylor, *Sport: Law and Practice*, 2nd edn (Tottel Publishing, 2008) ch F1.

name. Where the company is limited by shares, the shareholders are liable to the company only up to the amount unpaid on their shares; where limited by guarantee, the guarantors are liable only up to the amount of their guarantee.[3] Particular laws in the fields of taxation, insolvency and others apply to them.[4] It would go beyond our purpose to attempt any exposition here of the different types of body corporate encountered in the sporting world. Reference should be made to standard works on company law, the most comprehensive of which is Palmer's *Company Law*.[5]

2.9 For the purposes of our bird's eye view of the framework of sports law, it is sufficient here to mention only some of the principal attributes of a limited liability company. Its legal existence and the limited liability of its members are well known. Other important features of a company are its governing constitutional documents, the memorandum and articles of association; the fiduciary duties owed to it by its directors; its susceptibility to an administration order or to liquidation (compulsorily, in winding up proceedings, or voluntarily, by resolution); and the particular statutory remedy available to minority shareholders who may wish, and in certain circumstances are permitted, to complain about the manner in which the company's affairs are being conducted.[6]

2.10 These and other aspects of company law too numerous and complex to mention here are the subject of a vast tapestry of interlocking regulatory provisions enacted by statute and statutory instrument, all admirably expounded in Palmer's *Company Law* and other specialist works. Expert legal and accounting advice is given to administrators in sport to help them to determine which legal animal to select as the most appropriate form for the governing body in question. The choice of form has implications for accounting methods, tax liability regimes and other practical matters. It is not part of the exercise undertaken in this chapter to provide an explanation of those factors, or of the advantages and disadvantages of particular legal forms. The decision as to how best to create a body to administer a sport should be informed by the detailed circumstances of the case and specialist advice.

2.11 If a sporting body is not incorporated as a company, then, in English law, it will be classified as an unincorporated association. Such associations are now seldom if ever found at national level in professional sport, but continue to thrive in amateur sports played at district and county level. English law regards such associations as no more than a group of individuals comprising the members of the association, who have collectively agreed amongst themselves by contract to abide by the content of the rules of the association as amended from time to time. We will look further at this organisational model when considering the impact of contractual terms in sport, below.[7] Unincorporated

---

[3] Davies, *Gower and Davies: The Principles of Modern Company Law*, 8th edn (Sweet & Maxwell, 2008) para 1-5, p 8.

[4] It has been suggested that 'having a distinct stand alone entity, separate from committee and members alike, can make for clearer management and decision making structures': Woodhouse (n 2).

[5] Morse, *Palmer's Company Law* (Sweet & Maxwell, looseleaf).

[6] See, eg, s 994 of the Companies Act 2006, enabling a minority shareholder to petition the court for relief on the ground that the company's affairs are being managed in a manner prejudicial to the interests of the minority. Contrary to the decision of HHJ Weeks QC in *Exeter City AFC Ltd v The Football Conference Ltd* [2004] EWHC 831 (Ch), [2004] 1 WLR 2910, such a petition may be stayed under s 9 of the Arbitration Act 1996 to give effect to an arbitration clause such as that in Rule K of the rules of the Football Association: see *Fulham FC (1987) Ltd v Richards* [2011] EWCA Civ 855, overruling the decision in *Exeter City*.

[7] See para 2.36 ff.

associations are common inhabitants of the English law landscape. They are not confined to the sporting world; on the contrary they are very common outside it as well as within it. For example, most barristers' chambers operate as unincorporated associations of their members, although, like other associations, many have created a service company to employ staff, purchase supplies and perform other acts on behalf of the members, more conveniently done by an entity with distinct legal personality and limited liability.

2.12 Sports clubs often take the form of unincorporated associations as well. A common example is that of a village cricket club, an association with a simple written constitution providing for government by a committee, an annual general meeting and for certain major decisions to be taken only at such an annual general meeting or at an extraordinary general meeting. Such is the paradigm case in amateur sport.[8] Bodies concerned with the government of professional sport are more likely to be incorporated as limited companies. The essence of an unincorporated association is that its legal identity is no more than that of the sum of the individuals who are its members. Its constitution records its objects and method of decision making, and derives its force from the contract between them.

2.13 The common law supplements the normal express provisions commonly found in the constitutional documents of such associations by implying into the rules certain fundamental principles: in particular (subject to any contrary provision), the principle of decision by simple majority, and the right to resign from membership. Subjection to the court's jurisdiction in matters of law is also fundamental and cannot be negated by any contrary provision in the rules. A fuller account of the law relating to unincorporated associations and members' clubs would stray beyond the territory of sports law. The sports lawyer may be confronted—and not only in a disciplinary context of the type considered in chapter seven—with issues of construction and interpretation arising in this field of law. A useful account of that law can be found in *Halsbury's Laws of England*.[9]

2.14 As an example of a dispute in the context of sport over the meaning and effect of the rules of an unincorporated association, it is instructive to mention *Baker v Jones*.[10] A judge held that the central council of the British Amateur Weightlifters' Association did not, on the true construction of its rules, have the power to authorise the use of the Association's funds to pay the personal legal costs of some of its members in defending

---

[8] In Australian case law it has been held that the rules of an amateur sports club may not be legally enforceable, for want of intent to create legal relations, unless the players are paid (but not necessarily as professionals) to play, or unless a player's reputation would be affected by expulsion; but more recent decisions recognise legal enforceability of the rules where the sports organisation is large and influential and/or has a virtual monopoly in controlling participation in the sport; see eg *Smith v South Australian Hockey Association Inc* (1988) 48 SASR 263; *Rose v Boxing New South Wales Inc* [2007] NSWSC 20; cf *Kovacic v Australian Karting Association (Qld) Inc* [2008] QSC 344; *Rush v WA Amateur FC Inc* [2001] WASC 154, para 54; Sullivan, *The Role of Contract in Sports Law* (2010) 5(1) Australia and New Zealand Sports Law Journal 3, at 6–8.

[9] Mackay, *Halsbury's Laws of England*, 5th edn (LexisNexis, 2009) vol 13, paras 201–93. See also Cores, Pugh-Smith, Ruck Keene and Caulfield, *Shackleton on the Law and Practice of Meetings*, 12th edn (Sweet & Maxwell, 2012); Davies et al, *The Modern Law of Meetings*, 2nd edn (Jordans, 2009); Josling and Alexander, *The Law of Clubs*, 6th edn (Sweet & Maxwell, 1987); McNamara, *A Legal Guide for Clubs and Associations* (Bloomsbury Professional, 2005); *Ashton and Reid on Clubs and Associations*, 2nd edn (Jordans, 2011); Stewart, Campbell and Baughen, *The Law of Unincorporated Associations* (Oxford University Press, 2011).

[10] [1954] 1 WLR 1005, Lynksey J; but cf *Hill v Archbold* [1968] 1 QB 668, CA (trade union entitled to support libel action by officers; the decision casts some doubt on *Baker v Jones*); cf in a local government context *R (Comninos) v Bedford BC* [2003] EWHC 121 (Admin); [2003] BLGR 271 (local authority had power to fund libel action brought by officers, but decided on statutory grounds without citation of *Hill* or *Baker*).

proceedings brought against them in their personal capacity. The officers had been sued in actions alleging the torts of conspiracy and defamation. The reasoning of the judge was that a particular provision authorising the central council to act on behalf of the Association regarding any matters not dealt with by the rules, had to be read in conjunction with the object of the Association which was to promote weightlifting as a sport and weight training as a means of physical improvement.

2.15 Other disputes which have from time to time exercised us professionally have involved questions as to whether a dissentient member, unpopular with the leadership of the association in question, satisfied the conditions for establishing an automatic right to membership of a successor body to the association involved; whether a particular procedure proposed by the chairman of an international sporting body for the election of his or her successor was valid or invalid under the rules of the body in question; and other similar legal issues arising from clashes of personalities or politics within the internal administration of a sport. Such disputes can and do also arise in connection with incorporated sporting bodies operating as companies. In such cases, the dispute falls to be resolved by reference to the distinct, but to some extent related, body of principles which has grown up through case law dealing with the interpretation of successive company law statutes over the past few centuries, at present the Companies Act 2006, a Leviathan of a statute.

2.16 One important procedural point arises in relation to the nature of a sporting (or other) association. If the body is incorporated, and can therefore sue and be sued in its own name, ordinary legal procedures can be followed in the same way as where the party suing or being sued is an individual person and not a corporate person. If, however, the association is unincorporated, it cannot bring or defend legal proceedings in its own name, ie in the name of the association.[11] Instead, any action must be brought against, or defended by, individual representative defendants, being the officers of the association acting in their official capacity for and on behalf of all other relevant members for the time being of the association. Rules of court make specific provision for such representative proceedings. By rule 19.6(1) of the Civil Procedure Rules 1998[12] proceedings may be begun by or against any person or persons in the capacity of representatives of the interests of other persons, 'where more than one person has the same interest in a claim'.

2.17 In sporting cases it is consequently common for proceedings by a dissident member or members of an association to bring an action whose title describes the claimants in terms such as:

> X Y Z, suing on his own behalf and on behalf of all other members of the A B C Sports Association who voted in favour of a motion numbered 1 2 3 at the Annual General Meeting held on 18 January 2010

and the defendants are described as, for example:

> E F G and H J K, sued as, respectively, the Chairman and Secretary of the A B C Sports Association, on their own behalf and on behalf of all other members for the time being of that Association except the claimants.

---

[11] *R v Darlington BC, ex parte Association of Darlington Taxi Owners* [1994] COD 424 (Auld J). The court consequently had power to award costs enforceable against members of the association: [1995] COD 128.
[12] See *Civil Procedure (The White Book)* (Sweet & Maxwell, 2012); see also CPR Part 19.

This form of proceeding is not confined to litigation in sport but extends to any litigation in which representative proceedings are appropriate because numerous persons have the same interest in the subject matter of the litigation. It gets over the difficulty of absence of legal personality where an association is unincorporated. However, it can create complications in relation to legal costs, where an organisation is split and the powers to incur legal costs may themselves be in dispute—as shown by the decision in *Baker v Jones*.[13] Such complications do not arise so frequently in the case of corporate bodies, where the power to litigate and incur legal costs is normally provided for uncontroversially in the company's memorandum and/or articles of association, and can be exercised by the board of directors acting in the name of the company.

2.18 We have included in our overview brief mention of the consequences of legal personality, or the lack of it, in order to draw attention to the way in which legal forms may have practical effects on disputes arising in sport. The trend in professional sport is away from unincorporated associations, which still have something of the flavour of a private club, towards a modern corporate model conducive to sport being run on business lines. The Middlesex Cricket Club (MCC), founded in 1787 and at the time of writing (though perhaps not for much longer) still a private club, was formerly the governing body for cricket in England.[14] That would be difficult to contemplate now. The number of unincorporated associations is likely to diminish further in professional sport but will remain important in the amateur sports and in particular in the administration of sport at local level, exemplified by a village football team, perhaps sponsored by a local building company, playing in a local league within the county.

Constitution of International, National and Local Sports Bodies

2.19 What matters are regulated by the constitutional documents of a sports body? In England, if the body is incorporated as a company, its constitution must conform to Part 3 of the Companies Act 2006 (sections 17–38). In particular, it must have articles of association. If the body is unincorporated, its constitutional document or documents will have contractual effect, as already explained.

2.20 The constitutions of national and international sports bodies based in Switzerland or elsewhere outside England and Wales are governed by the law of the country where they are established. For example, the International Tennis Federation turns out to be ITF Limited (trading as the International Tennis Federation), a limited liability company with share capital of US $ 1,000, registered in New Providence, Bahamas under the International Business Companies Act 2000, a Bahamian statute; although its headquarters and

---

[13] [1954] 1 WLR 1005.
[14] In 1993 many of its international functions were transferred to the International Cricket Council, which now runs international cricket from Dubai. Its domestic functions passed to the then Test and County Cricket Board and then devolved on the England and Wales Cricket Board in 1997.

registered seat are in London and its constitutional documents, available on its website, contain all the usual provisions.[15]

2.21 The substantive content of a sports body's constitutional documents is likely to comprise or include the following. The list below is not a legal classification of types of constitutional provision; it is little more than a list, giving a non-technical account of the types of provision normally found.

Legal Nature of the Organisation: The constitution of a sports body will reveal what its legal nature is; whether incorporated or unincorporated, and if incorporated, whether it is a company limited by shares, or by guarantee, or some other legal entity such as (in England) an industrial and provident society, as the Rugby Football Union is.

Seat and Headquarters or Principal Place of Business: The constitutional documents normally include the geographical location of the organisation and—which may not be the same place—its juridical 'seat', ie the territory where it is based and whose laws will accordingly govern the operation of its constitutional documents.

The Organisation's Objects and Purposes: The objects and purposes for which the organisation is established will be stated: these are likely to include promotion and development of the sport concerned and advancement of its interests; preservation of its integrity and independence; performance of the functions of the sport's governing body; making, amending and enforcing the rules of the sport; and administering the organisation's finances.

Governing Organs: Normally, the organisation will have a governing council or assembly, typically consisting of the delegates of all the member associations or members, meeting in general meeting, either annually at the annual general meeting, or for a specific reason at an extraordinary general meeting. This body will have the function of voting on strategic matters and approving changes to the constitution by whatever majority is required, often two thirds. The day-to-day running of the organisation is typically undertaken by a much smaller executive body or board of directors, led by a President who acts as chairman, which meets more frequently, often monthly or when necessary. That body takes executive decisions and instructs the staff of the organisation as to their implementation.

Membership of the Organisation: The constitutional documents of the organisation will define those persons or other bodies eligible for membership or affiliation. There will often be different classes of member: for example, a national association might have in its membership regional bodies and smaller, local level bodies or individual clubs or players. An international governing body is likely to have different classes of member, often including confederations of national associations on a particular continent and their constituent national associations. Annual subscription fees are payable. The rights of different classes of members or affiliates are likely to differ according to their membership status. For example, in cricket, the test playing nations have greater control over decisions of the International Cricket Council than national cricket associations aspiring to join that élite but not yet granted the privilege. In tennis, there are classes of members with differential voting rights depending on whether they are regarded as sufficiently mature

---

[15] An unincorporated body, the International Tennis Federation, still exists; see Art 1 of the articles of association of ITF Ltd.

as tennis playing nations to have earned full voting rights, eg by being a 'Grand Slam' nation or having been a Davis Cup playing nation for a number of years.

2.22 Powers of the Governing Organs: The board of directors or executive is charged with management of the organisation, which it may delegate to committees and professional staff insofar as such delegation is provided for in the constitution. These powers include organisation, supervision and management of competitions; amending, upholding and enforcing the regulatory regime; determining access to competitions and any disciplinary issues arising from them; and administration of the organisation's finances.

Rules of the Organisation: The organisation's rules, according to which it is administered, are usually set out in a separate document called its rules, regulations, bye-laws, or some other similar term. These are not part of the constitutional structure of the organisation at its highest level. They sit beneath the constitutional provisions just outlined, and articulate the rights and obligations of the organisation's members as agreed in accordance with the organisation's constitutional procedures. They include the detailed content of the provisions governing access to competitions; the laws of the game; the organisation's anti-doping rules; the definitions of other disciplinary offences; the applicable range of sanctions where they are proved to have been committed; the methods of enforcing them, preferably by recourse to a tribunal independent of the organisation; the procedural rules governing proceedings before such a tribunal; its powers and duties; and any rights of appeal from it, at international level, often to the CAS; at domestic level, often to a tribunal specific to the sport concerned or (in this country) to a tribunal set up under the auspices of Sport Resolution UK, a dedicated sport dispute resolution organisation further mentioned in chapter eight.[16]

Governance in Sport: The Responsibilities of Governing Bodies

2.23 The responsibilities of sports governing bodies (SGBs) are so varied that they appear not so much a two faced Janus as a many-headed hydra. They are, whatever legal form they take, and whatever their origins, voluntary organisations. They were not created by or under statute (although as a matter of basic constitutional principle they could be regulated or even abolished by statute), and, although the Jockey Club, which controls horse racing in the United Kingdom, has a royal charter—the consequence of the exercise of a prerogative power—it could exist without it. Contract is the means by which they exert control over their members. Over non-members, they cannot exert control directly by contract, but do so by having a monopoly or near monopoly over a particular sport or competition. If a person wished to establish a rival body to the FA, he could in law do so; but the prospects of such body exercising any influence in the field of football would be nugatory.

2.24 The main consequence of this consensual basis for the authority of an SGB under English law—ie that its exercise of power is not amenable to judicial review, the procedure

---

[16] See para 8.168.

used to challenge the decisions of public authorities—is discussed in chapter eight.[17] But there is nonetheless judicial recognition that the similarities between SGBs and public authorities cannot be entirely overlooked. In *AEK Athens v UEFA*[18] a CAS Panel said:

> The Panel remarks that there is an evident analogy between sports-governing bodies and governmental bodies with respect to their role and functions as regulatory, administrative and sanctioning entities, and that similar principles should govern their actions.

However, Lord Denning MR stated:

> The rules of a body like this are often said to be a contract. So they are in legal theory. But it is a fiction. Putting the fiction aside, the truth is that the rules are nothing more or less than a legislative code, a set of regulations laid down by the governing body to be observed by all who are, or become, members of the association.[19]

Hence courts now apply public law standards to these private law bodies. They have a duty to act lawfully, rationally, fairly and proportionately in exercise of their plural powers, for whilst SGBs are autonomous bodies, they are nonetheless, also as a matter of basic constitutional principle, subject to the law of the land.

2.25 The first function of an SGB, its raison d'être, is to establish rules for the playing of the sport and to organise competitions in which participants will observe such rules. The rules will characteristically provide sanctions for their breach both internal to the match or competition (eg sending off, sin-binning, points docking) and subsequent to it (eg disqualification, suspension or fine). So SGBs also characteristically establish disciplinary machinery which has to pass the litmus test of natural justice.

2.26 The second function of an SGB, allied to the first, is the need to ensure the safety of both those who play the game and those who watch it. That function, conditioned by the law of tort, is also discussed in more detail in chapter five.[20]

2.27 National SGBs fit into a global sporting framework so that, for example, the FA is a member of and must be involved in the actions of the European body, UEFA, and the international body, FIFA. They also must liaise with various organs of government, which themselves have responsibilities embracing sport though not unique to it, with oft changing acronyms such as DCMS, DCSF, DCLG, and the Home Office and the Treasury; as well as quangos such as UK Sport.

2.28 Given that sport has graduated from a purely recreational activity to an economic one, SGBs will also be involved in the solicitation of sponsorship, and the sale of broadcasting rights.

2.29 While the tradition of self-governance is the hallmark of British sport, government is increasingly concerned about the way in which association football in particular is administered, prompting the FA to propose reforms, including a licensing system for clubs.[21]

---

[17] See paras 8.12–8.34.
[18] CAS 98/200, para 58.
[19] *Enderby Town FC v The FA* [1971] Ch 591, 606.
[20] See para 5.33 ff.
[21] *The Guardian*, 29 February 2012. See also *Football Governance: Response to the Culture, Media and Sport Committee Inquiry* (HC 792-1); *Government Reply to a Select Committee*, 12 October 2011 (Cm 8207).

Interpretation of the Rules of Sporting Bodies

2.30 Thus far we have concentrated, in our description of the framework of law regulating sport, on the legal nature of sporting bodies. We now consider briefly the way in which the rules of sporting bodies are and should be interpreted. Their interpretation is a matter of considerable importance. A court may have to determine the meaning and effect of contract terms found in the rules of such bodies. They are not necessarily interpreted in the same way as other kinds of contract terms found in other types of contract. The rules of sporting bodies are often drafted by lay people, not lawyers. This is changing, but many sports bodies, particularly smaller locally based ones, have not had their rules looked over by lawyers. Those which have are not guaranteed to have clearer rules, but may do. The CAS has on more than one occasion criticised a lack of clarity in the rules of a body appearing before it, referring in one case to 'drafting that engenders controversy'.[22] The task of construing the meaning of such rules is undoubtedly one for the court, and therefore cannot be left to the jury in an action for defamation.[23] The task of construction is not made any easier where additions and amendments have been made without reference to the structure as a whole.[24]

2.31 One thing at least is clear: the rules may not usurp the court's function of determining their meaning. Older rules of sporting and other associations, derived from times when such associations were less familiar with the risk of their rules being scrutinised in a court of law, frequently refer to the Chairman's decision on any matter of interpretation as 'final and binding', or some similar expression. Such provisions necessarily mean that the 'finality' of the association's own interpretation is subject to correct application of English law, if necessary determined by a ruling of the court.[25] The jurisdiction of the courts cannot be ousted save by statute. This does not prevent a body from providing in its rules that a dispute of a particular type must be submitted to arbitration. Such clauses have long been recognised as valid[26] and enjoy statutory recognition, most recently in the Arbitration Act 1996, as further explained in chapter eight.[27]

2.32 The rules of a sporting body should not be construed in too technical a manner, as though they are the words of a statute. They should be interpreted sensibly and in accordance with the spirit of the activity to which they apply. In the parallel field of trade union government, Lord Wilberforce commented:

---

[22] See *National Wheelchair Basketball Association v International Paralympic Committee*, CAS 95/122, paras 34–35. See also *Cullwick v FINA*, CAS 96/149, para 13; *Hall v FINA*, CAS 98/218, paras 19–20.

[23] See *Williams v Reason* [1988] 1 WLR 96, per Stephenson LJ at 104 (Welsh rugby union full-back's libel action in respect of an allegation that he had infringed the regulations of the International Rugby Football Board by writing a book for reward); cited also in Beloff, *Pitch Pool Rink ... Court? Judicial Review in the Sporting World* [1989] Public Law 95, 96–97.

[24] See also *Reel v Holder* [1981] 1 WLR 1226, per Lord Denning MR at 1231B–C ('one can argue to and fro on the interpretation of these rules ... the courts have to reconcile all the various differences as best they can').

[25] See *Chitty on Contracts*, 30th edn (Sweet & Maxwell, 2011) vol 1, para 16-045; *Lee v The Showmen's Guild of Great Britain* [1952] 2 QB 329, CA. Nor may CAS jurisdiction be ousted: *ITF v Korda*, CAS 99/A/223, applying an earlier decision of the English Court of Appeal in June 1999 (unreported) in the same case: *Korda v ITF*, CA, unreported, 25 March 1999, transcript, p 12E–F per Clarke LJ.

[26] *Scott v Avery* (1856) 5 HLC 811.

[27] See paras 8.128–8.147.

[Such rule books] are not drafted by parliamentary draftsmen. Courts of law must resist the temptation to construe them as if they were; for that is not how they would be understood by the members who are the parties to the agreement of which the terms, or some of them, are set out in the rule book, nor how they would be, and in fact were, understood by the experienced members of the court. Furthermore, it is not to be assumed, as in the case of a commercial contract which has been reduced into writing, that all the terms of the agreement are to be found in the rule book alone ...[28]

However, one should not take that proposition too far, for in another case Viscount Dilhorne took a more restrictive view:

I do not think that, because they are the rules of a union, different canons of construction should be applied to them than are applied to any other written documents. Our task is to construe them so as to give them a reasonable interpretation which accords with what in our opinion must have been intended.[29]

Although these two judicial statements of approach did not concern sporting bodies, the approach is similar in the sporting field. Thus, in *Cowley v Heatley*[30] Sir Nicholas Browne-Wilkinson V-C declined to interpret the French word 'domicil' in the sense of a legal term of art derived from the rules of private international law, preferring to treat it instead, in the context of its use in the rules of an international sporting body determining eligibility to compete in international competitions, as an ordinary word.[31] Likewise in the international sporting arena the CAS, interpreting anti-doping provisions contained in the rules of an international federation, adopted a 'purposive construction' of the relevant rules, stating that it was seeking to 'discern the intention of the rule-makers, and not to frustrate it'.[32]

2.33 From time to time the difficult question may arise as to what effect, if any, the legal form of a sporting association may have on the approach of the court required to interpret its rules. In principle, words used in the rules of such a body ought to mean the same thing irrespective of whether the body is a limited company or an unincorporated association; but allowance must be made for the tighter drafting often encountered in the case of the former than the latter. In one particular context the scope of the general duty to act fairly,

---

[28] *Heatons Transport v TGWU* [1973] AC 15, 100–1.

[29] *British Actors' Equity Association v Goring* [1978] ICR 791, 794–5. In *Burnley Nelson Rossendale and District Textile Workers' Union v Amalgamated Textile Workers' Union* [1987] ICR 69, at 74, Tudor Price J held that remarks of Lord Denning MR in *Goring* in the Court of Appeal did 'not suggest that the court should infer rules which do not exist, or assume that the parties intended something which, had they applied their minds to the problem, they might have intended'.

[30] *The Times*, 24 July 1986. See, more recently, *Irish Football Association v Football Association of Ireland, Kearns and FIFA*, CAS 2010/A/2071, [2011] ISLR, SLR 151, para 2: 'The interpretation of the statutes and rules of a sport association has to be objective and always start with the wording of the rule. The adjudicating body will have to consider the meaning of the rule, looking at the language used, and the appropriate grammar and syntax. The identification of the intentions of the association which drafted the rule will be further taken into consideration, as well as any relevant historical background and the regulatory context in which the particular rule is located ...'

[31] A similar approach was applied to the rules of the Rugby Football League in *Widnes RFC v Rugby Football League* (1995) unreported, Ch Div, Jonathan Parker J, 26 May. See also *R v British Basketball Association, ex parte Mickan* (1981) unreported, transcript 17 March, per Cumming-Bruce LJ at p 4: 'The ... Regulations ... have to be construed in the context of the object and structure of the Association.'

[32] *Cullwick v FINA*, CAS 96/149, paras 5.8–5.10, holding that prior notification of inhalation of a potentially permitted substance used to treat asthma was a precondition of its permitted status, and not merely a freestanding duty.

implied into the rules of sporting and other bodies exercising regulatory or disciplinary functions, has had to be considered with reference to the type of body exercising them. In *Gaiman v National Association for Mental Health*[33] Megarry J had to consider this issue in the context of a claim by scientologists that a resolution requiring them to resign, passed without complying with the principles of natural justice, was invalid, as was the provision in the Association's articles of association under which the resolution had been adopted. The Association was a company limited not by shares but by guarantee.

2.34 The judge rejected the submission that every member had a right to be heard before being expelled; an unusual and conclusion and one that is impossible to sustain as any kind of general proposition. His analysis proceeded mainly from consideration of the different types of body to which the tenets of natural justice have been held to apply or not to apply. He did not fully accept the scientologists' proposition that:

> … it would be odd if a club to which the principles of natural justice apply could be stripped of those principles merely because the club had been turned into a company limited by guarantee.[34]

He concluded that the position of corporations and clubs is different: in the former but not the latter case the governing council or directors of the corporation must exercise their powers bona fide in what they believe to be the interests of the corporation. However he added, importantly, that his conclusion might have been different if the case had been one in which the expelled members' livelihoods or reputations had been in question. That was not the position, since the Association's principal object was to work for the preservation and development of mental health, ie it operated in what would now be called the voluntary or third sector.

2.35 So far as Megarry J's conclusion turns on the proposition that the more is at stake for the person to whom the duty of fairness is owed, the more onerous is the duty, it is unobjectionable and consistent with a mass of other authority in fields as diverse as trade union law, the law relating to private clubs, and indeed sporting cases.[35] However, the decision was only one on a motion for interlocutory injunctions, not at full trial. So far as the judge's conclusion might turn on the proposition that a body could absolve itself from the obligation to observe natural justice by changing its legal form from that of a club to that of a company (whether limited by shares or by guarantee), the decision appears questionable. The committee of a club should be required as a matter of contract to act in the best interests of the club, as the directors of a limited company must act in support of the company's interests. We take the view that the content of the duty of fairness ought not to be influenced, particularly in sport, by the legal form of the body owing the duty; rather its content should depend on the subject matter under consideration and, especially, on whether a person's reputation or livelihood is at stake—as it clearly is in, for example, a case where doping, ball tampering or match fixing is alleged.[36]

---

[33] [1971] Ch 317.

[34] Ibid, 335D–E.

[35] The celebrated decision in *Russell v Duke of Norfolk* [1949] 1 All ER 109 was among the authorities cited, at p 336F of the decision.

[36] *Gaiman* was considered and applied without criticism or qualification by Lightman J in *Royal Society for the Prevention of Cruelty to Animals v Attorney General* [2002] 1 WLR 448, para 36, upholding the right of the RSPCA to operate a selective membership system which excluded from membership persons considered unlikely

Rights and Obligations Created by Contract

2.36 We now move away from the legal nature of the bodies that administer sport to consider the nature of the rules determining the content of rights and obligations in sport. Here we take a brief look at sports law from the perspective of a traditional 'horizontally minded' lawyer, dividing up the subject by reference to the well-known legal classifications of contract, tort and other renowned sources of law. We begin with the law of contract because it is the most important determinant of the content of variable legal relationships in sport. It is the legal tool with which the stage designers of sport create the scene; and it contains the script used by the sporting actors to play to the public.

2.37 Contract often, but not always, delineates the scope of rights of access to sporting competitions, which we consider in chapter three. It governs many aspects of the rights and obligations of players, coaches and officials vis-à-vis their club, as we shall discover in chapter four which is concerned with players' rights. Contract is usually the ultimate source of the regulatory jurisdiction of referees and governing bodies in sport, enabling the latter to determine the laws according to which sport is played (examined in chapter five), and the former to implement those laws on the field of play. The law of contract plays a pivotal role in determining the scope of rights to market and broadcast sporting competitions and associated merchandise. That aspect of the law is considered in chapter six. The law of contract is also of crucial importance in shaping and delimiting the punitive jurisdiction exercised by disciplinary bodies in sport, which we consider in some detail in chapter seven.

2.38 It is worth looking a little more closely at the nature of legal rules created by contract in the world of sport. Contractual relationships abound in sport. First, contracts of membership exist between individuals and the sports club or association of which they are members. If the body in question is unincorporated, then each of its members, by joining, will have entered into a contractual relationship—whether expressly, by signing a form, or perhaps impliedly, by conduct ie having notice of the rules and behaving as a member—on the terms of the rules of the club. Those rules may be amended from time to time in accordance with the proper constitutional procedures forming part of them. Provided that those procedures are properly followed, amendments to the rules will be binding in contract on the members without the need for express notice to each of them of any change.

2.39 In the case of an unincorporated members' club or association, the contractual relation of each member is with every other member of the club. There is thus a 'horizontal' matrix of contracts binding each member to all the other members. There cannot in such a case be a 'vertical' contract binding each member to the club itself, for the club itself has no legal existence, being unincorporated, as explained above. A simple example of such a body would be a local amateur golf club. There are probably hundreds of such clubs active in local sport throughout the United Kingdom. Indeed, until quite recently at least one of the top rugby union clubs, playing in the highest echelons of the game in England, was

to uphold and promote its aims and objectives; a conclusion unaffected by Art 11 of the European Convention (freedom of association) and the Human Rights Act 1998.

still an unincorporated club run on a traditional committee basis, underpinned in law by a horizontal matrix of contracts between the members.

2.40 We should note here the difference between an unincorporated sports club of the type just mentioned, and a proprietary club formed as a commercial venture to enable its members to take exercise at their leisure, for a price. There are now hundreds of fitness clubs in the private sector. Our readers will have noticed them and may have joined one.[37] Obviously, such an entity differs from a traditional sports club in that it exists not to promote competitive sport for its own sake, but to offer a service to its members in return for a subscription. A ten pin bowling club to which members resort for recreation and perhaps friendly competition, is another example of such a body. The difference between a members' club and a proprietary club is that a body of the latter type, such as a commercial sports club, is likely to be incorporated as a limited company and the members will enter into a contract of membership with that company 'vertically' and pay their subscriptions to it. They will not have any contractual obligations to fellow members unless and except to the extent that the rules so provide. Commercial sports clubs make an important contribution to social and leisure activity, but are not central to our account of sports law because they do not exist directly to promote any particular sporting competition.[38]

2.41 The notion of a 'web' or 'horizontal matrix' of contracts between persons with an interest in sport is not confined to the context of membership of a sporting association or club. The same contractual position may pertain in the case of participants in a particular sporting enterprise, or an individual competition. In *The Satanita*[39] the House of Lords ruled on a maritime collision claim between one competitor and another in the Mudhook Yacht Club regatta. The *Satanita* ran into and sank the *Valkyrie* in breach of the 18th rule of the competition. Their Lordships decided that the competitors were under a contractual liability, inter se, to observe the rules of the competition and, it followed, to make good all damage caused by a breach of those rules. This had the consequence that the crew of the *Satanita* could not avail themselves of a limitation of liability provision in section 54 of the Merchant Shipping (Amendment) Act 1862. The case is commonly cited as authority for the proposition that generally, in the case of a competition, 'competitors enter into multilateral contracts binding each to the others to observe the rules of the competition'[40]—despite the difficulty of analysing the process of entering into those

---

[37] Possibly on terms of the type ruled unfair by Kitchin J in *Office of Fair Trading v Ashbourne Management Services Ltd* [2011] EWHC 1237 (Ch), because designed to take advantage of the naivety and inexperience of the average consumer in overestimating predicated use of health and fitness facilities. Where contracts were for a minimum of 12–36 months, it was an unfair commercial practice contrary to the Consumer Protection from Unfair Trading Regulations 2008 (SI 2008/1277) to brand as 'defaulters', threatened by the club with registration of the default with credit reference agencies, those who terminated early. The payment terms were month by month. The judge noted, optimistically, that reasons for terminating early could include moving away from the area or other reasons besides sloth and loss of enthusiasm.

[38] Proprietary clubs are not required by law to be incorporated as companies, but frequently are. They are sometimes, under their rules, managed by a committee but the proprietor usually reserves to itself ultimate control; see *Halsbury's Laws* (n 9) vol 13, paras 209–10.

[39] Also sub nom *Clarke v Dunraven* [1897] AC 59, HL. The analysis in *The Satanita* was applied by the Supreme Court of New South Wales in *Raguz v Sullivan* (2000) 50 NSWLR 236 so as to hold a judoka bound into a matrix of contracts binding individuals, arising from a selection agreement between the Judo Federation of Australia and the Australian Olympic Committee, governing the selection of athletes for the 2000 Olympic Games in Sydney.

[40] *Chitty on Contracts* (n 25) vol 1, para 2-110.

contracts by reference to the traditional contract theory of offer and acceptance, familiar to first year law students.

2.42 So groups of people involved in sport may bind themselves to each other contractually, either in relation to the rules of a particular body or in relation to an individual competition administered by such a body. Yet in *Earl of Ellesmere v Wallace*[41] the Court of Appeal entertained a representative action in which representatives of the Jockey Club, then an unincorporated body,[42] successfully sought a declaration that contracts between entrants to horse races and the Club were not void as gaming and wagering contracts. The importance of that issue was that gaming and wagering contracts cannot be enforced, but if the contracts were valid, the Club would be able to recover the entry fee if an entrant did not pay it. By agreement the relevant contracts were treated as contracts between the race entrants and the Club, not between those entrants and other entrants, nor between all the members of the club inter se.[43] *The Satanita* was not cited to the Court of Appeal. However, 'on the pleadings questions were raised as to the party entitled to sue ... but these possible questions were not argued ...'[44] The case should not be regarded as authority for the mistaken proposition that an unincorporated club can sue in its own name; it cannot. The contracts under consideration were merely treated as having been made with the Jockey Club as a convenient shorthand to describe what, in strict legal analysis, should be described as a contract between the horse race entrant and each of the members of the Club.[45]

2.43 In the case of sporting bodies which are incorporated as companies, lack of contractual capacity does not arise. Consequently, directly enforceable horizontal contractual rights as between members to compel observance of the rules of the body do not assume the same analytical importance as in the case of unincorporated bodies. Mutual obligations between members may exist in relation to the rules of a particular competition or otherwise, depending upon the terms on which the body's rules are framed. In England, many of the most powerful governing bodies in sport are limited companies, including the Football Association (whose full title is the Football Association Limited) and the Premier League (the Football Association Premier League Limited). Under the corporate model, the incorporated sporting association can sue and be sued in its own name so that the representative action procedure described above is not necessary or permissible.

2.44 Each member of the body, by joining it, will enter into a 'vertical' contract with the limited company, agreeing by virtue of that contract to abide by the rules established from time to time pursuant to the constitutional documents establishing the company, namely its memorandum and articles of association.[46] Each member may also be a shareholder,

---

[41] [1929] 2 Ch 1, CA.

[42] The Jockey Club was founded in 1750 and was incorporated by royal charter in 1970 following a merger with the National Hunt Committee. It is the most influential commercial organisation in British horseracing. Its regulatory responsibilities were transferred to the Horseracing Regulatory Authority (now the British Horseracing Authority) in 2006.

[43] See *Earl of Ellesmere v Wallace* (n 41) pp 4–5: 'It was not disputed that the contracts made by nominating a horse were, so far as the plaintiffs or any of them were parties to them, contracts with the Jockey Club, and that the other plaintiffs between them could properly be treated as the Jockey Club for that purpose.'

[44] Ibid, 7, in the judgment of Clauson J.

[45] See also *Chitty on Contracts* (n 25) vol 1, paras 18-010 and 18-011 ('multilateral contracts'; 'sporting competitions').

[46] But in *Treherne v Amateur Boxing Association of England Ltd* [2002] EWCA Civ 381 the Court of Appeal upheld the refusal of an injunction to compel the ABAE to admit the Welsh Amateur Boxing Federation as a

often taking a nominal £1 share as a badge of membership, making him, her or it a member of the company in the company law sense of being a shareholder. All shareholders in a company are bound by contract to observe the company's rules, since its articles of association take effect as a contract between its members.[47] But the extent of the members' mutual obligations may be limited by the rules themselves. Thus where one club wishes to complain about another club in the league, there will normally be a contractual right to complain to the association about another member on specified grounds. The association may then have its own powers of adjudication; or it may have been given the power under its constitution to respond by taking disciplinary action against the member complained against; or both members may be bound by a rule of the association to submit the dispute to arbitration.

2.45 So much, then, for contracts binding sports bodies and their members. We move on to look briefly at contracts of employment between players and their club, and between other employees and their club. In individual sports such as tennis and boxing it would be highly unusual to encounter a contract under which the individual competitor is employed to practise his or her sport. Individual sportsmen and women are normally self-employed—like barristers, they work on a case-by-case, or tournament-by-tournament, basis. In team sports, however, the norm is that the players, the coach, the administrative and ground staff, and others such as catering staff, are all employed under contracts of employment requiring them to render service to their employer, the club, which will normally be a limited company.

2.46 At the highest level in professional team sports, particularly football, the terms of such contracts of employment dealing with remuneration have become highly favourable to players, whose negotiating position has become very strong. Negotiation of the terms of these contracts of employment is becoming something of a specialist legal discipline in its own right, ably offered by certain firms of solicitors in this country and elsewhere. Such contracts may be negotiated by players' agents, who themselves, if fortunate, will receive a lucrative cut often expressed as a percentage of the player's remuneration or of the fee for obtaining his services.[48]

2.47 The activities of players' agents in England are now the subject of detailed regulation, particularly in football, where agents are licensed on terms that bind them contractually to the rules of the Football Association, including its disciplinary rules incorporating mandatory arbitration provisions in 'rule K' which are effective to prevent an agent challenging the disciplinary process in the courts and do not infringe Article 6 of the European Convention on Human Rights.[49] Football agents are also regulated under regulations promulgated by FIFA, the world governing body for the sport. In *Piau v*

---

member, agreeing with the judge that the correspondence had not established a binding contract to admit the breakaway WABF. Both Garland J and the Court of Appeal would in any case have refused relief in the exercise of the court's discretion.

[47] Companies Act 2006, s 33(1): 'The provisions of a company's constitution bind the company and its members to the same extent as if there were covenants on the part of the company and of each member to observe those provisions.'

[48] As to agents' contracts see Miller, *Not Every Agent is a Bad Guy* (1996) 4(1) SLJ 36; Goldberg, *Football Contracts: Seeking the Best Deal for your Client* (1993) 1(3) SLJ 101.

[49] See *Stretford v The Football Association Ltd* [2007] EWCA Civ 238, [2007] ISLR, SLR 41, concerning disciplinary charges against the former agent of the footballer Wayne Rooney.

Commission of the European Communities and FIFA,[50] the Court of First Instance rejected a challenge by a French agent alleging that provisions in FIFA's rules regulating agents infringed competition law, in breach of (then) Article 81 of the EC Treaty, and were an abuse of FIFA's dominant position, contrary to (then) Article 82, in the market for the services of players' agents.

2.48 A contract of employment between a sports club and its playing and other staff brings into existence the ordinary common law obligations of the parties to such a contract to observe its terms. The employer's right to receive service, the employee's right to remuneration, the right of both parties in certain circumstances to treat the contract as terminated, on notice or by reason of a repudiatory breach of contract by the other party, are all normal incidents of the employment relationships found in the world of sport as elsewhere. These common law rights can be extremely valuable in the highest echelons of sport, where claims for very large sums may turn on whether the employee left of his or her own free will or was compelled to leave by the club; and if the latter, whether in circumstances entitling the employer to terminate.

2.49 These points may depend on the interpretation of conversations conducted in highly colloquial (and not always readily intelligible) language. Clubs wishing to dispense with their manager after a spell of poor results sometimes fail to appreciate the high threshold that must be reached before it can be said that the manager's conduct is 'gross misconduct' entitling the club to dismiss him. Without that threshold being reached, it is often very expensive to dismiss a manager, whose contract may entitle him to a substantial payout on a 'liquidated damages' basis, to compensate for loss of remuneration during the remainder of the fixed term. Recent well publicised examples of far-fetched allegations of misconduct failing miserably in legal proceedings can be found at Premiership level in football.[51]

2.50 Contracts of employment also act as the trigger for various statutory rights enjoyed by employees—ie by those employed under a contract of service—under English employment legislation, particularly the Employment Rights Act 1996. The scope of those statutory rights is a vast topic which it is not our task to explain in detail in this book.[52] Those statutory rights are, in the main, intended to benefit lower paid employees in more humble occupations in life than playing for Manchester United FC or managing Chelsea FC. The financial limits on compensation—with the important exception of cases involving discrimination on the ground of sex, race, disability, religious or philosophical belief, age and sexual orientation—are too low to be of more than passing interest to our most highly paid sporting figures. They are, however, of considerable interest to the lower ranking

---

[50] Case T-123/02, [2005] ECR II-209. For a detailed account of the regulation of players' agents, see chapter D4 in Lewis and Taylor (n 2), including the point made at D4.57 that a restraint of trade challenge to restrictions on players' agents' activities was left undetermined in the *Stretford* saga. A restraint of trade challenge to rules preventing 'tapping up' failed before a domestic tribunal in the *Ashley Cole* case (as determined by an FA Disciplinary Commission chaired by Sir Philip Otton on 1 June 2005).

[51] *Fulham FC (1987) Ltd v Tigana* [2004] EWHC 2585, Elias J, and [2005] EWCA Civ 895; *Kevin Keegan v Newcastle United FC Ltd*, Premier League Manager's Arbitration Tribunal, [2010] ISLR, SLR 1. Mr Keegan was awarded £2 million plus interest. Newcastle was also ordered to pay costs on an indemnity basis. A similar claim against Ipswich Town FC by its former manager, James Magilton, was taken out of the High Court Queen's Bench Division list a few days before the trial date in 2011.

[52] For a good detailed exposition, including the annotated text of the relevant statutes, see the looseleaf encyclopaedia, *Harvey on Industrial Relations and Employment Law* (LexisNexis, 1996).

members of staff employed by a club or league. Employment rights are touched upon in our discussion of the rights of players in sport (in the widest sense) in chapter four.[53]

2.51 In professional sport, contracts of employment between players and their club, and between officials and their club, often incorporate in their terms the rules under which the club operates within the sporting body of which it is a member. Indeed the rules of some sports require the contracts of players and managers to conform to the model prescribed by the rules. Thus, for example, football players, coaching staff and other club officials must abide by the rules of the FA and the league to which the club belongs. They must do so because the club that employs them is required by the rules of those bodies to which it in turn belongs to extract a contractual obligation on the part of its staff that they too undertake—though not themselves members of the FA or any league—to observe their rules. This is achieved by the promulgation of standard form contracts in a number of professional sports in the United Kingdom and elsewhere. Regulation of this type by the sporting body, limiting the freedom of the employing club and the player or official to negotiate their own terms, is common. However, the legal validity of such restrictions can sometimes be questioned, as we explain in chapter four.[54]

2.52 We have now mentioned two links in a chain of contracts—that between player and club, and that between club and league or association. We now move one link further up the chain and observe that the league or association may itself be connected by contract with other bodies, either within one country or operating internationally, namely leagues of leagues or associations of associations. The structure of the Olympic movement is a case in point. The National Olympic Committees are affiliated to the International Olympic Committee (IOC). Various national athletic federations are likewise members of the International Amateur Athletic Federation (IAAF).

2.53 A similar arrangement is found in football, in which the national associations in Europe are members of UEFA (a private limited company incorporated in Switzerland); those associations are bound to observe UEFA's rules and require observance of them by their own members; UEFA is in turn recognised by FIFA, along with the five other continental confederations representing, respectively, South America, Asia, Africa, North and Central America and the Caribbean, and Oceania. The national associations of those continental confederations are members of FIFA, and as such are bound by contract to require their member leagues and clubs at national and (where applicable) local level to adhere to the rules promulgated by FIFA.[55]

2.54 Such a chain of contractual obligations to observe rules emanating from the highest level within the sport concerned ensures the supremacy of the world governing bodies within their sphere of influence, and also marks out the territory of autonomy for

---

[53] See paras 4.52–4.72.

[54] See paras 4.40–4.44.

[55] An example of enforcement of a national association's duty to submit to the disciplinary regime of its continental confederation and international governing body occurred in April 2011, when FIFA and UEFA suspended the Football Federation of Bosnia-Herzegovina for non-adoption of new statutes replacing the system of a rotating presidency (under which the three ethnic groups in Bosnia—Serb, Croat and Bosniak—took turns to nominate a president) with a single president elected for four years. FIFA's statutes empowered removal from office of executive bodies of member associations 'under exceptional circumstances … in consultation with the relevant Confederation', and their replacement 'by a normalisation committee for a specific period'. The normalisation committee was charged with securing acceptance by the Federation's general assembly of revised statutes putting in place the single presidency model.

national and local or club level decision making in sport. Contract is the legal mechanism whereby local and national bodies in sport are obliged to comply with rules and rulings of their international sporting counterparts. In sports that are tightly structured, a matrix of interlocking contracts may need to be consulted by the sports lawyer in order to ascertain the extent of rights and obligations of a particular participant in the sport concerned.

2.55 It follows that a player or coach may be subject to the disciplinary jurisdiction of a sporting body with which he or she is not in a contractual relationship. The body may exercise jurisdiction by virtue of its contract with the player's club, and the player may owe a contractual obligation to the club to submit to the disciplinary jurisdiction of the sporting body. Or, alternatively, a direct contractual nexus between the two may, depending on the circumstances, be implied or inferred by treating the club as the agent of the individual for the purpose of constituting an ad hoc contract, inter alia, to submit to the body's disciplinary jurisdiction.

2.56 This phenomenon can lead to proceedings, of a type further discussed in chapters three and seven,[56] in which the player and his or her national association are on the same side of a dispute, pitted against the international association. The interests of the former may coincide with those of the player in a case where, for example, the national body has already acquitted the player of wrongdoing, and that acquittal is challenged on appeal by the international federation. This has occurred in several cases before the CAS in which national bodies have decided that players should not be banned in alleged doping cases, in circumstances where the player is shortly to compete in an international competition for his or her country; while the international federation concerned has sought to have the verdict overturned and secure a ban which will weaken the national side in a forthcoming competition.[57]

2.57 Alternatively, an international federation may simply disagree with the verdict of an independent arbitral tribunal established under its rules and appeal the decision to the CAS as provided for in the rules. Following the advent of the World Anti-Doping Code, discussed in chapter seven,[58] the World Anti-Doping Agency (WADA) now also has a right of appeal against decisions of sports arbitral tribunals applying its provisions.[59]

2.58 Lawyers and others involved in sport also need to be aware that contract law is of prime importance in the promotion of one-off or individual sporting events. This is particularly common in boxing, where attention is focused so closely on individual bouts between boxers that the sport lends itself to contracts governing particular fights rather than seasonally recurring competitions. An example of litigation arising out of such a contract can be found in *Lennox Lewis v World Boxing Council and Frank Bruno*.[60] A more

---

[56] See para 7.1 ff, *passim*.

[57] See, eg, *Quigley v Union Internationale de Tir*, CAS 94/129; *Lehtinen v FINA*, CAS 95/142. In *Quigley* the outcome directly affected the number of places open to the United States in an international shooting competition.

[58] See paras 7.213–7.224.

[59] For a recent example of such a challenge by a federation, see the International Tennis Federation and World Anti-Doping Agency's unsuccessful appeal to the CAS against the decision of an independent arbitral tribunal (chaired by one of the present authors) which had declined to impose a (disproportionate) two-year ban on a celebrated French tennis player inadvertently contaminated with a minute quantity of cocaine in a Miami night club, probably as a result of kissing a companion at the club: *ITF v Gasquet*; *WADA v ITF and Gasquet*, CAS 2009/A/1926 and 1930, 17 December 2009.

[60] (1995) unreported, Ch Div, 3 November, Rattee J. Mr Lewis attempted unsuccessfully to obtain an injunction preventing Frank Bruno and the World Boxing Council (WBC) from accepting a challenge to Mr Bruno made by Mike Tyson. Lennox Lewis subsequently became WBC world heavyweight champion.

recent falling out over money between the well-known boxing promoter Frank Warren and the sometime light heavyweight world champion Joe Calzaghe CBE set the stage for another round of litigation over contract based claims and counterclaims between Mr Calzaghe and Mr Warren, and a company controlled by him.[61]

2.59 Individual competitors will normally be found to have contractually bound themselves to abide by the rules of a competition, including disciplinary and anti-doping rules, by participating in the competition. The participant is normally required to sign appropriately worded undertakings to do so, as a condition of being allowed to compete. These are now likely to have the character of contractual obligations: see *Modahl v British Athletic Federation (in Administration)*.[62]

2.60 Still on the subject of contract in the law of sport, we now move away from contracts regulating the game itself, or employment within sport, and identify certain species of contract regulating commercial interests associated with sport. The first is the contract of sponsorship. Such a contract is found in two main forms. The first is a contract between a sportsman or woman, or a club, and a commercial body concerned to promote its products, whereby the sporting party undertakes certain obligations intended to assist in promoting the business of the commercial party, in return for financial support. The product of the sponsor may or may not be connected with sport. Examples of this type of contract are well known. Normally, they require a celebrated player or club to use exclusively the product of a particular manufacturer. Thus, the 1998 World Cup Final between France and Brazil was also, in a sense, between Adidas and Nike, with the victory going to France and Adidas at the expense of Brazil and Nike. The second type of sponsorship contract is one between two commercial bodies, of which at least one has some connection with sport, and each of which is concerned to promote its product. By the terms of the contract they agree to join forces in their promotion. For example, a radio sports commentator may be required to mention and endorse the product of the sponsor during the commentary, at intervals defined by the contract.[63]

2.61 Another species of commercial contract ancillary to sporting activity, but of critical importance to the financing of sport, is the contract regulating broadcasting rights. So important have these contracts become in relation to satellite television that they are now widely regarded as capable of determining the entire future, or lack of it, of particular sporting competitions, at least in highly paid professional team sports. A contract to allow broadcasting of a sporting event is, in its simplest form, no more than a licence to enter property coupled with the right to set up broadcasting equipment, and use it, on the

---

[61] *Calzaghe v Sports Network Ltd* [2009] EWHC 480 (QB), Wyn Williams J; *Warren v Calzaghe* [2010] EWCA Civ 1447, [2011] ISLR, SLR 147.

[62] [2002] 1 WLR 1192, CA. The reasoning of Latham LJ indicates that a contract will readily be inferred from participation in an event even if entry form formalities are not observed. See also the reported and unreported cases usefully gathered in Lewis and Taylor (n 2) A4.87–92, and in the CAS see also *Ohuruogu v UK Athletics Ltd*, CAS/2006/A/1165, 3 April 2007.

[63] See Steele, *Sponsorship Contracts; 'The Full Monty'* (1997) 5(3) SLJ 25; *Commercial Exploitation of Sport* (1998) 6(2) SLJ 59; Abramson, *Whose Rights Are They Anyway?* (1996) 4(3) SLJ 100; IAAF, *Sport and Law: Supplement*, ch 3 (Cooper: *Drafting of Sponsorship Contracts*), ch 5 (Barr-Smith: *Television*); Steele, *Personality Merchandising, Licensing Rights and the March of the Turtles* (1997) 5(2) SLJ 14; Ebsworth, *Reputations for Rent; Product Endorsement* (1997) 5(2) SLJ 34. *Conchita Martinez v Ellesse International SpA* (1999) CLY 861 (CA) involved the interpretation of a promotional contract for a sportswoman where payments were dependent upon world ratings.

property. However, allocation of broadcasting contracts has in the past been channelled through leagues and associations rather than individual clubs. The impact of this type of contract, and the subjection of such contracts to English and European Union law rules regulating competition and the freedom to provide services—in the economic, not the sporting sense—are examined in detail in chapter six of this book.[64]

2.62 Finally we must mention in passing the effect of contract on the rights of spectators at sporting events. The first important aspect of such contracts is that they determine whether, and on what terms, the spectator may have a right of admission, or a preferential right to purchase tickets for admission, to a sporting event. They may also determine the circumstances in which a club is entitled to refuse admission to a spectator who may believe he has a right of admission although he may arrive at the ground in possession of, say, numerous cans of lager or a wooden club. Secondly, the terms of a contract conferring a right of admission may have an effect on any claim the spectator may have in tort in the event that he or she is injured.[65] We will look further in chapter five at the effect such terms may have on claims in which personal injury is the cause of action.[66]

Sport and the Criminal Law

2.63 We now move away, at last, from the law of contract. The criminal law has a limited role to play in sport.[67] Those involved in it may be accused in disciplinary proceedings, or in criminal proceedings, or both, of conduct amounting to a criminal offence. Where crime and sport meet, the disciplinary function of the governing bodies overlaps with the state's role as enforcer of the criminal law. An example occurred in the 1990s when prosecutions were unsuccessfully brought in England against two goalkeepers and a businessman arising from an alleged plan to rig matches in return for money. At the time of writing, criminal prosecutions have recently led to convictions in London arising from alleged 'spot fixing' of test matches by Pakistan cricket players who have already received lengthy bans issued by an Anti-Corruption Tribunal (chaired by one of the authors).

2.64 Needless to say, criminal law is imposed and enforced by the state irrespective of any question of agreement between the parties. It is part of the general law of the land to which the most exalted sporting celebrities are as much subject as the humblest of hooligans.

2.65 The impact of the criminal law in sport is examined more fully in chapter five.[68] In all countries, the criminal law affects the practice of sport. However, even under a penal regime, what sporting participants have agreed is not wholly irrelevant. Perhaps the most important function of the criminal law in sport is to lay down distinctions

---

[64] See para 6.41 ff.

[65] See, eg, *White v Blackmore* [1972] 2 QB 651, CA, on the effect of an exemption clause where an accident occurred at a jalopy race meeting.

[66] See para 5.73.

[67] See R Beloff, *Fast Cars and Soccer Stars* [2000] ISLR 29. For an insight into corruption scandals afflicting sport in 2006, see Beloff, editorial [2006] ISLR 27.

[68] See para 5.87 ff.

between conduct which is tolerated in the context of sports involving physical contact—and would not necessarily be tolerated outside that context—and conduct sufficiently extreme as to transgress the criminal law irrespective of its sporting context[69] and, sometimes, irrespective of the consent of the victim. The criminal law also has a role to play in visiting with penal sanctions some very serious instances of violence on the field of play. Deliberate assault, as well as being a tort, is a criminal offence of varying gravity according to the seriousness of the injury inflicted.[70]

2.66 The criminal law also serves to outlaw corruption in sport, making punishable the fraudulent manipulation of sporting competition, including match fixing and other forms of corruption such as the payment of illegal 'backhanders' (in football parlance known as 'bungs', particularly if paid in cash, normally in an envelope and if so invariably a brown one). Criminal sanctions against offences involving corruption in sport are becoming increasingly important in an era of increasingly complex betting industry practices, high financial rewards and correspondingly greater temptations to err. Where the conduct complained of infringes the criminal law as well as any disciplinary rules to which the perpetrator is subject, the criminal courts have jurisdiction in the case additional to the jurisdiction of the relevant disciplinary bodies, and their powers of sanction are invariably greater. But obtaining a criminal conviction is difficult because of stretched state resources and the high standard of proof. Sports disciplinary bodies therefore have an important role to play in policing alleged wrongdoing and appointing independent tribunals to punish it where it is proved to the standard provided for in the rules—usually a lower standard than the criminal standard of proof beyond reasonable doubt.

2.67 The criminal law even prohibits some sporting activities altogether. We refer briefly in chapter five to some controversial forms of sport.[71] This leads naturally into a discussion *en passant* of the question of what a 'sport' actually is, a question which has not yet seriously taxed the intellectual powers of sports lawyers but may do so in the future when legal systems include fully developed doctrines of sports law.

The Law of Tort in Sport

2.68 Without the need for any contract, the law of tort imposes negative obligations on certain classes of persons for the protection of other classes of persons, creating a right in the victim to damages or, sometimes, an injunction in circumstances where the victim suffers injury or damage through the wrongful act of the other person, called the tortfeasor or wrongdoer. The law of tort is not particularly concerned with sport over and above

---

[69] See *R v Barnes (Mark)* [2004] EWCA Crim 3246, [2005] 1 WLR 910 (appeal against conviction for inflicting grievous bodily harm allowed; defendant was tackling opponent in football match; held, criminal prosecution of those who had inflicted injury on another in the course of a sporting event was reserved for those situations where the conduct was sufficiently grave to be properly categorised as criminal).

[70] See eg *R v Bowyer (David James)* [2001] EWCA Crim 1853; [2002] 1 Cr App R (S) 101: eight months' imprisonment for deliberate assault fracturing another rugby player's jaw, described by the recorder as 'off the ball thuggery'.

[71] See paras 5.13–5.15.

other forms of human activity, but an explanation of how tort law impacts on sporting activity is essential to a full account of the law relating to sport.

2.69 Torts occasioning personal injury require proof of deliberate assault or negligent infliction of injury. These are considered in chapter five.[72] The courts remain the final judges of conduct on and around the field of play, though where the conduct complained of occurs in the actual course of a match, judges have generally been reluctant to interfere, preferring to leave such matters in the hands of referees and disciplinary bodies. In the 1990s the English courts shifted away somewhat from their traditional pro-defendant approach, founded on the concept of acceptance of risk in the sporting arena, towards an approach which evinced a greater willingness than hitherto to hold participants in sport liable under the law of tort for physical injuries inflicted on the field of play. In the 2000s, a series of English judicial decisions involving recreational but not specifically sporting activities marked a swing of the pendulum back the other way, in the defendant's favour.

2.70 Economic torts are also relevant in sport. There the wrongdoing consists of a deliberate act, not involving a breach of contract towards the victim, causing economic loss. Claims of this type usually arise in the course of disputes over access to competitions and in that context are touched upon in chapter three,[73] or over transfers of players between clubs, dealt with in chapter four.[74] The essence of such a claim is usually the assertion that contractual relations are being interfered with. The relevant contract may be between a club and a player; between a league and a player; between a club and a league; or between any of the above and a commercial entity such as a sponsor or broadcasting company.

2.71 There are other torts which arise incidentally in the course of sport rather than as an intrinsic feature inherently likely to arise from the practice of sport. The best example is the tort of defamation, which is not specific to sport or different in the sporting field than in any other field, but which periodically gives rise to well publicised cases involving celebrated and notorious sporting figures. We do not consider that defamation merits separate treatment in its application to sport in a book such as this, and we therefore touch on it only in passing.

Public Law Principles in Sport

2.72 We consider in chapter eight the controversial question of the extent to which sports law is public in character, and thus deserving of inclusion within the framework of administrative law. In England, the development of legal doctrine in the sporting field has, in some of the most important cases, occurred at the very frontier between public and private law.[75]

---

[72] See para 5.33 ff.
[73] See paras 3.37–3.41.
[74] See para 4.18 ff.
[75] Examples are *Nagle v Fielden* [1966] 2 QB 633, CA; *McInnes v Onslow-Fane* [1978] 1 WLR 1520; *R v Disciplinary Committee of the Jockey Club, ex parte Aga Khan* [1993] 1 WLR 909, CA; *Stevenage FC Ltd v The Football League Ltd*, transcript, 23 July 1996, belatedly reported at [2006] ISLR, SLR 128, and CA (1997) 9 Admin

2.73 During the period in which the law of England and Wales came to include a developed system of administrative law, uncertainty dogged lawyers and the courts as to whether, and if so to what extent, rights of participation in sport and the right to fairness in sport, should form part of that body of administrative law, or should be treated as separate from it and concerned only with private rights. The present position, in England, is that the rights in question are treated as private in nature, but their content is the same as rights arising in public law. Therefore, they must be vindicated in a private law action and not in an administrative law judicial review. But it is not clear that the last word has been said on the subject.

2.74 It is no coincidence that sports cases made a major contribution to the debate over the nature of public rights during the formative period of English administrative law in the last 30 years or so of the twentieth century. The vitality and importance of sport as a force in modern society bears a direct correlation to the place occupied by celebrated sporting cases in the development of our conception of public and private rights—and what in some cases can now even be called human rights where the European Convention (to which we return very shortly) is engaged.

2.75 We set out more fully in chapter eight[76] our reasons for continuing to question the current orthodox view that rights in sport are merely private in character. If they were, they would principally arise merely as a matter of contract; yet in *Nagle v Fielden* there was no contract but the court was prepared to countenance the granting of relief against an unfairly discriminatory practice in sport affecting a woman's ability to ply her trade as a trainer of horses.

2.76 The question of whether and if so how sports law overlaps with public law is of great importance from the standpoint of a theoretical foundation for sports law.[77] But it is not just an academic question. We also consider in chapter eight the practical effects in sport of the present state of the law which normally denies judicial review as a remedy in sports law, with consequential ramifications for the form of proceedings, time limits and the types of remedy available.[78]

Statute Law and Sport

2.77 This is a short topic, for the role of legislation in sport is, in the United Kingdom, relatively slight. Indeed, we have already pointed out in chapter one that the absence of frequent legislative intervention in sport is one of the features that differentiate sports law from other activity based branches of the law. In England, domestic statute impacts

---

LR 109; *Flaherty v National Greyhound Racing Club Ltd* [2005] EWCA Civ 1117; [2006] ISLR, SLR 8; *R (Mullins) v Jockey Club Appeal Board (No 1)* [2005] EWHC 2197, [2006] ISLR, SLR 30; and *Mullins v McFarlane* [2006] EWHC 986 (QB), [2006] ISLR, SLR 65.

[76] See para 8.12 ff; see also brief mentions in chapters 3 and 7, paras 3.63 and 7.1–7.7.
[77] See Kerr, *Disciplinary Regulation of Sport: A Different Strand of Public Law?* in Bogusz, Cygan and Szyszczak (eds), *The Regulation of Sport in the European Union* (Edward Elgar, 2007) ch 5, pp 97–106; Kelly, *Judicial Review of Sports Bodies' Decisions: Comparable Common Law Perspectives* [2011] ISLR 71.
[78] See paras 8.12–8.34.

little on sporting activity. This reflects the traditional laissez-faire attitude of the state, which usually proceeds from the premise that politicians should not run sport and that self-regulation should prevail where possible.

2.78 It is elementary that rules created by statute are superior to all other sources of law in the United Kingdom; but our legislators are not disposed to use their powers to impose a code of sports law from the top downwards. There is no sign that Parliament is willing to take the lead in legislating widely in the sporting field. The role of government is that of facilitator, providing funding and helping to create the conditions for sport to take place with the participation of private capital, most notably for the 2012 Olympics in London. The other area of importance in which the state has, in this country, intervened in recent years, is that of public safety and public order. We consider briefly in chapter five such legislation as has been enacted in England in support of those policy objectives.[79] We are certainly no advocates of wholesale statutory regulation in sport. It does not follow that the lack of it leads to the conclusion that sport is a purely private matter.

Protection of Children in Sport

2.79 There is no specific legislation dealing with the protection of children who participate in sport.[80] At a statutory level, therefore, the protection of children is therefore governed by the law of obligations (tort and contract) and the body of legislation relating to the protection of children in general[81] and at a practical level to the codes of the SGBs. A decade ago it could be said that 'there is little quantitative evidence of the prevalence of sexual abuse in sport'.[82] The existence of the problem is now well recognised since sport provides ample opportunity for physical contact between adults and children.

2.80 The child protection regime in the United Kingdom is based around Part V of the Children Act 1989.[83] It makes provision for the protection of children at risk. It imposes specific duties on local authorities to investigate where they have reasonable cause to suspect that a child is suffering or is likely to suffer significant harm,[84] and in other circumstances[85].

2.81 If attempts to have a child examined or assessed voluntarily fail, an application may be made to the court for a child assessment order which will require the child to be produced and made available for assessment in accordance with directions given by the

---

[79] See paras 5.19–5.32.
[80] Boocock, *Child Protection in Sport*, WSLR 1/3, p 3; Gray, *Swimming and Child Protection: The Story So Far* (1994) 2(2) Sports Law Bulletin 8–9; Lewis and Taylor (n 2) D7; Gardiner, Felix, O'Leary, James and Welch, *Sports Law* (Cavendish, 1997) 140–8.
[81] For the principles of a child's right to freedom from harmful treatment and its foundations in international law, see MacDonald, *The Rights of the Child: Law and Practice* (Family Law, 2011) ch 15.
[82] McArdle, *From Boot Money to Bosman: Football, Society and the Law* (Cavendish, 2000) 215–17.
[83] Ie the Children Act 1989 Part V (ss 43–52) (as amended).
[84] Ibid, s 47(b).
[85] Ibid, s 47(a).

court.[86] The court may, in certain circumstances, make an emergency protection order authorising the removal of the child, or the prevention of the child's removal, along with the power to include an exclusion requirement and certain other ancillary powers, for a limited period.[87] A power is conferred on the police to take a child into protection,[88] and the Children Act 1989 confers powers of entry and search[89] and provides that the court may, in certain circumstances, make a recovery order in respect of a child.[90]

2.82 In support of these provisions the Children Act 1989 creates criminal offences relating to the wrongful removal of children.[91]

2.83 However, despite the obligation on local authorities to investigate where they have reasonable cause to suspect that a child is suffering or is likely to suffer significant harm,[92] there is no law in the United Kingdom that requires sports organisations, sports professionals or any other persons to report their suspicions to the authorities.

2.84 We look more closely at the content of the substantive law requiring the protection of children engaged in sport in the concluding part of chapter four.[93]

Application of European Union Law to Sport

2.85 European Union law is of considerable importance in the regulation of sport. Two aspects of its application should be distinguished.

2.86 First, various substantive provisions of EU law have had a substantial impact upon sport. Most notably, Article 45 TFEU[94] enacts the principle of the free movement of workers within the EU; Article 49 provides for a right of establishment of EU nationals in other Member States; and Article 56 prohibits restrictions on the freedom to provide and receive services. These provisions assume considerable significance in our narrative in chapter three concerning access to sporting competitions and chapter four on the law relating to players' rights. Also of great importance are the competition rules contained in Articles 101 and 102 TFEU, which are mirrored domestically in the Competition Act 1998. These provisions play a central role in the law relating to broadcasting and marketing, discussed in chapter six.

2.87 Second, the EU institutions have in recent years been developing their own policy in relation to the role of sport in the EU. Their efforts have been fortified by the enactment in the Lisbon Treaty of a new provision conferring for the first time on the EU a

---

[86] Ibid, s 43.
[87] Ibid, s 44, s 44A (as added), s 44B (as added), s 45 (as amended).
[88] Ibid, s 46.
[89] Ibid, s 48.
[90] Ibid, s 50.
[91] Ibid, s 49.
[92] Ibid, s 47(b).
[93] See para 4.73 ff.
[94] Treaty on the Functioning of the European Union, which came into force when the Lisbon Treaty was ratified and which resulted in a further renumbering of the Articles of the EC Treaty.

formal competence in relation to sport. Article 165 TFEU provides (so far as is material) as follows:

(1)   … The Union shall contribute to the promotion of European sporting issues, while taking account of the specific nature of sport, its structures based on voluntary activity and its social and educational function.

(2)   Union action shall be aimed at: … developing the European dimension in sport, by promoting fairness and openness in sporting competitions and cooperation between bodies responsible for sports, and by protecting the physical and moral integrity of sportsmen and sportswomen, especially the youngest sportsmen and sportswomen. …

(3)   The Union and the Member States shall foster cooperation with third countries and the competent international organisations in the field of education and sport, in particular the Council of Europe.

Article 165(4) goes on to provide for the institutions to adopt 'incentive measures' and 'recommendations' in order to contribute to the objectives set out in the Article. They are not permitted, however, to adopt measures harmonising the laws of the Member States.

2.88 This provision has resulted in the EU institutions having a legislative basis, albeit a 'soft' one, for implementing an EU sports programme supported by a budget. A blueprint for this programme is to be found in the White Paper on Sport published by the European Commission in July 2007. This was accompanied by a detailed Staff Working Document entitled *The EU and Sport: Background and Context.*[95] The purpose of the White Paper is summarised at paragraph 1 as being:

> … to give strategic orientation on the role of sport in Europe, to encourage debate on specific problems, to enhance the visibility of sport in EU policy-making and to raise public awareness of the needs and specificities of the sector. The initiative aims to illustrate important issues such as the application of EU law to sport. It also seeks to set out further sports-related action at EU level.

2.89 The White Paper goes on to highlight significant issues and set out further action under three headings. The first, 'The societal role of sport', canvasses various initiatives such as the encouragement of physical activity as a health enhancing measure;[96] the participation of the EU in the fight against doping;[97] enhancing the role of sport in education and training;[98] and strengthening the prevention of and fight against racism and violence.[99] The second, 'The economic dimension of sport', envisages information-gathering activities designed to measure the economic impact of sport,[100] as well as measures designed to place economic support for sport on a more secure footing, such as the maintenance of the possibility of reduced VAT rates for sport.[101] The third category of initiatives covers 'The organisation of sport'. The Commission expresses the view that it can play a role in promoting good governance in sport and, to that end, will combat discrimination based on nationality in sport through dialogue and infringement

---

[95] SEC(2007) 935.

[96] Para 2.1.

[97] Para 2.2. For example, by supporting the development of partnerships between the law enforcement agencies of the Member States.

[98] Para 2.3.

[99] Para 2.6. For example, by analysing the possibilities for new legal instruments and EU-wide standards to prevent public disorder at sports events.

[100] Para 3.1.

[101] Para 3.2.

procedures.[102] The Commission will also focus on player transfers and the promotion of transparency in that context,[103] as well as on the issues surrounding players' agents in relation to which it will carry out an impact assessment in order to evaluate whether action at EU level is warranted.[104] This category also covers the protection of minors within sport;[105] corruption, money laundering and other financial crime;[106] licensing systems for clubs;[107] and media.[108]

2.90 Paragraph 5 of the White Paper explains how the Commission intends to follow up on these various initiatives, through structured dialogue with sport stakeholders and cooperation with the Member States. All of the actions to be taken by the Commission under the White Paper form the 'Pierre de Coubertin' Action Plan, which will guide the Commission in its sport-related activities over the coming years.

2.91 To what extent does EU law apply to sport? Like English law, EU law recognises an area of autonomy for the organisers of sport, within which the law will not interfere. However, the effect of the ECJ's judgment in *Meca-Medina*[109] is that fewer sport-related cases will fall outside the scope of EU law. The case concerned a complaint by two professional long distance swimmers who challenged the compatibility with Articles 101 and 102 TFEU[110] of the anti-doping rules adopted by the International Olympic Committee (IOC) and implemented by the swimming governing body, FINA. Both the Commission and the Court of First Instance had held that the competition provisions did not apply because the anti-doping rules in question were rules relating to questions of purely sporting interest and had nothing to with economic activity.[111] The ECJ rejected this approach and set aside the CFI's judgment. It laid down the following principles, which are of great importance in determining when a sport-related case might fall outside the scope of EU law.

2.92 The ECJ began by referring back to its earlier case law concerning the free movement provisions. Those provisions apply to sport insofar as it constitutes an economic activity. However, they do not 'affect rules concerning questions which are of purely sporting interest and, as such, have nothing to do with economic activity'.[112] More specifically, the provisions concerning the free movement of persons and the freedom to provide services 'do not preclude rules or practices justified on non-economic grounds which relate to the particular nature and context of such sporting events'. However, 'such a restriction on the scope of the provisions in question must remain limited to its proper objective. It cannot, therefore, be relied upon to exclude the whole of a sporting activity from the scope of the Treaty.'[113] It follows that 'the mere fact that a rule is purely sporting in nature does

---

[102] Para 4.2.
[103] Para 4.3.
[104] Para 4.4.
[105] Para 4.5.
[106] Para 4.6.
[107] Para 4.7, including the promotion of dialogue with sports organisations in order to address the implementation and strengthening of self-regulatory licensing systems.
[108] Para 4.8.
[109] Case C-519/04P *Meca-Medina and Majcen v Commission* [2006] ECR I-6991.
[110] Then Arts 81 and 82 EC.
[111] The CFI's judgment is reported at [2004] ECR II-3291.
[112] Para 25.
[113] Para 26.

not have the effect of removing from the scope of the Treaty the person engaging in the activity governed by that rule or the body which has laid it down'.[114]

2.93 Having thus circumscribed the limits of the so-called 'sporting exception' in the context of the free movement provisions, the Court turned to Articles 101 and 102 TFEU. It held that the application of these provisions must be considered separately. Consequently, even if sport-related rules 'do not constitute restrictions on freedom of movement because they concern questions of purely sporting interest and, as such, have nothing to do with economic activity … that fact means neither that the sporting activity in question necessarily falls outside the scope of [Articles 101 and 102 TFEU] nor that the rules do not satisfy the specific requirements of those articles'.[115]

2.94 The scope of application of the free movement rules and the competition rules to sport are examined further in chapters four and six.[116]

European Convention on Human Rights

2.95 The Human Rights Act 1998 (HRA) enables victims of a breach of rights guaranteed by the ECHR to seek remedies in the domestic courts.[117] Claims can only be brought against public authorities, and the orthodox view is that sports governing bodies themselves do not satisfy the statutory definition, which includes any person 'certain of whose functions are functions of a public nature'.[118] The soundness of the view has yet to be tested at the level of the Supreme Court.[119]

2.96 The definition of public authorities includes courts and tribunals, the latter extending to 'any tribunal in which legal proceedings may be brought'.[120] The internal disciplinary tribunals of sports governing bodies are again unlikely to qualify because of an absence of a public dimension.[121] The National Anti-Doping Tribunal, however, may well do so because of the circumstances of its creation.[122] Courts certainly qualify and their consequent obligation to act compatibly with Convention rights itself means that those rights may fall to be considered in a sporting context.[123] The particular rights have (differing) potential relevance in sport.

---

[114] Para 27.

[115] Para 31.

[116] See paras 4.14 ff, 6.2 ff.

[117] See generally, for a prospective survey, UK Sport, *Human Rights Act—Implications for Sport*, 14 December 2000; Boyes, *The Regulation of Sport and the Impact of the Human Rights Act 1998* (2000) 6(4) European Public Law 517, 523–4; Boyes, *Regulating Sport after the Human Rights Act* (2001) 151 New Law Journal 444; Sithamparanathan and Himsworth, *Are Sporting Bodies Abusing Human Rights?* (2003) 11(3) SLJ 138; for an interim survey see Hedley-Dent and Wilde, *Sporting Rules and the Human Rights Act: Current Position*, WSLR 5/6.

[118] HRA, s 6(2): see Wood, *Sports Governing Bodies* (1993) 1(6) Sports Law Bulletin 5; *R v Jockey Club, ex parte Aga Khan* [1993] 1 WLR 909; *Bradley v Jockey Club* [2004] EWHC 2164 (QB), [2006] ISLR, SLR 1; *R (Mullins) v Appeal Board of the Jockey Club* [2005] EWHC 2197 (Admin).

[119] Beloff and Kerr, *Why Aga Khan is Wrong* [1996] Judicial Review 30; *R v Jockey Club, ex parte RAM Racecourses* [1993] 2 All ER 225.

[120] HRA, s 6.3(a).

[121] See also *Rubython v FIA*, transcript, 6 March 2003, QBD, Gray J.

[122] *Gibbs v National Anti-Doping Panel*, CAS 2010/A/2230, paras 4.1–4.14, 10.4, fn 5.

[123] *Stretford v The Football Association Ltd* [2007] EWCA Civ 238, [2007] ISLR, SLR 41.

2.97 Article 4 prohibits slavery and forced labour. This Article was, albeit unsuccessfully, relied upon in a Dutch case concerning the transfer system. The European Commission of Human Rights (ECommHR) dismissed the claim as manifestly ill-founded on the basis that the player's contract with his club, which denied him the right to play for another club during its subsistence, was not 'oppressive'.[124]

2.98 Article 6 provides for the right to a fair trial in both civil and criminal contexts. The concepts of 'criminal charge' and 'civil rights and obligations' are autonomous—ie the definitions are for the Strasbourg organs, not for the national law of Member States of the Council of Europe (which include the United Kingdom).[125] The touchstone for the latter is where the body against whom a claim is brought *determines* civil rights and obligations. Although the European Court of Human Rights has declined to rule on whether disciplinary charges *ratione materiae* fall into the civil or criminal category,[126] disciplinary charges, if of a sufficiently serious nature or with sufficiently serious consequences, may be treated as analogous to criminal charges[127] and hence the protections particular to criminal charges, ie freedom from self-incrimination,[128] the presumption of innocence,[129] and the Article 6.3 procedural guarantees, may be engaged. In any event, as a matter of common law sports disciplinary bodies are obliged to act fairly.[130]

2.99 The rights common to both the civil and criminal contexts are those of access to a court or tribunal,[131] which is independent[132] and impartial;[133] enjoys sufficient jurisdiction over fact and law;[134] provides, albeit subject to exceptions, for a public and hence oral hearing[135] within a reasonable time;[136] and pronounces judgment publicly. Overall the trial must be fair,[137] and must satisfy the principle of equality of arms.[138]

2.100 Article 8 guarantees, subject to listed exceptions, the right to respect for private and family life.[139] The concept of private life is extensive. In the sporting context it is relevant to the enforcement of anti-doping policy, including the obligation to submit to out-of-competition testing,[140] the tests themselves involving the taking of urine and

---

[124] Application 9322/81, *X v Netherlands* 32 DR 180.
[125] *Re Westminster Property Management Ltd (No 1), Official Receiver v Stern* [2000] 1 WLR 2230, CA.
[126] *Albert & Le Compte v Belgium* (1982) 5 EHRR 533; *Re Westminster Property Management Ltd*, ibid.
[127] Ibid.
[128] *Saunders v UK* (1996) 23 EHRR 313.
[129] *Salabiaku v France* (1988) 13 EHRR 379, para 28; *R v DPP, ex parte Kebeline* [2002] 2 AC 326, 378–80.
[130] For the fundamental ingredients of a fair disciplinary process for sporting bodies see *Dispute Guidance*, available at the time of writing at www.sportresolutions.co.uk. It is particularly important that their rules as to both substance and procedure in the disciplinary context should be clear: *USA Shooting and Quigley v UIT*, CAS 94/129, para 34. See also *Mullins v McFarlane* [2006] EWHC 986 (QB), [2006] ISLR, SLR 65.
[131] *Golder v UK* (1975) 1 EHRR 524.
[132] *Bryan v UK* (1995) 21 EHRR 342, para 37.
[133] *Piersack v Belgium* (1982) 5 EHRR 169, para 30.
[134] *Albert & Le Compte v Belgium* (1982) 5 EHRR 533, para 29.
[135] *Pretto v Italy* (1983) 6 EHRR 182, para 21.
[136] *Dyer v Watson* [2002] 3 WLR 1488, [2004] 1 AC 379, PC.
[137] *Barbera v Spain* (1988) 11 EHRR 360, paras 68 and 69.
[138] *De Has v Belgium* (1997) 25 EHRR 1, para 53.
[139] Art 8(2).
[140] See Pendlebury and McGarry, *Location, Location, Location: The Whereabouts Rule and the Right to Privacy* [2009] Cambrian Law Review 63.

blood samples,[141] methods used for gender identification[142] and the confidentiality of the names of sportspersons who are the subject of tests, unless and until any allegations against them have been proved. It is also engaged where the media or others seek to disclose details of a sportsperson's private, usually sexual, life and there is no countervailing public interest.[143] Specific rules of sports bodies restricting sexual relationships between coach and adult trainee have survived a challenge in arbitral proceedings.[144] Hunting, however, being a public activity, is not within the ambit of Article 8.[145]

2.101 Article 9 guarantees, subject to exceptions, the right to freedom of thought, conscience and religion; this right includes freedom to worship and manifest one's religion or belief alone or with others, in public or in private. Its impact on sport is limited: dress codes promulgated in the interests of safety must take account of religious sensibilities[146] and the scheduling of sporting events must take account of holy days. Sportsmen such as (historically) Eric Liddell and Jonathan Edwards who objected to competing on a Sunday might have had a prima facie, if defeasible, claim.

2.102 Article 10 guarantees, subject again to listed exceptions,[147] freedom of expression. Dress constitutes expression[148] so that the rules as to participants' clothing in competition would require justification, no doubt easily provided. Restrictions on managers, officials and players speaking to organs of the media in a manner calculated to bring the sport into disrepute, characteristic in many sporting contexts, would also require justification,[149] although it has been held that there is no interference where an individual has contractually agreed to limit such right.[150] The Jockey Club failed, because of public interest considerations, to restrain the BBC from broadcasting information by a former director of the Club.[151]

2.103 Article 11 guarantees, subject to listed exceptions, freedom of peaceful assembly and association. The right to form such bodies as the Professional Football Players Association is thus protected. The Article does not, however, protect the right to gather for sporting purposes.[152]

---

[141] Beloff and R Beloff, *Blood Sports—Blood Testing, The Common Law and Human Rights* [2000] 2 ISLR 43; Rigozzi, Kaufmann-Kohler and Malinverni, *Doping and Fundamental Rights of Athletes* [2003] ISLR 61; cf *O'Hallaren v University of Washington*, 679 F Supp 997 (1988); Hislox, *Anti-Doping Policy after the Human Rights Act* (2004) 12(2) SLJ 12.

[142] Worley, *An Alternative to the IOC's Gender Testing Policy*, WSLR 8/2, p 10—a plea for its abolition.

[143] *A v B plc* [2003] QB 195, CA; *John Terry v Persons Unknown* [2010] EMLR 16. Footballers are said to be the major beneficiaries of super injunctions. *JLH v Newsgroup Newspapers Ltd* [2011] EWCA Civ 42; Burnett and Smith, *Super Injunctions and Use of the Protection of Privacy*, WSLR 8/10, p 8; Felstead, *Public Figures and Private Lives*, WSLR 3/5, p 6.

[144] See Hedley-Dent and Wilde (n 117). In *A v B plc* [2003] QB 195 the Court of Appeal set aside an injunction restraining the Captain of Blackburn Rovers from disclosure of his extra-marital affairs on the ground that he was a role model and so there was a public interest in his off-field activities. The case has not proved to be a precedent.

[145] *R (Countryside Alliance) v Attorney-General* [2006] 1 AC 719.

[146] Cottrell, *Freedom of Religion and Rules on Safety*, WLSR 8/2 p 12.

[147] Grove and Parks, *Sanctioning Ex-Athletes for Autobiographical Revelations*, WSLR 8/2, p 4.

[148] Application 11674/85, *Stevens v United Kingdom* (1986) 46 DR 245 (European Commission).

[149] Ionnaides and Alderman, *Freedom of Expression and Public Criticism of Officials*, WSLR 9/4, p 11.

[150] Application 11308, *Vereniging Rechtswinkels Otvrecht v Netherlands* (1986) 46 DR 200.

[151] *Jockey Club v Buffham* [2003] QB 462, Gray J.

[152] *R (Countryside Alliance) v Attorney-General* [2008] 1 AC 719, per Lord Hope at paras 56–58, and Baroness Hale at paras 118–20.

2.104 The justification for any interference with qualified rights such as those guaranteed by Articles 8–12 has to satisfy three tests: being within the sphere of one of the specified exceptions; legality (in terms of compliance with both the domestic law and general principles of law such as accessibility and precision); and necessity in a democratic society. The test of necessity equates to one of 'pressing social need' and requires that the means employed must be proportionate to the specified aim pursued.[153]

2.105 Article 14 guarantees freedom from discrimination on grounds of status only insofar as it impinges on another Convention right.[154]

2.106 Article 1 of the First Protocol guarantees the right to property,[155] which includes a wide range of economic interests. In principle the grant (possibly) or removal (certainly) of permits, licences and other items connected with participation in sports-related activities falls within the ambit of this provision. However, it has been held in another jurisdiction that prevention of employment in a sport or hobby is not deprivation of a possession.[156]

---

[153] *Sunday Times v UK* (1979) 2 EHRR 245, para 59.

[154] In *R (Countryside Alliance) v Attorney-General* [2008] 1 AC 719 it was held that being a huntsman was not a status.

[155] *Sporrong & Lonroth v Sweden* (1992) 5 EHRR 35, para 61.

[156] *Re Chalmers Brown's Application for Judicial Review* (2003) NICA 7 per Carswell LJ. See too *R (Countryside Alliance) v Attorney General* [2008] 1 AC 719. The Hunting Act 2004 was not a confiscatory measure but insofar as eg landowners lost control over their land by their inability to hunt on it, this was justified by considerations of animal welfare.

3

Access to Sporting Competitions

Introduction: Entry Criteria in Sport

3.1 In this chapter we seek to explain the content of the law that determines directly whether or not a particular individual, or a particular club in the case of team sports, may or may not take part in a particular competition, or generally in competitions administered by a particular sporting body. We are not concerned in this chapter to give an account of the rules governing entitlement to participate in sport arising indirectly, through the medium of an employment or similar relationship between a player and a club. In those cases it is the club that is the primary competitor; the player's right to compete arises only indirectly, if he is selected to play by the club that employs his services and that itself is eligible to take part in particular competitions. Rights in sport arising indirectly in this way are examined below in chapter four, under the heading of players' rights.

3.2 We are concerned here to consider the existence or otherwise of direct rights to compete (and in some cases, obligations to compete) which the law, in certain circumstances, gives to individual players or, in the case of team sports, to clubs. The question of whether and when such rights exist is a matter of profound importance to competitors and sports administrators alike. It is often taken for granted that, for example, the winner of the football Championship is entitled to compete in the Premier League the following season, or that the winner of the Grand National was eligible to enter it. But such commonplace propositions are derived from a set of rules establishing entry criteria for particular competitions, or for tournaments played under the auspices of a particular sporting association.

3.3 It is self-evident that such rules must exist, for access to sporting competitions must be controlled if organised sport is to be conducted in an orderly fashion. The public's enjoyment of sport would be negated if competitions were a shambolic free-for-all. The Olympics would not command the attention of millions across the globe if participation were not restricted to those with proven ability to perform to a high standard through rigorous selection processes at national level. And it would be absurd to suppose that the Oxford versus Cambridge boat race could take place if the dark blues and the light blues had to contend with other motley crews aboard craft of rotten planks and differing shapes and sizes. Sport must be well organised if it is to be entertaining, as the public demands it must be. An important aspect of good organisation is that competitions should pitch against each other participants of potentially similar ability in comfortable and safe conditions, and on (figuratively and sometimes literally) a level playing field. A major contribution to the achievement of that objective is made by the application of entry criteria.

3.4 It falls, then, to the administrators of sport to devise, promulgate and apply the sets of rules that must govern rights of entry to sporting competitions, if the public demand for entertainment from sport is to be satisfied. Such rules must separate those eligible to participate from those excluded from competing, a process which by its nature is likely, on occasion, to generate disputes over the application of entry criteria and even legal challenges brought by disappointed aspiring entrants to a particular competition or a particular type of sporting activity regulated by an association. These challenges may call into question either the validity of the relevant entry criteria themselves, or the manner in which they are applied to the aspiring participant in a particular case, or both.

3.5 Sometimes, as in the case of professional boxing in England, a licence issued by the organiser of the sport is a precondition of entitlement to compete in all competitions organised or recognised by that body. If the body has quasi-monopolistic powers, failure to obtain such a licence may in practice prevent participation in the sport concerned entirely. Where professional men and women earn their living from sport, either by direct competitive participation or through sport-related employment regulated by a sporting association, difficult questions may arise as to the extent to which the law is prepared to protect their livelihood.

3.6 Access to sporting competitions may be sought not only by aspiring entrants who are not yet members of the organising body. Those already eligible to compete, by virtue of membership of the body, possession of a licence, or performance on the field of play, may have to fulfil further criteria set by the organising body in order not to lose their eligibility. Once a person or club has fulfilled the relevant entry criteria, rules generally regulate continuing eligibility to participate in the following season or tournament. Simple examples are rules providing for the bottom clubs in a division of a league to be relegated or, if already in the bottom division, excluded from the league. Failure to win sufficient points to rise above bottom place in the table means failure to meet one of the criteria for entry to the same division the following season.

3.7 A sportsman or woman, or a club, may wish to assert a legal right to participate in a particular competition or sport. The legal form of such a claim depends on the circumstances. One of several causes of action may be open to such a claimant, all founded on the assertion that the claimant fulfils the necessary entry criteria. The most likely types of proceeding are: (1) a claim by an existing member of the organising body to enforce an existing contractual right to participate; (2) a claim by a non-member of the organising body for a declaration to enforce a freestanding non-contractual right to participate, or expectation of being permitted to participate; or (3) a claim in tort by or against a third party—ie not the body that runs the competition—seeking to prevent inducement of a breach by the players or by the body that runs the competition of contractual rights to participate or to require participation.

3.8 Some attempts have also been made to establish rights of participation founded on the competition law provisions of the EC Treaty, Articles 81 and 82 of which are now Articles 101 and 102 of the Treaty on the Functioning of the European Union; or under English domestic competition law previously enacted in the Restrictive Trade Practices Act 1976 and replaced by the Competition Act 1998. However, no such attempt has yet, so far as we are aware, succeeded.

3.9 We consider these various causes of action below. We begin by considering the content of the duty of fairness owed by sporting bodies to aspiring entrants who are not, but who seek to become, members of the body. Next, we consider the position where there is, or there is alleged to be, a pre-existing contractual relationship establishing continuing eligibility rules between the aspiring entrant and the sporting body. We will then look at non-contract based claims in which an outsider attempts to surmount a more difficult hurdle by asserting a right to join a competition or take part in a competition or sport without prior membership of the organising body. Finally, we will consider in brief certain related topics, including the potential for reliance on the restraint of trade doctrine and for asserting rights of access to sporting competitions in reliance on domestic and European competition law.

3.10 Necessarily, there is a potential overlap between this chapter and chapter seven, which deals with the exercise of disciplinary jurisdiction in the sporting field. Disciplinary sanctions can include match bans or loss of the right to enter or apply to enter particular competitions. However, in this chapter we are concerned with the law regulating entry to a competition other than as a disciplinary measure. The distinction between exclusion from a competition as a punishment and exclusion from a competition through non-compliance with entry criteria may be a fine one to draw on the facts of a particular case. But the two phenomena are conceptually distinct, for the former presupposes that the person excluded possessed a right (or at least a contingent right) to compete which he has lost as a punishment, while the latter entails that he never possessed such a right in the first place.

3.11 The Court of Arbitration for Sport (CAS) has also had to consider questions of eligibility to compete. We mention some of them below. The analysis in the CAS case law is different from that of the English courts, since in CAS cases English law is not usually the law governing the merits of the dispute; and the starting point may be not the presence or absence of contractual rights, but the rules of the organisation concerned, the way in which they are applied in the case in question, and the way in which the governing law— often Swiss law (and particularly the Swiss law of associations)—applies to the question of eligibility to compete. The CAS also applies EU law, although based in Switzerland which is outside the EU, if the measure under consideration will be applied within the territory of the EU.[1]

The Duty of Fairness Owed by Sporting Bodies to Outsiders

3.12 The right to take part in particular competitions may hinge on membership of the body organising them, as in the case of the Football League and the Premier League in association football. Or it may depend on possession of a licence issued by a controlling authority. This is the case with professional boxing in Britain, in which challengers for the various titles, as well as promoters and managers, must possess a licence issued by the British Boxing Board of Control, which administers those competitions under

---

[1] *Ahlstrom v Commission (Woodpulp)* [1988] ECR 5193; *AEK Athens FC and Slavia Prague FC v UEFA*, CAS 98/200, paras 71 ff.

its auspices. Applications for such a licence, or for membership of a sporting body, are usually dependent on the fulfilment of entry criteria. If a dispute arises as to whether those criteria have been met, the applicant may wish to obtain a finding to that effect in legal proceedings and, relying on that finding, seek an order compelling the body to admit the applicant as a member.

3.13 But such a claim may invite the retort that the applicant for membership has no pre-existing relationship with the body he (or it) seeks to join, and therefore no right—not even a contingent right—to join, even on the footing that the relevant entry criteria have been met. This issue is an important one, since an applicant for membership of a sporting body, or an applicant for a licence issued by such a body, will be able to achieve little through litigation if even a successful claim to have fulfilled the necessary criteria does not generate the legal remedy necessary to confer entitlement to participate. We therefore consider the question here.

3.14 Historically, the courts have declined to compel an association by injunction to admit a member it is unwilling to admit. The law's reluctance to enforce admission against the will of the association's existing members is firmly grounded in the notion of freedom of contract. Given that, as we saw in chapter two,[2] a club is regarded as a combination of individuals who voluntarily associate together in a common activity (whether by contract only, or as an incorporated body), traditional freedom of contract would point to the conclusion that it is for the existing members, and not the courts, to decide whether to accept new applicants. However, the possibility of a court being prepared to depart from that position and, in an extreme case, compel a sporting body to accept a new member against its will, cannot be excluded.

3.15 In *Stevenage Borough FC Ltd v The Football League Ltd*[3] the issue was whether Stevenage was entitled to membership of the Football League, having won the Vauxhall Conference and having thus fulfilled the playing requirement for promotion to the League, but having failed to meet the League's criteria relating to its ground and finances by the date set by the League. As we shall see shortly, Stevenage challenged the validity of the criteria which it had failed to meet, but the League argued that, on authority,[4] the court ought not to order it to admit Stevenage as a new member against the will of the League even if the allegedly offending criteria were struck down as invalid. Carnwath J noted:

> [N]o case has been cited in which the court has forced a private organisation to admit a member against its will, even where the organisation controls the member's right to work,[5]

but concluded that it was unnecessary to decide the point. If, as we believe, sporting bodies should be viewed as bodies which sometimes exercise public or quasi-public

---

[2] See paras 2.2–2.18.

[3] Transcript, 23 July 1996, Carnwath J; reported a decade later at [2006] ISLR, SLR 128; Stevenage's appeal was dismissed but on the ground of delay (1997) 9 Admin LR 109, CA.

[4] *R v Master and Warden of the Company of Surgeons in London* (1759) 2 Burr 893; *R v Dr Askew et al* (1768) 4 Burr 2185 (both decisions of courts presided over by Lord Mansfield); *R v Benchers of Lincoln's Inn* (1825) 4 B and C 854; *Faramus v Film Artistes Association* [1964] AC 925, 941–2 (Lord Evershed) and 944–8 (Lords Hodson and Pearce); *Lee v The Showmen's Guild of Great Britain* [1952] 2 QB 329, CA, per Denning LJ at 342–4, citing *Baird v Wells* (1890) 44 Ch Div 661, per Stirling J at 676.

[5] para 56, at [2006] SLR 139.

functions,[6] the objection to enforced admission based on freedom of contract is less than compelling.

3.16 The related question of whether a body which issues licences to participate in professional sporting activity could be compelled by injunction to issue such a licence would probably yield the same answer. We do not, in principle, agree with the view that a body which controls the right to work in a particular profession and can therefore make or break people's livelihoods, can—as a matter going to the court's jurisdiction—never be compelled to admit as a member or issue a licence to a person who fulfils the criteria announced in advance by the body as qualifying that person for membership or a licence. In an appropriately strong case there seems to be no objection in principle to the court asserting jurisdiction to require the existing members of the association to stand by their word; though we recognise that such cases would be rare.

3.17 The cases in which it has been said that an injunction will not be granted to compel membership of a club are best viewed as authority only for the proposition that the discretion to grant such an injunction will be exercised sparingly and with extreme caution, in view of the lack of a pre-existing legal relationship between the parties. Indeed, in *Nagle v Feilden*[7] a Court of Appeal presided over by Lord Denning MR pointedly refused to strike out a claim which included a claim for an injunction ordering the stewards of the Jockey Club to grant the plaintiff a licence to train horses, which she said had repeatedly been refused, affecting her livelihood, for no other reason than that she was a woman. *Nagle's* case therefore establishes that our view is arguable.[8]

3.18 *Nagle's* case has been cited dozens of times in subsequent case law, without any subsequent court giving an authoritative ruling on what proposition it stands for. When the *Stevenage* case reached the Court of Appeal, Millett LJ commented[9] that 'the absence of a contractual nexus is not fatal to the claim'; but, as he made clear, that was in the context of a restraint of trade based challenge. In *R v Disciplinary Committee of the Jockey Club, ex parte Aga Khan*,[10] Hoffmann LJ in the Court of Appeal said obiter that the possibility that Mrs Nagle could have obtained an injunction has probably not survived *The Siskina (Owners of cargo lately laden on board) v Distos Compania Naviera SA*.[11] But in *The Siskina* the refusal of an injunction followed from the absence of any cause of action that could have founded a claim for one. It is now recognised more clearly than in the early 1990s that an action may lie for a freestanding private law declaration, without reliance on contract, applying principles analogous to judicial review principles.[12]

3.19 Whatever the precise limits of the law, it is, at least, extremely difficult to gain access to sporting competitions as an outsider without prior membership of the body

---

[6] A view we discuss further in chapter 8, which draws strong support from, inter alia, Carnwath J's judgment in *Stevenage* (n 3) paras 49–64.

[7] [1966] 2 QB 633, CA.

[8] See Lord Denning's judgment at p 647F ('she may have a good case to ask for a declaration and injunction').

[9] (1997) 9 Admin LR 109, CA, per Millett LJ at 115G–H, cited by Pumfrey J in *Hearn v RFU* [2003] EWHC 2690 (Ch), transcript, para 16.

[10] [1993] 1 WLR 909, CA, at 933.

[11] [1979] AC 210.

[12] *R (on the application of Mullins) v Jockey Club Appeal Board (No 1)* [2005] EWHC 2197 (Admin), [2006] ISLR, SLR 31, Stanley Burnton J.

controlling access, and against its will. The question that next arises is the extent to which the outsider can achieve the lesser objective of requiring the sporting body to conduct itself in a fair manner when considering applications for participation rights and compelling the body by court order to reconsider a failed application for participation rights. Here we encounter the now well-known duty of domestic tribunals to act fairly. That duty has evolved through a series of cases, mainly (in the case of sporting bodies) concerning disciplinary decisions. These are discussed more fully in chapter seven.[13]

3.20 But there have also been non-disciplinary cases raising the question of the scope of the duty to act fairly, in which access to sporting competitions or professional activities in the sporting field has been at stake. In the USA, the courts have regarded failure to observe fair procedures in adopting and enforcing the rules of sporting associations as a ground for holding them invalid. Failure to entertain comments on a proposed change of rule by those affected, prior to adopting it, can lead to invalidation of the rule.[14] Even a rule which is reasonable in itself and adopted after fair consideration can be invalidated if it fails to set forth guidelines for its application or fails to allow the affected party a hearing.[15]

3.21 In England, the content of the duty owed to an 'outsider' to act fairly includes at least an obligation not to refuse an application for membership or a licence on grounds which can be characterised as arbitrary and capricious. The best known authority for this proposition is *McInnes v Onslow-Fane*,[16] a case brought in private law which has profoundly influenced English public law both within and outside the sporting field. Within that field, Megarry J's decision can fairly be regarded as the first English judicial development in the shaping of a corpus of law particular to sport; a process now, arguably, sufficiently advanced to warrant use of the term 'sports law'. Mr McInnes was a former amateur boxer who had become a professional promoter and had held a promoter's licence issued by the British Boxing Board of Control which had expired. He had also held a Master of Ceremonies' licence which had been withdrawn following a disagreement. After applying and reapplying for a manager's licence several times, he brought an action asserting the right to be informed of the 'case against him' and requesting an oral hearing of his application, while the Board maintained that it had considered his application and rejected it, and that he was not entitled to a hearing.

---

[13] Eg *Russell v Duke of Norfolk* [1949] 1 All ER 109, CA; *Breen v Amalgamated Engineering Union* [1971] 2 QB 175 (especially the celebrated passage from Lord Denning MR's dissenting judgment at pp 189–91); *Colgan v The Kennel Club* (2001) unreported, 26 October (Cooke J); *Modahl v British Athletic Federation Ltd (No 2)* [2002] 1 WLR 1192, CA. See chapter 7, para 7.101 ff.

[14] *Linseman v World Hockey Association*, 439 F Supp 1315, 1322 (D Conn 1977) (rejection of league rule prohibiting persons under 20 years of age from playing hockey); *Gunter Harz Sports, Inc*, 511 F Supp at 1122 ('... in order to avoid liability under Section 1 of the Sherman Act ... [a league's] notice and comment procedure concerning the proposed rule [must be] sufficient to inform those potentially affected by the rule ... as well as to allow interested parties to be heard regarding the proposed rule').

[15] *Los Angeles Memorial Coliseum Commission v National Football League*, 726 F 2d 1381, 1397 (9th Cir 1984), US Court of Appeals (rule against team relocation held contrary to Sherman Act because, inter alia, it lacked an 'objective set of guidelines' as well as any 'procedural mechanism' for applying such guidelines); similarly, *Denver Rockets v All-Pro Management*, 325 F Supp 1049 (CD Ca 1971) (NBA rule prohibiting teams from signing players until at least four years after their high school graduation struck down as there was 'no provision for even the most rudimentary hearing before the four-year college rule is applied to exclude an individual player').

[16] [1978] 1 WLR 1520, Megarry J.

3.22 The judgment of Megarry J broke new ground by drawing attention to three categories of cases, which he termed application cases, forfeiture cases and expectation cases. In straightforward application cases, where 'nothing is being taken away',[17] an applicant for membership of a body has no right to observance of the tenets of natural justice or fairness; the body is free to admit him or deny him membership on whatever grounds it wishes. In forfeiture cases, where there is a threat to take something away, as in the case of an existing member subject to disciplinary sanctions, the member has the right to be treated fairly by being given notice of the allegations, an opportunity to speak in defence against them, and an unbiased tribunal to consider them.[18] In an intermediate category of cases, which the judge termed 'expectation' cases, the applicant is seeking membership or a licence but in circumstances giving him the right to expect that it will be granted unless there is reason to the contrary, as where he has previously been considered suitable to hold a licence. The judge held that Mr McInnes' case was not an expectation case, since he had never before held a manager's licence, only a promoter's licence and a Master of Ceremonies' licence, which were insufficient to establish the expectation.

3.23 He went on to consider the extent of the duty owed to an applicant in a pure application case. The Board accepted a limited duty to reach a conclusion honestly and without caprice or bias,[19] but denied any more extensive duty to give the applicant notice of the reasons why it was minded to refuse his application, and an opportunity to make representations in support of his application and in rebuttal of those reasons. The judge agreed, noting that the courts had recently brought about 'a marked expansion of the ambit of the requirements of natural justice and fairness, reaching beyond statute and contract',[20] but pointing out that refusal of the licence did not entail any finding of dishonesty or reprehensible conduct; and doubting that the notion of a 'right to work' could be said to include the right to begin a new career of the worker's choice, as distinct from continuing an existing career. However, it may be doubted whether the judge's limitation of the duty owed to an applicant represents the modern law: in particular where refusal impacts upon a person's reputation, he may have an entitlement to make representations, having been told the substance of the decision maker's concerns.[21]

3.24 Megarry J's exposition in *McInnes* has been overtaken by important public law cases articulating the requirement of fairness in each case by reference to the concept of a 'legitimate expectation' possessed by a claimant who claims to have good reason to continue enjoying a benefit previously bestowed; or good reason not to have it withdrawn without

---

[17] Ibid, 1529D–G.

[18] Ibid; the content of the duty of fairness in disciplinary cases is considered more fully in chapter 7 at para 7.101 ff.

[19] In the US, a court has refused to uphold summarily a hockey league's decision to bar a team from competition, on the ground that the league was 'motivated by financial considerations to eliminate [the team] as a competing amateur hockey team', an allegation that had to be balanced against the league's assertion that the decision was made 'in order to develop American amateur hockey and improve the quality of young American hockey players' (*Tondas v Amateur Hockey Association of the US*, 438 F Supp 310 (WDNY 1977) 314). Similarly in *Heldman v US Lawn Tennis Association*, 354 F Supp 1241, 1252 (SDNY 1973) the court held that a rule barring players who had participated in tournaments sanctioned by other leagues would 'cross the line of legality' if the rule were 'intended to or [had] the natural effect of defeating competition', such as an intent to prohibit the plaintiff, a tennis promoter, from establishing a competing tennis circuit.

[20] Ibid, 1528A–B, citing *Nagle v Feilden* (n 7).

[21] See Woolf, Jowell and Le Sueur, *De Smith's Judicial Review*, 6th edn (Sweet & Maxwell, 2007) para 7-057 (and 1st Cumulative Supplement (2009) at 7-057); *R v Gaming Board for Great Britain, ex parte Benaim* [1970] 2 QB 417, CA, per Lord Denning MR at 430–1.

an opportunity to make representations. These developments go beyond the law relating to participation in sport, but practitioners in sports law need to be aware of them, if only because in *R (on the application of Niazi) v Secretary of State for the Home Department*[22] May LJ pointed out that Simon Brown LJ in *R v Devon County Council, ex parte Baker* had said that Lord Diplock's analysis in the *GCHQ* case 'supersedes, as I believe, all earlier attempted expositions of this doctrine such as that found in *McInnes v Onslow Fane*'.

3.25 However, the analysis in *McInnes* remains relevant, especially in pure application cases, where a claimant in an equivalent public law situation (for example, an applicant for a permit) would have difficulty establishing any public law legitimate expectation except to the extent conferred by any relevant statutory provisions. The concession made in *McInnes*, accepted by Megarry J, that in such a case the sports body deciding whether to grant access to the sport must not act in a manner that is arbitrary and capricious, has taken root and was applied to the facts (unsuccessfully for the claimant in both cases) by two first instance judges both subsequently elevated to the Court of Appeal: Carnwath J in *Stevenage FC Ltd v The Football League Ltd* and (in a different factual context) Stanley Burnton J in *Mullins v McFarlane*.[23]

3.26 In New Zealand, the Court of Appeal decided *Stininato v Auckland Boxing Council*[24] three months before Megarry J's decision in *McInnes*. The New Zealand Boxing Council had acquitted the plaintiff boxer of breaches of its rules but decided not to revoke his licence to compete. When the licence had expired and renewal was applied for, it was refused without a hearing. The claim was for damages and a declaration, not an injunction, and the Court of Appeal upheld the judge's exercise of discretion to refuse relief on the ground that a hearing would have made no difference, and because of delay, the plaintiff having waited several years before bringing his claim. The Court of Appeal was clear that any breach of duty did not sound in damages, and the plaintiff had not claimed an injunction.

3.27 In *Wayde v New South Wales Rugby League Ltd*[25] the High Court of Australia had to consider a claim brought by representatives of the Western Suburbs District Rugby League Football Club to set aside the decision of the League to reduce from 13 to 12 the number of clubs allowed to participate in the following season's premiership competition, and for an injunction restraining the League from implementing the decision. The Board of the League, which was a limited company operating under New South Wales

---

[22] Per May LJ at para 32 of *R (Niazi) v Secretary of State for the Home Department* [2007] EWHC 1495 (Admin); affirmed on appeal, [2008] EWCA Civ 755 (on appeal, see the seminal passage in Laws LJ's judgment, paras 26–39); *Council of Civil Service Unions v Minister for the Civil Service* [1985] AC 374 (*GCHQ*); *R v Devon CC, ex parte Baker* [1995] 1 All ER 73, 91 LGR 479. Simon Brown LJ said at p 90: 'Thus the only touchstone of a category 2 interest emerging from Lord Diplock's speech is that the claimant has in the past been permitted to enjoy some benefit or advantage. Whether or not he can then legitimately expect procedural fairness, and if so to what extent, will depend upon the court's view of what fairness demands in all the circumstances of the case. That, frankly, is as much help as one can get from the authorities. Lord Diplock's analysis supersedes, as I believe, all earlier attempted expositions of this doctrine such as that found in *McInnes v Onslow Fane* ...'

[23] [2006] EWHC 986 (QB), [2006] ISLR, SLR 65, Stanley Burnton J.

[24] [1978] NZLR 1, Cooke J and Woodhouse J. English case law confirms that damages are not available for unfair conduct of a disciplinary process: see the discussion of another Cooke J in *Colgan v Kennel Club* (2011) unreported, 26 October 2011, transcript, paras 32–36, also citing the Court of Appeal's decision to the same effect in *Modahl v British Athletic Federation Ltd (No 2)* [2002] 1 WLR 1192.

[25] (1985) 61 ALR 225.

company law statutes, had made the decision in what it considered to be the interests of the company, ie of the League. The excluded club, represented by the plaintiffs, was aggrieved at the decision, being the unfortunate recipient of notification that its entry for the 1985 competition had been refused. The plaintiffs had initially obtained an order from Hodgson J restraining the League from implementing the decisions on the ground that they were oppressive[26] to the plaintiffs, but the League had obtained a reversal of that decision by the Court of Appeal.

3.28 On a further appeal to the High Court of Australia, five judges rejected the claim, accepting the League's reasons for reducing the size of the premiership competition—in essence, too many matches in a too long season—observing that the League was expressly constituted to promote the best interests of the sport and empowered to determine which clubs should be entitled to participate in competitions conducted by it, and distinguishing sharply between adverse impact on the complainant club, and oppressive or unfairly prejudicial conduct which was not made out.[27] Thus, recourse to company law procedures did not enable the disappointed aspiring entrant to narrow the width of the discretion allowed to sporting bodies by the courts in administering sporting competitions. The decision was an important vindication of the power of sporting bodies to control access to their own competitions.

3.29 In *Ray v Professional Golfers Association Ltd*[28] a golfer excluded from certain competitions as a result of failing golf related examinations set by the Association of which he was a provisional, or trainee, member, optimistically sought access to golfing competitions relying, inter alia, on denial of an opportunity to be heard by the Association. The claim failed. The right to continued participation in golfing competitions under the Association's auspices was subject, under its rules, to success in the examinations. The duty of fairness was satisfied by giving the plaintiff the opportunity to show his suitability by sitting the examinations. Fairness did not require any right to make further representations.

3.30 In *Fraser v Professional Golfers Association Ltd* a differently framed claim for breach of contract and resulting loss of earnings was considered in Scotland in both the Outer House and the Inner House of the Court of Session.[29] The Lord Ordinary, Lord Wheatley, was prepared to accept that the examinations the pursuer had to pass in order to obtain full membership (without which a professional career in golf was well nigh impossible) generated an implied contractual obligation on the defenders to 'assess the pursuer's performance in this test fairly and reasonably and by the application of the standards of a reasonably competent golf repairer'.[30] The Lord Ordinary considered the technical evidence in detail and strongly criticised the defenders' assessment of the pursuer's examination performance, but found that it could not be shown that but for the 'blunders' in marking, Mr Fraser would have passed the test. Damages were contingently assessed at

---

[26] Under s 320 of the New South Wales Companies Code, a statutory variant, with common ancestry, of our own s 994 Companies Act 2006.

[27] Noted in Beloff and Kerr, *Judicial Control of Sporting Bodies: The Commonwealth Jurisprudence* (1995) 3(1) SLJ 5.

[28] (1997) unreported, 15 April, HHJ Dyer QC.

[29] [2006] CSOH 129, 25 August 2006.

[30] Ibid, para 40 of Lord Wheatley's Opinion. The implied obligation was inferred as the common intention of the parties from the relevant rules and held necessary to give business efficacy to the contract.

£100,000 for loss of earnings. An appeal to the Extra Division of the Inner House was unsuccessful.[31]

3.31 The cases just discussed show the importance of the forms of action and the remedies sought by a frustrated entrant wishing to practise a sport but rebuffed by a governing body which controls entry to the sport and, often, a person's ability to make a living from it. Claims are more likely to succeed if a contract can be shown, for then a breach can be relied upon if it can be proved. Contract based claims to take part in sport are discussed below. A contract will more readily be inferred if the aspiring entrant has to undergo a procedure designed to prove his worth—as in *Ray* and *Fraser*—than in a simple licensing context where the governing body simply decides applications, as in *McInnes* and *Stininato*. In a pure application case without any contract, the content of the duty to act fairly depends on the context in which it arises.[32] Where access to a sporting competition or a livelihood derived from sport is in issue, the English courts are sympathetic to claims where arbitrary or capricious conduct is genuinely shown, or where a willingness to listen to representations is absent in circumstances where it should be present. But the sympathy of the court will always be tempered by proper respect for autonomy in decision making by sporting bodies best placed to regulate access to competitions, and also by the various ways of earning a living that such competitions generate.

Contractual Claims Asserting a Right to Participate

3.32 Having considered the mainly procedural duty of sporting bodies not to treat outsiders arbitrarily or capriciously, we turn next to consider the substantive law determining whether or not, in a particular case, the aspiring entrant can establish his right to enter the fray. We deal with this aspect of the law by looking first at claims to participation rights which depend in some way on assertion of a contractual right, whether directly against the administering body or in a tort claim against a third party charged with procuring a breach by the administering body of the aspiring entrant's contractual right to participate. We then go on to consider non-contract based claims founded on alleged fulfilment of valid eligibility criteria, conferring an expectation or alleged 'right' to compete. We recognise that the divide between claims founded on contract and those not founded on contract is not always fundamental: it is more important in common law jurisdictions than civil law ones; and it is less important in cases where the court is prepared to treat the actions of a governing body as quasi-public in nature and attracting the application of principles derived from administrative law. Still, the importance of contract in the common law sporting jurisprudence is such that it merits separate consideration.

3.33 In a simple case, there may be a contractual right to compete in a certain competition by virtue of a pre-existing contract of membership between an individual or club and

---

[31] [2008] CSIH 53 (11 September 2008).
[32] See also, for an account of further Australian case law, Sullivan, *The Role of Contract in Sports Law* (2010) 5(1) Australia and New Zealand Sports Law Journal 3, 5–7 ('Situations in which there is no enforceable contract').

a sporting body, on terms which confer a right to compete on fulfilment of entry criteria. An example would be the right of a football club to compete in the second division of a football league after winning the third division championship the previous season. In that example, the club has a contract of membership of the league on terms set out in the league's rules, as properly amended from time to time. Those rules include the normal rule that the winner of the third division championship shall be promoted to the second division. Winning the third division championship thus converts the club's contingent right to compete in the second division into an accrued right to do so.

3.34 The winning club's right of access to the second division could be enforced in the normal way, by obtaining an injunction to restrain breach of contract. If the league attempted to block the promotion of the winning club, it would be in breach of the club's contractual right to promotion unless some other rule entitled the league to prevent the promotion from taking effect. In that example, the respective rights of the parties are clear. Precisely because they are clear, the practitioner of sports law is not confronted with numerous authorities to support the existence of enforceable contractual rights to promotion. Such rights are deduced from established principles of ordinary contract law.

3.35 But in other cases contractual rights to compete are less clear. In *Lennox Lewis v World Boxing Council and Frank Bruno*,[33] the well-known boxer Lennox Lewis claimed against the promoters of the WBC world heavyweight title a contractual right to challenge the holder, Frank Bruno, for that title, and sought an injunction restraining Bruno from accepting a challenge instead from the notorious boxer Mike Tyson, which Lewis claimed would be a breach of his contractual right to challenge for the title. Lewis relied on his status as 'designated official mandatory challenger' under the WBC's rules, which defined the challenger as:

> the number one rated contender, or the next higher rated if the number one cannot or will not participate in the bout, or if he is the winner of an official tournament to determine an official challenger.

Lewis had defeated Lionel Butler in an official WBC 'elimination bout' shortly before the hearing, only to find that the WBC proposed to pit Tyson and not Lewis against Bruno for the title. The parties agreed that Lewis was in a contractual relationship with the WBC arising out of the arrangements for the final eliminator bout, even though he was not a member of the WBC, whose members were associations, not individuals, but the scope of the WBC's obligation to Lewis was in issue. The WBC and Bruno denied that Lewis had a contractual right to challenge for the title by virtue of having won the eliminator bout, claiming that the only obligation was to 'officially sanction' the eliminator bout, without any right in the winner to challenge for the world title. In the event the court did not determine what Lewis's rights were because it decided that England was not the appropriate forum for the dispute, the claim against Frank Bruno in England being merely ancillary to the main claim against the WBC. But the case throws up an interesting example of direct contractual relations arising between a competitor and a federation in relation to rights to compete.

---

[33] (1995) unreported, 3 November, Rattee J. Lewis lost the application for an urgent injunction, but later became the WBC world heavyweight champion.

3.36 Another case in which disputed rights of participation were ventilated in an English court was *Widnes v Rugby Football League*.[34] The RFL had decided to start a new league competition, with the benefit of monies helpfully provided by a company controlled by Mr Rupert Murdoch, in return for broadcasting rights. Widnes, a traditionally great club which had suffered from poor form, was not offered a place in the new league, having finished poorly at the end of the previous season. Widnes argued, inter alia, that it had a contractual right by virtue of its membership of the RFL to a place in the new league, and went so far as to seek an injunction, in a representative action against officers of the RFL, restraining the RFL from proceeding with the new league at all unless Widnes were accommodated within it. The claim failed on the facts, as Widnes could not show that the RFL had acted outside its rules in adopting a structure for the new league which excluded Widnes from it. The *Widnes* case was an instance of administrative realignment in sport prompted by commercial sponsorship in pursuit of profit from broadcasting, causing a disappointed club, left out in the cold, to attempt a forced entry via the court to the newly constituted league.

3.37 Litigation over rights of access to sporting competition may take the form of a battle between sporting bodies seeking to preserve their role in administering competitions, and commercial interests determined to supplant them, using financial muscle to attract the players and legal proceedings, or the threat of them, to induce the sporting body to negotiate. In *News Ltd v Australian Rugby Football League Ltd*,[35] the League responded to rumours that News Limited was preparing to establish a new superleague, to replace the national competition, by offering 20 clubs admission to the national competition for five seasons on condition that each agreed to participate for those seasons, and not in any other competition unless conducted or approved by the League. The 20 clubs signed a contractual commitment to that effect. News Limited sought to bring the League on board, but the League rejected overtures that would have given it control over the proposed new superleague. News Limited then signed up large numbers of players and coaches for new clubs, which it intended to constitute as the members of a competing superleague of 12 clubs. It also sued the League, seeking to set aside the latter's agreements on competition law grounds. The League, and clubs aligned with it and not with News Limited, counterclaimed against the clubs aligned with News Limited for breach of those latter clubs' contractual duties. Coaches and players who promised services to new clubs aligned with News Limited would plainly be acting in breach of their duty of fidelity to the clubs that employed them if they fulfilled those promises. The League and its allied clubs also claimed against News Limited for inducing breach of those contractual duties by enticing away coaches, players and rebel clubs.

3.38 The trial judge, partly applying Australian competition law and partly on common law contractual principles, held that the League's contracts were valid, were not vitiated by economic duress and were consequently enforceable. It followed that News Limited was liable for inducing breach of those contracts. The judge made orders the effect of which was to prevent the News Limited interests from setting up a superleague until the year 2000. However, the full Federal Court allowed an appeal brought by the News

---

[34] (1995) unreported, High Court (Manchester), 26 May, Parker J.
[35] (1996) 135 ALR 33; and on appeal to the Full Court of the Federal Court of Australia, see (1997) 139 ALR 193.

Limited interests (except as to the economic duress argument which was not pursued on appeal), set aside the judge's orders, declared some of the relevant contracts void on competition law grounds and restrained the League from enforcing them, but held that certain other limited contractual rights were valid and enforceable, had been breached, and that News Limited had induced breaches of them. The Court commented that the orders made at trial had had the practical effect of reducing substantially, if not removing altogether, whatever competitive advantage and head start the News Limited interests might have gained from its tortious conduct.[36]

3.39 For present purposes, the case illustrates no more significant legal principle than that a club may not gain access to a competition if to do so would be inconsistent with its prior contractual commitment owed to the organiser of another competition to participate in that other competition. The organiser of the first competition can prevent this by injunction. This is merely an example of the *pacta sunt servanda* principle: prior contractual obligations (if valid) take precedence over subsequent ones—a simple point but one worth restating in an epoch in which substantial financial rewards may tempt not just players away from their clubs, but clubs away from their allegiance to their governing bodies.

3.40 Similar upheavals threatened rugby union in England in the 1990s. The advent of professional rugby union gave rise to a notorious dispute in the 1990s in which players threatened to break away from the Rugby Football Union. That dispute did not lead to litigation. There was another well-publicised dispute in 1996 between the Rugby Football Union in England and the unions of France and the Celtic nations over the future of the (then) Five Nations Championship.[37] It was eventually settled, but not before France and the Celtic nations had publicly threatened to exclude England from the tournament, again over a dispute involving broadcasting rights. Had the threat been carried out, litigation would have been a near certainty.

3.41 At national level, the RFU found itself in the position of defendant rather than potential claimant. It brokered a complex reorganisation of the game in England, involving a matrix of companies and contracts and an increase in the size of the first and second divisions from 12 to 14 clubs. Rotherham RUFC was unsuccessful before Ferris J in establishing legal entitlement to be one of the two new clubs admitted to the first division of the Premier League in 1999, despite having finished second in the second division at the end of the previous season. The contractual structure did not give Rotherham the right to a year's notice to changes in the promotion and relegation system; nor did the changes require the consent of the second claimant, the company administering the second division.[38]

3.42 International tournaments such as the Six Nations Championship usually take place by virtue of a contractual arrangement between the promoters of each country's team. The same type of contract may establish the rights of sporting clubs within one country

---

[36] *News Ltd v Australian Rugby Football League Ltd* (1997) 139 ALR 193, 293.

[37] The dispute briefly flared up again in early 1999; see eg *The Sunday Times*, 17 January 1999 ('England threatened with Five Nations Axe').

[38] *Rotherham RUFC Ltd and ESDR Ltd v EFDR Ltd and RFU* [2000] ISLR 33, Ch Div. In Wales, a club had no greater success at first instance or in the Court of Appeal against the Welsh Rugby Union: *Aberavon & Port Talbot RFC v WRU Ltd* [2003] EWCA Civ 584, (2003) 2 SLJ 185.

to participate in competitions run by different sporting bodies, as in the case of the English league football clubs which take part in league and cup competitions established under a set of contractual rules regulating relations between the clubs, their players (and other staff) and the governing organs, the Football Association, the Football League, the FA Premier League and other less prominent bodies such as the Football Conference. The existence of contractual rights which would ground a possible injunction to restrain exclusion of a club from a competition is usually evidenced by documents such as the rulebooks of the relevant sporting bodies and minutes of meetings of those bodies.

3.43 Litigation over access to competitions can take place in an international setting as well as in the domestic courts. The dispute before the CAS involving football clubs controlled by the English National Investment Company plc (ENIC) is a major example.[39] In May 1998 UEFA adopted a rule which prevented two or more clubs in common ownership from participating in the same UEFA administered competition. At the time UEFA organised the Champions' League, the European Cup Winners' Cup and the UEFA Cup. One of the three clubs controlled by ENIC, AEK Athens FC, had already qualified for the UEFA Cup before the rule was adopted; another, SK Slavia Prague, qualified shortly after the rule had been announced. UEFA purported to exclude AEK Athens from the UEFA Cup, adopting a 'points coefficient' system to determine which of the two clubs should be excluded. But the clubs successfully obtained an interim ruling from the CAS, applying Swiss and EC law, preventing UEFA from excluding AEK Athens, mainly on the ground that AEK had already qualified and UEFA could not lawfully deprive it retroactively of its place in the competition.[40]

3.44 The President of the Ordinary Arbitration Division of the CAS did not found her decision on conventional contractual principles as a court in a common law jurisdiction might have done. The clubs were not direct members of UEFA; they were 'indirect members', in that they were members of their respective national associations which in turn were members of UEFA. The Swiss law of associations protects the rights of indirect members in certain circumstances, in particular by imposing a duty of good faith on the association's governing organs. But the same result could have been reached on a common law analysis by inferring the existence of limited direct contractual relations between the clubs and UEFA, from the clubs' membership of their national associations, the obligations of the clubs and those national associations to comply with UEFA's competition rules, and from subjection of the clubs to UEFA's disciplinary regime. The following year, the final hearing took place and the claim was ultimately unsuccessful on the facts. In its detailed decision, the CAS panel accepted UEFA's contention that the rule in question was a proportionate means of achieving a legitimate objective, namely (in summary) protecting the integrity of the sport and avoiding any risk to the principle of uncertainty of results that might result from clubs in common ownership playing each other.

---

[39] *AEK Athens FC and Slavia Prague FC v UEFA*, CAS 98/200, interim order of 17 July 1998.

[40] The foundation in Swiss law for this proposition was Art 2 of the Swiss Civil Code, as applied in the decision of the Swiss Supreme Court in *Grossen* (ATF 121 III 350) where the Swiss Wrestling Federation was ordered to pay damages to a wrestler whom it had excluded from a competition after he had qualified, by imposing a late change to the admission requirements designed to favour another wrestler. The Association was held to have breached its duty of good faith. (After winning one round, AEK Athens was knocked out by Vitesse Arnhem of the Netherlands.)

3.45 A club threatened with exclusion from a competition in breach of its contractual right to participate may in principle obtain an injunction preventing its exclusion, though this would be subject to the discretion of the court, which may be reluctant to interfere in the face of clear evidence that the club is not wanted by the other competitors; especially if the plaintiff club has been guilty of any delay.[41] Depending on the facts, the court might well decide to leave the wrongfully excluded club to its remedy in damages, by analogy with cases in which the courts have refused to grant injunctions whose effect is to compel close cooperation between parties at loggerheads with each other.[42]

3.46 That is essentially what happened, by a roundabout route, in the notorious proceedings between Sheffield United and West Ham Football Clubs. West Ham obtained the services of a gifted striker, Carlos Tevez, in breach of Premier League rules. Sheffield United finished below West Ham at the end of the 2006–7 season and was relegated, while West Ham, against all expectation, achieved what was called the 'Great Escape' and avoided relegation. A disciplinary commission of the Premier League fined West Ham heavily but did not deduct points, which meant that West Ham remained in the Premier League. Nor did it annul Tevez's registration with West Ham. Sheffield United's challenge to that decision failed.[43]

3.47 Sheffield United then brought arbitration proceedings under rule K of the Football Association's rules, seeking damages against West Ham for its breaches of Premier League rules which, Sheffield United claimed, had caused it to be relegated by reason of Tevez's firepower having saved West Ham and condemned Sheffield United. Perhaps inevitably, there was an argument about whether the relevant rules, on a correct reading, created mutually enforceable obligations sounding in damages for breach. The panel found that they did.[44] It went on to decide that on the evidence, including expert evidence from doyens of the football world, Tevez's contribution had been an effective cause of West Ham's survival and of Sheffield United's relegation. While noting that in logic the second proposition was not a necessary consequence of the first, it was sufficient on ordinary principles of causation for the breach to be *an* effective cause of the claimant's loss, and it need not be the only cause if both causes were 'co-operating and of equal efficacy'.[45]

3.48 *Raguz v Sullivan*[46] was another case, this time concerning judo in Australia, where a multipartite contract between potential competitors, and between them and the governing

---

[41] See *Newport AFC v The Football Association of Wales Ltd* (1995) unreported, 12 April, Blackburne J, discussed further below at paras 3.62, 3.64, 3.83–84; and in chapter 8, paras 8.71–74, 8.84 and 8.95.

[42] The scope of injunctive relief to secure participation rights in sport is further discussed in the context of remedies in chapter 8 at paras 8.62–8.91.

[43] *Sheffield United FC Ltd v Football Association Premier League Ltd*, FA Premier League arbitration panel, 3 July 2007, reported at [2007] ISLR, SLR 77. The panel held that the decision challenged, though generous to West Ham, was not perverse and capricious and was within the permissible range of conclusions open to it, albeit that (see para 38 of the decision) the panel would have decided the matter differently.

[44] *Sheffield United FC Ltd v West Ham United FC plc*, FA Arbitration under Rule K [2009] ISLR, SLR 25, paras 52–63. Part of the argument was over whether *The Satanita, Clarke v Earl of Dunraven* [1897] AC 59, HL, was authority for a general proposition that competitors mutually bind themselves contractually to obey the rules of the competition, or whether that decision turned (as West Ham contended) on the specific wording of the rules governing the Mudhook Yachting Regatta. The panel seemed inclined to agree with West Ham's position on this issue but decided that in the case before it the rules did give Sheffield United a cause of action, noting that the right to recover damages for breach would have to be expressly excluded, and was not.

[45] See para 80 of the panel's decision, quoting the orthodox proposition on dual causes as expressed in the then 29th edition of *Chitty on Contracts*; see now 30th edn (Sweet & Maxwell, 2011) at 26-041.

[46] (2000) 50 NSWLR 236.

body, was inferred from the circumstances, and held to include selection procedures even though those procedures were set out in an agreement between the governing body, the Judo Federation of Australia, and the Australian Olympic Committee. The latter two bodies had entered into a selection agreement determining who would compete at the 2000 Olympic Games in Sydney, which included an arbitration clause making the CAS sole arbiter of disputes arising from it. A dispute arose as to whether Ms Raguz or Ms Sullivan should be preferred under the selection agreement. The Australian Federation selected Raguz, but Sullivan's appeal to the CAS was successful and she was substituted.[47]

3.49 Raguz's attempt to appeal to the New South Wales Court of Appeal could only succeed if that court had jurisdiction to hear it, which in turn depended on whether the selection agreement bound Raguz as well as the immediate parties to it. The Court of Appeal held that it did bind Raguz, even though she was not a direct party to it, relying on Lord Herschell's speech in *The Satanita*[48] and proving the durability of that venerable authority in the context of modern sport. The selection agreement was made binding on Raguz (and Sullivan and other judoka) by various nomination forms and team membership forms which together amounted to a multipartite selection agreement complete with its CAS arbitration clause, including a contract between individual athletes to the same effect.[49]

3.50 In *Phoenix Finance Ltd v Fédération Internationale de l'Automobile*[50] a new Formula One team sought interim relief to support its alleged right to compete in the 2002 championship, after missing the opening Australian Grand Prix, asserting that it had acquired the right to do so (including rights to revenue from taking part in the competition under the 'Concorde Agreement') from the French liquidator of its insolvent predecessor. The judge held that under the relevant rules the entitlement of Phoenix to take part as a constructor turned on two things: first, whether as at the relevant date it 'currently races' a rolling chassis in which it owns intellectual property rights; and second, what was the reason for it having missed the Australian Grand Prix, which was only fatal if the failure was 'due to the insolvency' of the predecessor team.

3.51 Phoenix failed to persuade the judge that there was a serious issue to be tried on the first of those two issues, and accordingly failed to obtain interim relief. However, the judge went on to say that, had he found a serious issue to be tried, he would have held that damages were not an adequate remedy for any of the parties, that he was not satisfied that Phoenix could honour its cross-undertaking in damages, and that the balance of convenience favoured refusal of an injunction, to preserve the status quo (given that Phoenix was an aspiring new entrant and not an existing competitor and had missed the first race of the season) and because of the wide powers given to the governing body under the rules.[51] Finally, the judge would in any case have stayed the matter by reason of an arbitration clause in the rules, there being no effective challenge to the validity of the arbitration clause.

---

[47] *Sullivan v Judo Federation of Australia Inc and others*, CAS/2000/A/284.
[48] See para 2.41 above.
[49] (2000) 50 NSWLR 236, paras 65–82.
[50] [2002] EWHC 1028 (Ch), Sir Andrew Morritt VC.
[51] Ibid, paras 65–72.

3.52 Claims brought to overturn selection decisions refusing to select the claimant have been known to succeed. On the current state of the authorities, it seems that individuals are more likely to succeed than clubs or teams. We will return to some of them in the context of non-contractual claims, considered below.[52]

3.53 Where the selection criteria are objective and stated to be so, there is no room for implying any overriding discretion in the selecting body if its exercise would be contrary to the objective criteria. This is established in England by a brief but strong decision of Eady J[53] granting a final declaration in interim proceedings because he felt there was no room for doubt. A champion figure skater had been wrongfully excluded from selection for the 2009 World Championships, in clear breach of objective selection criteria based on past performance. A lower performing skater had been selected instead. Eady J rejected the suggestion of the governing body that it had an 'overriding discretion', expressed sympathy for the displaced skater, but granted a final declaration in favour of the claimant. It appears he would have granted a mandatory injunction but this was unnecessary as the association undertook to abide by the declaration.

3.54 Selection disputes are both more likely and more difficult where there is a subjective element to the selection process, rather than a strictly objective points system based on past results. In a case with a subjective element, the selectors must not act arbitrarily, capriciously or unreasonably (in what many lawyers still call the *Wednesbury* sense).[54] A colourful example was *D'Arcy v Australian Olympic Committee*:[55] a swimmer was held to have been properly de-selected from the Australian Olympic team for striking another man in a Sydney bar, inflicting serious injury during a drunken fracas. The all-Australian CAS panel upheld the decision both exercising its own judgment *de novo* (as provided for by CAS procedural rules) and upholding the exercise of discretion by the decision maker, which was not *Wednesbury* unreasonable.

Restraint of Trade and the Right to Participate

3.55 In a number of cases in which a claimant asserts a right (whether contractual or not) to compete, the obstacle sought to be overcome is an inconvenient provision or decision barring entry which the claimant considers unreasonable, or unreasonably relied upon by the relevant governing body. In the traditional common law analysis, such provisions in contract were often attacked as constituting an unreasonable restraint of trade. More recently,

---

[52] See para 3.76 ff.

[53] *Hilton v National Ice Skating Association of the United Kingdom Ltd* [2009] ISLR, SLR 75. There were challenges made to non-selection for the British team for London 2012 in a variety of sports: fencing, judo, swimming, diving, taekwondo, and rhythmic gymnastics. See eg the decisions of the SDRP in *Hutchinson v BFA*, 29 May 2012; *Couch v British Diving*, 29 June 2012.

[54] See Sullivan (n 32) 20–22, citing *Australian Football League v Carlton FC Ltd* [1998] 2 VR 546, and *Zusman v Royal Western Australian Bowling Association Inc* [1999] WASC 86; *Yachting New Zealand v Murdoch*, CAS 2004/A/582, 2 April 2004, at 6.11–6.42: 'In the absence of the Nomination Criteria specifying the relative weight to be attached to various considerations then, as a matter of general law, that was a matter for the Panel alone … On the facts of the present case it could not be said that "it is clear that the weight given to the matters so considered is so lop-sided that in truth no appropriate weighting process has been conducted".'

[55] CAS 2008/A/1574.

EU and domestic competition law grounds of challenge (considered at the end of this chapter—see paragraphs 3.106–3.123) have to some extent overtaken common law restraint of trade as a ground of challenge, but it is not unusual for the two to be combined.

3.56 In sports law, it has been suggested that the development of case law in England has now reached the point where restraint of trade may no longer usefully be regarded as distinct ground of challenge; the question may be better framed as simply whether the governing body's decision can be sustained as lawful applying a proportionality test more suitable as a standard of review than the restraint of trade standard.[56]

3.57 We believe it is still helpful and necessary for sports law practitioners to be aware of the restraint of trade doctrine and that it is not yet an anachronism of historical interest only. There is, as yet, no one universal and immutable standard of review applicable to the decision of a sports body to bar access to a competition. Until high authority ordains the application of a universal standard, restraint of trade needs to be understood. It cannot yet be dispensed with. It has played an important role in the development of sports law principles in the common law world since the 1960s. We will discuss below[57] the two seminal English cases from the last century concerning access to competitions, where the restraint doctrine has been considered in detail, with differing results: *Eastham v Newcastle United FC Ltd*[58] and *Greig v Insole*.[59]

3.58 First, then, a claimant may seek to avoid a term of a contract which would negate his, her or its right to compete, or would subject it to the judgment of an unfavourably disposed sporting body. Unless the terms of an existing contract entitle the would-be participant to argue that he qualifies to compete under them, it is necessary for him first to get rid of other terms which, on their face, constitute a bar to entry.[60] Most commonly, the claimant club or player seeks to achieve this by arguing that terms which block entry constitute an unreasonable restraint of trade and as such are unlawful and void, or, more accurately, voidable at the claimant's option.

3.59 The restraint of trade doctrine is a well-known creature of the common law of contract. It is not our purpose here to give a detailed exposition of its nature and scope.[61] The doctrine evolved as an aspect of a broader public policy bar to the enforcement of certain contract terms considered offensive, such as contracts to commit crime, to promote immoral purposes, and so forth. Contracts in unreasonable restraint of trade developed as a category of contract terms looked upon with disfavour by the common law courts on the ground that they inhibit freedom of trade and prevent the party restrained from exercising his talents and earning a living from them.

---

[56] See Lewis and Taylor, *Sport: Law and Practice*, 2nd edn (Tottel Publishing, 2008) A4.131–3. The authors note the decision of Langley J in *Days Medical Aids* [2003] EWHC 44 (Comm) stating that the court should reach the same conclusion applying restraint of trade principles to the facts as it would applying competition law principles. They recognise, however (rightly, in our respectful view) that for the present the doctrine retains some value for claimants seeking to frame their case.

[57] See paras 3.79–3.80.

[58] [1964] 1 Ch 413, Wilberforce J.

[59] [1978] 1 WLR 302, Slade J.

[60] In the litigation against UEFA involving clubs controlled by ENIC, as already mentioned at para 3.43 (*AEK Athens FC and Slavia Prague FC v UEFA*, CAS 98/200), the clubs sought to achieve this but, the claims proceeding under Swiss not English law, without using the common law restraint of trade doctrine considered here.

[61] See *Chitty on Contracts*, 30th edn (Sweet & Maxwell, 2011) ch 16 for a comprehensive account of the doctrine, at 16-075–16-141.

3.60 It is sufficient for our purposes to set out the salient features of the doctrine that figure where it is relied upon in sports law cases. First, the leading authority of *Nordenfelt v Maxim Nordenfelt Guns and Ammunition Co Ltd*[62] established that a contractual term embodying a restraint prohibiting the exercise of a trade was prima facie void as an interference with individual liberty of action, but might be valid and justified if shown to be reasonable by reference to the interests of the parties concerned and the interests of the public. This requirement has since, in ordinary commercial restraint of trade cases, sometimes been expressed by the proposition that the restraint must go no further than is reasonably necessary to protect a legitimate interest of the party in whose favour it operates.[63]

3.61 Second, the courts are more inclined to strike down as unreasonable some forms of restraint than others. A contract term restraining an employee after the end of his contract of employment will be more jealously scrutinised and less readily allowed to stand than a similar contract term exacted by the purchaser from the vendor on a sale of the goodwill of a business.[64] This is important in the context of sport, for it is inherent in arrangements regulating sporting competition that governing bodies must have powers to determine criteria for entry to competitions. If such criteria were subject to the degree of scrutiny practised in relation to restraining clauses in employment contracts preventing ex-employees from working for competitors or soliciting customers, few sporting restraints would survive and the orderly regulation of sport would be severely hampered. Consequently, as we shall see, eligibility criteria are viewed with relative tolerance by the English courts.

3.62 Thirdly, the onus of proving the reasonableness of a contractual restraint as between the parties to it, is on the party seeking to justify and benefit from the restraining term in the contract; whereas the onus of proving that a contractual restraint operates in a manner contrary to the public interest is on the party seeking to strike down the provision. The latter question is one of public policy, not merely one of fact, and the onus is 'no light one'.[65] In sporting cases it had been thought by practitioners until the mid-1990s that the onus of proving unreasonableness lay with the sporting body seeking to rely on a restraint. This view proceeds from the perceived applicability of orthodox commercial law principles to sporting contracts (and, as we shall see below, also to non-contractual arrangements).[66]

3.63 However, in *Stevenage Borough FC Ltd v The Football League Ltd*[67] Carnwath J accepted the League's submission that the doctrine as applied in the sporting context brought into play the public interest aspect of the test as expounded in the *Nordenfelt* case, despite the case law[68] normally ruling out the availability of judicial review of decisions of sporting bodies. Carnwath J drew on that case law, coupled with other authorities in which the Court of Appeal, presided over by Lord Denning MR, had developed the duty

---

[62] [1894] AC 535, HL.
[63] See, eg, *Esso Petroleum Co Ltd v Harper's Garage (Stourport) Ltd* [1968] AC 269, HL.
[64] See *Herbert Morris Ltd v Saxelby* [1916] AC 688, HL.
[65] Per Lord Parker in *Attorney-General of Australia v Adelaide Steamship Company* [1913] AC 781, 796–7.
[66] See *Eastham v Newcastle United FC Ltd* [1964] 1 Ch 413, Wilberforce J; *Greig v* Insole [1978] 1 WLR 302, Slade J; *Newport AFC Ltd v The Football Association of Wales Ltd* (1995) unreported, 12 April, Blackburne J.
[67] Reported at [2006] ISLR, SLR 128, but decided in July 1996.
[68] Considered in chapter 8, para 8.12 ff.

of fairness owed by domestic tribunals,[69] and concluded from his scholarly analysis that the orthodox view 'gives insufficient weight to the distinction between the private and the public aspect' and that:

> where the restraint is part of a system of control imposed by a body exercising regulatory powers in the public interest … [and] the system of control itself can be seen as in the public interest then … the onus lies on those seeking to challenge it to show that the particular rules under attack are unreasonable in that narrow sense.[70]

Importantly, Carnwath J's reference to the 'narrow sense' of unreasonableness reflected his view that the standard to be applied was probably that applicable in judicial review of public law decisions; thus requiring a claimant to show that the rule under challenge was arbitrary or capricious (the standard apparently considered correct by the Court of Appeal in *Nagle*'s case), or that it operated so harshly that its adoption was wholly outside the scope of the discretion of any reasonable sporting body. This conclusion tallied with the comment made by Megarry J in *McInnes v Onslow-Fane*,[71] which has been cited in several judgments since:

> I think that the courts must be slow to allow any implied obligation to be fair to be used as a means of bringing before the courts for review honest decisions of bodies exercising jurisdiction over sporting and other activities which those bodies are far better fitted to judge than the courts. This is so even where those bodies are concerned with the means of livelihood of those who take part in those activities. Concepts of natural justice and the duty to be fair must not be allowed to discredit themselves by making unreasonable requirements and imposing undue burdens. Bodies … which promote a public interest by seeking to maintain high standards in a field of activity which otherwise might easily become degraded and corrupt ought not to be hampered in their work without good cause. Such bodies should not be tempted or coerced into granting licences that otherwise they would refuse by reason of the courts having imposed on them a procedure for refusal which facilitates litigation against them … The individual must indeed be protected against improprieties; but any claim of this or anything more must be balanced against what the public interest requires.[72]

3.64 The upshot of the preceding discussion is that it is not always clear (1) where the onus of proof lies in a restraint of trade case involving a sporting body, or (2) precisely how the applicable standard of reasonableness should be formulated. Richards J in *Bradley v Jockey Club* deliberately left the open the question of onus of proof, as it was unnecessary for him to decide it.[73] Blackburne J at the trial in *Newport AFC Ltd v The Football Association of Wales Ltd*[74] treated the issue in the orthodox way, placing the onus on the body relying on the restraint to justify it, and applying the orthodox contractual test rather than a test inspired by public law principles.

3.65 A practical consequence of such uncertainty in this area of sports law is that, in preparing a restraint of trade challenge, or in preparing to resist such a challenge, a party would be well advised to plead and prove his or her case by identifying the specific factors

---

[69] *Nagle v Feilden* [1966] 2 QB 633; *Enderby Town FC v The Football Association* [1971] Ch 591; *Breen v Amalgamated Engineering Union* [1971] 2 QB 175.

[70] [2006] ISLR, SLR 128, para 60.

[71] [1978] 1 WLR 1520.

[72] Ibid, 1535F–H.

[73] [2004] EWHC 2164, para 35. Richards J's decision was upheld on appeal: [2005] EWCA Civ 1056.

[74] (1995) unreported, 12 April (full trial, Blackburne J; Jacob J's decision granting an interlocutory injunction is reported at [1995] 2 All ER 87).

which go to establish, or, as the case may be, undermine, the reasonableness of the rule or decision under attack.[75]

3.66 It is striking that cases concerning access to sporting competitions, as distinct from those involving employment related players' rights against their clubs, have for the most part failed insofar as they are founded on avoidance of rules alleged to operate in unreasonable restraint of trade. Thus in *Gasser v Stinson*[76] it was held that an automatic disqualification rule of the International Amateur Athletic Federation (IAAF) applicable to any athlete, regardless of guilty intent, whose urine should contain a banned substance, was justified by the need for certainty and the avoidance of evidential difficulties even though 'the morally innocent may have to suffer in order to ensure that the guilty do not escape'.[77] The strict liability principle in doping cases is now unexceptionable but at the time was controversial. The restraint of trade doctrine was held not to apply because of the amateur nature of the sport of athletics.

3.67 Again, in *Ray v Professional Golfers Association Ltd*,[78] a challenge to golfing related examination requirements as a precondition of eligibility to compete in certain tournaments was rejected. Although the learned judge appeared to hold (in our respectful view wrongly) that the restraint of trade doctrine did not apply at all because Mr Ray's contract was a training contract and not a trading contract, the judge clearly felt that any restraint in the contract was justified and referred to very full evidence from the Association showing why it was justified: namely, in order to protect the Association's legitimate interest in maintaining high standards by encouraging the concept of the well-rounded professional, versed not only in playing golf but in knowledge of other golf related matters.

3.68 In *Williams v Pugh*,[79] the Cardiff and Ebbw Vale rugby football clubs alleged against the Welsh Rugby Union that the latter's insistence that clubs wishing to be part of the Union must commit themselves to membership of it for at least 10 years, was in unreasonable restraint of trade. Refusal to enter the 10-year commitment meant not being allowed to play in a European competition the following season. Popplewell J considered the Union's evidence supporting its submission that the 10-year requirement was incontestably reasonable and that the decision to adopt it was neither arbitrary nor capricious. He did not have to decide whether the submission would succeed at a full trial, since the application was for an interim injunction, which the clubs obtained on the basis that their restraint of trade argument was not doomed to fail, and that the injunction should be granted to allow the clubs the chance to compete in Europe, and in the Premier League, the following season, applying classical principles governing interlocutory injunctions.[80]

3.69 But in *Chambers v British Olympic Association*,[81] application of those same principles led to the opposite result. Mackay J refused an injunction to enable Dwain Chambers to compete for Britain at the 2008 Beijing Olympics. Chambers had served a two-year ban

---

[75] Cf *Pharmaceutical Society of Great Britain v Dickson* [1970] AC 403, HL, where the claim succeeded on the basis that justification for the Society's strictures on new entrants to the pharmacist's profession had not been pleaded or proved. Cf *Conteh v Onslow Fane* (1) TLR, 5 June 1975; (2) TLR, 26 June 1975.

[76] (1988) unreported, 15 June, Scott J.

[77] Transcript, p 39G.

[78] (1997) unreported, 15 April, Judge Dyer QC.

[79] (1997) unreported, 23 July.

[80] See *American Cyanamid v Ethicon Ltd* [1975] AC 397, HL.

[81] [2008] EWHC 2028 (QB), [2008] ISLR, SLR 115.

for taking a banned substance, and on his return his performance on the track was good enough to earn him a place in the British team. However a bye-law provided that any athlete who had been found guilty of doping was ineligible for selection. Chambers asserted that the bye-law was an unreasonable restraint of trade and should be disapplied: he had served his time and should not have his two-year ban increased by the back door.

3.70 The judge disagreed. He held that since the Olympic Games was an amateur event offering no financial rewards and only medals, the prospects of establishing at trial (and a trial was most unlikely) that the doctrine did apply were poor;[82] and that even if it did, the test was whether the Association's bye-law went further than was reasonable or necessary to achieve the legitimate aims of the Association. He held that it was not a disproportionate measure. It only applied to the Olympic Games; it was not a worldwide ban. It was widely supported by athletes as appropriate to send a message to the public that doping was a blot on sport.

3.71 Wimbledon Football Club was more successful in achieving its objective of moving stadium through use of the restraint of trade doctrine. In *Wimbledon FC Ltd v The Football League Ltd*[83] the club successfully argued that it had a pressing need to move its ground to Milton Keynes in order to trade effectively. The League had a rule requiring clubs not to move outside their area of origin without permission, and refused to grant permission to Wimbledon. The League argued that the rule was justified because it was essential to maintain the pyramid structure of football in England. The arbitrators held that it was a restraint of trade which must be weighed against the harm that would be caused to the club if permission to move were refused. A subsequent FA Commission held that the risk of harm to the pyramid structure was outweighed by Wimbledon's need to move its ground.

3.72 Another instance of a claimant sportsman successfully removing a restraint was *Hendry v World Professional Billiards and Snooker Association*.[84] The judge decided that a rule requiring players to obtain the Association's permission to play in any snooker competition (other than in certain specified circumstances) was void and could not be enforced. He decided the claim mainly on competition law grounds (as further explained below), but also noted that the Association could not 'justify this restriction as being no more than is reasonably required for the protection of its own legitimate interests'.[85] This expresses the issue in the language of the classical orthodox doctrine and not in its alternative public law infused formulation preferred by Carnwath J in the *Stevenage* case,

---

[82] Applying the reasoning of O'Connor LJ in *Currie v Barton*, *The Times*, 12 February 1988 (an amateur tennis case where the restraint doctrine was held not to apply); and of Richards J in *Bradley v Jockey Club* [2004] EWHC 2164 (a 'right to work' case where the severity of a five-year ban from the sport was unsuccessfully challenged) (upheld on appeal, [2005] EWCA Civ 1056). At para 43 Richards J stated: 'The court's role, in the exercise of its supervisory jurisdiction, is to determine whether the decision reached falls within the limits of the decision-maker's discretionary area of judgment. If it does, the penalty is lawful; if it does not, the penalty is unlawful. It is not the role of the court to stand in the shoes of the primary decision-maker, strike the balance for itself and determine on that basis what it considers the right penalty should be.'

[83] FA arbitration, 29 January 2002.

[84] [2002] ISLR, SLR 1, [2001] Eu LR 770, Lloyd J (Ch Div).

[85] At para 116 of his judgment.

which was cited to the court but not analysed in the judgment, the judge commenting that nothing turned on the burden of proof in the case before him.[86]

3.73 The courts continue to adjudicate on conventional restraint of trade issues in commercial and employment related contracts in the sporting field. These are not cases concerned with criteria for entry to particular competitions but show the normal operation of the doctrine in the sports context. In *Watson v Prager*[87] Scott J decided that the British Boxing Board of Control's standard form manager's contract for professional boxers, of three years' duration but with an option for the manager to extend it by another three years if a certain level of successful results were attained, was an unreasonable restraint of trade and unenforceable. He granted relief to a boxer freeing him from the contract. Similarly, in *Proactive Sports Management Ltd v Rooney and others*[88] it was held that an 'image rights' contract relating to the footballer Wayne Rooney was too onerous and an unreasonable restraint on ordinary principles.

3.74 The occasional appearance of conventional restraint of trade cases in sport reminds us of an important and largely unanswered question: whether salary caps in sport should be regarded as unlawful as an unjustified restraint of trade, or whether they can be justified by the need to conserve funds for the development of the sport which otherwise are consumed in seemingly uncontrollable wage inflation, as is the case with Premier League football at present. The answer is likely to be fact sensitive, depending on conditions in the particular sports concerned. Salary caps can take various forms. They have already been introduced, without challenge, in several sports in this country and are an established feature of professional sport in the United States and Australia. The test would seem to be whether the cap is necessary to secure the continued existence and competitive balance of the sport and whether it is a proportionate means of attaining that objective.[89]

3.75 Challenges to contractual or other provisions operating in restraint of trade, including those setting criteria for entry to sporting competitions, sometimes bring into play the question whether an offending term can be severed from other valid parts of the document. The law relating to severance of unlawful terms is well established from case law in the commercial field, and we do not propose to treat it in detail here.[90] The guiding principles are as follows: (1) the court will not rewrite a contract (or other document) by altering its nature; (2) the court will not sever unenforceable parts of the document

---

[86] The Australian courts have been prepared to find restraints justified where measures are adopted to satisfy the demands of media organisations whose funding is essential to the commercial viability of the competition: *South Sydney District Rugby League FC v News Ltd* [2000] FCA 1541, [2001] FCA 862.

[87] [1991] ICR 603, [1991] 1 WLR 726; cf Gray J's decision in *Leeds Rugby Ltd v Iestyn Harris* [2005] ISLR, SLR 91 where clauses in a release agreement between a club and a player, taken together with other interlocking agreements, were valid and reasonable restraints (nor void for uncertainty or lack of consideration).

[88] [2011] ISLR, SLR 36, a truly epic 821 paragraph judgment of Judge Hegarty QC; see paras 620–731. The Court of Appeal ([2011] EWCA Civ 1444) dismissed the appeal on this aspect (partially allowing it on other grounds relating to construction of the contract at issue), holding that whether a contract was oppressive required an evaluation of all relevant factors by the judge and since the judge's evaluation was not clearly wrong, the appellate court would not interfere.

[89] See Lewis and Taylor (n 56) A3.19 and B2.194–9, expressing the view that in top flight European football a cap would not be held justified; see also (among the many articles on the subject) Harris, *Salary Caps* (2002) 10(1) SLJ 120; and Davies, *Salary Cap Scandals in Australian Professional Team Sports* [2011] ISLR 30. The temptation secretly to overpay creates the potential for disciplinary proceedings.

[90] For a useful exposition in the leading standard work on contract law, see *Chitty on Contracts* (n 61) vol 1 ch 16, paras 16-194 ff.

unless it accords with public policy to do so; and (3) it must be possible to excise the offending parts of the document without affecting the sense of the remaining valid parts—a process usually explained by reference to use of a 'blue pencil' which can be used to delete portions of the document but not to write in corrections on it. The question of severance arose in the *Stevenage* case,[91] but did not have to be decided because both the judge and the Court of Appeal decided to refuse any relief in the exercise of discretion despite criticisms of the Football League's entry criteria.

Non-Contractual Claims Asserting a Right to Participate

3.76 Having set out the fundamentals of the restraint of trade doctrine, in this next section we take a closer look at cases in which aspiring entrants to sporting competitions have attempted, sometimes in reliance on that doctrine and sometimes independently of it, to achieve access to the competition through litigation in the absence of any contractual right to participate. We have already mentioned the difficulty faced by a non-member of an organisation seeking to compel the organisation to accept the non-member as a member. However, a claimant whose private rights are affected by the operation of a restraint may seek a declaration from the court that the restraint is invalid, and possibly an injunction preventing it from being acted upon. It used to be supposed that a declaration could not be obtained for want of any underlying cause of action. But it is now established that, where private rights are affected, the freestanding right to a declaration is itself a cause of action sufficient to found declaratory relief.[92]

3.77 The restraint of trade doctrine has taken migratory steps into the quasi-regulatory field, having begun life as quintessentially a creature of nineteenth century contract law. This expansion of the doctrine occurred with the advent of an increasingly regulated society leading to a developed system of administrative law. A feature of this development was the extension of the doctrine to non-contractual cases.[93] Sporting cases were among the non-contractual cases but the doctrine had already been applied to non-contractual cases before judges applied it in a sport context. Carnwath J has rejected the argument that the doctrine is too blunt an instrument with which to judge the conduct of a sporting body in setting and enforcing standards governing entry to sporting competitions, preferring instead to adapt the doctrine, putting the onus of proof on the claimant and affording a considerable margin of appreciation to the sporting body.[94]

---

[91] Mentioned above, paras 3.18, 3.25, 3.63, 3.72, 3.75.

[92] See *Eastham v Newcastle United FC Ltd* (n 66) 443, Wilberforce J; Zamir and Woolf, *The Declaratory Judgment*, 4th edn (Sweet & Maxwell, 2011) 237–45 (paras 5-21–5-42); *Greig v Insole* [1978] 1 WLR 302 (Slade J).

[93] *Pharmaceutical Society v Dickson* [1970] AC 403 at 440C, per Lord Wilberforce ('The "doctrine" of restraint of trade has never been limited to contractual arrangements …'). Sullivan (n 32) 8 speaks in terms of *property* rights rather than private rights ('a sufficient right of property to give the members standing to seek a declaration [or] injunction, or … some other circumstance which gives the members standing to seek those remedies'); citing *Dixon v Esperance Bay Turf Club Inc* [2002] WASC 110; *McClelland v Burning Palms Surf Life Saving Club* (2002) 191 ALR 759; and *Rose v Boxing NSW Inc* [2007] NSWSC 20.

[94] *Stevenage Borough FC v Football League Ltd* (n 3).

3.78 Scott J rejected a similar argument in *Gasser v Stinson*,[95] pointing out that authority favoured applicability of the doctrine to the rules of the International Amateur Athletic Federation, of which the plaintiff athlete was not a member.[96] We do not accept the suggestion[97] that Carnwath J in the *Stevenage* case inappropriately elided the restraint of trade doctrine with applicability of public law derived principles against which to judge the actions of a sports governing body. It is indeed true that in *Mullins v McFarlane*[98] Stanley Burnton J stated that he did not regard the supervisory jurisdiction to grant a declaration against a governing body as confined to cases of unreasonable restraint of trade. It does not follow that public law principles have no useful part to play in cases where the doctrine is engaged, or that it should be applied in the same way to a sports body as to other relationships which themselves attract application of the doctrine nuanced according to the relationships in play, such as those of vendor and purchaser of a business, employer and employee, principal and agent, and so forth.

3.79 The court's jurisdiction to grant a declaration at the suit of an employee not only against his employer but also against 'the association of employers whose rules or regulations place an unjustifiable restraint on his liberty of employment' was established by the judgment of Wilberforce J in *Eastham v Newcastle United FC Ltd.*[99] George Eastham was able to obtain a declaration not merely against his employer, Newcastle United Football Club, but against the Football League, of which Newcastle, but not he, was a member. That approach was followed by Slade J in *Greig v Insole*,[100] in which the plaintiff cricketers succeeded in obtaining declarations against the International Cricket Council (ICC) and the Test and County Cricket Board (TCCB) (in each case through their representatives), though the plaintiffs were members of neither body.

3.80 In *Eastham*, the restrictive retention and transfer system embodied in rules of the Football Association and of the Football League were declared invalid as an unreasonable restraint of trade. In *Greig*, rule changes intended to prevent English county cricketers from signing contracts to play in test matches organised outside the auspices of the ICC and TCCB, and promoted by Mr Kerry Packer, were held to constitute a tortious inducement to players to break their contracts with Mr Packer's company (which also sued) and an unlawful interference with those contracts, which were not themselves an unreasonable restraint of trade. The cricketers obtained declarations of invalidity in relation to the ICC and TCCB's rule changes similar to that obtained by George Eastham. Thus he secured access to league football (his club in fact consenting to his transfer to Arsenal before the trial) after refusing to contract with Newcastle on expiry of his previous contract. And the cricketers in *Greig* vindicated their right of access to Mr Packer's competition which the established cricketing powers had sought to deny them.

3.81 However, a swimmer named Cowley was less fortunate in litigation she undertook against officers of the Commonwealth Games Federation, which had sought to declare

---

[95] (1988) unreported, 15 June, Scott J.

[96] See also Scott J's subsequent decision in *Watson v Prager* [1991] 1 WLR 726, 745D–F, where, however, the restraint was contained in a contract between a professional boxer and his manager.

[97] See Lewis and Taylor (n 56) A4.124, esp at fn 3.

[98] [2006] EWHC 986 (QB), [2006] ISLR, SLR 65.

[99] [1964] 1 Ch 413, 440–6. The passage cited from p 446 follows a useful review of prior non-sporting authority.

[100] [1978] 1 WLR 302, see 345E–H.

her ineligible to represent England in the Commonwealth Games. She challenged the decision of the officers of the Federation that she was not 'domiciled' in England, within the meaning of that word in the relevant rule requiring that the competitor must be domiciled in the country she represents. The decision turned on the meaning of the French word 'domicil' in its context. Sir Nicholas Browne-Wilkinson V-C said that it was not necessary for the court to decide the further question of whether Miss Cowley had the necessary standing to bring an action for a declaration against a body with which she had no contractual relationship. He held that, if he had jurisdiction to grant the declaration in question, he would not do so in any event, citing the abstentionist approach embodied in the dictum of Megarry J already quoted above.[101] He is also famously reported in the only report of his judgment, in *The Times* of 24 July 1986, as having said:

> Sport would be better served if there was not running litigation at repeated intervals by people seeking to challenge the decisions of the regulating bodies.

But the jurisdiction to entertain such proceedings and grant relief is not seriously in doubt, whether the challenge is founded on restraint of trade or, as in *Cowley v Heatley*, on alleged misconstruction by the sporting body of its own rules.

3.82 Indeed in one New Zealand case the right to bring proceedings for a declaration was stretched to its very limits, the plaintiffs having remarkably tenuous links to the defendant body, the New Zealand Rugby Football Union Inc. In this celebrated litigation two members of local rugby football clubs in Auckland sought an injunction to prevent the defendant Union from accepting an invitation to the All Blacks to tour South Africa. Initially they failed on the ground of lack of standing to bring the action, but on appeal the Court of Appeal in Wellington decided that they had sufficient standing as they were linked through a chain of contracts to the defendant Union. An interim injunction was granted and the tour of South Africa became administratively impossible as a result, though an appeal was pending. The plaintiffs therefore achieved their objective of stopping the tour, although their private rights were affected only to the extent that their local clubs had the right to appoint delegates as members of the Auckland Union which in turn was affiliated to the defendant New Zealand Union which had accepted the invitation. Thus the plaintiffs were members of clubs whose delegates were members of a member of the defendant.[102]

3.83 Mention should be made of the successful action by Newport Football Club and two other clubs against the Football Association of Wales in which the clubs succeeded in obtaining both an interim injunction and, at the full trial in 1995, a declaration that the Welsh FA's resolution preventing Welsh football clubs from playing in the English Football League, and to prevent them playing home matches in Wales other than within the Welsh FA, was invalid as an unreasonable restraint of trade. The interim injunction allowed them, pending the full trial, to play home matches in Wales during the 1994–5

---

[101] *Cowley v Heatley*, *The Times*, 24 July 1986; see above, para 3.81. For an up-to-date account of CAS cases on eligibility restrictions based on nationality and the increasing phenomenon of athletes seeking to compete for adopted countries, see Beloff, editorial [2011] ISLR 27.

[102] *Finnigan v New Zealand Rugby Football Union Inc* [1985] 2 NZLR 159, noted in Beloff and Kerr (n 27). For an example of an Antipodean case similar to *Eastham* (n 66) see *Kemp v New Zealand Rugby Football League Inc* [1989] 3 NZLR 463, HC.

football season. At the full trial Blackburne J held, applying orthodox restraint of trade principles, that the decisions under attack went further than was reasonably necessary for the protection of the Welsh FA's legitimate interest in promoting and administering football in Wales.[103]

3.84 The *Newport* challenge predictably succeeded because the Welsh FA had overestimated the scope of its power to allow its member clubs (and indeed ex-member clubs, for the three clubs resigned from the FA of Wales before commencing proceedings) to play football in Wales, and to prohibit them from doing so, on grounds unrelated to either performance on the field of play or the quality of facilities available. By contrast, Stevenage Borough Football Club, and before it, Enfield Town Football Club, failed to gain access to higher level competitions administered by bodies of which they were not members, but whose entry criteria relating to performance on the field of play they had satisfied by winning the lower level competition.[104]

3.85 In *Bradley v Jockey Club*[105] Richards J had to consider a claim that a five-year ban (reduced on appeal from eight years) imposed on a former jockey for wrongfully providing inside information for reward over a long period was excessive and unlawful. The Jockey Club provided for an appeal board under its rules and agreed to act as the appropriate defendant rather than require separate joinder of the appeal board, but the jockey had a contract only with the Club and not with the appeal board as such, which was a separate and independent body. The former jockey turned bloodstock agent sought what could be termed a private law judicial review of the appeal board's decision to impose a five-year ban, which would prevent him from earning his living during that period. He therefore invoked the jurisdiction of the court to intervene irrespective of contract, and asserted that the penalty imposed was excessive and an unreasonable restraint of trade. He failed on all counts. The importance of the case for present purposes lies in Richards J's, and the Court of Appeal's, endorsement of the proposition that the test to be applied to the decision was essentially the same as that which would be applied to a public body in a judicial review application.[106]

3.86 Not long afterwards, in *Mullins v McFarlane*, a case of inadvertent horse doping (the horse's feed being contaminated with poppy seeds containing small amounts of morphine) leading to the horse trained by the claimant being stripped of its victory in the Cheltenham Gold Cup, Stanley Burnton J considered the authorities including *Bradley* and expressed the provisional view that the court's jurisdiction to intervene was 'unrestricted' except by discretionary factors including, importantly, 'the respect and caution appropriate when considering the decision of an impartial qualified tribunal whose knowledge and experience of the subject matter in question is likely to exceed those of the Court.'[107]

---

[103] *Newport AFC Ltd v The Football Association of Wales Ltd* [1995] 2 All ER 87, Jacob J (interim injunction); ibid, unreported, transcript 12 April 1995 (full trial, Blackburne J).

[104] See *Stevenage Borough FC Ltd v The Football League Ltd*, at first instance, Carnwath J (n 3); cf *Enfield Town FC*, arbitration (1995), Sir Michael Kerr and two senior QCs, referred to at paras 63–64 of Carnwath J's judgment. Enfield Town's restraint of trade based challenge to the Conference's financial criteria, which it had failed to meet, was unsuccessful on the facts.

[105] [2004] EWHC 2164, upheld on appeal [2005] EWCA Civ 851 but better known for Richards J's admired analysis at first instance, fully endorsed in the Court of Appeal.

[106] See Richards J's judgment, paras 37 ff.

[107] [2006] EWHC 986 (QB), [2006] EWHC 986 (QB), [2006] ISLR, SLR 65. The challenge failed on the facts; it was not made out that the Appeal Board's decision was arbitrary and capricious. The claimant contended that

3.87 Such a wide formulation could be said to have gone beyond even the submission made on the claimant's behalf, founded on Carnwath J's decision in the *Stevenage* case and Richards J's in *Bradley*, which the judge correctly recorded as 'the Court will interfere with a decision of a body such as the Appeal Board of the Jockey Club if that decision is arbitrary or capricious or is based on a misinterpretation of the applicable rules of the sporting body in question'.[108] Nonetheless, it is to be doubted whether Stanley Burnton J intended to expand the grounds for intervention beyond the judicial review test sanctioned by Richards J and the Court of Appeal in *Bradley*, even if he did appear to re-cast restrictions going to jurisdiction as considerations going to discretion only.

3.88 Finally under this heading we mention some of the cases brought before the CAS in which access to sporting competition has had to be adjudicated upon. The CAS jurisprudence does not place contractual rights and obligations centre stage in the analysis. The rules under consideration often have contractual force, but not necessarily directly between the claimant seeking access to a competition and the body disputing the right of access. Much of the case law has been concerned with either individual selection challenges, or eligibility challenges turning on questions of nationality or citizenship. We consider nationality cases first.

3.89 An important and relatively early such case was heard in Montreal in March 1996.[109] The issue was whether José Cruz, a baseball player born in Puerto Rico and a Puerto Rican national but with US citizenship, was entitled to choose to play baseball for the USA national team, or whether the Puerto Rican federation was entitled to insist that he should play exclusively for Puerto Rico. The International Baseball Federation had been unable to resolve the dispute and had initiated a reference to arbitration before the CAS.

3.90 The Puerto Rican Federation argued that nationality and citizenship are not synonymous; that Cruz had US citizenship only, not US nationality; and that he should not be allowed to play against his own country. The respondent federation contended that the Olympic Charter recognised the right of an athlete to choose between playing for his country of birth and his country of citizenship, and, Cruz having chosen the USA, his choice must be respected. The panel decided that the source of applicable law was the Olympic Charter to which express reference was made in the rules of the International Baseball Association. Applying the relevant provisions of the Olympic Charter,[110] it decided that Cruz possessed two nationalities; that the Olympic Charter recognised dual nationality; that an athlete could choose which country he wished to represent in such cases, but could not elect more than one country; that Cruz had elected to play for the USA and had not played for Puerto Rico; and that his choice to play for the USA was valid.

---

the concentration of morphine in the sample was below a de facto threshold of 50ng/ml established in certain emails, but the judge accepted that the emails did not establish such a threshold, only a 'limit of detection' or 'reporting level'.

[108] See paras 37–39 of Stanley Burnton J's judgment.

[109] *Puerto Rico Amateur Baseball Federation v USA Baseball*, CAS 95/132, 15 March 1996.

[110] Rules 45 and 46 and their respective bye-laws, concerning eligibility and nationality of competitors.

3.91 The CAS Ad Hoc Division sitting at the Sydney Olympics in 2000 considered several cases of disputed eligibility based on nationality and citizenship.[111] The Olympic Charter now provides[112] that:

> A competitor who has represented one country in the Olympic Games, in continental or regional games or in world or regional championships recognised by the relevant IF, and who has changed his nationality or acquired a new nationality, may participate in the Olympic Games to represent his new country provided that at least three years have passed since the competitor last represented his former country. This period may be reduced or even cancelled, with the agreement of the NOCs and IF concerned, by the IOC Executive Board, which takes into account the circumstances of each case.

3.92 The kayaker Angel Perez nonetheless succeeded in a trilogy of cases[113] in establishing his right to compete for his adopted country, the USA, rather than his native Cuba, which sought vainly to prevent him from doing so. Perez had acquired US citizenship in the year before the 2000 Olympic Games and had been ruled ineligible to compete for the USA by the International Olympic Committee (IOC). His national federation and the US Olympic Committee appealed, initially unsuccessfully, but Perez then applied to reopen the matter, relying on a legal opinion that he had become a stateless person after defecting from Cuba, which had denied him fundamental civic rights and could not therefore be heard to assert any claim to his allegiance. Cuba failed to contradict the legal opinion and her subsequent attempt to reopen the matter a third time was refused on the ground of estoppel because Cuba had declined the opportunity to contest the second set of proceedings.

3.93 The Ad Hoc Panel interpreted the expression 'who has changed his nationality' as including the notion of becoming a stateless person, and held that to permit Cuba to assert dominion over an athlete whose civic rights it had denied would offend against the principles that the interests of athletes are paramount, and that competition is between athletes and not countries.[114]

3.94 The Panel distinguished its decision in *Miranda v IOC*[115] on the basis that the diver Arturo Miranda, who had obtained Canadian citizenship the year before the Sydney Olympics, had maintained his Cuban citizenship and passport and travelled annually to Cuba, maintaining his links with that country up to the moment of obtaining Canadian citizenship. He could not show any loss of civic rights. The Panel therefore upheld the IOC's refusal to let him dive for Canada.[116]

---

[111] See Beloff, *The CAS Ad Hoc Division at the Sydney Olympic Games* [2001] ISLR 105.

[112] Bye-law 2 to Rule 41; at Sydney in 2000, bye-law 2 to the then Rule 46 made provision in similar terms.

[113] CAS OG 00/001, 00/005 and 00/009 (Sydney). The substantive decision was *Perez v IOC*, CAS OG 00/005.

[114] Olympic Charter, then rr 3(1) and 9(1) respectively; now rr 1(3) and 6(1) respectively.

[115] CAS, OG 00/003 (see also the sequel at OG 00/008). The same result was reached at the 2008 Beijing Olympics in *Moldova National Olympic Committee v IOC*, CAS, OG 08/006, a bizarre case arising from a swimmer's purported change of 'sport nationality', to which the Moldovan and Romanian NOCs had apparently consented but the international federation (FINA, which took no part in the hearing) had not. The athlete was Moldovan but had, irregularly, represented Romania in a previous competition. CAS upheld the IOC's refusal to let him represent Moldova at Beijing.

[116] The CAS Ad Hoc Division at Sydney in 2000 also gave two decisions on the right to participate not based on nationality: *Comité Olympique Congolais, Kibunde v AIBA*, CAS JO 00/004 (Sydney) (boxer who missed weigh-in and medical examination because of travel and visa difficulties unable to overcome unequivocal rule barring participation, despite not being at fault, because principle of equality of treatment would be infringed if allowed to compete); and *Samoa NOC and Sports Federation Inc v IWF*, CAS OG 00/002 (Sydney) (Samoan weightlifter accused of sex with minor allowed to compete where alleged offences had not been examined on merits and athlete entitled to presumption of innocence).

3.95 A more recent nationality case came before the CAS in September 2010.[117] The case concerned the application of FIFA rules on eligibility to play for national teams, and the impact of those rules on the case of Daniel Kearns, a professional footballer who had held dual Irish and British nationality from birth, and had grown up in Northern Ireland. He had played for Northern Ireland several times at junior level but never in the top flight team. The Single Judge of FIFA's Players' Status Committee had acceded to his request to change his national association to that of the Republic of Ireland. The football governing body in Northern Ireland unsuccessfully challenged this conclusion before the CAS.

3.96 The relevant rules were complex and the outcome turned on their true construction. They allowed a change of association on a single occasion in the case of players with dual nationality, provided they had not played for their previous association at the highest level. Dual nationality cases were different from 'shared nationality' cases in which a player with a single nationality is eligible to play for more than one association. On a correct interpretation of the complex rules in issue, the Irish Football Association of Ireland (the Northern Ireland governing body) was unable to prevent the Football Association of Ireland (the Republic of Ireland's governing body) from acquiring the services of Mr Kearns, who at the time of writing plays for Peterborough United and has not yet represented the Republic of Ireland at full international level.

3.97 We turn next to some of the CAS cases where the challenge related to an individual selection decision. In two Australian decisions of the CAS, decided in July 1996 within 10 days of each other with opposite outcomes,[118] cyclists challenged their exclusion from selection for the Australian Olympic team due to compete in Atlanta in the 1996 Olympics. In the first case, Lynette Nixon argued that the selectors had not followed the criteria for selection set out in the Federation's document issued in January 1996, by failing to take into account performance in certain races in Europe in which she had taken part, and by failing to take account of psychological and physiological test results. She sought an order that the selectors should be required to reconsider the selection of the Australian Olympic team taking account of those factors. The jurisdiction of the CAS was established by an appeal agreement and was accepted by the parties. The applicable law was not dealt with in the brief written decision. The claim failed on the facts and on the construction of the selection criteria.

3.98 In the other case, Kathryn Watt sought to quash a decision of the same Federation to select another cyclist ahead of her to represent Australia in the women's 3,000 metres track cycling event, and further requested an order that the Federation honour a written guarantee that Watt would be selected. The parties agreed to submit the dispute to arbitration at very short notice. Four days later Winneke J, President of the Court of Appeal of Victoria, gave his decision in favour of Ms Watt. The case was unusual in that the Federation had actually announced to the media that it had 'guaranteed Kathy Watt's nomination as the rider in the Women's 3000m individual pursuit at the Atlanta Olympic Games in July', though the 'guarantee' was qualified in the event of illness or a 'unique ride' by another competitor 'equal or near to the new world record'.[119]

3.99 The judge noted the caution that courts exercise in interfering with decisions of domestic bodies (citing *McInnes v Onslow-Fane*) but held that the CAS was not a court

---

[117] *Irish Football Association v FA of Ireland and FIFA*, CAS 2010/A/2071.
[118] *Nixon v Australian Cycling Federation Inc*, CAS 96/152, *and Watt v Australian Cycling Federation Inc*, CAS 96/153.
[119] CAS 96/153, transcript at pp 8–9.

of law but an arbitral body whose very purpose was to entertain disputes referred to it, inter alia, by agreement. He regarded the agreement to submit the matter to arbitration by way of an appeal as requiring him to determine whether the decision was arrived at fairly and with due and proper regard to the interests of the appellant.[120] He found in favour of the appellant cyclist, on the basis that her legitimate expectation of selection had been unfairly denied by the Federation in that the guarantee had been reneged upon without cause, and that Watt had relied on the guarantee by spending time, effort and money preparing herself in accordance with a training schedule set by the Federation's coach and agreed to by the Federation.

3.100 In a strong decision reminiscent of Lord Denning, yet not one apparently founded on any contract, Winneke J held that the Federation was 'duty bound to honour its commitment to the Appellant unless circumstances of the type which qualified that commitment came to pass'.[121] He declined to remit the matter back to the Federation for further consideration and directed it to nominate Watt instead of the other cyclist. For good measure, he stated as an apparently general proposition that:

> Where a sporting organization, in circumstances deemed by it to be appropriate, chooses to depart from its established rules of selection procedure and to nominate, in advance, a particular athlete as its selected choice for a particular event and, in doing so, creates expectations in and obligations upon that individual, then in my view it should be bound by its choice unless proper justification can be demonstrated for revoking it.[122]

Winneke J's decision represented, at the time, the high water mark of judicial interventionism in the affairs of sporting bodies exercising discretion in the selection of competitors. Australian judges have been slightly less reticent than English ones about interfering with decisions of sporting bodies. But the facts were very strong in *Watt*, an unusual case of withdrawal of a pre-selected athlete. Winneke J did say that the decision should be regarded as confined to its own facts, and it should not be assumed that the proposition above could necessarily be applied to other factual situations in other jurisdictions.

3.101 In the first case to be heard before the Ad Hoc Division of the CAS at the 1996 Olympic Games in Atlanta,[123] the US Swimming Federation, supported by the German and Netherlands swimming teams, challenged a decision of the International Swimming Federation (FINA) to allow the Irish gold medallist Michelle Smith to compete in the 400 metres freestyle. Had the challenge succeeded, a formidable rival to the celebrated US swimmer Janet Evans would have been eliminated while still on dry land. The basis of the complaint was that Ms Smith's entry had been submitted too late. In a swift decision given the night before the race, the panel of arbitrators decided that as late entries for specific events were frequent in many sports, and as FINA's rules did not impose a stricter regime than in other sports, it would be unfair to single out one late entrant and penalise her with disqualification. Ms Smith won the gold medal the following day.

3.102 We have already mentioned that challenges to selection decisions are likely to be more straightforward where the selection criteria are purely objective, based on results

---

[120] Ibid, 12–13.
[121] Ibid, 18.
[122] Ibid, 27.
[123] *US Swimming v FINA*, CAS Ad Hoc Division, 21 July 1996, reported in *Mealey's International Arbitration Report*, February 1997, pp 25–26, by Gabrielle Kaufmann-Kohler, President of the Ordinary Arbitration Division of CAS, and President of the Ad Hoc Division in Atlanta.

only, than in cases where there is a subjective element in the selection criteria. This was never better demonstrated than by the contrasting results in two cases heard by the CAS Ad Hoc Division at the 2006 Olympic Winter Games in Turin.

3.103 In the first case[124] a snowboarder's challenge failed where five snowboarders, excluding Fraülein Schuler, had been selected on the basis of criteria which were a mix of objective facts and subjective judgments. Her failure to show that she been wrongfully excluded was not surprising, for she was asked at the hearing which of the other five she should have replaced, and was unable to say.

3.104 In the second case,[125] an Italian snowboarder's challenge succeeded. The selection criteria were purely objective, and were altered by the national federation to the detriment of the claimant without informing her of the change, after she had already earned one of the four places to which she had established her entitlement under the unaltered previous criteria. Thus the effect of the change was unfairly to take away her accrued right to participate, as in the case of the cyclist Kathryn Watt. The Ad Hoc Panel distinguished the *Schuler* case and declared the claimant duly selected to the Italian snowboard team.[126]

3.105 The Beijing Olympics of 2008 saw a selection dispute relating to the German tennis player Rainer Schüttler, whom the German National Olympic Committee (NOC) had nominated to take part on the basis of its nationally set criteria, even though that excluded another player with higher world ranking points, following the withdrawal of other higher ranked players through application of other rules, injury and other valid causes. The International Tennis Federation argued that the matrix of rules required NOCs to nominate players strictly in accordance with the ITF's order of ranking. The CAS Panel disagreed,[127] acknowledging that while there were powerful arguments on both sides, autonomy of selection was not removed from the NOC under the rules on their true construction. Herr Schüttler's selection was therefore upheld.

EU Law and Access to Sporting Competitions; Competition Law and the Right to Participate

Applicable Provisions of EU Law

3.106 The access of players employed by clubs to sporting competitions is addressed in chapter four below in the context of the player/club relationship. This chapter is concerned with the access of teams and self-employed sportsmen and women to competitions.

3.107 Both the EU free movement rules (particularly Article 56 TFEU, which protects the freedom to provide services) and the EU rules on competition are potentially applicable to rules and regulations governing access to sporting competitions. Article 56 TFEU

---

[124] *Schuler v Swiss Olympic Association*, CAS OG 06/002.
[125] *Isabella Dal Balcon v CONI and FISI*, CAS OG 06/008.
[126] For commentary on the two cases see [2006] ISLR 50–52.
[127] *Schüttler v ITF*, CAS OG 08/003.

prohibits restrictions on the freedom to provide and receive services in other Member States. It provides materially as follows:

> Within the framework of the provisions set out below, restrictions on freedom to provide services within the Union shall be prohibited in respect of nationals of Member States who are established in a Member State other than that of the person for whom the services are intended.

Restrictions falling within this provision may nonetheless be justified if they are proportionate to one of the legitimate public interest objectives set out in Article 52 TFEU,[128] namely public policy, public security or public health. Restrictions may also be justified as being proportionate to one of the many additional legitimate public interest objectives recognised by the ECJ in its case law so long as the restrictions are not discriminatory.

As explained further below,[129] the free movement provisions apply to sport insofar as it constitutes an economic activity. This has been interpreted broadly by the ECJ. Thus, the application of the free movement provisions extends to participants in amateur sports who receive any indirect remuneration, even if they are not directly paid for their sporting activities.[130] However, the ECJ has also recognised that certain rules are of 'purely sporting interest' such as not to attract the application of the free movement provisions.[131] This principle has survived the Court's judgment in *Meca-Medina*,[132] though it is likely that the so-called 'sporting exception' will henceforth be more narrowly construed. Certainly, the Court made clear in *Meca-Medina*[133] that it cannot be relied upon to exclude the whole of a sporting activity from the scope of the Treaty.

3.108 The EU competition rules are contained in Articles 101 and 102 TFEU and their domestic equivalents are the Chapter I and Chapter II prohibitions in the Competition Act 1998, which fall to be interpreted in accordance with the EU rules. A fuller introduction to the general scope of these provisions will be found in chapter six, since they have been applied more often to the marketing of sport than to rules regulating the actual practice of sport.[134]

3.109 It is self-evident, however, that rules regulating access to a sporting competition by definition have the effect of preventing some players or clubs from playing in the competition and that this, in turn, may restrict or distort competition in the economic sense. As explained above,[135] the ECJ's judgment in *Meca-Medina* establishes that a rule is not immune from the application of the competition provisions simply because it is concerned with the organisation of sport. The 'sporting exception' applicable to the free movement provisions does not therefore apply; instead, it is necessary to examine the requirements of Articles 101 and 102 TFEU in each individual case. But, equally, the fact that a rule restricts the freedom of action of athletes or clubs does not necessarily mean that it will infringe Articles 101 and 102. The Court recognised in *Meca-Medina* that a sporting rule may be

---

[128] Applicable by virtue of Art 62 TFEU.
[129] See paras 4.8–4.49 below.
[130] See Joined Cases C-51/96 and C-191/97 *Deliège* [2000] ECR I-2549.
[131] See, eg, Case 36/74 *Walrave and Koch* [1974] ECR 1405, para 4; Case 13/76 *Donà v Mantero* [1976] ECR 1333, para 12.
[132] Case C-519/04P *Meca-Medina* [2006] ECR I-6991, para 25.
[133] Ibid, para 26.
[134] See para 6.2 ff.
[135] See para 3.107 above.

compatible with those provisions to the extent that it pursues a legitimate objective and its restrictive effects are inherent in that objective and proportionate to it.[136] The latter principle is particularly relevant in the context of rules governing access to sporting competitions. This is because legitimate objectives of sporting rules will normally relate to 'the organisation and proper conduct of competitive sport'[137] which may include rules relating to access.

Selection Rules

3.110 In *Deliège*,[138] the ECJ held that the selection rules applied by a judo federation to govern participation in an international competition inevitably limited the number of participants, but that such a limitation was 'inherent in the conduct of an international high-level sports event, which necessarily involves certain selection rules or criteria being adopted'.[139] It followed that the selection rules did not constitute a restriction on the freedom to provide services within the meaning of Article 56 TFEU.[140] Although the Court did not apply Articles 101 and 102 TFEU in that case, it is likely that the rule in question would also meet the *Meca-Medina* test for those provisions as its effects would be inherent in the pursuance of a legitimate objective (proper organisation of the sport event) and would not be disproportionate.[141]

3.111 The Court has also considered selection rules which are based on the nationality of teams or participants and has held that it is not an infringement of EU law to require that national teams include only persons of the same nationality. Thus, in *Walrave*,[142] two Dutch nationals who acted as paid pacemakers in cycling races brought an action against the Union Cycliste Internationale whose rules provided that, for the purposes of the medium-distance World Championships, the pacemaker had to have the same nationality as the cyclist. The ECJ held that the prohibition against discrimination based on nationality did not affect the composition of national teams, the formation of which is a question of purely sporting interest. In other words, it applied the sporting exception. Although the Court did not apply the competition rules, it is likely that the rule in question would also meet the *Meca-Medina* test for the application of Articles 101 and 102 as it was inherent in the legitimate objective it pursued (organisation of sports competitions with national teams).[143]

---

[136] *Meca-Medina* (n 132) para 42. See also Case C-309/99 *Wouters* [2002] ECR I-1577.
[137] *Meca-Medina* (n 132) paras 45–46. See also the Commission's Staff Working Document (SWD) at para 2.1.5.
[138] Joined Cases C-51/96 and C-191/97 *Deliège* [2000] ECR I-2549.
[139] Ibid, para 64 of the Court's judgment.
[140] Then Art 59 EC; though the Court rejected the argument that Art 56 did not apply on the basis that Ms Deliège was an amateur sportswoman who was not engaging in an economic activity. The Court noted that Ms Deliège had received grants and sponsorship and, whilst leaving the determination of the question to the national court, noted at paras 56 and 57 that a high-ranking athlete's participation in an international tournament was capable of involving the provision of a number of separate but closely related services, such as advertisement and sponsorship.
[141] Commission's SWD, para 2.2.1.1.
[142] Case 36/74 *Walrave and Koch* [1974] ECR 1405.
[143] This is the Commission's view: see the SWD at para 2.2.1.4.

3.112 Similarly, in *Donà v Mantero*[144] the Court of Justice held that rules excluding foreign players from participating in football matches between national teams were excluded from the scope of the free movement provisions because they 'relate to the particular nature and context of such matches and are thus of sporting interest only'.[145] The Court takes a very different approach in relation to nationality restrictions outside the context of selection for national teams and has, for example, declared rules that limited the number of players from other Member States that a football club could field at any time to be invalid.[146]

The Organisation of Sport on a Territorial Basis

3.113 Most sports in Europe are organised primarily on a national basis such that clubs or athletes present in one Member State compete in the national competitions organised by the national federation. One aspect of this is that it is common to provide that access to national competitions is not open to clubs or individual athletes based in another Member State or belonging to a different national federation.

3.114 In the *Mouscron* case[147] the Commission received a complaint under Articles 101 and 102 concerning UEFA's refusal to permit the Belgian football club, Excelsior Mouscron, to play its home match in the 1997–8 UEFA Cup against FC Metz in Lille rather than Mouscron. UEFA refused permission on the basis that to grant it would be incompatible with its 'home and away' rule. The Commission rejected the complaint on the ground that the 'home and away' rule constituted a sporting rule which did not fall within the scope of Articles 101 and 102. The Commission found further that 'the case had to be assessed within the context of the national geographic organisation of football in Europe, which is not called into question by Community law'.[148] Although this case would now be analysed differently in the light of *Meca-Medina*, it seems likely that the outcome would be the same given the Commission's conclusion that the rule pursues a legitimate objective (equality of chances between clubs). The restrictions caused by the rule appear to be inherent in the organisation of club competitions and the Commission found that the rule was proportionate to its objective.[149]

3.115 The Commission also received a complaint from Clydebank, which wanted to move to Dublin whilst continuing to play in the Scottish football league. The complaint alleged that a league rule preventing this contravened Article 49 TFEU, which protects freedom of establishment. The Commission did not reach a final decision but said in response to a question in the European Parliament that it 'seems at first sight that the organisation of national football leagues on a territorial basis is not related to the economic issues in this sport but to the very nature of the sport in question'. Again, although the analysis would be different now in the light of *Meca-Medina*, it is likely that the outcome would be the same.

---

[144] Case 13/76 *Dona v Mantero* [1976] ECR 1333, para 12.

[145] Ibid, para 14 of the Court's judgment.

[146] This is discussed at paras 4.45–4.49 below.

[147] Commission decision of 9 December 1999, Case 36851, *CU de Lille/ UEFA (Mouscron)*, decision not published; see Commission press release IP/99/965 of 9 December 1999.

[148] See the Commission's press release.

[149] See the Commission's SWD at para 2.2.1.2.

Promotion Criteria

3.116 Access to a league or a division within a league is often dependent on attaining certain standards. These may be confined to sporting achievement (eg, whether a team has won the championship in the division below) but they may also relate to matters such as financial soundness, ground facilities or the equipment used. There seems little doubt that the *Meca-Medina* approach would apply to such rules.

3.117 In the *Stevenage FC* case[150] it was argued by the claimant club that the requirement that clubs that win the Vauxhall Conference must fulfil certain criteria relating to the quality of their ground facilities and their financial soundness, before being admitted to the League, was contrary to Article 101 TFEU.[151] The Court did not, in the event, decide the point because it held that there was no effect on trade between Member States. This would be no answer today as a club in an equivalent position would now be able to rely on the Chapter I prohibition in the Competition Act 1998 which requires simply an effect on trade within the UK or a substantial part of it. Indeed, it must be doubted whether the rule would have passed the *Meca-Medina* test. The fact that the criteria were more onerous than those imposed on clubs which were already members of the Football League makes it very difficult to conclude that it was proportionate.

3.118 The Office of Fair Trading (OFT), in the *England Rugby Ltd Entry and Ongoing Criteria* case, upheld a complaint from First Division Rugby that the criteria applied by England Rugby Limited (ERL) (i) were discriminatory in favour of clubs incumbent in the Premiership, and (ii) contained disproportionate rules concerning the ownership of grounds.[152] It was alleged in particular that some First Division clubs would be denied promotion to the Premiership, even if they finished the previous season at the top of Division One, because they failed to meet the 'Primacy of Tenure' requirements set down by ERL. The Primacy of Tenure rule required a Premiership club to have first call on use of its own ground. According to the complaint, the fact that most successful non-Premiership clubs tended to share grounds with football clubs, who have first call on their own grounds, meant that, in practice, this rule restricted membership to existing Premiership clubs. The OFT was concerned that this requirement could raise the costs of aspirant clubs relative to at least some incumbent clubs and that this could distort competition between those clubs. It therefore required ERL to revise its criteria such that aspirant clubs were no longer required to have first call over the ground at which they played. Instead, all clubs had to demonstrate that they were able to provide a venue with certain minimum facilities for home matches.

Common Ownership of Competing Clubs

3.119 Returning to the *AEK Athens* litigation before the CAS,[153] UEFA's rule preventing commonly owned clubs from taking part in the same competition was challenged

---

[150] First instance (n 2), Carnwath J, transcript, 23 July 1996.
[151] Then Art 85 EEC.
[152] Case closed on 6 August 2003.
[153] CAS 98/200.

by AEK Athens and Slavia Prague, which were both controlled by ENIC and which had both qualified for the 1998 UEFA Cup. They alleged that the rule infringed Articles 101 and 102 TFEU in that it was not necessary to protect the integrity of European football competitions and was disproportionate in its impact to the attainment of that objective, in particular because it applied in blanket fashion and did not allow for exceptions in cases where, for instance, the common owner would pass a 'fit and proper person' test.[154] The clubs further argued that UEFA enjoys a position of dominance in the market for European football competitions, and that the decision to adopt the rule under challenge constituted an abuse of that dominant position. An interim order in July 1998 preventing UEFA from excluding AEK Athens from the 1998–9 UEFA Cup was made on other grounds.[155] However, following the substantive hearing, the CAS found that the rule appeared to 'have the effect of preserving competition between club owners and between football clubs rather than appreciably restricting competition on the relevant market or on other football markets'.[156]

Restrictions on the Organisation of New Competitions

3.120 Such restrictions have been discussed in the context of the application of the restraint of trade doctrine,[157] but they are also prime material for the application of the competition rules. The Commission, at paragraph 2.2.2.1 of its Staff Working Document, cites rules shielding sports associations from competition as an example of sporting rules that may infringe Articles 101 and 102 TFEU. It discusses, in that paragraph, the *FIA* case relating to Formula One racing. It concerned a complaint considered by the Commission in 1999 concerning FIA rules which prohibited drivers and race teams that held an FIA licence from participating in non-FIA authorised events. Furthermore, circuit owners were prohibited from using their circuits for races that could compete with Formula One. The Commission issued a Statement of Objections which reached the preliminary conclusion that these rules violated Articles 101 and 102. It was concerned about the conflict of interest inherent in the fact that the FIA was not only the regulator of the sport but also its commercial exploiter. The Commission considered that the rules in question enabled the FIA to block the organisation of races which the FIA organised and from which it derived a commercial benefit. The Commission also objected to certain terms of the contracts between Formula One Administration Ltd (FOA), the company that administered the TV rights to Formula One races, and broadcasters because they also made it possible to block competing events, eg by imposing a severe financial penalty on broadcasters if they showed anything deemed by FOA to be a competitive threat to Formula One.

3.121 The Commission closed the case after a settlement was reached in 2001. The settlement provided that the FIA would limit its role to that of a regulator without influence

---

[154] As in, for example, the case of the rules of the English Premier League and the Scottish Football Association, both of which restrict multiple shareholdings in clubs except with the prior consent of the association or league.

[155] Viz, a prima facie violation of the principle of good faith through retroactive effect on AEK Athens after that club had fulfilled pre-existing qualification criteria.

[156] *AEK PAE and SK Slavia Praha v UEFA*, CAS 98/2000, award dated 20 August 1999, *Digest of CAS Awards II, 1998–2000* (2002, Kluwer) paras 150–1.

[157] See para 3.55 ff above.

over the commercial exploitation of the sport, through the appointment of a commercial rights holder for 100 years in exchange for a one-off fee. It also provided that the FIA would no longer prevent teams from participating in or circuit owners from organising other races, provided that the requisite safety standards were met. The FIA also agreed to waive its TV rights or transfer them to the promoters concerned and to remove the anti-competitive terms from agreements between FOA and broadcasters.

3.122 Similar issues relating to a conflict of interests came before the European Court in the *MOTOE* case.[158] That case concerned the role of ELPA, the Greek Automobile Club, in approving applications to organise motorcycling competitions in Greece in circumstances where the Club itself also organised such competitions. MOTOE, an organisation which wished to organise such competitions, complained that Greek legislation conferring the power to authorise such events on ELPA, with no restrictions on its power and no right for applicants to seek review of its decisions, was contrary to Article 102 TFEU. The Court held that ELPA was an undertaking for the purposes of the application of Article 102. Further, Articles 102 and 106[159] TFEU both precluded the Greek legislation in question because it placed ELPA at an obvious advantage over its competitors and was liable to lead it to deny other operators access to the market.[160]

3.123 *Hendry v World Professional Billiards and Snooker Association Ltd*[161] was a case decided under what are now Articles 101 and 102 TFEU (previously Articles 81 and 82 of the EC Treaty) and under the Competition Act 1998. The WPBSA is the world governing body for snooker and acts as the regulator as well as the organiser and promoter of professional snooker tournaments. At issue was the compatibility with the competition provisions of one of its rules, pursuant to which members were precluded, without the prior consent of the WPBSA, from entering tournaments or participating in matches organised by anyone else. Although the WPBSA did sanction other matches and tournaments, its policy was not to do so on dates which conflicted with WPBSA tournaments or matches or in circumstances where they might be televised at the same time as WPBSA tournaments or matches. Lloyd J held that this rule was an abuse of WPBSA's dominant position and thus a breach of the Chapter II prohibition. The scope in the calendar for sanctioning rival events to the WPBSA was very limited,[162] and its effect was to prevent competition 'by limiting the sources to which players can have recourse in order to earn their livelihood'.[163]

---

[158] Case C-49/07 *MOTOE* [2008] ECR I-4863. See [2009] CML Rev 1327; [2008] ISLJ 13.

[159] Which precludes Member States, in relation to public undertakings and undertakings to which it grants special or exclusive rights, from enacting or maintaining in force any measure contrary to the rules of the Treaty and, in particular, the competition provisions.

[160] See, in particular, paras 51–53 of the Court's judgment.

[161] [2001] Eu LR 770 (Lloyd J, 5 October 2001). For case comment see, eg, Veljanovski, *Markets in Professional Sports: Hendry v WPSBA and the Importance of Functional Markets* [2002] ECLR 273; Harris, *Abusive Sports Governing Bodies: Hendry and others v World Professional Billiards and Snooker Association* [2002] Competition Law Journal 101; Stoner, *Competition Matters: The Rules of Snooker under Scrutiny in English Courts* (2002) 9(3) Sports Law Administration and Practice 8.

[162] See para 109.

[163] Para 112.

4

Players' Rights

Introduction: Relations between Players and Clubs Generally

4.1 This chapter concerns the rights and obligations of players vis-à-vis their employers. We are concerned not only with players in the narrow sense of sportsmen and women, but also with 'players' in the world of sport, in the wider sense of those who work alongside the individual and team competitors: coaches, managers, team doctors, physiotherapists and the like. Most of the principles discussed here are applicable to persons employed by sports bodies in those capacities as well as actual competitors. For convenience, in this chapter we refer to employers of players as 'clubs'. Unless otherwise stated, that term should be taken to include any other type of sporting body which may employ players.

4.2 The chapter examines players' rights in two stages. We deal, first, with the *formation* of the relationship between player and club, and, second, with the *content* of that relationship. The latter includes the circumstances in which the relationship can be terminated; but it is not central to our purpose to dwell on the law governing dismissals in sport, which do not occupy a position of prominence in sporting jurisprudence.

4.3 In the majority of team sports, a player must be employed by a club in order to participate professionally. Thus, a player's freedom to join a club is closely connected with his ability to play in sporting competitions and, therefore, to work. The first section of this chapter focuses on the nature of that freedom and the legality of restrictions placed upon it. The other side of the same coin is the freedom of a player to leave a club by which he or she is employed and join another. We have already, in chapter three, covered the related issue of access to competitions outside the employment context, in respect of sports where employment by a club is not a prerequisite to competition.

4.4 If the main theme of the first section of this chapter is freedom of movement, that of the second is employment rights. We do not attempt to summarise the law of employment; where appropriate the reader is directed to specialist works on the subject. Our aim is to illustrate how that area of law applies to the particular features of employment in the context of sport.

4.5 We also include at the end of this chapter an account of the developing law relating to the protection of children as it applies to the practice of sport.

Formation of the Player/Club Relationship

4.6 In most professional sports there is not a perfectly free market in players. In other words, the ability of a club to purchase and sell players and the corresponding ability of players to join and move clubs is not unconstrained. There are a number of potential obstacles. Some of these are imposed by the rules of leagues and/or governing bodies to which the clubs belong. Thus, a league may prescribe that its member clubs have to pay a transfer fee when buying a player from another member club; or it might lay down transfer 'windows' outside of which clubs are not permitted to buy or sell players. Others stem from the contractual nature of the player/club relationship. For example, it may be difficult for a player to leave a club before the contract between them has expired. Obstacles may also be imposed by legislation. An example of this is the requirement imposed by immigration legislation on most foreign players to obtain a work permit before they can play for a British club.[1]

4.7 The EU free movement rules and competition rules and the restraint of trade doctrine are all potentially applicable to restrictions on movement between clubs. The scope, structure and general application of the free movement rules are considered below before we discuss how they apply to matters affecting the formation of the player/club relationship. The EU and domestic competition rules are explained in chapter six below in the context of the commercial exploitation of sport; and the restraint of trade doctrine is discussed in chapter three in the context of access to sporting competitions. This chapter addresses the application of those legal provisions and principles to restrictions on the formation of the player/club relationship.

The EU Free Movement Rules

4.8 In chapter two above, we summarised the application of EU law to sport. Of great importance are the free movement provisions of the Treaty and especially, so far as this chapter is concerned, Article 45 TFEU on the free movement of workers.[2] Article 45 provides as follows:

(1)   Freedom of movement for workers shall be secured within the Community.
(2)   Such freedom of movement shall entail the abolition of any discrimination based on nationality between workers of the Member States as regards employment, remuneration and other conditions of work and employment.
(3)   It shall entail the right, subject to limitations justified on grounds of public policy, public security or public health:
   (a)   to accept offers of employment actually made;
   (b)   to move freely within the territory of Member States for this purpose;

---

[1] See *R v Secretary of State for Education and Employment, ex parte Portsmouth FC Ltd* [1998] COD 142.
[2] Art 49 TFEU, which provides for freedom of establishment, and Art 56 TFEU on the freedom to provide services, are both important in relation to the rights of clubs and of self-employed sportsmen and women. For a recent statement of the Commission's view of the application of the free movement provisions to sport, see the Commission Staff Working Document, *Sport and Free Movement* SEC(2011) 66/2.

    (c)   to stay in a Member State for the purpose of employment in accordance with the provisions governing the employment of nationals of that State laid down by law, regulation or administrative action;

    (d)   to remain in the territory of a Member State after having been employed in that State, subject to conditions which shall be embodied in implementing regulations to be drawn up by the Commission.

(4)   The provisions of this Article shall not apply to employment in the public service.

Scope of Application

4.9 The first question that needs to be addressed is the extent to which Article 45 and the other free movement provisions are applicable to sport. The free movement rules are, in the main, applicable to action taken by the state and not private parties.[3] However, the European Court of Justice (ECJ, or now the renamed Court of Justice of the European Communities, the CJEU) has made it clear that they extend to certain actions of private law sports governing bodies. Thus, in *Walrave* the Court held that the prohibition of discrimination contained in the free movement provisions[4]

> does not only apply to the action of public authorities but extends likewise to rules of any other nature aimed at regulating in a collective manner gainful employment and the provision of services.

Consequently, those provisions were to be taken into account by the national court 'in judging the validity or the effects of a provision inserted in the rules of a sporting federation'.[5]

4.10 Who may rely on the free movement provisions and in respect of what kind of act? The ECJ has held that 'sport is subject to Community law only in so far as it constitutes an economic activity'.[6] Consequently, in its early *Donà v Mantero* judgment,[7] the Court held that the free movement rules apply to professional or semi-professional football players who are providing services for remuneration or have signed an employment contract. In *Deliège*,[8] the Court held that the mere fact that a sports federation unilaterally classifies its members as amateur athletes does not in itself mean that they do not engage in economic activities.[9] Although Ms Deliège did not receive direct remuneration for her participation in judo competitions, the Court noted that she had received sponsorship from a bank and a car manufacturer as a result of her sporting achievements.[10] As regards specifically the provision of services (now Article 56 TFEU), the Court held as follows at paragraphs 56–57 of its judgment:

> [S]porting activities and, in particular, a high-ranking athlete's participation in an international competition are capable of involving the provision of a number of separate, but closely related,

---

[3] Though the ECJ has given a much more expansive scope of application to Art 45 TFEU, which has been held to have horizontal as well as vertical direct effect: see Case C-281/98 *Angonese* [2000] ECR I-4139.

[4] Case 36/74 *Walrave and Koch v Union Cycliste Internationale* [1974] ECR 1405, para 17.

[5] Ibid, para 25.

[6] Ibid, para 4.

[7] Case 13/76 *Donà v Mantero* [1976] ECR 1333.

[8] Joined Cases C-51/96 and C-191/97 *Deliège v Ligue Francophone de Judo et Disciplines Associées ASBL* [2000] ECR I-2549. See Turner-Kerr and Bell, *The Place of Sport within the Rules of Community Law: Clarification from the ECJ? The Deliège and Lehtonen Cases* [2002] European Competition Law Review 256.

[9] *Deliège*, ibid, para 46.

[10] Ibid, para 51.

services which may fall within the scope of [Article 56] even if some of those services are not paid for by those for whom they are performed ...

For example, an organiser of such a competition may offer athletes an opportunity of engaging in their sporting activity in competition with others and, at the same time, the athletes, by participating in the competition, enable the organiser to put on a sports event which the public may attend, which television broadcasters may retransmit and which may be of interest to advertisers and sponsors. Moreover the athletes provide their sponsor with publicity the basis for which is the sporting activity itself.

4.11 The *Deliège* judgment shows that the scope of application of the free movement provisions is potentially very broad. However, the outer bounds in relation to amateur sport are still not clear. On the one hand, the Services Directive[11] which applies, inter alia, to sport activities states at Recital 35 that 'Non-profit making amateur sporting activities ... often pursue wholly social or recreational objectives. Thus, they might not constitute economic activities within the meaning of Community law and should fall outside the scope of this Directive.' On the other hand, the Commission's Staff Working Document states the view that 'amateur sport must not remain outside the scope of the fundamental principles of free movement' because 'access to sport is a social advantage [with] ... high popularity and importance for the social integration of citizens'.[12] Thus, the position of someone in Ms Deliège's situation who was competing in amateur competitions but had not attracted sponsorship remains an open question as regards the application of the free movement provisions.

4.12 Without prejudice to the principles set out above, the European Court has also held that sporting rules are not subject to EU law where they concern issues of purely sporting interest; this has often been referred to as the 'sporting exception'.[13] This is the case, for example, as regards the application of nationality conditions when selecting a national team. Thus, in *Donà*[14] the Court held that rules excluding foreign players from participating in football matches between national teams were excluded from the scope of the free movement provisions because they 'relate to the particular nature and context of such matches and are thus of sporting interest only'.

4.13 However, as confirmed in the *Meca-Medina* case, in order to benefit from the sporting exception, a rule must 'remain limited to its proper objective' and cannot 'be relied upon to exclude the whole of a sporting activity from the scope of the Treaty'.[15] The Court went on to state at paragraph 27 that:

> [I]t is apparent that the mere fact that a rule is purely sporting in nature does not have the effect of removing from the scope of the Treaty the person engaging in the activity governed by that rule or the body which has laid it down.

Substantive Application of Article 45 TFEU and the Other Free Movement Provisions

4.14 The European Court tends to apply the same principles in the context of Articles 45, 49 and 56 TFEU. These provisions represent the application, in the specific fields of

[11] 2006/123/EC.
[12] Staff Working Document (n 2) para 4.2.1.
[13] Mentioned in chapter 2: see paras 2.91–2.93.
[14] *Donà v Mantero* [1976] ECR 1333, para 12.
[15] Case C-519/04 P *Meca-Medina* [2006] ECR I-6991, para 26.

employment, establishment and services, of the fundamental rule contained in Article 18 TFEU prohibiting discrimination on grounds of nationality. These provisions are themselves directly effective and have also been amplified by secondary legislation which clarifies their scope.[16] A two-stage analysis applies when considering whether there has been a breach of the free movement provisions. The court will, first, examine whether there has been a restriction on free movement; second, it will determine whether that restriction is nonetheless objectively justified.

4.15 There will be a restriction on free movement if a rule (a) directly discriminates on grounds of nationality;[17] (b) indirectly discriminates on grounds of nationality (ie is neutral on its face but has a discriminatory impact in practice; or (c) though not discriminatory is liable to hamper or render less attractive the exercise of free movement rights.[18] Such restrictions are unlawful unless they can be objectively justified. A restriction will only be objectively justified if (a) it is an appropriate means of attaining a legitimate objective, and (b) it is proportionate to that objective in that it goes no further than is necessary to achieve it. A slightly different approach to justification applies depending on whether or not the restriction is directly discriminatory.

4.16 Directly discriminatory restrictions may only be justified pursuant to one of the express derogations set out in the Treaty. Article 45(3) TFEU permits derogations from the principle of the free movement of workers on the grounds of public policy, public security and public health. Articles 52 and 62 TFEU contain the same derogations for establishment and services. The burden of proof is on the defendant to demonstrate that one of the derogations justifies its rule or action.

4.17 Indirectly discriminatory and non-discriminatory restrictions may be justified on these grounds, but may also be saved by a broader category of public interest objectives which have been recognised by the European Court. For example, in *Bosman* the European Court recognised that restrictions on free movement were capable of being justified in that 'the aims of maintaining a balance between clubs by preserving a certain degree of equality and uncertainty as to results and of encouraging the recruitment and training of young players must be accepted as legitimate'.[19]

Transfer Rules

4.18 Transfer fee systems are extremely common. They are generally administered through the rules of a particular sport's league or governing body. Transfer rules are, thus, contractually enforceable as between clubs either directly or indirectly through their common membership obligations, as direct or indirect members of the organising body. Transfer fee systems are peculiar to the context of sport. It is difficult to think of another context in which prospective employers are subject to financial disincentives to

---

[16] For example, Regulation 1612/68 elaborates on the equal treatment principle in the context of free movement of workers, setting out many of the substantive rights or workers and their families.

[17] Eg the rules of the Italian football federation providing that only Italian players could take part in matches, considered in *Donà v Mantero* [1976] ECR 1333.

[18] Eg the transfer rules considered in Case C-415/93 *Bosman* [1995] ECR I-4921, discussed further below at para 4.22 ff.

[19] Case C-415/93 *Union Royale Belge des Sociétés de Football Association ASBL v Jean-Marc Bosman* [1995] ECR I-4921, para 106.

recruitment. The rationale is said to be that they provide compensation for the training and development of players.

4.19 Transfer systems may differ in their detail from one sport to another but they all share common features. Essentially, they impose a scheme of player registration such that a player becomes registered with a particular club upon joining it. Registration confers the right to play and must relate to a single club at any one time. Any other club wishing to employ that player must pay the first club a transfer fee in order to purchase the player's registration.

4.20 Although transfer rules govern the business relationships between clubs rather than the employment relationships between clubs and players, they clearly affect a player's chances of finding employment and the terms on which such employment is offered.[20] The transfer system may impede the ability of a player to join the club of his or her choice if a transfer fee cannot be agreed. Thus, players may be prevented from simply selling their labour freely to the employer willing to pay the most once their employment has come to an end. Further, it has been said that high transfer fees have a deflationary effect on players' wages.

4.21 Leagues and governing bodies are not, however, unrestricted in terms of the transfer rules they impose. The law is astute to ensure that transfer systems do not unduly curtail three important freedoms. They are, first, the freedom of movement of players within the European Union;[21] second, the right of clubs freely to compete in the labour market, a right protected by competition law, notably Articles 101 and 102 TFEU as well as analogous provisions of UK law; thirdly, it is important that the operation of transfer systems does not unduly restrict the right of players to work. This right is protected by the common law doctrine of restraint of trade. These three areas of law and their impact on the operation of transfer systems are discussed in turn below.

Application of the EU Free Movement Provisions to Transfer Rules

4.22 In the celebrated *Bosman* case, the Court of Justice held that (what is now) Article 45 TFEU precludes the application of rules whereby a professional footballer who is a national of one Member State may not, on the expiry of his contract with a club, be employed by a club of another Member State unless a transfer, training or development fee is paid.[22]

4.23 Jean-Marc Bosman was a Belgian footballer who had been employed by FC Liège, a Belgian first division club. His contract expired at the end of June 1990. In April 1990 the club offered him a new one-year contract at a very unattractive salary. Bosman refused this offer and was transfer listed at a 'compensation' fee of BFR 11,743,000. Interest in Bosman was shown by US Dunkerque, a French second division club. In July 1990 the two clubs agreed a contract for the transfer of the player for one year only at a price of BFR 1,200,000, including an option allowing Dunkerque subsequently to buy the player at an additional cost of BFR 4,800,000. Both the contract between the two clubs and that between Dunkerque and the player were subject to the receipt by the French Football

---

[20] Ibid, para 5.
[21] Discussed above; see para 4.8 ff.
[22] *Bosman* (n 19) para 114.

Federation of the transfer certificate issued by the analogous Belgian federation. FC Liège entertained doubts as to US Dunkerque's solvency and did not ask the Belgian federation to forward the certificate in question. As a result, neither contract took effect. On 31 July 1990, FC Liège suspended Mr Bosman, thereby preventing him from playing for the entire season.

4.24 The Court held that the transfer rules in question constituted an obstacle to freedom of movement for workers prohibited in principle by Article 45 TFEU. It reasoned that Article 45 precludes measures which might place Community citizens at a disadvantage when they wish to pursue an economic activity in the territory of another Member State. That includes measures which preclude or make it more difficult for a Community national to leave one Member State and enter another in order to work. The transfer rules clearly fell within that category.[23] The fact that the transfer rules applied also to transfers of players between clubs within the same Member State, and therefore did not discriminate on nationality grounds, did not mean that they were consistent with Article 45. This is because Article 45 prohibits not only measures which are directly or indirectly discriminatory, but also measures which hinder movement between Member States of the European Union.

4.25 Having found that the transfer rules were prima facie contrary to Article 45, the Court went on to consider whether they were capable of justification on any of the public interest grounds contained in Article 45. The parties resisting Mr Bosman's claim argued that the transfer rules were justified by the need to maintain a financial and competitive balance between clubs, and to support the search for talent and the training of young players. These arguments were rejected by the Court. It held that the application of transfer rules does not achieve the first of those aims since they do not prevent the availability of financial resources from being a decisive factor in competitive sport. As regards the second aim, the Court accepted that the prospect of receiving transfer fees is likely to encourage clubs to seek new talent and train young players. However, bearing in mind that it is impossible to predict the sporting future of young players with any certainty, and that transfer fees do not reflect the actual cost of training players, the Court found that the prospect of receiving such fees was not a decisive factor in encouraging recruitment and training, and the infringement of Article 45 was therefore not objectively justified.[24]

4.26 Several observations may be made as to the scope of the *Bosman* judgment. First, it goes without saying that the Court's ruling is not limited to football but applies equally to similar rules in the context of other sports. Second, the TFEU confers rights only on nationals of EU Member States. However, analogous principles apply under the European Economic Area (EEA) agreement to the additional EEA Member States (Norway, Iceland and Liechtenstein). Further, the ECJ has held that a player who is a national of a third country also benefits from similar rights where the EU has entered into an international agreement with that country in circumstances where the agreement includes rights of non-discrimination in employment that have direct effect.[25]

---

[23] Ibid, paras 94–97.
[24] Ibid, paras 105–14.
[25] Case C-438/00 *Kolpak* [2003] ECR I-4135, discussed further below at para 4.48.

4.27 Third, the purpose of Article 45 is to facilitate movement between Member States of the European Union. Therefore, it does not bite upon the application of transfer rules to players who are EU nationals moving between a club within and a club outside the European Union. Nor does it apply to transfer rules within the purely domestic sphere, as discrimination within a Member State against a national of that state, known as 'reverse discrimination', does not come within the scope of the Treaty.[26] This does not, however, mean that domestic transfer rules are necessarily compatible with EU law as there remains the question of the impact of the competition rules discussed below.

4.28 Following the *Bosman* ruling, FIFA amended its regulations to abolish the payment of transfer fees for out-of-contract players who were EU or EEA nationals and who moved from one EU or EEA Member State to another. This left a number of situations in which transfer fees still did have to be paid. Although these situations were not covered by Article 45 TFEU, the Commission addressed them pursuant to the competition rules as discussed below.[27]

4.29 *Bosman* was concerned with the impact of Article 45 on the requirement for transfer fees once a player's contract with the selling club has ended. There remained, however, other aspects of transfer fee systems which were potentially susceptible to challenge under Article 45. An obvious example is where a transfer system treats transfers to clubs in other Member States less favourably than transfers within the national association. In his opinion in *Bosman*, Advocate General Lenz referred to the system then in place in Denmark where the rules governing the calculation of transfer fees led to a higher fee where a player was moving to a club abroad than where he was moving between clubs in Denmark.[28] Such rules would infringe Article 45 as their effect is to hinder the free movement of players between Denmark and other Member States of the EU.

4.30 Similar reasoning applies where the rules of the national association, in conjunction with the rules of UEFA or FIFA lead to unequal treatment. Advocate General Lenz pointed to a feature of the system then operating in France where under the rules of the French association a transfer fee was payable only if it was a professional player's first change of club. Further transfers within France could therefore take place without payment of a fee. However, if a player wished to move to a club abroad, the UEFA and FIFA rules, which assumed the payment of a transfer fee, applied. This too constituted a breach of Article 45.[29] A similar rule in Spain was disapplied to the benefit of the Brazilian forward, Ronaldo. He was under contract with Barcelona and wanted to join Inter Milan. Under the Spanish league rules he could buy himself out of his contract with Barcelona, provided he went to another club in Spain. As it seemed clear that the rule in question in principle breached Article 45 Ronaldo was eventually able, even though not himself a

---

[26] *Bosman* (n 19) para 89. For the purposes of EU law (though not for football administration), movement between England and Scotland is viewed as purely internal. Therefore, Art 45 of the Treaty does not prohibit the application of transfer rules to British players moving between England and Scotland, though *quaere* whether it would prohibit the application of transfer rules to nationals of other EU Member States moving between English and Scottish clubs.

[27] See para 4.33 ff, below.

[28] *Bosman* (n 19) para 156.

[29] Ibid, para 160.

national of any EU state, to buy himself out of his contract in the same way as he would
have done had he gone to another Spanish club.

4.31 Many transfer systems have a transfer window in the season or a transfer deadline after which transfers may not take place. The compatibility of such deadlines was
considered by the European Court in the *Lehtonen* case. The Court held that a transfer
deadline or window engages the application of Article 45 because a rule which restricts
participation in matches to persons transferred before the relevant deadline 'obviously
also restricts the chances of employment of the player concerned'.[30] However, in principle such rules could be objectively justified on the ground that they meet the objective of
ensuring the regularity of sporting competitions. In particular, the Court recognised that
late transfers might be liable to change the sporting strength of one or more teams in the
championship, something which could call into question the functioning of the championship as a whole if they occurred at a late stage of the season or in advance of a decisive
match.[31] Whether a rule which restricts free movement is objectively justified is a question of fact in each case; the rule must be proportionate to its legitimate objective. In this
case, the Court noted that the deadline for transfers from teams located outside Europe
was a month later. In those circumstances—though the question of proportionality was
ultimately for the national court—the ECJ expressed the view that the earlier deadline
therefore went beyond what was necessary to achieve the aim pursued.[32]

4.32 In its *Olympique Lyonnais* judgment, handed down some 15 years after *Bosman*, the
Court reaffirmed the principles it had laid down in the earlier judgment.[33] *Olympique
Lyonnais* concerned a rule applicable to professional football players in France which
provided that young players employed by professional clubs under a fixed term training
contract (*joueurs espoir*) could be required by their club to sign a professional contract
at the end of the training period, failing which they could be ordered to pay damages to
the club. The question for the Court was whether this rule breached Article 45 TFEU. It
held that the rule restricted a player's free movement rights and that, in principle, such
a rule might be justified by the objective of encouraging the recruitment and training of
young players. In particular, the Court recognised that clubs might be discouraged from
training young players if they could not obtain reimbursement of the amounts spent for
that purpose.[34] However, the rule must be proportionate to that objective and, in the
present case, it was not proportionate because it provided for the payment of damages
by the player which were unrelated to the real training costs incurred by the club.[35] The
Court indicated that the scheme would have been proportionate and therefore compliant
with Article 45 TFEU had it provided for damages which were related to the costs borne
by the club 'in training both future professional players and those who will never play
professionally'.[36]

---

[30] Case C-176/96 *Lehtonen v ASBL* [2000] ECR I-2681, para 50.
[31] Ibid, paras 53–55.
[32] Ibid, para 58.
[33] Case C-325/08 *Olympique Lyonnais v Olivier Bernard and Newcastle United FC* [2010] ECR I-2177. See
Pijetlovic, *Another Classic of EU Sports Jurisprudence* [2010] European Law Review 857.
[34] *Olympique Lyonnais*, ibid, paras 38–45.
[35] Ibid, paras 45–49.
[36] Ibid, para 45.

Articles 101 TFEU and the Chapter I Prohibition of the Competition Act 1998

4.33 The meaning and effect of these provisions are discussed in chapter six. This section focuses on their application to transfer rules. Although this question was argued in *Bosman*, the Court did not perceive the need to decide it given that the case could be determined on the basis of Article 45. However, it was considered in some detail by Advocate General Lenz. The first issue to consider is whether a set of transfer rules constitutes either an agreement between undertakings or a decision by an association of undertakings. As explained in chapter six, there is little difficulty in classifying clubs as undertakings and governing bodies as either undertakings or associations of undertakings.[37] The European Commission and Courts have adopted a broad approach to the meaning of 'undertaking' such that the word includes any entity carrying on activities of an economic nature. In *Distribution of Package Tours during the 1990 World Cup*[38] the Commission explained that an activity of an economic nature is one that involves economic trade whether or not profit-making. This broad definition means that Article 101 TFEU is applicable not only to large and profitable sports clubs, but also to smaller clubs which carry on only minor commercial activities. It also follows that national and international sports governing bodies are themselves undertakings to the extent that they carry on economic activities. Indeed, in its decision on *Distribution of Package Tours during the 1990 World Cup*, the Commission held that FIFA, the Italian Football Association and the local organising committee were each undertakings for the purposes of Article 101 TFEU.

4.34 Further, there is little difficulty in establishing that a system of transfer rules constitutes either an agreement between clubs or a decision taken by a governing body which is itself an association of undertakings. The precise analysis may depend on the structure of a particular league. For example, if the governing body is monolithic and independent in structure, then any transfer system is more likely to be deemed a decision taken by an association of undertakings. However, if a governing body provides in effect no more than a talking shop for its members, then the analysis is likely to be that of an agreement between the clubs themselves. Which of these two characterisations is adopted matters little, as it does not affect the substantive issue of whether the transfer system is caught by Article 101 TFEU. However, the issue is important as far as enforcement is concerned, as it will dictate whether it is a club or its governing body that is liable for any infringement of the competition rules.

4.35 The next and important question is whether transfer rules can have the effect of restricting or distorting competition. The view of both the Commission and Advocate General Lenz is that rules requiring the payment of a fee after the expiry of a player's contract, such as those at issue in *Bosman*, clearly can. In particular, they deprive clubs of the possibility of competing freely with respect to the signing of players. If there was no obligation to pay transfer fees, then a player would be free at the end of his contract to choose the club which offered him the best terms.[39] Thus, an obligation to pay a transfer fee in respect of an out-of-contract player is very likely caught by Article 101(1) TFEU.

---

[37] See paras 6.13–6.16 below.
[38] See para 255 of AG Lenz's opinion in *Bosman* (n 19).
[39] Ibid, para 262 of AG Lenz's opinion.

4.36 Would such a restriction benefit from exemption under Article 101(3)? This would depend upon the precise details of the transfer rules in question. Advocate General Lenz thought that those in issue in *Bosman* would not. He acknowledged that professional football is substantially different from other markets in that clubs are mutually dependent on each other; football cannot be played if there are no other teams to play against. Therefore each club has an interest in the health of other clubs and generally does not aim to exclude its competitors from the market. Likewise, the economic success of a league depends on the existence of a certain balance between its clubs.[40] Advocate General Lenz could envisage the possibility of certain restrictions on competition being necessary in order to maintain that balance. However, the transfer rules at issue could not benefit from exemption under Article 101(3) as they were not indispensable to the attainment of such objectives. Less restrictive alternatives existed, such as the redistribution of a proportion of income.[41]

4.37 *Bosman* did not address the wider issue of the legality of transfer fees for players who are still under contract. Following the Court's ruling, FIFA amended its regulations to abolish the payment of transfer fees for out-of-contract players who were EU or EEA nationals and who were moving cross-border in the EEA. But it left all other aspects of its transfer regime intact. In December 1998, the Commission sent FIFA a statement of objections in which it took issue with the transfer regime and, amongst other things, expressed the view that the rules applicable to in-contract players also fell within the scope of Article 101(1) TFEU.[42] The Commission raised four main concerns. The first related to the FIFA rule which provided that a player who unilaterally terminated his contract would not be able to play for a new club even if he paid whatever damages were due for breach of contract. The second concerned the rule which provided that the buying club, selling club and player were all free to agree on a transfer fee which need not bear any relation to the actual costs that the transferring club had incurred in relation to developing or training the player. Thirdly, the Commission objected to the rule that obliged national associations to organise their domestic transfer regimes in accordance with the principles set out in the FIFA rules. And finally, the Commission objected to the provision in the FIFA statutes that prevented parties taking disputes concerning transfers to the civil courts.

4.38 After months of negotiations, the Commission announced in March 2001 that it was satisfied with the new set of principles proposed by FIFA for the international transfer of players.[43] The main principles agreed upon were: (i) measures to support the training of players, eg through training compensation for young players and a solidarity mechanism in order to redistribute a significant proportion of income to clubs involved in the training of the player; (ii) establishing a transfer period per season; (iii) the specification of contractual arrangements between players and clubs, eg requiring contracts to have a minimum one-year and maximum five-year duration; and (iv) ensuring that arbitration

---

[40] Ibid, para 227.
[41] Ibid, para 270.
[42] The Commission also takes the view that transfer fees for players still under contract have 'the potential to severely restrict freedom of movement between UK states for players': see the Staff Working Document (n 2) para 2.2.2.4.2.
[43] Commission Press Release IP/01/314.

was voluntary and did not preclude recourse to national courts in the event of disputes. The agreement reached brought the competition proceedings to an end, though the Commission did not issue an exemption, thus leaving open the possibility of challenge before the national courts.[44]

4.39 It may be surmised from the outcome of these negotiations that, in the Commission's view, transfer windows or deadlines raise no issue under Article 101(1)[45] but, conversely, very high transfer fees might well do so.

Restraint of Trade

4.40 The application of the restraint of trade doctrine to sport is discussed in chapter three in the context of access to sporting competitions. Here we deal with the application of the doctrine to transfer rules.[46] The restraint of trade doctrine has always been applied to covenants contained in contracts of employment which limit the freedom of the employee to work following termination of employment.[47] A feature of transfer systems is that they almost always have this restrictive effect, and so the main question is whether the restraints inherent in the transfer system are reasonable with reference to the interests of the parties concerned and of the public.

4.41 This question was addressed in respect of the then transfer rules of the FA in *Eastham v Newcastle United FC*.[48] The transfer rules were at that time coupled with powers of retention whereby a club could debar a player joining another club at the end of his contract simply by continuing to pay him a reasonable wage. Wilberforce J held that the transfer and retention systems, when combined, operated in restraint of trade, that the defendants had not discharged the onus on them of showing that the restraints were no more than was reasonable to protect their interests, and, as such, they were unenforceable.[49] In assessing whether the restraints were capable of justification, the judge held that it was unnecessary to consider whether the justifications put forward by the defendants corresponded to categories of interests, such as goodwill and trade secrets, which the law recognised as constituting interests which employers were entitled to protect. Rather, he acknowledged that the context of sport in which the restraints operated was different from that of industrial employment, and found that those concerned with the organisation of professional sport had legitimate interests worthy of protection.[50] The judge went on to consider the various justifications put forward, including that they enabled clubs to be maintained in smaller towns and that, in the absence of transfer rules, clubs would

---

[44] See Egger and Stix-Hackl, *Sports and Competition Law: A Never-Ending Story?* [2002] European Competition Law Review 81. For an analysis of the approach taken by the Commerce Commission in New Zealand to the application of competition law to transfers in rugby union, see Ahdar, *Professional Rugby, Competitive Balance and Competition Law* [2007] European Competition Law Review 36.

[45] See also para 2.4 of the Commission's Staff Working Document (n 2).

[46] See, generally, McCutcheon, *Negative Enforcement of Employment Contracts in the Sports Industries* (1997) 17(1) Legal Studies 65; Bailey, *The Tie that Binds: Restraint of Trade in Sports*, conference paper presented at Chelsea FC, 25 November 1996.

[47] See *Chitty on Contracts*, 30th edn (Sweet & Maxwell, 2011) (incorporating 3rd Cumulative Supplement) para 16-081.

[48] *Eastham v Newcastle United FC Ltd* [1964] Ch 413.

[49] Ibid, 446–7.

[50] See ibid, 433–7. It is notable that the justifications put forward bear a striking similarity to those invoked in *Bosman* over 20 years later.

be dissuaded from spending money on training players. He held, however, that insofar as these concerns were made out as legitimate on the evidence, they could be met by less restrictive means.

4.42 Similar issues were at stake in *Greig v Insole*,[51] a case which concerned not transfer rules but rules of the International Cricket Council (ICC) and the then Test and County Cricket Board (TCCB) which, in effect, prevented cricket players taking part in competitions organised by another body to which they had already signed up.[52] After finding that the rules were such as 'substantially [to] restrict the area in which it will be open to professional cricketers to earn their livings',[53] Slade J went on to consider whether they were nevertheless justifiable. Applying what was essentially a proportionality test,[54] Slade J found that though the defendant had legitimate interests worthy of protection, the restraints went further than was necessary to protect them. Both of these cases also establish that an action for restraint of trade may be brought by a third party. The plaintiffs in *Eastham* and *Greig* were not themselves in a contractual relationship with the organising body whose rules they sought to challenge. This was not, however, a bar to relief.[55]

4.43 That the necessity for transfer rules must be carefully assessed if they are to pass muster under the restraint of trade doctrine is also well established in Commonwealth jurisprudence. In one Australian case,[56] 154 rugby league players challenged the validity of rules of the New South Wales Rugby League providing that players wishing to be transferred at the end of the 1990 season had to nominate terms and conditions on which they were prepared to play. Thereafter the clubs had the right to select any particular player, provided it was willing to meet the terms asked, in an order of precedence which was the reverse of that in which the teams were ranked at the end of the preceding competition. There were to be several such 'drafts' during the season, so that if a player was not selected in the first draft, he could submit himself at the next draft, and so on. The last such draft was in June, the relevant competition having already begun in March. The Federal Court declared these rules unenforceable as an unreasonable restraint of trade, commenting that the 'draft' system did little to protect the interests of the League but much to infringe the freedoms and interests of players.[57]

4.44 It can be seen from the above discussion that transfer fees and other rules of sports federations which restrict freedom of employment will generally fall to be considered both under competition law rules and under the restraint of trade doctrine. Usually, the focus of competition law is different to that of restraint of trade, being more concerned with the public interest question of competitiveness in the marketplace generally, as opposed to the private law question of the effect of a particular contract on one person's ability to trade. However, transfer systems—by their nature—are implemented via rules

---

[51] *Greig v Insole* [1978] 1 WLR 302.
[52] This case arose from Kerry Packer's attempts to set up a rival series of test matches.
[53] *Greig* (n 51) 345B–C.
[54] Ibid, 347H.
[55] A significant case in this context is *Faramus v Film Artistes Association* [1964] AC 925, in which it was held that an organisation with effective monopolistic power over a particular field of activity, such that compliance with membership rules is a prerequisite to earning a living in that field, is subject to the restraint of trade doctrine at the suit of individuals whom it prevents from earning a living.
[56] *Adamson v New South Wales Rugby League Ltd* (1991) 103 ALR 319.
[57] See also *Buckley v Tutty* (1971) 125 CLR 353.

affecting a large number of participants in a sport. For this reason, whilst they impact upon each individual's freedom to trade, they are also liable to have a much wider impact on the competitiveness of the market.

Nationality-Related Restrictions

4.45 The EU free movement rules obviously have something to say about rules or quotas applied by leagues or governing bodies which contain restrictions on players based on nationality. Following *Bosman*, it is clear that leagues may not restrict the number of EU nationals that may be employed by a club or may be fielded by the club in any one team.[58] At issue in that case was the legality of the '3+2' rule adopted by UEFA whereby clubs could field three foreign players and two 'assimilated' players.[59] The Court held that the rule did restrict the free movement of workers within the meaning of Article 45 TFEU of the Treaty. The fact that it concerned not so much the employment of other EU nationals but the extent to which their clubs could field them in official matches was irrelevant, given that participation in matches is the essential purpose of a professional player's activity. A rule which restricts participation also restricts the chances of employment of the player concerned.[60] The Court went on to consider whether the '3+2' rule was justified on non-economic grounds but held that it was not. The arguments put forward by the football federations were that such rules serve to maintain the traditional link between each club and its country, are necessary to create a sufficient pool of national players to provide the national team with top players, and help to maintain a competitive balance between clubs by preventing the richest clubs from appropriating the services of the best players.

4.46 The Court doubted the legitimacy of the first of these arguments. It reasoned that a club's links with the Member State in which it is established cannot be regarded as any more inherent in its sporting activity than its links with its locality, town or region and, even though national championships are played between clubs of different regions, there is no rule restricting the right of clubs to field players from other regions. As to the second argument, the Court made the point that whilst national teams must be made up of players with the nationality of that country, those players need not necessarily play for clubs in that country. Thirdly, it stated that the nationality rule did not maintain a competitive balance between clubs as there was nothing to prevent the richest clubs recruiting the best national players.

4.47 Nationals of states belonging to the EEA (that is, Norway, Iceland and Lichtenstein) benefit from similar rights.[61] And in a line of cases, the ECJ has established that nationals of third countries which have an international agreement with the EU containing an equal treatment clause prohibiting discrimination on grounds of nationality in the context of

---

[58] Contrast the position in relation to selection for national teams discussed in chapter 3 above, where the ECJ has held in several cases that rules excluding foreign players from playing in matches between national teams are excluded from the free movement provisions because they fall within the sporting exception.

[59] The rule was the result of a compromise between UEFA and the Commission in 1991. 'Assimilated' players are those who have played in the country of the relevant association for an uninterrupted period of five years, including three years as a junior.

[60] See para 120 of the Court's judgment in *Bosman* (n 19).

[61] The European Economic Area Act 1993.

employment cannot be excluded on the basis of their nationality from a team sent out on the field. Consequently, in its Order in *Nihat Kahveci*[62] the Court held that a rule of the Spanish Football Federation whereby clubs could only field three non-EU nationals could not be applied to a Turkish player who played for Real Sociedad. In so ruling, the Court followed its earlier judgments in *Kolpak*[63] (where it held that similar nationality restrictions could not be applied by the German handball federation to a Slovak player because of a non-discrimination provision in the Association Agreement with Slovakia) and in *Simutenkov*,[64] another case concerning the rules of the Spanish football association but this time their application to a player of Russian nationality.

4.48 Since *Bosman*, both FIFA and UEFA have attempted to introduce modified nationality restrictions, no doubt motivated by the fact that clubs rarely nowadays reflect their country, let alone their locality.[65] FIFA, at its Congress in May 2008, decided to try to implement a '6+5' rule whereby each club must field at least six players eligible to play for the national team of the country of the club. The European Commission swiftly declared that such a rule would be directly discriminatory on grounds of nationality and thus in breach of EU law.[66] Following unsuccessful attempts to persuade the Commission to the contrary, FIFA announced in 2010 that it would abandon the proposal and look at other options.

4.49 The Commission has, however, so far taken a different view of UEFA's 'home-grown player' rule, stating that this is capable of justification and, unlike the rule at issue in *Bosman*, does not constitute direct discrimination. The 'home-grown player' rule was introduced in 2005 and requires that clubs participating in the Champions League and Europa Cup[67] must have a minimum number of 'home-grown' players in their squads. 'Home grown players' are defined by UEFA as players who have been trained by their club or by another club in the national association for at least three years between the ages of 15 and 21. UEFA's rule provided for a gradual implementation such that in the 2006–7 competition, a club had to name four home-grown players from a squad of 25 and this would increase to eight out of 25 in the 2008–9 season. In its 2008 press release,[68] the Commission noted that the practical effects of the rule would therefore not be totally clear for a number of years and that it intended to monitor its implementation closely and undertake a further analysis of its consequences by 2012. The rule is one which may well end up being challenged in court. It seems very likely to be indirectly discriminatory as it is likely that more young players being trained in a particular Member State are nationals of that state. The question for a court would therefore be whether the rule is a proportionate to a legitimate objective.[69]

---

[62] Case C-152/08 *Nihat Kahveci* [2008] ECR I-6291.

[63] Case C-438/00 *Kolpak* [2003] ECR I4135.

[64] Cae C-265/03 *Simuntenkov* [2005] ECR I2579.

[65] Of the 24-member first team squad of Chelsea FC, only seven were UK nationals at the time of writing. The proportion selected for the first eleven is often lower. Similarly, only six members of Arsenal's 36-man squad are currently British.

[66] See Press Release of 28 May 2008, IP/08/807.

[67] Previously, the UEFA Cup.

[68] IP/08/807.

[69] In October 2011 the Belgian lawyer who represented Bosman, Jean-Louis Dupont, asserted that he doubted the legality of the Premier League's '100% ownership rule' whereby the right to a player's services may not be shared between more than one club (at issue in the Carlos Tevez affair involving West Ham and Sheffield United,

Contracts Involving Minors

4.50 Contracts are generally not binding on minors, that is, those under the age of 18. However, an exception applies in relation to contracts for 'necessaries'.[70] This extends to contracts for the minor's benefit and in particular to contracts of training and service. In *Roberts v Gray*[71] the Court of Appeal held that a minor who had entered into a contract to go on a tour with a professional billiards player was liable in damages for failing to proceed with that tour. The court considered that once it had been decided that a contract was one for necessaries not qualified by unreasonable terms, then it was binding on the minor.

4.51 The question whether particular services are necessaries is one of fact in each case. In *Aylesbury FC v Watford Association FC*[72] Poole J held that the claimant club, which had purported to contract with a player when he was 16, could not recover damages from the defendant club for signing him as a 17-year-old because the claimant's contract was not for the minor's benefit and therefore did not bind him. There was a similar result in litigation concerning an agent's signing of the mercurial footballer Wayne Rooney when he was just 15.[73] The agent he moved to subsequently was not liable for inducing breach of contract as the original contract had been entered into when Rooney was a minor and was therefore voidable.

Content of the Player/Club Relationship

4.52 This section deals with some of the ways in which the relationship between player and club is regulated once the player has become employed by the club. First, we consider the extent to which some of the terms and conditions that might form part of a player's contract may be challengeable, and, second, we address the issue of discrimination in sport. These are the areas where we consider that the particular context of sport throws up interesting questions. There are, of course, many other ways in which the relationship between players and their employers is regulated. There is a raft of employment legislation providing protection, for example in the event of unfair dismissal, redundancy and failure to pay wages. The interpretation of such legislation is not affected by the fact that an employee is a sportsperson. As a matter for general employment law, it goes beyond the scope of this book and is not dealt with here.[74]

---

mentioned at paras 3.46 and 8.96); see www.bbc.co.uk/sport/0/football/15386863. However, no challenge to the rule has yet been brought, so far as we are aware.

[70] See, generally, *Chitty on Contracts* (n 47) ch 8.

[71] *Roberts v Gray* [1913] 1 KB 520. See also *Doyle v White City Stadium Ltd* [1935] 1 KB 110, CA (contract binding on infant boxer including rule whereby he forfeited prize money for hitting below the belt); and in the CAS anti-doping jurisprudence *ITF v Karatantcheva*, decision of the ITF Anti-Doping Tribunal (presided over by one of the authors), 11 January 2006 (anti-doping rules governed by English law binding on 16-year-old Bulgarian tennis player; appeal to CAS on other grounds dismissed: CAS/2007/A/1032; both decisions available on the ITF's website subject to redaction of parts of the judgment dealing with sensitive evidence).

[72] (2002) unreported, 12 June.

[73] *Proform Sports Management Ltd v Proactive Sports Management Ltd* [2006] EWHC 2812 (Ch).

[74] For a comprehensive guide to employment law see *Harvey on Industrial Relations and Employment Law* (Butterworths, looseleaf).

Terms and Conditions of Work

4.53 As already noted, a term in a player's contract—or for that matter a federation rule—which places restrictions on his or her ability to participate in their sport may well be unenforceable as an unlawful restraint of trade. An example is afforded by the *Greig v Insole* case[75] in which the court found that ICC and TCCB rules preventing players from taking part in test matches organised by a rival body went further than was necessary to protect the legitimate interests of the governing bodies and were, therefore, unenforceable as an unreasonable restraint of trade.

4.54 Similar issues were raised in *Kemp v New Zealand Rugby Football League*.[76] Mr Kemp wanted to play rugby league for the Newcastle Knights in New South Wales but the New Zealand League refused 'clearance' for Mr Kemp's transfer overseas with the consequence that the League in New South Wales would not authorise him to enter into the contract offered by the Newcastle Knights. The relevant rule gave the New Zealand League complete discretion to grant or approve any transfer to an overseas league. Henry J decided that the New Zealand League had a legitimate interest to protect, and that public policy justified reasonable restrictions on overseas employment of players under the League's jurisdiction. However, he granted a declaration that the rule was void as an unreasonable restraint of trade. The rule was unlimited as to time and place and envisaged the possibility of being operated worldwide in a preventive way throughout the working life of a professional player. Such a wide power went beyond what was reasonable to protect the interests of the League.

4.55 Other rules limiting the conduct of players which have been struck down as unreasonable restraints of trade include a rule of the Australian Cricket Association providing for automatic disqualification of a player taking part in an unauthorised match,[77] and rules of the Australian Rules Football Authority in Victoria which tied players to the club in the area in which they resided unless the club consented to their release.[78]

4.56 The restraint of trade doctrine is also relevant to terms dealing with the duration of a player's contract. In our discussion of transfer rules, we pointed out that clubs have attempted to mitigate the effects of the *Bosman* ruling by entering into longer term contracts with young players, thereby ensuring that they retain much of the player's value. However, long-term contracts themselves have a restrictive impact on a player's freedom, preventing him from moving from one club to another in the event that he becomes dissatisfied with his employer. The question arises as to whether long-term contracts in the context of sport may in principle be subject to the restraint of trade doctrine, and therefore subject to investigation by the courts as to their reasonableness.

4.57 The courts have recognised that every contract may, in one sense, be said to restrict trade since by contracting with a particular party a person is restricting himself from contracting inconsistently with someone else. However, it would be inappropriate if all

---

[75] *Greig v Insole* [1978] 1 WLR 302.
[76] *Kemp v New Zealand Rugby Football League Inc* [1989] 3 NZLR 463, HC.
[77] *Hughes v Western Australian Cricket Association (Inc)* (1987) 69 ALR 660.
[78] *Hall v Victorian Football League* [1982] VR 64. See also *Adamson v West Perthshire FC* (1979) 27 ALR 475; *Blackler v New Zealand Rugby Football League Inc* [1968] NZLR 547.

contracts were to fall within the restraint of trade doctrine. In attempting to provide a demarcation, the courts have in the past drawn a distinction between post-termination restraints, which are subject to the doctrine, and restraints during the currency of employment, which, the courts have said, are not. Terms governing the duration of a contract, *ex hypothesi*, fall into the latter category and so might be said to fall outside the restraint of trade doctrine. However, in recent years this approach has not found favour with the courts.[79]

4.58 The matter was discussed in *Watson v Prager*,[80] which concerned the duration of a contract between a professional boxer and his manager. The contract in question was in the form prescribed by the British Boxing Board of Control. It was of three years' duration, but contained a provision giving the defendant manager the option to extend the period for a further three years if the plaintiff should win one of several specified championships during the initial period. This did happen and the defendant exercised his option to extend the contract. The plaintiff became dissatisfied and sought to establish that the contract was unenforceable as an unreasonable restraint of trade. Scott J considered the attempts that had been made in the authorities to distinguish between contracts subject to the restraint of trade doctrine and those which fell outside it.[81] He concluded that the contract in issue did fall within the scope of the doctrine because it was not negotiated freely but was prescribed by the governing body. It was not, in the judge's view,

> satisfactory that an entity such as the board, which controls all aspects of professional boxing should be regarded as free from judicial supervision in so far as its rules and regulations impose commercial restrictions on participators in the sport.[82]

Scott J therefore went on to consider whether various restrictions contained in the contract were justified in the interests of the parties and the public. He held, as to its duration, that three years was reasonable, but that the manager's option to extend its duration for as much as three years was of doubtful reasonableness. Although there was an interest in ensuring that managers were able to take some share of the large financial rewards that would be available to a boxer if he won a major championship, this interest could be met by an option to extend the contract for 18 months rather than three years.[83]

4.59 *Watson v Prager* establishes that restraints during the currency of a contract in the context of sport may be subject to the restraint of trade principle. It only addresses the issue of terms governing duration of the contract where those terms have been imposed by the sport's governing body. However, authority in the context of the music industry suggests that, even where the rules of the governing body say nothing about duration and the parties have in principle been at liberty to negotiate freely, contracts of long duration may fall to be assessed for reasonableness under the restraint of trade doctrine in some

---

[79] See *Chitty on Contracts* (n 47) para 16-115: 'It now appears probable that even restraints which operate only during the currency of employment are subject to the doctrine of restraint of trade, at any rate if they have as their objects the sterilising rather than the absorption of a man's capacity for work, or perhaps are such that one of the parties is so unilaterally fettered that the contract loses its character of a contract for the regulation and promotion of trade and acquires the predominant character of a contract in restraint of trade.'

[80] *Watson v Prager* [1991] 1 WLR 726.

[81] Ibid, 742F–745F.

[82] Ibid, 746C.

[83] The judge did not have to reach a final view on the reasonableness of the contract's duration as there were other restrictions which were more obviously offensive and which rendered the agreement as a whole unenforceable.

circumstances. This will be the case where the courts perceive the contractual restrictions to be unnecessary or oppressive. Lord Reid put it this way in *Instone v Shroeder Music Publishing Ltd*,[84] a case in which the House of Lords held a 10-year exclusive contract between a young songwriter and his music publisher to be an unreasonable restraint of trade:

> Any contract by which a person engages to give his exclusive services to another for a period necessarily involves extensive restriction during that period of the common law right to exercise any lawful activity he chooses in such manner as he thinks best. Normally the doctrine of restraint of trade has no application to such restrictions: they require no justification. But if contractual restrictions appear to be unnecessary or to be reasonably capable of enforcement in an oppressive manner, then they must be justified before they can be enforced.

4.60 In reaching its conclusion, the House of Lords took account of the fact that the publishing house was not bound, under the contract, to publish or promote the songwriter's work if it chose not to. This might lead to him earning nothing and to the sterilisation of his talents contrary to the public interest.[85]

4.61 The courts are astute to prevent unfairness resulting from inequality of bargaining power and will, if necessary, invoke the restraint of trade doctrine to achieve this. We would submit that there is no difference in principle between a young sportsperson and a young musician without an established reputation. Both are often placed in a weak bargaining position against a large, powerful organisation. Further, as was the case with the songwriter in *Shroeder*, a long-term contract may lead to the sterilisation of a player's talents. One can envisage a young footballer signed up to a 10-year contract with a rich club content to carry on paying him his weekly wage who never sees any first team play. For these reasons, we consider that the applicability of the restraint of the trade doctrine should be taken into account by clubs when negotiating contracts with players.[86]

Salary Caps

4.62 A salary cap[87] is a limit on the amount of money a team can spend on player salaries, expressed as a per-player limit, as a total limit for the entire team, as a percentage of the team's income, or some combination of these options. Salary caps are reasonably well

---

[84] *Instone v Shroeder Music Publishing Ltd* [1974] 1 WLR 1308 per Lord Reid at 1314G–H. The other Law Lords agreed. See also *ZTT Ltd v Holly Johnson* [1993] EMLR 6 in which the Court of Appeal held that a recording contract entered into by the parties was unenforceable as an unreasonable restraint of trade, and *Panayiotou v Sony Music Entertainment (UK) Ltd*, *The Times*, 30 June 1994, where the singer George Michael failed to show that his contract with Sony was an unreasonable restraint of trade although Parker J accepted that the contract fell to be examined for reasonableness under the doctrine.

[85] *Instone*, ibid, 1313C–1314B.

[86] Absent any restraint of trade argument, players' employment contracts may be enforced by injunction in the same way as other contracts, subject always to the discretion of the court, as we discuss in chapter 8 by reference to cases such as *Julian White v Bristol Rugby Ltd* [2002] IRLR 204, HHJ Havelock-Allan QC, where the employee is prevented from leaving the club in breach of contract on the basis that the club is willing and able to let him continue playing for it. See para 8.85.

[87] This topic is also touched upon in chapter 3 above, in the context of restraint of trade and the right to take part in sporting competition. See para 3.55 ff.

established in some North American and Australian sports, such as American football and Australian Rules football. English Rugby League (the Super League) adopted a salary cap system in 1998. Initially, this permitted clubs to spend a maximum of 50 per cent of their net income on all player payments. This was later changed to address the resulting advantage conferred on richer clubs so as to introduce an overall cap. In 2010, this provided that clubs could not spend more than £1.65 million on their top 25 earners. In 2011, it was announced that clubs which develop and deliver talent for the national teams are to be given a dispensation to spend up to £100,000 more than the £1.65 million limit on players. The English Rugby Union Premiership also operates a salary cap, which currently stands at £4.2 million, though teams also now receive an additional £30,000 credit for each home-grown player in their senior squads. The salary cap system appears to be growing in popularity given the current economic climate. In November 2011, Wales' four rugby union regions announced a cap to be implemented from July 2012 according to which each of the four teams will spend a maximum of £3.5 million on squad members for the two European club cup competitions.[88]

4.63 Salary cap systems potentially raise questions under free movement rules, competition rules and the restraint of trade doctrine. In its Staff Working Document,[89] the Commission specifically refers to the compatibility with the competition rules of salary caps as a pending and undecided issue. The existence of a salary cap would, in our view and whether viewed in terms of free movement, competition or restraint of trade, constitute a restriction and so its legality would depend on whether it was reasonably justified. This in turn would depend on factors such as the level at which the cap is set and the need for a cap in terms of the continued viability of the championship concerned.

Discrimination

4.64 Arbitrary discrimination in some forms is arguably contrary to public policy in the common law. The Equality Act 2010 prohibits discrimination on grounds of sex, race, disability, age, sexual orientation, gender reassignment, marriage and civil partnership, pregnancy and maternity, and religion or belief, subject to the exceptions contained therein. The Human Rights Act 1998 prohibits discrimination falling within the ambit of other rights secured by the Convention on any ground amounting to a 'personal characteristic' including sex, race, language, religion, and political and other opinion. Finally, discrimination is also prohibited under EU law. Article 18 TFEU prohibits discrimination on the grounds of nationality in areas covered by the Treaty, while Article 19 enables the EU, within the areas covered by the Treaty, to enact measures to prohibit discrimination on grounds of sex, racial or ethnic origin, religion or belief, disability, age or sexual orientation. Two major legislative instruments have so far been enacted under Article 19: the Race Directive 2000/43 and the Framework Employment Directive 2000/78.

---

[88] Currently known as the Heineken Cup and the Amlin Challenge Cup.
[89] (n 2) Annex 1, para 2.3.

Common Law

4.65 In *Constantine v Imperial Hotels*, the famous West Indian cricketer bringing proceedings was awarded a mere £5 damages following a hotel proprietor's refusal to offer him accommodation on the ground of his race, and then only because innkeepers were a 'common calling'. Exemplary damages were refused, although Mr Justice Birkett found that there had been 'unjustifiable humiliation and distress'.[90] However, in *Nagle v Fielden* the Court of Appeal declined to strike out an action brought by the plaintiff based on the refusal of the Jockey Club to allow her a trainer's licence, holding it to be arguable that the practice of refusing a trainer's licence to women was void as contrary to public policy. Lord Denning MR said: '[T]he Jockey Club's unwritten rule may well be said to be arbitrary and capricious. It is not as if the training of horses could be regarded as an unsuitable occupation for a woman like that of a jockey or speedway rider.'[91]

4.66 It has been suggested that the common law protection of the right to work may be engaged 'where a person was refused admission to an association, and so deprived of the opportunity of exercising a profession, on political grounds that had no bearing on his competence in that profession'.[92] For this purpose professional sport would presumably qualify as a profession. Further, a contract or rules with discriminatory effect may be in restraint of trade. Contracts in unreasonable restraint of trade are unenforceable, as already discussed.[93] Discrimination may make the restraint unreasonable.

The Equality Act 2010

4.67 The Equality Act 2010 replaced previous anti-discrimination statutes such as the Sex Discrimination Act 1975 and the Equal Pay Act 1970. There are three forms of discrimination under the Equality Act: direct discrimination, indirect discrimination, and discrimination by way of victimisation.

— **Direct discrimination** occurs where a person treats another less favourably than they treat or would treat others because of a protected characteristic.[94] The characteristics protected by the Act are age, disability, gender reassignment, marriage and civil partnership, pregnancy and maternity, race, religion or belief, sex, and sexual orientation.[95] Direct discrimination is unlawful unless expressly permitted by statute; with the exception of discrimination on grounds of age, there is no possibility of justification. Direct discrimination includes harassment, and employers, eg clubs, can be liable for taking insufficient steps to prevent it.

— **Indirect discrimination** is concerned with treatment which may be neutral on its face but which discriminates in practice against members of a group who share a protected characteristic.[96] Such treatment is unlawful unless it can be shown to be

---

[90] [1944] KB 693, 708.
[91] *Nagle v Fielden* [1966] 2 QB 633, 647C–E.
[92] *Chitty on Contracts* (n 47) 27-075.
[93] *Ibid*, ch 16.
[94] Equality Act 2010, s 13.
[95] Ibid, s 4.
[96] Ibid, s 19.

a proportionate means of achieving a legitimate aim—in other words, unless it can be objectively justified.

— **Discrimination by way of victimisation** occurs when a person is treated less favourably on the ground that he has carried out a 'protected act', which includes bringing proceedings against alleged discrimination and alleging (unless falsely and in bad faith) prohibited discrimination by another.[97]

4.68 Section 195 of the Equality Act replaces exceptions relating to sporting activities in earlier legislation. It allows separate sporting activities to be organised for men and for women where such activities are 'gender-affected', in that 'physical strength, stamina or physique are major factors for determining success or failure, and in which one sex is generally at a disadvantage in comparison with another', eg in football, rugby and athletics but not chess or bridge. Section 195(4) concerns children and provides that 'in considering whether a sport, game or other activity is gender-affected in relation to children, it is appropriate to take account of the age and stage of development of children who are likely to be competitors'.

4.69 This provision suggests that *Bennett v FA*[98] (in which the sporting exception was successfully relied upon to prevent an 11-year-old girl from playing in a league match under the auspices of the FA, which prohibited mixed teams) may well be decided differently today.[99] Special provision is also made for sports clubs which may restrict access to facilities or services to prevent serious embarrassment to male users at the presence of women, eg changing rooms. Section 195(2) permits organisers of competitions to restrict the participation of a transsexual person in sporting activity but only if it is necessary to ensure fair competition or the safety of the competition. Because of the controversy over Caster Semenya, winner of the women's 800m in the Berlin IAAF World Championships 2009, the IOC and IAAF have introduced new rules based on androgen levels to define who will be eligible for women's events.[100]

Examples of Discrimination Cases in the Context of Sport

4.70 An example of a successful discrimination claim in the context of sport is provided by *Hassamy v Chester City FC*,[101] where the claimant relied on the fact that the manager had called him a 'black cunt', and that he had subsequently been refused a professional contract, and in which the club was also held vicariously liable.[102] In *Hargreaves v FA*,[103] the successful female complainant was refused a coaching certificate by the FA when, out of 1,500 successful applicants, only two had been women and her performance on the advanced course outranked her victorious male rivals.[104]

4.71 Discrimination in sport may also occur in the area of employment. This encompasses the discriminatory award of qualifications by governing bodies in circumstances

---

97 Ibid, s 27.
98 *Bennett v FA* (1978) unreported, 29 July, CA.
99 s 196 Equality Act 2010 and Sched 3, Part 7, para 27(6).
100 See Worley, *An Alternative to the IOC's Gender Testing Policy*, WSLR 8/2, pp 10–11.
101 IT Case 2102426/97.
102 SLB, vol 1 no 1, p 4.
103 IT Case 2320451/96.
104 SLB, vol 1 no 1, p 4.

where the qualification in fact facilitates employment. In *Petty v British Judo Association* a female judo referee was granted a national referee certificate by the British Judo Association (BJA). However, she was told that she could not referee men's competitions at national level. The Employment Appeal Tribunal (EAT) found that, as the BJA both granted certificates and selected referees for matches, its conduct amounted to the granting of a certificate on discriminatory terms, ie on the basis that the applicant was not eligible to referee men's national events. In so holding, Browne-Wilkinson J said:[105]

> In our view section 13 [of the Sex Discrimination Act 1975] covers all cases where the qualification in fact facilitates the woman's employment, whether or not it is intended by the authority or body which confers the authorisation to do so.

Likewise, the British Boxing Board of Control, in *Couch v BBBC*,[106] and the FA, in respect of a coaching course,[107] have been held to be qualifying bodies, but the Kennel Club has been held not to be such a body.[108]

4.72 Allegations of race discrimination in sport have recently given rise to some high profile cases, such as the decision of the FA's Regulatory Commission upholding the complaints made by Manchester United's Patrice Evra against Liverpool's Luis Suarez and the pending prosecution of John Terry for alleged racist abuse of Anton Ferdinand. The Equality Act and its predecessors also prohibit nationality-based discrimination. In *Ice Hockey Super League v Henry*,[109] a successful challenge was made to the inclusion of a probationary period in a player's contract in circumstances where a player originating outside the EU/EEA would not have had a similar clause in their contract.[110] As explained above, age is a protected characteristic under the Equality Act. A claim against a company for imposing a retirement age of 48 for football referees was upheld under the predecessor legislation.[111]

Child Protection in Sport

4.73 In chapter two, we referred in our overview to the core provisions of the Children Act 1989 dealing with promotion of the welfare of children and their application to the practice of sport. We now set out in more detail the content of the law relevant to the protection of children engaged in sporting activities.

---

[105] [1981] ICR 660, 664.
[106] IT Case No 2304231/97. See Felix, *The 'Fleetwood Assassin' Strikes a Blow for Female Boxers* (1998) 1(3) SLB 1.
[107] *Hargreaves v FA*, IT Case 220651/96.
[108] *Nagle v Kennel Club* (IT, reference unavailable).
[109] EAT 1167/99, unreported, 2 March 2001. On the position in Canada cf Eaton, *Gender Equity in Canadian Ice Hockey: The Legal Struggle* (2012) 12(2) LIM 121.
[110] Other successful claims include: *Singh v FA* IT5203593/99 2002 ISLR 141 (Asian referee in English Football League); *Sterling v Leeds Rhinos Rugby Club* LC 2000 Case No 11 1802453/00 (Afro-Caribbean rugby player refused opportunity to play for first team); see also the related appeal in *Leeds Rhinos Rugby Club v Sterling*, EAT/267/01, Judge Robert Reid QC presiding.
[111] Employment Equality (Age) Regulations 2006; see *Martin v Professional Game Match Official Ltd* (2010) unreported, 13 April, ET; Scott, *Referees Win Case against Mandatory Retirement Age*, WLSR 8/9, pp 8–9.

4.74 We start with the Rehabilitation of Offenders Act 1974, which provides that in certain circumstances criminal convictions are spent after a certain period.[112] This statute is relevant to the employment, in the sport sector, or the withholding of employment, of persons who have been convicted of crimes in the past. In most circumstances, a conviction which has become spent or any circumstances ancillary thereto, or any failure to disclose a spent conviction or any such circumstances, is not a proper ground for dismissing or excluding a person from any office, profession, occupation or employment, or for prejudicing him in any way in any occupation or employment[113] unless the employment is by a youth club, local authority or other body concerned with the promotion of leisure or recreational activities for persons under the age of 18, which is of such a kind as to enable the holder to have access to such persons in the course of his normal duties. In those special circumstances the employer is allowed to take both spent and unspent convictions into account when filling those positions.[114]

4.75 The law is in a state of flux. The Protection of Children Act 1999 was designed to create the framework for a single coherent cross-sector system for identifying people who are unsuitable to work with children,[115] and requires the Secretary of State to keep a list of individuals who are considered unsuitable to work with children.[116] However, the scheme has been replaced by provisions of the Safeguarding Vulnerable Groups Act 2006.[117]

4.76 Part II of the Criminal Justice and Court Services Act 2000 sets up an integrated statutory system to prevent unsuitable people from working with children, with a statutory ban enforced by criminal sanctions.[118]

4.77 Section 35(1) of the Criminal Justice and Court Services Act 2000 provides that an individual who is disqualified[119] from working with children is guilty of an offence if he knowingly applies for, offers to do, accepts or does any work in a regulated position.[120] Section 35(2) provides that an individual is guilty of an offence if he knowingly (a) offers work in a regulated position to, or procures work in a regulated position for, an individual who is disqualified from working with children, or (b) fails to remove such an individual from such work.

[112] Rehabilitation of Offenders Act 1974, s 1.
[113] Ibid, s 4(3)(b).
[114] Rehabilitation of Offenders Act 1974 (Exceptions) Order 1975, Sched 1, Part II, para 14.
[115] Combining two lists of criminal records maintained by the police, namely (i) the previous Department of Health's 'Consultancy Index List' and (ii) the list commonly known as 'List 99' maintained by the Department of Education and Skills under s 142 of the Education Act 2002, which contained details of teachers considered unsuitable or banned from working with children in education.
[116] Protection of Children Act 1999, s 1 (repealed). See the DfES publication *The Protection of Children Act 1999: A Practical Guide to the Act for All Organisations Working with Children*, September 2005.
[117] Safeguarding Vulnerable Groups Act 2006, s 63, Sched 10. As to transitional provisions see s 62, Sched 8.
[118] For a detailed summary of disqualification orders under the Criminal Justice and Court Services Act 2000, see *Criminal Justice and Courts Services Act 2000: Protection of Children Guidance* (Home Office, 2000).
[119] An individual is disqualified from working with children for the purposes of Part II of the Criminal Justice and Court Services Act 2000 if (a) he is included (otherwise than provisionally) in the list kept under s 1 of the Protection of Children Act 1999 (individuals considered unsuitable to work with children); (b) he is subject to a direction under s 142 of the Education Act 2002 (prohibition from teaching etc), given on the grounds that he is unsuitable to work with children; (c) he is included, on the grounds that he is unsuitable to work with children, in any list kept by the Secretary of State or the National Assembly for Wales of persons disqualified under s 470 or s 471 of the Education Act 1996; or (d) he is subject to a disqualification order.
[120] As defined in the Criminal Justice and Court Services Act 2000, s 36.

4.78 The 'regulated positions' defined in section 36 of the Criminal Justice and Court Services Act 2000 include positions which may be held by individuals working in sports governing bodies, clubs etc, such as a position whose normal duties include caring for, training, supervising or being in sole charge of children, or which involve unsupervised contact with children under arrangements made by a responsible person, or which involve caring for children under the age of 16 in the course of the children's employment, or include supervising or managing an individual in his work in a regulated position, or a position a substantial part of whose normal duties includes supervising or training children under the age of 16 in the course of the children's employment.[121] Therefore, by way of example, coaches, trainers, referees, match officials and drivers who provide transport arranged by a sports organisation could all be considered to hold regulated positions.

4.79 The Sexual Offences Act 2003 provides that it is an offence for a person (A) aged 18 or over intentionally to behave in certain sexual ways in relation to a child aged under 18, where A is in a position of trust.[122] The abuse of trust offences currently only apply to adults working in the public sector;[123] they do not apply to sports coaches in the private sector, for example.

4.80 Relations between sports coaches and child athletes are expressly provided for in the Home Office booklet *Caring for the Young People and the Vulnerable? Guidance for Preventing Abuse of Trust*.[124] The guidance, which has no statutory force but contains principles of good practice, states that the government believes that all organisations which work with young people or vulnerable adults should have in place guidance or principles of good practice for the protection of those in their care from sexual and other forms of abuse.

4.81 The Children Act 2004 establishes a Children's Commissioner for England, with the function of promoting awareness of the views and interests of children in England having regard to the UN Convention of the Rights of the Child 1989;[125] a power for the Secretary of State by regulations made by affirmative resolution procedure to require local authorities to establish and operate a database or databases of information about all children and other young people to whom arrangements under section 10, 11 or section 175 of the Education Act 2002 may relate;[126] and Statutory Local Safeguarding Children's Boards with the aim of ensuring that each local area takes a coherent and effective approach to safeguarding children based on contributions from all key agencies.[127]

4.82 The strategy document accompanying the Children Act 2004, *Every Child Matters: Change for Children*, states that everyone delivering services for children and young people has an important role to play in working towards the objectives of the Act, including those working in sports and play organisations.[128] Section 10 of the Children Act 2004 places an obligation on children's services authorities to make arrangements to promote

---

[121] Ibid, s 36(1)(c), (d), (e), (h) and (f), respectively.
[122] Sexual Offences Act 2003, ss 16–19.
[123] See the definition of 'position of trust' in ibid, s 21.
[124] Published in 1999.
[125] See Part 1 of the Children Act 2004, ss 1–9, for a detailed summary of the role and powers of the Children's Commissioner.
[126] Ibid, s 12.
[127] Ibid, ss 13–16.
[128] Para 1.10.

cooperation between the authority, each of the authority's relevant partners, and such other persons or bodies as the authority considers appropriate, being persons or bodies of any nature who exercise functions or are engaged in activities in relation to children in the authority's area.[129] This will include sports coaches and sporting bodies.

4.83 The Safeguarding Vulnerable Groups Act 2006 provides a legislative framework for a centralised national vetting and barring scheme in relation to regulated activity for people who work with children and vulnerable adults.[130] The Act has been brought partially into force by a series of commencement orders, while at the same time being subject to a new legislative initiative resulting from a change of government and policy, as discussed below.[131] The law as stated in the Act cannot be guaranteed to endure. We include a brief account of the main provisions here, but it is necessary to check the up-to-date position for changes subsequent to publication of this book.

4.84 Individuals who work closely, or apply to work, with children or vulnerable adults are required to make an application to the Secretary of State to be 'subject to monitoring'.[132] This will cover everyone engaging in 'regulated activity'[133] with the permission of a 'regulated activity provider'.[134] The Secretary of State, using the Criminal Records Bureau, will then search the Police National Computer for cautions and convictions and make enquiries of local police forces to obtain other relevant information.[135] Where the Secretary of State's enquiries reveal that a person satisfies one of the criteria that lead to automatic inclusion on a barred list, he will refer the matter to the Independent Safeguarding Authority (ISA) so that the person can be included on the relevant barred list. The Secretary of State will also pass details of relevant cautions and convictions together with all information received from local police forces to the ISA, which the ISA can then consider in relation to inclusion on a barred list.[136] Where a person is included on a barred list, he ceases to be subject to monitoring (if he was previously so subject) and is not able to engage in regulated activities. Those who have been convicted of or cautioned for certain specified offences will be included on the list automatically; those convicted of or cautioned for other specified offences will be included subject to the right subsequently to make representations to the contrary. Others may be included if the ISA decides in the light of relevant information assembled from the police or other organisations that they should.[137]

4.85 At a non-statutory level, the protection of children in sport has generated a significant body of regulation. The vast majority of sports governing bodies now include a child protection policy in their rules and regulations and issue guidance to their members setting out the appropriate course of action if they are concerned about the welfare of a child

[129] Part 1 of the Children Act 2004, s 10(1).
[130] Safeguarding Vulnerable Groups Act 2006.
[131] See para 4.113 ff.
[132] Ibid, s 8, not in force, and s 24, only partially in force.
[133] By s 5(1) of the Safeguarding Vulnerable Groups Act 2006, a reference to a regulated activity relating to children must be construed in accordance with Part 1 of Sched 4.
[134] As defined in ibid, s 6.
[135] Ibid, s 24(3).
[136] Ibid, Sched 3, Part 1.
[137] Ibid.

with whom they come into contact and the procedures for dealing with transgressors.[138] This will assist in showing that all reasonable steps were taken to safeguard children by way of a defence to any possible subsequent claims for negligence.[139]

4.86 In 2001, following a series of high profile cases of abuse of young athletes by those in positions of trust such as coaches, the Child Protection in Sport Unit (the Unit) was established as a partnership between the National Society for the Prevention of Cruelty to Children, Sport England, Sport Northern Ireland and Sports Wales. Such bodies would in principle owe a duty of care in tort, and the establishment of the Unit is part of their performance of that duty.[140] The purpose of the Unit is to work with UK sports councils, national governing bodies, county sports partnerships and other organisations to help them minimise the risk of child abuse during sporting activities.[141] The Unit provides guidance to sports organisations regarding child protection, and has developed the Standards for Safeguarding and Protecting Children in Sport.[142] The Standards provide a national benchmark of good practice for sports organisations to work towards. Their purpose is to help create a safe sporting environment for children and young people to protect them from harm; to provide a benchmark to assist those involved in sport to make informed decisions; and to promote good practice and challenge practice that is harmful to children. The 10 areas covered in the Standards are: policy, procedures and systems, prevention, codes of practice and behaviour, equity, communication, education and training, access to advice and support, implementation and monitoring, and influencing.

4.87 Whilst legislation has long regulated the employment of children and young persons, there are few statutory provisions specifically dealing with the employment of children[143] and young persons[144] in the sports industry. The main sources of legislation governing the employment of children in general are the Employment of Women, Young Persons and Children Act 1920 (as amended), the Children and Young Persons Act 1933

---

[138] For useful websites, functional at the time of writing, see:
LTA (tennis): Safeguarding and Child Protection Resources and Forms: www.lta.org.uk/players-parents/Supporting-your-child/Safeguarding--Child-Protection/Safeguarding-and-Child-Protection-Resources
Child Protection Guidance: www.lta.org.uk/NewWebsite/LTA/Documents/Players%20and%20Parents/Safeguarding%20and%20%20Child%20Protection/Child%20Protection%20Guidance.doc
FA (football): safeguarding pages: www.thefa.com/TheFA/WhatWeDo/FootballSafe
FA—Safeguarding Children and Young People in Football: Child Protection Policy, Procedures and Implementation Guidance for Grassroots Football: www.thefa.com/Leagues/Respect/Safeguarding/~/media/Files/PDF/TheFA/ChildProtectionPolicyProceduresandImplementationGu.ashx
UK Athletics: www.uka.org.uk/governance/welfare-and-safeguarding/guidance-documents-and-resource
Policies: www.uka.org.uk/governance/policies
ASA (swimming): Safeguarding Children & Vulnerable Adults pages: www.swimming.org/asa/clubs-and-members/safeguarding-children-vulnerable-adults
ECB (cricket): Safe Hands: Cricket's Policy for Safeguarding Children, www.ecb.co.uk/ecb/safeguarding-children-and-child-protection/safe-hands
[139] Although taking reasonable care will not provide a defence to an action in trespass brought in respect of an employee for child abuse: *Lister v Hesley Hall* [2002] 1 AC 215.
[140] See further the useful account in Lewis and Taylor, *Sport: Law and Practice*, 2nd edn (Tottel Publishing, 2008) D7.46 and D.7.57.
[141] See www.thecpsu.org.uk
[142] The Standards were approved by the National Society for the Prevention of Cruelty to Children, Sport England and the Sports Minister in 2002, and published in 2003.
[143] 'Child', for the purposes of any enactment relating to the prohibition or regulation of the employment of children or young persons, means any person who is not over compulsory school age: Education Act 1996, s 558.
[144] For the purposes of the Education Act 1996, 'young person' means a person over compulsory school age but under 18: s 579(1).

Part II (sections 18–30) (as amended), the Children and Young Persons Act 1963, Part II (sections 34–44), and the Education Act 1996 (section 560) (as amended). In addition to the statutory framework, local authorities also have the power to issue byelaws limiting the conditions, hours and nature of employment that a child is permitted to engage in.

4.88 Part V of the Police Act 1997 (as amended) established a scheme whereby certain employers and bodies in the voluntary sector may obtain a certificate containing information from the criminal records of prospective employees and volunteers. Since 2002 this scheme has been administered by the Criminal Records Bureau (CRB). Under the 1997 Act there is no legal obligation on sports organisations such as clubs and governing bodies to apply for disclosure from the CRB in the context of child protection; this is because only 'childcare organisations', as defined, are legally obliged to make checks on applicants through the CRB for any paid or unpaid work,[145] and sporting and leisure groups fall outside this definition.[146] However, government guidance makes it clear that such background checks are strongly recommended for sports organisations,[147] and it is easy to see why a sports organisation would be well advised to take such steps to protect children, which could be used (if necessary) to prove that all reasonable steps had been taken to safeguard children by way of a defence to any possible subsequent claim for negligence.

4.89 It is possible to apply for three different types of disclosure under the 1997 Act: a criminal conviction certificate ('Basic Disclosure');[148] a criminal record certificate ('Standard Disclosure');[149] and an enhanced criminal record certificate ('Enhanced Disclosure').[150] Each type contains a different level of detail: criminal conviction certificates simply record unspent convictions, whereas criminal record certificates (CRCs) and enhanced criminal record certificates (ECRCs) record the details of all convictions (unspent as well as spent), as well as cautions, that are held in central records. In addition, an ECRC may contain non-conviction or caution information in consequence of the requirement that before issuing an ECRC the CRB must request the chief officer of every relevant police force to provide any information which in the chief officer's opinion (a) might be relevant to the 'prescribed purpose' identified in the application, and (b) ought to be included in the certificate. A relevant police force is that where the applicant resides or resided during the five years preceding the application.

4.90 In addition, the relevant chief officers are asked to provide separately any information which might be relevant to the purpose of the application and ought not to be disclosed in the certificate in the interests of the prevention or detection of crime, but which can, without harming those interests, be disclosed to the registered person. This information is disclosed by way of a separate side letter from the relevant chief police officer, which is not shared with the applicant, and no reference is made to its existence in the certificate. Authoritative guidance on deciding whether information ought to be

---

[145] As well as the Protection of Children Act (PoCA) list, which combines the Department of Health's 'Consultancy Index List', the Department for Education and Skills' 'List 99' (which contains details of teachers who are considered unsuitable or banned from working with children in education under PoCA), and police criminal records.

[146] See the DfES publication *The Protection of Children Act 1999* (n 116).

[147] See *Criminal Justice and Court Services Act 2000: Protection of Children Guidance* (Home Office, 2000) para 9.8.

[148] Police Act 1997, s 112.

[149] Ibid, s 113A.

[150] Ibid, s 113B.

included in an ECRC has been given by the Supreme Court in *R (L) v Commissioner of the Metropolis*.[151]

4.91 Whichever type of disclosure is applied for, the applicant in every case is the individual *about* whom disclosure is sought. However, the requirements of such applications differ. An application for a criminal conviction record (CCR) is simply made by the individual applicant and no reason need be given for requesting it.[152] Thus, any sports organisation could potentially ask an applicant (or volunteer) for any sort of post to request such a certificate. By contrast, an application for a Criminal Records Check must be countersigned by a 'registered person' and be accompanied by a statement by the registered person that the certificate is required for the purpose of an exempted question.[153] A 'registered person' is a person or body who has registered with the Secretary of State as a person likely to ask 'exempted questions', that is, questions in respect of which relevant provisions of the Rehabilitation of Offenders Act 1974 (which would otherwise have precluded reference to spent convictions and cautions) have been disapplied.[154]

4.92 Thus, the sports organisation must be seeking the information in order to assess the suitability of the particular applicant or volunteer to work with children,[155] defined to include any work which is in a 'regulated position',[156] including positions whose *normal* duties involve caring for, training, supervising or being in sole charge of children, or which involve unsupervised contact with children under arrangements made by a responsible person (eg a parent, guardian or primary carer). There is no requirement that the 'work' is paid: this exclusion therefore applies both to potential employees and to volunteers.

4.93 Where an application for an ECRC is made, not only must it be countersigned by a registered person; it must be accompanied by a statement from the registered person that the certificate is required for the purposes of an exempted question asked for a 'prescribed purpose'. The purposes that have been prescribed include 'considering the applicant's suitability for a position which involves regularly caring for, training, supervising, or being solely in charge of, persons aged under 18',[157] as well as (following the changes brought about by the Safeguarding Vulnerable Groups Act 2006 (SVGA)) 'considering the applicant's suitability to engage in any activity which is a regulated activity relating to children within the meaning of Part 1 of Schedule 4 to the [SVGA]'.[158]

4.94 Whether Standard or Enhanced (or any) Disclosure should be applied for under the 1997 Act effectively depends upon the frequency of potential contact between the job holder and children; ie whether the contact is 'normal' or occurs 'regularly'. Accordingly,

---

[151] [2009] UKSC 3, [2010] 1 AC 410.
[152] Police Act 1997, s 112(1).
[153] Ibid, s 113A(2).
[154] Ibid, s 113A(6): an exempted question is a question in relation to which (so far as it applies to convictions) s 4(2)(b) or (b) of, and (so far as it applies to cautions) para 3(3) or (4) of Sched 2 to, the Rehabilitation of Offenders Act 1974 has been excluded.
[155] The Rehabilitation of Offenders Act 1974 (Exceptions) Order 1975/1023 disapplies the above provisions in relation to any question asked by or on behalf of any person in the course of his work, in order to assess the suitability of a person to work with children, where the question relates to the person whose suitability is being assessed (Art 3(aa)(i)).
[156] As defined in the Criminal Justice and Court Services Act 2000, s.36.
[157] Para 5A(a)(ii) of the Police Act 1997 (Criminal Records) Regulations, SI 2002/233 (as amended).
[158] Ibid, para 5A(a)(i).

it is important that before recruiting employees or volunteers a sports organisation has clearly identified the role to be performed by that person. The Cabinet Office has issued guidance in the context of volunteers[159] which emphasises that it is bad practice for an organisation to apply for checks on all volunteers without properly evaluating risk, and where there is no legal or other reason to do so. An organisation should not simply apply for Enhanced rather than Standard Disclosure under the Police Act 1997 in every case.

4.95 Sports bodies' rules or constitutions should therefore provide that an applicant for employment will consent to the making of an application to the CRB by the organisation, as a condition of participation or licensing. A sports governing body (SGB) can require all clubs and all members of such clubs to participate in and take reasonable steps to comply with CRB procedures, and provide that a failure to do so may constitute a disciplinary matter, potentially warranting suspension pending compliance.

4.96 Under the Data Protection Act 1998 (DPA), data consisting of information as to the commission or alleged commission by a person of any offence constitutes 'sensitive personal data'.[160] In order to process such data fairly and lawfully it must be processed in accordance with the data protection principles set out at Schedule 1 to that Act, and one of the conditions set out in Schedule 3 must be met. The first and in this context only relevant such condition is that the data subject has given his 'explicit consent' to the processing of the personal data.[161] It is therefore necessary (and in any event clearly prudent) that the individual expressly gives his consent to Enhanced rather than Standard Disclosure if that is to be applied for.

4.97 Guidance on how to handle information disclosed is provided in the CRB's document, *Code of Practice for Registered Persons and other Recipients of Disclosure Information* (revised in April 2009) made pursuant to section 122(2) of the Police Act. That Code makes clear that sports organisations should have a written policy on the handing of such information, including storage, dissemination and disposal. The policy should also include the organisation's stance on the suitability of ex-offenders and suspected offenders for positions, and should be made available to the persons concerned. When deciding whether to employ a person, a sports body is entitled to take a precautionary approach which recognises the importance of protecting children as the paramount consideration, while recognising also that the rights of individuals concerned must also be considered. Sports organisations must be careful to ensure that they consider each case individually and on its own merits; they should not make hasty decisions based on the disclosure or apply a blanket policy; they must act fairly respecting the rights to natural justice of the individual concerned; and decisions taken must be proportionate.

4.98 Sports organisations should, therefore, consider the circumstances of each case individually alongside the relevant policies, so that they can judge whether any exception should be made if the policy indicates that a particular individual should not be

---

[159] *Criminal Records Bureau Checks: Guidance for Volunteering*, June 2008.

[160] Data Protection Act 1998, s 2.

[161] The Information Commissioner's *Guidance on the Conditions for Processing* considers the requirement that consent be 'explicit' in the case of sensitive personal data as follows: 'This suggests that the individual's consent should be absolutely clear. It should cover the specific processing details; the type of information (or even the specific information); the purposes of the processing; and any special aspects that may affect the individual, such as any disclosures that may be made.'

employed. Factors to be considered include the nature of the work that the individual concerned is or would be undertaking; the degree of contact with children; whether such contact is supervised or unsupervised; the age and sex of the children; whether the individual is applying for a new position or has worked in that position for some time; the precise nature of the information disclosed, such as whether it relates to possible offences against children at all, and, if it does, the age and sex of the children and the context of the alleged offence (in particular whether it is a sexual offence); whether there is an apparent pattern of offending; and the reliability of the disclosed information. In particular, Enhanced Disclosure may reveal allegations that have not been tested and which the CRB recognises are not always accurate; the length of time that has passed since the incident or incidents in question; and whether there has been a change in circumstances since the offence.

4.99 Sports organisations must ensure that they have afforded the individual concerned a fair opportunity to comment on matters which concern him or her and must take the individual's account into consideration. If a sports organisation has to act with particular urgency, the reason for such urgency must be explained and the individual's account must be sought at the earliest opportunity. The individual should also be afforded the opportunity to provide explanations or undertakings which might satisfy the sports body for the time being. For example, an individual who is working as a sports coach may be able to explain that he does not carry out work with children or undertake not to do so. That may be sufficient to avoid a suspension.

4.100 It is an offence for information supplied to a sports organisation by way of disclosure to be disclosed to any person who is not a member, officer or employee of the registered body, unless a relevant legal exception applies. Such information must not in any event be disclosed where it is not related to the proper performance of that person's duties.[162] Where information is supplied to a sports organisation by way of a separate letter that is not also supplied to the individual concerned, it would be an offence for even the existence of the letter to be disclosed to that individual. When considering how much, if any, weight is to be placed on such a letter, the sports organisation should have particular regard to the fact that the individual is denied an opportunity to respond to the information contained in the letter.[163]

4.101 The SVGA establishes the Vetting and Barring Scheme (VBS), administered by the ISA.[164] As noted above, the SVGA is only partially in force, having been planned for a 2010 start but suspended following a review by the new government and the introduction of proposed amendments in the Protection of Freedoms Bill, now the Protection of Freedoms Act 2012 (outlined below). Its framework is nevertheless relevant to the basis of the proposed regime. In short, the purpose of the SVGA is to create a centralised national monitoring scheme in relation to 'regulated activity' connected with children and vulnerable adults.

---

[162] See para 8 of the CRB's *Code of Practice for Registered Persons and other Recipients of Disclosure Information* (revised April 2009).

[163] See further the Chartered Institute of Personnel and Development document, *Employing Ex-Offenders: A Practical Guide.*

[164] SVGA, s 1 and Sched 1. The Protection of Freedoms Act 2012 makes provision to abolish the ISA and for its functions to be carried out by a new body, the DBS: chapter 3 (ss 87–91) and see below, para 4.115.

4.102 First, the SVGA requires the ISA, and in future the Disclosure and Barring Service (DBS),[165] to keep lists of individuals who are barred from working (a) with children, and (b) with vulnerable adults.[166] Those who have been convicted of or cautioned for certain specified offences are included on the list automatically; those convicted of or cautioned for other specified offences are included subject to a subsequent right to make representations in support of their removal from the list; others may be included if the ISA[167] decides in light of relevant information assembled from police and other organisations that they should be so included.[168]

4.103 Second, the SVGA uses those lists as a basis for a regime governing who is and who is not allowed to undertake 'regulated activity'. This concept of 'regulated activity' lies at the heart of the SVGA regime. Under provisions not yet in force, an individual (a) may not engage in regulated activity if he is barred from doing so by virtue of having been included on the children's barred list,[169] and conversely (b) may only engage in regulated activity if he is 'subject to monitoring'.[170]

4.104 These provisions are mirrored for a 'regulated activity provider' (a person responsible for the management or control of regulated activity),[171] in that he commits an offence if (a) he permits an individual to engage in a regulated activity from which he is barred, and the provider knows or has reason to believe that he is barred from that activity, and the individual engages in the activity,[172] or (b) he permits an individual to engage in a regulated activity in relation to which he is not subject to monitoring, and the provider knows or has reason to believe that he is not subject to monitoring in relation to that activity, and the individual engages in the activity.[173]

4.105 However, in addition the SVGA provides that a regulated activity provider commits an offence if he permits an individual to engage in a regulated activity, the individual engages in it, and the provider fails to ascertain whether the individual is subject to monitoring in relation to the activity.[174] A regulated activity provider is taken to ascertain whether a person is subject to monitoring if he either (a) obtains relevant information relating to the individual pursuant to an application for vetting information under section 30 of the SVGA or (b) obtains a copy of an ECRC relating to the individual issued in relation to the regulated activity provider.[175]

4.106 Accordingly, these provisions, to the extent that they survive future repeal, represent a major change from the previous regime whereby sports bodies had a discretion to obtain CRB disclosure, to one where they are obliged to ascertain whether an

[165] Ibid.

[166] Ibid, s 2.

[167] or DBS.

[168] SVGA, Sched 3.

[169] Ibid, s 7 (in force at the time of writing).

[170] Ibid, s 8 (not in force at the time of writing). A person becomes subject to monitoring by his (a) not being barred from engaging in the regulated activity, (b) making an application to the Secretary of State, (c) satisfying the prescribed requirements, and (d) paying such fee as prescribed (SVGA, s 24).

[171] Ibid, s 6(2)(a).

[172] Ibid, s 9.

[173] Ibid, s 10.

[174] Ibid, s 11.

[175] Ibid, Sched 5, Part 1, para 1. Schedule 5 also provides for a situation where an ECRC is issued where the application was countersigned by the registered person on behalf of the regulated activity provider (para 2).

individual is 'subject to monitoring'. The Protection of Freedoms Act 2012 (discussed below) repeals the requirement that a regulated activity provider must ascertain whether an individual is subject to monitoring but replaces it with a statutory duty to check whether that individual is barred. Again, one way in which this duty can be fulfilled is by obtaining an ECRC under the 1997 Act.[176] Therefore, it will no longer be sufficient for a sports body simply to consider whether (having regard to whether contact with children will be 'normal' or 'regular' in the particular post) Enhanced Disclosure should be applied for; the body will have to consider whether, having regard to the definition of 'regulated activity', it must be applied for, or an application for disclosure made otherwise under the SVGA itself.

4.107 The term 'regulated activity' is defined in a number of ways under the SVGA. The most pertinent definition for sports bodies is that an activity constitutes a 'regulated activity' if it is an activity of a prescribed type (described in the explanatory notes to the Act as 'types of close contact activity') and it is carried out frequently by the same person or the 'period condition' (see below) is satisfied.[177] An activity is also a regulated activity if it is carried out in a specified establishment (such as a school) for or in connection with the purposes of that establishment, and it is carried out frequently by the same person or the 'period condition' is satisfied.[178]

4.108 The types of activity prescribed include:

(a) any form of teaching, training or instruction of children, unless the teaching, training or instruction is merely incidental to teaching, training or instruction of persons who are not children;

(b) any form of care for or supervision of children unless the care or supervision is merely incidental to care for or supervision of persons who are not children;

(c) any form of advice or guidance provided wholly or mainly for children, if the advice or guidance relates to their physical, emotional or educational well-being;

...

(f) driving a vehicle which is being used only for the purpose of conveying children and any person supervising or caring for the children pursuant to arrangements made in prescribed circumstances.[179]

In addition, 'any activity which consists in or involves on a regular basis the day to day management or supervision of a person carrying out an activity mentioned [above] ... is a regulated activity relating to children'.[180]

4.109 These activities will constitute 'regulated activities' where they are carried out 'frequently by the same person' or where the 'period condition' is satisfied. The term 'frequently' is not defined under the SVGA but 'it is intended to take its normal, everyday meaning'. The 'period condition' (also referred to as the 'intensive contact test') is satisfied if the person carrying out the activity does so at any time on more than three days in any period of 30 days.[181] In relation to certain activities (including those set out

---

[176] The relevant provisions of the Protection of Freedoms Act 2012 are briefly touched upon below.
[177] SVGA, Sched 4, Part 1, para 1(1).
[178] Ibid, Sched 4, Part 1, para 1(2). Relevant establishments are specified at para 3(1).
[179] Ibid, Sched 4, Part 1, para 2(1).
[180] Ibid, Sched 4, Part 1, para 2(14).
[181] Ibid, Sched 4, Part 3, para 10(1).

at paragraph 2(1)(a)–(c) inclusive, as above) the period condition is also satisfied if the person carrying out the activity does so at any time between 2 am and 6 am and the activity gives the person the opportunity to have face-to-face contact with children.[182]

4.110 A person is not a regulated activity provider if he is an individual and the arrangements he makes are private arrangements (arrangements being private arrangements if the regulated activity is for, or for the benefit of, a child who is a member of that person's family or a friend of that person).[183] Equally, the SVGA does not apply to any activity which is carried out in the course of a family relationship or in the course of a personal relationship for no commercial consideration.[184]

4.111 In addition to the concept of a 'regulated activity', section 23 created the parallel concept of a 'controlled activity'. Much of the law on controlled activities was left to be established in secondary legislation, and is now found in the Safeguarding Vulnerable Groups Act 2006 (Controlled Activity and Miscellaneous Provisions) Regulations 2010.[185]

4.112 However, even before those regulations entered into force, and before the change of government in May 2010, amid concerns that the regime would require some 11 million people to register, in September 2009 Sir Roger Singleton was commissioned to review the VBS and in particular to assess whether the government had 'drawn the line in the right place' in relation to the frequency of contact which would trigger the obligation to register. He reported in December 2009, recommending that the 'frequency test' be set at a level of once per week (contrary to the then government's intention of setting it at once per month), and that the period condition be raised from 'three times in 30 days' to 'four times in one month'.[186] He also recommended that the 'controlled activity' element of the scheme be reviewed and possibly abolished. The Home Office estimated that his recommendations would reduce the number of people requiring registration to between 9 and 9.5 million.

4.113 In May 2010, the new Coalition Government pledged in its 'Programme for Government' to scale back the vetting and barring regime to 'common sense levels'. It announced that the introduction of voluntary applications would be suspended pending a further review. A report was published on 11 February 2011, recommending among other things that the monitoring requirement be abolished.[187]

4.114 In March 2011, the Home Secretary (Theresa May) introduced to Parliament the Protection of Freedoms Bill. She criticised the SVGA for being 'disproportionate and over-reliant on the state', stressing the need to encourage volunteers rather than 'treat them like criminals', and proposed a new regime 'whereby employers will be given a much more central role in ensuring safe recruitment practices, supported

---

[182] Ibid, Sched 4, Part 3, para 10(2).

[183] Ibid, s 6(6) and 6(7).

[184] Ibid, s 58.

[185] SI 2010/1146, in force since 30 March 2010, and including amendment to the Safeguarding Vulnerable Groups Act 2006 (Prescribed Criteria and Miscellaneous Provisions) Regulations 2009 (SI 2009/37), which entered into force the following day.

[186] *Drawing the Line: A Report on the Government's Vetting and Barring Scheme*, 14 December 2009; see (functional at the time of writing) www.education.gov.uk/publications/eOrderingDownload/DCSF-01122-2009.pdf

[187] *Vetting and Barring Scheme Remodelling Review—Report and Recommendations*; see (functional at the time of writing) www.homeoffice.gov.uk/publications/crime/vbs-report

by a proportionate central barring scheme' which does not require registration or monitoring.

4.115 The Protection of Freedoms Act 2012 received royal assent on 1 May 2012.[188] Part 5 of the Act addresses the VBS and criminal records, essentially implementing the results of the February 2011 review. Part 5 is split into four sections:

(a) Chapter 1 (sections 64–78), concerning the VBS;
(b) Chapter 2 (sections 79–86), concerning criminal records;
(c) Chapter 3 (sections 87–91), making provision for the abolition of the ISA and the transfer of its powers to the DBS;[189]
(d) Chapter 4 (sections 92–101), allowing individuals to apply to have certain convictions for now-repealed homosexual offences disregarded (not dealt with here).

Chapter 1: The VBS

4.116 The main change introduced by the Protection of Freedoms Act is the scrapping of the registration and monitoring regime for individuals engaging in a regulated activity.[190] The regime will operate by means of barring only, with the regulatory burden shifted from the state onto the employer or organisation.

4.117 New arrangements are established to enable regulated activity providers (with the individual's consent) to receive information about the individual from the ISA (or the DBS), and to register an interest to receive updates regarding his status.[191] Consent to the initial check suffices as consent for registration for such updates. In parallel with this, a statutory duty is placed on regulated activity providers to check whether a person is barred before allowing him or her to engage in a regulated activity.[192]

4.118 The Act also narrows the definition of 'regulated activity' itself. It is no longer to include any form of teaching, training or instruction of children which is regularly subject to day-to-day supervision by another person who is engaged in a regulated activity.[193] A number of other categories are removed, such as those which encompassed the provision of legal advice to a child, working in a schools or children's inspectorate, and temporary or occasional work in a specified place which has the consequence of bringing the person into contact with children (eg maintenance work in a school).[194] In respect of one area—namely certain types of personal care and health care which take place in a specified place (such as a school)—the definition is expanded so that the activity need not be undertaken regularly in order to be regulated.[195]

---

[188] However, as of 29 May 2012 none of Part 5 is in force save for parts of Chapter 3.
[189] On 19 June 2012 Adrienne Kelbie and Bill Griffiths were appointed Chief Executive and Chair of the DBS respectively. It is intended that the DBS will replace the ISA from 1 December 2012.
[190] Protection of Freedoms Act 2012, s 69.
[191] Ibid, s 72.
[192] Ibid, s 73.
[193] Ibid, s 64(7)(c).
[194] Ibid, s 64(6), (5).
[195] Ibid, s 64(3).

4.119 The period definitions, defining the threshold of regularity before an activity becomes regulated, are unchanged in relation to children.[196] The parallel category of 'controlled activities' is abolished altogether.[197]

4.120 There are also changes to the circumstances in which a person will be barred. Whereas previously any person convicted of or cautioned for a specified offence would automatically be included on the register, the Act provides that such a person will only be barred if he or she 'is or has been, or might in future be, engaged in the regulated activity'.[198] In other words, those who have not undertaken and have no intention of undertaking a regulated activity will not be barred. Wherever the SVGA provided that a person would be automatically barred with a subsequent right to make representations, it is provided that the ISA (or the DBS) be required to seek representations first. The process in relation to offences simply justifying an automatic barring is unaffected.[199] There is also no change to the representations procedure; representations must still be made in writing only.

4.121 As a result of the above, the SVGA offences relating to the monitoring scheme will be repealed. It will remain an offence for (a) a barred person to work with vulnerable groups in a regulated activity, and (b) an employer or voluntary organisation knowingly to employ a barred person in a regulated activity role.

4.122 Finally, a number of changes have been made to the ISA's powers: it is now able to review a person's inclusion on the barred list at any time, rather than after a specified period;[200] it is given the power to obtain relevant police information about an individual where the automatic or discretionary barring provisions appear to apply;[201] and those holding such information are required to disclose it if they reasonably believe it to be relevant. The ISA is no longer required to notify an employer of its intention to bar an individual before representations have been received and a final decision made.[202] In other words, the employer will only be notified once a decision has been made.

4.123 Certain provisions require the ISA to inform a professional body that somebody on the body's register is on the barred list, and to allow such bodies to apply for barred list information.[203]

Chapter 2: Changes to the CRB Regime

4.124 The Act repeals the requirement that a CRB certificate be sent to the registered body as well as to the individual to whom it relates, however the registered body must be informed whether or not a certificate has been issued if it requests this information.[204]

---

[196] Ibid, s 66(9).
[197] Ibid, s 68.
[198] Ibid, s 67(1).
[199] Ibid, s 67(2)–(6).
[200] Ibid, s 71.
[201] Ibid, s 70(1).
[202] Ibid, s 77.
[203] Ibid, ss 75–76.
[204] Ibid, s 79.

The intention is to put the individual in control of the information that is disclosed and to allow him to contest any disclosure before it goes to his employer.

4.125 In addition, the test for disclosing information under an ECRC is raised from what 'might be relevant' to what the chief police officer 'reasonably believes to be relevant'.[205] This aims to give expression to the Supreme Court's decision in *R (L) v Commissioner of Police of the Metropolis*[206] that Article 8 rights are engaged in relation to the decision whether or not to disclose non-conviction related information.

4.126 The Act restricts CRB checks to those aged 16 years and over.[207] Finally, a mechanism is created for employers to register an interest in an individual so as to receive notification when new information has made it necessary for a new certificate to be obtained.[208]

Consequences

4.127 While the definition of 'regulated activity' is being narrowed, the Home Office expects that around 4.5 million people will still fall within it. The main purpose of the reform is not to end regulation but to shift the main regulatory burden from the state to the organisation providing the regulated activity.

4.128 In practice, the Act's regime in relation to regulated activity may not be substantially different from that proposed by the SVGA as originally enacted. Since the regulated activity provider must check with the ISA whether a person is barred before allowing them to engage in such an activity, and it will be very good practice to register an interest in order to receive updates as to status, the practical effect will be very similar to that of a monitoring regime.

4.129 The area of danger for organisations is activities which are no longer regulated but which nevertheless involve contact with children. This includes the extremely large number of people who provide teaching, training or instruction subject to day-to-day supervision by somebody who is regulated. Sports-related organisations are very likely to be affected by this; one of the categories of person identified in the Government's February 2011 review as being freed from formal regulation was 'a volunteer touchline judge at a children's football match'.

4.130 Where the activity is not formally regulated, it will be for the provider to form a decision as to the person's suitability to work with children. In effect, the decision whether or not to let the individual work with children is being devolved from the state to the recruiter. The recruiter may be exposed to negligence claims if it does not approach this decision with great thoroughness and care. It is still be able to seek criminal record checks in respect of such people, and it will remain good practice to do so.

4.131 The changes in Part 5 Chapter 2 mean that the practicalities of doing so will be slightly more complex than before. In particular, when a criminal record certificate is

---

[205] Ibid, s 82(1).
[206] [2009] UKSC 3.
[207] Protection of Freedoms Act 2012, s 80(1).
[208] Ibid, s 83.

required it will now go to the individual, who will pass it on to the organisation if content to do so. The Government seems confident that this carries little risk of tampering or interference, but providers will have to be careful to ensure that they have adequate procedures in place for requesting, receiving and checking such certificates in the absence of any power to receive them directly.

4.132 The fact that the threshold for disclosing information as part of a criminal records check has been raised, and that the affected individual has the opportunity to challenge the disclosure of any such information before it reaches the recruiter, is likely to mean in practice that recruiters can be relatively comfortable relying on such information as a reason not to employ or otherwise engage the individual to whom it relates. The likeliest litigation arising out of a refusal to employ a person on the basis of such information is a judicial review by the affected individual of the police's decision to disclose it.

4.133 Liability for negligence remains an issue where a recruiter is insufficiently cautious about employing or engaging an individual. With disclosure of an enhanced certificate and a reasonably robust recruitment procedure, however, such liability can be guarded against.

4.134 There is a tension between the interests of the child who requires protection and those of the person accused of abuse. The proper approach to this sensitive issue is summarised in the judgment of Lord Woolf MR in *R v Broxtowe BC, ex parte Bradford*,[209] in which the Council barred the applicant from tennis coaching of young people on the basis of allegations of sexual abuse by three pupils without giving him an opportunity to comment:

> It is very important that, although every appropriate step is taken to protect vulnerable children from improper attentions, particularly from somebody who is in a position of authority such as a teacher, that [sic] the person who is the subject of allegations is also given a proper degree of protection[210] ... [T]he council is entitled to attach the greatest importance to the protection of the children. So far as that protection is concerned, it can take any appropriate action as long as that action is not disproportionate or unreasonable in relation to its conclusions on the relevant facts.[211]

---

[209] [2000] IRLR 329, CA.
[210] Ibid, para 29.
[211] Ibid, para 31.

5

The Regulation of Play

Introduction

5.1 In the two preceding chapters we considered the existence of rights to participate in sport from two different standpoints. First, in chapter three we looked at direct rights of participation in sporting competition established by satisfying entry criteria. Second, in chapter four we examined the rights and duties of players (in the broadest possible sense) and their clubs (or governing bodies) towards each other. In this chapter we move on to consider the extent and content of rights and obligations governing the conduct of sport itself. For the purposes of this chapter, our enquiry has gone beyond the stage of ascertaining whether a right to participate exists at all, and, if it does, what are the pre-competition conditions subject to which that right may be exercised, and whether they have been fulfilled or not. Our account of sports law has now reached the point of examining the content of sporting rights and obligations once all the pre-conditions for participation in a sporting competition have, from the perspective of the organisers of the competition, been satisfied.

5.2 It follows that, for the purposes of the current enquiry, we may assume that the players are entitled and permitted to play; that the club they play for is eligible to enter the competition; and that no other objection to participation is forthcoming from the organisers of the competition. On those assumptions, we now look at the rules to which participation in sport is subject. Those rules are established partly by the organisers of the competition and partly by the general law of the state in whose territory the competition takes place. Their content may affect spectators and officials as well as players and clubs. They include rules requiring safety measures to be taken, rules prohibiting criminal conduct in the course of sport, and rules establishing the scope of liability, on the part of players and clubs, to others who may be participants, officials, spectators or indeed members of the public affected by a sporting event.

5.3 This rather amorphous collection of rules may, loosely, be referred to as rules regulating play. The notion of the regulation of play is considered, in our exposition, to denote rules which directly affect participation in sport and the organisation of sporting competition once eligibility to compete has been established. These rules are thus different in character from pre-competition eligibility rules of the type considered in chapter three. They also differ, conceptually, from rules governing relations between players and clubs which operate, so to speak, horizontally and do not, in principle, affect the actual conduct of sporting competition.

5.4 Rules which regulate play are also different, in their nature, from disciplinary rules which apply to the course of the game itself but are not enforced until after the competition is over. Disciplinary regimes occupy an important position in sports law. Their functioning merits separate treatment, and is discussed in chapter seven. The operation of such disciplinary rules may require bodies exercising punitive jurisdiction to look back at events on the field of play. But such rules do not apply to the course of the game itself while it is actually being played. The distinction is well illustrated by the example of a referee exercising the power to show a red card to a player, sending him off for misconduct. The referee's power to do so arises in the course of the game, as it is a rule of the game that a player to whom a red card is shown must leave the field. This is a rule which regulates play and falls within the scope of our enquiry in this chapter. The same player may later face disciplinary charges as a result of having been sent off. These are applied to him *a posteriori*, and consequently do not fall within the scope of this chapter, but under the heading of disciplinary proceedings, considered in chapter seven.

5.5 Certainly in England and Wales, and it may be assumed in every country in the world, subject to any relevant special rules of law, the general principles of the criminal law and the law of tort or delict apply to participants in sport as they apply to everyone else. It goes without saying that the shooting of a player by another player during a game (as unfortunately happened once at a football match in El Salvador) is as much a crime as if it were committed anywhere else. Similarly, if a rugby player makes a dangerous tackle, causing his opponent physical injury, the perpetrator may be guilty of a criminal offence such as common assault, or may be liable in tort for assault or negligence. It is not left solely to the laws of the game to penalise the perpetrator and to compensate the victim. And sporting rules empowering adjudicators to award compensation for dangerous play are rare or non-existent.

5.6 However, the application of common law principles in the context of sport throws up different issues from cases involving, say, a bar-room brawl or a road traffic accident. This is because in contact sports, participants consent to a degree of physical contact. How far that consent extends is a frequent issue in litigation following injuries sustained on the field of play. The related issue of importance is that of the standard of care in negligence in the course of a sport whose rules permit and envisage physical contact. Furthermore, statute may affect the manner in which sport is conducted. Match fixing would be unlawful as a criminal conspiracy at common law or under the Criminal Law Act 1977, and would be likely also to contravene the Theft Act 1968 and the Fraud Act 2006. Legislation requires measures to ensure safety and public order in some cases. And a raft of statutory provisions regulates betting on the outcome of horse races and other sporting competitions—as part of the specialist field of law relating to betting, gaming and lotteries.[1]

5.7 It is beyond our purpose to give a comprehensive account of all rules regulating play, in the sense described above, applicable in England and Wales; still less do we seek to describe fully those that apply in other countries. Our aim is the more limited one of identifying the nature of such rules, subdividing them into categories which we estimate will be helpful,

---

[1] See Monckom, *Smith and Monckom: The Law of Gambling*, 3rd edn (Tottel Publishing, 2009) for a helpful account of that branch of the law.

and giving a brief account of some of the more important legal developments within those categories.

5.8 As a starting point, we ought just to pause to consider first what we mean by the notion of 'play', when we speak of rules which regulate play. This requires us to consider, though only briefly, the nature of sport itself and its limits. Immediately we are struck by the sheer variety of human activities which, down the ages, have been treated as sport. The founders of the Olympic Games in 776 BC[2] would probably have rejected synchronised swimming as inappropriate for inclusion in the Games. Those espousing the Corinthian ideal might have difficulty accommodating snooker and darts as sport; yet some purists, initially sceptically inclined, now accept them as legitimate sporting activities. Intellectual games such as chess are generally thought to test purely mental rather than physical prowess, but science now increasingly regards cerebral activity as physiological, so it may be that chess tests stamina as well as intellect.[3]

5.9 This sort of musing is mildly entertaining but does not point in the direction of a precise legal definition of sport. Indeed in no legal system, so far as we are aware, has it been found necessary to embrace a conceptual approach to the nature of sport or to adopt a legal definition of the term—though in the familiar field of betting, gaming and lotteries the English courts have had to consider what is meant by a game of chance, and so forth. For the purposes of this book, we content ourselves with the easy proposition that sports law does not, or does not yet, attempt to impose limits on the definition of what a sport is.

5.10 If we had to offer such a definition, we suggest that it would contain the following four elements: (i) an activity, human or animal (ii) in which two or more players, human or animal, compete against each other (iii) according to predetermined rules (iv) pursuant to which someone wins, and which determine who wins.[4] Such a definition focuses on competitive rather than recreational sport, and would exclude 'blood sports' such as hunting and coursing where the winner is determined crudely by the survival or otherwise of the pursued, rather than by the application of rules of the game. This is an appropriate exclusion in our view since such sports are now illegal in England, Wales and Scotland (but not Northern Ireland).[5]

---

[2] Also the foundation date of the calendar based on the recurrence of the Olympic Games every fourth year; see Bernard Knox's introduction to Homer's *Iliad* (Penguin Classics, 1996) 23.

[3] See *Chess: A Sport or Just a Game?* (1999) 2(2) Sports Law Bulletin 16, recounting the British Chess Federation's efforts to get chess adopted as an Olympic sport and citing Michael Adams, Britain's number one chess player: 'You need a lot of stamina ... being in good shape helps to keep you focussed mentally ... chess can be very draining.' The same applies to legal practice, which however is *not* a sport. For a useful and entertaining account of recognised and unrecognised sports, including an alphabetical table showing the status of sports or potential sports from Abseiling to Yoga, see Lines, *Six Degrees of Sports Participation: Are the Olympics the Common Denominator for All Sports?* [2008] ISLR 53.

[4] Cf Grayson in All ER Annual Review 1987 at p 239 ('The categories [of sport] are never closed').

[5] Hunting Act 2004, extending (by s 17) only to England and Wales, criminalising the hunting of wild mammals with dogs; Protection of Wild Mammals (Scotland) Act 2002 (Act of Scottish Parliament). Both have limited exceptions for rabbits and rodents. A Hunting Bill was introduced in the Northern Ireland Assembly, but was rejected in December 2010. Optimistic challenges to the validity of the legislation predictably failed in *R (Countryside Alliance) v Attorney General* [2008] 1 AC 719 and *Adams v Scottish Ministers* [2004] SC 665. The ECtHR rejected as inadmissible two applications alleging violation of various articles of the European Convention: *Friend v United Kingdom; Countryside Alliance v United Kingdom* (2010) 50 EHRR SE6.

5.11 With those preliminary thoughts, we turn to consider the different types of rules regulating play. We began in chapter one with the premise that sports law is by nature international and non-governmental in character.[6] Insofar as rules regulating play are derived from the general law of the state in which a competition is taking place, it is naturally a matter for the national law of that state to prescribe rules governing both the organisation of sports and liability arising from events in the course of play. The extent to which the general law of a particular state impacts on the conduct of sport, and the content of the relevant rules, will vary from sport to sport and from state to state. Our account of rules regulating play in this chapter is mainly specific to the law of England and Wales, though its common law content is also relevant in other common law jurisdictions across the world.

5.12 Before addressing the manner in which the law intervenes to regulate play, we consider a logically prior question with which the law is concerned: whether the game may be played at all.

Prohibited Sports

5.13 The question here is whether the general law of the land, as opposed to the law governing relations between the parties involved in sport, permits the sport in question to be played. An answer to this question requires an account of prohibited sports. Under the still mainly unwritten libertarian constitution of the United Kingdom, activities which are not specifically made illegal by statute or judicial precedent may lawfully be undertaken. Chariot racing is therefore not banned in the United Kingdom (though it has lost much of its popular appeal). We do not need a law permitting chariot racing; we would need a law to ban it. Under the written constitutions of other nations, sport is permitted by virtue of express constitutional guarantees of freedom of association.

5.14 A distinction can be drawn between sports which the state prohibits as such, and sports which are prohibited only if practised using unlawful means. For example, bear baiting, popular in Elizabethan times, would now by its very nature infringe legislation protecting animals against cruelty. So, probably, would dog fighting, which is known to have taken place clandestinely in recent times, in the East End of London. Professor Grayson's picturesque account of some of the legislation and litigation affecting rural and water sports, including hunting, shooting and fishing,[7] reminds us that our proposed definition of sport offered above excludes non-competitive sports pursued for pleasure. We have already mentioned the prohibition against hunting wild mammals with dogs everywhere in the United Kingdom except Northern Ireland. If and insofar as such hunting could be termed a 'sport'—a minefield we prefer not to tread—it is a prohibited one.

5.15 Sports prohibited per se may also include sports in our sense of the term. Swordfights to the death between gladiators would infringe criminal laws banning offensive weapons, and would probably amount to a conspiracy to commit grievous bodily harm or murder, and possibly to corrupt public morals as well. But martial arts and wrestling are

---

[6] See paras 1.16–1.18.
[7] See Grayson, *Sport and the Law*, 2nd edn (Butterworths, 1994) 112–17; 3rd edn (Butterworths, 2000) 208–13.

not criminal by definition. Contact sports in this latter category are commonplace. The application to them of the criminal law is considered below.[8]

Organisation and Competition

Introduction

5.16 In the remainder of this chapter we consider how the law regulates the practical organisation of and participation in sporting events. Jurisdiction over such activity is conferred principally in four ways: by statute, by the law of tort, by the criminal law, and by the rules of the game itself. A fifth and extremely rare type of intervention consists in a challenge to the result of a game in a court of law, on the basis of applying the rules of the game. As to the latter, these include both primary rules determining how the game must be played (for example, the prohibition against handling the ball in association football, the rule that a cricketer is out if the ball is caught straight from the bat without bouncing, and so forth) and secondary rules conferring power on officials to disqualify a horse, to send a player off for misconduct, and so on. Such rules form a category narrower in scope even than that of rules which are 'of sporting interest only' in the EU law sense mentioned in chapter three and explained further in chapter four;[9] since that latter category includes some pre-competition eligibility criteria.

5.17 Jurisdiction conferred by the rules of the game is exercised summarily during the game by the designated officials on the spot, and is virtually certain to be held non-reviewable by the courts. One could not realistically suppose that a court would ever overturn a decision to award a try or a penalty. The referee or umpire's exercise of discretion and judgment is beyond challenge, except to the extent that the rules of the game so provide, as they do in the case of an assistant referee in football whose provisional decision may be summarily reversed by the referee. The possibility of increased use of immediate video replays in refereeing may provide for summary appeal procedures in certain cases but, subject to that point, the risk of unfairness to a player is conclusively outweighed by the overwhelming sporting imperative of immediate certainty.

5.18 So obvious is the above proposition that one ought not to need authority to support it; it simply goes without saying.[10] We need therefore look no further at summary jurisdiction over play exercised pursuant to the rules of the game. We turn next to the

---

[8] See para 5.87 ff.

[9] See ch 3 paras 3.108–3.112; ch 4 paras 4.12–4.13, 4.69. See Case 38/74 *Walrave and Koch v Association Union Cycliste Internationale* [1974] ECR 1405; Case 13/76 *Donà v Mantero* [1976] ECR 1333; Case C-415/93 *Union Royale Belge des Sociétés de Football Association ASBL v Jean-Marc Bosman* [1995] ECR I-4921; *AEK Athens FC and Slavia Prague v UEFA*, CAS 98/200.

[10] However, there is authority to support the proposition: *Machin v FA* (1993) unreported (CA), referred to in Grayson 3rd edn (n 7) 409; *Mendy v IABA*, CAS Ad Hoc Division, 96/006 (Atlanta), referred to in Beloff, *CAS at the Olympics* (1996) 4(3) SLJ 5, 8; *Segura v IAAF*, CAS Ad Hoc Division, OG 00/013 (Sydney); *Birmingham City v Football League* (2001) unreported, 18 May.

more substantial matter of legal intervention through statute, through the law of tort and under the criminal law.

Statute

5.19 The European Union has in recent times shown a greater willingness to contemplate involvement in the regulation and development of sport. Following a path which can be traced through declaration 29 of the Amsterdam Treaty, the 2000 Nice Declaration and the European Commission's 1997 *White Paper on Sport*, the Treaty of Lisbon introduced provisions relating to sport into the main body of the Treaty on the Functioning of the European Union (TFEU). Article 165 TFEU states:

> The Union shall contribute to the promotion of European sporting issues, while taking account of the specific nature of sport, its structures based on voluntary activity and its social and educational function.

And Union action shall be aimed at:

> developing the European dimension in sport, by promoting fairness and openness in sporting competitions and cooperation between bodies responsible for sports, and by protecting the physical and moral integrity of sportsmen and sportswomen, especially the youngest sportsmen and sportswomen.

The Article, however, specifically excludes harmonisation of laws and regulations of Member States as a means of achieving these objectives and instead envisages the adoption of incentive measures.[11] The competence provided in respect of sports is therefore soft and, whilst it may represent the development of a sports policy within the European Union, in reality it falls short of establishing the regulation of sport at a Community level.[12]

5.20 It is therefore to national legislation that one must look to discern how sporting activity is regulated by statute. In the United Kingdom statutory regulation intrudes relatively little into the sporting world. In contrast to other countries where an interventionist approach has been adopted, and government introduces specific legislation to regulate and coordinate sports, the majority of statutory regulation in England and Wales is undertaken primarily in support of non-sporting objectives, principally public safety and order. We include in our account some of the main statutes currently regulating the organisation of sports, which covers spectators as well as clubs and players. The claim of such legislation to form part of sports law properly so called, in our conception of the term, is a little doubtful.

5.21 However, the legislation is of great practical importance to sports administrators. It may be considered to merit inclusion in this book on practical grounds and, for the purist theoretician, as a set of mere examples of statutory and judicial intervention in the course and context of sport rather than in or over sport itself.

---

[11] TFEU Art 165(4).
[12] See further and generally Weatherill, *Fairness, Openness and the Specific Nature of Sport: Does the Lisbon Treaty Change EU Sports Law?* (2010) 3/4 ISLJ 11.14–17; Griffiths and Drew, *Developing the European Dimension in Sport* (2011) 22(5) Entertainment Law Review 136.

5.22 Successive disasters at football stadia through the last century at Wembley, Bolton Wanderers, Ibrox (Glasgow), Bradford and Hillsborough led to commissions of enquiry presided over by distinguished judges whose subsequent reports led to legislation. It is fair to say that the legislature has reacted to these well-publicised tragedies rather than anticipating them. The most recent and authoritative reports are still those of Mr Justice Popplewell[13] and Lord Justice Taylor.[14] A fuller account of legislative and administrative measures against football violence and in pursuit of safety can be found in the second edition of Professor Grayson's *Sport and the Law*.[15]

5.23 The relevant legislative weapons in the state's armoury are, briefly, the following. The Safety of Sports Grounds Act 1975 enacted a regulatory regime whereby sports grounds designated by the Secretary of State require a safety certificate issued by the local authority in whose area the ground is located. Detailed provisions govern the power of the local authority to determine the terms and conditions for issue of such a certificate and the procedure for obtaining it.[16] Section 10 of the Act[17] empowers the relevant local authority to issue a prohibitive notice limiting the number of spectators who can lawfully be admitted to a particular ground, if the authority forms the view that admission of a greater number will involve a sufficiently high degree of risk to them to warrant such a limit until steps have been taken to reduce the risk to a reasonable level.

5.24 The 1975 Act marked the start of a general public supervisory function specific to sports grounds, over and above pre-existing regulatory powers applying to buildings generally, such as fire protection legislation. In 1987 the requirement for a safety certificate was extended specifically to stands at sports grounds holding 500 or more spectators.[18] The detailed procedure governing applications for such a safety certificate is prescribed by regulations.[19]

5.25 Parliament has also enacted legislation specific to sport for the purpose of promoting public order, in response to public concern about hooliganism. These statutory provisions supplement the general law relating to public order, which applies in and around sporting events as it does anywhere else.

5.26 Thus the Sporting Events (Control of Alcohol etc) Act 1985 makes it an offence to cause or permit intoxicating liquor to be carried on a train or coach being used principally to carry passengers to or from a sporting event designated by the Secretary of State, which may be a sporting event abroad as well as in England and Wales.[20] Other offences of being drunk in a private vehicle adapted to carry more than eight passengers to or from such an event, or causing or permitting intoxicating liquor to be carried on such a vehicle, were added by a new section 1A of the 1985 Act the following year.[21] Section 2A made it an offence to possess, during a designated sporting event or while entering or trying to enter

---

[13] Interim and Final Reports of the Committee of Inquiry into Crowd Safety and Control at Sports Grounds, Cmnd 9585 and Cmnd 9710 respectively (Final Report November 1985).

[14] *Inquiry into Crowd Safety and Control at Sports Grounds*, Cmnd 962 (January 1990).

[15] Grayson 2nd edn (n 7) 125–44.

[16] See ss 1–7 of the 1975 Act.

[17] As substituted by the Fire Safety and Safety of Places of Sport Act 1987, s 23(1).

[18] Ibid, ss 26–30.

[19] Safety of Places of Sport Regulations 1988, SI 1988/1807.

[20] See ss 1 and 9(3) of the Act.

[21] S 1A was added by the Public Order Act 1986, s 40(1) and Sched 1, Part I.

it, 'any article or substance whose main purpose is the emission of a flare for purposes of illuminating or signalling (as opposed to igniting or heating) or the emission of smoke or a visible gas ... [including] distress flares, fog signals, and pellets and capsules intended to be used as fumigators or for testing pipes, but not ... matches, cigarette lighters or heaters'.[22] An offence is also committed if the article carried is a firework.[23]

5.27 The Public Order Act 1986 contained wide ranging revisions to the general law of public order, including the creation of certain new offences not specific to sport but influenced by specific behaviour of, among others, individuals attending sporting events. Part IV of the Act also enacted provisions specific to football matches, empowering courts before which offenders are convicted of certain football related offences (as defined in section 31 of the Act) to impose exclusion orders prohibiting such offenders from attending football matches.

5.28 The provisions were made subject to prospective repeal by the Football Spectators Act 1989,[24] following the enactment of that Act which created a more wide ranging regulatory regime for football, including the concept of a national football membership scheme administered by a newly created Football Membership Authority, and a Football Licensing Authority with the function of issuing licences to organisers of designated football matches to admit spectators subject to such terms and conditions as the Authority should consider appropriate.[25] However, the membership scheme was not implemented and the provisions relating to it have now been repealed.[26]

5.29 The provisions in Part IV of the Public Order Act 1986 have been repealed by provisions in the Football (Disorder) Act 2000, and replaced by similar powers to impose restriction orders which can apply to football matches outside as well as inside England and Wales.[27] The added element was the duty on the offender to report to a specified police station on the occasion of designated football matches, so that the subject of the order cannot go to the match.[28]

5.30 The Football (Offences) Act 1991 created an additional offence of throwing anything at or towards the playing area or any area where spectators or others are or may be present, at a designated football match.[29] Further offences were created by the same Act, of indulging in 'chanting of an indecent or racialist nature';[30] and of going onto the playing area or an area adjacent to it.[31]

---

[22] S 2A(3).
[23] S 2A(4).
[24] See s 27(5) of the 1989 Act.
[25] See generally ss 1–9 as originally constituted.
[26] By the Violent Crime Reduction Act 2006.
[27] S 14A of the 1989 Act as amended by the Football (Disorder) Act 2000 requires the court to impose a football banning order on anyone convicted of a football related offence, if the court is satisfied that there are reasonable grounds for believing that the order would help prevent violence or disorder at or in connection with any regulated football match.
[28] S 14 of the 1989 Act; in the case of overseas matches the offender must surrender his passport. The 1989 Act was also substantially amended by the Football (Offences and Disorder) Act 1999, making the present scheme of statutory regulation something of a patchwork quilt, demonstrating the penchant of politicians of all hues to be seen to tackle the ugly side of the beautiful game.
[29] Football (Offences) Act 1991, s 2.
[30] See ibid, s 3.
[31] Ibid, s 4.

5.31 Finally, the Criminal Justice and Public Order Act 1994, which like the Public Order Act 1986 enacted various revisions to public order law generally, included a section creating a new offence of ticket touting at a designated football match, committed where a person unauthorised by the home club or the match organisers sells or offers to sell or exposes for sale a ticket, or something purporting to be a ticket, in any public place or place to which the public has access, or, in the course of a trade or business, in any other place[32] including over the internet.[33]

5.32 Numerous regulations supplement the statutory regime outlined above, a detailed account of which is beyond the compass of this book. The legislation banning and restricting the sale and use of guns is likewise not described here. It is clearly a measure designed to enhance public safety, enacted without sporting considerations in mind and indeed in spite of them, for it has a considerable impact on competitive shooting contests.[34]

Tort and Sport

Generally

5.33 Whereas obligations which arise out of contract are derived from the choice of the parties, obligations which arise out of tort are derived from the law of the land. It is for the law of tort to determine in what circumstances, and with what consequences, one person may be liable for injury, physical, psychological, psychiatric, financial or to reputation, which he has caused to another person, otherwise than under terms and conditions to which he has agreed.

5.34 The law of tort sometimes makes the standard of behaviour of the person who caused the injury determinative of whether liability arises. Assault and battery, respectively the threat of and the actual infliction of physical injury, require intent in the tortfeasor. Negligence requires the infliction of injury in circumstances where the person has no intent, but his action or omission falls short of an appropriate objectively set standard.[35]

5.35 The law of tort sometimes makes the nature of the action determinative of whether liability arises. Nuisance is constituted by an interference with another's enjoyment of land.

5.36 These general propositions (which require elaboration and qualification) are applicable to all forms of human activity. Therefore tort applies to sport: Swift J in *Cleghorn v Oldham*,

---

[32] S 166(1) Criminal Justice and Public Order Act 1994.

[33] Ibid, s 166A as amended by s 53 Violent Crimes Reduction Act 2006; similar protection was given to the 2012 Olympic Games by the London Olympic Games and Paralympic Games Act 2006.

[34] Firearms (Amendment) Act 1997; the government has had to make an exemption for the 2012 London Olympics to allow pistol shooting competitions to take place, as it did for the 2002 Manchester Commonwealth Games.

[35] See generally Felstead and Kingsley-Miller, *Forms of Legal Action when On-Pitch Remedies Fail*, WSLR 6/12, pp 10–11.

in giving judgment for the plaintiff who had been injured when struck by the defendant's golf club during a demonstration swing, stated:

> Games might be and [are] the serious business of life to many people. It would be extraordinary to say that people could not recover from injuries sustained in the business of life, whether that was football, or motor racing, or any other of those pursuits which were instinctively classed as games but which everyone knew quite well to be serious business transactions for the persons engaged therein.[36]

Negligence

5.37 Negligence is the dominant tort; indeed in the views of some it threatens to absorb or outflank almost every other tort in the field. The tort of negligence has three elements: the claimant must establish that the defendant (i) owed him a common law duty of care, (ii) breached that duty, and (iii) damage resulted. The primary aspect of the common law duty of care that is relevant to sport is the need to avoid foreseeable risks which result in foreseeable physical injury.[37] Three main issues arise: first, whether there is a duty of care; second, if so, what standard of care is required; and third, where the claimant is a participant, whether and—if so—to what extent such voluntary participation provides a defence.

5.38 As to the duty of care, it is elementary that a duty is owed to those who ought reasonably to be in contemplation as being affected by a particular act (the so called 'neighbour' principle).[38] Further, the duty itself is to take *reasonable* care to avoid injury to another person or property. Finally, since both the identification of the individuals to whom the duty is owed and the existence and extent of the duty are substantially determined by conceptions of reasonableness, the facts of and relating to any given case will determine whether or not a duty is established and, if so, whether or not breach of such duty can be shown.

Duty of Participants to Each Other

5.39 The existence of a duty of care between competitors in sports is well established. It follows from the propositions adumbrated above that where a participant in a game or other sporting pastime is injured by the act or omission of another participant, whether or not there exists a duty of care and, if so, to what extent, are both questions to be determined in the light of all the circumstances.

---

[36] (1927) 43 TLR 465, 466.
[37] Duff, *Civil Actions and Sporting Injuries* (1994) 144 New Law Journal 639. For a fascinating perspective from the ancient world, see Ibbetson, *Athletics in Ancient Law* (2012) 12(2) LIM 98: '[a] number of texts of Roman law are concerned with injuries arising in the course of athletics. The are particularly concerned with blameworthy killings, and constitute some of the most fundamental texts at the historical base of modern negligence liability.'
[38] See *Donoghue v Stevenson* [1932] AC 562.

5.40 In *Rootes v Shelton*,[39] the plaintiff was an experienced water skier temporarily blinded by spray who as a result swung wider than usual, colliding with a stationary boat. Kitto J said:

> I cannot think that there is anything new or mysterious about the application of the law of negligence to a sport or a game. Their kind is older by far than the common law itself. And though water skiing may be slightly faster than chariot-racing it is, like every other sport, simply an activity in which participants place themselves in a special relation or succession of relations to other participants so that adjudication under the common law upon a claim by one participant against another for damages for negligence in respect of injuries sustained in the course of the activity requires only that the tribunal of fact apply itself to the same kind of question of fact as arises in other cases of personal injury by negligence.

> … the conclusion to be reached must necessarily depend, according to the concepts of the common law, upon the reasonableness, in relation to the special circumstances, of the conduct which caused the plaintiff's injury … the tribunal of fact may think that in the situation in which the plaintiff's injury was caused, a participant might do what the defendant did and still not be acting unreasonably, even though he infringed the 'rules of the game'. Noncompliance with such rules, conventions or customs (where they exist) is necessarily one consideration to be attended to upon the question of unreasonableness; but it is only one, and it may be of much or little or even no weight in the circumstances.[40]

This approach was followed in the Court of Appeal in *Condon v Basi*,[41] where a foul tackle by the defendant during a game of soccer resulted in the plaintiff sustaining a fractured leg.[42] The court concluded that the duty of care between players in competitive sports was a duty to take all reasonable care, taking into account the particular circumstances in which the completing players were placed. If one player injured another, either because he had failed to exercise the degree of care which was appropriate in all the circumstances, or because he had acted in a way to which the other could not have been expected to consent, he would be liable for damages in an action in negligence brought by the injured player.[43] In *Pearson v Lightning*[44] the plaintiff recovered damages after being hit in the eye by a golf ball hit by the defendant. Sir Christopher Slade said: 'in any case concerning a golf course injuries must depend upon its particular facts.'

---

[39] *Rootes v Shelton* (1967) 41 ALJR 172; [1968] ALR 33, High Court of Australia. See also *McComiskey v McDermott* [1974] IR 75: where a racing car driver and his passenger are acting as a team, the duty of care owed by the driver to the latter is to drive the car as carefully as a reasonably prudent competitive rally driver would be expected to drive in the circumstances.

[40] *Rootes*, ibid, 387.

[41] *Condon v Basi* [1985] 1 WLR 866.

[42] See Grayson, *Revisiting the Field of Play* (1985) 135 New Law Journal 628; MJH, *Standard of Care in Competitive Sports* [1985] 4(8) 4 Litigation 337; Khan and Wolfgarten, *Liability for Foul Play*, 29 Solicitors Journal 859; McEwan, *Playing the Game: Negligence in Sport*, 130 Solicitors Journal 581.

[43] See *Ridder v Thaler* (1990) unreported; (1998) 1(1) Sports Law Bulletin 3 (scrum half ordered to pay compensation for high tackle); see also *McCord v Swansea City AFC Ltd*, *The Times*, 11 February 1997 (a tackle constituted 'an error which was inconsistent with his taking reasonable care towards his opponent') (see also the cases of tackles settled out of court: Moore, *Sports Law and Litigation* (CLT Professional Publishing, 1997) 51 and 2nd edn (2000)). A 'reckless disregard' test applies in the USA in a player vs player situation (*Nabozay v Barnhill*, 334 NE 2d 258 (Illinois Appellate Court, 1975)). The English test seems more stringent from the defendant's point of view. Recklessness necessarily involves negligence, but absence of recklessness does not disprove it: see Duff, *Reasonable Care v Reckless Disregard* (1997) 7(1) SLJ 44; Duff, *Reasonable Care v Reckless Disregard Revisited* (2002) 10(2) SLJ 156.

[44] (1998) unreported, 1 April (CA).

5.41 In recent years several cases have revisited the concept of a standard of reckless disregard[45] in the sporting context.[46] In *Blake v Galloway*,[47] a case involving horseplay between youths rather than an organised game,[48] Dyson LJ stated:

> In a case such as the present there is a breach of the duty of care owed by participant A to participant B only where A's conduct amounts to recklessness or a very high degree of carelessness.

This followed *Caldwell v Maguire*,[49] where at first instance the court suggested that a breach of duty in a case where a jockey sought damages against fellow competitors for injuries caused by a fall during a race might only be found where conduct on the part of the defendants amounted to a reckless disregard[50] for a fellow contestant's safety. The Court of Appeal concluded that what was referred to was the practical evidential requirement necessary to satisfy the claimant's legal burden, and not legal principle.[51] There remains, we suggest, no modified or special duty of care in actions founded in negligence in the sporting arena. However, consideration of the relevant circumstances may often have the result that actions that would amount to negligence in other contexts do not do so in a sporting situation. A momentary error of judgment is likely to lead to liability in road traffic cases, where such errors are not tolerated, but not on the field of play, where such errors are to be expected.

5.42 The clear implication from *Condon v Basi* is that, in the case of contact sports, such as football and rugby, it will be almost impossible to establish liability unless the actions of the defendant are outside the rules of the game. Indeed the Court of Appeal appeared to be saying that a breach of the rules is virtually a necessary, albeit not a sufficient, requirement for liability to attach. Again, there is nothing special about sports cases in this regard. In various fields it has regularly been held that the rules and standards laid down by professional bodies provide a good guide as to the standards of reasonableness expected of those who operate in the fields governed thereby. Not every foul will constitute a tort,[52] but something short of a foul will not do so.[53]

5.43 What, then, are the relevant circumstances to be taken into account? These may, in our view, include the following. First, whether the sport is a contact or a non-contact sport. Different standards apply to boxing (where the object of the exercise is to engage in bodily contact), to rugby (where it is an incidental but inevitable feature of the sport) and to bowls (where such contact should not occur). Second, whether the accident is caused in

---

[45] First enunciated in *Wooldridge v Sumner* [1963] 2 QB 43 but much criticised at the time; see eg Goodhart, *The Sportsman's Charter* (1962) 78 Law Quarterly Review 490. It is noteworthy that a 'reckless disregard' test applies in the USA in a 'player v player' situation (*Nabozay v Barnhill* (n 43)).

[46] See James and Deeley, *The Standard of Care in Sports Negligence Cases* (2004) 1(1) Entertainment Law 104; Charlish, *A Reckless Approach to Negligence* (2004) 4 Journal of Personal Injury Law 291.

[47] [2004] 1 WLR 2844.

[48] The court however recognised that there was a close analogy between the two in a legal context; per Dyson LJ at 2850.

[49] [2002] PIQR P6.

[50] See further *Gaynor v Blackpool FC* [2002] CLY 3280; *Richardson v Davies* [2006] 1 CLY 405.

[51] Per Tuckey LJ at para 23.

[52] See, eg, *Pitcher v Huddersfield Town FC* (2001) unreported, 17 July.

[53] Although adherence to Codes of Conduct will not in all circumstances enable a defendant to escape negligence; *Woodroffe-Hedley v Cuthbertson* (1997) unreported, 20 June.

the heat of the moment or in a quiet passage of play.[54] Third, the level of risk necessarily accepted as inherent in the sport. Fourth, as explained above, whether the rules of the game have been broken. Fifth, the cost and availability of precautions. Sixth, the level of risk involved.

5.44 These last two tests were applied in *Lewis v Buckpool Golf Club*,[55] where a high-handicap golfer was held to have been negligent in failing to wait before driving off the fifth tee. When he drove he mishit the ball, which struck and injured the pursuer, who was fully visible to him. The court stated that the mishit was something a reasonable man would have had in contemplation as a risk that was reasonably likely to happen, ie more than merely possibly, but less than probably, and it was negligent to run such a risk in a situation where it could be avoided without difficulty, disadvantage or expense. This may be contrasted with *Feeney v Lyall*,[56] where the pursuer failed in a claim arising out of the circumstance that during a round of golf he was struck by a golf ball when he was in an unexpected fairway and invisible to the striker.

5.45 A controversial issue is whether different standards of care apply at different levels of the game, for example depending on whether the game is professional or amateur.[57] In *Condon v Basi* it was stated: 'The standard is objective but objective in a different set of circumstances. Thus there will of course be a higher degree of care required of a player in a First Division football match than of a player in a local league football match'.[58] A contrary approach is, however, illustrated by *Elliott v Saunders and Liverpool FC*,[59] where Drake J said:

> The fact that the players are top professionals with very great skills, is no doubt one of the circumstances to be considered, but in my judgment the fact that the game is in the Premier League rather than at a lower level, does not necessarily mean that the standard of care is different.

5.46 The skill of individual golf players has been considered relevant in golfing cases particularly with regard to the foreseeability of injury caused by stray golf balls.[60] However, the application of different standards of care could potentially lead to difficulties in team sports. In football cup matches teams from significantly different levels of the game often

---

[54] Where, during a motorcycle race, the sidecar passenger was injured when the machine crashed, caused partly by the failure of the rear brakes as a result of a known defect that ought to and could have been rectified by its rider before the race began, his action for damages succeeded. It was held that the rider owed his passenger the normal standard of care and not the modified one, which usually applied to competitors in a sport, because the negligence had occurred in the relative calm of the workshop and not during the flurry and excitement of the race: *Harrison v Vincent* [1982] RTR 8. However, it was said in *Agar v Canning* (1965) 54 WWR 302 at p 304: 'The conduct of a player in the heat of a game is instinctive and not to be judged by standards suited to polite social intercourse.'
[55] *Lewis v Buckpool Golf Club* 1993 SLT (Sh Ct) 43.
[56] *Feeney v Lyall* 1991 SLT 156; *Leatherhead v Edwards* (1998) unreported, 28 November. Where a defendant breached a cardinal safety rule at the heart of the game of uni-hockey, he was negligent when the high follow-through of his stick caused the plaintiff to lose sight in one eye.
[57] In *Vowles v Evans* [2003] 1 WLR 1607 at 1618 Lord Phillips MR considered this point as one where there was 'scope for argument'.
[58] Ibid, 868, per Sir John Donaldson MR. Moore notes at p 48 of the 1st edn of *Sports Law and Litigation* (n 43), in support of Sir John Donaldson MR, that 'a variable standard of care is applicable in other areas of the law, most notably the medical profession'.
[59] *Elliott v Saunders and Liverpool FC* (1994) unreported, 10 June.
[60] *Lewis v Buckpool Golf Club* (n 55); *Brewer v Delo* [1967] 1 Lloyd's Rep 488; *Phee v Gordon* [2011] CSOH 181.

play each other. It has been suggested that it would be anomalous that one team should owe a higher standard of care to their opponents than vice versa.[61]

5.47 It may, however, be that the standard of care required in each case is the same, although the nature and level of the match in question (and, accordingly, the standard of skill to be expected from the players) would form part of the factual context within which such standard fell to be applied. From a practical point of view, sports injury cases often raise evidential problems. In particular, it may be difficult to assess whether a player has breached the duty of care he owes to another player given that this type of assessment will often involve analysing an occurrence whose duration can be measured in seconds.[62]

Duty of Participants Towards Spectators

5.48 In *Wooldridge v Sumner*,[63] in which a horse ridden by the defendant collided with the plaintiff, Diplock LJ referred to 'an almost complete dearth of judicial authority as to the duty of care owed by the actual participants to the spectators'. The judgment sought to fill the vacuum. Diplock LJ's main points were as follows.

5.49 First, Lord Atkin's statement of principle in *Donoghue v Stevenson*

> does not purport to define what is reasonable care and was directed to identifying the persons to whom the duty to take reasonable care is owed. What is reasonable care in particular circumstances is a jury question and where, as in a case like this, there is no direct guidance or hindrance from authority it may be answered by inquiring whether the ordinary reasonable man would say that in all the circumstances the defendant's conduct was blameworthy ... The law of negligence has always recognised that the standard of care which a reasonable man will exercise depends upon the conditions under which the decision to avoid the act or omission relied upon as negligence has to be taken.[64]

Second,

> If ... in the course of the game or competition, at a moment when he really has not time to think, a participant by mistake takes a wrong measure, he is not, in my view, to be held guilty of any negligence ... In such circumstances something in the nature of a reckless disregard of the spectator's safety must be proved.[65]

Third,

> The matter has to be looked at from the point of view of the reasonable spectator as well as the reasonable participant; not because of the maxim *volenti non fit injuria*, but because what a reasonable spectator would expect a participant to do without regarding it as blameworthy is as relevant to what is reasonable as what a reasonable participant would think was blameworthy conduct in himself.[66]

---

[61] See Moore, 2nd edn (n 43).
[62] See Lewis and Taylor, *Sport: Law and Practice*, 2nd edn (Tottel Publishing, 2008) 720–1; *Wooldridge v Sumner* [1963] 2 QB 43, 52 per Sellers LJ and 60 per Diplock LJ.
[63] *Wooldridge*, ibid.
[64] Ibid, 66–67.
[65] Ibid, 68, 72.
[66] Ibid, 67.

Fourth,

> A person attending a game or competition takes the risk of any damage caused to him by any act of a participant done in the course of and for the purposes of the game or competition notwithstanding that such act may involve an error of judgment or a lapse of skill, unless the participant's conduct is such as to evince a reckless disregard of the spectator's safety.[67]

There is in short a difference between a Carling colliding with a spectator and a Cantona kicking one. Watching sport is not without risk and competitors are entitled to be all but oblivious to spectators whilst intent on winning a contest in the 'heat of battle'.[68] A spectator who is injured by the actions of the participants can have no valid complaint if their actions are those normally to be expected of competitors pushing themselves. In *Wilks v Cheltenham Homeguard Motor Cycle & Light Car Club*[69] the plaintiffs were spectators at a motorcycle scramble and were lined up against the rope of the spectators' enclosure, when one of the competitors, riding at between 25 and 30 mph, suddenly left the track and ploughed into them. It was held that a competitor in a race, who was going all out to win, owed a duty to spectators not to show a reckless disregard for their safety or (per Edmund Davies LJ) to cause injury 'by an error of judgment which a reasonable competitor, being a reasonable man of the sporting world, would not have made' and which could not, in the stress of the circumstances, reasonably be regarded as excusable.[70]

Duty of Participants to Passers-By

5.50 A person merely passing by a sporting venue may, if they are aware of it, be considered to accept the risk of injury from stray balls, for example. The test as to whether a duty of care has been breached in the event that injury is caused remains the same, taking account of all of the circumstances as usual. In such circumstances the extent and likelihood of foreseeable harm is likely to be the paramount consideration.[71]

Duty of Referees

5.51 In appropriate circumstances those refereeing or otherwise controlling dangerous sports may themselves be liable for any failure to display reasonable competence resulting in injury to a player, including failure to implement relevant rules, designed to protect against injury. For example, in *Smoldon v Whitworth*[72] the referee of a game of rugby was held liable to a player who was injured when a scrum collapsed dangerously.[73] The level of care required of an official towards a player was that appropriate in all the circumstances, taking full account of the factual context in which he was exercising his functions as

---

[67] Ibid, 68. Sellers LJ gave judgment to the same effect.
[68] *Smolden v Whitworth* [1997] ELR 249 per Bingham LCJ.
[69] *Wilks v Cheltenham Homeguard MotorCycle and Light Car Club* [1971] 1 WLR 668; [1971] All ER 369 (CA).
[70] Ibid, 674. See also *Payne and Payne v Maple Leaf* (1949) 1 DLR 369 in which ice hockey players were held liable when they started a fight and injured a spectator with a hockey stick.
[71] In *Bolton v Stone* [1951] 1 AC 580 no negligence was found when injury was caused by a cricket ball struck so far that it travelled outside the cricket ground, when such instances had previously been rare. In contrast, in *Miller v Jackson* [1997] QB 966, where the same had occurred regularly, the defendant was found liable.
[72] *Smoldon v Whitworth* [1997] ELR 249, CA.
[73] *The Liability of The Official* (1998) 1(2) Sports Law Bulletin 8.

referee. Lord Bingham LCJ declined to equate the duty owed by a referee to players with that owed by a participant to a spectator:

> In [the latter] cases it was recognised that a sporting competitor, properly intent on winning the contest, was (and was entitled to be) all but oblivious of spectators. It therefore followed that he would have to be shown to have very blatantly disregarded the safety of spectators before he could be held to have failed to exercise such care as was reasonable in all the circumstances. The position of a referee vis-à-vis the players is not the same as that of a participant in a contest vis-à-vis a spectator. One of his responsibilities is to safeguard the safety of the players. So, although the legal duty is the same in the two cases, the practical content of the duty differs according to the quite different circumstances.[74]

Lord Bingham LCJ then set out the way in which the duty of care was to be applied in this context:

> Full account must be taken of the factual context in which a referee exercises his functions and he could not be properly held liable for errors of judgment, oversights or lapses of which any referee might be guilty in the context of a fast moving and vigorous contest. The threshold of liability is a high one. It will not easily be crossed … [The learned trial judge] did not intend to open the door to a plethora of claims by players against referees, and it would be deplorable if that were the result. In our view that result should not follow provided all concerned appreciate how difficult it is for any plaintiff to establish that a referee failed to exercise such care and skill as was reasonably to be expected in the circumstances of a hotly contested game of rugby football …[75]

Similarly, in *Vowles v Evans*[76] an amateur referee was held liable for injuries caused when a scrum collapsed.[77] The Court of Appeal confirmed that the threshold of liability was high.[78] Lord Phillips MR considered that there were clear policy reasons for imposing a duty even on amateur referees, and stated:[79]

> Rugby football is an inherently dangerous sport. Some of the rules are specifically designed to minimise the inherent dangers. Players are dependent for their safety on the due enforcement of the rules. The role of the referee is to enforce the rules. Where a referee undertakes to perform that role, it seems to us manifestly fair, just and reasonable that the players should be entitled to rely upon the referee to exercise reasonable care in so doing. Rarely if ever does the law absolve from any obligation of care a person whose acts or omissions are manifestly capable of causing physical harm to others in a structured relationship into which they have entered.

Duty of Coaches

5.52 Because a claim in negligence is founded upon the principle that the law requires the exercise of reasonable care to avoid injuring one's 'neighbour' and identifies one's neighbour as anyone who ought reasonably to be in contemplation of being affected by one's acts or omissions, it follows that coaches, other supervisors and the like will be expected to exercise reasonable care in imparting their knowledge and skills to their charges. It is

---

[74] *Smoldon* (n 72) 256F–H.
[75] Ibid, 256E–F.
[76] [2003] 1 WLR 1607.
[77] Bellamy, *Who would be a Referee?* [2004] ISLR 9.
[78] For example, in *Allport v Willbraham* (2004) unreported, 15 December, the referee was held not to be liable.
[79] *Vowles* (n 76) 1617–18.

submitted that a coach owes a duty to take reasonable care in all the circumstances to avoid physical injury[80] but that a claim that deficient coaching resulted in economic loss (eg as a result of non-selection for a lucrative event) would only succeed in the unlikely event that the coach had expressly undertaken that his protégé would achieve a particular standard of excellence.[81]

5.53 Coaches may be liable for sins of omission as well as commission, for failing to give right advice as well as for giving wrong advice. Thus, for example, a weightlifting coach who fails to advise how to lift heavy weights so as to minimise the risk of back injury may find himself exposed to liability when his charge sustains injury through the use of an unsafe technique. Hence, a schoolboy who broke his neck when diving from a starting block into the shallow end of a swimming pool succeeded in a claim for damages against his PE teacher who had failed to give him appropriate instruction on how safely to effect such a dive.[82] He also succeeded against the Amateur Swimming Association for failing to issue (to instructors) appropriate warnings as to relevant dangers. Similarly, in *Woodroffe-Hedley v Cuthbertson*,[83] a professional mountain guide was held liable for the death of his fellow climber because of his failure to take adequate safety precautions when proceeding with a manoeuvre.

5.54 The failure of a coach to follow appropriate safety codes may give rise to liability.[84] A relevant circumstance will also be the experience[85] or the age of those under supervision. In a contact sport, where an adult coach participates in a demonstration or a practice game, his duty of care must take appropriate account of the difference in size and strength between himself and his students.[86]

Duty of Schools

5.55 The duty of a school to take reasonable care is the same: the fact that those to whom the duty is owed are children intensifies its content.[87] In *Van Oppen v Clerk to the Bedford*

---

[80] Norris, *The Duty of Care Owed by Instructors in a Sporting Context* [2010] Journal of Personal Injury Law 183.

[81] Gardiner, *Should Coaches Take Care?* (1993) 143 New Law Journal 1598. See *Van Oppen v Clerk to the Bedford Charity Trustees* [1990] 1 WLR 235 where, in the context of an injury to a pupil on the rugby field, it was held that the circumstances did not give rise to a duty on the school to have regard to its pupils' economic welfare by advising on the dangers of rugby football or by taking out insurance and that, in the absence of such a duty on the school, it could not be said voluntarily to have assumed a duty to advise parents on the question of insurance against injury.

[82] *Gannon v Rotherham Metropolitan Borough Council* (1991) unreported, 6 February.

[83] *Hedley v Cuthbertson* (1997) unreported, 20 June, Dyson J.

[84] *Bacon v White and Chartfield Associates* (1998) unreported, 21 May.

[85] Ibid, where a novice scuba diving pupil died.

[86] See, eg, *Affutu-Nartoy v Clarke* (1984) *The Times*, 9 February.

[87] The particular duties of school and local authorities are discussed in Grayson 2nd edn (n 7) 103–8: see in particular the valuable summary of relevant decisions at pp 105–7 which illustrates how the courts have approached duties of supervision and guidance. See, eg, *Gibbs v Barking Corp* [1936] 1 All ER 115; *Ralph v LCC* (1947) 111 JP 548; *Wright v Cheshire County Council* (1952) 2 All ER 789; *Conrad v Inner London Education Authority* (1967) 111 Sol Jo 684; *Fowles v Bedfordshire County Council* (1996) ELR 51; and *Thornton v Trustees of School District No 57* (1976) 57 DLR (3d) 438. See also *A (a minor) v Leeds City Council* (1999) unreported, 2 March (unstructured gym activity negligent). There are however clear limits: in *Chittock v Woodbridge School* [2002] ELR 735 a school was held not liable for injuries sustained by a schoolboy who was skiing unsupervised with parental consent to do so; and in *Woodland v Swimming Teachers Association* (2012) unreported, 9 March, the Court of Appeal declined to extend a non-delegable duty to a school where a swimming lesson had been arranged by the school but provided by others.

Charity Trustees,[88] where a schoolboy was injured by a rugby tackle but not insured, it was held that there was no duty on the school to insure. Nor was there a duty on the school to advise the boy's parents to arrange insurance. In *Mountford v Newlands School*[89] the school was held liable for injuries caused in a rugby game by a pupil the school had allowed to take part, who was well above the age group for the match and whose superior size and strength had contributed to the claimant's injury.

Duty of Organisers and Promoters

5.56 Organisers and promoters may be liable for injuries caused to spectators at a sporting event. The most likely cause of action is in negligence, and in addition under the Occupiers Liability Act 1957 (as amended by the 1984 Act of the same name), which imposes a statutory common duty of care not differing materially, as to the standard of care, from that which obtains in common law negligence. Whether or not the club or event organisers are liable for injury to spectators or others injured at the event, such as officials, naturally depends upon the facts. The authorities have tended to involve claims by spectators, but the principles should not differ according to whether the claimant is a spectator or an official or other person lawfully present at the game.

5.57 The Court of Appeal in 1932, the same year as the report of *Donoghue v Stevenson*,[90] had to consider a case in which a car at a race track had careered over a barrier and struck a spectator.[91] The Court of Appeal reversed a jury's finding in favour of the plaintiff and entered judgment for the defendants. The court drew a distinction between exposure to the ordinary risks associated with presence at an event which the spectator must expect to run, and extraordinary perils to which he or she is additionally exposed in cases where the organisers or competitors act without proper regard to the safety of spectators. The latter, but not the former, will entail liability. Scrutton LJ described the test as applying generally to cases 'where landowners admit for payment to their land persons who desire to witness sports or competitions carried on thereon, if these sports may involve risk of danger to persons witnessing them'.[92] Thus he commented that 'those who pay for admission or seats in stands at a flying meeting run a risk of the performing aeroplanes falling on their heads';[93] and gave other more prosaic examples such as a spectator at Lord's or the Oval being hit by a cricket ball.

5.58 The principle has not changed, but has been applied on a number of occasions since. It is usually easy to predict the result of its application by using plain common sense. It is most unlikely that there will be liability unless the rules of the competition are breached, for compliance with them is the very thing which the claimant pays to watch. Such breach is a necessary but not a sufficient condition for liability. It is another matter altogether if safety is compromised by malfunctioning equipment provided by the event organiser, such as a collapsing grandstand at the Cheltenham Races.[94] In such a case no

---

[88] [1990] 1 WLR 235.
[89] [2007] ELR 256, discussed by Stout in (2007) 8(3) Education Law Journal 191–3.
[90] *Donoghue v Stevenson* [1932] AC 562.
[91] *Hall v Brooklands Auto-Racing Club* [1933] 1 KB 205, CA.
[92] Ibid, 209.
[93] Ibid, 213.
[94] *Francis v Cockerell* (1820) 5 QB 501; see also *Brown v Lewis* (1896) 12 TLR 455 (stand collapsed at Blackburn Rovers FC).

question arises of breach of the rules of the game. Indeed the cases only very rarely reveal examples of liability being established where injury was caused through the actions of competitors. Defendants have been successful in cases where spectators were injured by a polo player on a pony running through a hedge;[95] a racing car leaving the track;[96] an ice hockey puck;[97] the winning horse at a horse show which collided with a photographer;[98] a motorcycle at a scramble meeting;[99] and a discus thrown at an athletics ground.[100]

5.59 But where ice hockey players started a fight and injured a spectator with a hockey stick, the players were liable.[101] In one case competitors themselves recovered damages for injuries resulting from a defect in a race track controlled by a local authority, which caused horses and jockeys to stumble and fall.[102] And in *Cunningham v Reading FC Ltd*[103] Drake J held that the company which owned Reading Football Club was liable to police officers for injuries caused to them by football hooligans indulging in violence. The judge noted that the club's exoneration by a Football Association Commission of Inquiry was irrelevant to his finding that the common duty of care under the Occupiers Liability Act 1957 had been breached in circumstances where the visiting supporters were known to include an element with a propensity for violence.

5.60 It is also theoretically possible that promoters and organisers may be liable to persons who suffer harm as a result of a sporting event even though they were not actually present at the ground. In *Alcock v Chief Constable of South Yorkshire*,[104] a case arising out of the Hillsborough disaster where 96 football fans were crushed to death as a result of overcrowding in the stadium, the House of Lords considered whether a duty was owed to persons who suffered psychiatric injury as a result of the disaster. It was held that such a duty could be owed where a plaintiff fulfilled the following conditions. First, the plaintiff must have close ties of love and affection with the victim. Second, the plaintiff must have been present at the accident or its immediate aftermath. Third, the psychiatric injury must have been caused by a direct perception of the accident or its immediate aftermath and not upon hearing about it from someone else. This test does envisage the possibility of a duty to a person who was not at the scene at the time the disaster happened.

5.61 However, it is in practice extremely difficult for a bystander to recover damages for psychiatric injury. This is demonstrated by the fact that, in *Alcock*, the House of Lords dismissed all the claims brought by relatives, including the claim of a plaintiff who himself witnessed the scenes at the football ground where two of his brothers died. Further, in *White v*

---

[95] *Piddington v Hastings, The Times*, 12 March 1932.
[96] *Hall v Brooklands* (n 91).
[97] *Murray v Harringay Arena* [1951] 2 KB 529.
[98] *Wooldridge v Sumner* [1963] 2 QB 43.
[99] *Wilks v Cheltenham Home Guard MotorCycle and Light Car Club* [1971] 3 All ER 369, CA; [1971] 1 WLR 668.
[100] *Wilkins v Smith* (1976) 73 Law Soc Gaz 938. However, organisers of a football match do not owe a duty of care to a spectator for its cancellation: *MacDonald v FIFA/SFA* (1999) unreported (Court of Session, Outer House).
[101] *Payne and Payne v Maple Leaf* (1949) 1 DLR 369.
[102] *Cook, Cochrane and Hampson v Doncaster Borough Council*, Sporting Life, 16 July 1993.
[103] *The Times*, 20 March 1991. For further cases on sport facilities management liability see *Glenic v* Slair (1999) unreported (HHJ Graham Jones); *Davis v Feasey* (1999) unreported, 14 May (CA); *Greening v Stockton on Tees BC* (1998) unreported, 6 November; *Hosie v Arbroath FC Ltd* 1978 SLT 122.
[104] *Alcock v Chief Constable of South Yorkshire* [1992] 1 AC 310.

Chief Constable of South Yorkshire[105] the House of Lords dismissed claims brought by police officers who suffered psychiatric injury as a result of witnessing the tragic scenes.

5.62 Organisers and promoters may be liable to participants in sporting events who suffer harm.[106] However, in such cases the assumption of risk on the part of the participants is likely to be highly relevant. In cases where a participant has freely accepted the risks inherent in the sport, an organiser or promoter is unlikely to be liable for harm he sustains[107] and overly harsh safety standards should not be imposed.[108] As May LJ stated in *Portsmouth Youth Activities v Poppleton*:[109]

> Adults who choose to engage in physical activities which obviously give rise to a degree of unavoidable risk may find they have no means of recompense if the risk materialises so that they are injured.

Duty of Governing Bodies

5.63 Where a governing body assumes a regulatory rather than an advisory role, they owe a duty of care to competitors.[110] In *Watson v British Board of Boxing Control*[111] a boxer was injured during a fight. There was a lack of adequate medical facilities at the ringside with the result that the boxer suffered serious brain damage, which could otherwise have been averted. The defendant had not itself provided the ringside medical facilities but had set down minimum mandatory requirements, which had been followed by the fight promoters. Nevertheless the Court of Appeal held that by reason of its imposition of mandatory rules there was sufficient proximity[112] for a duty to be owed, and found that:[113]

> The board set out by its rules, directions and guidance to make comprehensive provision for the services to be provided to safeguard the health of the boxer. All involved in a boxing contest were obliged to accept and comply with the board's requirements.

And,

> ... by reason of the effective absolute control over boxing that the board assumed, the board was in a position to determine, and did in fact determine, the measures that were taken in boxing to protect and promote the health and safety of boxers.

---

[105] *White v Chief Constable of South Yorkshire* [1998] 3 WLR 1509.

[106] See Norris, *Duty of Care and Personal Responsibility: Occupiers, Owners, Organisers and Individuals* [2008] Journal of Personal Injury Law 187; Gardiner, *Liability for Sporting Injuries* [2008] Journal of Personal Injury Law 16.

[107] *Sims v Leigh RFC* [1969] 2 All ER 923; *Wattleworth v Goodwood Road Racing Co Ltd* [2004] PIQR P25; *Gillmore v LCC* [1938] 4 All ER 331; and see para 5.67 below on *volenti non fit injuria*. See also *Harrison v West of Scotland Kart Club* (2008) CSOH 33; Junor, *Suing a Club: Substance and Procedure* (2008) 80 Civil Practice Bulletin 2.

[108] *Sutton v Syston RFC Ltd* (2011) unreported, 20 October.

[109] [2009] PIQR P1 at P3.

[110] See Opie, *Negligence Liability of Rule-Making Bodies in Sport* [2002] ISLR 60; Lines, *Thinking Outside the Box (-ing Ring): The Implications for Sports Governing Bodies following Watson* [2007] ISLR 4, 67–75.

[111] [2001] QB 1134.

[112] See generally *Caparo Industries v Dickman* [1990] 2 AC 605.

[113] *Watson* (n 111) 1146.

It is clear from *Watson*, however, that it is only where a governing body has tight, if not absolute, control over safety of participants will a duty be found.[114] As Lord Phillips MR stated:[115]

> In my judgment there is a difference in principle between making rules and giving advice, but it is not one which assists the board. Had the board simply given advice to all involved in professional boxing as to appropriate medical precautions, it would be strongly arguable that there was insufficient proximity between the board and individual boxers to give rise to a duty of care. The board, however, went far beyond this. It made provision in its rules for the medical precautions to be employed and made compliance with these rules mandatory.

5.64 The need to protect participants against neglect of duty by governing bodies must, we suggest, be balanced against practicalities; successful claims against them are likely to be rare. Most sports could be made safer, but the failure of a governing body to do so when it would alter the fundamental nature of the sport will not give rise to a breach of duty to participants.[116]

Defences

Contributory Negligence

5.65 On occasion a participant's own lack of care may contribute to harm suffered and they will suffer a deduction in compensation for contributory negligence. In *Craven v Riches*,[117] whilst the organisers of an amateur motorcycle racing event were held to be liable for a racer's accident in allowing riders of different standards to use the track at the same time, the defendant's own careless riding was held to be two-thirds contributorily negligent.

5.66 There may well be occasions where the claimant, as an ordinary prudent participant in the game and calling upon his experience in the sport generally, will foresee dangers and will anticipate the likelihood of negligence of his fellow players. Just as in rescue cases, a court ought to make proper allowances where the speed of the activity on the playing field has reduced the time available to the claimant to take stock of his situation and, hence, his opportunity to take evasive action either to avoid the accident or to reduce the degree of damage suffered. In *Feeney v Lyall*,[118] during a round of golf, the pursuer had hooked his drive from the ninth tee onto the adjacent sixth fairway. In order to play his second shot he crossed over to the sixth fairway, where he was struck and seriously injured by a golf ball driven off the sixth tee by another golfer, who could not see the presence of the pursuer on that fairway. Liability in negligence was not established but, if

---

[114] For example, in *Wattleworth v Goodwood Racing Company Ltd* [2004] PIQR P25 the Fédération Internationale de L'Automobile was held not to owe a duty in respect of a fatal motor racing crash as their safety role was only advisory; in contrast the Royal Automobile Club Motor Sports Association was held to owe a duty of care as it issued licences to tracks that met safety standards, although on the facts of the case that duty had not been breached.

[115] *Watson* (n 111) 1160.

[116] See, eg, the Australian case of *Agar v Hyde* [2000] 201 CLR 552 where claims against the International Rugby Football Board for their failure to revise scrummage rules to reduce the risk of injury failed.

[117] (2001) unreported, 27 February; in *Fowles v Bedfordshire County Council* [1996] ELR 51 a parachutist was held to be 50% contributorily negligent for failing to keep a proper lookout and in *C (A Child) v W School* [2002] PIQR P13 an unsupervised child skier's damages were reduced by 50% on account of his own lack of care.

[118] *Feeney v Lyall* 1991 SLT 156.

it had been, the opinion was expressed that the pursuer would have been held 25 per cent contributorily negligent.

Volenti non fit injuria

5.67 The maxim *volenti non fit injuria* is used to describe a defence which operates where it can be shown that the claimant had consented to the breach of the duty of care alleged. Such consent may be express but it is usually implied from the particular circumstances of the case. There have been some cases concerning sport which have been analysed in terms of this defence or in which the court has commented on the potential availability of the defence. Thus, in *Lane v Holloway*, where the defence was held not to apply, Lord Denning said the following:[119]

> I agree that in an ordinary fight with fists there is no cause of action to either of [the participants] for any injury suffered. The reason is that each of the participants in a fight voluntarily takes upon himself the risk of incidental injuries to himself. But he does not take on himself the risk of a savage blow out of all proportion to the occasion. The man who strikes a blow of such severity is liable in damages unless he can prove accident or self defence.[120]

5.68 Further, in *King v Redlich*[121] the plaintiff, who was not yet wearing his protective helmet, suffered a severe head injury during the warm-up period prior to the start of an ice hockey match. As the plaintiff was skating out from behind the goal the defendant, who had delayed his shot momentarily to enable the plaintiff to get clear, took a practice shot at goal but the puck hit the post and ricocheted, striking the plaintiff. The Court of Appeal of British Columbia held that the plaintiff should be deemed to have accepted the risk of injury in all the circumstances, because practice shots at goal during warm-up were a normal part of the game. Although the defendant had realised that there was a higher risk in that he had seen the plaintiff, he had increased his level of care appropriately by the delay in making his shot and could not be expected to have foreseen that the puck would ricochet. Accordingly, the plaintiff's claim failed.

5.69 However, in our view the defence of *volenti non fit injuria* will rarely be of relevance in the context of sport.[122] This is because the acceptance of risk by the participant or spectator is already taken into account in determining the content of the duty of care.[123] As shown above, the duty to exercise reasonable care does not usually require the competitor, the referee or the coach to avoid risks which are inherent in the game itself. A court is unlikely to imply consent to risks which go beyond those inherent in the sport. It is only in rare cases that a defendant will be found to have acted in breach of his duty of care but is absolved of liability because of the consent of the claimant.

5.70 Thus in *Rootes v Shelton*[124] a water skier brought an action against the driver of the towing speedboat, where he, one of a group of skiers which included the driver, was

---

[119] *Lane v Holloway* [1968] 1 QB 379 at 386, 387.
[120] See also *R v Coney* (1882) 8 QBD 534.
[121] *King v Redlich* (1986) 4 WWR 567 (Court of Appeal, British Columbia).
[122] See further Kevan, *Sports Personal Injury* [2005] ISLR 61.
[123] See further Kevan, *Sports Injury Cases: Footballers, Referees and Schools* [2001] Journal of Personal Injury Law 138; Adams, *Volenti non fit injuria or Contributory Negligence? A Comparative Review of Three Football Cases* (1994) 2(2) European Review of Public Law 329.
[124] *Rootes v Shelton* (1967) 41 ALJR 172.

performing a complicated manoeuvre and was injured by a collision with a stationary obstruction of which the driver had given him no warning. It was held that the onus was on the driver to establish voluntary acceptance of a risk not inherent in the pastime. In another case, where a spectator did not know of the risk of injury caused by the failure of the organisers of a 'jalopy' car race meeting to take proper safety precautions in roping off enclosures, it was held that the doctrine did not apply at all.[125] And in *Smoldon v Whitworth*,[126] *volenti* was held inapplicable: there was no consent to a breach of duty by the referee. The Court of Appeal said:

> … this argument is unsustainable. The plaintiff had of course consented to the ordinary incidents of a game of rugby football of the kind in which he was taking part. Given, however, that the rules were framed for the protection of him and other players in the same position, he cannot possibly be said to have consented to a breach of duty on the part of the official whose duty it was to apply the rules and ensure so far as possible that they were observed.

5.71 The scope of the defence in the context of sport was also addressed by Diplock LJ in *Wooldridge v Sumner*.[127] An experienced horseman, while taking part in a competition for heavyweight hunters at a horse show, galloped his horse called 'Work of Art' so fast around a corner of the arena that centrifugal force caused it to follow a wide arc, sweeping out towards the edge of the course. The rider temporarily lost control of the horse, which plunged down a line of potted shrubs, bordering the arena, to a point where the plaintiff, a photographer, was standing. He, having no experience of horses, took fright, stepped back, stumbling into the path of the animal, and was injured. Diplock LJ stated:

> The practical result of this analysis of the application of the common law of negligence to participant and spectator would, I think, be expressed by the common man in some such terms as these: 'A person attending a game or competition takes the risk of any damage caused to him by any act of a participant done in the course of and for the purposes of the game or competition notwithstanding that such act may involve an error of judgment or a lapse of skill, unless the participant's conduct is such as to evince a reckless disregard of the spectator's safety.'
>
> The spectator takes the risk because such an act involves no breach of the duty of care owed by the participant to him. He does not take the risk by virtue of the doctrine expressed or obscured by the maxim volenti non fit injuria. … In my view, the maxim in the absence of expressed contract has no application to negligence simpliciter where the duty of care is based solely upon proximity or 'neighbourship' in the Atkinian sense. The maxim in English law presupposes a tortious act by the defendant. The consent that is relevant is not consent to the risk of injury but consent to the lack of reasonable care that may produce that risk … and requires on the part of the plaintiff at the time at which he gives his consent full knowledge of the nature and extent of the risk that he ran.

5.72 A competitor in a race 'is expected to go as fast as he can, so long as he is not foolhardy'.[128] This modified standard of care does not apply unless the circumstances are such that the acts complained of are done in the flurry and excitement of the sport, for

---

[125] *White v Blackmore* [1972] 2 QB 651.

[126] *Smoldon v Whitworth* [1997] ELR 249; the Court of Appeal went on to suggest that where a player was the prime culprit in the collapse of a scrummage it might be arguable that his actions may have amounted to consent to the risk of injury.

[127] *Wooldridge v Sumner* [1963] 2 QB 43, 68–69. The case was distinguished in *Quire v Coates* [1964] SASR 294 and *Rootes v Shelton* (1947) 41 ALJR 172.

[128] Per Lord Denning MR in *Wilks v Cheltenham Homeguard MotorCycle and Light Car Club* [1971] WLR 668, 670; [1971] 3 All ER 369 (CA).

instance where a motorcycle rider failed to change gear when approaching a hairpin bend in a race and crashed, having failed to get around the trace.[129]

5.73 However, the position is slightly different in relation to occupiers' liability. The defence of *volenti non fit injuria* was always a defence available to the occupier, and section 2(5) of the 1957 Act expressly preserves it:

> The common duty of care does not impose on an occupier any obligation to a visitor in respect of risks willingly accepted as his by the visitor (the question whether a risk was so accepted to be decided on the same principles as in other cases in which one person owes a duty of care to another).

So, where a visitor knowingly exposes himself, while on another's premises, to a particular physical risk, the occupier may raise the defence against him. In *Tomlinson v Congleton Borough Council*[130] the House of Lords considered that such a defence would have wide application, Lord Hoffmann said:

> I think it will be extremely rare for an occupier of land to be under a duty to prevent people from taking risks which are inherent in the activities they freely choose to undertake upon the land. If people want to climb mountains, go hang gliding or swim or dive in ponds or lakes, that is their affair.

Thus in *Simms v Leigh RFC*[131] Wrangham J held that a visiting rugby league football player willingly accepted the risks necessarily involved in playing on a field with a concrete wall running at a distance of seven feet three inches from the touchline, such walls being permitted under the rules of the game.

Of course, the *volenti* maxim only applies where the danger that causes injury is the one which the claimant has willingly accepted; and this usually means that he must have known the precise risk in advance. Thus in *White v Blackmore*[132] it was held that the defence was not available against a spectator watching stock-car racing who was fatally injured when he was catapulted into the air by safety ropes in which the wheel of a car had become entangled. The relevant risk did not arise from participation in a dangerous sport but from the organisers' failure properly to lay out the safety arrangements, a failure of which the plaintiff clearly did not knowingly take the risk.[133]

Nuisance

5.74 Members of the public in the vicinity of a sporting activity may sustain injury or suffer damage to their property as a result of the activity. Such persons may have a cause of action in nuisance. Private law nuisance requires proof of interference with the reasonable use and enjoyment of land in which the claimant has a proprietary or possessory interest. Where such interest is lacking, the claim must be brought in public nuisance or negligence. Actions in public nuisance may arise from activity on sports grounds which causes danger on a highway nearby. Thus, where the hole of a golf course was placed

---

[129] *Harrison v Vincent* [1982] RTR 8, CA. See Kovats, *Sportsman's Charter Revoked*, 115 Solicitors Journal 824.
[130] [2004] 1 AC 46.
[131] *Simms v Leigh RFC Ltd* [1969] 2 All ER 923.
[132] [1972] 2 QB 651.
[133] See also *Latchford v Spedeworth International, The Times*, 11 October 1983; *Gillmore v LCC* [1938] 4 All ER 331; *Horton v Jackson* [1996] CLR 4475. In *White v Blackmore* the organisers' liability was held to have been successfully excluded (Lord Denning MR dissenting) by notices excluding liability for accidents 'howsoever caused'.

adjoining the highway, so that players habitually drove out of bounds on to the road, that was held to be a nuisance, rendering the club liable to a person on the highway who was injured.[134] That case should be compared to *Potter v Carlisle and Cliftonville Golf Club Ltd*[135] where it was held that the playing of cricket on a ground, from which cricket balls were hit out of the ground on rare occasions only, was not a nuisance and the club was not liable to a person who was injured by a ball in the highway.[136]

5.75 An example of a claim brought in private nuisance is the case of *Miller v Jackson*.[137] The law of private nuisance was applicable because the plaintiff's house adjoined a cricket ground. The Court of Appeal held that the defendants had committed a nuisance since their use of the land involved an unreasonable interference with their neighbour's use of their house and garden. However, Lord Denning MR and Cumming Bruce LJ refused an injunction on the basis that the public interests of the village in recreation should be preferred to the private interests of the plaintiff in his property.[138] In *Kennaway v Thompson*,[139] on the other hand, an injunction was granted against a watersports club on orthodox principles that the discretion to award damages should only be exercised where the nuisance was 'trivial and occasional'.[140] Where a sporting activity is well established and a dominant feature of the locality, no actionable nuisance will be caused to those who move to the locality.[141]

Assault

5.76 The torts of assault and battery, sometimes called trespass to the person, are further possible causes of action in sports injury cases although in practice with a far narrower application than negligence. They require the intentional or reckless infliction of injury, or the threat of it. It is therefore insufficient for this tort to prove merely negligent behaviour.[142]

---

[134] *Castle v St Augustine's Links* (1922) 38 TLR 615. The player who struck the golf ball would also be liable if he had failed to take reasonable care to keep his ball from going where it did: see *Cleghorn v Oldham* (1927) 43 TLR 465.

[135] *Potter v Carlisle and Cliftonville Golf Club Ltd* [1939] NI 114.

[136] See further *Bolton v Stone* [1951] AC 850; *Calson Gillon v Chief Constable of Strathclyde Police* (1996) *The Times*, 22 November.

[137] *Miller v Jackson* [1977] QB 966.

[138] See also *Goode v Owen and Four Ashes Golf Centre Ltd* [2002] 02 LS Gaz R 29 where an injunction requiring a golf driving range operator to erect a 40 foot high fence was overturned by the Court of Appeal on the ground that it was unjustified given the nature of the nuisance.

[139] *Kennaway v Thompson* [1981] 1 QB 88.

[140] For other examples of claims brought in nuisance see: *Hilder v Associated Portland Cement Manufacturers Ltd* [1961] 1 WLR 1434 (footballs regularly kicked out of field); *Lamond v Glasgow Corporation* 1968 SLT 291 (liability established in circumstances where there were 60,000 golf shots over fence each year); *Stretch v Romford FC* (1971) 115 Sol Jo 742 (liability for noise caused by speedway racing at a football stadium); *Lacay v Parker and Boyle (sued on behalf of Jordans Cricket Club)* (1994) *The Times*, 15 May, (1994) 144 New Law Journal 485 (injunction refused on the basis that the plaintiff came to the nuisance—which is, however, not a defence, see *Miller v Jackson* (n 137); *Watson v Croft Promosports Ltd* [2009] 3 All ER 249; *East Dorset DC v Eaglebeam Ltd* [2007] Env LR D9. See also *Sheler v City of London Electric Lighting* (1895) 1 Ch 287; *AG v Hastings Corporation* (1950) 94 Sol Jo 225; *Barr v Biffa Waste Services Ltd* [2012] 3 All ER 380, CA; *Coventry (t/a RDC Promotions) v Lawrence* [2012] EWCA Civ 26.

[141] *Coventry (t/a RDC Promotions) v Lawrence* [2012] EWCA Civ 26.

[142] See *Letang v Cooper* [1964] 2 All ER 929; *Lane v Holloway* [1968] 1 QB 379; *Bici v Ministry of Defence* [2004] All ER (D) 137 (Apr). On vicarious liability of a club for assault see *Gravil v Caroll* [2008] ICR 1222 (CA), discussed in (2008) 32(18) Company Secretary's Review 139, Gore (2008) 4 Journal of Personal Injury Law 182;

Damages

5.77 It is not our intention to deal in detail here with the principles governing awards of damages in tort cases involving sport. Those principles do not differ from the general principles applicable in cases of personal injury outside the sporting context. The measure of damages will, in the ordinary way, be that which is necessary to put the claimant in the position he would have been in—so far as money can do it—if the tort had not been committed. The award will cover pain and suffering, and any financial loss.[143]

5.78 Those representing participants in sport who are injured should bear in mind the possibility of claiming damages for loss of a chance.[144] In *Mulvaine v Joseph*[145] the plaintiff, an American club professional golfer, suffered a hand injury as a result of a taxi driver's negligence. He was awarded damages for loss of the opportunity to compete in tournaments, the ensuing loss of experience and prestige which might have resulted in him becoming a tournament professional in America, and loss of the chance of winning prize money. Arguably such loss is equivalent to the loss of the opportunity of competing at the Olympics and the loss of a chance of winning a medal, albeit these losses are more difficult to quantify. The principle in *Mulvaine* extends to loss of a chance to do something which attracts no monetary prize.

5.79 In assessing the value of the lost chance, the usual civil standard of the balance of probabilities does not apply. In *Davies v Taylor*,[146] Lord Reid said as follows:

> When the question is whether a certain thing is or is not true—whether a certain event did or did not happen—then the court must decide one way or the other. There is no question of chance or probability. Either it did or it did not happen. But the standard of civil proof is a balance of probabilities. If the evidence shows a balance in favour of it having happened, then it is proved that it did in fact happen ... You can prove that a past event happened, but you cannot prove that a future event will happen and I do not think that the law is so foolish as to suppose that you can. Sometimes it is virtually 100 per cent: sometimes virtually nil. But often it is somewhere in between. And if it is somewhere in between I do not see much difference between a probability of 51 per cent and a probability of 49 per cent.

Damages for loss of a chance are therefore to be assessed in proportion to that chance, subject to the *de minimis* principle that no account is to be taken of possibilities which are very small, speculative or fanciful. The assessment process must take uncertain events into account. As a matter of fact, an athlete's chances of winning a competition turns on many contingencies: his form at the time of the competition, the form of his competitors, and avoidance of injury. It is immaterial that such contingencies render the assessment of

---

Parpworth, *Vicarious Liability on the Rugby Union Field* (2008) 172(35) Justice of the Peace and Local Government Law 572.

[143] *Watson v Bradford* (1999) unreported (HC) (almost £1 million damages awarded for a vicious tackle); see also Farrow, *Injury Compensation: Collett v Smith; Compensation for Future Earnings*, WSLR 6/9.

[144] See *Chaplin v Hicks* [1911] 2 KB 786, CA; *Kitchen v RAF Association* [1958] 2 All ER 241, CA; *Collett v Smith* [2008] ISLR 125; see also McGregor, *McGregor on Damages*, 18th edn (Sweet & Maxwell, 2011) paras 18-031 ff. Damages can be awarded for loss of opportunity to enjoy sport: *Tsipoloudis v Donald* (1998) unreported, 11 December, CA; *H West & Son v Shephard* [1964] AC 326 at 365, per Lord Pearce.

[145] *Mulvaine v Joseph* (1968) 112 SJ 927.

[146] *Davies v Taylor* [1974] AC 207, 213.

damages uncertain. In the leading case of *Chaplin v Hicks* the plaintiff lost the chance of winning a prize. Vaughan Williams LJ stated:[147]

> It was said that the plaintiff's chance of winning a prize turned on such a number of contingencies that it was impossible for anyone, even after arriving at the conclusion that the plaintiff had lost her opportunity by the breach, to say that there was any assessable value of that loss. It is said that in a case which involves so many contingencies it is impossible to say what was the plaintiff's loss. I am unable to agree with that contention. I agree that the presence of all the contingencies upon which the gaining of the prize might depend makes the calculation not only difficult but incapable of being carried out with certainty or precision … I do not agree with the contention that, if certainty is impossible of attainment, the damages for a breach of a contract are unassessable.

However, negligent actions which interfere with a participant's contract are not sufficient to give rise to damages for that interference;[148] only where there has been an intentional interference will such a claim succeed.[149] A professional sportsman who is unable to carry on his career due to injury may be able to recover damages for loss of congenial employment.[150]

Practical Issues Arising in Sporting Injury Claims

5.80 Apart from a sound grasp of the legal principles involved, the sports lawyer also needs a finely tuned understanding of the practical issues that are likely to arise when representing clients in such claims. Particularly difficult problems may confront a club which is sued in its capacity as employer of a player who injures another player.

5.81 Take the straightforward case of a rugby player claiming in respect of injuries arising from an unlawful high tackle, contrary to the rules of the game. Liability of the player may not be seriously in doubt, for example because he is caught on video making the tackle in a plainly dangerous manner long after the ball has been passed away and is immediately shown a red card by the referee. But suppose, further, that the real issue in the case is whether the club and not just the player is liable. This may depend on whether infliction of injury on the claimant was deliberate, reckless or merely negligent. If it was deliberate, the defendant player will be guilty of the tort of assault and it is unlikely that the club will be held vicariously liable.[151] If, however, the injury was inflicted negligently or recklessly—in the sense that the guilty player showed reckless disregard for the safety of the victim, but without deliberate intent to injure him—the club will be vicariously liable on ordinary principles as the employer of the guilty player.[152]

---

[147] *Chaplin* (n 141) 791–2.
[148] *Watson v Gray*, *The Times*, 26 November 1998.
[149] *OBG Ltd v Allan* [2008] 1 AC 1, 31 per Lord Hoffmann; see also Cox, Schuster and Costello, *Sport and the Law* (Firstlaw, 2004) 210–13.
[150] See, eg, *Appleton v El Safty* (2007) unreported, 23 March, where a professional footballer recovered damages of £25,000 for loss of congenial employment; see also Allen, *Loss of Congenial Employment* [2009] Journal of Personal Injury Law 135.
[151] See, eg, *Racz v Home Office* [1994] 2 AC 45; *Makanjuola v Commissioner of Police for the Metropolis* [1989] 2 Admin LR 214; however, cf more recently *Weir v Chief Constable of Merseyside* [2003] ICR 378, CA; *Lister v Hesley Hall Ltd* [2002] 1 AC 215, HL. The Court of Appeal expressed a contrary view in *Gravil v Carroll* [2008] ICR 1222 CA, where a rugby club was found vicariously liable for an assault by one of its players on the basis that such violence was part and parcel of the game, the nature of the assault and sport must therefore be taken into consideration.
[152] See Dugdale and Jones, *Clerk and Lindsell on Torts*, 20th edn (Sweet & Maxwell, 2010) paras 6-03ff.

5.82 The club may find itself in a difficult position. It may wish to stand behind its player, whom it may, for example, have defended in disciplinary proceedings subsequent to the incident. If it does that, it is likely to support the proposition that the injury was caused by accident, not design. However, that outcome is detrimental to the club's economic interests, since it will find itself liable. The club's financial position may be better served by 'disowning' the player, and supporting the proposition that he deliberately inflicted the injury, with the consequence that the club is not vicariously liable. However, as a matter of employee relations, that may not be a tenable position in practice.

5.83 One must add to the above equation two further practical considerations: (i) the club is likely to have liability insurance under a policy which, typically, would cover liability for accidentally inflicted but not deliberately inflicted injury; and (ii) the governing body of the sport in question may take a dim view of a club which adopts inconsistent positions in, respectively, disciplinary proceedings and subsequent litigation. The relevant governing body may also be unimpressed with one of its member clubs taking a stance in litigation which appears to espouse a lenient view of, if not actually to condone, violence on the field of play.

5.84 We offer the above example as a convenient illustration of the application of the principle of vicarious liability in sports law, as well as an instance of the difficulties which clubs may face when seeking to reconcile sometimes divergent and conflicting interests.

5.85 In all sporting injury claims clear evidence of the incident complained of is likely to prove critical. For professional sports which are televised, such evidence may be readily available.[153] Where they are not, both claimants and defendants may face substantial difficulties in producing evidence to demonstrate what may have occurred in a fraction of a second.

5.86 Further careful consideration needs also be given in many situations to proving that the actions of a defendant fall outside the rules of the game or what might be expected of a reasonable person in his or her situation.[154]

The Criminal Law

5.87 It is only in the most serious cases of sports injuries that criminal prosecutions will be warranted.[155] As Lord Woolf LCJ succinctly put it in *R v Barnes*:[156]

> In determining what the approach of the courts should be, the starting point is the fact that most organised sports have their own disciplinary procedures for enforcing their particular rules and standards of conduct. As a result, in the majority of situations there is not only no need for criminal proceedings, it is undesirable that there should be any criminal proceedings. Further, in addition to a criminal prosecution, there is the possibility of an injured player obtaining damages in a

---

[153] Although such evidence was held to be of limited use in *Elliott v Saunders and Liverpool FC* (n 59).

[154] Experts are a frequent feature of such cases, eg Jimmy Hill in *Watson v Gray, The Times*, 26 November 1998.

[155] For useful examples of such cases see Lewis and Taylor (n 62) 757–63; Anderson, *Playing by the Rules* (2011) 175(4) Criminal Law & Justice Weekly 40; Gardiner et al, *Sports Law*, 4th edn (Routledge, 2012) 517.

[156] [2005] 1 WLR 910, 912–13; see also Parsons, *Contact Sports and Criminal Law* (2011) 175(4) Criminal Law & Justice Weekly 40; Barnes, *Crime and Punishment on the Sports Field*, WSLR 3/9, pp 6–7.

civil action from another player, if that other player caused him injuries through negligence or an assault. The circumstances in which criminal and civil remedies are available can and do overlap. However, a criminal prosecution should be reserved for those situations where the conduct is sufficiently grave to be properly categorised as criminal.[157]

5.88 There are a number of offences against the person which may be applicable in cases of violence on the sports field, ranging from assault at one end of the spectrum to manslaughter at the other. We do not attempt here to provide a guide to the constituent elements of these offences. For that, the reader should consult a specialist criminal law textbook.[158]

5.89 However, one issue that is of particular relevance to sport is the defence of consent. Consent provides a defence to the offences most commonly found in sport, for example common assault, battery and assault occasioning actual bodily harm contrary to section 47 of the Offences against the Person Act 1861.[159] Consent will not be a defence in the absence of 'good reason'. Thus, in *R v Brown*,[160] the House of Lords held that the defence did not avail the defendants who had consensually engaged in sado-masochistic practices as the satisfaction of sado-masochistic desires does not constitute good reason.[161] In *Attorney-General's reference (No 6 of 1980)*[162] Lord Lane, the then Lord Chief Justice, in addressing the question whether persons engaged in a fight outside the context of the sport could avail themselves of the defence of consent and concluding that most fights will be unlawful regardless of consent, emphasised that:

> nothing which we have said is intended to cast doubt upon the accepted legality of properly conducted games and sports.[163]

5.90 Thus, consent to injury deriving from the fact of participation in a sport will be consent for 'good reason'. However, this does not mean that every injury inflicted in the course of sporting activity is lawful. In *R v Barnes* the Court of Appeal identified a variety of factors that should be considered in deciding whether an act inflicting injury was lawful. Whether a participant can be taken to have consented to the risk of an injury will depend on the nature of the sport, the type of injury and the manner in which it was inflicted.[164] A common sense approach must be taken to this type of assessment. The nature of the sport will often be determinative. Take the case of boxing. Its very essence is the 'assault' of one's opponent and each competitor will be taken to have consented to

---

[157] See, eg, *R v Evans* (2006) unreported, 15 June, where a jury was directed to acquit the defendant who had caused slight bruising to an opponent during a game of rugby.

[158] Such as *Archbold* (Sweet & Maxwell, a new edition of which comes out each year) or Ormerod, *Smith and Hogan: Criminal Law*, 13th edn (Oxford University Press, 2011).

[159] Though not to the more serious offences against the person.

[160] *R v Brown* [1994] 1 AC 212, HL.

[161] In *Laskey, Jaggard and Brown v UK* (1997) 24 EHRR 39, the European Court of Human Rights ruled that the conviction of the defendants was an interference in their private lives which was 'necessary in a democratic society' and was therefore not contrary to Art 8 of the European Convention on Human Rights.

[162] *Attorney-General's Reference (No 6 of 1980)* [1981] QB 715.

[163] As early as *R v Canniff* (1840) 173 ER 868 the courts drew a distinction between properly conducted sporting contests and fights resulting from anger.

[164] See also the Canadian cases of *R v Cey* (1989) CCC (3d) 480; *R v Cicarelli* (1989) 54 CCC (3d) 121; *R v Leclerc* (1991) 67 CCC (3d) 563; and *R v Jobidon* (1991) 25 SCR 714, where an objective test based upon similar factors was set out.

the level of injury that is inherent in the sport itself.[165] Compare that to a tennis match in which there is no physical contact between competitors. No defence of consent will be available to the tennis player who leaps over the net and hits his opponent.

5.91 Apart from the nature of the sport, the issue of whether or not the injury has been inflicted within the rules of the game will also be important.[166] Thus, even in the context of a boxing match, there are types of injury to which the participants cannot be said to have consented because they are not envisaged by the rules of the sport. The biting by Mike Tyson of Evander Holyfield's ear is a case in point. The intention of the aggressor is also important. A sportsperson can be said to have consented to the risk that a contact sport may have unintended effects of such severity that they may amount to a serious injury not envisaged by the rules of the game. However, the law does not permit that type of injury to be inflicted deliberately or recklessly.[167]

5.92 The criminal law has been used increasingly in recent years to resolve disputes on the field of play. In Scotland, the Lord Advocate has issued a series of *Instructions* to Chief Constables which provide guidance on when and why the police ought to take action.[168] These *Instructions* state, for example, that the Lord Advocate wishes the police to investigate in circumstances 'where the violence used by the participant goes well beyond that which would be expected to occur during the normal run of play and which the rules of the sport concerned are designed to regulate. In deciding which incidents to investigate the police should pay particular regard to incidents where the violence or disorderly conduct has occurred after the whistle has blown and whilst the ball is dead and to incidents where the violence or disorderly behaviour has occurred in circumstances designed or liable to provoke a disorderly or violent response from spectators.' The Lord Advocate's intervention followed a number of high profile prosecutions in Scotland involving violence on the field. These included the conviction of Duncan Ferguson, then of Glasgow Rangers FC, for an assault by headbutting John McStay of Raith Rovers FC.[169]

5.93 In England and Wales the Crown Prosecution Service and Association of Chief Police Officers produced a series of draft guidelines in 2005 dealing with how and when the police and Crown Prosecution Service should act in relation to conduct on the field

---

[165] Boxing, along with other contact martial arts, has been regarded by the courts as a legal activity only on the basis of public policy so that consent is extended to actions which in other situations, due to the severity of the harm caused, could not be consented to: see *R v Brown* (n 160) per Lord Mustill at 262–5; Anderson, *The Legality of Boxing: A Punch Drunk Love* (Taylor and Francis, 2007).

[166] See Livings, *'Legitimate Sport' or Criminal Assault? What are the Roles of the Rules and the Rulemakers in Determining Criminal Liability for Violence on the Sports Field?* (2006) 70(6) Journal of Criminal Law 495; see also *R v Bradshaw* (1878) 14 Cox CC 83 and *R v Moore* (1898) 14 TLR 229.

[167] See *R v Brown* (n 160) and Singh, *Consent to Violence in Sport* (1994) 2 SLJ 7; Law Commission Consultation Paper No 134, *Consent and Offences against the Person* (HMSO, 1994); Gardiner, *The Law and the Sports Field* [1994] Crim LR 513; and *R v Billinghurst* [1978] Crim LR 553 where, despite evidence of common practice, punches thrown during a rugby game could not be rendered lawful by consent.

[168] See Gardiner, *Touchlines and Guidelines: The Lord Advocate's Response to Sportsfield Violence* [1997] Crim LR 41; Miller, *Criminal Law and Sport in Scotland* (1996) 4(2) SLJ 40.

[169] Duncan Ferguson was sentenced to three months in prison and received a 12 match ban from the Scottish Football Association. The increasing number of criminal prosecutions in sport has been a feature throughout the UK. See, eg, *R v McHugh* (1998) unreported, 20 February. McHugh was convicted of causing grievous bodily harm under s 20 Offences against the Person Act when he kicked an opposing player, Darren Smith, in the head, causing him severe injuries: SLB vol 1 no 2, March/April 1998, p 3.

of play.[170] The guidelines recognise that the police have wide discretion in dealing with any given incident but note that 'any conduct on the field of play which breaches the criminal law cannot be tolerated'. If the police consider that an offence has been committed, which merits referral to the Crown Prosecution Service, then the normal dual test of whether there is a realistic prospect of conviction and whether it is in the public interest to prosecute will be applied. The draft guidelines set out a number of criteria to be applied in considering the second limb of the test in the sporting context. These include the nature of the conduct in the context of the particular sport; any degree of pre-meditation; whether the offender sought to carry out the act out of sight of match officials; who the conduct was directed at; what was the impact of the conduct on other people and their subsequent behaviour; previous incidents of a similar nature; and any action taken by match officials or governing bodies in relation to the incident.[171]

5.94 The draft guidelines have not to date been adopted as a formal policy and in many respects they simply enunciate those factors considered relevant by the courts in *Barnes* and elsewhere. Nevertheless they highlight the strong public policy considerations that are to be considered in the application of the criminal law so that in some instances a criminal sanction will be appropriate even where disciplinary steps have been taken and the seriousness of the conduct derives not from the nature of any injury that may have been caused but from its wider effects.[172]

---

[170] CPS and ACPO draft, *Guidance to Prosecutors and Police Officers: Crime in Sport* (2005).

[171] The issue of who bears the cost of policing football matches has been most recently explored in *Leeds Utd Football Club v Chief Constable of West Yorkshire Police* 2012 EWHC 2113 (QB).

[172] For example, the footballer Lee Bowyer was charged with, and pleaded guilty to, a public order offence arising out of a relatively minor scuffle with a teammate in 2005; the match was televised and reached a large audience.

6

The Commercial Exploitation
of Sport

Introduction

6.1 This chapter is concerned with selling sport to the public. The manner in which sport is sold has undergone a rapid transformation in recent years and sport, as an industry, has grown immensely in stature. The sale of broadcasting and media rights, sponsorship and merchandising now make up a very significant proportion of the income of sports clubs and organisations. At the time of writing, FIFA had sold the United States broadcasting rights for the 2018 and 2022 World Cups for a reported $1.2 billion and had announced further agreements in Australia, Canada and the Caribbean, bringing the total thus far to $1.85 billion.[1] Over the three financial years from April 2010, the value of the broadcasting rights for the Premier League has reportedly increased to around £3.6 billion from £2.8 billion.[2] In this chapter we introduce the EU and domestic competition rules that play an important role in regulating the sale of broadcasting rights; we go on to address the regulation of broadcasting; and, finally, we consider various other methods of marketing sport.

Competition Law

Introduction

6.2 It is convenient to discuss at this juncture the application in general terms of competition law to sport.[3] This section is of relevance not only to the substantive issues of broadcasting dealt with in this chapter but also to access to competitions (which forms the subject of chapter three), employment rights (chapter four) and discipline (chapter seven). We focus here on EU competition law (ie Articles 101 and 102 TFEU).

---

[1] www.sportbusiness.com

[2] Deloitte Sports Business Group, *Annual Review of Football Finance*, 2011. At the time of writing, the rights for the last of those three financial years (April 2012–March 2013) have recently been sold.

[3] For a comprehensive commentary on competition law see Bellamy and Child, *Common Market Law of Competition*, 6th edn (Sweet & Maxwell, 2008).

These provisions are directly applicable in the UK. The Competition Act 1998 contains domestic equivalents of these rules, referred to respectively as the Chapter I and Chapter II prohibitions, because they are set out in, respectively, Chapters I and II of the Competition Act 1998. Given that there is a large substantive coincidence between the two regimes, all discussion in this book of the substantive application of Articles 101 and 102 TFEU to sport can also be taken as demonstrating the probable application of UK law. There is one significant jurisdictional difference between the two regimes. In order for EU law to apply, an effect on inter-state trade must be demonstrated; the same restriction does not apply in respect of UK law.

Article 101 TFEU

6.3 Article 101 TFEU provides as follows:

(1) The following shall be prohibited as incompatible with the common market; all agreements between undertakings, decisions by associations of undertakings and concerted practices which may affect trade between member states and which have as their object or effect the prevention restriction or distortion of competition within the common market, and in particular those which:
  (a) directly or indirectly fix purchase or selling prices or any other trading conditions;
  (b) limit or control production, markets, technical development, or investment;
  (c) share markets or sources of supply;
  (d) apply dissimilar conditions to equivalent transactions with other trading parties, thereby placing them at a competitive disadvantage;
  (e) make the conclusion of contracts subject to acceptance by the other parties of supplementary obligations which, by their nature or according to commercial usage, have no connection with the subject of such contracts.
(2) Any agreements or decisions prohibited pursuant to this Article shall be automatically void.
(3) The provisions of paragraph 1 may, however, be declared inapplicable in the case of:
  any agreement or category of agreements between undertakings;
  any decision or category of decisions by associations of undertakings;
  any concerted practice or category of concerted practices; which contributes to improving the production or distribution of goods or to promoting technical or economic progress, while allowing consumers a fair share of the resulting benefit, and which does not:
  (a) impose on the undertakings concerned restrictions which are not indispensable to the attainment of these objectives;
  (b) afford such undertakings the possibility of eliminating competition in respect of a substantial part of the products in question.

Thus, for Article 101(1) to apply, the following features must be present. First, there must be an agreement, decision or concerted practice between undertakings. Second, it must affect competition within the common market. Third, there must be an effect on inter-state trade. Even if these factors are all present, the agreement may benefit from exemption pursuant to Article 101(3). EU law also makes provision for more general or 'block' exemptions. Of particular importance is Regulation 330/2010/EU, the block exemption for vertical restraints. If an agreement falls within Article 101(1) and is not exempt under Article 101(3), then Article 101(2) renders it, subject to possible severance, automatically void.

Article 102 TFEU

6.4 Article 102 TFEU provides:

Any abuse by one or more undertakings of a dominant position within the common market or in a substantial part of it shall be prohibited as incompatible with the common market in so far as it may affect trade between member states. Such abuse may, in particular, consist in:

(a) directly or indirectly imposing unfair purchase or selling prices or unfair trading conditions;

(b) limiting production, markets or technical development to the prejudice of consumers;

(c) applying dissimilar conditions to equivalent transactions with other trading parties, thereby placing them at a competitive disadvantage;

(d) making the conclusion of contracts subject to acceptance by other parties of supplementary obligations which, by their nature or according to commercial usage, have no connection with the subject of such contracts.

6.5 An undertaking acts in contravention of Article 102 if (i) it occupies a dominant position in the marketplace, and (ii) it abuses that dominant position by acting anti-competitively. It is important to emphasise that occupying a dominant, ie monopolistic, position does not of itself constitute an infringement of Article 102. The dominance or otherwise of an undertaking can only be assessed in the context of a defined market. Careful market definition is crucial. The more narrowly a market is defined, the more likely the conclusion that a particular undertaking is dominant in it. Conversely, the same undertaking is less likely to be found dominant in a widely construed market. The ECJ has defined dominance as 'a position of economic strength enjoyed by an undertaking which enables it to prevent effective competition from being maintained on the relevant market by giving it the power to behave to an appreciable extent independently of its competitors, customers and ultimately of consumers'.[4]

6.6 The competition rules are enforced both publicly by the Commission and the Office of Fair Trading (OFT)[5] and privately by means of litigation. The Commission and the OFT can investigate a potentially anti-competitive practice either of their own motion or following a complaint. They have wide-ranging powers to seek information and to impose fines on offending undertakings.[6] Where they carry out an investigation, they must issue a Statement of Objections to which the parties have a right of reply and a right to an oral hearing. The Commission and the OFT have the power to order interim measures and, if they find that an infringement has occurred, to impose (often substantial) fines. There is a right of appeal against a Commission Decision to the EU General Court and against a decision of the OFT to the Competition Appeal Tribunal.

6.7 Private proceedings may also be brought in the English courts by victims of breaches of the EU or domestic competition rules, seeking declarations, injunctions or damages.

---

[4] Case 27/76 *United Brands v Commission* [1978] ECR 207.
[5] See Bellamy and Child (n 3) ch 13.
[6] Ibid.

Application of the Competition Rules in the Sports Sector

The Specific Nature of Sport

6.8 As explained in chapter three above,[7] the ECJ in *Meca-Medina*[8] established that a rule or agreement is not immune from the application of the competition rules simply because it is concerned with the organisation of sport. The 'sporting exception' applicable to the free movement provisions does not, therefore, apply. It is thus necessary to examine the application of Articles 101 and 102 TFEU in each individual case. Equally, however, the courts will take account of the sporting context of a rule or agreement when assessing whether or not the competition provisions have been infringed. Thus, a sporting rule may be compatible with those provisions to the extent that it pursues a legitimate objective and its restrictive effects are inherent in that objective and proportionate to it.[9]

6.9 In particular, sport has a characteristic which differentiates it from other industries and which may justify a somewhat more sensitive application of the competition rules. That characteristic is that it is not in a sports participant's interest to eliminate its rivals from the market. A sports event depends on there being several competitors. Whereas in other industries the elimination of inefficient businesses from the market is an aim of effective competition, the same is not the case in the sports sector. The elimination or economic weakening of its rivals is not in a sports club's interests because it could lead to less even-handed competition on the sports field, and therefore present less of an attraction to spectators. Thus, measures which tend to restrict competition between sports undertakings *may* be justifiable as necessary to the maintenance of sporting competition whilst analogous measures would be unlawful in other industries.

6.10 Following the ECJ's judgment in *Meca-Medina*, the Commission produced in its Staff Working Document, a methodological approach for assessing whether a rule adopted by a sports association relating to the organisation of sport infringes Article 101 or Article 102 TFEU.[10] The methodology is as follows:

> Step 1. Is the sports association that adopted the rule considered to be an '*undertaking*' or an '*association of undertakings*'?
> The sports association is an 'undertaking' to the extent it carries out an 'economic' activity itself (e.g., the selling of broadcasting rights).
> The sports association is an 'association of undertakings' if its members carry out an economic activity. In this respect, the question will become relevant to what extent the sport in which the members (usually clubs/ teams or athletes) are active can be considered an economic activity and to what extent the members exercise economic activity. In the absence of economic activity [Articles 101 and 102] do not apply.
>
> Step 2. Does the rule in question *restrict competition* within the meaning of [Article 101(1) TFEU] or constitute an abuse of a dominant position under [Article 102 TFEU]?
> This will depend, in application of the principles established in the *Wouters* judgment, on the following factors:

---

[7] See paras 3.108–3.116.
[8] Case C-519/04 P *Meca-Medina* [2006] ECR I-6991. See eg Subiotto, *How a Lack of Analytical Rigour has Resulted in an Overbroad Application of EC Competition Law in the Sports Sector* [2009] ISLR 21.
[9] Ibid, para 42 of the Court's judgment. See also Case C-309/99 *Wouters* [2002] ECR I-1577.
[10] Annex 1, para 2.1.2.

the *overall context* in which the rule was adopted or produces its effects and its *objectives*; whether the rule is *proportionate* in light of the objective pursued.

Step 3. Is *trade between Member States affected?*

Step 4. Does the rule fulfil the conditions of *[Article 102(3) TFEU]?*

Market Definition

6.11 The proper definition of the relevant market is of critical importance in Article 102 cases and is also important in many cases concerning the application of Article 101 TFEU. There are two principal elements to market definition: the product market and the geographical market. Regard must be had to the twin concepts of demand and supply substitutability. This means the extent to which other products are deemed to be substitutable for that under consideration from the point of view of consumers and suppliers respectively. The Commission has stated that:

> Basically, the exercise of market definition consists in identifying the effective alternative sources of supply for the customers of the undertakings involved, in terms both of products/services and of geographic location of suppliers.[11]

6.12 The retail of replica football shirts affords a good example of how these tests are applied. To assess whether a particular shirt manufacturer is dominant, the market must first be defined. Is the market the retail of Manchester United shirts or is it the retail of football club shirts generally? There is likely to be almost no demand substitutability. In other words, Manchester United fans would not switch to Liverpool shirts if there was a change in their respective price. Supply substitutability is more complicated. At first sight it might be thought easy for manufacturers of other shirts to start producing Manchester United shirts. However, football clubs enter into exclusive contracts with one shirt manufacturer. Furthermore, shirts bear at least three trade marks: those of the club, shirt manufacturer and sponsor. Manchester United is therefore able to prevent other shirt manufacturers producing its replica kit. This is not to say that a shirt manufacturer does not face any competitive pressure; once its contract with the club has expired it must compete with other manufacturers for another contract. However, it does seem that supply substitutability is fairly limited. The Commission has stated that where, as in this example, supply substitutability would entail time delays, it will not be considered at the stage of market definition.[12] Instead, it will be relevant, once the position of the undertaking in the market has been established, to determine whether the action complained of is anti-competitive.

Undertakings, Associations of Undertakings

6.13 The term 'undertaking' has been construed broadly to extend to any entity, regardless of legal form, which carries on an economic activity. EU law takes a broad view of what constitutes an economic activity. It includes the provision of services as well as

---

[11] Commission Notice on the definition of relevant market for the purposes of Community competition law, 1997 OJ C372/5, para 13.

[12] Ibid, para 23: 'When supply-side substitutability would entail the need to adjust significantly existing tangible and intangible assets, additional investments, strategic decisions or time delays, it will not be considered at the stage of market definition.'

the supply of goods. Thus, it is well established that entities which transmit television broadcasts are undertakings within the meaning of the competition rules.[13] Further, it is immaterial whether or not the undertaking is profit-making.

6.14 Professional and semi-professional sports clubs will almost always be 'undertakings'. Even if their main purpose is sporting, they will generally be engaged in economic activities such as the sale of tickets for matches, sports merchandise such as replica shirts, television broadcasting rights and advertising. As regards individual athletes, the ECJ found that a high-level judoka participating in an international competition was exercising an economic activity, even though she was not remunerated by the organiser, due to the fact that such services are normally remunerated and that participation in the event generates economic activity (eg the sale of tickets, transmission by broadcasters, sponsoring agreements).[14]

6.15 Sports governing bodies may be both undertakings and associations of undertakings. They are undertakings where they themselves carry out an economic activity, for example, by commercially exploiting an event. In *Distribution of Package Tours During the 1990 World Cup*,[15] the Commission considered agreements between FIFA, the Italian Football Association and the local organising committee. All three entities were held to be 'undertakings' for the purposes of (what is now) Article 101 TFEU. The Commission noted that although FIFA carries out sporting activities, it also carries out activities of an economic nature, such as the sale of advertising and television broadcasting rights.[16] Similarly, the Italian Football Association was responsible for the organisation of the World Cup and, for the purpose of financing its expenditure, had a share in the net profits of the competition.[17]

6.16 It may be that sports governing bodies are better described as associations of undertakings where they constitute groupings of clubs or athletes which themselves are carrying out an economic activity. As far as the application of Article 101 is concerned, it makes no real substantive difference whether a governing body is found to be an undertaking in its own right or an association of undertakings, as both are caught. However, the characterisation of a governing body may be of tactical significance to a potential claimant as it may well have an impact upon the choice of defendant. Thus, where a league has engaged in an anti-competitive practice and a claimant wishes to proceed against an individual club rather than against the body itself, then it will be in that claimant's interest to argue that the league comprises an association of undertakings and is not itself an indivisible undertaking. The choice of defendant will of course dictate whether it is the club or the governing body that is fined or liable in damages if the action is successful. Article 102 TFEU does not include the concept of an 'association of undertakings'. However, the General Court has held that, even where a sports association is not itself active on a given market, it may be considered an undertaking under Article 102 TFEU to the extent that the association is the emanation of its members which are active on the market.[18]

---

[13] See, eg, Case 155/73 *Sacchi* [1974] ECR 409, [1974] 2 CMLR 177.
[14] Joined Cases C-51/96 and C-191/97 *Deliège* [2000] ECR I-2549, paras 56–57.
[15] OJ 1992 L326/31, [1994] 5 CMLR 253.
[16] Ibid, paras 47–49 of the Commission's decision.
[17] Ibid, paras 50–33. See also Case T-46/92 *Scottish Football Association v Commission* [1994] ECR II-1039 in which the Scottish FA did not dispute before the CFI the power of the Commission to rely against it on Regulation 17/62 implementing Arts 85 and 86 (subsequently 81 and 82, now TFEU Arts 101 and 102).
[18] Case T-193/02 *Piau v Commission* [2005] ECR II-209.

Agreements, Decisions, Concerted Practices

6.17 Agreements, decisions and concerted practices overlap and are treated fluidly by the courts. No formality is required; the concept of 'concerted practices' covers informal cooperation not recorded in any agreement or decision. The ECJ has defined 'concerted practice' as:

> a form of co-ordination between undertakings which, without having reached the stage where an agreement properly so called has been concluded, knowingly substitutes practical co-operation between them for the risks of competition.[19]

Thus, any form of cooperation between undertakings falls within Article 101(1) if it significantly affects competition and has an effect on trade between Member States.

6.18 As far as associations of undertakings are concerned, Article 101 covers all activities which produce anti-competitive effects and have an impact on inter-state trade. So, although Article 101 expressly refers to decisions, nothing will really turn on the precise form of the measure taken. This is particularly important to appreciate in the context of sports law given that associations in the form of leagues and governing bodies are common in the sports sector. Thus, agreements between such associations may be caught by Article 101(1)[20] and so may their rules, constitutions and statutes.

Restrictions on Competition under Articles 101(1) and 102 TFEU

6.19 The next question to consider is whether the rule, agreement or act in question restricts competition within the meaning of Article 101(1) or constitutes an abuse of a dominant position contrary to Article 102 TFEU. Article 101(1) and the Chapter I prohibition contain the following examples of agreements that restrict competition: agreements that fix prices, limit production, share markets, apply dissimilar conditions to similar transactions with other trading parties, and/or tie unrelated obligations together. The restriction on competition must be appreciable.[21] Commercial agreements may be horizontal (ie between undertakings at the same level of supply in the market) or vertical (ie between undertakings at different levels, such as manufacturers and retailers). Common examples of horizontal agreements caught by Article 101(1) are price-fixing and market-sharing agreements. The Commission and European Courts view price-fixing and market-sharing-agreements as anti-competitive by their very nature so they will almost certainly be caught by Article 101(1).

6.20 Examples of vertical agreements which may fall within Article 101(1) are exclusive distribution, exclusive purchasing and trade mark licensing agreements. Broadly, the effect on competition of agreements of this type must be assessed with regard to the whole economic context of the agreement. For example, in assessing whether an exclusive purchasing beer-tie agreement restricted competition, the ECJ held that it was necessary to examine the extent of other barriers to entry or to growth for participants on the

---

[19] Case 48/69 *ICI v Commission* [1972] ECR 619, [1972] CMLR 557, para 64.
[20] Case 71/74 *Frubo v Commission* [1975] ECR 563, [1975] 2 CMLR 123, para 30.
[21] See the Commission Notice on agreements of minor importance which do not appreciably restrict competition: OJ C368, 22 December 2001, p 13.

market and consider the cumulative effect of the agreement and others like it.[22] However, where restrictions in a vertical agreement have the effect of preventing imports or exports between Member States of the EU or otherwise segregating the market, then such restrictions by their nature are likely to be caught by Article 101(1).

6.21 Article 102 TFEU and the Chapter II prohibition contain examples of conduct which constitutes an abuse of a dominant position, including the imposition of unfair trading terms, limiting production to the prejudice of consumers, applying dissimilar conditions to equivalent transactions with other trading parties, and tying unrelated obligations together. Essentially, conduct is abusive where it distorts competition. The ECJ has explained it as follows:[23]

> The concept of abuse is an objective concept relating to the behaviour of an undertaking in a dominant position which is such as to influence the structure of a market where, as a result of the very presence of the undertaking in question, the degree of competition is weakened and which, through recourse to methods different from those which condition normal competition in products or services on the basis of transactions of commercial operators, has the effect of hindering the maintenance of the degree of competition still existing on the market or the growth of that competition.

6.22 In the context of sport, conduct which is potentially abusive includes collective selling of television rights,[24] the application of non-objective entry criteria to leagues or competitions, charging unfairly high prices for merchandise, and selling tickets only as part of expensive package holidays.

6.23 As explained above, an agreement, rule or measure relating to the organisation of sport will not contravene Article 101 or 102 TFEU where it pursues a legitimate objective whose effects are inherent and proportionate to that objective.

Effect on Inter-State Trade

6.24 This is a threshold test. Articles 101 and 102 TFEU will not apply unless there is an appreciable effect on trade between Member States. The test as to whether an agreement has the requisite effect, as consistently laid down by the ECJ, is as follows:

> … it must be possible to foresee with a sufficient degree of probability on the basis of a set of objective factors of law or fact that it may have an influence, direct or indirect, actual or potential, on the pattern of trade between member states …[25]

6.25 The term 'trade' is construed broadly and covers the activities of professional sports bodies. In *Bosman*[26] UEFA argued that the transfer of players did not amount to 'trade'. Advocate General Lenz disagreed, stating that 'trade' 'is not restricted to trade in goods but covers all economic relations between the member states'.[27] This is consistent with the Court's case law which shows that the test is a relatively easy one to satisfy.

---

[22] Case C-234/89 *Delimitis* [1991] I ECR 935, [1992] 5 CMLR 210.
[23] Case 85/76 *Hoffmann-La Roche v Commission* [1979] ECR 461, [1979] 3 CMLR 211.
[24] Discussed below: see paras 6.46–6.52.
[25] Case 56/65 *Société Technique Minière v Maschinenbau Ulm* [1966] ECR 235, [1966] CMLR 357.
[26] Case C-415/93 *Union Royale Belge des Sociétés de Football Association ASBL v Jean-Marc Bosman* [1995] ECR I-4921.
[27] Ibid, para 261 of AG Lenz's opinion.

Thus, agreements between sports leagues (or clubs) located in different Member States will certainly affect inter-state trade. So too might an agreement which determines the manner in which a sport is organised in one Member State if this in turn affects the ability of clubs to participate in competitions with clubs from other Member States.

6.26 However, in such a case, if the possibility of clubs playing in European competitions is remote then the inter-state trade hurdle will not be surmounted. In *Stevenage Borough FC Ltd v The Football League Ltd*,[28] Stevenage argued at first instance that the League rule preventing its promotion from the Vauxhall Conference to the League was contrary to the then equivalent of Article 101 TFEU and that there was an effect on inter-state trade because entry into the League enabled it to compete for a place in one of the UEFA competitions. This argument was rejected on the ground that this eventuality was unlikely.

6.27 This question only arises under the EU competition rules. Under the domestic provisions, the relevant test is whether there is an effect on trade within the UK.

Broadcasting

What are Broadcasting Rights?

6.28 Organisers of sporting events may spend significant resources to make them happen. Likewise, a club with a large support base will need to make a considerable ongoing investment in maintaining and increasing its popularity. Where a sporting event is televised, are the organisers automatically entitled to the television revenues? Where a match between popular clubs is televised, attracting a large audience, are those clubs entitled to share in the proceeds? The issue at the root of these questions is the extent to which the law recognises a 'right', akin to a property right, in a sporting event.

6.29 Different legal systems take very different approaches to this fundamental question.[29] In the United States, quasi-property rights in sporting events are recognised as part of the doctrine of commercial misappropriation. In an early case a radio station was sued for broadcasting play-by-play commentaries of Pittsburgh Pirates games. The necessary information was obtained from observers whom it paid to watch the games from premises that the radio station leased and which overlooked the ball park. The court held that the plaintiff, Pittsburgh Athletic Co, had a property right in the news disseminated by the defendant and the right to control that news for a reasonable period following each game. This 'right' derived from the fact that the plaintiff organised the games and controlled the ball park. The defendant's conduct constituted unfair competition and an interim injunction was granted to the plaintiff to restrain radio broadcasts of the games.[30]

---

[28] *The Times*, 1 August 1996.
[29] For a helpful summary of US and Commonwealth case law see Wise, *A 'Property Right' in a Sports Event: Views of Different Jurisdictions* (1996) 4(3) SLJ 63.
[30] *Pittsburgh Athletic Co v KQV Broadcasting Co*, 24 F Supp 490, 492 (WD Pa, 1938). On the misappropriation doctrine generally, see the decision of the US Supreme Court in *International News Service v Associated Press*, 248 US 215 (1918).

6.30 Essentially, the test for intervention by the courts seems to be whether a third party is 'free-riding' on the plaintiff's efforts. In a recent case involving the legality of transmitting data about basketball games in progress via Motorola's 'Sportstrax' device, the Second Circuit Court of Appeals reversed the District Court's finding that Motorola had misappropriated the National Basketball Association's (NBA's) 'property right' in NBA games, holding that the NBA had failed to show that the defendants were 'free-riding' on its efforts.[31] In France, the organisers of some sports events own statutory rights enabling them to exploit those events. In Italy, there is case law recognising that a sports event organiser has a 'right' in the event, and in Germany and Japan, though no such right is recognised as a distinct legal concept, nonetheless broad unfair competition laws usually have the effect of protecting the organiser of an event against appropriation of the benefits by a third party.[32]

6.31 In English law there is no property right in sports events, nor does it recognise a tort of unfair competition which prevents third parties exploiting the business developed by others. Thus, someone who had bought supposedly exclusive rights to photograph a dog show was unable to prevent others from taking and publishing their own photographs, the Court of Appeal holding that the promoters of the dog show had no property right capable of assignment.[33] Nonetheless, 'broadcasting rights' in sports events are routinely negotiated and sold. Since such rights do not exist as such, what is it that is actually sold? The answer is that the ability to broadcast is often dependent upon a recognised proprietary right.

6.32 For example, if a match is to be held at a cricket ground, a television company will require a licence, ie permission, from the owner of the ground in order to enter it and film the event. If such a licence is granted, the company may loosely be described as owning a 'broadcasting right' in respect of the match in question. The broadcaster would be unable to film the event without such a licence because it would be committing the tort of trespass as against the owner (or person entitled to possession) of the premises where the event is held, and the person in control of the premises would be able to obtain an injunction to prevent the trespass.

6.33 Ultimately, then, where the ability effectively to televise an event is dependent upon access to the sports ground where the event is held, the owner of that ground may be said to own broadcasting rights which it may sell to television companies either on an exclusive or non-exclusive basis. Practically, however, market power may well lie not with the owner of the ground but with the organiser of the event or with the teams competing. Thus, a company wishing to organise a high profile international athletics meeting in the UK will have a choice of venue at which to stage it. Conversely, owners of the available

---

[31] *National Basketball Association and NBA Properties Inc v Motorola Inc and Sports Team Analysis and Tracking Systems Inc*, 105 F 3d 841, (1997) 25 Media L Rep 1385.

[32] Wise and Meyer, *International Sports Law and Business*, Part IV, *Broadcasting and Sports in Selected Jurisdictions*, para 5.9.1.A (Kluwer, 1997).

[33] *Sports and General Press Agency Ltd v 'Our Dogs' Publishing Co Ltd* [1917] 2 KB 125, CA. Most Commonwealth jurisdictions take a similar approach. Thus, the leading Australian decision on the issue is *Victoria Park Racing and Recreation Ground Company Ltd v Taylor* (1937) 58 CLR 479 in which the plaintiff racecourse operator sought to prevent the defendant from broadcasting a radio commentary of a race by using scaffolding erected on the defendant's own property near the racecourse. The plaintiff argued that it had a quasi-property right in the races. The Australian High Court rejected this argument, holding that 'a spectacle cannot be owned'.

venues will compete for the contract to hold the event. An important part of the selection and negotiation process will undoubtedly be the issue of broadcasting rights. Where there are many potential venues, the event organiser will be in a powerful position to negotiate a favourable agreement in respect of television rights. Thus, though a broadcasting right stems from a licence to enter property, as a matter of commercial reality its value derives from the event itself and it is the organiser of or participants in that event that will usually gain most of the profit. Broadcasting rights are, therefore, a commercial rather than a legal concept.

6.34 Where sports clubs are members of a league, it is common to find that the rules of the league deal expressly with the sale of broadcasting rights. Often such rules provide that the league will be responsible for selling rights to broadcast matches played within the league structure. The rules of a league are generally contractually binding upon clubs and this means that clubs subject to such a rule have no latitude to sell rights to their own matches individually to the highest bidder. Thus, though Manchester United, Manchester City and Chelsea can undoubtedly command larger television audiences than, say, Swansea, Norwich or Wigan, they are precluded by the Premier League Rules from capitalising on that by individually selling broadcasting rights to their games at a higher price. This type of joint selling has competition law implications which are discussed below.[34]

How are Broadcasting Rights Regulated?

6.35 In common with other commercial agreements, broadcasting contracts must comply with competition law. This impacts upon the content of such contracts, affecting issues such as exclusivity and joint selling. Second, broadcasting relationships must comply with the statutory framework that is in place to regulate broadcasting. Before moving on to discuss the limitations imposed by competition law, the main subject of this chapter, it is appropriate to make some brief observations regarding statutory regulation.

Statutory Regulation

6.36 Ofcom is the regulator for all UK commercial television and radio services. It has wide ranging powers and functions under the Broadcasting Acts of 1990 and 1996 and under the Communications Act 2003. These include licensing functions as well as functions in relation to the content of programmes.[35]

6.37 Sports broadcasting is subject to the regulatory scheme in the same way as any other broadcasting. However, it is singled out for special treatment by Part IV of the Broadcasting Act 1996 which is entitled 'Sporting and Other Events of National Interest'. The concern addressed by this Part of the Act is the limitation placed by the growth of satellite and other forms of subscription television on the general accessibility of popular sporting events. This concern was underlined by a general resolution passed in 1996, in which the European Parliament declared that it 'considers it essential for all spectators to have a right of access to major sporting events' and that:

---

[34] See paras 6.46–6.52.
[35] See the Ofcom Broadcasting Code.

exclusive broadcasting rights for certain sports events which are of general interest in one or more Member States must be granted to channels which broadcast in non-encrypted form so that these events remain accessible to the population as a whole.[36]

To this end, the Audiovisual Media Services Directive expressly permits Member States to take measures:[37]

to ensure that broadcasters under its jurisdiction do not broadcast on an exclusive basis events which are regarded by that member state as being of major importance for society in such a way as to deprive a substantial proportion of the public in that member state of the possibility of following such events via live coverage or deferred coverage on free television. If it does so, the Member State concerned shall draw up a list of designated events, national or non-national which it considers to be of major importance for society ...

Accordingly, section 97 of the Broadcasting Act 1996[38] permits the Secretary of State to draw up and publish a list of sporting or other events of national interest. The list must be divided into two categories, Group A and Group B. Before exercising any such power the Secretary of State must consult.[39] The right to broadcast listed events, live rights in the case of Group A events or highlights in the case of Group B events, must be offered to 'qualifying broadcasters'. Qualifying broadcasters are those whose channels are available without payment to at least 95 per cent of the UK population.[40]

6.38 The current list includes, in Group A, the Olympic Games, the FIFA World Cup Finals tournament, the FA Cup Final, the Scottish FA Cup Final (in Scotland), the Grand National, the Derby, the Wimbledon Tennis Finals, the European Football Championship Finals tournament, the Rugby League Challenge Cup Final, and the Rugby World Cup Final. In Group B are cricket test matches played in England, non-finals play in the Wimbledon tournament, all other matches in the rugby World Cup Finals tournament, Six Nations rugby tournament matches involving home countries, the Commonwealth Games, the World Athletics Championship, the final, semi-finals and matches involving home nations' teams in the Cricket World Cup, the Ryder Cup, and the Open Golf Championship.[41]

6.39 The listed events rules were considered by the House of Lords in the *TV Danmark* case.[42] TV Danmark, a UK-based broadcaster, acquired exclusive rights to broadcast in Denmark live qualifying matches played by Denmark in its FIFA 2002 World Cup qualifying campaign. The Independent Television Commission (the predecessor of Ofcom) refused it permission to do so because the matches were included in Denmark's own list of protected events and TV Danmark was a subscription based broadcaster. TV Danmark brought a claim for judicial review against the ITC claiming that it had outbid Denmark's free-to-air broadcasters for the rights. It lost at first instance, succeeded in the Court of Appeal but the House of Lords then allowed the ITC's appeal and held that the ITC's

---

[36] European Parliament Resolution of 22 May 1996, 1996 OJ C166/109.
[37] Directive 2010/13/EU of 10 March 2010, Art 14.
[38] As amended by s 299 of the Communications Act 2003.
[39] See sub-s (2).
[40] See ss 98–101 of the Broadcasting Act 1996, as amended.
[41] In the UK, the governing bodies that are the rights owners of the listed events have signed up to a voluntary code of conduct entitled *Broadcasting of Major Sporting Events: A Voluntary Code of Conduct for Rights Holders*, dated 14 August 2011, committing themselves to reinvesting in their sport at least 30% of revenue from sales of listed events broadcasting rights.
[42] *R v Independent Television Commission, ex parte TV Danmark I Ltd* [2001] UKHL 42, [2001] 1 WLR 1604.

refusal of consent had been correct. In particular, the objective of the Directive could not be attained simply by ensuring that public broadcasters had a right to bid for the rights at an open auction. If that was all that was required, there would be no restriction on free market forces and the Directive would serve no purpose.

6.40 More recently, FIFA and UEFA sought to challenge the Commission's approval of the listing by the UK of all World Cup and European Championship matches and by Belgium of all World Cup matches.[43] They argued that only certain 'prime' matches should be listed as this was the approach adopted by some Member States. The General Court held that the UK (and hence the Commission) was entirely justified in treating the World Cup as a single event for listing purposes rather than as a series of individual events. The General Court also rejected other arguments raised by FIFA and UEFA alleging lack of adequate reasons and infringement of the Treaty provisions on freedom to provide services and the freedom of establishment. Appeals to the ECJ against these judgments are currently pending.[44]

Broadcasting and Competition Law

6.41 Broadcasting contracts in the context of sport, in common with other commercial agreements, must comply with Articles 101 and 102 TFEU. The exponential commercial growth of sport and rapid technological developments in the broadcasting sector have given this area of competition law a high profile. There are various characteristic features of broadcasting agreements, and sports broadcasting agreements in particular, which invite particular scrutiny under Article 101 TFEU.[45] However, the compatibility of any such agreement with the competition provisions will largely depend on the market definition adopted. It is only by defining the market that it is possible to identify an undertaking's competitors and potential competitors and then assess whether competition is being restricted.

The Relevant Market in Sports Broadcasting Cases

6.42 The Commission's Staff Working Document contains a very helpful guide to market definition at para 3.1.2 of the Annex. In a number of decisions, the Commission has identified particular upstream product markets for the acquisition of sports events. This was done on the basis of specific criteria, such as brand image, the ability to attract a particular audience, the configuration of that audience, and revenues from advertising or sponsorship. In 1996, the Commission identified for the first time the acquisition of the rights to broadcast sports events as constituting a separate market.[46] Since then, it

---

[43] Case T-385/07 *FIFA v Commission*; Case T-68/08 *FIFA v* Commission; Case T-55/08 *UEFA v Commission*.
[44] Case C-201/11P *UEFA v Commission*; Case C-204/11P *FIFA v Commission*; Case C-205/11P *FIFA v Commission*; see also Case C-283/11 *Sky Österreich*, a pending reference raising the compatibility of Art 15 of the Audiovisual Media Services Directive with the Charter of Fundamental Rights and with Art 1 of Protocol No 1 to the ECHR. Art 15 is an analogous provision to Art 14 and concerns access by broadcasters to short news reports.
[45] These are dealt with below: see paras 6.46–6.69.
[46] Case M779 *Bertelsmann/CLT*, OJ 1996 C364/3.

has identified narrower markets. For example, in *Eurovision*,[47] the Commission took the view that there was a strong likelihood that distinct markets existed for the acquisition of broadcasting rights for some major sporting events such as the Olympic Games.[48] Further, in *UEFA Champions League*, the Commission held as follows:[49]

The Commission's market investigation in the case regarding the merger of the sports rights trading subsidiaries, Sport+ SNC and UFA Sports GmbH with the Groupe Jean-Claude Darmon demonstrated that although sports broadcasting rights may constitute a distinct field from other television programming, that market ought to be further subdivided into other separate product markets and that, at least within the EEA, football broadcasting rights may not be regarded as substitutes to other sports broadcasting rights. The Commission therefore concluded that there is a separate market for the acquisition and resale of football broadcasting rights to events that are played regularly throughout every year. In practice this involves matches in the national leagues (primarily the first division) and cups, the UEFA Champions League and the UEFA Cup. It was concluded that events that take place more intermittently are not part of that market definition.

In the present case, the Commission also considers that the relevant product market can be defined as the market for the acquisition of TV broadcasting rights of football events played regularly throughout every year. This definition would in practice mainly include national first and second division and cup events as well as the UEFA Champions League and the UEFA Cup. The TV rights of football events create a particular brand image for a TV channel and allow the broadcaster to reach a particular audience at the retail level that cannot be reached by other programmes. In pay-TV football is the main driver of subscriptions. As regards free TV, football attracts a particular consumer demographic and hence advertising, which cannot be attracted with other types of programming.

6.43 In its *CVC/SLEC* decision,[50] the Commission left open the question, with respect to Italy and Spain, whether an upstream market for major sporting events (Formula One and Moto Grand Prix) exists or whether the relevant market includes all regular major sporting events excluding football. In the same decision, the Commission confirmed that regular major sporting events, ie sport events that take place throughout the year or throughout a significant time period each year such as Formula One races, are not in the same market as major sport events such as the Olympic Games which do not take place every year.

6.44 As regards the main downstream product markets, the Commission has repeatedly held that separate markets exist for pay-TV and free TV.[51] With regard to new media, the Commission found in its *UEFA Champions League* Decision and in *Joint Selling of the*

---

[47] Commission Decision of 10 May 2000, Case 32150 *Eurovision*, OJ 2000 L151/18, para 43.

[48] Although this Decision was annulled by the General Court, it accepted the Commission's approach to market definition.

[49] Commission Decision of 23 July 2003, Case 37398, OJ 2003 L291/25, paras 62–63. See also the Commission Decision of 2 April 2003 *Newscorp/Telepiù*, OJ 2004 L110/73, in which the Commission defined as a separate market the acquisition of broadcasting rights for football events which do not take place regularly where national teams participate, such as the FIFA World Cup or the European Championships.

[50] Decision of 19 January 2006, Case M4066, OJ L134/46.

[51] See Commission Decision of 15 September 1999, *BIB/Open*, OJ 1999 L312/1, para 24; Commission Decision of 21 March 2000, Case JV.37 *BSkyB/Kirch Pay TV*, para 24; *Newscorp/ Telepiù*, paras 18–47; Commission Decision of 29 December 2003, Case 38287 *Telenor/Canal+/Canal Digital*, para 28.

Media Rights to the German Bundesliga[52] separate downstream markets for on-demand sport content services delivered via wireless mobile devices or via the internet.

6.45 With regard to the geographic markets, the Commission has held thus far that the downstream markets are of a national character or at least confined to geographic regions. Its Staff Working Document goes on to say that the upstream geographic markets also tend to be national 'not only for national events (e.g. rights for national football leagues) but also for international sports events since such rights are normally also sold on a national basis. This is due to the national character of distribution as a result of national regulatory regimes, language barriers and cultural factors.' It may be that the Commission will now have cause to review this approach in light of the ECJ's ruling in the *FAPL* and *Murphy* cases (discussed below)[53] in which it held that EU law does not permit rights holders to license broadcasting rights in a manner which partitions the internal market by conferring territorial exclusivity on national licence holders.

Collective Selling

6.46 It is currently very common for television rights to all matches played by teams in a league to be marketed centrally by that league rather than individually by its member clubs. Many leagues and associations contain a rule to this effect. The Commission takes the view that collective selling may affect competition in several ways.

6.47 First, collective selling may restrict competition between clubs *inter se*. In the absence of a collective selling rule, clubs which are members of a league may decide that it is in their interests to sell rights to their matches on an individual basis. Thus, a football team such as Manchester United or Chelsea will clearly attract larger television audiences for its matches than many smaller, less popular clubs in the Premiership. However, because the Premiership collectively sells broadcasting rights to all matches, that advantage in the popularity stakes cannot be translated into greater broadcasting revenues. There is therefore a distortion in the competition between clubs. Furthermore, as one price is applied to all rights collectively, this amounts to price-fixing. Second, collective selling rules have an impact on competition between broadcasting companies. In the absence of collective selling, a greater number of individual rights are available for broadcasters, meaning that more broadcasters have the possibility of entering the market. Collective selling, on the other hand, acts as a means of foreclosing the market to potential entrants by tying rights up together.

6.48 However, the Commission has also recognised that joint selling may create efficiencies and has accepted joint selling arrangements under Article 101(3) TFEU. It has in its decisions identified three types of benefits. First, the creation of a single point of sale provides efficiencies by reducing transaction costs for football clubs and media operators. Second, branding of the output creates efficiencies as it helps the media products gain a wider distribution. Third, the creation of a league product is attractive to many viewers. Indeed, joint selling may be pro-competitive, as was found to be the case in *Bookmakers'*

---

[52] Commission Decision of 19 January 2005, Case 37214, OJ 2005 L134/46.
[53] See paras 6.67–6.69 below.

Afternoon Greyhound Services Ltd v Amalgamated Racing Ltd[54] where the Court of Appeal considered the collective selling of certain media rights in relation to horse racing, specifically the rights to show live coverage of races in licensed betting offices. The claimants alleged that the collective selling by the racecourses of their rights to a joint venture established by them and the 'closed' selling of the rights to the joint venture constituted a restriction by object and effect of competition within the meaning of Article 101 TFEU and the Chapter I prohibition of the Competition Act 1998. The High Court and then the Court of Appeal begged to differ, dismissing the claim and holding that the object of the agreement was to sponsor the joint venture's entry into a hitherto monopolistic market. Prior to the agreement, the racecourses faced a monopoly purchaser. The creation of the joint venture and its purchase from the racecourses of live coverage broadcasting rights, was a means of introducing competition to the market.

6.49 In its decisions on the issue, the Commission has sought to ensure that the positive effects of joint selling outweigh the negative effects on competition. Its decision in each case has depended on the particular facts, including the degree of market power enjoyed by the parties. The Commission's analysis has largely been conducted under Article 101 TFEU but, should media rights be owned by the league itself rather than by its constituent clubs, then the proper analysis will be under Article 102 TFEU.

6.50 The Commission has taken three major decisions involving joint selling of rights to broadcast football matches. In the *UEFA Champions League* decision,[55] the Commission's intervention resulted in a change to UEFA's original arrangements which were to sell the UEFA Champions League fee and pay-TV rights on an exclusive basis to a single broadcaster in each territory for a period of several years. UEFA subsequently unbundled the rights into several packages such that more than one broadcaster per territory could acquire rights. Restrictions remained, however. The joint selling arrangement prevented individual clubs from competing with each other or with UEFA in the sale of rights.[56] This meant that UEFA determined a single price and a single set of sales conditions. The arrangements therefore plainly fell within Article 101(1) TFEU.

6.51 However, the Commission found them to be exempt under Article 101(3) for several reasons. First, there were advantages for media operators in having a single point of sale of a packaged league product. This enabled the acquisition of coverage for the entire Champions League season, something which would be very difficult and uneconomic if broadcasters were dealing with individual clubs as they could not know in advance which clubs would make it through to the end of the competition. Second, consumers benefited directly from the improved distribution of rights and increased coverage.[57] Further, the efficiencies created by the single point of sale enabled broadcasters to invest more in improving production and transmission.[58] The Commission found that the restrictions on competition were indispensable to the creation of a UEFA Champions League branded

---

[54] [2009] EWCA Civ 750; see also Brown, *Bookmakers' Afternoon Greyhound Services Ltd v Amalgamated Racing Ltd: Anti-Competitive Agreements—Sports Media Rights* [2009] European Competition Law Review N184.
[55] Case 37398, Commission Decision of 23 July 2003, OJ 2003 L291/25.
[56] Ibid, para 114.
[57] Ibid, para 172.
[58] Ibid, para 171.

product sold via a single point of sale and the related benefits.[59] Finally, the joint selling arrangements were not likely to eliminate competition in respect of a substantial part of the football rights market because substitutable rights to other football events taking place regularly throughout the year were also available (eg national football league rights).[60]

6.52 Similar issues arose in relation to the sale of the FA Premier League rights[61] and the rights to the German Bundesliga.[62] In both cases, commitments were made to amend the original selling arrangements by the respective leagues on behalf of their club members. These included the unbundling of rights into separate rights packages for TV broadcasting and mobile platforms and the possibility for individual clubs to exploit certain unsold rights and rights unused by the initial purchaser. Rights were to be sold by means of a public tender procedure and exclusive rights contracts were not to exceed three football seasons. In addition, the competitive bidding process for the acquisition of the FA Premier League's rights was made subject to independent scrutiny by a Monitoring Trustee. Furthermore, no single purchaser was allowed to acquire all the live rights packages as from the 2007–8 season. This commitment was negotiated by the Commission in order to end BSkyB's monopoly over rights to the FAPL in the United Kingdom. The Commission's concern was that, given the importance of football for pay-TV services, a restriction on competition on the upstream market for the acquisition of media rights is likely to have significant effects on the downstream market.

Collective Purchasing

6.53 Broadcasting companies sometimes join forces in order to acquire rights to televise sports events. One of the reasons why this may be attractive is that collective selling is currently commonplace. It gives sellers of rights strong bargaining strength, thus often making television rights expensive to buy. Moreover, in addition to the cost of the rights, sports programmes may be costly and risky to broadcast. As the Commission has noted, the cost of production of the television signal is high. This applies in particular to tournaments or championships which take place over a number of days with several events taking place at the same time. While only a fraction can be broadcast, most if not all must be covered in order to be able to offer a meaningful selection. Further, the broadcasting of sports events may be risky in that rights must be acquired well in advance of the event but its appeal to audiences may change considerably depending, for example, on how a particular team performs. The expense and risks are reduced if several television companies contribute to the purchase of rights.[63]

6.54 Although joint purchasing agreements do not automatically fall within Article 101(1) TFEU, they will do so if they lead to foreclosure and output restrictions as a result of vertical restraints in agreements between seller and buyer or by horizontal agreements between different buyers.

---

[59] Ibid, paras 174–80.
[60] Ibid, paras 193–6.
[61] Commission Press Release IP/06/356; the Decision is available at http://ec.europa.eu/competition/antitrust/cases/dec_docs/38173/38173_134_9.pdf
[62] Case 37214, Commission Decision of 19 January 2005, OJ 2005 L134/46.
[63] See *EBU/Eurovision System*, OJ 1993 L179/23, paras 17–18.

6.55 The Commission explains in its Staff Working Document[64] that foreclosure issues are especially relevant in arrangements concerning 'premium' content such as the broadcasting rights for live football matches. Such content is important in the downstream market, and competition in that market can be adversely affected by monopolisation of the acquisition of the rights to the content. In other words, if access to premium sports content is available only to one or more TV operators, further operators will find it very difficult to access the market. There is also a concern that powerful purchasers may try to restrict competition in neighbouring markets, eg the mobile phone market, by acquiring exclusive audiovisual rights for all platforms.[65]

6.56 In several decisions the Commission has required remedies to be implemented in order to address these competition issues. Thus, in *Newscorp/Telepiù*[66] the Commission considered a merger between Italy's two satellite pay-TV operators, one of which (Telepiù) was already dominant in the market. The new merged entity would have almost 100% of the Italian pay-TV market and would therefore have been able to put together an unrivalled portfolio of exclusive rights for premium content, thereby foreclosing third parties from accessing the premium content needed to establish competing pay-TV offers downstream. The merger was only cleared after substantial commitments were given by the new entity, ensuring access to its technical platform, limiting the exclusivity of its rights to its satellite platform and limiting the duration of its rights to premium (including football) content to two years.[67]

6.57 Similar concerns underpinned Ofcom's pay-TV decision,[68] appeals against which have been heard by the Competition Appeal Tribunal.[69] Although not concerned with joint purchasing as such, Ofcom's investigation focused on competition between pay-TV providers in the downstream market and concluded that Sky, through the acquisition of exclusive rights to the most sought after premium sports, has market power in the wholesale of certain channels including this content. Ofcom concluded that Sky exploits that market power by limiting the wholesale distribution of its premium channels, with the effect of restricting competition from retailers on other platforms. This is prejudicial to effective competition, reducing consumer choice and holding back innovation by operators other than Sky. Ofcom consequently decided to require Sky to offer Sky Sports 1 and 2 to retailers on platforms other than Sky's at prices set by Ofcom.

6.58 A collective purchasing agreement which is caught by Article 101(1) may nonetheless be exempted under Article 101(3) where its purpose is pro-competitive and where it does not have the effect of excluding competitors from the market.

6.59 This, indeed, was the approach adopted by the Commission when it adopted its decision in *EBU/Eurovision System*.[70] The European Broadcasting Union (EBU), an association of public broadcasting companies facing increasing competition from commercial

---

[64] Para 3.1.4 of the Annex.
[65] See, eg, Papaloukas, *Competition Rules and Sports Broadcasting Rights in Europe* [2010] ISLJ 81.
[66] Case M2876, Decision of 2 April 2003, OJ 2004 L110/73.
[67] See also the Commission's *AVS* decision, Press Release IP/03/655 of 8 May 2003.
[68] Announced on 31 March 2010. See, eg, *Ofcom Orders Sky Sports to Make their Coverage More Widely Available* [2010] ISLJ 148.
[69] Judgment had not been handed down at the time of writing.
[70] OJ 1993 L179/23, [1995] 4 CMLR 56.

broadcasters, notified its statutes and rules to the Commission. These provided, amongst other things, for the joint acquisition of rights to international sports events. In particular, television rights for international sports events were normally acquired jointly by all interested members who then shared the rights and the fee between them. Whenever EBU members from two or more countries were interested in a specific sports event, they requested coordination from the EBU. As a result, negotiations were carried out on behalf of all interested members either by a member or by the EBU itself. Once negotiations for Eurovision rights had been commenced and until they were formally declared to have failed, members were required not to engage in separate negotiations for national rights. Where rights were jointly acquired, coverage was normally carried out by a member of the country where the event was taking place if the event was within the Eurovision area, and the signal would be offered free of charge to other EBU members on the understanding that in return it would receive corresponding offers from other members in respect of events taking place in their respective countries.[71]

6.60 The Commission held that this arrangement did distort competition within the meaning of Article 101(1) TFEU. Although members from different countries normally acquired rights only for those respective countries and so did not compete directly with each other, competition between them was nevertheless restricted because (i) some countries had more than one EBU member which would normally compete with each other for coverage of international sports events, and (ii) there was an increasing number of members broadcasting via satellite and cable into each other's countries who would, therefore, normally have to acquire the rights for those countries in competition with the national members. Further, competition with commercial channels was distorted, since those channels were disadvantaged in not being able to participate in the rationalisation and cost savings that joint purchasing permitted. The Commission further held that there was an effect on trade between Member States in that the Eurovision system concerned cross-border acquisition and use of television rights. The impact on competition and trade was appreciable given that sports programmes are indispensable for any generalist channel; they cannot be totally replaced by any other type of programme.

6.61 However, the Commission went on to hold that the agreement merited exemption under Article 101(3). It provided a number of benefits. In particular, it led to an improvement in purchasing conditions by, for example, reducing the transaction costs that would be associated with a multitude of separate negotiations and guaranteeing that the negotiations were carried out by the most competent negotiator. Further, the exchange of the television signal resulted in considerable rationalisation and cost savings and provided smaller countries with coverage which they would otherwise find very difficult to afford. Consumers received these benefits in that the system enabled the EBU's members to view more and higher quality sports programmes than they would otherwise be able to do. The money saved could be used for the acquisition of other attractive programmes. The Commission went on to find that the arrangement contained no restrictions which were not indispensable to its purpose. Finally, the EBU's rules did not allow participating members to eliminate competition for a substantial part of the products in question as

---

[71] See paras 27–40 of the Commission's decision.

the joint negotiation rules concerned only international and not national events, which constituted the majority of sports on television.

6.62 The Commission's decision was, however, annulled by the Court of First Instance[72] on appeal, an appeal brought by private commercial television companies that were not entitled to membership of the EBU.[73] One of the restrictions on competition identified by the Commission was that 'competition vis-à-vis purely commercial channels, which are not admitted as members, is to some extent distorted' by the EBU's membership rules since those channels cannot participate in the rationalisation and cost savings achieved by the Eurovision system. In order for Article 101(3) to apply, the restrictions on competition caused by the membership rules must be indispensable. The CFI found that the Commission had not adequately considered this issue. In particular, it had failed to examine whether the membership conditions were 'applied in an appropriate, reasonable and non-discriminatory way'.[74] The CFI found further that it was a misinterpretation of Article 101(3) to treat fulfilment of a particular public mission as a criterion for granting exemption. The Commission's Staff Working Document states that it is currently reviewing the Eurovision rules under Article 101 TFEU.

Exclusivity

6.63 The sale of exclusive rights to broadcast sports events has until recently been an accepted commercial practice. From the point of view of the sports organisers, the price paid for exclusivity by one broadcaster is probably higher than the sum of the amounts that would be paid by several broadcasters for non-exclusive rights. For the broadcaster, it represents the best way of realising the value of the purchase of expensive broadcasting rights. Further, exclusive rights bring to the broadcaster greater opportunities to gain advertising or sponsorship revenue, since the broadcaster can be confident that a particular audience will be watching. For pay-TV channels, exclusivity of rights to very popular sports events is crucial in order to be able to attract new subscribers. The sale of exclusive rights is typically organised on a territorial, Member State by Member State, basis and so this practice raises questions under both the free movement provisions and Article 101 TFEU.

6.64 The hitherto permissive approach taken by the Commission and the ECJ to this practice is demonstrated by the Court's judgments in *Coditel I*[75] and *Coditel II.*[76] These cases concerned the right to broadcast a film which was licensed separately in Belgium and Germany. The film was broadcast by the German licensee and picked up by Belgian broadcasters and distributed to their cable subscribers. The ECJ held, in *Coditel I*, that the free movement provisions did not prevent the Belgian licensee from asserting its intellectual property rights to prevent the broadcast.

---

[72] Now the General Court.

[73] Joined Cases T-528/93, T-542/93, T-543/93 and T-546/93 *Metropole Television SA v Commission* [1996] ECR II–649.

[74] Ibid, paras 94–103 of the CFI's judgment. The reference to uniform and non-discriminatory application of membership criteria is drawn from the jurisprudence of the European Courts on selective distribution, as indeed is expressly acknowledged by the CFI at para 95 of its judgment with its reference to Case 26/76 *Metro v Commission* [1977] ECR 1875, [1978] 2 CMLR 1.

[75] Case 62/79 *Coditel* [1980] ECR 881.

[76] Case 262/81 *Coditel* [1982] ECR 3381.

6.65 In *Coditel II*, the ECJ held that the grant of an exclusive territory for each licensee was compatible with the competition rules. In particular, the Court held that: [77]

> The mere fact that the owner of the copyright in a film has granted to a sole licensee the exclusive right to exhibit that film in the territory of a Member State and, consequently, to prohibit during a specified period its showing by others, is not sufficient to justify the finding that such a contract must be regarded as the purpose, the means or the result of an agreement, decision or concerted practice prohibited by the Treaty. The characteristics of the cinematographic industry and of its markets in the Community, especially those relating to dubbing and subtitling for the benefit of different language groups, to the possibilities of television broadcasts, and to the system of financing cinematographic production in Europe serve to show that an exclusive exhibition licence is not, in itself, such as to prevent, restrict or distort competition.

6.66 There was until recently much to suggest that, in determining whether the sale of exclusive rights is compatible with Article 85 (now Article 101 TFEU), the Commission and Courts would take an economically analytical approach and would not take the view that such a sale falls per se within Article 101 TFEU.[78] Parallels can be drawn between the sale of exclusive broadcasting rights and the grant of exclusive copyright licences, and it was considered that a similar approach would be taken to the former as to the latter. The *Coditel* cases on exclusive copyright licensing were therefore considered instructive.

6.67 Recently, however, in the *FA Premier League/Karen Murphy* joined cases,[79] the Court took a different view when considering the grant of exclusive territorial licences. The cases arose out of civil and criminal proceedings brought by the FA Premier League against importers of satellite decoder cards and a pub landlady respectively, in an effort to prevent live Premier League matches broadcast by FAPL's Greek licensee from being shown in the United Kingdom. The broadcasts were made in Greece by encrypted signals via satellite and the Greek broadcaster supplied satellite decoder cards to its customers within Greece. It was precluded by its licence from supplying cards for use in other countries. The FAPL relied upon sections 297 and 298 of the Copyright, Designs and Patents Act 1988.

6.68 In its ruling, the ECJ accepted the defendants' submission that the provisions of the 1988 Act constituted a restriction on the freedom to provide services protected by Article 56 TFEU in that their effect was to prevent consumers in the UK from receiving satellite services broadcast from Greece. Further, this restriction could not be objectively justified either by the objective of protecting intellectual property rights or by that of reinforcing UEFA's 'closed period' rules which are designed to encourage attendance at football stadiums and which consequently prohibit the broadcasting in the UK of football matches on

---

[77] Ibid, paras 15–16.

[78] See, eg, 'Broadcasting of Sports Events and Competition Law', Commission orientation document, *Competition Policy Newsletter No 2*, June 1998. For a general survey of the law see Fleming, *Exclusive Rights to Broadcast Sporting Events in Europe* [1999] European Competition Law Review 143.

[79] Joined Cases C-403/08 and C-429/08 *FAPL v QC Leisure; Karen Murphy*. See, eg, Batchelor and Jenkins, *FA Premier League: The Broader Implications for Copyright Licensing* [2012] European Competition Law Review 157; Geey, Burns and Akiyama, *Live Premier League Football Broadcasting Rights: The CJEU Judgment* [2012] Entertainment Law Review 17; Smith and Maxwell, *Premier League Football Cases: Linguistic Tactics, Non-Naked Match Feeds and the Away Goals Rule* [2012] Computer and Telecommunications Law Review 33; Hyland, *The Football Association Premier League Ruling: The* Bosman *of Exclusive Broadcasting Rights?* [2012] Communications Law 7; Wood, *The CJEU's Ruling in the Premier League Pub TV Cases: The Final Whistle Beckons* [2012] European Intellectual Property Review 75.

Saturday afternoons. As to the former potential justification, the Court held that holders of broadcasting rights were entitled to appropriate remuneration but were not entitled to charge a premium in order to guarantee absolute territorial exclusivity such as to result in artificial price differences between the partitioned national markets:

> Such partitioning and such an artificial price difference to which it gives rise are irreconcilable with the fundamental aim of the Treaty, which is completion of the internal market. In those circumstances, that premium cannot be regarded as forming part of the appropriate remuneration which the right holders concerned must be ensured.[80]

6.69 The Court went on to consider the application of Article 101 TFEU, holding that a right holder may, in principle, grant to a sole licensee the exclusive right to broadcast particular content, during a specified period from a single Member State or from a number of Member States. However, agreements 'which are aimed at partitioning national markets according to national borders or make the interpenetration of national markets more difficult must be regarded, in principle, as agreements whose object is to restrict competition within the meaning of Article 101(1) TFEU'.[81] It followed that the obligations in the FAPL's licence agreement with broadcasters designed to ensure compliance with the territorial limitations in those licences (ie the obligation on broadcasters not to supply decoding devices with a view to their use outside their territory) restricted competition within Article 101(1) and did not meet the criteria for exemption under Article 101(3).[82]

6.70 It follows from this judgment that, although it is lawful in principle for broadcasting right holders to grant exclusive licences, they may not impose requirements designed to guarantee or reinforce territorial exclusivity.

Ticketing Arrangements

6.71 The competition law principles that apply to the broadcasting of sports also apply to the ways in which sports may be marketed. Most obviously, sports are marketed directly to the public through ticket sales to view the actual sporting event as it takes place. A ticket for a sporting event is, essentially, a licence to occupy a place on the stadium owner's property for a limited period of time and is, usually, restricted to a particular part of that property. Normally, the main problems encountered in relation to ticket sales are touting and counterfeiting. Both are dealt with in the UK under the criminal law, the former being, in the context of football tickets, the subject of a specific criminal prohibition.[83]

---

[80] *Murphy*, ibid, para 115.
[81] Ibid, para 139.
[82] Ibid, para 145.
[83] S 166 Criminal Justice and Public Order Act 1994. In *RFU v Viagogo Ltd* [2011] EWCA Civ 1585, [2012] FSR 11, the Court of Appeal upheld a *Norwich Pharmacal* (third party disclosure) order against an online ticket retailer requiring it to disclose details of those who had advertised tickets for rugby matches at Twickenham at inflated prices, thereby allegedly committing actionable wrongs—namely breach of contract, conversion and trespass; and in particular, breach of a contract term whereby distributors (allegedly) agreed not to sell tickets at more than the face value determined by the RFU.

6.72 However, in relation to major sporting events it is also important to ensure that distribution arrangements comply with competition law.[84] Article 102 TFEU has played an important role in cases involving ticketing arrangements because tickets for sports events are often sold through a single entity (eg the organising committee for the World Cup). It follows that market definition is important. In general, the relevant product market is the market for the sale of tickets for the sports event in question as tickets for particular sports events (eg the Olympic Games) are not normally substitutable by tickets for other sports events. Depending on the particular context, separate sub-markets may be identified. For example, in the *1998 World Cup* decision,[85] the Commission found two separate markets for (i) the sale of 'Blind Pass France 98' tickets (entitling the buyer to view all first round matches at a particular stadium and one match, in the same stadium, of the eight matches played by the last 16 teams at the start of the knock-out phase), and (ii) the sale of 'blind' individual tickets (relating to the opening match, quarter and semi-finals, third place play off and final). The definition of the geographic market will depend on the type of sport event. The Commission has stated that, for important international sport events (Olympic Games, football World Cup, etc), the geographic market will be at least EEA-wide in scope because of the widespread demand for tickets.[86] For sports events of primarily national interest (eg national track and field championships) the geographic market may be national or even regional (eg ticket sales for football clubs with mainly local fans).

6.73 The Commission has paid particular attention in its decisions to exclusive distribution agreements, territorial restrictions on ticket sales and restrictions in payment methods (credit card exclusivity).

6.74 In *Distribution of Package Tours During the 1990 World Cup*[87] the Commission investigated and condemned under the predecessor to Article 101 ticket distribution arrangements for the 1990 World Cup in Italy. The international governing body for football, FIFA, had appointed the Italian Football Association (the Federazione Italiana Gioco Calcio) as organiser of the World Cup and jointly they set up a local organising committee for the event. The organising committee granted a joint venture, set up by two Italian travel agencies, exclusive worldwide rights to sell tickets for matches as part of package tours. These tickets accounted for at least 30 per cent of the total capacity of the grounds used in the tournament. Otherwise tickets were to be sold through national football and sport associations, UEFA, the tournament sponsors and an Italian bank, and under those arrangements were not to be resold.

6.75 A Belgian travel agent complained to the Commission that it could not obtain tickets for sale as part of package tours it wished to sell for Italia 90, and the Commission upheld this complaint under Article 101. It held that the grant of exclusive rights to sell tickets as part of package tours distorted competition between tour operators. The Commission refrained from imposing fines due to the (then) novelty of some of the legal issues involved.

---

[84] See, eg, Bailey, *Ticketing: Meeting the Challenges of a Cross-Border Ticketing Programme* [2010] Sports Law Administration & Practice 4.
[85] Case 36888 *1998 Football World Cup*, Commission Decision of 20 July 1999, OJ 2000 L5/55.
[86] Staff Working Document, Annex, para 3.2.2.
[87] OJ 1992 L326/31, [1994] 5 CMLR.

6.76 The principal justification advanced in defence of the exclusive arrangements was that of safety. It was claimed that the separation of spectators within grounds by nationality and the need for safety around the grounds meant that only one tour operator could be authorised to put together the package tours comprising entrance tickets for sale at world level. This was rejected by the Commission on the ground that a restriction of ticket sales through one operator was a disproportionate means of achieving this objective. There were other less restrictive means of ensuring spectator segregation. Indeed, evidence was given by a representative of the local organising committee that the computerised ticketing arrangements operated by one of the main distributors within Italy, an Italian bank, could with the appropriate coordination have enabled the selection of 'two, fifteen or twenty' tour operators.[88]

6.77 It is important to understand the limits of this decision. It did not establish a principle that any tour operator was entitled to tickets for a major sporting event. The Commission acknowledged the need for ticketing arrangements to ensure crowd safety and stated:

> [T]he Commission considers it justified that travel agencies not controlled by the organisers, such as the agency which has brought the complaint in this case, should not have been able to acquire blocks of entrance tickets with a view to putting together package tours that would have been sold in a way that was not controlled.[89]

However, it stressed that those particular exclusive arrangements were unnecessarily restrictive, disproportionate and therefore contrary to EU law.

6.78 Despite the problems identified with regard to ticket distribution for Italia 90, further difficulties were encountered when ticket distribution for the France 1998 World Cup was entrusted to the organising committee, the Comité Français d'Organisation de la Coupe du Monde de Football 1998 (CFO). The CFO decided to restrict sales of 60 per cent of the tickets for the World Cup to people with a verifiable French address,[90] which led to a high profile European Commission investigation. This was clearly discriminatory against non-French EU citizens and the Commission found that it constituted an abuse under (what is now) Article 102 TFEU. The outcome of that investigation was a symbolic fine of 1,000 euros,[91] a decision which outraged the British tabloid press. The pitfalls that the affair highlights for ticket distribution are clear. A ticket distribution policy should not be based on criteria which discriminate between EU citizens on the basis of nationality or equivalent tests such as residence. Whatever the need to ensure crowd segregation, a restriction on sales of tickets which offends the fundamental EU principle of non-discrimination on the grounds of nationality cannot be permitted.

6.79 The Commission has, in two cases, examined credit card exclusivity arrangements for sports events: the 'Visa exclusivity' for ticket sales via the internet for the Athens Olympic Games in 2004, and the 'MasterCard exclusivity' for direct sales of tickets for

---

[88] Ibid, para 115.

[89] Ibid, para 118.

[90] In *Italia 90*, it appears that some 50% of tickets were distributed in Italy; it is not clear from the Commission Decision whether there was a requirement of a particular address. The complaint in that case did not concern any nationality requirement. See OJ 1992 L326/31, [1994] 5 CMLR 253, para 27.

[91] Again, because of the legal uncertainty at the time concerning ticket arrangements, a factor that the Commission says in its Staff Working Document is 'unlikely to play a role in future Commission cases'.

the World Cup in 2006. In the former case,[92] the Commission took the view that the exclusivity did not constitute a breach of Article 101 or Article 102 TFEU if consumers in the European Economic Area (EEA) had reasonable access to tickets via alternative sales channels that did not require payment with Visa cards. Such an alternative supply channel was available, in that tickets could be bought from any National Olympic Committee in the EEA and these did accept other payment methods. The organising committee for the 2004 Athens Games also agreed to improve the information available to consumers about their options for purchasing tickets.

6.80 The *2006 Germany World Cup* case was triggered by a complaint by the UK consumer organisation *Which?* against FIFA and the German Football Association under Article 102. The Commission applied the same principle as in the *Athens Olympics* case that there should be reasonable access to tickets for all consumers in the EEA. Tickets could be paid for by MasterCard, direct debit from a German bank account or international bank transfer. However, the latter option would involve considerable costs. In light of the enormous demand for tickets and the high incidence of sales by the organising committee direct to the public, the Commission took the view that there needed to be a viable alternative to ensure adequate access to tickets for consumers who did not have a MasterCard. As a result, the organising committee set up local currency accounts enabling fans to pay for tickets by making domestic bank transfers. The complaint was subsequently withdrawn and the case was closed without a decision.[93]

Merchandise Sales

6.81 The terms of a merchandise licence agreement need to be examined for their compatibility with competition law. Such agreements in the context of sports merchandise are treated in the same way as for other goods. This was underlined by the fines imposed by the Commission in *Dunlop Slazenger International*.[94] The infringement of Article 101 consisted of the imposition of an export ban in order to protect the company's exclusive distribution network.[95]

6.82 Vertical agreements are common between manufacturers of sporting brands and their licensees. These must be examined in accordance with Article 101 TFEU and the Vertical Restraints Regulation.[96]

---

[92] Commission Press Release IP/03/738 of 23 May 2003.
[93] Commission Press Release IP/05/519 of 2 May 2005. In March 2011, the OFT decided that it would not open a formal investigation into Visa's sponsorship arrangements with the London Organising Committee for the London 2012 Olympics given, in particular, the availability of pre-paid cards and other alternative payment methods.
[94] OJ 1992 L131/32; appeal dismissed by CFI in Case T-43/93 *Dunlop Slazenger International v Commission* [1994] ECR 2441.
[95] See also *Tretorn*, Commission Decision of 21 December 1994, 1994 OJ L378/45.
[96] Regulation 330/2010.

Sponsorship Agreements

6.83 Sponsorship agreements have not tended to raise many competition law concerns, primarily because sponsorship competes with a wide range of methods for promoting a particular brand. It follows that an exclusive vertical arrangement is unlikely to restrict competition.

6.84 Horizontal agreements may be more likely to have anti-competitive effects. Thus, an agreement between a league or competition organiser on behalf of all participating clubs or athletes to use only a particular supplier's kit may have such effects. In the *Danish Tennis Federation* case,[97] the DTF's tennis ball sponsorship arrangements were investigated by the European Commission for their compatibility with the competition rules. The DTF had been following the practice of nominating a particular tennis ball supplier as its official supplier and requiring all tournaments to obtain their balls only from that supplier's official outlets in Denmark. Following Commission intervention, these arrangements were amended to require the DTF only to award the sponsorship contract after an objective tender procedure open to all suppliers, to award the contract for no more than two years at a time, to allow the nominated balls to be bought anywhere throughout the EU and, surprisingly from a competition point of view, to cease describing the nominated balls as 'official' DTF balls, because consumers were being misled into thinking that the term denoted superior quality.[98]

6.85 Rules affecting sponsorship applied by a league or competition organiser may offend the competition rules if they are discriminatory. *Adidas-Salomon*[99] concerned a rule of the Grand Slam Committee of the Lawn Tennis Association requiring competitors to comply with a dress code which restricted the display of a manufacturer's logo to below a specified size. Four of Adidas's competitor manufacturers complained that the use by Adidas of its three stripe motif constituted a logo which exceeded the permitted size. The LTA amended its rules so as to include the Adidas three stripe as a logo. Adidas succeeded in obtaining an interim injunction against the LTA on the basis that it had a real prospect of successfully establishing that the LTA had breached Article 101 TFEU by failing to apply its dress code to other manufacturers and thereby discriminating against Adidas. The case was settled after the interim injunction was granted and did not therefore proceed to a full trial.

---

[97] European Commission Press Release IP/98/355, 15 April 1998.

[98] However, a rule banning a particular type of equipment for purely sporting reasons would not be caught. A challenge under antitrust law in the US courts to a ban on double strung tennis rackets failed in *Gunter Harz Sports Inc v US Tennis Association*, 511 F Supp 1103 (D Neb 1981). A challenge to the ban imposed by the cricket authorities on Dennis Lillee's infamous aluminium cricket bat would doubtless similarly have failed.

[99] *Adidas-Salomon v Lawn Tennis Association* [2006] EWHC 1318.

7

Disciplinary Proceedings in Sport

Introduction

7.1 As we explained in chapters two and three, the English courts have frequently professed themselves reluctant to intervene in sporting disputes and, generally, are only prepared to do so at a relatively high threshold, when confronted with a clear case of an unfair or otherwise unlawful operation of the domestic machinery for the resolution of sporting disputes. In chapter three we looked at the validity and effect of rules determining eligibility to participate in sporting competition. As we saw, the aspiring entrant seeking to satisfy entry criteria, or to persuade a court that he or it has done so, may or may not be in a pre-existing contractual relationship with the sporting body charged with applying and enforcing those criteria. Disciplinary proceedings occupy an important place in sports law, for without them it would be unfair to punish wrongdoing by those involved in sport, and it is essential that misconduct should be visited with appropriate punishment where it is proved, unless we are prepared to run the risk of violent behaviour, cheating and unfair sporting advantage being tolerated.

7.2 That would be as unacceptable in sport as in other forms of social life, but except in cases of serious criminal conduct it is usually sufficient for sport to manage its own disciplinary regime, without involving the general law enforcement machinery of the state. Notable exceptions include two notorious ear biting cases in the late 1990s (involving rugby in England and boxing in the USA), showing that there must be limits to the principle of self-regulation in sport. Both could have involved criminal proceedings. Recent instances of spot fixing in cricket in England by Pakistan cricketers have led to criminal convictions. Match fixing and illegal betting for gain also test the limits of self-regulation.[1] In England, racist abuse on the field of play can attract the attention of the police and prosecuting authorities as well as disciplinary bodies.[2]

7.3 In this chapter we shall consider the nature and scope of the punitive jurisdiction exercised by sporting organisations over sportsmen and women and clubs accused of violating disciplinary rules applying to the sport practised by the accused.[3] Such a person

---

[1] See generally Gardiner, *Match Fixing in Sport: Recent Developments* (2010) 18(2) SLJ 28; Gardiner and Naidoo, *On the Front Foot against Corruption* (2007) 15(2) SLJ 16.

[2] *R v John Terry*: Chief Magistrate Howard Riddle, Westminster Magistrates Court, 13 July 2012.

[3] See generally Parker, *Disciplinary Proceedings from the Governing Bodies' Point of View*; Bitel, *Disciplinary Procedures from the Point of View of the Individual*; Wearmouth, *No Winners on the Greasy Pole; Ethical and Legal Frameworks for Evaluating Disciplinary Processes in Sport*; Stewart, *Judicial Control of Sporting Bodies in Scotland*, all in (1995) 3(3) SLJ; Kerr, *Disciplinary Regulation of Sport: A Different Strand of Public Law?* in Bogusz, Cygan and Szyszczak (eds), *The Regulation of Sport in the European Union* (Edward Elgar, 2007) ch 5, pp 97–106.

or club, accused in disciplinary proceedings, must necessarily have a prior legal relation of some sort with the body exercising disciplinary jurisdiction. Without such a prior relationship there would be no foundation for the sporting body's punitive powers, with the consequence that any disciplinary proceedings and any penalty imposed would be wholly void in the same way as would be a 'trial' of an alleged burglar detained by a self-appointed group of vigilantes, conducted in the back garden of one of them.

7.4 However, disciplinary jurisdiction exercisable by a sporting body does not necessarily exist by virtue of a direct contractual relationship between that body and the accused. The relationship may be indirect, in the sense that the accused may have contracted with his club to submit to the jurisdiction of the governing body within the sport concerned; and the club may in turn have contracted with the governing body that its players will abide by the disciplinary regime established by that body from time to time. Thus in *Haron bin Mundir v Singapore Amateur Athletic Association*[4] the Court of Appeal of Singapore had no difficulty entertaining a private law action brought by an athlete disciplined by the Singapore Amateur Athletic Association, which had suspended him for prematurely returning from a training trip to Japan.

7.5 The athlete won his action (other than his claim for special damage) in that the Court of Appeal upheld the decision of the High Court to quash the Association's decision to suspend him.[5] Mr Mundir achieved his victory without being a member of the Association, which was made up of several sports clubs and had no individual members at all. In the event, the High Court held that an ad hoc contract should be implied, and based its decision on contract; though it is not clear from the brief report whether the Court of Appeal upheld that aspect of the reasoning of the court below. Similarly, in *Modahl v British Athletic Federation (in administration)*[6] Latham LJ was prepared to infer the existence of a contract to abide by the relevant rules from participation in an event, even if entry form formalities are not observed. However, the existence of a direct contractual nexus between the accused and the adjudicating body is not a necessary prerequisite of the latter's obligation to act fairly, or of its other common law obligations examined further below.[7] In most cases there will be, at least, an indirect legal relation between the parties, both of which are likely to have a contract with another body, usually the club or other organisation of which the accused is a member and which, in its turn, is a member of the disciplining body.

7.6 Even without any element of contract at all, where a sporting body asserts control over a particular sport or particular competitions, and the accused is a participant, or potential participant, in that sport or in such a competition, the accused ought in principle to be entitled to, at least, a declaration to enforce the duties of fairness, and the other common law obligations, of the disciplining body by virtue of its control over the sport or competition

---

[4] (1994) 1 SLR 47, CA.

[5] See *Haron bin Mundir v Singapore Amateur Athletic Association* (1992) 1 SLR 18; *Commonwealth Law Bulletin*, April 1992 p 444, and April 1994 p 437.

[6] [2002] 1 WLR 1192, CA. Jonathan Parker LJ dissented on the issue of whether a contract existed, but Mance LJ agreed with Latham LJ.

[7] Our view, now well established, received early support from Pilcher J in *Davis v Carew-Pole* [1956] 2 All ER 524, who held that contractual relations are not necessary to found the jurisdiction of the court to grant a declaration or injunction in a case where an association exercising disciplinary jurisdiction (the Stewards of the National Hunt Committee over a livery stable keeper) exceeds its jurisdiction; but decided in the event that an ad hoc contract could be implied from submission to the association's jurisdiction.

concerned, and its subjection of participants to disciplinary rules applying to the activity in question. A person or club entitled to take part in sporting competition has a stronger right to such a declaration than a mere stranger seeking to gain entry, in the circumstances examined above in chapter three.[8] In the disciplinary context a remedy ought to be available, irrespective of the separate question, which we consider in chapter eight,[9] whether the nature of the right allegedly infringed is such that it properly arises in private or public law. Subordination to a disciplinary regime, with or without contract, is itself, in our view, a sufficient pre-existing legal relation between accuser, accused and adjudicating body.

7.7 We are concerned in this chapter to give a brief outline of the law governing the exercise of punitive jurisdiction by domestic sporting bodies over individuals or clubs. Our account will inevitably overlap to some extent with the discussion in chapter three of rights of access to competitions, since the punitive measures open to the disciplining body may include imposing a ban from taking part in a particular competition, or over a particular period. But we observe here the distinction between ineligibility and expulsion: the latter, imposed as a disciplinary measure, presupposes the prior fulfilment of entry criteria, which, in a case of alleged ineligibility, is the very question under consideration. This chapter deals with the content of the law, not with the ways in which breaches of it may be enforced, which are the subject of chapter eight below.

7.8 An intellectually rigorous approach to the subject of disciplinary proceedings in sport does not involve treating particular types of misconduct separately. Doping cases, which occupy a large part of the sporting jurisprudence in this area, are not conceptually distinct from cases involving other types of misconduct such as swearing at a referee or failing to play a scheduled fixture. Nevertheless the World Anti-Doping Code (WADC) and the Court of Arbitration for Sport (CAS) have established principles in doping cases which, though capable of application outside that field, are particularly relevant within it, and can be seen as an important part of the international *lex sportiva*.

7.9 In recognition of the practical importance of doping cases and of the work of the CAS in balancing the twin objectives of aiding the fight against drugs and safeguarding the right to fair treatment, we end this chapter with a separate account of those principles.

7.10 We begin our general account with the following observations. Sporting disciplinary bodies, like other domestic tribunals, are not required to conduct themselves as if they were amateur courts of law. This proposition is the traditional starting point for any exposition of their obligations. They are not bound by strict rules of procedure and evidence which apply in courts of law (but normally not in statutory tribunals), except to the extent that their rules so provide. However, they must not misinterpret the meaning of the rules they are applying; nor must they conduct themselves other than in conformity with well-recognised principles of fairness. Examples of unlawful conduct in the course of disciplinary proceedings, of the type examined more closely below, include:

(1)   Finding guilt on the basis of a defective charge; defective because what it accuses of is not a disciplinary offence at all. An extreme example would be a charge of ingesting aspirin where aspirin is not a banned substance under the relevant rules. Another, less extreme, example drawn from our own experience in a case which

---

[8] See para 3.12 ff.
[9] See para 8.12 ff.

confidentiality prevents us from explaining more fully, is that of a charge of failure to report certain wrongdoing where the rules in play placed no duty on the accused club to do so, but only on individuals.

(2) Misconstruction or misapplication of the disciplinary rule being applied, as in a case where the disciplining body purports to find the accused guilty of a disciplinary offence on the basis of findings of fact which do not amount to such an offence. For example, where a player is charged with knowingly receiving an illegal payment, it would be unlawful for the disciplining body to find him guilty where its finding of fact was that the payment was made into his bank account without his knowledge.[10]

(3) Making a finding of fact which is unsupported by any evidence at all. An example, again extreme, would be a case where an athlete is charged with deliberately taking a banned steroid, and the tribunal finds that he has done so, despite unanimous expert evidence agreed upon by all the scientists in the case that the substance found in his body was not a steroid at all but a permitted substance.

(4) Acting in bad faith: for example, making a finding of guilt without genuine belief in its rectitude, in order to achieve an ulterior purpose unrelated to the exercise of disciplinary jurisdiction. An example would be a ban imposed on a racing driver for a disciplinary offence, imposed predominantly for the improper purpose of leaving the field clear for a rival competitor. Such a decision would be tainted by bad faith, if that predominant purpose could be proved, whether or not the disciplining body regarded the driver as guilty; but if it did not, the case would be the more heinous.

(5) Deciding a disciplinary case without hearing the accused, in breach of the celebrated duty to comply with natural justice, or, as it is now more commonly known, the duty of fairness.[11] Other forms of unfairness, drawn from case law on the subject, would include the making of a decision on the basis of information undisclosed to the accused, and the giving of insufficient time to prepare a defence.

(6) The adjudication of a disciplinary case in which the decision making body, or an individual sitting on it, has an interest, financial or otherwise, in the outcome, to an extent giving rise to a real possibility of bias against the accused; whether or not there is actual bias.

(7) Cases in which the disciplining body purports to impose a penalty for a disciplinary offence outside the range of sanctions open to it. A very simple example would be imposition of a £10,000 fine where the rules provide for a maximum fine of £5,000. More difficult cases arise where the body seeks to impose a penalty said to be impliedly outside the range of available sanctions, where the rules are silent or confer ostensibly unfettered discretion. Clearly a sporting body cannot impose a prison sentence on a sprinter for leaving the blocks early. Nor could it order an individual found guilty of receiving illegal payments to leave her husband or to have his head shaved.

---

[10] Various instances of this type of error can be found in Beloff, *Pitch, Pool, Rink ... Court? Judicial Review in the Sporting World* [1989] Public Law 95, 98.
[11] See ibid, 101 for a number of examples.

Specific Features

Subject Matter

7.11 In the last two decades, the handling of disciplinary cases by sports bodies has become more professional and better managed. The rules of many sports bodies have been brought up to date and now make better provision than in the last century for basic standards of procedural justice to be observed. In consequence, instances of elementary unfairness—such as failure to hear the accused at all—are now rare. The rules are now usually published on the website of the governing body concerned, and are intelligible and mainly clear. They are now likely to make provision for some sort of recourse to a panel independent of the disciplining body, often now chaired by a lawyer. Allegations of bias arising from panel members being too close to the governing body of the sport in question have likewise become a rarity. Governing bodies and players alike have largely accepted the need to be subject to the rule of law like everyone else. There has been a welcome improvement in standards of disciplinary justice in the world of sport since the first edition of this book was published late in the last millennium.

7.12 The disciplinary rules of sports bodies have also changed. Scientific and forensic evidence is becoming more complex and sophisticated. Doping cases now include charges founded on 'biological passport' evidence.[12] The reliability of such evidence was upheld by the CAS in *Pechstein v International Skating Union (ISU)* and *Deutsche Eisschnelllauf Gemeinschaft eV (DESG) v International Skating Union (ISU)*.[13] In a paper presented by the distinguished CAS arbitrator Professor Massimo Coccia, to a conference at Montreux on 16–17 November 2011, he referred to the 'Athlete's Biological Passport' (ABP) as 'an indirect system to detect anti-doping violations through the longitudinal profiling of some biological markers, ie by collecting and monitoring some athletes' individual values for a given period of time'.[14] Professor Coccia's main point, emerging from the jurisprudence, is that the standard of proof (comfortable satisfaction) can be met by any reliable means, including through innovations in scientific detection techniques, provided the expert testimony is sufficiently credible. The novelty of such evidence does not necessarily enable the athlete to rely on the maxim *in dubio pro reo*; as pointed out in the *Valjavec* case, the panel 'cannot abdicate its adjudicative role'; it is *iudex peritus peritorum*, a Roman law maxim meaning, in English, the expert judge of the experts.

---

[12] Defined on *Wikipedia* thus: 'an individual, electronic record for professional athletes, in which profiles of biological markers of doping and results of doping tests are collated over a period of time. Doping violations can be detected by noting variances from an athlete's established levels outside permissible limits, rather than testing for and identifying illegal substances.'

[13] Respectively, CAS 2009/A/1912 and CAS/2009/A/1913. Ms Pechstein's appeal to the Swiss Federal Tribunal was dismissed on 10 February 2010.

[14] See also the rulings in the following cases cited in Professor Coccia's learned paper: *Caucchioli c CONI & UCI*, TAS 2010/A/2178 (8 March 2011 (in French)); *De Bonis v CONI & UCI*, CAS 2010/A/2174 (15 April 2011); *UCI v Valjavec & OCS*, CAS 2010/A/2235 (21 April 2011); *Pellizotti v CONI*, CAS 2010/A/2308; *UCI v Pellizotti*, CAS 2011/A/2335 (in French)).

7.13 The rules of some governing bodies now include specific anti-corruption provisions specifying penalties for attempts to fix or wrongly influence the outcome of matches.[15] For example, in 2010 the four international governing bodies in the sport of tennis[16] established a Uniform Anti-Corruption Program, enforced by the Tennis Integrity Unit, pursuant to which two players had been banned for life. The rules include detailed provisions requiring players to cooperate by attending for interview when requested, and to disclose documents such as financial and mobile telephone records.

7.14 Following a confidential hearing presided over by one of the authors, the Austrian tennis player Daniel Köllerer received a life ban. The Association of Tennis Professionals' (ATP) press release of 31 May 2011 stated that Köllerer had been banned for life and fined US $100,000 after being found guilty of three charges: contriving or attempting to contrive the outcome of an event; soliciting or facilitating a player not to use best efforts in an event; and soliciting, offering or providing money, benefit or consideration to another covered person with the intention of negatively influencing a player's best efforts in any event. On 23 March 2012 the CAS upheld the life ban but set aside the fine.[17] The Serbian player David Savic was also banned for life and fined US $100,000 in a similar proceeding in October 2011. At the time of writing, his appeal to the CAS has been argued and the judgment is awaited.

7.15 The International Cricket Council's independent Anti-Corruption Tribunal, chaired by one of the authors, imposed substantial bans on three Pakistan players found to have engaged in 'spot fixing' in test matches played at the Oval and Lords in August 2010.[18] Since 2004, the World Anti-Doping Agency (WADA) has imposed controversial 'whereabouts' requirements, now (since the revisions to the WADC effective from 1 January 2009) requiring athletes to select one hour per day, seven days a week to be available for drug testing without prior notice.

7.16 In the first edition of this book we made only brief reference to corruption. It is a feature of the changing face of sport over the intervening decade that such brevity would now betray a lack of balance. Jacques Rogge, President of the IOC in 2011, identified corruption as a greater threat to the integrity of sport than doping; and there are few major sports which have not suffered from a scandal.[19]

---

[15] See generally Naidoo, *On the Front Foot against Corruption* [2004] ISLR 1.

[16] The International Tennis Federation, ATP Tour, Inc, WTA Tour, Inc and the Grand Slam Committee.

[17] See CAS 23 March 2012 and CAS 2011/A/2490, so heavily redacted by reason of confidentiality that parts of the judgment are difficult to follow.

[18] Decision dated 5 February 2011, available (in redacted form) on the ICC's website. The players were subsequently convicted of criminal charges in London and imprisoned. At the time of writing one of the players, Mohammed Asif, has lodged an appeal to the CAS against his seven-year ban (for two years of which the ban was suspended). The appeal was lodged while he was serving his prison sentence. See Ross, *Corrupting Cricket* SLJ 2(10) 28; Ross, *Corruption in Cricket: Using the Law to Cull the Crooks from a Gentleman's Game* (2010) 18(3) SLJ 28.

[19] Carpenter, *Match Fixing: The Biggest Threat to Sport in the Twenty First Century?* [2012] 2 ISLR 13; Heron and Jiang, *The Gathering Storm: Organised Crime and Sports Corruption* (2010) 5(1) Australian and New Zealand Sports Law Journal (online); Beloff, editorial [2006] ISLR 27; Gardiner, *Match Fixing in Sport: Recent Developments* (2011) 18(2) SLJ 28; Cairns, *Corruption Watch* (2010) 18(3) SLJ 53; Barak, *Illegal Betting: Match Fixing and CAS Case Law*, CAS Conference, Montreux, November 2011 (for tennis, see also the website of the Tennis Integrity Unit: *David Savic Banned for Life and Fined US $100,000 for Three Violations of Uniform Tennis Anti-Corruption Program*, press release of 1 October 2011 *Savic v ITF* CAS 2011/A/2621). The Gambling Commission, established under the UK 2005 Gambling Act, has considered cases from, inter alia, horse racing, football and snooker: Annual Report 2009/10 HC 199. See too Gardiner et al, *Sports Law*, 3rd edn (Routledge) 314–48; Lewis and Taylor, *Sport: Law and Practice*, 2nd edn (Tottel Publishing, 2008) D6.5. The IOC and WADA have called for a global betting watchdog: WSLR 9/4, p 1.

7.17 In *Oriekhov v UEFA* a CAS panel said:

> ... it is essential in the panel's view for sporting regulators to demonstrate zero tolerance against all kinds of corruption and to impose sanctions sufficient to serve as an effective deterrent to people who otherwise might be tempted through greed or fear to consider involvement in such criminal activities,[20]

referring specifically to match fixing[21] and other corruption offences. It also noted that:

> ... the very essence of sport is that competition is fair; its attraction to spectators is the unpredictability of the outcome.[22]

7.18 There are two methods by which the law combats corruption, which in this context means improperly influencing the outcome or any dimension of a sports event for financial or personal benefit:[23] the public law of the land and the domestic law of the sports governing body (SGB).[24] In the United Kingdom the common law offence of conspiracy to defraud was specifically retained under the Fraud Act 2006 to deal with cases where the interest of justice cannot be achieved by charging a series of statutory offences.[25]

7.19 Section 42 of the Gambling Act 2005 provides that a person commits an offence if he cheats at gambling or assists another to cheat at gambling. Section 42(3) includes within the concept of cheating at gambling actual or attempted deception or interference in connection with a real game, race or other event to which gambling relates. Since the most obvious motive for match or spot fixing is to promote a gambling coup, these offences are apt to embrace the most prevalent features of sporting corruption.[26] Acceptance of corrupt payments can also breach the provisions of the Bribery Act 2010, which from 1 July 2011 replaced provisions in the Prevention of Corruption Act 1906.[27]

7.20 The domestic law of the SGB will often cast its net more widely, since its object is to ensure the fairness of sporting competition rather than to frustrate unlawful betting coups. The penalties imposed by SGBs for match or spot fixing are enforceable against

---

[20] CAS 2010/A/2172, para 80.

[21] See also *Grobbelaar v News Corporation* [2002] UKHL 40, [2002] 1 WLR 3024.

[22] *Oriekhov* (n 20) para 78.

[23] But there are other forms, eg bungs: Goldberg and Pentol, *Football Bungs Preventing an Inherent Problem*, WSLR 4/10, p 8.

[24] Of international SGBs only UEFA refers specifically to 'match fixing' in its current regulations: Art 5, 2011 UEFA disciplinary regulations (see too Art 11.38), although others have rules which embrace it in different formulae. FIFA Statutes 2011, Art 2. FIFA Disciplinary Code 2011, Arts 62, 69, 136; FIFA Code of Ethics 2009, Art 13. See Winner, *FIFA's Code of Ethics: Rules of Conduct and Sanctions*, WSLR 8/1, p 4. FIBA General Statutes 2010, Art 15.1.1; International Regulations 2012, Art 28; FINA Code of Conduct, Art 2; IRB Regulation 20; Uniform Tennis Anti-Corruption Programme, Arts D and E; IAAF Rule 9 of Competition Rules; and the entirety of the ICC Anti-Corruption Code. See also Anderson, Regulations: *The FC Sion Case and its Effects: Part Two* (2012) WSLR.

[25] See generally Nicholls, Daniel, Bacarese and Hatchard, *Corruption and the Misuse of Public Office*, 2nd edn (Oxford University Press, 2011). For the potential relevance of the Bribery Act 2010 see Cogman, Hunt and Blake, *The Bribery Act 2010, Applications to Sport* (2010) 18(2) SLJ 23 and (less significantly) Brightling, *The Impact of the Bribery Act 2010 on Corporate Hospitality*, WSLR 9/3, p 15.

[26] Problems can arise in terms of difficulty establishing a link between the bet and the incident that caused the match fixing: *Forest Green v Grays Athletic*, 23 April 2010. The link was successfully made in *R v Butt, Asif and Amir*, Southwark Crown Court, October 2011. See generally Monckom, *Smith and Monkcom: The Law of Gambling* (Tottell Publishing, 2009) 299–300.

[27] This offence was admitted by Mervyn Westfield, the cricketer, who admitted receiving a bribe of £6,000 for promising to give away 12 runs in an over in a 40-over game between Essex and Durham in September 2009: *The Times*, 13 January 2012. He was the first England player to be convicted of cheating in a cricket case. See a further story in the *Sunday Times* of 11 March 2012, on betting related corruption in India.

its members by reason of their contractual relationship with the SGB, and consequent acceptance of its rules and liability to disciplinary action if the rules are broken.

7.21 Cricket is an example of a sport where prominent sportsmen,[28] notably in South Africa (Hansie Cronje) and Pakistan (Mohammad Azharuddin), as well as in other cricket playing countries, have been involved in highly publicised corrupt activities of various kinds. This prompted the International Cricket Council (ICC) to publish an anti-corruption code supported by an Anti-Corruption Unit headed first by Sir Paul (now Lord) Condon and then Sir Ronnie Flanagan, and a Code of Conduct Commission headed first by Lord Griffiths, the former Law Lord, and then by Michael J Beloff QC with a tribunal to adjudicate upon charges of breach and power to impose penalties up to and including a life ban.[29]

7.22 The two systems of law can be used consecutively. The three Pakistani cricketers—Salman Butt, Mohammed Asif and Mohammad Amir—charged with and convicted of breaches of the code for involvement in spot fixing in the Lords test between England and Pakistan in 2010,[30] were subsequently charged (along with the fixer Mazhar Majeed), convicted of criminal offences arising out of the same incident and sentenced to terms of imprisonment.[31] The Sentencing Remarks of Mr Justice Cooke epitomised the concerns:

> The gravamen of the offences committed by all four of you is the corruption in which you engaged in a pastime, the very name of which used to be associated with fair dealing on the sporting field. 'It's not cricket' was an adage. It is the insidious effect of your actions on professional cricket and the followers of it which make the offences so serious. The image and integrity of what was once a game, but is now a business is damaged in the eyes of all, including the many youngsters who regarded three of you as heroes and would have given their eye teeth to play at the levels and with the skill that you had. You procured the bowling of three no balls for money, to the detriment of your national cricket team, with the object of enabling others to cheat at gambling. Now, whenever people look back on a surprising event in a game or a surprising result or whenever in the future there are surprising events or results, followers of the game who have paid good money to watch it live or to watch it on TV, in the shape of licence money or TV subscriptions, will be led to wonder whether there has been a fix and whether what they have been watching is a genuine contest between bat and ball. What ought to be honest sporting competition may not be such at all.

These were echoed and endorsed by the Lord Chief Justice in the unsuccessful appeals against sentence of Butt and Amir. He said that the corruption had been 'carefully prepared' and the cricketers had betrayed their team, their country, their sport, 'and the followers of cricket throughout the world'. If corruption continued, the enjoyment of those who watch cricket would 'eventually be destroyed'.[32]

7.23 On the international plane the CAS has had to deal with cases from tennis and football, involving both players and officials.[33] The burden of proof lies with the SGB.

---

[28] Nafziger, *International Sports Law* (Transnational Publishing, 2004) 33–37; Speed, *Sticky Wicket: A Decade of Change in World Cricket* (HarperSports, 2011), esp chs 2, 3 and 9.

[29] Naidoo, *On the Front Foot against Corruption* [2004] ISLR 1; Joshi, *Combating Spot Fixing in Cricket: The Role of the ICC*, WSLR 9/1, p 6.

[30] Joshi, *Tribunal's Verdict in Spot Fixing Case*, WSLR 9/2, p 11.

[31] Three years for Butt, one year for Asif, and six months in a Youth Offenders Institution for Amir.

[32] Court of Appeal Claimant Division, 23 November 2011.

[33] *M v APT Tour Inc*, CAS 2007/A/1427; *M Montcourt v ATP*, CAS 2008/A/1630; *N Mezaros v UEFA*, CAS 2010/A/2266; *Oriekhov v UEFA*, CAS 2010/A/2172; *Pobeda v UEFA*, CAS 2009/A/1920; see Cairns, *Corruption in Football: The Saga Continues* (2010) 18(2) SLJ 61; *FC Nouadhibou v FFRIM*, CAS 2011/A/2529.

The standard of proof is comfortable satisfaction.[34] How the standard is applied depends upon the private law of domicile of the SGB.[35] Whistleblowing witnesses can be protected subject to satisfactory safeguards as permitted under the European Convention on Human Rights.[36] Sanctions must be proportionate but reflect the importance of what is at stake.[37]

7.24 The difficulties in identifying spot, or even match fixing are obvious: it is no coincidence that the Pakistani cricketers were only inculpated as the consequence of a journalistic sting. The methods used themselves raise difficult legal problems;[38] and it is obvious that prevention is better than cure.[39]

7.25 Below the level of actual corruption is a far larger sphere of cheating, of which examples are as various as they are legion.[40] Apart from on-the-field sanctions imposed by match officials, eg sending to the 'sin-bin', there can be subsequent disciplinary action; and all major sports have their own codes to define the wrong, provide the penalty, and set out the machinery for determination. Various catch-all phrases capture the former.[41] Here the boundary between morality and legality is blurred: the ambiguous phrase 'the professional foul' itself illuminates the problem for all SGBs and clubs.[42]

Jurisdiction of Disciplinary Panels

7.26 We now return to our exposition of the functions of sports disciplinary tribunals, starting with the question of jurisdiction. To render a valid decision, a sports disciplinary body must have jurisdiction to determine the case before it. This means not only that the rules it is applying must be valid in law, but also that it must be the body properly charged with applying them. The jurisdiction of a sports body to apply rules is distinct from the

---

[34] *Pobeda v UEFA*, ibid, para 85; except in tennis, where the CAS accepted in the appeal of Daniel Köllerer in March 2012 (press release, 23 March 2012) that the standard of proof was the lower standard of proof on a 'preponderance of the evidence' in accordance with Florida law, which governs the Tennis Uniform Anti-Corruption Programme. This is essentially no different from proof on a balance of probabilities.

[35] *Mezaros v UEFA* (n 33).

[36] *Pobeda v UEFA* (n 33).

[37] *Mezaros v UEFA* (n 33) para 93; see further *M v APT Tour Inc* (n 33).

[38] Room, *The Use of Personal Data when Investigating Corruption*, WSLR 3/5 p 7; Burrows, *Assessing the Reliability and Legality of Lie-Detector Tests*, WSLR 9/6, p 11.

[39] Taylor and Foley-Train, *Preventing Match Fixing: Player Education is Fundamental*, WSLR 9/6, p 6; Morgan and Sherill, *Integrity: Tackling Sporting Fraud* (Parts 1, 2 and 3) (2012) WSLR 2, 3, 4 and 5.

[40] Judge Blackett, *2010 Obolensky Lecture* (2010) 8(2) ISLR 38 (on 'Bloodgate'); Cutting, *Feigning of Blood Injuries and Rugby Union: Implications*, WSLR 8/2, p 14. See also Connolly, *A Warning to Disciplinary Panels of Regulatory Bodies: The Impact of 'Bloodgate' Goes Beyond Sport* ((2010) 18(2) SLJ 6. Fraser, *Cricket and the Law: The Man in White is Always Right* (Routledge, 2005) has chapters on Chuckling (chs 15–16), Bouncers (ch 17) Ball-tampering (chs 18–19), Slow Over Rates (ch 20), Sledging (ch 22) and (not) walking (ch 23). See also Barnes, *Changing Face of Cheating: A Handy Reminder, The Times*, 24 June 2011, referring to such notorious incidents as Maradona's 'Hand of God' goal in the 1986 World Cup and Ben Johnson's use of steroids at the Seoul Olympics 1978, ending with the salutary words, 'we accept that players no longer even try to play sport entirely by the rules. But there is a point at which law breaking breaks cover and becomes cheating: I suspect that if we no longer believe that cheating mattered sport would no longer have a reason to exist.'

[41] The ASA judicial regulations define 'serious misconduct' as 'any action, behaviour or practice liable to bring the sport into disrepute' (at 102.4.2).

[42] Blakeley, *Governance: Tackling Sports Cheats*, WSLR 4/7, p 12; Findlay, *Harmonising Punishment for Cheats*, WSLR 4/8, p 11.

issue whether the rules are valid. Rules may be valid in themselves but enforced by the wrong body.

7.27 The following are examples of arguments that could be deployed by an accused in support of a case of lack of jurisdiction. First, it might be contended that the rules in play had not been properly adopted and were consequently unconstitutional and wholly void. That would be a case of absence of jurisdiction arising from invalidity of the rules. If the argument were well founded, the disciplining body would have no jurisdiction to hear the case at all, and its decision would be of no more effect than that of any member of the public; the resulting decision would simply be a nullity.

7.28 Next, there can be cases in which the panel is improperly constituted. Such an argument may go to the heart of the jurisdiction of the disciplining body, as in a case where that body assumes a jurisdiction which it does not possess. A simple example would be a hearing conducted, and a penalty imposed, by committee A where the rules vest in committee B the power to conduct the hearing and impose penalties.[43] In such a case, self-evidently, committee A will have to rule on the accused's objection to its jurisdiction to hear the case and, if it did hear the case, it would be found to have impliedly ruled against the accused whether or not it gave an express ruling on the point.[44] Where jurisdiction is conferred by contract, the parties can cure jurisdictional problems by agreement; for example, by agreeing to a determination by a panel of two members where the rules provide for a three-member panel.

7.29 In *Karatantcheva v ITF*[45] an independent anti-doping tribunal had to rule on a submission from the player that the tribunal lacked jurisdiction because the player, who had tested positive for metabolite of nandrolone,[46] was a minor and thus, the player submitted, she was not subject to the contractual obligations in respect of anti-doping to which adult competitors were subject because the contract was not in the class of contracts recognised in English law (the governing law) as being ones that can be enforceable against an infant if the contract is for the infant's benefit. The tribunal (chaired by one of the authors) held that the contract to participate in the relevant competitions was sufficiently analogous to a contract of employment so as to fall within the class of contracts recognised as binding on minors if of benefit to them;[47] and that, manifestly, the player benefited from the contract since it enabled her to achieve fame and fortune.

7.30 A challenge to the tribunal's jurisdiction also failed in a football related confidential arbitration, where a former Premier League club challenged the jurisdiction of

---

[43] As in the *Anderlecht* case (*l'affaire Anderlecht*); *Royal Sporting Club Anderlecht v UEFA*, CAS/A/98/195: the CAS quashed the decision of the UEFA Executive Committee to ban Royal Sporting Club Anderlecht from UEFA competitions for one season in consequence of revelations of corruption of the referee in respect of a cup tie between Anderlecht and Nottingham Forest in the 1983–4 season. The decision was taken without jurisdiction because UEFA's rules vested disciplinary powers exclusively in its juridical organs, not its Executive Committee.

[44] In England, in proceedings governed by the Arbitration Act 1996, the arbitral tribunal has power to rule on its own substantive jurisdiction, unless otherwise agreed between the parties: Arbitration Act 1996, s 30. The London Court of International Arbitration Rules 1998 make similar provision (Art 23).

[45] Decision of 11 January 2006, available (in redacted form) on the ITF's website: see paras 50–51; unsuccessfully appealed to CAS, 2006/A/1032, 3 July 2006.

[46] For an earlier account of cases involving positive tests for nandrolone and its metabolites, see Kerr, *Doped or Duped? The Nandrolone Jurisprudence* [2001] ISLR 97.

[47] Cf the contractual obligations of the young boxer in *Doyle v White City Stadium* [1935] 1 KB 110, CA, relied on by the ITF.

the tribunal to determine an employment related claim by its former manager, on the ground that the Premier League Managers' Arbitration Tribunal only had jurisdiction over a dispute if the club was a member of the Premier League at the date of the request for arbitration and that if—as in the instant case—the club after suffering relegation was a member of the Football League and not the Premier League at the date of the request for arbitration, jurisdiction rested with any managers' arbitration tribunal established under the Football League's rules. The tribunal preferred the submission of the former manager that on a correct reading of the rules as incorporated by the former manager's service agreement, the Premier League Managers' Arbitration Tribunal had jurisdiction to determine a dispute between club and manager, at least, where the cause of action relied upon arose while the club was a Premier League member; and perhaps (though it was unnecessary so to decide) in every case where the club was a member of the Premier League when the service agreement was entered into.

Validity of Disciplinary Rules

7.31 Next, the rules that are being applied must be valid in themselves. Broadly, this means that the rules must be within the law and must not claim to be above it. In recent decades, a familiar refrain in sporting circles has been the complaint made by administrators in sport that they and the bodies they administer are over-susceptible to legal attack. Conferences in the sporting field often used to include, and sometimes still do include, discussion about ways of fortifying such bodies against legal challenge. Indeed, some such bodies, particularly international ones, would wish to be immune from such challenge in the courts altogether, which explains certain historic provisions in the rules of international sporting bodies (which no English court would enforce) purporting to prohibit recourse to the law at all, and seeking to confine all disciplinary jurisdiction within the sporting arena.

7.32 As already observed in chapter two, any attempt in the courts of England and Wales to oust the jurisdiction of the courts is necessarily doomed to fail, for the constitutional right of access to the courts cannot be removed or bargained away except by Parliament.[48] Sports administrators therefore have to lower their sights and concentrate not on immunising their governing bodies from legal attack, but on fortifying them against challenges, recognising that such challenges cannot be stopped but seeking to ensure that, if made, they will not succeed.

7.33 In the preceding section we looked at the preliminary point that the tribunal must have jurisdiction to deal with the case, if its decision is be valid and binding. If it does, that must necessarily mean that the rules giving it power to do so are valid, and that they are applicable. It does not necessarily follow that all the rules said by the party bringing the charge to be applicable, are valid and enforceable. The court ultimately retains the power to decide whether the allegedly applicable rules are valid. However, the first body to decide the point should not be the court, but the disciplinary body itself.

---

[48] See para 2.31.

7.34 So the first question to confront that body may be the question whether the disciplinary rules it is applying are valid in law or not. It may seem surprising at first blush that a domestic tribunal should be put in the position of adjudicating upon the validity of the very rules which it is its task to apply. It is sometimes thought that the accused may not impugn the validity of a rule relevant to his case before a disciplinary tribunal. But that is not correct. There is no theoretical difficulty with the adjudicating body accepting the jurisdiction to rule on the validity of its own rules. Indeed it could be an instance of unfairness to abdicate responsibility for adjudicating upon a submission of invalidity. A body exercising punitive jurisdiction must act in accordance with the rules constituting it. If one or more of those rules is in law void, then the disciplining body may not apply that rule. It follows, logically, that the body must decide whether to apply it and, in order to do so, must decide whether it is valid or not.

7.35 It is not fanciful to envisage accused athletes, clubs or other sportsmen and women making such a submission to a body entertaining disciplinary proceedings against them. Indeed, the authors are aware of more than one instance in which a sporting body (chaired by one of them) was specifically invited to treat as wholly void a rule providing for an automatic two-year ban for a first doping offence, and an automatic life ban for any subsequent offence. The basis of the unsuccessful submission was that such a rule would be in unreasonable restraint of trade, according to the principles discussed above in chapters three and four.[49] In the case in question it was unnecessary for the tribunal to decide the point. Where a sporting disciplinary tribunal does decide such an issue, its decision will be subject to review in point of law by a court or other tribunal in which a subsequent challenge is brought, as we shall see in chapter eight.

7.36 An example would be an argument that the body concerned is 'making up the rules as it goes along'; in other words that it is seeking to enforce rules of its own invention which have not properly been adopted under the constitutional instruments of the body concerned, rather than applying the body's rules to a new situation. For instance, if that body's constitution required disciplinary rules to be adopted by a two-thirds majority at an annual meeting, then a disciplinary tribunal could not lawfully apply disciplinary rules which, on a vote at the last annual meeting, had obtained the support of only one-third of the membership.

7.37 Such was one of the successful arguments of Mr Henry Andrade in his contest against the Cape Verde National Olympic Committee which was arbitrated by the CAS at Atlanta in July 1996.[50] His National Olympic Committee had purported to remove his accreditation at the Atlanta Olympic Games, with the consequence that he was prohibited from entering the heats of the 110 metres hurdles. The Committee had purported to impose this penalty by way of a disciplinary measure on the ground that Mr Andrade had disrupted the organisation, questioned the authority of its President and Secretary General and, in particular, carried the flag at the opening ceremony contrary to a decision of the Committee that the flag bearer would be the Chef de Mission of the Committee.

7.38 The panel applied the relevant rules promulgated for the occasion of the 1996 Olympics by the International Council for Arbitration in Sport (ICAS), the Swiss Private

---

[49] See para 3.55 ff and para 4.40 ff.
[50] *Andrade v Cape Verde NOC*, CAS 96/002 and 96/005.

International Law Act of 1987 and the Olympic Charter. It noted that Article 17 of the ICAS rules required the panel to apply those legal provisions and 'general principles of law and the rules of law, the application of which it deems appropriate'. Having done so the panel held that the decision to exclude Mr Andrade was void for want of consent of the International Olympic Executive Board. A few days later it went on to hold once again that the decision was void even though the consent of the International Olympic Committee (IOC) had been obtained in the interim, because Mr Andrade had not had an opportunity to make any representations prior to his exclusion, in breach of the duty of fairness discussed further below.

7.39 As already mentioned, an accused person or club might argue that a disciplinary rule is void as an unreasonable restraint of trade. This point was taken in the High Court in *Gasser v Stinson*,[51] although there is no suggestion that the point was taken, as it could have been, by way of submission to the International Amateur Athletic Federation (IAAF) prior to that body's announcement of Miss Gasser's two-year ban. The rule in that case operated by way of ineligibility rather than as a disciplinary measure, so that there appears to have been no hearing at which Miss Gasser could have sought a ruling (which she failed to obtain in court afterwards in any event) that the relevant rule was void. In principle, such a contention could be advanced before a disciplinary panel in relation to disciplinary penalties imposed for misconduct, such as the automatic bans already mentioned.

7.40 There is no reason why the restraint of trade doctrine should not be applied to such rules, although harsh penalties for doping offences will be easily justified by the need for a level playing field and the grave mischief of drug taking in sport. Allied to the restraint of trade doctrine as a potential ground of invalidity is the broader principle that a domestic tribunal may not impose a penalty so radically out of proportion to the offence charged as to be irrational, or so manifestly excessive that it is outside the permitted range of discretionary responses to the offence.[52] It follows from that principle that a disciplinary rule providing for a manifestly perverse penalty necessarily out of all proportion to the seriousness of the offence to which it applied, would itself be void on public policy grounds. That consideration appears to have influenced the decision of the IAAF to reduce from four years to two years the length of its mandatory ban for serious doping offences.[53]

---

[51] (1988) unreported, 15 June, Scott J.

[52] See *R v Barnsley MBC, ex parte Hook* [1976] 1 WLR 1052; *R v Brent LBC, ex parte Assegai, The Times*, 18 June 1987; *R v Secretary of State for Transport, ex parte Pegasus Holdings (London) Ltd* [1988] 1 WLR 990, 1001; *R v General Medical Council, ex parte Colman* [1989] 1 Admin LR 469, 489; and note the well publicised outcome of the arbitration proceedings in *Tottenham Hotspur v Football Association*, briefly reported in Grayson [1994] All ER *Annual Review*, 389.

[53] See *The Independent*, 1 July 1997, referring to restraint of trade legislation in Germany, Russia and Spain, and to successful applications for reinstatement by German athletes halfway through four-year suspensions. In *Blalock v Ladies Professional Golf Association*, 359 F Supp 1260 (1973), the Atlanta Division of the US District Court (District Judge Moye) held that an agreement to suspend a professional golfer from the Association for one year for alleged cheating was an unlawful restraint of trade and illegal under the Sherman Anti-Trust Act in that the suspension had been imposed in the exercise of the Association's unfettered subjective discretion, as was evident from the fact that it had initially imposed only probation and a fine, and had subsequently, without hearing from the golfer, decided to impose the one-year suspension. However, in *ITF v Burdekin*, Anti-Doping Tribunal decision dated 4 April 2005, a challenge to the validity of the mandatory two-year ban in a case where the player tested positive for cocaine predictably failed (para 64).

7.41 The following are examples of challenges to the validity of disciplinary rules in the sporting context. In *Chambers v British Olympic Association*,[54] the notorious sprinter Dwain Chambers failed to persuade Mackay J to grant an injunction to enable him to compete for Britain at the 2008 Beijing Olympics. Having served a two-year ban for a doping offence, he performed well enough to earn a place in the British team but was prevented from competing by a rule providing that any athlete who had been found guilty of doping was ineligible for selection. The athlete sought to impugn the validity of the rule as an unreasonable restraint of trade. But the judge upheld the rule on the basis that the Olympic Games was an amateur event; that the claimant would therefore probably fail at trial to establish that the doctrine applied; and that even if it did, the rule was reasonable and proportionate: it applied to the Olympic Games and was not a worldwide ban, and was widely supported by athletes as an appropriate means of conveying the message that doping was not acceptable.

7.42 However, the CAS held in *USOC v IOC*,[55] applying Swiss law, the Olympic Charter and the WADC, that the International Olympic Committee's rule (rule 45) barring any athlete banned for more than six months for a doping offence from taking part in the next Olympics, was void and unenforceable. The United States Olympic Committee succeeded in its various arguments which, reduced to their simplest form, amounted to the assertion accepted by the CAS panel that rule 45 illegitimately increased the sanctions provided for under the WADC, and could not be characterised as an eligibility rule rather than a rule providing for imposition of a sanction. The panel noted that eligibility rules, properly so called, were not rules designed to penalise undesirable behaviour by athletes.[56] On 30 April 2012 the CAS decided that the rule under which Mr Chambers was prevented from taking part in the 2008 Beijing Olympics is non-compliant with the WADC, upholding WADA's determination to that effect.[57]

7.43 In the sport of tennis, an issue arose in *Gasquet v ITF*[58] which gave rise to a wide ranging debate about the validity of a rule dealing with the point at which a player could be said to have withdrawn from a competition, on which depended the question whether a doping test had been administered in or out of competition. A small quantity of cocaine metabolite was found in the player's body, cocaine being banned in competition but not out of competition. The player submitted[59] that as he had withdrawn from the relevant tournament in Miami before playing a match, the test could not be treated as in competition and, if the true meaning of the rules was that the test was an in competition test, the rules must be disapplied as they would infringe the player's rights under EU and English competition law, English and international human rights law and common law restraint

---

[54] [2008] EWHC 2028 (QB), [2008] ISLR, SLR 115.

[55] CAS 2011/O/2422, 4 October 2011.

[56] At para 8.9, citing *RFEC & Alejandro v UCI*, CAS 2007/O/1381, para 76; and see the panel's conclusion at para 8.19. At para 8.27, the panel noted that a rule such as rule 45 could, however, in principle be validly incorporated into the WADC. The panel commented that any issue as to proportionality would then have to be considered by the first instance tribunal, subject to review on appeal.

[57] *BOA v WADA*, CAS 2011/A/2658.

[58] Anti-Doping Tribunal decision, 15 July 2009; in effect (with varied reasoning) upheld on appeal, CAS 2009/A/1926 and 1930.

[59] Anti-Doping Tribunal, paras 66–71 (upheld on appeal at paras 5.3–5.7 of the CAS's decision).

of trade, and would infringe the principle of proportionality developed in the jurisprudence of the CAS based on general principles of law.

7.44 The player submitted that it would be unlawful for the ITF to impose such rules on a player, and therefore unlawful for the tribunal to apply them to the player. He relied on numerous authorities including, most notably, *Meca-Medina v Commission*,[60] asserting that the ECJ's decision marked a fundamental departure in the applicability of competition law to sports anti-doping rules. The ITF countered with authorities in which the courts have recognised the high degree of autonomy accorded to sports governing bodies when formulating the rules under which sporting competition should take place, insisting that the burden was on the player to show that the ITF's rules were invalid and should be struck down; that the burden was a heavy one; that it would be a serious thing for a domestic tribunal appointed by a sports governing body to disapply the very rules it was appointed to apply; and that it was not unfair to the player to subject him to an anti-doping regime which treated as in competition a test carried out on his withdrawal from a competition without playing in it, or which extended the period regarded as 'in competition' beyond the period during which a player had played.

7.45 In answer to the player's contention that *Meca-Medina* is authority for the application of EU competition law to anti-doping rules in sport, the ITF submitted that the private rules of conduct that the ITF imposes on its players do not engage EU competition rules, and relied in this regard on *UK Athletics v Ohuruogu*:[61]

> There must be at least a question whether the principles expressed [by the ECJ in *Meca-Medina*, applying the EC competition rules to FINA's anti-doping rules] are capable of being applied to anti-doping provisions imposed under the World Anti-Doping Code. The Code represents an international consensus, supported by, inter alia, the member states of the EU, setting out an agreed mechanism for the operation of an anti-doping regime. There can be no doubt that the antidoping rules have a legitimate aim and are intended to be limited to what is necessary to ensure the proper conduct of competitive sport.

7.46 Neither the tribunal in *Gasquet* nor the CAS panel on appeal needed to decide whether *Meca-Medina* was authority for the application of EU competition law rules to anti-doping provisions enacted in accordance with the Code. No unfairness or illegality was found in adopting a rule which treats as 'in competition' a test administered to a player who is scheduled to take part in a tournament but withdraws before hitting a ball.

7.47 We consider it likely, however, that a rule purporting to reverse the traditional onus of proof in a sporting disciplinary context, so as to require the accused to prove his innocence, rather than the other way round, would be regarded by an English court as invalid by reason of public policy as informed by our criminal law and indeed the principle that in civil proceedings also the party asserting a fact must, generally, prove it. Such a rule must be distinguished sharply, however, from the commonplace provision in the rules of sporting bodies creating a presumption, in doping cases, that ingestion of a banned substance was voluntary unless the athlete should prove the contrary. Such a provision is unobjectionable since it does not, in truth, require the athlete to prove innocence: the onus of proving the presence of the banned substance in the athlete's body remains on the accuser.

---

[60] Case C-519/04P, [2006] ECR I-6991, ECJ.
[61] Disciplinary Committee (Charles Flint QC, chairman), 15 September 2006, para 34.

7.48 Similarly, rules making positive test results prima facie evidence of the presence of a banned substance in the body are not open to objection on policy grounds. But a rule purporting to render a positive test result 'conclusive' as to the presence of the substance in the body would go too far. An English court would require, at least, the player to have the opportunity to prove that the sample tested was not hers at all,[62] as do the rules of sports bodies that have signed up to the WADC.

7.49 A related issue surfaced in *ICC v Tharanga*[63] but did not, in the event, need to be decided: whether it is lawful for a sports body to enact a rule requiring a player to prove a negative—in the instant case, lack of intent to enhance sport performance (for the purpose of reducing the otherwise applicable sanction)—to the tribunal's comfortable satisfaction, rather than to the lesser standard of proof on the balance of probabilities. The tribunal was, in the event, comfortably satisfied that the player did not intend to enhance his sporting performance when he imbibed a potion, given to him by a revered healer calling himself a doctor, which the player thought contained only natural herbs, but which in fact contained a banned steroid. The player had reserved for argument elsewhere the contention that the rules could not properly impose so high a standard on a player. The point was not argued before the tribunal.[64]

7.50 We consider below in more detail the question of standard of proof in sports disciplinary rules. Traditionally, burdens imposed on defendants are to prove facts (or negatives) on the balance of probabilities. The *Tharanga* case raised, but did not resolve, the issue whether higher standards can be imposed on players, perhaps even the highest standard in use: that of proof beyond reasonable doubt. We are not aware of any authority bearing on the point, which may one day have to be looked at by the CAS or a national court.

Interpretation of Disciplinary Rules

7.51 Assuming, then, that the rules in question are valid and that the disciplinary body charged with enforcing them is properly constituted, the next question is what the rules mean on their true construction. Again, the interpretation of valid rules is a matter, in the first instance, for the sporting body applying them, but always subject to the non-excludable power of the court to review the correctness of that body's interpretation.[65] The body considering the meaning of the rules it is applying must arrive at the correct interpretation of them, on pain of correction by a court. It follows that such a body must necessarily entertain submissions as to the true meaning of its disciplinary rules. This can create difficulty in cases where that meaning is opaque and the tribunal lacks a legally

---

[62] As the former world number one tennis player Martina Hingis unsuccessfully attempted to do after testing positive for cocaine, leading to a two year disqualification: see *ITF v Hingis*, Anti-Doping Tribunal, 3 January 2008.

[63] Anti-Doping Tribunal, 15 July 2011, para 81.

[64] The relevant ICC rule mirrors the WADC at 10.4: 'To justify any elimination or reduction, the Athlete or other Person must produce corroborating evidence in addition to his or her word which establishes to the comfortable satisfaction of the hearing panel the absence of an intent to enhance sport performance or mask the use of a performance-enhancing substance ...'

[65] See *Lee v The Showmen's Guild of Great Britain* [1952] 2 QB 329, CA.

qualified member or access to legal advice, while the player may be legally represented or, if not, may nonetheless be advancing submissions formulated by a lawyer.

7.52 Thus in *Stewart v Judicial Committee of the Auckland Racing Club Inc*[66] the question arose as to whether, in a three-tier system with two successive rights of appeal, the function of the appellate bodies was confined to reviewing the fairness of the initial hearing, or whether the appeals, or either of them, should proceed as a full re-hearing and, if so, whether the appellate bodies should receive fresh evidence. Hillyer J held that the rules must be construed so as to accord fairness to the accused overall and that, in view of time constraints preventing full examination of the issue at the initial hearing, any appeal should be by way of re-hearing and not merely review. In consequence he set aside the decisions of all three domestic bodies, the effect of which was to impose a three-month ban on a jockey for failing to ride a horse on its merits. Incidentally, the relevant rule empowered the stewards to disqualify the horse as well as the rider; a point of potential significance since horses can change jockeys just as jockeys can change horses. It is possible to envisage a jockey arguing that his horse was unruly and that it, not the jockey, was responsible for a disciplinary offence being committed.

7.53 The case shows how a domestic body may have to rule on a procedural submission by the accused. He sought to introduce two affidavits not available at the initial hearing which had taken place shortly after the race. The first appeal body refused to admit the affidavits and declined even to read them. Had its role been confined to a review of the fairness of the initial hearing, that position would have been tenable. But the court subsequently held that the initial hearing was too cursory to warrant interpretation of the rules governing appeal in that restricted way. Not for the first time a sporting body fell into the error of interpreting its own rules less favourably to the accused than was consistent with fairness.

7.54 A more straightforward example of a sporting tribunal misunderstanding and misapplying its own rules occurred in *Jockey Club of South Africa v Forbes*.[67] The Transvaal and Orange Free State Stipendiary Stirrups Board had charged a racehorse trainer with being party to the administration of a prohibited substance to a horse. An alternative, less serious charge was being the trainer of a horse in respect of which an analytical test disclosed the presence of the prohibited substance. Under what the court described as 'an elaborate system of inter-meshing measures', the rules provided for urine samples taken from the horse to be split into two. The trainer could insist on analysis of one of the two samples at a laboratory selected by him so that the rules made the analyst's certificate conclusive proof of the result of the analysis. But no such 'conclusive proof' provision applied to the other sample, which it fell to the Board's scientists to analyse.

7.55 Both specimens were apparently found to contain naproxen, a banned substance. But the Board's decision to convict of the more serious offence of being party to the administration of a banned substance was quashed. The court observed that in the case of the more serious offence, the correctness of the analysis of the sample had to be proved, and the Board could not rely on the conclusiveness of the certificate provided

---

[66] [1992] 3 NZLR 693.
[67] (1993) (1) SA 648; the Appellate Division of Witwatersrand said that the tribunal had 'fundamentally misconceived the scope of the inquiries and hearings to be conducted', per Kriegler AJA at 633.

by the analyst nominated by the trainer, as it could have done to support a conviction for the lesser offence. The court was sympathetic to the trainer's contention that he had been charged under the wrong rule and that as a result the Board had not considered the substance of his defence, namely his denial that the specimens contained naproxen. The result may seem favourable to the trainer, but the principle is sound. The difference between knowingly administering a banned substance to a horse, and unwittingly training a horse to which someone else has administered a banned substance, may mean the difference between destruction of a livelihood and reputation, and mere technical liability. If the Board had accepted the certificate of its scientists as merely prima facie, rebuttable evidence instead of regarding it as conclusive, the trainer might well have had grave difficulty refuting the proposition that the samples did indeed contain naproxen.

7.56 In a case involving top level football in England, a disciplinary commission of the Football Association, and a subsequently convened board of appeal, wrongly interpreted a rule allowing the Football League (as then constituted) to order compensation to be paid by one club to another in a case of unlawful lack of transparency in a player's contract of service. The FA's disciplinary organs had purported to impose disciplinary sanctions on the offending club, while the rule in question, as an ad hoc arbitration panel subsequently held, created a civil remedy in favour of one club and against another and was not a disciplinary rule at all. It followed that the disciplinary bodies had erred in law in taking into account such lack of transparency when deciding upon the penalties to be imposed; which penalties the arbitrators subsequently reduced substantially.[68] The result of the subsequent arbitration proceedings was critical to the club's future and that of its players and staff. No case, in our experience, better illustrates the necessity for intellectual rigour, application of legal principle, and access to sound advice, when a sporting tribunal has to construe its own rules in the exercise of its punitive jurisdiction.

7.57 In a series of pre-WADC cases decided by the CAS the correct interpretation of anti-doping provisions has been debated. The principal issue has been whether particular rules under consideration create a 'strict liability' offence of ingesting a banned substance, or whether knowledge of ingesting and/or intention to ingest the substance must additionally be proved. Strict liability doping offences are not necessarily invalid as contractual terms on public policy grounds, since performance-enhancing drugs confer an unfair advantage even if taken accidentally or without intent to gain advantage.[69] The uniform regime in the WADC has diminished the importance of these early cases as precedents, but they helped to mould the CAS's approach to the interpretation of disciplinary rules and remain of importance in non-doping cases or in the increasingly rare doping cases where the Code does not apply.

7.58 The precise elements of a doping offence, like any other offence, must be derived from a correct construction of the rules in play. It follows that differently drafted rules may produce different results on the same or similar facts. In *USA Shooting and Quigley v Union Internationale de Tir*[70] the CAS, applying Swiss law, overturned the decision of the UIT to ban Mr Quigley for three months and to strip his team of its victory in one of the

---

[68] Two of the authors were instructed for the successful club, but are not free to write about the details.
[69] See para 7.39.
[70] CAS 94/129.

shooting events at the 1994 Cairo World Cup. The UIT had accepted that Mr Quigley had not intended to take ephedrine and other banned substances present in certain medication prescribed for his bronchitis. But it acted on a misconstruction of the UIT's anti-doping rule which included a definition of doping that included reference to 'the aim of attaining an increase in performance'. The case is best known for the dictum which the CAS has itself subsequently cited many times:

> The fight against doping is arduous, and it may require strict rules. But the rule-makers and the rule-appliers must begin by being strict with themselves. Regulations that may affect careers of dedicated athletes must be predictable. They must emanate from duly authorised bodies. They must be adopted in constitutionally proper ways. They should not be the product of an obscure process of accretion. Athletes and officials should not be confronted with a thicket of mutually qualifying or even contradictory rules that can be understood only on the basis of the de facto practice over the course of many years of a small number of insiders.

7.59 An asthmatic Finnish swimmer named Lehtinen also succeeded in having a two-year ban set aside by the CAS, though he failed in his claim for damages. Again applying Swiss law, the CAS appeared to accept that the rule in question could properly be characterised as one of strict liability. Despite that, it held that the mere presence of salbutamol in urine or blood was insufficient to establish a doping offence in view of the limited exception in the international association's rules where salbutamol is inhaled. The CAS held that the association must prove additionally that the use of salbutamol was not justified by medical necessity, or that it had not been taken by inhalation. The argument mainly centred on the effect of a requirement on team doctors wishing to administer, inter alia, salbutamol to notify the Medical Commission of the IOC in writing. The CAS held that the requirement of prior notification was a precondition of the player's right to invoke the exception to the ban on salbutamol. On the facts, that requirement had been complied with. Interestingly, this had the consequence that 'there is no need to examine whether the [association's] doping rules themselves comply with the applicable (ie Swiss) law'.[71]

7.60 But the National Wheelchair Basketball Association of the USA was less fortunate in its challenge to the decision of the predecessor body to the International Paralympic Committee to disallow the victory of the US basketball team over the Netherlands at the 1992 Barcelona Paralympic Games. One of the US team took a painkiller containing a banned substance and tested positive immediately after the championship final. The CAS distinguished the *Quigley* case on the ground that the rules there created an offence of intention, while those applying in the case before it did not and 'no one subject to the [relevant] Rules could come to the conclusion that they would excuse the *inadvertent* ingestion of banned substances'.[72] The CAS interpreted the relevant rules as creating strict liability even though there was no explicit definition of doping at all and the rules provided only for sanctions in respect of those 'guilty of doping'. The CAS commented adversely on such an example of 'drafting that engenders controversy'[73] and refused the IPC its costs.

---

[71] *Lehtinen v Fédération Internationale de Natation Amateur*, CAS 95/142, para 59 at p 19.
[72] *National Wheelchair Basketball Association v International Paralympic Committee*, CAS, 95/122, para 32 at p 9; emphasis in original.
[73] Ibid, para 35, p 10.

7.61 An intermediate position is occupied by rules which, on their true construction, contain a rebuttable presumption of guilt arising from the presence in the body of a prohibited substance. Such was the conclusion of the CAS in the case of a French swimmer, Mlle Chagnaud, who appealed against a two-year ban imposed by the international federation (FINA) of which the French Swimming Federation was a member. The relevant anti-doping provision contained an explicit definition unmistakably couched in the language of strict liability.[74] The CAS approved the use of strict liability rules irrespective of any question of guilty intent.[75] Despite this, the CAS construed the rules in favour of the swimmer, relying on previous flexibility exercised by FINA in applying them. There was evidence that FINA had previously allowed a swimmer to adduce exculpatory evidence disproving fault, deliberately ignoring the letter of its rules. Accordingly the CAS would have allowed Mlle Chagnaud to rebut the presumption of deliberate ingestion, but held on the facts that she had failed to do so.

7.62 The previous case which the CAS had in mind related to another swimmer, Samantha Riley. Ms Riley had escaped with a warning after testing positive for propoxyphene metabolite. FINA instead imposed a two-year ban on her coach, a Mr Volkers, who admitted giving Ms Riley the analgesic painkiller which caused her positive test. The ban was then shortened to one year. Mr Volkers appealed against it. The CAS applied 'the rules of FINA and … general principles of law', having heard citations of Swiss and Australian law in argument. It decided that the rule created strict liability for a coach as well as a swimmer, and dismissed Mr Volkers' appeal against FINA's finding of guilt.[76]

7.63 The decision is difficult to square with that in *Chagnaud*. The former case is best seen as an interesting example of the effect that prior custom and practice may have on the correct interpretation of disciplinary rules. FINA's failure to discipline Ms Riley on the basis of strict liability was invoked in support of a construction favourable to the swimmer and at odds with the plain meaning of the words creating a strict liability offence. Similarly, in English law, the interpretation of contractual terms, including disciplinary rules, may be informed by past custom and practice, but only to the extent that the meaning of the words in question is unclear or ambiguous.

7.64 Then in *Cullwick v FINA*,[77] a New Zealand water polo player tested positive for salbutamol at Dunkirk in July 1995 and appealed against a two-year ban, again on the basis of ingestion by inhalation pursuant to medical necessity. The CAS considered Mr Cullwick's submission that prior notification to a relevant authority of the medical necessity to inhale salbutamol was a freestanding obligation but not a precondition of the swimmer's right to invoke the exception to the ban on salbutamol. But the submission was rejected in favour of a purposive construction which drew inspiration from the *Quigley* case. The *Lehtinen* case was held distinguishable in that there had been evidence in that case of prior written notification to the relevant authority by the athlete's doctor.[78]

---

[74] See *Chagnaud v FINA*, CAS 95/141, para 4, p 7: 'the identification of a banned substance … in a competitor's urine or blood sample will constitute an offence …'

[75] Citing Dallèves, Conférence Droit et Sport, CAS 1993, p 26.

[76] *Volkers v FINA*, CAS 95/150.

[77] CAS 96/149, presided over by one of the authors.

[78] Ibid, paras 5.7 and 5.9, pp 19 and 20; evidencing the early growth of an incipient body of precedent, now much more developed, in the CAS jurisprudence. See now *Mrs Michelle Smith de Bruin v FINA*, CAS 98/211.

7.65 The cases just mentioned established that strict liability doping offences are accept-able and indeed regarded as appropriate by the highest international sporting judicial authorities. This is now a commonplace in the many cases governed by the WADC. But those same authorities are loath to allow such rules to operate unfairly so as to punish the innocent in a case where the rules themselves are unclear or their applicability to the facts of the case doubtful. Questions of interpretation will continue to be raised in non-doping cases, and in doping cases too despite the advent of the WADC with its system of uniform offences and defences. The following more recent examples demonstrate the continuing relevance of rule interpretation in sports disciplinary jurisprudence.

7.66 In certain disciplinary proceedings not in the public domain, a male coach was charged with breaching the terms of his coaching licence by conducting what was said to be an inappropriate sexual relationship with a female athlete, coached by him, who was aged 22 at the relevant time. The conditions attached to the licence included a prohibition against conducting inappropriate intimate relationships with child athletes aged under 18, and 'strongly recommended' that a coach should not conduct such a relationship where the athlete is aged over 18. A disciplinary panel banned the coach for 10 years, which was reduced to five years on appeal.

7.67 The appeal panel rejected the coach's arguments that sexual relations fall within the sphere of private life to which respect must be accorded under Article 8 of the European Convention—indeed, he could have married the athlete since, as it happened, he was unmarried; that it was not the governing body's business to interfere in the private lives of coaches and athletes engaging in sexual relations between consenting adults; and that the rules did not support the charge because they only recommended refraining from intimate relationships in the case of adults, and did not (and indeed could not) prohibit such relationships. The case was complicated by a bitter factual dispute about the extent to which the athlete remained a willing sexual partner, but was not decided on the basis that she was coerced.

7.68 The decision was controversial and its correctness is not beyond all doubt, but funding problems prevented a further challenge, which could ultimately have led in the direction of the Strasbourg court. The case shows how difficult it can be to define the scope of general provisions making it a disciplinary offence to engage in conduct likely to bring a sport into disrepute, or which bring discredit on the accused. It is not sug-gested that such general forms of disciplinary offence are impermissible. Indeed they are often thought necessary to protect the reputation of sport. It is not wrong in princi-ple for a sports body to condemn a player under a rule prohibiting him from bringing his sport into disrepute, where the player has (for example) taken part in an unseemly bar brawl after a match. The disciplinary system would be unworkable if the rules had to create a specific offence for every type of conduct having the effect of bringing the sport into disrepute.

7.69 Where the alleged misconduct is on the border between acceptable and unacceptable behaviour, a disciplinary panel may have a difficult task deciding the breadth of a general prohibition on misconduct. In a borderline case the athlete may have to resort to invoking the *contra proferentem* principle, whereby in a case of ambiguity a rule—particularly one with penal consequences—should be construed against the drafter of the rule. However, in our experience that principle is much more frequently relied on by accused sportsmen and women than used as a basis for decisions of disciplinary panels.

7.70 Other issues of rule interpretation have had to be decided in the context of doping. In *Puerta v ITF*,[79] the CAS upheld the ITF's submission that a second doping offence for the purposes of the WADC, which carried a higher period of ineligibility, included an offence which was the first committed under the Code itself, but where a previous doping offence had been committed by the same player under the predecessor provisions of the then disciplinary code of the ATP. In *ITF v Bogomolov*,[80] the anti-doping tribunal accepted that the question whether results subsequent to the event producing a positive test should be disqualified (with loss of prize money and ranking points), while requiring a factual enquiry in each case, must start from the premise that such disqualification is the norm and not the exception, for otherwise the relevant rule would have been drafted the other way round, so as to make non-disqualification the norm unless the tribunal considers that fairness requires disqualification.[81]

7.71 Another vexed question of interpretation in the anti-doping field is whether under the WADC a player can intend to enhance sport performance (which he must prove he did not intend, if he is to benefit from reduced sanction provisions in cases of 'specified substances') through the ingestion of a prohibited substance if the athlete is unaware that he has ingested the substance in question; for example, because it is concealed within a dietary supplement of whose ingredients the player is ignorant. The submission that the player cannot so intend is founded on the controversial decision of the CAS in *Flavia Oliveira v USADA*[82] but is inconsistent with the subsequent decision of the CAS sitting in Sydney in *Kurt Foggo v National Rugby League*, where the court declined to follow *Oliveira*.[83]

7.72 Domestic anti-doping tribunals faced with that inconsistent CAS authority have gone both ways.[84] Most recently, in *UCI v Alexander Kolobnev and Russian Cycling Federation*[85] the CAS concurred with the reasoning in *Oliveira*, largely exonerating a Russian cyclist who had taken a dietary supplement without knowing that it contained a banned substance. In *ITF v Kutrovsky* a tribunal presided over by one of the authors

---

[79] 2006/A/1025, 12 July 2006; [2006] ISLR, SLR 149.

[80] Anti-Doping Tribunal decision, 26 September 2005, para 109.

[81] A subsequent rule amendment required the tribunal not to found its decision solely on the absence of unfair sporting advantage to the player when deciding whether to disqualify results in events subsequent to that which produced the positive test: see *ITF v Dupuis*, Anti-Doping Tribunal, 29 September 2006; cf the discussion in *Hipperdinger v ATP Tour Inc*, CAS 2004/A/690, paras 93–101: the CAS panel expressed concern (para 97) that a player should not be penalised for exercising, without any abuse of rights, the right to continue competing where the rules do not provide for provisional suspension and that 'the application of the fairness exception must not be weakened by the application of a very stringent standard of proof'; otherwise there would be a risk of a period of ineligibility which is de facto longer than the maximum provided for under the relevant rules.

[82] CAS 2010/A/2107, given in Lausanne on 10 December 2010 (see at paras 9.9–9.21).

[83] CAS A2/2011: see paras 35–36 and 45–47.

[84] See *IRB v Duncan Murray*, Board Judicial Committee, 27 January 2012, para 47–75, preferring the approach in *Oliveira* and, at para 58, applying the 'principle of interpretation ... that where words may bear two constructions, the more reasonable one, that which produces a fair result, should be preferred' and noting at para 75 that the *Oliveira* approach 'has found favour with at least one other CAS panel, in *WADA v FIV & Berrios*, CAS 2010/A/2229 (at §83); ... and in *UKAD v Dooler*, UKNADP (2010) ...'. The point was deliberately left open in *ICC v Tharanga*, Anti-Doping Tribunal, 15 July 2011, where it was unnecessary to resolve it (see paras 78–79); and in *UKAD v Gleeson*, National Anti-Doping Panel, 13 June 2011 (Charles Flint QC, chairman), where, however, at para 61 the panel expressed the strong view (obiter) that: 'If a player takes a tablet intending that it will enhance his sport performance then he has the intent to use whatever is in the tablet for that purpose. He is not required to have in mind the chemical composition of what he ingests.'

[85] CAS 2011/A/2645, 29 February 2012, see paras 79–83.

commented that while the *Oliveira* approach had the edge at present in the CAS case law, the issue was not concluded and was not yet firmly established jurisprudence.[86]

7.73 Two further examples of difficult interpretation questions confronting disciplinary tribunals will suffice to illustrate the types of issue that can arise. The first concerns the troublesome question of backdating of periods of ineligibility in doping cases, where a player has voluntarily abstained from competition after being notified of a positive test result, during the run-up to the hearing before an anti-doping tribunal. In *ICC v Tharanga*[87] this question arose because the ICC Code, modelled on the WADA Code, provided that where the player promptly (and before competing again) admits the doping offence after being confronted with it, the tribunal may backdate the start of the period of ineligibility as far back as the date of the sample collection, provided that the commencement date may not be backdated such that the player 'actually serves less than one-half of that period', ie the period of ineligibility.

7.74 Does that mean that where the preconditions are met, a tribunal may backdate the start of a ban so that it covers a period while the player was still playing, but only if the player does not play competitively for at least half the total period of the ban? Or does it mean that where the preconditions are met, a tribunal may backdate the start of a ban but only so that it covers a period at least half of which predates the tribunal's decision and during no part of which the player was actually playing? In *Tharanga* the tribunal ultimately did not need to decide the point but noted that the former interpretation would remove some of the obscurity of certain earlier similar rules which left unclear the question whether a tribunal could or should ban a player retrospectively in respect of a period when he was still playing, which in turn leads to complications and artificiality with regard to performance statistics, prize money and ranking points; while the latter interpretation appears to give too much significance to the date of the tribunal's decision, delay in production of which is also (by other provisions) relevant.[88]

7.75 Secondly, tribunals interpreting the WADC and its derivatives in individual sports have had to contend with the provision that the sole criterion for determining the length of a ban for ingesting a specified substance, the player having proved how it entered his or her body and that it was ingested without intent to enhance sport performance, is the degree of the player's fault. This has the surprising consequence that a player's contrition or otherwise is irrelevant to the length of the ban she must serve in such a case. Nothing is gained by apologising except the goodwill of the tribunal and the governing body and, possibly, an earlier start date for the period of ineligibility.[89]

---

[86] ITF Anti-Doping Tribunal, 15 May 2012 (Tim Kerr QC sitting alone), para 71.

[87] Anti-Doping Tribunal, 15 July 2011, see paras 98–104.

[88] The equivalent provisions in the WADC are differently phrased and also difficult to follow. They include a separate article (Art 10.9.4) which corresponds approximately to Art 10.9.3 of the ICC Code and gives an athlete credit for time voluntarily served before the tribunal's decision. The commentary to the WADC indicates that Art 10.9.2 'shall not apply where the period of ineligibility already has been reduced under Article 10.5.4'.

[89] The tribunal in *ICC v Tharanga* (n 84) accepted 'with some reluctance' the ICC's submission to that effect: see para 97. See also *ICC v Smartt*, Anti-Doping Tribunal, 14 December 2011, paras 86–89, holding that it was a matter 'of very limited weight' that the player must, on her own evidence, have been doped in a match prior to that which produced the positive test result, in respect of which she had not been charged, having taken the offending single dose of the prohibited substance before *both* matches.

Evidence and Proof

7.76 In the first part of this chapter we looked at the legal requirement that the rules operated by a disciplining body must be valid, and that the body applying them must be properly constituted and must interpret them correctly. In this next section, we consider the factual material on which a sporting tribunal exercising punitive jurisdiction may lawfully rely in support of a finding of guilt. In some cases disciplinary tribunals have sought to make findings of guilt and impose penalties in consequence, on the basis of evidence whose nature and sufficiency is subsequently put in issue in a legal challenge before the courts.

7.77 The starting point here is the proposition that the disciplinary tribunal, like all domestic tribunals, must have some evidence before it supporting a finding of guilt, if such a finding is to be lawful; but that the weight to be placed on such evidence is a matter for the tribunal and not the court.[90] English law insists on autonomy of decision making for domestic tribunals, including those concerned with discipline in the sporting field, provided the tribunal has some evidence before it to support its finding, and provided (as explained above) it applies valid rules correctly interpreted.[91]

7.78 Nor is such a tribunal likely to be bound by the strict rules of evidence that apply in English courts. This has the consequence that a sporting disciplinary tribunal may accept hearsay evidence without the procedural requirements of the Civil Evidence Acts 1968 and 1995, and of rules of court.[92] Thus the tribunal may generally receive evidence in written form without cross-examination, even in the case of expert evidence. However, the latitude allowed to such disciplinary tribunals is always qualified by the duty to act fairly. If the nature of evidence received and relied upon by the tribunal is such as to compromise the duty of fairness, the resulting decision could later be set aside in court; for example, where evidence relating to the scientific appropriateness of laboratory procedures in a doping case is given by a secretary at the laboratory with no scientific qualification.

7.79 Expert evidence is particularly important in doping cases, but can also bear on other issues. A notorious example was the expert evidence of Mr Bob Wilson, the famous broadcaster and former Arsenal goalkeeper, on the issue whether video footage supported the contention that another goalkeeper had or had not deliberately failed to save certain goals. Any expert called upon to give evidence before a sporting disciplinary tribunal should bear in mind the requirements of impartiality and independence, in England now set out in the form of the declaration of independence and impartiality found in Part 35

---

[90] *Dawkins v Antrobus* (1881) 17 Ch Div 615, CA, per James LJ at 626–8, Brett LJ at 630 and 633, Cotton LJ at 633–4; *Faramus v Film Artistes Association* [1964] AC 925 at 941–2 per Lord Evershed, and at 944–8 per Lords Hodson and Pearce; *Lee v The Showmen's Guild of Great Britain* [1952] 2 QB 329, CA, per Denning LJ at 342–4.

[91] Thus, in *N, J, Y, W v FINA*, CAS 98/208, para 40, the CAS panel commented: 'In reaching the conclusion that the offence was committed, and that the Appellants had not discharged the burden which lay upon them to mitigate the maximum sanction of two years, the Panel have borne in mind that all the swimmers have denied on affidavit that they took Triamterene. The Panel has treated that evidence as if it had been given on oath. However, it is regrettable that the currency of such denial is devalued by the fact that it is the common coin of the guilty as well as of the innocent.' At a hearing in June 2006 behind closed doors, a sports disciplinary body likened that passage to an earlier obiter dictum of Miss Mandy Rice-Davies, whose celebrated comment in the witness box when told that Lord Astor had denied having an affair with her was: 'Well he would [say that], wouldn't he.'

[92] See Part 33 of the Civil Procedure Rules 1998.

of the Civil Procedure Rules 1998, which were influenced by the seminal guidance of Cresswell J on the duties of an expert: to be and be seen to be independent; to provide an objective unbiased opinion; to state the facts or assumptions on which that opinion is based; to volunteer material facts which detract from his opinion; to delineate clearly his area of expertise and identify any issue falling outside it; to distinguish between concluded opinions and provisional ones; and to communicate to the other side and the tribunal any change of view on a material point, arising, for example, from availability of new material.[93]

7.80 The practicalities of obtaining expert evidence are of vital importance to both sides in sporting disciplinary proceedings. The duty of the tribunal to act fairly and impartially, and to decide the case on the evidence before it, may mean that the absence of any, or of adequate, expert evidence leads to the acquittal of the guilty or, worse, the conviction of the innocent. In a doping case, for instance, expert evidence may be necessary to determine whether a sample has been taken properly so as to exclude the risk of contamination from outside; or to establish whether subsequent testing procedures are scientifically adequate. Expert evidence is not, however, necessary to establish whether a sample subsequently tested is that of the accused athlete at all. That issue can be determined by examining the chain of custody of the sample and, if the chain is a long one and the sample has passed through several hands, the absence of a lay witness through whose hands it has passed may be telling. Among the disciplines involved in doping cases we may find chromatography, mass spectrometry, pharmaceutical science, toxicology and steroid endocrinology. Such narrowly focused specialisms require great care in the choice of expert.

7.81 The next question that may arise is this: which party bears the onus of proving guilt, or of proving a particular factual point relevant to guilt? We have already commented that an outright reversal of the presumption of innocence, written into the rules of a sporting body, would be unlikely to survive a judicial challenge in English law. We now look more closely at the incidence of the burden of proof in sporting disciplinary proceedings. The starting point is the normal rule that a party asserting the existence of a particular fact bears the onus of proving that fact. But that rule may be modified or displaced by the effect of disciplinary rules creating presumptions or reversing the onus of proof on a particular issue, provided that the effect of any such modification is not to create a presumption of guilt. Thus in a doping case, the onus must be on the association bringing the case to prove the presence of a banned substance in the athlete's body. But the association's disciplinary rules may also require that ingestion of the substance occurred voluntarily and/or with intent to gain advantage, so that the case is not one of strict liability. In that event, the rules may also create a presumption that ingestion occurred voluntarily and with intent to gain advantage, arising on proof of the presence of the substance in the body, unless the athlete can show the contrary—for example, by producing a witness who says he 'laced' the athlete's drink, or similar evidence.

---

[93] *The Ikarian Reefer* [1993] 2 Lloyd's Rep 68 (reversed on appeal on an unrelated point). On video evidence see Gardiner, *The Third Eye: Video Adjudication in Sport* (1994) 2(1) SLB. Video evidence is standard in disciplinary cases. Witness evidence is often taken by video link across frontiers, oceans and continents. In *Rezaeipoor v Arabhalvai* [2012] EWHC 146 (Ch), Kevin Prosser QC (sitting as a deputy judge of the High Court) upheld the decision of a Master to permit the giving of evidence via Skype link from Iran, with an interpreter.

7.82 English law does not find objectionable *per se* the placing on the accused of the onus of proving a specific factual defence.[94] Nor, as already explained, need the rules afford such a defence at all.[95] The WADC now provides for strict liability offences subject to uniform defences which are considered separately below.[96] In an early case, the IAAF established that its rules create a strict liability doping offence.[97] The Federation, in its argument in support of a strict liability construction, assured the tribunal that if an athlete was bound and gagged and forcibly injected with a prohibited substance, the Federation would not prosecute. However, if the knowledge and intention of the athlete are truly irrelevant, and if the justification for strict liability is the gaining of unfair advantage, then it is difficult to see why an 'innocent' athlete in whose body the prohibited substance is present should not suffer disqualification on the reasoning in *Gasser v Stinson*.[98]

7.83 There was a debate during the 1990s as to whether the presence of a prohibited substance in a player's body itself provided prima facie evidence of fault or of intent to gain a sporting advantage.[99] Where the WADC applies, this debate is now redundant as the Code clearly distinguishes between presence of a substance in the body, and the separate issues of fault and intent to gain advantage. It is well established, in any case, that presence or otherwise of a substance in an athlete's body is a question of pure fact and has no necessary connection with intent or fault. Thus the IAAF panel dealing with the issue of presence stated without any misdirection that 'no mental element of intent or negligence has been taken into consideration'.[100]

7.84 The importance of the question of where the onus of proving a particular point lies is not confined to doping cases. For example, where a Premiership football club admitted cancelling a fixture with another club, which constituted a disciplinary offence under the relevant rules unless there was 'just cause' for cancelling the match, an issue arose as to the onus of proof in respect of 'just cause'. The gist of the offence was cancellation of the fixture, which the association would have to prove in the normal way. In the event it did not have to do so since cancellation of the match was admitted by the club. The onus clearly lay on the club to show just cause, though the rules in question did not explicitly say so. It was because the club was asserting 'just cause' that it had to prove it. It was not for the association to show lack of 'just cause' for cancelling the fixture. The club's attempt to discharge the onus upon it failed and it suffered a penalty in consequence.[101]

7.85 Finally on this topic, we should mention one other point. The concept of the onus of proof is not wholly apt in the context of bodies which exercise inquisitorial, as opposed to adversarial, disciplinary jurisdiction. Some sporting bodies' rules still make provision to the effect that a committee of enquiry shall enquire into the matters alleged and may, if

---

[94] Malek, *Phipson on Evidence*, 17th edn (Sweet & Maxwell, 2010) paras 6-12, 6-33–6-48; *Wilander v Tobin (No 1)* (1996) unreported, 26 March, CA.

[95] See para 7.57.

[96] See para 7.222.

[97] *Re Dean Capobianco*, Arbitration Award of 17 March 1997.

[98] (1988) unreported, 15 June, Scott J.

[99] See Tarasti, *Strict Liability in Doping Cases in the Light of Decisions made by the Arbitration Panel of the IAAF* (conference paper, 1997).

[100] *Re Dean Capobianco*, Arbitration Award of 17 March 1997.

[101] *Middlesbrough FC Ltd*, Premier League disciplinary proceedings and appeal, 1997, in which two of the authors were involved; see also the *Lehtinen* case, CAS 95/142, in which the athlete accepted the onus of rebutting the prima facie case against him arising from his admission of a positive test.

of the view that they are well-founded, impose appropriate sanctions. Other bodies' rules provide for the classical English adversarial model of proceedings, with a 'prosecutor' and a 'defence'. To the extent that such a tribunal conducts itself in an inquisitorial manner, in the tradition of the civil law jurisdictions, the utility of the concept of onus of proof may be undermined. A fact finding body conducting an enquiry as to the truth of matters under investigation will decide for itself where the truth lies, and may do so without necessarily engaging in a comparison of the relative strengths of the cases presented by each party. Thus it may decide the issue without recourse to the question of onus at all. Subject always to the duty to hear both sides, there is nothing objectionable in such an approach.[102]

Standard of Proof

7.86 The next question to consider is that of the standard of proof, a question which arises whether the body concerned is conducting itself adversarially, inquisitorially or somewhere between the two. In proceedings conducted adversarially, the civil standard of proof on the balance of probabilities expresses the weight of evidence required to succeed in making good the charge. To the extent that proceedings are conducted in an inquisitorial manner, the civil standard of proof is a measure of the standard imposed by the disciplinary tribunal on itself.

7.87 Here the position in English law is tolerably clear. Unless the relevant rules provide otherwise, the standard of proof under disciplinary or other rules administered by sporting bodies is the normal civil standard, that is to say, proof on the balance of probabilities or, to put it another way, that it is more likely than not that the factual state of affairs in question obtains. The standard of proof before a domestic tribunal in proceedings governed by English law, including proceedings before sporting disciplinary or other tribunals, is not the criminal standard of proof beyond reasonable doubt. The contrary view once appeared to have some currency[103] but is inconsistent with the weight of authority in England.[104]

7.88 Application of the criminal standard of proof is unnecessary; the view that fairness calls for the criminal standard confuses the standard of proof with the weight of evidence required to meet that standard. In English law, the courts may accept that in a particular factual context, the more serious the misconduct alleged, the more cogent must be the evidence required to meet the civil standard of proof and thus to discharge the onus of proof. That view proceeds from the common sense proposition that it is inherently less likely—or so we must hope—that a person will commit a grave wrong than a trivial

---

[102] Cf *R (CJ) v Cardiff City Council* [2011] EWCA Civ 1590 (onus of proof not an appropriate concept in the context of an enquiry into the age of an illegal entrant to the UK, ie whether over or under 18).

[103] See, eg, Morton-Hooper, *Sporting Disciplinary Proceedings in Practice—the Participant's View*, Sports Forum 1996, conference paper, pp 15–17.

[104] See *Phipson on Evidence* (n 93) para 6-55; *Re B (Children)* [2009] 1 AC 11, HL, and the cases therein cited; *R (A) v Independent Appeal Panel for the London Borough of Sutton* [2009] ELR 321 (Hickinbottom J); *Dadourian Group International Inc v Sims* [2009] 1 Lloyd's Rep 601, per Arden LJ at para 32; and *Wanjiku v Secretary of State for the Home Department* [2011] EWCA Civ 264; cf the now doubtful authority of *Campbell v Hamlet* [2005] UKPC 19.

wrong. The practice of the civil courts in England of recognising a connection between the gravity of the charge and the weight of the evidence required to prove it on the balance of probabilities, has on occasion led to the fallacious proposition that the criminal standard of proof must be met even in civil proceedings (which sporting disciplinary proceedings are) where the conduct of which the accused stands charged is a criminal or other gravely wrongful act.

7.89 In international sports disciplinary tribunals the standard is now formulated differently. In one of the early cases heard by the Ad Hoc Division of the CAS at Atlanta in 1996, the CAS referred to a requirement of 'comfortable satisfaction' as the standard necessary to establish commission of a doping offence with which two Russian athletes stood charged. The CAS went on to reiterate the proposition that the more serious the allegation, the greater the degree of evidence required to achieve 'comfortable satisfaction'.[105] This is a higher standard than the civil standard applicable in English law domestic proceedings, and is now frequently found expressed in the disciplinary rules of sports bodies, including rules providing for English law to apply to the proceedings. It is also the standard of proof required in the WADC to prove that a doping offence has been committed. English law does not require such a high standard unless the relevant rules so provide.

7.90 Applying the 'comfortable satisfaction' standard may not, for a common lawyer initially unfamiliar with it, be comfortable at all, but familiarity breeds contentment. The standard of comfortable satisfaction has taken root in international sports jurisprudence and is now the standard most commonly applied by the CAS where the burden is on a body bringing an accusation. It is not, however, the universal standard. Usually, but not always, burdens imposed on the defence are to prove the relevant fact or matter on the balance of probabilities. And in relation to an accusation of corrupt behaviour, the Uniform Tennis Anti-Corruption Program, governed by Florida law, requires proof of a corruption offence 'by a preponderance of the evidence'.

7.91 In corruption cases, the standard of proof may be of critical importance because the allegations are likely to be of very serious wrongdoing and the evidence relied on may well, unless covertly obtained evidence such as sound recordings is relied upon, consist principally of reports of conversations between the accused and those he has, allegedly, tried to corrupt. Anti-corruption rules often place a duty on innocent players to report corrupt approaches such as invitations to fix a match. On examination, the standard of proof 'by a preponderance of the evidence', familiar to lawyers in Florida and elsewhere in the USA, does not appear to differ in substance from the ordinary English law civil standard of proof on the balance of probabilities.[106]

7.92 This state of affairs means that in the fight against corruption and match fixing in sport, arguably a greater scourge even than doping, proof to a lesser standard than that required to prove a doping offence is regarded as acceptable. The contrary proposition

---

[105] *Korneev and Russian NOC v IOC; Gouliev and Russian NOC v IOC*, reported in *Mealey's International Arbitration Report*, February 1997, pp 28–29; applied in *Wang v FINA*, CAS 98/208 (22 December 1998), para 5.6, describing the standard (as CAS has frequently done in other cases since) as 'less than criminal standard, but more than the ordinary civil standard'. Also, in *Mrs Michelle Smith de Bruin v FINA*, CAS 98/211, the CAS adopted the *Korneev* test at 10.2.

[106] See Broun, *McCormick on Evidence* (a reputable United States work), 6th edn (Thomson/West, 2006) paras 339–41.

is unlikely to be accepted: that in the context of a penal regime involving sanctions which threaten a player's livelihood and reputation and are likely to include allegations of criminal wrongdoing, the standard of proof should, however expressed, be akin to that of proof beyond reasonable doubt, applying the principle *in dubio pro reo*.

7.93 In the context of doping, the CAS in *Pechstein v International Skating Union*,[107] a case involving new methods for detecting prohibited substances, rejected the submission that allegations of doping are akin to criminal allegations and that the standard of 'comfortable satisfaction' must therefore be very close to the criminal standard of proof beyond reasonable doubt. Yet in some jurisdictions including that of England and Wales, and also in some states in the United States, it has been suggested, as already noted, that where the allegations of wrongdoing are particularly serious, more cogent evidence than usual is required even to satisfy the ordinary civil standard of proof on the balance of probabilities, or in Florida, by a preponderance of the evidence. As we have already pointed out, this should not be taken as illegitimately raising the standard in civil cases.[108]

7.94 The sport of cricket has recently seen penalties imposed on players in respect of allegations connected with match fixing or attempted match fixing. The Anti-Corruption Code for Players and Player Support Personnel, adopted by the International Cricket Council and governed by English law, expressly provides for the standard of 'comfortable satisfaction' to be applicable.[109]

7.95 Interestingly, the rules of the International Amateur Athletic Federation formerly included a provision requiring proof beyond reasonable doubt in doping cases. It was that provision which led Athletics Australia, a member of the IAAF, to acquit Mr Dean Capobianco of a doping offence in July 1996, shortly before the Atlanta Olympics in which he was due to compete. Athletics Australia dismissed the charge despite a positive test result, because of defects in the chain of custody of the relevant samples. The national tribunal held that it had not been shown beyond reasonable doubt that a doping offence had been committed.

7.96 However, following a reference to arbitration by the Federation, the arbitrators found (in the light of certain fresh evidence not previously available) that the chain of custody was complete and that there was no reasonable doubt that a doping offence had been committed. As the offence was one of strict liability, there was no room for the athlete to mount a defence of innocent ingestion through contaminated products. The

---

[107] CAS/2009/A/1912; see paras 123–6.

[108] Cf Lewis and Taylor, *Sport: Law and Practice*, 2nd edn (Tottel Publishing, 2008) A2.101, stating that while rules should define the standard of proof, '[t]he concept of satisfaction to the civil standard in the context of disciplinary offences involves a sliding scale: the more serious the offence, the greater the degree of satisfaction required. It has been argued that where the disciplinary offence discloses a criminal offence, the standard should be the equivalent of the criminal standard, but this may be putting it too high.' In the appeal of the Austrian tennis player Daniel Köllerer against his life ban, the CAS rejected the player's submission that the standard of proof should be higher than that of the preponderance of the evidence (press release of 23 March 2012 and CAS judgment, CAS 2011/A/2490).

[109] Para 3.1 of the ICC's Anti-Corruption Code adds the following gloss: '… the standard of proof in all cases brought under the Anti-Corruption Code shall be whether the Anti-Corruption Tribunal is comfortably satisfied, bearing in mind the seriousness of the allegation that is being made, that the alleged offence has been committed. This standard of proof in all cases shall be determined on a sliding scale from, at a minimum, a mere balance of probabilities (for the least serious offences) up to proof beyond a reasonable doubt (for the most serious offences).'

Federation also relied on the English law principle embodied in the Latin maxim *omnia rite praesumuntur esse*, otherwise known as the presumption of regularity, which holds that official acts are deemed to have been properly carried out unless the contrary can be shown.[110] However, the applicability of the presumption to official acts of an international sporting association is open to doubt and is not established authoritatively in English law.

7.97 If the sporting association in a disciplinary case is able to prove the primary fact constituting the offence (for example, presence of a banned substance in an athlete's body), but the accused seeks to discharge the onus of proving facts constituting a defence (for example, the means of innocent ingestion, absence of significant fault and absence of intent to enhance performance), the rules of many sports bodies now make express provision for what standard is to apply. Absent such express provision, the default standard must be that of proof on the balance of probabilities.[111] The exception, already noted, is that the WADC and its derivatives provide that an athlete must prove to the tribunal's comfortable satisfaction that he did not intend to enhance sport performance when ingesting a 'specified substance', for the purpose of achieving a reduction in the otherwise mandatory two-year period of ineligibility, for a first offence.

7.98 The importance of the point is evident, for an athlete may be able to show a *possibility* of innocent ingestion, yet be unable to prove that this possibility was more than just that, ie that innocent ingestion is more likely than not to be the explanation for a positive test result. In the pre-WADC jurisprudence the point arose, but was not tested fully on the facts, in *Wang Lu-Nuyeta v FINA*.[112] Chinese swimmers who had tested positive for triamtarene, a banned substance, appealed to the CAS against a two-year ban imposed by FINA, contending, inter alia, that a health food called actovegin could have been responsible for a false triamtarene reading. Rule DC9.3 of FINA's doping control rules provided that a finding of a banned substance present in the body 'shall shift to the competitor the burden of establishing why he or she should not be sanctioned'.

7.99 The majority of the CAS, applying Swiss law but with power to find the facts as well as the law and thus with 'its main focus ... on evidence before it', found that the evidence as to laboratory procedure was unimpeachable and that the swimmers could not raise a reasonable doubt that the substance detected might, in truth, be a substance other than triamtarene such as actovegin not containing triamtarene. The panel found that the presence of the banned substance was established beyond any reasonable doubt. The next question was whether triamtarene could actually be present in actovegin and thus be present as a result of innocently ingested actovegin, whose manufacturers denied that it contained triamtarene. On that question, the onus lay on the swimmers, but the panel held that rule DC9.3 was relevant to penalty, not to liability, and that in any case the swimmers would have to prove the point on the balance of probabilities, ie they would have to show that it was more likely than not that the presence of triamtarene in actovegin was the explanation for the positive test. On the facts, they failed to discharge this onus.

---

[110] See *R v Inland Revenue Commissioners, ex parte P C Coombs and Co* [1991] 2 AC 283, per Lord Lowry at 300C–F.

[111] See also to the same effect *Phipson on Evidence* (n 94) para 6-52.

[112] CAS 98/208, 22 December 1998.

7.100 Since the advent of the WADC, the CAS has emphasised many times that an athlete cannot discharge the onus of proving how a 'specified' prohibited substance entered his or her body merely by reasoning from a bare denial of having ingested the substance deliberately. The athlete must show by positive evidence, not merely speculation or deduction from a protestation of innocence, how the substance entered the player's system; and, the standard of proof being the balance of probabilities, must show that the innocent explanation advanced is more likely than not to be the correct one. To discharge that burden the player must show the factual circumstances in which the prohibited substance entered his or her system and not merely the route of administration.[113]

Procedural Fairness

7.101 Our account of the law relating to disciplinary procedures in sport continues with a brief exposition of the content of the rules of natural justice, or the duty of procedural fairness.[114] We have observed already that this duty can inform and influence the interpretation of disciplinary rules, which generally must be construed in conformity with the duty of procedural fairness and not in conflict with it, where the words so permit. If a disciplinary rule is itself, on its correct construction, inconsistent with the duty of fairness—for example, a rule which explicitly provides that an accused should have no right to be heard before determination of the charge against him—the rule will probably be held invalid by an English court on the basis that the rule making body cannot lawfully and constitutionally adopt unfair rules.

7.102 The point is not entirely clear since most disciplinary rules, as already explained, take effect as contractual terms. A duty of fairness is implied into contracts containing such terms, but in English contract law implied terms may be displaced by express ones. To preserve the integrity of the duty of fairness in disciplinary rules, the law may regard such rules as more than contractual terms, but as quasi-legislative in character. This approach protects the duty of fairness and accords with the celebrated analysis of Lord Denning MR in a seminal dissenting judgment.[115]

7.103 Putting aside the unlikely case of an attempt expressly to exclude the implied duty of fairness, we consider next what the true scope of that duty is. In one interlocutory appeal, the Court of Appeal declined to give a definitive answer to that difficult

---

[113] *WADA v Stanic and Swiss Olympic Association*, CAS 2006/A/1130, para 39; *Karatantcheva v ITF*, CAS 2006/A/1032, paras 98 and 117; *ITF v Karol Beck*, Anti-Doping Tribunal, 13 February 2006, paras 14 and 24; *ITF v Jamie Burdekin*, Anti-Doping Tribunal, 4 April 2005, para 76; *International Rugby Board v Keyter*, CAS/2006/A/1130, paras 6.10–6.12; *CCES v Lelièvre*, Sport Dispute Resolution Centre of Canada, 7 February 2005, para 51; *ITF v Martina Hingis*, Anti-Doping Tribunal, 3 January 2008, paras 151–3.

[114] See generally Parpworth, *Sports Governing Bodies and the Principles of Natural Justice: An Australian Perspective* (1996) 4(2) SLJ 5; Griffiths, *Procedural Fairness and Regulation of Sport: Lessons from the Common Law* [2009] ISLR 69.

[115] *Breen v Amalgamated Engineering Union* [1971] 2 QB 175, 189–91. However, Alan Sullivan QC, in *The Role of Contract in Sports Law* (2010) 5(1) Australia and New Zealand Sports Law Journal 3, points at p 23 to the words of Campbell J in the vividly named case of *McClelland v Burning Palms Surf Life Saving Club* (2002) 191 ALR 759, at 785: 'In Australia, the preferable view is that natural justice comes to operate in [sporting bodies] by the rules of those private organisations being construed on the basis that fair procedures are intended, but *recognising the possibility that express words or necessary implication in the rules could exclude natural justice in whole or in part*' (emphasis added).

question, but contemplated that the answer would vary according to the surrounding factual circumstances, including the rules of the body in question.[116] The celebrated athlete Diane Modahl sued the (then) British Athletic Federation for damages of about half a million pounds after samples she had given were reported to contain an impermissibly high ratio of testosterone to epitestosterone. She was initially suspended and subsequently banned following a hearing before a disciplinary committee of the Federation, but in 1995 her appeal was allowed by an Independent Appeal Panel and the ban was lifted. She alleged wrongful use of an unaccredited laboratory to test the samples and bias on the part of two members of the disciplinary committee. She claimed the expenses incurred in connection with the disciplinary hearing and the subsequent appeal, and loss of earnings during the period of her allegedly wrongful suspension from competition.

7.104 As Ms Modahl had been successful in her appeal, the Federation was able to argue that the disciplinary system had functioned correctly in protecting an athlete whose guilt could not be proved, the Independent Appeal Panel having accepted, on the basis of evidence not before the disciplinary committee, the possibility of degradation of the samples. The Federation applied on that ground, amongst others, to strike out the claim. The question of what term should be implied to give effect to the duty of fairness was among the points at issue. The Federation contended that the disciplinary proceedings would only be flawed if the proceedings as a whole, including the appeal, were unfair. On that basis there could not be a breach in view of the athlete's successful appeal. The athlete, however, contended for an implied term that the members of the disciplinary committee would act in good faith and would not be biased, a term she alleged was breached in the course of the initial hearing, the unfairness of which she submitted could not be cured by an appeal.

7.105 Lord Woolf MR mentioned the well-known case law establishing the proposition, in public as well as private law, that an appeal can cure defects in earlier proceedings if the result of the appeal is that the process, taken as a whole, was fair;[117] and the general reluctance of the English courts to become embroiled in sporting disputes.[118] He strongly hinted (in our respectful view correctly) that the Federation was correct in submitting that the court will not imply a term which goes beyond requiring the disciplinary process to be fair as a whole. He pointed to the structure of the Federation's rules, and those of the International Federation to which it was affiliated.

7.106 It was inherent in that structure that an innocent athlete might suffer suspension between an initial disciplinary hearing and a successful appeal from its outcome. He noted the lack of any financial remedy under the rules, and contrasted that with the contention that the alleged implied term could found such a financial remedy. Finally,

---

[116] *Modahl v British Athletic Federation Ltd*, CA transcript, 28 July 1997, per Lord Woolf MR at pp 20–26; per Morritt LJ at pp 36–39; and per Pill LJ at pp 43–44.

[117] *Calvin v Carr* [1980] AC 575, PC; *Lloyd v McMahon* [1987] 1 AC 625, HL.

[118] Citing *Cowley v Heatley*, *The Times*, 24 July 1986; *McInnes v Onslow-Fane* [1978] 1 WLR 1520, 1535. See too *British Wheelchair Sports v British Paralympic Association*, 5 November 1997, Scott V-C ('What is unnecessary and to be avoided in my judgment is spending scarce resources of these charitable associations in conducting litigation when a solution that can be lived with by all concerned can surely be reached by sensible discussion').

he observed that if the claim had been sustainable in public law,[119] damages would not be available, only the setting aside of the decision which would be otiose as the appellate body had already done this. But as this was an interlocutory application and not a trial, he felt unable to strike out the claim on that issue, accepting as arguable the proposition that each step in the disciplinary process must be individually fair. Morritt LJ regarded as 'well arguable' the existence of the implied term for which the athlete contended.

7.107 The approach of the Master of the Rolls is, in our respectful view, to be preferred, for it avoids an artificially sharp differentiation between private and public law approaches to decisions of sporting bodies. As we explain in chapter eight, we question the rationale for denying a public law remedy to challenge decisions of sporting bodies.[120] There is strong support in principle and in authority[121] for the view that the result of a claim should not differ according to whether it is available by way of private or public law procedure. In public law, damages for unlawful administrative action are only recoverable in case of misfeasance, which requires a finding of bad faith, in the sense of conduct going beyond bias or an appearance thereof in the form of a predisposition against the athlete, but without malice, arising from a genuinely held belief in her guilt.

7.108 The athlete's argument in *Modahl* entails a dilution of the strong requirement of malice or bad faith necessary to recover damages in public law, but in circumstances not conceptually different from a public law claim. We therefore agree with the view that the scope of the implied term as to fairness should, absent any specific term modifying it, be the narrow one advanced by the Federation in *Modahl*: that the disciplinary process taken as a whole must be fair, but nothing more. In the trial of Ms Modahl's subsequent claim for breach of contract, which failed, the Court of Appeal subsequently confirmed that view of the law in *Modahl v British Athletic Federation (No 2)*.[122]

7.109 The general duty of fairness applying to sports disciplinary tribunals should not detract from the wide discretion they enjoy as to the manner in which they may, without unfairness, conduct their proceedings. Thus in *Justice v South Australian Trotting Control Board*,[123] the Supreme Court of South Australia refused an application for review, under a form of public law procedure not available in England, alleging injustice in the conduct of disciplinary proceedings following which the plaintiff had been suspended for five weeks for failing to take all reasonable and permissible measures to ensure that his trotting horse was given full opportunity to win or obtain the best possible place in the field. The Court rejected the submission that the investigating stewards must be available for cross-examination by the accused, pointed to the wide discretion of a domestic tribunal as to the manner of its proceedings and the lack of any obligation to adopt the formalities of a court of law, and found that no other form of unfairness was made out.

---

[119] Ie, by application for judicial review, a remedy not currently available as English law stands, as we explain in chapter 8 below, at para 8.12 ff.

[120] See para 8.22 ff. See, eg, Beloff and Kerr, *Why Aga Khan is Wrong* [1996] Judicial Review 30; Pannick, *Judicial Review of Sports Bodies* [1997] Judicial Review 150.

[121] Eg Carnwath J's judgment at first instance in *Stevenage Borough FC Ltd v The Football League Ltd*, transcript, 23 July 1996.

[122] [2002] 1 WLR 1192, CA.

[123] (1989) 50 SASR 613.

7.110 That authority does not appear to have been cited to Ebsworth J in *Jones v Welsh Rugby Union*,[124] in which the judge found arguable the proposition that unfairness had tainted disciplinary proceedings against a rugby player because the system was one which 'in effect prohibits a party from challenging by question or by evidence the factual basis of the allegations against him'.[125] The judge's approach was unusually interventionist in that the proposition she found arguable was, in effect, that an adversarial system was necessary to comply with the duty of fairness, and that an inquisitorial one could not do so unless it included the adversarial elements of live evidence and cross-examination.

7.111 This approach goes beyond previous authority in circumscribing the discretion of the disciplinary body as to the conduct of its proceedings. The decision still resonates even though it was only an interlocutory application which required the judge to apply tests that can make the law appear more favourable to the claimant than it actually is.[126] Ebsworth J described the issue as being whether the association had applied its rules with undue rigidity and whether the rules themselves were unfair. She did not have to resolve that issue but was impressed by the contention that it was unfair for the disciplining body to view a video of the incident in question in private, despite a specific request to the contrary.

7.112 The general law relating to fair procedure outside the sporting field has continued to develop in the days since *Jones v Welsh Rugby Union*, under the influence of Article 6 of the European Convention on Human Rights and, in England, the Human Rights Act 1998. In *Ogbonna v Nursing and Midwifery Council*[127] a midwife had been struck off for misconduct at least partly on the basis of crucial evidence from a witness who was absent abroad and whose written statement was admitted without cross-examination. The Court of Appeal (deciding to remit the matter to the disciplinary body, constituted differently) held that whether cross-examination was required to achieve fairness was a fact sensitive issue and that in the circumstances, it was unfair not to have secured the attendance by live evidence or video link of the absent witness whose whereabouts abroad were known.

7.113 And in *R (Bonhoeffer) v General Medical Council*[128] a male doctor accused of criminal sexual impropriety involving alleged abuse of boys was found to have been unfairly and unreasonably refused permission to cross-examine an alleged victim who was the principal witness against him, on the inadequate ground that though willing to travel from Kenya to the United Kingdom to give oral evidence, the witness would face an increased danger of reprisals from homophobic elements in Kenya, or persons loyal to the accused, than if his statement were read to the panel hearing the case in England.

7.114 Neither of these decisions, ultimately, does much more than illustrate that what is fair or unfair is a question of fact in each case. Sports bodies' procedural rules, and

---

[124] (1997) unreported, 27 February, upheld on appeal, *The Times*, 6 January 1998, CA.

[125] Ebsworth J, transcript 27 February 1997, p 20. In the Court of appeal Potter LJ remarked: 'In the days of professional sport now upon us, the requirements of natural justice in relation to disciplinary proceedings may well require further development.'

[126] This is because of the low threshold required of a claimant in an interlocutory injunction application, on the authority of *American Cyanamid v Ethicon* [1975] AC 396, HL (and subsequent cases including *Leisure Data v Bell* [1988] FSR at 367, CA).

[127] [2010] EWCA Civ 1216.

[128] [2011] EWHC 1585 (Admin), [2012] IRLR 37, DC.

video conferencing technology, have developed in recent years to the point where procedural arguments of the type ventilated in *Jones v Welsh Rugby Union* are less likely to be ventilated now; there is a tendency to allow oral evidence and cross-examination more frequently than in the past. But the courts will continue to exercise vigilant supervisory jurisdiction over the procedural fairness of sports disciplinary procedures and will not hesitate to intervene where unfairness is made out.

The Right to a Fair Hearing

7.115 Our next task is to focus more closely on some of the characteristics of the duty of fairness. These can be readily identified. The first is the well-known proposition that an accused has the right to be informed in clear terms of the allegations against him or her. In practice this may mean that the sporting association must accede to a request by the accused for further and better particulars of the allegations, before they are considered by the body exercising punitive jurisdiction. It would not be fair merely to allege that a sportsman or woman had engaged in conduct likely to bring his or her sport into disrepute, without condescending to inform the accused when, where and how he or she is alleged to have committed that conduct. If those particulars could be shown to be already well known to the accused and the request for them merely tactical, then doubtless no relief would be available from a court in respect of failure to provide them; but as so often in this field, the sporting body is usually best advised to opt for caution and provide more information than necessary, rather than less.

7.116 Equally well known and now only rarely disregarded by sporting bodies is the right of an accused to make representations by way of defence against the charge, or if the charge is admitted, by way of mitigation of the penalty. Early outré examples of outright failure to hear the sportsman in his defence are found in *Keighley FC v Cunningham*[129] and *Angus v British Judo Association*.[130] More recently, the bizarre tale of Nathan Baggaley, Australian canoeist, Olympic medallist and ingester of stanozonol, banned for nine months at 'the stroke of a pen', without a hearing, shows that sports bodies cannot always be trusted to respect the right of a player—albeit believed on strong grounds to be a steroid cheat—to due process.[131]

7.117 As an established principle, this right requires no elaboration, despite still occasionally being breached; but we will consider further below the extent to which the exercise of the right may include the making of representations in a particular way in certain cases.[132] We deal below with the circumstances in which the accused may have a right to be represented by a lawyer at the hearing of the charge.

---

[129] *The Times*, 25 May 1960 (rugby player sent off the field and subsequently suspended without notice either to him or his club).

[130] *The Times*, 15 June 1984 (judoka banned after positive drug test not allowed opportunity to explain that the prohibited substance was found in a sinus decongestant taken under a lawful medical prescription).

[131] See Marshall and Hale, *Unilateral Unappealable Doping Sanctions* [2007] ISLR 39, recounting the story leading to *Baggaley v International Canoe Federation*, CAS/2006/A/1168; *Baggaley v Australian Canoeing Inc*, CAS/2007/A/1201. Baggaley lost his case because he failed to appeal in time an *additional* nine-month ban imposed unilaterally by his federation without a hearing, in defiance of a 15 month ban imposed by an arbitrator. The article includes the poignant subheadings 'Would you believe ...' and 'Why does no one seem to care?'.

[132] See paras 7.126–7.130.

7.118 The law does not require, necessarily, that there should even be an oral hearing of a disciplinary charge at all. For example, in *Currie v Barton*[133] the Court of Appeal held that an amateur tennis club did not breach its duty of fairness when its committee decided to ban a player from the amateur county team for three years, for refusing to play a match and walking off the court, without inviting him to appear before the committee in person. He had learned from press reports that he might be facing a ban, and had written a long letter to the secretary giving his side of the story. Importantly, his ban from the county team did not affect his livelihood earned from coaching, sponsorship and professional tournaments. The restraint of trade doctrine was therefore not engaged.[134]

7.119 The rules of many sports bodies now include provision for an oral hearing to be requested as of right by the accused, if the charge is denied, but it is quite common for oral hearings to be dispensed with by consent, particularly where the offence is admitted and the issue is what sanction should be imposed. An example of the latter is *ITF v Karic*,[135] where the tribunal felt constrained to impose a full two-year ban on a player who could not show that she was without significant fault in failing to ascertain the contents of prescription medication, even though it was agreed that the medication containing a prohibited stimulant (not being a specified substance) was taken for therapeutic purposes by a disabled tennis player.

7.120 In *USA Shooting and Quigley v Union Internationale de Tir*,[136] an early case of alleged doping, the UIT had held a meeting of its executive to decide Mr Quigley's fate. Neither Mr Quigley nor his national association were permitted to attend that meeting despite requests to do so. However, a detailed written presentation on Mr Quigley's behalf was submitted and considered by the executive. The relevant rules provided that the accused person should have the right to present evidence, comment on the accusation, defend himself and be represented. In the event, the CAS did not need to rule on his alternative contention that he had not received a fair hearing, since he was successful in establishing that the offence was not one of strict liability. However, the CAS commented that it was obvious that Mr Quigley's argument would have failed, since the right to be heard does not include a right to an oral hearing. The CAS added that even if the procedure had initially been insufficient to comply with natural justice, 'as long as there is a possibility of full appeal to the [CAS] the deficiency may be cured'.[137]

7.121 It appears to be frequently assumed in the jurisprudence relating to the conduct of sporting disciplinary proceedings that the right to a fair hearing has some existence independent of contract. In civil law systems contract is not needed in order to found procedural rights to be treated fairly; for example, the Swiss law of associations, influential in the development of the CAS's jurisprudence, accords such rights independently of contract to members of the association, whether direct or 'indirect', the latter not necessarily having contractual relations with the association. In English law, the question may

---

[133] *The Times*, 12 February 1988, CA.
[134] *Currie v Barton* was followed by Mackay J in *Chambers v British Olympic Association* [2008] EWHC 2028, QB, when he held that the restraint of trade doctrine was not engaged in relation to exclusion from the Olympic Games.
[135] Anti-Doping Tribunal, 19 December 2006.
[136] CAS 94/129.
[137] Ibid, paras 74–80; cf *Calvin v Carr* [1980] AC 574, PC.

now be of less importance than formerly, since the Contracts (Rights of Third Parties) Act 1999 can, absent an express exclusion, secure the right to fair treatment enforceable at the suit of a player who is not a party to, say, the contract between his club and the association providing for disciplinary jurisdiction to be exercised in respect of the player.

7.122 Much juristic energy has been devoted to the question whether an employment relationship confers a right in an employee to be treated fairly. This is well travelled ground in employment law. Orthodox contract law held that a right to a fair hearing could not be implied into an employment contract, and that statutory provisions were needed to create the right, subject to procedural conditions. The development of the 'trust and confidence' term—more long-windedly expressed as the employer's fundamental implied obligation not without good cause to conduct itself so as to undermine or destroy the relationship of trust and confidence subsisting between employer and employee—went a long way towards the creation of a contractual right to fair treatment.[138] Until recently, this was thought by some to include a right to damages for procedural breaches forming part of a dismissal process, but it is now clear that damages at large are not available (though other remedies may be) independently of statutory unfair dismissal law, to compensate an employee for procedural breaches forming part of a dismissal process.[139]

7.123 In the sporting context the right to procedural fairness has been less closely anchored in contract law; the rules of a sporting association have long been seen as quasi-legislative in nature[140] and, where a livelihood is at stake in professional sport, the content of the right to fairness is now seen as co-terminous with the right to fair treatment in the context of public law, even though public law remedies are not available to enforce it. The common law is astute to prevent unfair treatment. In *Jones v Welsh Rugby Union*[141] the suggestion that the rules being applied could themselves be unfair, and, presumably, unenforceable as a result, treats such rules as *par excellence* legislative in character. Ebsworth J's interlocutory judgment, already mentioned several times, appeared to treat subjection to unfair rules as an infringement of a right apparently arising independently of contract.

7.124 Similarly inspired by public law doctrines, in *Stewart v Judicial Committee of the Auckland Racing Club Inc*[142] the High Court in Auckland, New Zealand, entertained a motion for statutory review, which is a public law form of proceeding, in respect of a challenge to the fairness of certain disciplinary proceedings in which a jockey was accused of failing to ride his horse on its merits. Hillyer J set aside a three-month suspension, inter alia, on the ground that the appeal body had declined to receive two affidavits in support of the defence, without looking at them.

7.125 But in *Justice v South Australian Trotting Control Board*,[143] the plaintiff trainer and driver of trotting horses failed to establish unfairness in the conduct of a quasi-inquisitorial process in which the stewards enquired into whether the plaintiff had failed

---

[138] The 'trust and confidence implied term means, in short, that an employer must treat his employees fairly': per Lord Nicholls in *Eastwood v Magnox Electric plc* [2005] 1 AC 503, 523G.

[139] *Edwards v Chesterfield Royal Hospital NHS Foundation Trust* [2012] 2 WLR 55, [2012] ICR 201, [2012] IRLR 129, SC.

[140] *Breen v Amalgamated Engineering Union* [1971] 2 QB 175, per Lord Denning MR (dissenting) at 189–91, cited above at para 7.102, n 115.

[141] (1997) unreported, 27 February.

[142] [1992] 3 NZLR 693.

[143] (1989) 50 SASR 613.

to give his horse a full opportunity to win or obtain the best possible place. Among the contentions rejected by O'Loughlin J was that the stewards were investigating and giving evidence at the same time, but had not been subject to cross-examination, and that this was unfair. The judge noted that they were available for questioning and that Mr Justice had to some extent questioned them, but they were not required to present evidence formally and be cross-examined on it.[144]

7.126 Can a player insist on exercising the right to make representations in his defence through a solicitor or counsel, rather than on his own or with help from a friend or colleague? Disciplinary rules frequently make provision as to representation; often it is explicitly permitted, particularly in cases with potentially serious adverse consequences for the accused. In other instances it is explicitly prohibited or limited, for example by allowing representation but not by a solicitor or not by counsel. In an intermediate category of cases, the rules in question are either silent on the point or confer a discretion on the adjudicating body to permit or prohibit legal representation, or legal representation of a particular type, as it thinks fit.

7.127 English law does not require the rules of sporting bodies to confer an absolute right to legal representation of a person accused of a disciplinary offence. If the rules do confer such a right, then obviously it will be irregular to deny representation. If the rules are silent, the adjudicating body has a discretion arising from the general proposition that it may regulate its own proceedings in such manner as it thinks fit. Lord Denning MR pithily pointed out that in domestic tribunals 'justice can often be done … better by a good layman than by a bad lawyer'.[145] But there can be cases in which the charge is so serious that it would be a wrong exercise of discretion and unfair to disallow representation, for example in a doping case or, but more doubtfully, in a case arising from a fracas on the field of play.[146]

7.128 The status of the sport related cases dealing with the qualified right to representation may now have to be reassessed in the light of recent human rights based jurisprudence outside the field of sport, analysing a line of Strasbourg cases starting with *Ringeisen v Austria (No 1)*[147] in which the Court of Human Rights held that Article 6 of the European Convention was engaged where the proceedings in question were 'proceedings the result of which is decisive for private rights and obligations'. After an extensive discussion of domestic and Strasbourg authority in *R (G) v Governors of X School*,[148] Lord Dyson JSC noted that whether that test is satisfied on the facts of a particular case depends on the context, and he concluded that Article 6 was not engaged in the case of a teacher dismissed for sexual misconduct with an underage boy, where subsequent proceedings would allow another body, the 'Independent Safeguarding Authority', to exercise independent judgment on the separate question of whether G should be barred from

---

[144] Decisions such as these would now be reviewed in England through the prism of recent ECHR Art 6 influenced case law such as *Ogbonna v Nursing and Midwifery Council* [2010] EWCA Civ 1216, and *R (Bonhoeffer) v General Medical Council* [2011] EWHC 1585 (Admin); [2012] IRLR 37, DC, both discussed above at paras 7.112–7.113.

[145] *Enderby Town FC v The Football Association Ltd* [1971] 1 All ER 215, CA, at 218.

[146] See, as to the former, *Pett v Greyhound Racing Association Ltd (No 2)* [1970] 1 QB 46, CA (the 'unruly horse' case); and as to the latter, *Jones v Welsh Rugby Union* (n 141) pp 9 and 20 of the transcript.

[147] (1971) 1 EHRR 455.

[148] [2011] 3 WLR 237, SC.

teaching in future. Therefore, G was not entitled to be represented by his solicitor at the disciplinary hearing before the school governors, following which he was dismissed.

7.129 On the other hand, *Kulkarni v Milton Keynes Hospital NHS Trust*[149] indicates that a doctor will be entitled to legal representation in disciplinary proceedings brought by his employer where the doctor faces 'charges which are of such gravity that, in the event they are found proved, he will be effectively barred from employment in the NHS'.[150] This is because the National Health Service is in practice the single employer of doctors for the whole country; thus loss of the particular job would mean a de facto bar to employment as a doctor. If dismissal from a particular job is at stake, Article 6 will not be engaged, but if what is at stake is prevention from practising one's profession, it will be engaged.[151]

7.130 There is room for argument as to how this line of cases might apply in the context of sport related disciplinary proceedings. It seems likely that Article 6 would be engaged in the case of a professional sportsman or woman accused of an offence where the penalty could include a lengthy ban that could in practice snuff out his or her career, often a relatively short career in the many sports where top level competition ceases from the age of about 30. In practice, legal representation is now normally allowed in such cases. Lesser offences, such as a fracas on the field of play that could lead to a much shorter ban, would appear to fall short of the requirements for engagement of Article 6. The impact of the latest non-sport cases may well be to leave unaffected the authority of Lord Denning's pre-Convention judgments in the *Enderby Town* and *Pett* cases.[152]

7.131 A closely related question is whether the right to make representations includes the right to call witnesses and, often more importantly, the right to cross-examine witnesses appearing for the other side. Rights to the attendance of witnesses to give oral evidence may be more valuable if the accused has the services of a qualified lawyer to put questions to those witnesses. These difficult questions raise again the tension between adversarial and inquisitorial procedure, between formality and informality in disciplinary proceedings, and between traditional judicial abstentionism and recent interventionism corresponding to higher stakes in an increasingly professionalised sporting world.

7.132 In *Jones v Welsh Rugby Union* the court was invited to grant an injunction on the basis of, inter alia, denial of legal representation. The argument was that rugby union football was now a professional sport and consequently representation could not lawfully be denied, as livelihoods were at stake. The practice of the Union was not to allow representation, but to allow a 'shoulder to lean on', which in the particular case was a distinguished Queen's Counsel who, at one point, was allowed to speak for the accused uninterrupted for a period estimated variously as being from 10 minutes to 20 minutes. Ebsworth J,

---

[149] [2010] ICR 101, CA.

[150] Per Smith LJ (obiter) in *Kulkarni v Milton Keynes Hospital NHS Trust*, ibid, para 67. But cf *Mattu v University Hospitals of Coventry and Warwickshire NHS Trust* [2012] EWCA Civ 641.

[151] See also *R (Wright) v Secretary of State for Health* [2009] 1 AC 739, HL, concerning the procedure for provisionally listing a worker on the Protection of Vulnerable Adults (POVA) list under statutory provisions. The House of Lords held that some interim measures 'have such a clear and decisive impact upon the exercise of a civil right that article 6.1 does apply' (per Baroness Hale of Richmond, at para 21). Provisional listing in the POVA list was a determination of the civil right to work because it had 'detrimental' and 'often irreversible and incurable' effects (ibid, para 25). Both *Kulkarni* and *Wright* were cited without disapproval by Lord Dyson JSC in the *G* case (n 146) at paras 60 and 61.

[152] See above, para 7.127, n 145 and n 146.

granting the injunction, did so apparently not in reliance on denial of legal representation, but because of the Union's refusal to allow the parties to view a video of the incident and make representations on it, and its refusal to allow both cross-examination of the referee and the calling of witnesses.

7.133 The judge made copious reference to sport having become 'big business' from which many people now earn their living, and commented that it would be 'naive to pretend that the modern world of sport can be conducted as it used to be not very many years ago'.[153] Had the case been decided after the entry into force (in October 2000) of the Human Rights Act 1998, the arguments would have centred on the content of the Convention right just mentioned, as well as contractual or other implied common law rights, but the result and the reasoning would not necessarily have been very different, and the case retains a relevance which is out of proportion to its interlocutory character and relative antiquity.[154]

7.134 While the learned judge's observations are, in themselves, correct, they do not differentiate between a merely temporary effect on the livelihood of a player, which was the worst that could happen to Mr Jones; and utter destruction of a player's livelihood, for example through a life ban for drugs offences or horse doping. There will be cases falling somewhere in the middle; a two-year ban imposed on a professional footballer may or may not in practice extinguish his career and, on any view, is serious enough. But the true principle ought still to be that enunciated by Lord Denning MR in the *Pett* case, namely that it is a question of fact, having regard to the seriousness of the charge, whether natural justice requires a right to legal representation. The same logic should dictate that a parallel principle applies where the right to call or cross-examine witnesses is at issue.

7.135 So the *Jones* case ought not to be regarded as authority supporting an absolute right to call and cross-examine witnesses, still less an absolute right to legal representation, in every case where the outcome may have an economic impact on the accused. For example, a professional footballer facing a possible ban after receiving one too many yellow cards should not expect to succeed in restraining the Premier League or the Football Association from proceeding with a hearing without allowing him to be represented by counsel and to call a panoply of witnesses.

7.136 A related issue that occasionally arises is whether a third party with an interest adverse to the accused should be allowed to appear at a disciplinary hearing to speak against him, or against a club. A rule conferring a right on such a third party would not be objectionable in principle. If the rules are silent, the discretion as to the manner of conducting disciplinary proceedings is broad enough to allow an appearance by an adversely interested third party.

7.137 The objection that an accused ought not to face 'two prosecutors' or, in relation to penalty, a 'plea in aggravation', is not compelling, and was rejected in the disciplinary case involving Middlesbrough Football Club in which Blackburn Rovers Football

---

[153] Transcript, 27 February 1997, p 25.

[154] The sports cases, namely *Enderby*, *Pett* and *Jones*, were not cited in the appellate judgments in *Wright*, *G* and *Kulkarni*, though *Enderby* was mentioned in *Kulkarni* at first instance by Penry-Davey J, whose decision the Court of Appeal reversed.

Club was allowed to appear by leading counsel (now Leveson LJ) to argue in support of Middlesbrough's guilt, and in support of a particular form of punishment—forfeiture of the match and award of the points to Blackburn—favourable to Blackburn's interest.

7.138 As has since been remarked, to say that an accused faces two prosecutors is a vivid phrase, but does not mean the accused faces more than one case to answer. However, if the proceedings comprise an arbitration governed by the Arbitration Act 1996, arbitrators have no power to permit the joinder of third parties to an arbitration in the absence of an agreement or a power in the contract, ie the sports body's rules, under which they are appointed.[155] Similarly, the CAS's procedural rule R41.4 provides that '[a] third party may only participate in the arbitration if it is bound by the arbitration agreement or if itself and the other parties agree in writing'.

The Rule Against Bias

7.139 The next, likewise very well known, aspect of the duty of fairness is the rule against bias, which, broadly, requires the adjudicating tribunal to be free from any bias or appearance of bias against the accused, and free from any vested interest, particularly a financial interest, in the outcome of the proceedings in which it is adjudicating. The modern law is now to be found in the speech of Lord Hope in *Porter v Magill*.[156] 'The question is whether the fair-minded and informed observer, having considered the facts, would conclude that there was a real possibility that the tribunal was biased.'[157]

7.140 The fair-minded and informed observer has largely replaced the man on the Clapham omnibus as the personification of all that is reasonable, but it is becoming increasingly obvious that he or she is in truth the court, for he displays all the admirable attributes of a good judge. Thus the fair-minded observer 'can be assumed to have access to all the facts that are capable of being known by members of the public generally ... is neither complacent nor unduly sensitive or suspicious when he examines the facts ... is able to distinguish between what is relevant and what is irrelevant, and ... is able when exercising his judgment to decide what weight should be given to the facts that are relevant'.[158]

7.141 In the sporting context, the Court of Appeal in *Flaherty v National Greyhound Racing Club Ltd*[159] overturned a decision of Evans-Lombe J, reached after a 10-day hearing, that apparent bias had tainted a hearing before the club stewards which had fined the claimant £400 and reprimanded him for breaches of the rules of racing after his greyhound was found to have a banned substance, hexamine, in its body. The Court of Appeal found it unsatisfactory that the court proceedings had been so protracted; reminded itself

---

[155] *The Eastern Saga* [1984] 3 All ER 835. It is suggested in Lewis and Taylor (n 108) at A6.63 that the Premier League Rules include a case management power wide enough to permit joinder, and that this is supported by an unpublished arbitration decision in the dispute between Sheffield United and West Ham arising out of the notorious Carlos Tevez affair, but other arbitrators (in proceedings not in the public domain) have considered the power not wide enough to permit such joinder in the absence of consent from both parties to the arbitration clause.

[156] [2002] 2 AC 357, HL, followed in countless cases since, including (to name but a few) *R (on the application of Condron) v National Assembly for Wales* [2006] EWCA Civ 1573, [2007] BLGR 87; *Gillies v Secretary of State for Work and Pensions* [2006] UKHL 2, [2006] 1 WLR 781; *Lawal v Northern Spirit Ltd* [2003] UKHL 35, [2003] ICR 856; and *R v Abdroikov* [2007] UKHL 37, [2007] 1 WLR 2679.

[157] *Porter v Magill* (n 145) per Lord Hope at para 103.

[158] *Gillies v Secretary of State for Work and Pensions* (n 156) per Lord Hope at para 17.

[159] [2006] ISLR, SLR 8, [2005] EWCA Civ 1117, Scott-Baker LJ giving the leading judgment.

of Mance LJ's admonition in *Modahl v British Athletic Federation Ltd*[160] that 'a conclusion that the disciplinary process should be looked at overall matched the desirable aim of affording to bodies exercising jurisdiction over sporting activities as great a latitude as is consistent with the fundamental requirements of fairness';[161] and roundly rejected the submission that one of the stewards had an appearance of bias (not actual bias) by reason of his prior relationship with the stadium in question, his prior professional contacts with the accusers, and the robust manner in which he expressed views on certain evidential points at the disciplinary hearing.

7.142 Despite the abject failure of the bias allegations in cases such as *Flaherty*, the rule against being 'judge in one's own cause'[162] makes it most unwise for sporting bodies to appoint to disciplinary panels persons who have had prior involvement in a matter, especially if they have been involved in formulating charges or have expressed a view, on or off the record, as to the merits of a disciplinary case. The expression of such views may be extremely tempting in a case where there appears to be no conceivable defence to the charge, where its existence has already received wide publicity and the press is clamouring for a reaction from the sporting body responsible for determining the charge.

7.143 It is understandable that a sporting association which finds itself in such a position might feel the need to send strong signals to others at once, without waiting for the case to be completed. Indeed the body may risk criticism for failing to speak out against the conduct with which the accused is charged. The two cardinal rules to follow are, first, to ensure that any such statement condemns the conduct complained of only in general terms and with the caveat that no reference is being made to the individual case in question, which has yet to be determined; and, second, that any such statement should emanate from a person who will have no part to play in the subsequent disciplinary process. If these rules are carefully followed, allegations of bias engendered by considerations of public relations can be avoided, for bias is not established by showing a predisposition against the conduct complained of, which *ex hypothesi* is unlawful under the relevant rules, as distinct from a predisposition against the person charged with that conduct.

7.144 Other cases in the sporting field in which allegations of bias have been aired mainly predate the decision of the House of Lords in *Porter v Magill* and indeed what was previously the leading English case, *R v Gough*.[163] But it is unlikely that they would have been decided differently following the shift of emphasis from a 'real likelihood' of bias to a 'real danger' of bias, and more recently to a 'real possibility' of bias. Thus as long ago as 1979 members of a tribunal of the Football Association who had spoken critically of the former England team manager Don Revie before hearing charges against him, were held by Cantley J to have acted unlawfully in subsequently imposing a 10-year ban from

---

[160] [2002] 1 WLR 1192, para 115.

[161] Per Scott-Baker LJ at para 19. Allegations of 'at least' apparent bias similarly failed in *McKeown v British Horseracing Authority* [2010] ISLR, SLR 87, per Stadlen J in his principal judgment (there is also an additional judgment reported in the same place) at paras 284–352.

[162] Or, for those who prefer Latin, the maxim *nemo iudex in causa sua*.

[163] [1993] AC 646, HL, establishing the previously applicable test, namely whether there is a real danger of bias. The word 'danger' was dropped in *Porter v Magill* [2002] 2 AC 357 after debate over whether 'real danger' and 'real possibility' were the same, as Lord Phillips MR suggested in *Re Medicaments and Related Classes of Goods (No 2)* [2001] 1 WLR 700, para 85.

footballing activities on Mr Revie.[164] By falling into the trap of speaking out, they had demonstrated a likelihood of bias. The plaintiff had objected to the constitution of the tribunal, but the members had refused to stand down. The result would surely be no different today.

7.145 For well over a century English law has regarded any person with a direct pecuniary or proprietary interest in the outcome of proceedings as disqualified from adjudicating in such proceedings.[165] But if such an interest is merely indirect and tenuous, the person concerned may not be disqualified, a proposition best illustrated by the case of the judge who was held not disqualified from trying a defendant alleged to have conspired to rob several banks, including one in which the judge held shares.[166]

7.146 A notable illustration of the principle in the sporting field can be found in *Barnard v Jockey Club of South Africa*,[167] an alleged horse doping case in which a member of one of the disciplinary bodies which found against the accused horse trainer fatally impaired the validity of the proceedings by declining to recuse himself after being invited to do so by the accused. His good faith was not impugned, and he had very properly disclosed that he was a partner in the firm of attorneys representing the respondent Jockey Club. His apparent financial interest, which was not contradicted by evidence, arose by inference from the fact of being a partner in that firm, and the drafting by another partner in the same firm of the reply to the grounds of appeal to the body on which he sat. Gordon J went on to hold that the same evidence also established a very real likelihood of bias which should have disqualified the partner concerned irrespective of his financial interest. But it is possible that this latter conclusion might have been overcome by adducing evidence of an effective 'Chinese wall' between the two partners.

7.147 Needless to say, personal hostility against the accused will readily lead a court to apprehend a real possibility of bias.[168] But the cases may go either way as the question is one of fact and degree, and the courts are particularly reluctant to hold that the judgment of professionals is likely to be impaired by personal motives. It is beyond our purpose to give a full account of the copious case law on the subject. Reference should be made to specialist works.[169]

7.148 A player's entitlement to have disciplinary charges determined by an independent and impartial tribunal can be waived. The player may not wish to undergo a hearing in a case where the disciplinary charge is admitted. The rules of at least one international sports governing body, the International Tennis Federation (ITF), now provide for a player charged with a doping offence to have the opportunity to agree that the offence was

---

[164] *Revie v Football Association, The Times,* 14 December 1979.

[165] *Dimes v Grand Junction Canal Co Proprietors* (1852) 3 HLC 759; and the useful account in Woolf, Jowell and Le Sueur, *De Smith's Judicial Review,* 6th edn (Sweet & Maxwell, 2007) ch 10, pp 499 ff.

[166] *R v Mulvihill* [1990] 1 WLR 438.

[167] (1984) 2 SALR 35 (W).

[168] See analogously the trade union cases, *Taylor v National Union of Seamen* [1967] 1 WLR 532 and *Roebuck v National Union of Mineworkers* [1977] ICR 573.

[169] A good account is found in Woolf, Jowell and Le Sueur (n 165) 499 ff; see also Holly Stout's snappily titled *Bias,* at [2011] Judicial Review 458, suggesting that actual bias can be unconscious and is therefore not as heinous an allegation as sometimes thought; and annexing the celebrated exchange between Peter Smith J and counsel in *Howell v Lees Millais* (from Anthony Clarke MR's judgment in the Court of Appeal in the same case); see [2007] EWCA Civ 720.

committed and to submit to a sanction (publicly announced on the Federation's website) imposed by a non-independent officer of the ITF, as an alternative to the more expensive and time consuming process of requiring a hearing before an independent and impartial anti-doping tribunal chaired by a lawyer and including a medical and scientific expert. There can be no objection to such a provision in the rules provided that such a fast track procedure is voluntary and provided that the player retains the alternative option of requiring a hearing before an independent tribunal.[170]

7.149 CAS rule S.18 provides that 'CAS arbitrators and mediators may not act as counsel for a party before the CAS'. Rule R.34 provides that 'An arbitrator may be challenged if the circumstances give rise to legitimate doubts over his independence. The challenge shall be brought within seven days after the ground for the challenge has become known. Challenges are in the exclusive power of the ICAS [International Council of Arbitration for Sport] Board ...'

Conclusion

7.150 Our brief survey of some of the case law delineating the scope of the duty of fairness shows that each case depends upon its own facts. This is consistent with the administrative law proposition that there is no such thing as a technical breach of natural justice. Running through the case law, however, is a constant tension between the traditional latitude and autonomy afforded to domestic tribunals, encouraging an abstentionist judicial line, and a more formal approach reflecting a growth of legalism in sport coinciding with the growth of professionalism. This tension was very marked in *Jones v Welsh Rugby Union*, in which the respective parties' submissions reflected the traditional and the modern approach. Ebsworth J attempted to steer a course between the two, but gave a fillip to the modern formalist approach in a dictum which stands uneasily with the courts' normal policy of non-interventionism:[171]

> There are likely to be many people who take the view that the processes of the law have no place in sport and the bodies which run sport should be able to conduct their own affairs as they see fit and that by and large they have done so successfully and fairly over the years. It is a tempting and attractive view in many ways, particularly to those (and I almost said those of us) who grew up on windy and often half deserted touchlines. However, sport today is big business. Many people earn their living from it in one way or another. It would, I fear, be naive to pretend that the modern world of sport can be conducted as it used to be not very many years ago.

Since those words were written in February 1997, the rules of many sports disciplinary bodies have been upgraded, those bodies are more frequently chaired by lawyers, and their proceedings are on a more professional footing and less easy to challenge on appeal. Sports administrators have heeded the invitation implicit in Ebsworth J's words to improve the fairness of decision making by modernising procedures.

---

[170] The need to raise a procedural objection, which would include an application to recuse a panel member on the ground of bias, was highlighted by Neuberger J's decision in the Haverfordwest County Court, *Lovell v Marchant and Phillips* [2003] ISLR, SLR 38 (reported as *Lovell v Pembroke County Cricket Club* but in fact a representative action against the club's officials). The judge would have granted relief for procedural irregularities but for the player's omission to accept an offer of a five-person appeal hearing before a panel of whom only two would be members of the executive committee, which could have cured the defects.

[171] See transcript, 27 February 1997, p 10.

7.151 However, there is as yet no clear duty on sporting disciplinary bodies to give reasons for their decisions, unless the relevant rules so provide. In administrative law generally, decision makers are under no general duty to give reasons for a decision, but reasons may be required if a statutory scheme so provides, and absence of reasons may contribute to a finding of irrationality.[172] In *Dundee United Football Co Ltd v Scottish Football Association*[173] Dundee United purported to terminate the contract of a player who appealed to the appeals committee of the Scottish Football League. The League upheld the appeal but did not give reasons. Dundee appealed to the Scottish FA appeals committee, which dismissed the appeal. Dundee then petitioned for judicial review of that decision, seeking, inter alia, a remission to the League appeals committee for an explanation of the reasons for its decision. The Outer House held that since the League appeals committee had been represented before the Scottish FA appeals committee, the former committee was able to provide in that forum whatever explanation was necessary for its decision. The court noted that while a right of appeal was a strong indication that reasons should be given for a decision that could be appealed, the existence and scope of any duty to give reasons was a question of fact dependent on the circumstances in which the decision was made, and the rules under which it was made.

7.152 In the sporting context, as in other contexts, it is a salutary discipline on those who discipline others to provide explanations for their decisions. There is no doubt that having to give reasons concentrates the mind and is likely to improve the quality of decision making. It cannot be said that in the English law relating to sport there is necessarily any duty on sporting disciplinary bodies to give reasons. But where reasons are given, they can be analysed and used to support a case for setting aside an allegedly unlawful decision, if the reasons given are thought to disclose a misapplication of the rules, or unfair treatment of the accused. This does not mean that the law should encourage decision makers exercising disciplinary jurisdiction in sport deliberately to refrain from giving reasons in order to protect themselves against subsequent criticism of the reasons they give. The rules of many sporting bodies have now been modernised to the point where they routinely require reasons for disciplinary decisions. In doping cases and other disciplinary and arbitral proceedings, often presided over by lawyers, quite detailed reasons in the form of written judgments are now the norm rather than the exception.

Penalties

7.153 We consider next the jurisdiction of disciplinary bodies to impose penalties on those they have lawfully found guilty of misconduct. The jurisdiction to penalise is derived from the relevant rules. It is usual for there to be a provision setting out the powers of the disciplining body to impose sanctions. Among the powers commonly found in the rules of sporting associations are powers to impose fines, and to suspend players

---

[172] See *R v Secretary of State for Home Department, ex parte Doody* [1994] 1 AC 531, per Lord Mustill at 564; *Stefan v General Medical Council (No 1)* [1999] 1 WLR 1293, PC; *R (Hasan) v Secretary of State for Trade and Industry* [2009] 3 All ER 539, paras 7 and 8; *R v Secretary of State for Education, ex parte G* [1995] ELR 58, at 67; *R v Higher Education Funding Council, ex parte Institute of Dental Surgery* [1994] 1 WLR 242, per Sedley J at 258 and 261.
[173] 1998 SLT 1244.

from particular competitions or for a particular period; powers of expulsion from the association; and the ubiquitous power to impose such other penalty as the tribunal shall think fit. As we have already noted, punitive powers, though derived from contract, may not constitute contractual terms directly binding the accuser and the accused. Each may contract with another body to abide by the outcome of the exercise of those punitive powers.

7.154 From time to time the question arises as to whether a disciplining body has gone beyond the powers of punishment possessed by it in a case where it has lawfully found an accused guilty. In other cases, a penalty imposed partly in respect of findings of guilt validly reached, and partly in respect of invalid findings of guilt which are erroneous in law, may be successfully challenged on the basis that the disciplining body took into account the invalid as well as the valid matters, resulting in an excessive penalty. It is desirable, therefore, for a disciplinary tribunal to indicate, when passing sentence, which punishment corresponds to which offence, lest a court should subsequently overturn the decision, not being able to sever any unobjectionable parts from the objectionable parts of the sentence.

7.155 A contractual power to penalise a person must, naturally, be exercised in accordance with the true meaning, scope, spirit and intent of the power. In a case where the rules provide an apparently unlimited discretion, the discretion must be exercised in a manner which is rational and within the range of reasonable sanctions with which the misconduct found may be visited. In the context of association football, an open-ended power to penalise does include a power to deduct points previously earned by winning or drawing matches. This was the fate suffered by Middlesbrough Football Club when it wrongly cancelled a fixture in late 1996 without just cause.[174]

7.156 However, the obligation to exercise powers of punishment rationally and in accordance with the spirit and intent of the power may mean that an exercise of penal power can be set aside, in an extreme case, even where the penalty imposed is one which is within the scope of the power on the true construction of the rule in play. Thus deduction of points from a football club's total may be within the range of penalties open to the relevant association where its rules allow it to impose such penalty as it thinks fit in respect of a particular transgression. It does not follow that the association's disciplinary organs may validly deduct any number of points, however great, in respect of any misconduct, however venial.

7.157 The discretion must be exercised within the four walls of the rule so as to give effect to its purpose. The protection of the discretion against subsequent interference by a court, though great, is not absolute; there must be some relationship of proportionality between the offence and the penalty with which it is visited. This principle flows from the

---

[174] An eccentric sequel to the Middlesbrough case was a county court action, *Arnolt v Football Association* (1998) unreported, 2 February, in which the plaintiff Middlesbrough supporter unsuccessfully argued that he was deprived of Premier League football by the deduction of three points, which in the event propelled the club into the relegation zone at the end of the season, giving Coventry City FC a windfall reprieve and condemning Middlesbrough to a season in what was then the First Division of the Football League. The London Wasps rugby club was more fortunate: it succeeded in showing that it had 'just cause' not to play a fixture against the Sale Sharks after the referee had failed to appreciate that it was for him, not the club, to decide whether the pitch was unsafe: *Wasps v Premier League Rugby*, PRL Designated Panel, reported at [2010] ISLR, SLR 44.

normal approach to the interpretation of contractual terms. They are presumed to bear a meaning in harmony with, and not at odds with, the inferred intention of the parties. A similar principle applies to the imposition of disciplinary penalties pursuant to statutory or other non-contractual powers of punishment or sanction.[175]

7.158 The principle is clear; applying it in a particular case may be more difficult. The view of a court subsequently considering the validity of a penalty imposed by a sporting body will necessarily depend to an extent on the outlook of the particular judge. In England, the court will not substitute its view for that of the disciplining body on the question whether the penalty imposed was right or wrong, provided it is within the range of responses open to a rational disciplinary body acting within its powers.[176] But the court will have to form a view as to where the upper and lower limits of that range lie in order to determine whether the sanction imposed falls within the range or outside it. To that extent, the court cannot avoid engaging in an assessment of the gravity of the misconduct found. Thus Tottenham Hotspur Football Club was able to achieve restoration of its rights to compete in the 1995–6 FA Challenge Cup, and restoration of 12 points which an appeal panel of the Football Association had purported to deduct from its Premiership tally.

7.159 In *McKeown v British Horseracing Authority*,[177] a complex saga of alleged corruption in the world of racing, Stadlen J remitted back a limited issue to a disciplinary panel where an Appeal Board had refused to remit back the same issue, it being common ground that the first panel had proceeded on the mistaken factual basis that certain horses had been moved to another location in December 2005 rather than, as was the fact, July 2005, a point that was potentially relevant to the severity of the penalty. The judge stated that he was taking this unusual course because it was not for him to substitute his view of the appropriate penalty.[178] The matter went back before the panel, which stated that it had power to *increase* the penalty but decided in the exercise of its discretion not to do so and to keep the same penalty of a four-year disqualification.[179]

7.160 In *Bradley v Jockey Club*[180] the Court of Appeal and Richards J upheld a decision of the club's appellate disciplinary body to reduce from eight years to five a ban imposed on a jockey for imparting sensitive information to a racing gambler in return for presents and money. The failure of the appeal was not surprising given that the appellant did not criticise Richards J's approach to the law, and given that the Appeal Board had directed itself expressly by reference to the definition of proportionality propounded by Lord Clyde in *De Freitas v Permanent Secretary of Agriculture, Fisheries, Lands and Housing*[181]

---

[175] See *R v Barnsley MBC, ex parte Hook* [1976] 1 WLR 102; *R v Secretary of State for Transport, ex parte Pegasus Holidays (London) Ltd* [1989] 2 All ER 481 at 490h–j. Cf Mummery J's decision in *Swindon Town FC v The Football Association Ltd, The Times,* 20 June 1990. It is now standard for football clubs to suffer a points deduction for going into administration, as has happened to several League One, League Two and Conference clubs, and, twice, to Portsmouth FC in the Championship.

[176] An exception was Cooke J's decision in *Colgan v The Kennel Club*, transcript, 26 October 2001, at para 49, where Cooke J indicated what he thought the correct (proportionate) sanctions were and said he would hear counsel further on the question of remedy.

[177] [2010] ISLR, SLR 87, Stadlen J.

[178] See para 378 of the long principal judgment.

[179] See the sequel at [2010] ISLR, SLR 157.

[180] [2005] EWCA Civ 1056, [2006] ISLR, SLR 1.

[181] [1999] 1 AC 69, at 80. The most important third part of the test is that the means used to impair the accused's right or freedom (ie by imposing a disciplinary sanction) must be no more than is necessary to accom-

and the adaptation of that test to the sports disciplinary context by Cooke J in *Colgan v The Kennel Club*,[182] in which dogs accidentally left in a vehicle by the club member died of heatstroke in hot weather.

7.161 The CAS has also had occasion, from time to time, to consider the validity of sanctions imposed for misconduct. In *National Wheelchair Basketball Association v International Paralympic Committee*,[183] the US paralympic basketball team had been disqualified and ordered to forfeit its gold medal gained by beating Spain in the 1992 Barcelona Paralympics, in consequence of a doping offence by one of its members. The CAS, applying Swiss law, upheld the decision to find misconduct proved, since it construed the rule as one imposing strict liability (as already explained above).[184] The CAS went on to consider the contention that the penalty of withdrawal of the gold medals from the entire team was grossly disproportionate to the infringement by one member of it (who was also personally banned for six months).

7.162 It held that an infringement by one team member necessarily must lead to forfeiture of the match, competition or event during which the infringement took place, by the entire team. It was able to leave open the separate question whether the rule in play conferred discretion to apply the forfeiture only to the match following which detection of the infringement took place, or whether the rule automatically applied to the entire competition leading up to the point of the infringement. The difference between these two interpretations was that, according to the former, the US team might have been able to have the silver medals instead of the gold; whereas according to the latter, the team would get nothing at all. In the event the CAS did not have to decide this subsequent issue of interpretation since the team abandoned its alternative case that it should be declared the silver medallists.

7.163 However, in *Football Association of Wales v UEFA*[185] the Welsh FA failed in its ambitious attempt to secure the disqualification of the Russian national team from the Euro 2004 competition, which would have meant qualification for Wales. A Russian substitute who was unused in the first of the two legs (a 0-0 draw in Moscow) played between Wales and Russia was tested after the first match, found to have taken bromantan, and sanctioned. Not knowing the test result, he played in the second leg in Cardiff until the 59th minute, when he was substituted, with Russia leading 1-0, also the final score. The CAS assumed, without deciding, that he would still have tested positive during the second leg, but even on that assumption refused to disqualify the Russian team, holding that on a correct reading of the rules the national team had to be implicated in the doping offence

---

plish the objective of the rule providing for the sanction to be imposed. The claimant had received an absolute discharge in criminal proceedings in the magistrates' court.

[182] Transcript, 26 October 2001, at para 42. Cooke J stated that various five-year suspensions and disqualifications imposed by the club's disciplinary organs were disproportionate and should be reduced to two and three years (for different elements of the offences), but rejected a claim that the procedure was unfair and held that damages could not be recovered, there being no duty to reach a correct result.

[183] CAS 95/122.

[184] As already explained above at para 7.60.

[185] CAS 2004/A/593.

and it was not enough for the player to be away from his club on international duty and under the control of the national federation.[186]

7.164 In *Chagnaud v FINA*,[187] a relatively early case, the CAS dealt with a two-year ban in a case of doping by a swimming coach without the swimmer's knowledge. The CAS explained the tension between the need for strict anti-doping measures, and the unfairness of a system that fails to differentiate between athletes doped without their knowledge and those who deliberately dope themselves. It came down in favour of a compromise position between the two extremes, which helped to lay the foundations for what is now the WADA Code. It considered that automatic disqualification from the competition in question should follow without any opportunity to disprove intent or fault. However, as to suspension from competitions over a period, the CAS stressed that the rules on sanctions should make allowance for 'an appreciation of the subjective elements in each case … in order to fix a just and equitable sanction'.[188] Thus the athlete should be presumed guilty where the banned substance is found present, but should be allowed to provide exculpatory evidence showing lack of fault or knowledge, in mitigation of the penalty to be imposed. The CAS pointed out that another swimmer had previously escaped with a strong warning in a similar case, and relied upon this precedent as showing that the Federation itself had refrained in the past from applying its doping rules strictly and rigidly. The rule in question merely stated: 'sanction recommended is 2 years for the first offence'.

7.165 The CAS therefore went on to consider whether Mlle Chagnaud had succeeded in rebutting the presumption of fault on her part, and found that she had not done so. Nevertheless it intervened to shorten the length of the ban from two years to a period of some 13 and a half months ending with the date of the hearing. The panel commented that the penalty was not in proportion to the circumstances of the case and pointed to the evidence of the 'excellent morality and exemplary conduct' of Mlle Chagnaud in general.[189] The CAS was prepared to substitute its own penalty for that of the Federation whose decision it overturned, rather than remitting the matter back for reconsideration by the Federation as an English court would do. But that was because the rules of the Federation provided for the CAS to hear the matter by way of appeal and not merely as a reviewing tribunal.

7.166 In *Cullwick v FINA*[190] a division of the CAS presided over by one of the authors entertained an appeal and held the offence to be one of strict liability of which the athlete was guilty in a technical sense only and without fault on his part. The power of the CAS under its regulations was, and still is, a 'full power to review the facts and the law'.[191]

---

[186] The panel rejected UEFA's contention that it lacked jurisdiction to deal with the case but held at para 53: '[I]t is impossible for a federation or club to control a player every day for 24 hours; the player will always have a chance sooner or later to hide and take by himself a forbidden substance.' For a fuller account of the case see Kerr, *Sanctioning of a Football Team*, ch 9 in Wild (ed), *CAS and Football: Landmark Cases* (Asser Press, 2012). See also Charlish, *Football Association of Wales v UEFA: Only Dopes Don't Cheat* [2004] ISLR 73; Kiener, *Consequences of Doping in Collective Team Sports: Review of Institutional Regulations and Case-Law* [2011] ISLR 67.

[187] CAS 95/141.

[188] Ibid, para 4(d) at p 9.

[189] Ibid, para 5 at p 12.

[190] CAS 96/149.

[191] See now CAS Procedural Rules as amended (version effective from 1 January 2012), reg R57.

In considering what sanctions to impose, the panel pointed out that since the offence was committed, the rules of the Federation had been amended so as to provide for a maximum two-year suspension for a first offence, rather than—if such were previously the correct interpretation—a mandatory two-year suspension for a first offence. The panel went on to invoke the doctrine of *lex mitior*,[192] which, in the civil law jurisdictions, permits a disciplinary tribunal to apply current sanctions to the case before it, if those current sanctions are less severe than those which existed at the time of the offence.[193] The offence being technical only, the upholding of the Federation's finding of liability was sufficient penalty in itself. No further penalty was imposed.

7.167 However, in an almost tragic case, *Raducan v IOC*,[194] a gold medal winning 16-year-old Romanian gymnast had taken a Nurofen tablet given to her by her team doctor for cold and headache symptoms and tested positive for pseudoephedrine without any proven competitive advantage. She was stripped of her gold medal by the IOC, which decided to impose no further disciplinary sanction such as a fine or period of ineligibility. The CAS Ad Hoc Panel saw no basis for impugning the validity of the decision: it was not necessary to show that competitive advantage had been obtained; the disqualification of results was automatic, and the player's young age could not alter that conclusion; nor could the fact that she had acted on medical advice.

7.168 We have already observed that powers to impose automatic or lengthy bans for certain types of misconduct can, in principle at least, be the subject of a challenge on the ground of restraint of trade.[195] Such challenges would be unlikely to succeed before the English courts, unless the penalties provided for were so manifestly excessive and disproportionate as to go beyond all reason. Automatic life bans for a first offence without possibility of mitigation or exculpation, applying in a case of innocent ingestion without fault or intention to gain, might be regarded as so harsh as to merit being struck down.

7.169 Strict and severe penalties short of that may be expected to be upheld, for the English courts would be loath to hand down rulings which would undermine the fight against drugs in sport. But even the WADC has produced cases in which the bounds of proportionality have been found to have been exceeded. As mentioned in chapter one of this book, in *Mariano Puerta v International Tennis Federation*[196] a CAS panel refused to apply a rule providing for a mandatory eight -year ban for a second doping offence committed without 'significant fault or negligence', reasoning that 'its decision in the present case does not involve the exercise of a discretion, but is a filling of a gap or lacuna in the WADC in circumstances which will rarely arise'.[197]

7.170 This reasoning was applied by an ITF tribunal, presided over by one of the authors, in *ITF v Richard Gasquet*,[198] when it refused to impose a two -year ban provided for a first

---

[192] Further mentioned below at para 7.171.

[193] See, eg, Art 2 para 2 of the Swiss Penal Code, and cf Art 2 of the Italian Penal Code; applied in *International Cycling Union and Italian National Olympic Committee*, CAS Advisory Opinion, February 1995, CAS 94/128, para 33, pp 48–49.

[194] CAS OG 00/011.

[195] See chapter 3, para 3.55 ff.

[196] CAS 2006/A/1025, 12 July 2006; [2006] ISLR, SLR 149.

[197] See para 11.7.29 of the judgment.

[198] Anti-Doping Tribunal, 15 July 2009. The tribunal imposed only a short ban, being time served pending the hearing.

doping offence involving a non-specified substance committed without significant fault or negligence. The tribunal agreed with the player that the likely cause of ingestion of the extremely small amount of cocaine in the player's body was contamination in a Miami nightclub by kisses from a woman who had ingested cocaine. Importantly, the governing body did not submit that this explanation was implausible and the expert scientists agreed that it was not inconsistent with the evidence. The decision was upheld by the CAS, which went further and actually found that the player had committed no fault or negligence, but dismissed the appeal on the basis that it was bound by the principle *ne eat iudex ultra petita partium* (the tribunal cannot grant relief going beyond the relief that is sought).[199]

7.171 As already noted, the WADC and the CAS jurisprudence includes the doctrine of *lex mitior*. The doctrine has not featured in the common law of England and is not familiar in the practice of the English speaking jurisdictions of the world, but is now frequently encountered in sports jurisprudence under the influence of the CAS. Sports bodies' rules frequently make express provision for its application, including bodies whose rules are governed by English law, and it is now applied frequently by sports disciplinary tribunals in England, as well as by international arbitral tribunals and the CAS, to the benefit of players and athletes who are able to rely on more favourable rules in relation to penalties, superseding those in force at the time the rules were breached.[200]

7.172 Since we wrote the first edition of this book, the sports jurisprudence has developed to such an extent that there is now available to practitioners a body of judicial precedent serving as a useful guide to the appropriate penalty in a given case. Where in the past there was a marked absence of consistency, sports tribunals now routinely cite—and have cited to them by lawyers—previous decisions considered useful as a guide to the appropriate penalty. While the appropriate penalty is a question which turns on the facts of each case, common threads have begun to emerge: for example, a likely ban of around three months for recreational cannabis consumption, absent any aggravating factors;[201] and a ban of between around two and seven months for accidental ingestion of a specified substance for medical purposes without sufficiently checking ingredients or asking a doctor to do so.[202] In *UCI v Alexander Kolobnev and Russian Cycling Federation*[203] there is a useful compendium of 'reprimand', 'warning' and various other such short ban cases.

7.173 Sometimes a punishment will be mitigated under the relevant rules by the giving of assistance to the governing body by the miscreant. For example, the ITF announced in December 2010 that one Wayne Odesnik, a US player serving a two -year ban for a doping

---

[199] Para 64 of the CAS award.

[200] See eg *Filippo Volandri v ITF*, CAS/2009/A/1782, para 50; *UCI v CONI*, CAS/94/128; *CONI*, CAS/2005/C/841, p 14; and in nationally based tribunals, see *Duckworth v UK Anti-Doping*, National Anti-Doping Appeal Tribunal, 10 January 2011 (David Phillips QC chairing); *UK Anti-Doping v Wallader*, National Anti-Doping Appeal Tribunal, 29 October 2010 (Charles Flint QC chairing); *South African Rugby Union v Ralepelle*, SARU Judicial Committee, 27 January 2011; *Luis Bernabé v ATP Tour Inc*, ATP Tour Anti-Doping Tribunal, 7 April 2005 (Professor Richard McLaren presiding).

[201] *Coutelot*, ATP Anti-Doping Tribunal, 10 August 2004; *ITF v Fischer*, Anti-Doping Tribunal, 30 January 2006; *ITF v Buck*, Anti-Doping Tribunal, 28 February 2006.

[202] *Koubek v ITF*, CAS/2005/A/828; *ICC v Smartt*, Anti-Doping Tribunal, 14 December 2011; *Drug Free Sport New Zealand v Chalmers*, Sports Tribunal of New Zealand, 11 March 2010; *Dos Santos*, Presidential Commission of the International Gymnastic Federation (FIG), 27 January 2010; *WADA and FIG v Melnychenko*, CAS 2011/A/2403, 25 August 2011; *WADA v Van Jaarsveld*, Anti-Doping Appeal Tribunal of South Africa, 22 September 2011; *ICC v Tharanga*, Anti-Doping Tribunal, 15 July 2011.

[203] CAS 2011/A/2645, 29 February 2012; see at para 92.

offence after human growth hormone was found in his luggage by Australian customs officials on his entry to that country to play in the Australian Open in January 2010,[204] had had
the second year of his ban suspended 'on account of ongoing Substantial Assistance provided by Mr Odesnik in relation to the enforcement of professional rules of conduct'.[205]

7.174 This form of after-the-event plea bargaining is permitted under the WADC, and
encourages players to rehabilitate themselves early by helping to root out misconduct by
others. In similar vein, the rugby player Tom Williams, who had faked injury to allow
another player to re-enter the field of play, had his suspension reduced on appeal from 12
months to four months, with the concurrence of the disciplinary officer. He claimed that
he had given false evidence under duress to the first instance disciplinary enquiry, and
on appeal changed his evidence so as to 'come clean' and give different evidence which
the disciplinary officer found credible and had allowed the disciplinary body to 'pursue
other culpable individuals'.[206]

7.175 At the other extreme, disciplinary bodies' rules may permit provisional suspension to be imposed on a player before the full hearing takes place. For example, the
International Cricket Council's rules confers on the ICC a discretion to impose provisional suspension where it charges a player with an offence and considers that the integrity of the sport could otherwise be seriously undermined. In doping cases governed by
the ITF's rules, the Federation can impose provisional suspension following a positive
test result where a review board determines that there is a case to answer, but the player
can apply to the independent chairman of the anti-doping tribunal to have the suspension lifted. Periods of provisional suspension invariably count towards any subsequently
imposed ban on competition; as do periods of voluntarily self-imposed abstention from
competition, provided that due notice is properly given by the player.

7.176 Court challenges in pending or unsatisfactorily completed cases are not unknown.
In *Tyrrell Racing Organisation v RAC Motor Sports Association and FIA*,[207] a rare injunction was granted requiring a governing body to permit a racing team to take part in a
lucrative grand prix, on the ground that the team had a strong case suggesting a breach of
natural justice in disciplinary proceedings leading to a ban. But the jockey Kieren Fallon
was not successful in overturning a provisional ban imposed on him by an independent
panel chaired by a former High Court judge (and an unsuccessful appeal to a similarly
eminent independent appellate body), preventing him from racing until the conclusion
of criminal proceedings against him for alleged conspiracy to defraud. Davis J upheld the
decisions, holding that they were within the margin of appreciation afforded by the law to
sports governing bodies, and rejected the arguments that Mr Fallon had not been heard
on the issue of the weakness of the charges, and that the ban was disproportionate in the
absence of proven wrongdoing.[208]

---

[204] ITF press release of 19 May 2010, published on its website.
[205] ITF press release of 22 December 2010, also on its website.
[206] *Tom Williams*, Appeal Committee of the European Rugby Cup, 17 August 2009, arising from the notorious
'Bloodgate' affair and reported at [2009] ISLR, SLR 122; see also Connolly, *A Warning to Disciplinary Panels of
Regulatory Bodies: The Impact of 'Bloodgate' Goes Beyond Sport* (2010) 18(2) SLJ 6; also at [2012] ISLR 3.
[207] (1984) unreported, 20 July, Hirst J.
[208] *Fallon v Horseracing Regulatory Authority* [2006] EWHC 2030 (QB). Fallon was acquitted of conspiracy to
defraud at the Old Bailey in December 2007.

7.177 We conclude our observations on penalties in sports disciplinary proceedings by returning to the most serious offences of all, involving corruption. We touched on some such cases from the world of horse racing above, where bans of the order of five years have ensued from cases of imparting information about horses useful to a gambler, for valuable consideration.[209] In match fixing or spot fixing cases, heavy punishments are handed out. We have already mentioned the cases of the Pakistani cricketers given lengthy bans for spot fixing,[210] and the two tennis players banned for life for corruption offences involving financial inducement to contrive the outcome of matches.[211]

7.178 In *Oleg Oriekhov v UEFA*,[212] evidence obtained by telephone tapping circumstantially implicated the Ukranian referee of a Europa League match between Basel and Sofia in 2009 in a possible corrupt attempt to fix the match. He was provisionally suspended and subsequently banned for life by UEFA's disciplinary body (upheld on internal appeal) for failing to report, in breach of a clear express duty to do so, repeated contacts with a criminal betting syndicate. It was not proved that he had actually fixed the match or accepted money for doing so. FIFA then extended the ban to give it worldwide effect. Before the CAS, the decisions were upheld on the basis that a life ban was within the rules and

> the Panel has to remind itself that match-fixing, money-laundering, kickbacks, extortion, bribery and the like are a growing concern, indeed a cancer, in many major sports, football included, and must be eradicated …[213]

Faced with such a scourge, sports governing bodies are increasingly concerned that the science of cheating in sport may be outflanking the science of detecting cheats. Doping scandals are perhaps less heinous than they were 20 years ago. The scandal of a Ben Johnson crudely taking banned steroids, or certain nations routinely doping their national athletes, is now less frequently encountered. Doping cheats are now more likely to get caught than they were in the 1970s and 1980s because of improvements in detection techniques. But match fixing, spot fixing and corrupt betting are cause for increasing concern. Unfortunately, sports such as cricket and tennis lend themselves to such activities because of the increasing complexity of betting practices: bookmakers may now offer odds on a double fault in a certain game and set, a no ball in a certain over, and so forth.

Governing bodies have responded by employing ex-detectives to investigate suspected corrupt practices and devising rules requiring compulsory cooperation in interviews, compulsory reporting of corrupt approaches, mandatory disclosure of mobile telephone records, bank statements and other documents, and severe punishment for transgressors, coupled with a policy of virtual zero tolerance and recognition that such corruption offences are by definition grave and never trivial, as shown by the CAS panel's decision in *Oriekhov*.[214]

---

[209] Eg the five -year ban imposed on appeal in *Bradley v Jockey Club* [2005] EWCA Civ 1056, [2006] ISLR, SLR 1, discussed above.

[210] Above, paras 7.15, 7.22. See Ross, *Corruption in Cricket: Using the Law to Cull the Crooks from the Gentleman's Game* (2010) 18(3) SLJ 28.

[211] Above, para 7.14.

[212] CAS 2010/A/2172 (CAS panel presided over by our senior author).

[213] Para 78 of the CAS award, 18 January 2011.

[214] Notorious examples of past corruption scandals include the cases of Hansie Cronje, South African cricket captain (life ban, 2000); Mohammed Azharuddin, Indian cricketer (life ban, 2000); Robert Hoyzer, German

Costs

7.179 This subject may be briefly disposed of. The rules of sporting bodies may or may not provide for awards of costs. In the absence of such provision, it is often thought that the tribunal concerned will not have any power to make an award of costs, so that each party will bear its own legal costs, if any. However in England, if the proceedings are arbitration proceedings arising from an arbitration agreement,[215] and the rules are silent on the question of costs, the effect of sections 4(2), 59 and 61–65 of the Arbitration Act 1996 is that the arbitral tribunal will have power to award costs recoverable and specify the amount recoverable in respect of the arbitrators' fees and as between the parties.

7.180 The rules of sporting bodies frequently, and increasingly, do confer a discretion on their disciplinary tribunals to make awards of costs if they think fit. The regulations of the CAS also provide for jurisdiction to award costs.[216] The duty on domestic tribunals to act fairly does not require there to be a jurisdiction to award costs. Indeed, as we have already seen, there are cases in which representation need not be allowed, even where it is provided at the expense of the represented party.[217] In doping cases, governing bodies may recover forfeited prize money in amounts which—depending on the case—may far exceed the governing body's legal costs, or may represent only a small fraction of them.

Appeals

7.181 Likewise, it is not necessary, as part of the duty of fairness, for the rules of a sporting body, or its practice in disciplinary matters, to allow for an appeal, whether internally or to an external independent body, against the determination of a properly constituted disciplinary body established under the association's rules. Whether such an appeal lies will depend entirely on the content of the rules in play.[218]

7.182 If the rules do provide a right of appeal and the appeal itself, or the hearing leading to the decision appealed against, is conducted in an unlawful manner, then the accused may be entitled to relief from the court, subject to the possibility of an initial defect being cured by means of an appeal, in accordance with the principles established by the Privy Council in *Calvin v Carr*.[219]

---

football referee (life ban and imprisoned, 2005); Edilson Pereira de Carvalho, Brazilian football referee (life ban, 2005); and see also *FK Pobeda, Aleksandar Zabrcanec, Nikolce Zdraveski v UEFA*, CAS/2009/A/1920 (life ban for club president but club captain acquitted of involvement, 2010).

[215] Defined in s 6(1) of the Arbitration Act 1996 as 'an agreement to submit to arbitration present or future disputes (whether they are contractual or not)'.

[216] See the current CAS Procedural Rules, rule R64.5: 'In the arbitral award, the Panel shall determine which party shall bear the arbitration costs or in which proportion the parties shall share them. As a general rule, the Panel has discretion to grant the prevailing party a contribution towards its legal fees and other expenses incurred in connection with the proceedings and, in particular, the costs of witnesses and interpreters. When granting such contribution, the Panel shall take into account the outcome of the proceedings, as well as the conduct and the financial resources of the parties.'

[217] See above, para 7.126.

[218] See *Jones v Welsh Rugby Union*, transcript 27 February 1997, p 21, applying *Ward v Bradford Corporation* (1972) LGR 27, CA. The relevant rules may permit an appeal by the governing body as well as the player.

[219] [1980] AC 574, per Lord Wilberforce at 592–6.

7.183 In the CAS appeal arbitration procedure, the panel has 'full power to review the facts and the law'.[220] This has been widely interpreted as empowering the panel to reopen questions of fact and effectively allows a *de novo* hearing, a provision which has the advantage of allowing eccentric findings of domestic sports tribunals to be revisited, though it can encourage speculative appeals since it does not exclude even reversal of findings of fact made by a sport specific independent tribunal which has heard oral evidence not called on appeal before the CAS.[221]

7.184 In *Volandri v ITF*[222] the CAS panel held that its scope of review is 'basically unrestricted' and rejected a submission from the ITF that the jurisdiction of the panel was restricted by the agreement between the parties reflected in a rule of the ITF providing that the CAS may overturn a decision and substitute its own decision only if it considers that the decision appealed against is 'erroneous or legally unsound'. The reasoning is not completely clear, but it appears the CAS panel decided, first, that this provision was effectively overridden by other provisions in the rules themselves, but also that the WADC, which the rules mirrored, itself provides for appeal exclusively to the CAS and requires the full applicability of the CAS's procedural rules including the power to revisit all issues of fact and law *de novo*. It is therefore doubtful, at any rate in doping cases, whether a WADC signatory body could, by clear words, limit the applicability of the CAS's procedural rules.

The Practical Management of Disciplinary Issues

7.185 It is now no longer possible to do without lawyers in sport, in the age of media moguls, competition law, transfer fees running to many millions of pounds, satellite broadcasting, cable television, business sponsorship and the inexorable growth of professionalism. Disciplinary issues in sport are particularly likely to give rise to legal controversy. The accused in disciplinary proceedings is usually no less, and sometimes more, in need of good legal support than his, her or its accuser. For example, many athletes faced with a adverse analytical finding indicating the presence of a banned substance may feel at a loss as to the options open to them. Should they accept a long period of suspension, even if they have not consciously taken anything stronger than cough medicine for bronchitis? Is the positive test conclusive evidence? Is the offence committed without knowledge, intention or fault?

7.186 These are issues which could bemuse any intelligent lay person. If the WADC applies, there is little excuse for not knowing what to do: the Code itself makes players responsible for knowledge of its contents and is accompanied by educational measures to familiarise athletes with its contents. It is probably easier for most players to understand the Code than for most lawyers to run as fast as, or jump as high as, an Olympian. But players required by the rules themselves to understand those same rules still need good legal advice on what to do when confronted with an allegation of breach.

---

[220] CAS Procedural Rule R57.

[221] As in *Mariano Puerta v ITF* 2006/A/1025, 12 July 2006; [2006] ISLR, SLR 149, where the CAS panel, without hearing oral evidence, replaced a finding of fact that the player had not explained the source of a prohibited substance with a finding that he had done so.

[222] CAS/2009/A/1782, see para 57.

7.187 In the case of sporting bodies, legal advice is relevant at the following stages:

(1) The drafting of rules: some sporting associations still have rules which have not been drafted or even vetted by lawyers. Drafting by lawyers, or scrutiny by lawyers of draft rules, ought not to mean that the rules become more complicated and technical. It should mean the opposite. They should be clear, simple and free from technicality, and should avoid legal pitfalls so that they can survive robust consideration by a court or arbitral panel in the event of challenge.

(2) The composition of adjudicating bodies, and the administrative arrangements for disciplinary hearings or other potentially contentious matters, including procedures for selecting participants for particular competitions, which may in some cases engage the duty to act fairly.

(3) The conduct of domestic disciplinary hearings, including the exercise of discretion as to procedural matters. If a lawyer is not sitting on the panel, adjournments to obtain advice quickly may be preferable to the risk of a legal mistake by a lay tribunal member when reacting to, for instance, a request to be allowed to call a particular witness, or to be granted access to confidential documents regarding the case.

(4) Consideration of the function of the adjudicating body in deciding on guilt or innocence: for example, whether a particular finding is open to the tribunal on the basis of the evidence, or on the basis of the correct construction of rules at issue.

(5) Consideration of the merits of any dispute as to the conduct of disciplinary matters after their conclusion but before the issue of proceedings to challenge the outcome. As we shall see shortly, sporting bodies can sometimes be protected against successful claims even after they have made mistakes of law or treated a sportsman or woman or a club unfairly.

(6) Finally, advice on the prospects of success of proceedings to challenge the outcome of a disciplinary case, and if necessary representation as an advocate in such proceedings.

7.188 One obvious way of achieving good legal decision making in the conduct of disciplinary proceedings is to appoint a lawyer to chair the disciplinary panel. This already happens in many cases. An alternative is to ensure that the rules provide for or permit the presence of a lawyer to act as an adviser to the disciplinary panel. In the latter case it is important to ensure that the lawyer does not stray beyond his or her brief by becoming involved in the factual merits, as opposed to the legal issues, in the case.

7.189 Good practical management of disciplinary issues by a sporting body requires experience and legal knowledge. In the case of the accused, the objective will be to assert procedural rights so as to prevent any risk of prejudice, and in order to allow presentation of the defence, and if necessary mitigation, at its strongest. It is often helpful for the chairman to issue a procedural order giving directions for the fair disposal of the case. A major purpose of this is to record matters of agreement and, where possible, avoid later factual disputes about what actually happened during the disciplinary process. A further purpose is to isolate matters of disagreement in point of law so as to enable legally unimpeachable rulings on points of procedure, evidence and construction to be given before, or in some cases during, the substantive hearing of the factual disciplinary issues.

7.190 In setting the procedural framework, it is important that the tribunal or chairman avoids stating views on contentious factual or legal issues, unless they are explicitly described as provisional and subject to consideration of further representations from the parties. A procedural framework document may also usefully contain a brief account of the anticipated procedure, to assist the parties and the tribunal, for example under the following headings, which may be useful as a checklist:

(1) the constitution of the disciplining body; and confirmation that there is no objection to any of the members sitting;

(2) the name and contact details of the representatives;

(3) the date, time and venue of the hearing and the time estimate;

(4) the role of any adviser to the panel, making clear the distinction between the adviser and the members;

(5) whether the disciplinary offence charged is admitted, denied or admitted in part;

(6) the nature of the hearing, ie whether it is an initial hearing or an appeal, and whether, if an appeal, it is by way of rehearing *de novo* or by way of review only;

(7) the onus of proof in relation to each issue, under the rules, or at common law, to the extent that onus is relevant, ie particularly in an adversarial procedure;

(8) the standard of proof in relation to each issue, which will usually be proof on the balance of probabilities, or 'comfortable satisfaction';

(9) the deadlines for any exchange of written statements of the parties' cases and submissions, written witness statements and documents (often in accordance with specific procedural provisions in the relevant rules);

(10) any issues in relation to disclosure of documents or any order for production or disclosure of documents;

(11) any directions for exchange or service of written evidence from any expert witness or witnesses;

(12) the arrangements for production of the bundle of relevant documents, usually by the governing body bringing the charge;

(13) the procedure for the giving of evidence orally (if applicable) at the hearing, including any arrangements for evidence to be given by an interpreter, by telephone or by video link;

(14) the order in which the parties will make closing submissions at the conclusion of the evidence;

(15) the means by which the decision is likely to be announced, if known: whether orally or in writing, and whether in a reserved or *extempore* decision;

(16) the position as to costs, ie whether there is power to award them; if not it is as well to warn the parties that each side will bear their own whatever the outcome;

(17) the range of penalties open to the disciplining body in the event of a finding of liability in whole or in part, but this may only be appropriate where there is an exhaustive list of available penalties;

(18) any rights of further appeal from the decision of the disciplining body, eg to the CAS.

7.191 Needless to say, a record should be kept, as accurately as possible, of the oral hearing of a disciplinary issue. Some governing bodies provide recording and transcription services for this purpose. The involvement of an independent person as a member of a disciplinary panel may or may not be provided for in the rules. The inclusion of such a person helps to ensure the exercise of independent judgment, which minimises the risk of procedural or other unfairness to the accused and consequential legal challenge. The avoidance of prior discussion of the merits by any panel member is an essential discipline. So is the avoidance of any appearance of bias or the risk of bias, such as may be even innocently conveyed by private discussions held in corridors during a hiatus in a hearing.

7.192 In some cases it may be desirable, in addition, to draw up a 'list of issues' arising in the hearing. If the parties are legally represented, their representatives can be expected to use their professional skill and experience to assist in this process and if possible agree the list of issues. The objective is to focus everybody's minds on that which is relevant and away from that which is irrelevant. The following is an example of issues that could arise in a doping case: (i) Did the sample tested contain a banned substance? (ii) If so, was the sample tested the same sample as that provided by the athlete? (iii) If so, was the athlete aware of the presence of a banned substance in his body? (iv) If not, is the offence of doping nevertheless made out? (v) If so, what penalty may be imposed?

7.193 Where documents of the type suggested are available, it is a useful discipline to invite each party or representative to indicate the extent to which they are in agreement as to the points set out in the procedural framework document, and to what extent they are in agreement that the list of issues truly states the relevant issues. A procedure document along the lines suggested above, intended to secure agreement to procedural matters, will be very difficult for a party to challenge in any subsequent legal proceedings, if no challenge to what it records is made at the time of the hearing. Unnecessary later disputes arising from nothing more than simple misunderstandings in a tense atmosphere, perhaps compounded by linguistic difficulties, may frequently be avoided by these simple expedients.

7.194 If a contentious procedural issue arises at a hearing before a disciplining body, of a type which might later become the subject of a legal challenge, then it is advisable to give clear, brief and legally correct rulings on those points, recorded on tape or at least in note form. An example would be a brief ruling on the panel's interpretation of a particular rule; or on whether an adjournment should be granted to allow more time to prepare; or on whether the accused should be allowed to cross-examine a laboratory technician who packed certain samples which later tested positive. Such rulings should include brief and cogent reasons, and should be sound in law; the reasons given should be good ones, since the record of the decision and the reasons for it will be admissible in any later court proceedings.

7.195 A vexed question that can arise in legal challenges to disciplinary proceedings is whether a party who has omitted to take a particular objection, or who has actively acquiesced in a particular procedural course, is precluded from subsequently taking the objection not previously taken, or from resiling from his acquiescence to the particular course. For the accused's representative, a dilemma may arise between wishing to reserve the accused's position for a later legal challenge in the event of a disagreement with the disciplining body on a particular procedural issue, and the risk that the disciplining body may look with ill favour upon such a reservation of the accused's position, perceiving it as an expression of less than full confidence in the disciplining body's ability to conduct itself properly. For the sporting association, and the disciplinary panel established under its rules, the objective is normally to achieve something as close as possible to finality. The steps mentioned above constitute an important safeguard against later legal proceedings.

7.196 The extent to which a party has, or has not, availed himself of his right to take a particular objection at a disciplinary hearing, or has acquiesced in a certain course later challenged, is always relevant to the exercise of the court's discretion as to the grant of relief, a subject to which we shall return in the next chapter on remedies. A more difficult question concerns the circumstances in which a court will hold that a party is barred from advancing a contention at all by reason of having taken a previous inconsistent position. In *Modahl v British Athletic Federation Ltd*[223] the plaintiff alleged, among other things, bias against two members of the disciplinary committee which initially found her guilty of a doping offence, a verdict against which she then successfully appealed. On the assumption that the appeal had not cured any defect arising from such bias (which was assumed but not at that stage proved), the Court of Appeal went on to consider whether it was open to Ms Modahl to complain in court of bias on the part of one committee member, to whose presence on the panel objection had been taken prior to the hearing but not at the hearing.

7.197 Insofar as reliance was to be placed solely on that member's alleged bias, Lord Woolf MR held[224] that Ms Modahl's claim for breach of contract would have failed because her failure to object was a representation by silence which prevented the disciplinary committee considering the basis of her objection, ie alleged bias. Morritt LJ considered that Ms Modahl's conduct in forbearing to object to the particular panel member at the hearing was capable of creating an estoppel of the type exemplified in *Central London Property Trust Ltd v High Trees House Ltd*,[225] or a waiver as described by Lord Denning MR in *WJ Alan & Co v El Nasr Export*.[226] However, the Court of Appeal declined to strike out the allegations of bias because they included a further, different objection of which the plaintiff athlete had, on the assumed facts, been unaware at the time of the hearing when she failed to make her objection.

7.198 Likewise in *Jones v Welsh Rugby Union*,[227] Ebsworth J, on an interlocutory application, stated that the omission of the plaintiff rugby player's accompanying friend to request specifically leave to question witnesses 'cannot estop the plaintiffs from complaining of the unfairness of the procedure'.[228] The reasoning in support of that proposition is not elaborated in the judgment. In the same case, the judge considered an argument advanced by the Union that Ebbw Vale Rugby Football Club had acquiesced in the procedural disciplinary rules of which it was complaining in court by omitting to take any constitutional step to alter them in a general or special meeting of the Union that had promulgated them, of which the Club was a member. On that point, the judge reserved her conclusion to trial, holding that the question of acquiescence was a matter of factual dispute on which it would be wrong to draw conclusions on affidavit evidence. At best, such an argument is likely to influence the exercise of a court's discretion to grant relief, rather than fulfilling the stricter requirements of estoppel or waiver.

7.199 Even in a case where unfairness has tainted disciplinary proceedings, for example owing to a failure to take into account exculpatory material relevant to the defence, there remains still the possibility of a further hearing curing the defect and preventing the other party from obtaining a remedy from the court since, as always, it is open to the court in the exercise of its discretion to refuse relief. If the conduct of the proceedings has been fair overall, taking into account the curative effect of any appeal, then relief may

---

[223] Transcript, 28 July 1997, CA.
[224] Ibid, p 28.
[225] [1947] KB 130.
[226] [1972] 2 QB 189, CA, at 213.
[227] Transcript, 27 February 1997.
[228] Ibid, p 19.

well be refused. If the rules of the body concerned provide no mechanism for an internal appeal, that is in itself no bar to a sporting body deciding voluntarily to revisit a decision which it believes may otherwise be challenged in court—whether successfully or otherwise (and even an ill-founded challenge has nuisance value and may generate irrecoverable cost). It is often overlooked that reconsideration of a disputed or contentious ruling can be undertaken by means of a rehearing, or some other form of renewed and further consideration of the matter, perhaps by a differently constituted body, and perhaps using a more rigorous procedure.

7.200 This is because there is no effective doctrine of *functus officio* in contract law, unless the contract itself so provides. Once a sports disciplining body has changed its allegedly unfair procedure it is, in our view, at liberty to hold a second hearing and impose a new and valid penalty.[229] However, one inhibiting factor is the consideration that the sporting body may not want to be seen to admit any failing in its prior handling of the matter of which complaint is made. It need not make any such admission, since further consideration of the matter can take place on the basis that this will occur without prejudice to the body's contention that the handling of the matter to date has been impeccable.[230] The other party, if well advised, is likely to respond by agreeing to such further consideration, but without prejudice to the contention that the first consideration of the matter was invalid and unlawful; and that any subsequent reconsideration is not admitted to be capable of curing the defect.

Principles Applied in Disciplinary Proceedings Before the CAS

7.201 Fundamental to the idea of fairness to sportsmen and honesty of results is the strict liability rule in doping offences, in which even inadvertent absorption of banned substances is penalised,[231] it is no defence to an athlete to claim that he was the victim of mislabelling, contaminated stock or faulty advice:[232]

> It is the trust and reliance of clean athletes in their sports and not the trust and reliance of athletes in their physicians and coaches which merit the highest priority in the weighing of the issues in the case at hand … At the starting line a doped athlete remains a doped athlete regardless of whether he or she has been victimised by his physician or coach.[233]

---

[229] See *Jones v Welsh Rugby Union* in the Court of Appeal, *The Times*, 6 January 1998 (appeal from Potts J).

[230] See by analogy in the context of trade union disciplinary proceedings *McKenzie v NUPE* [1991] ICR 155, QBD, in which Popplewell J reviewed previous authorities.

[231] The strict liability was described as part of the emerging *lex sportiva* in CAS 2002/0/373, *COC v IOC*, para 14. See Blackshaw, *Why Strict Liability is Essential to Policing Doping*, WSLR 4/11, p 4. There is a luminous analysis of the main ingredients of the rule in *L v IOC*, CAS 2000/A/310, paras 21–26, *N v FEI*, CAS 94/126, Reeb 2 137. The strict liability rule applies to horses as well as humans and coaches. Cf *H v FINA*, CAS 98/218, Reeb 2 325. The strict liability rule applies to coaches: *V v FINA*, CAS 95/150, Reeb 1 265.

[232] See eg *Vencil v USADA*, CAS 2003/A/484, paras 54–62. See however the counter case: Savulescu, Foddy and Clayton, *Why We Should Allow Performance Enhancing Drugs in Sports* (2004) 38 BVJ Sports Law 666; Cox, *Legalisation of Drug Use in Sport* [2002] ISLR 27; Smith, *WADA Should Not Ban Athletes for Recreational Drug Use*, WSLR 4/9, and the riposte: Blackshaw, *WADA Should Ban Athletes Who Take Recreational Drugs*, WSLR 5/1, p 16.

[233] *D v FEI*, CAS 2002/A/432, para 44.

As was said in *Quigley v UIT*:[234]

> ... the vicissitudes of competition, like those of life generally, may create many types of unfairness, whether by accident or the negligence of unaccountable persons, which the law cannot repair ... It appears to be a laudable policy objective not to repair an accidental unfairness to an individual by creating an intentional unfairness to the whole body of other competitors.

In this instance the interests of the many have to be preferred to the interests of the one.[235] There were further pragmatic considerations. Proving guilty intent would be difficult when all the key facts were known only to the athlete. Proving actual enhancement of performance would necessitate adduction of expert evidence. Litigation in which *mens rea* or efficacy was in issue would be damaging to the finality of results and destructive of the budgets of many sports bodies. Principled objections founded on such positive concepts as the presumption of innocence, natural justice and the right to work, and negative ones such as restraint of trade and anti-competitive practice, have proved sufficient to undermine the rule.

7.202 The European Court of Human Rights has held that strict liability offences do not violate Article 6(2) of the Convention (presumption of innocence in criminal cases),[236] and still more recently the European Court of Justice has accepted the compatibility of such offences with the pro-competition provisions of the Treaty of European Union.[237] Although the sometime President of the IAAF Tribunal Judge Laurens Tarasti appears to have taken the view that proof of due care and attention might exculpate an athlete in whose bodily fluids prohibited substances were found,[238] this article of belief has been roundly denounced as heresy by the CAS.[239] Nor will much heed be paid to technical points only.[240]

> If the Panel is satisfied the sample tested came from the person or horse in question, and that the chain of custody is established, that no question of contamination arises, that the equipment used to test was appropriate and that the results were correctly interpreted, then it should not be deterred from upholding a verdict as to the presence of a prohibited substance merely because some departure from procedure may be proven, still less because of matters inherent to the validity of the test.[241]

But the rigours of the rule are tempered by a number of considerations, each of which operates as a quid pro quo. First, the CAS has demanded that a strict liability standard must be clearly articulated.

> The fight against doping is arduous and it may require strict rules. But the rule makers and rule appliers must begin by being strict with themselves. Regulations that may affect the careers of dedicated athletes must be predictable. They must emanate from duly authorised bodies. They must be adopted in constitutionally proper ways. They should not be the product of an obscure process

---

[234] CAS 94/129 (paras 14–15). See generally McLaren, *CAS Doping Jurisprudence: What Can We Learn?* [2006] ISLR 4.

[235] See eg *D v FINA*, CAS 2002/A/432, para 44 for a strong statement to this effect.

[236] *Salabiaku v France*, decision of 7 October 1998, para 27 A114-A.

[237] Case C-519/04 P *Meca-Medina* [2006] ECR I-6991, ECJ.

[238] Tarasti, *Legal Solutions in International Doping Cases* (SEP Editrice, 2000).

[239] *Baxter v IOC*, CAS 2002/A/376, paras 7–9.

[240] *P v PEI*, CAS 98/184, Reeb 2 197 (para 19). But where a person charged with doping a horse did not ask for confirmatory analysis of a positive urine sample, but was kept in ignorance of a negative blood test (itself *not* necessarily inconsistent with a positive urine test), she was held not to have waived her right to ask for such analysis because she was not given the material on which to make an informed choice: ibid, paras 23–24.

[241] *H v FIM*, CAS 2000/A/281, Reeb 2 410, para 16. There is, however, a defence of act of ill-will of third party: *A v FEI*, CAS 91/56, Reeb 1 93, para 4.

of accretion. Athletes and officials should not be confronted with a thicket of mutually qualifying or even contradictory rules that can be understood only on the basis of de facto practice over the course of many years by a small group of insiders.[242]

7.203 For example, the CAS reinstated the gold medal of the winner of the snowboarding giant slalom at the 1998 Winter Games in Nagano, the Canadian Ros Rebagliatti, who had tested positive for the use of marijuana, since under the relevant code marijuana was not then—though it is now—listed as a banned substance.[243]

7.204 And at the Sydney Olympics, the US 4 x 400 metre men's relay team retained their gold medals although one of their squad, Jerome Young, who competed in a preliminary round, was ineligible because of a doping offence; as the rule in place at that time targeted individuals and not teams:[244]

> To take a rule that plainly concerns individual ineligibility and the annulment of individual rights, and then to stretch and complement and construe it in order that it may be said to govern the results achieved by teams is the sort of legal abracadabra that partisans in the fight against doping in sport love, but in which athletes should not be required to engage in order to understand the meaning of the rules to which they are subject.[245]

The CAS, however, used

> the fundamental principle upon which the IOC is based and the IOC's corresponding duty to fight doping and promote sports ethics [to override an IOC interpretation of one of their rules] which would allow an athlete excluded from the Olympics and banned for doping to retain any medals gained at such Games.[246]

Second, the SGB has to establish the element of the offence to the level of 'comfortable satisfaction'.[247] Moreover, the CAS proceeds on the basis that 'the fight against doping is no excuse for the conviction of innocent persons'[248] and that it 'considers only the evidence before it and pays no attention to media hyperbole'.[249] Third, a bright line has been drawn between the sanctions relevant to the competition in which the athlete is proved to have had the presumed benefit of drugs and those relevant to the athlete's long-term future. In respect of the latter, all circumstances may be taken into account, and here the degree of fault, if any, of the athlete comes into critical focus.

A highly controversial disqualification at the Sydney Olympics was that of the Romanian gymnast Raducan, who underwent a doping test after the event on 21 September 2000

---

[242] *Quigley*, CAS 94/129, para 34. On obligations on regulators to make clear rules, see further *C v FINA*, CAS 96/149, Reeb 1 25, para 34. There is also 'a duty of all those sporting bodies involved in the important fight against drugs in sport to likewise keep up to date and to ensure the steady dissemination to athlete and their coaches … of information which is unambiguously correct': *AOC v ABUA*, CAS A/2/99, para 29; *C v FINA*, CAS 96/149, Reeb 1 25, para 32.

[243] *R v IOC*, CAS OG 98/002 (Nagano), Reeb 1 419.

[244] *USOC v IOC and IAAF*, CAS 2004/A/725.

[245] See too Charlish (n 186), criticising *FAW v UEFA*, CAS 2004/A/593, [2004] ISLR, SLR 62, for not disqualifying a Russian team for playing with a footballer who failed a drugs test because the Football Union of Russia was not implicated; Tolman and Rugbynok, *Disqualification for Doping: The Marion Jones Case*, WSLR 8/9, p 6.

[246] *Beckie Scott and COC v IOC*, CAS 2002/0/373, para 51; see also *B v FIJ*, CAS 99/A/230, Reeb 2 39.

[247] *B v FINA*, CAS 2001/A/337, para 26; *Korneev and Gouliev v IOC*, CAS OG 96/003 and 004 (Atlanta), the *fons et origo* of the phrase. See also Davis, *Expert Evidence Before CAS: A Question of Weight* (2012) 2(12) ISLR 24.

[248] *N, J, Y and W v FINA*, CAS 98A//208, para 8.

[249] Ibid. For the problems caused by nandrolone, an endogenous as well as exogenous substance, see *B v ITU*, CAS 98/A/222.

which revealed the presence of pseudoephedrine.[250] The IOC Executive Board decided to disqualify her from the women's (athletic) individual all-round event and to withdraw her gold medal. The CAS panel said:

> The anti-doping code considers doping as a strict liability offence. This means that no intentional element is required to establish a doping offence. The mere presence of the forbidden substance in the urine sample is sufficient.

Raducan had therefore committed a doping offence pursuant to the Anti-Doping Code of the Olympic Movement, which provides (Article 3 paragraph 3) that:

> Any case of doping during a competition automatically leads to invalidation of the result obtained (with all consequences, including forfeit of any medals and prizes), irrespective of any other sanction that may be applied.

As to that the panel stated:

> It supports the strict consequence of an automatic disqualification—severe as it may be in that it affects the gold medal winner—in a matter of fairness to all other athletes ... This is why factors such as the athlete's age (she was 17 on September 30), her weight, the need for medication (there were other medicines available, as well as procedures to be followed, where medication with a banned substance is required for health reasons), the fact the drug may not have enhanced the performance, and the gymnast's reliance on the team's doctor were all held irrelevant. Such matters were, however, taken into account in not imposing a sanction beyond disqualification.[251]

In *A v FILA*[252] the CAS panel emphasised the importance of respecting the athlete's right of personality and allowing him or her the opportunity to disprove negligence or intent and so escape suspension. The panel referred to the fact that the suspension 'clearly affect the honour and social standing of the athlete concerned and [was] a stigma on his future'.[253] However:

> The unintended consumption of foodstuffs or supplements responsible for the presence of a prohibited substance in an athlete's body is hardly an unusual occurrence, let alone a 'truly exceptional circumstance' justifying a lowering of the usual time of a suspension.[254]

Fourth, the fundamental human rights of athletes must be respected.[255] Fifth, due account will be taken, depending of course on the particular rules in play, of bona fide medical use.[256]

7.205 Underlying all these strands of a *lex sportiva* is a vital consideration: in sport, results should not only be fair, but be seen to be fair. In another context where the panel upheld the rules prohibiting multi-club ownership within the same competition, the panel spoke of:

[250] CAS OG 00/11 (Sydney), Reeb 2 665; see generally McLaren, *Doping Sanctions: What Penalty* [2002] ISLR 23.
[251] For the distinction between disqualification and other sanctions in doping offences, see *C v FINA*, CAS 95/A/141, Reeb 1 25. For an example of mitigating circumstances being called into play see *L v FILA*, CAS 2000/A/312 (a nandrolone case), paras 44–47. See also *H v FIM*, CAS 2000/A/281, Reeb 2 410; *N, J, Y and W v FINA*, CAS 98/A/208, Reeb 2 24. Lack of intent goes to mitigation, ditto if persons responsible for team management have analysed a particular food product and cleared it (para 43).
[252] CAS 2000/A/317; see also *T v FIG*, CAS 2002/A/385, para 8.
[253] See paras 25–37.
[254] *IAAF v CAR*, CAS 2003/A/48, paras 11–12.
[255] Rigozzi, Kaufmann-Kohler and Malinverni, *Doping and Fundamental Rights of Athletes* [2003] ISLR 61.
[256] See eg *L v FINA*, CAS 95/142, paras 19–23 and 39 (salbutamol).

... the connection between the notion of integrity in football and the need for authenticity and uncertainty of results from both a sporting and an economic angle

and mentioned that the integrity

has a critical core which is that, in *the public's perception*, both single matches and entire championships must be a true test of the best possible athlete, technical, coaching and management skills of the opposing sides ... This particular requirement is inherent in the nature of sports ...[257] (emphasis in original)

The drugs jurisprudence since the coming into force of the first WADC is chiefly concerned with interpretation and application of the provisions of that global instrument, and is dealt with below.

Disciplinary Cases Involving Alleged Doping

7.206 The objects of doping control are clear. The essence of a sporting contest is that it should be fairly conducted, with success or failure depending on competitors' natural talents and qualities, speed, strength (physical and mental), flexibility, sense of rhythm, endurance, tactical awareness, honed as they may be by instruction, training and body maintenance (in the widest sense). The use of drugs inserts an unwarranted factor into this equation, offers an unfair advantage to the user, and offends against notions of equality and the sporting concept of the level playing field.

7.207 The 2009 WADA Code now sets the benchmark for doping control, but there are general considerations in play. Charges of breach of applicable regulations raise a number of factual issues. Was the positive sample that of the athlete charged? Was the chain of custody from the taking of the sample, transport, storage before reaching the laboratory, and during testing sound? Was the sample exposed to outside elements that may have impaired its integrity prior to testing? Was the testing equipment properly functioning? Was the prohibited substance found exogenous or endogenous? If exogenous, was it the result of taking a legitimate supplement or food which had become contaminated?[258] What was the athlete's degree of fault in taking an endogenous prohibited substance?[259]

7.208 Indeed, was the substance prohibited at all? This question was raised in the *bromantan* case in Atlanta,[260] the *Rebagliatti* case in Nagano,[261] the *Baxter* case in Salt Lake City[262] and by Dwain Chambers who—as it was held—used a designed steroid, chemically related to specified prohibited substances.[263] Was the test taken in circum-

---

[257] *AEK Athens v UEFA*, CAS 98/200, Reeb 2 38, paras 24 and 25.
[258] Barnes, *Doping: Liability for Ingesting Contaminated Products*, WSLR 3/12; Charlish, *Drugs in Sport* (2012) 12(2) LIM 109.
[259] Charlish, *Tennis: When Liability is Not So Strict* [2004] ISLR 64, criticising the Rusedski case in which the player was exonerated because the tablets that were the source of elevated nandrolone were given to him by the ATP. Charlish, *Drugs and Sport* (2012) 12(2) LIM 109–20.
[260] CAS OG 96/003 and 004 (Atlanta).
[261] *R v IOC*, CAS OG 98/002 (Nagano), Reeb 1 419.
[262] *Alain Baxter v IOC*, CAS 2002/A/376.
[263] *UK Athletics v Chambers* [2004] ISLR, SLR 7 (see also the sequel before Mackay J: [2008] EWHC 2028 (QB), [2008] ISLR, SLR 115).

stances permitted by the rules? In *Krabbe* the German Federation had not incorporated a provision for out of competition testing so allowing the sprinter to walk—albeit temporarily—away scot free.[264] Is the laboratory where the test was carried out authorised? Have the testing rules been followed, for example, has the athlete been given the required opportunity to be present by him or herself or a representative at the testing of the B sample?

7.209 Proof can be of various kinds: laboratory tests, non-analytical positive evidence (eg inculpating documents), or athletic profiling (eg the biological passport).[265]

7.210 There are also policy questions: in broad terms, on the one hand has the fight against drug use in sport gone too far? On the other, has it not gone far enough? Some argue that there is no moral difference between use of carefully selected expensive foods and use of performance enhancing drugs. Not everyone can make use of either because of economic considerations. The moral picture becomes still more blurred when altitude training, advantageous to stamina-based events, is considered; some have access to it because of the topography of their place of birth, eg Kenyans and Ethiopians; others because they can afford to travel to places offering similar benefits, such as Font Romeu in the Pyrenees or Colorado, or can simulate it, like Novak Djokovic and his travelling capsule.[266]

7.211 Some argue more modestly that there should be a distinction drawn between performance enhancing and recreational drugs.[267] Others suggest that the fight against doping, which has a health protection dimension, should be fortified by criminalising the use of performance enhancing drugs, as has occurred in other jurisdictions.[268]

7.212 It may be doubted whether spectators would themselves continue to patronise a sport where it was perceived that drug use was endemic and records were broken simply because of its use.

The World Anti-Doping Agency and the World Anti-Doping Code

7.213 The World Anti-Doping Agency (WADA) was established in 1999 to coordinate and harmonise anti-doping testing programmes at an international and national level.[269] On 1 January 2004 the first World Anti-Doping Code (WADC) came into effect; this has

---

[264] *IAAF v Krabbe* (1992) unreported, 28 June, IAAF tribunal.

[265] Nafziger, *Circumstantial Evidence of Doping: Balco and Beyond* (2005) 16(1) Marquette Sports Law Review 45; Coccia, *The Athlete's Biological Passport*, paper presented by Professor Massimo Coccia at Montreux conference, 16–17 November 2011.

[266] Cox, *Legalisation of Drug Use in Sport* [2002] ISLR 27; Owen, *Chemically Enhanced*, FT Magazine, 11–12 February 2006. See more generally McNamee and Tarasti, *Judicial and Ethical Peculiarities in Doping Policy* (2010) 36 Journal of Medical Ethics 165.

[267] Smith, *Why WADA Should Not Ban Athletes for Recreational Drug Use* [2007] ISLJ 119.

[268] Ionnaides, *Legal Regulation of Doping in Sport and the Application of Criminal law in Doping Infractions* [2006] ISLR 2.

[269] See the Lausanne Declaration (1999) 26(25) Olympic Review 17–18 and the preamble to the World Anti-Doping Code 2009. See Tarasti, *Some Juridical Questions in the Revised WADC* [2008] ISLR 17. See generally Ljungqvist, *Doping's Nemesis* (Sports Books, 2011). He was not the only one but one of the begetters of the Code.

been superseded by the 2009 WADC.[270] WADA's stated roles are to adopt and implement policies and procedures which conform with the WADC,[271] to monitor compliance by signatories to the Code,[272] to approve international standards concerning the implementation of WADC,[273] to accredit drug testing laboratories,[274] to approve models of best practice,[275] to promote anti-doping research and education,[276] to conduct an independent observer programme for anti-doping control,[277] and to conduct anti-doping controls when authorised to do so by other anti-doping organisations.[278] The majority of sports federations are now signatories to the WADC, including all international federations of Olympic sports.[279] The UK Anti-Doping Rules are also modelled on the WADC.[280]

7.214 The role of international federations, major event organisations, the British Olympic Association and UK-Anti Doping is to adopt and implement anti-doping policies and controls which comply with the WADC.[281] International federations and the British Olympic Association are also required to ensure that national federations[282] and individual athletes and coaches[283] comply with the provisions of the Code. Major event organisations are similarly required to ensure that athletes and coaches at their events agree to comply with anti-doping rules.[284]

7.215 Doping is defined under the WADC as the occurrence of one or more of eight anti-doping violations.[285] These are: presence of a prohibited substance or method,[286] use or

---

[270] See WADC Art 23 for acceptance, compliance and modification and Art 24 for interpretation. The main differences between old code and new are summarised in *FINA v Cesar Augusto Cielo Filho & CBDA*, CAS 2011/A/2495, at para 8.40. For the 2003 Code see David, *A Guide to the World Anti-Doping Code* (Cambridge University Press, 2008); see also Rigozzi, Kaufmann-Kohler and Malinverni, *Doping and Fundamental Rights of Athletes* [2003] ISLR 61 giving a human rights audit; Pound, *The World Anti-Doping Agency: An Experiment in International Law* [2002] ISLR 52. McLaren, *Exceptional Circumstances: Is it Strict?* [2005] ISLR 32; McLaren, *A New Era in the Control of Performance Enhancing Drugs* WSLR, 1/2, p 7. The 2009 Code is not retroactive, but *lex mitior* applies: *WADA v Hardy and USA*, CAS 2009/A/1870, para 16. Adolphsen, *Challenges for CAS Decisions Following the Adoption of the New WADA Code 2009* (2010) 1 CAS Bull 10.
[271] WADC, Art 20.7.1.
[272] Ibid, Art 20.7.2.
[273] Ibid, Art 20.7.3.
[274] Ibid, Art 20.7.4; see for a solitary case (to date) of de-accreditation *Doping Control Centre, Universiti Sains Malaysia v WADA*, CAS 2010/A/2162.
[275] WADC, Art 20.7.5.
[276] Ibid, Art 20.7.6.
[277] Ibid, Art 20.7.7.
[278] Ibid, Art 20.7.8.
[279] Even those that are not, such as FIFA, have anti-doping policies which comply with the WADC. See for a CAS advisory opinion on the compatibility of the then FIFA rules with the then WADC, CAS 2005/C/976 and 986 as to how Swiss law applies to a Swiss association such as FIFA; see paras 124–7. WADC Art 16 concerns doping control for animals competing in sport. Equestrian sports are for obvious reasons sui generis as far as the horses are concerned: see, on the regime, Blakely, *A New Era for Equestrian Sports* WSLR 815, p 12; see too Dickerson, Pheasant and Shaw, *Equine Supplement: No Fault and No Negligence Finding* WSLR 810, p 5 (on the *Yeoman* case).
[280] See, eg, *International Wheelchair Basketball Association v UK Anti-Doping and Gibbs*, CAS 2010/A/2230.
[281] WADC, Art 20.2–20.6. The IAAF banned any athletes who refused to take drug tests from participation in the 2011 World Championships: WSLR 9/8; see Benedetti and Bunting, *There's a New Sheriff in Town: A Review of the USADA* [2003] ISLR 17.
[282] WADC, Art 20.3.2 and 20.4.2.
[283] Ibid, Art 20.3.3–20.3.5 and 20.4.3–20.4.5.
[284] WADC, Art 20.6.4: the involvement (and obligations) of governments are dealt with in WADC, Art 22.
[285] WADC, Art 1.
[286] WADC, Art 2.1; Morgan, *WADA's Prohibited List and Similar Substances*, WSLR 9/2, p 3; 9/3, p 6. It has been argued that the inclusion of recreational drugs such as cannabis, cocaine and ecstasy 'defies logic': Smith (n 267). Drugs which have caused particular controversy are nandrolone (which can be endogenous) and clenbuterol

attempted use of a prohibited substance or method,[287] refusing or failing to give a sample collection,[288] violations of applicable requirements regarding availability for out of competition testing,[289] tampering or attempting to tamper with any part of the doping control process,[290] possession of prohibited substances or methods,[291] trafficking or attempting to traffick prohibited substances or methods,[292] and administration or attempted administration of a prohibited substance.[293]

7.216 A list of prohibited substances and methods is published at least annually by WADA,[294] containing substances or methods that have the potential to enhance performance in competition or have masking potential.[295] The list may be expanded by WADA for any particular sport.[296] Methods or substances can be included on the list if they meet any two of the criteria[297] of having the potential to enhance or enhancing sports performance,[298] representing an actual or potential health risk to athletes,[299] and violating the spirit of the sport.[300] Athletes are able to obtain an exemption for therapeutic use of prohibited substances or methods from the international federation for their sport.[301]

7.217 Failure to submit to doping control can also constitute an offence.[302]

7.218 Proof of doping is dealt with in Article 3. The burden of proof lies with the anti-doping organisation (ADO).[303] The standard of proof is greater than a mere balance of probabilities but less than proof beyond reasonable doubt.[304] This equates to the classic sports law test of comfortable satisfaction. Methods of establishing facts and presumptions are presumed[305] to be in conformity with the International Standard for Laboratories (ISL); an athlete must show not only a departure from the ISL, but that such departure could reasonably have caused the adverse analytical finding (AAF), in which

---

(which can be found in men of Chinese or Mexican origin). On clenbuterol see the newsletter issued by the Swiss law firm Lenz & Stählin, January 2012, pp 7–8.

[287] WADC, Art 2.2.

[288] Ibid, Art 2.3.

[289] Ibid, Art 2.4; see Kemp, *Doping: Athlete Impact and Whereabouts Information*, WSLR 3/12.

[290] Ibid, Art 2.5.

[291] Ibid, Art 2.6.

[292] Ibid, Art 2.7.

[293] Ibid, Art 2.8.

[294] Ibid, Art 4.1.

[295] Ibid, Art 4.2.1; see Morgan (n 286). The classification of a substance as 'similar' to one of the listed substances made by the WADA administration can be challenged: *Wawrrzyniak v HFF*, CAS 2009/A/1918, para 27.

[296] WADC, Art 4.2.1.

[297] Ibid, Art 4.3.1.

[298] Ibid, Art 4.3.1.1.

[299] Ibid, Art 4.3.1.2.

[300] Ibid, Art 4.3.1.3; see also *Fundamental Rationale for the World Anti-Doping Code* in the introduction to the Code.

[301] Ibid, Art 4.4.

[302] See Morgan, *Sample Collection: Failure to Submit to Doping Control*, WSLR 7/11, p 8. This is a particularly controversial issue for team sports where it is thought that the incidence of doping is lower; see Farrow, *Team Sports' Issues with WADA Code*, WSLR 7/6, p 4.

[303] WADC, Art 3.1.

[304] Ibid. See Mavromati, *The Athlete's Biological Passport Programme*, CAS Bulletin 2/11, p 35. An offence can be established without the necessity for a positive laboratory test. See also Coccia, *The Athlete's Biological Passport* [2012] ISLR (forthcoming); *Pellizotti v CONI*, CAS 2010/A/2308; *UCI v Pellizotti*, CAS 2011/A/2335 (in French).

[305] WADC, Art 3.2.

case the burden reverts to the ADO to show that it did not do so.[306] There are analogous provisions where departures from other standards, policies or rules are established.[307]

7.219 Facts established by an unappealed decision of a competent court or tribunal are irrebuttable evidence against the athlete unless reached in violation of the principle of natural justice.[308] Adverse inferences may be drawn from refusal by the athlete to answer questions from an ADO or disciplinary panel.[309] Article 8 provides (critically) for the right to a fair hearing.[310]

7.220 Testing is dealt with in Article 5; analysis of samples in Article 6; and results management in Article 7.

7.221 Where a doping infraction concerns the presence of a prohibited substance or method, the WADC adopts a rule of strict liability. The reasons behind the presence of the prohibited substance or method cannot provide a defence to the infraction but may be relevant to the appropriate level of sanction. This rule does not exempt an anti-doping organisation from the requirement to prove that an anti-doping rule violation has occurred, and the organisation is required to establish that the violation has occurred to the comfortable satisfaction of the hearing panel.[311]

7.222 Sanctions for doping infractions include automatic disqualification of individual results,[312] provisional suspension,[313] and a period of ineligibility from competition ranging from one year for a first offence[314] to lifetime ineligibility for subsequent offences.[315] Where an athlete can establish how a prohibited substance entered the body and that its purpose was not to enhance sporting ability or for masking purposes by means of corroborating evidence, the period of ineligibility may be reduced or, exceptionally,[316] be replaced with a reprimand.[317] Where an athlete establishes that he or she bears no fault

---

[306] Ibid, Art 3.2.1.

[307] Ibid, Art 3.2.2.

[308] Ibid, Art 3.2.3.

[309] Ibid, Art 3.2.4.

[310] WADC Art 13 provides for appeals; Art 14 deals with confidentiality and reporting in a manner designed to respect the principles of coordination of anti-doping results, transparency, accountability, and respect for the privacy interests of individuals.

[311] Ibid, Art 3.1; there may in fact be little to distinguish the required standard from the criminal standard of proof: *USADA v Montgomery*, CAS 2004/O/645. The composite award in *Contador v RFCC*, CAS 2011/A/2384, *WADA v Contador*, CAS 2011/A/2386 has complicated the issues of burden and standard of proof: paras 241–65. See also Ibarrola, *Contador: Burden of Proof and Presumption of Culpability*, WSLR 4/12.

[312] WADC, Art 9.

[313] Ibid, Art 7.5.

[314] Ibid, Art 10.2 and 10.3. See Hesse, *The Status of an Athlete during a Period of Ineligibility*, WLSR 9/5, p 6.

[315] WADC, Art 10.7; a third violation will always result in lifetime ineligibility except where it relates to an infraction under WADC Art 2.4 (the obligation to be available for out of competition tests), or where Art 10.4 is engaged. See Mavromati, *Lifetime Ineligibility According to the WADA Code* (2010) 1 Cas Bull 42.

[316] See *D v International Dance-Sport Federation*, CAS 2006/A/1175, and *P v ITF*, CAS 2008/A/1488.

[317] WADC, Art 10.4. The relationship between Art 10.4 and 10.5 is analysed in *Kendrick v ITF*, CAS 2011/A/2518: 'The fact that the language is effectively identical confirms that the analysis required is the same: ie under each article it is necessary to ascertain by how far the athletes departed from the standards expected of him or her under the WADC' (para 10.18).

or negligence,[318] or no significant fault or negligence,[319] or provides substantial assistance in discovering or establishing anti-doping infractions against others,[320] or voluntarily admits an offence in the absence of other evidence,[321] the period of ineligibility may be reduced or replaced with a reprimand.[322] In wholly exceptional cases it has been held that the doctrine of proportionality can override (and lessen) the sanctions provided by the rules.[323] The consequences for team sports are dealt within Article 11.[324]

7.223 Under IOC Rule 45 (the so-called Osaka rule) a period of ineligibility for a doping offence of greater than six months results in an athlete being ineligible for the next Olympic Games. The validity of these rules has been considered by the CAS in the case of *USOC v IOC*,[325] where it held the Osaka rule to be invalid because it was in excess of the WADC sanction by which the IOC had agreed to be bound and also contravened the principle *ne bis in idem* (double jeopardy). Doubt, therefore, was cast on the still more draconian British Olympic Association (BOA) 'bye-law 25' (now bye-law 7.2) resulting in lifetime ineligibility for selection for Team GB at the Olympic Games. The bye-law was applied in respect of the sprinter Dwain Chambers[326] and has itself been challenged before the CAS.

7.224 The CAS decided on 30 April 2012 that the BOA's rule was invalid; a result that came as no surprise to these authors.[327] The BOA had appealed to the CAS following WADA's determination that the bye-law providing that any British athlete 'who has been found guilty of a doping offence ... shall not ... thereafter be eligible for consideration as a member of a Team GB ... in relation to any Olympic Games' was non-compliant with the WADC. The CAS's reasoning is clear: the BOA did not act in compliance with the WADC by purporting to increase by the back door, under the colour of an eligibility rule, the uniform sanctions prescribed by the WADC, to which the BOA is a signatory. The BOA's rule could not therefore be enforced. The CAS panel rejected the BOA's argument that the rule fell outside the WADC regime because it only applied to deliberate doping cheats and because it was restricted to a single event (the Olympics) intended to set an example to youth.[328]

---

[318] WADC, Art 10.5.1; see, eg, *P v IIHF*, CAS 2005/A/990-O, where the prohibited substance resulted from emergency medical treatment. See generally on duties of athletes to check medication *P v ITF*, CAS 2008/A/1488, para 26; on an athlete's inability simply to rely on a doctor's advice and the need to consider all circumstances, see *Koubek v ITF*, CAS 2005/A/828, para 57. See generally *IWBF v Gibbs* CA 2010/A/2330.

[319] WADC, Art 10.5.2; see, eg, *ITF v Gasquet*, CAS 2009/A/1926, and *WADA v ITF and Gasquet*, CAS 2009/A/1930, where the prohibited substance resulted from kissing a woman in a nightclub. Age and experience (or lack thereof) may be relevant: *WADA v USADA and Thompson*, CAS 2008/A/1490, para 88.

[320] WADC, Art 10.5.3.

[321] Ibid, Art 10.5.4.

[322] A reprimand may only be given where WADC Art 10.5.1 or 10.5.2 applies. See also Art 10.5.5 for situations where multiple sections of Art 10.5 apply.

[323] *Mariano Puerta v ITF*, CAS/2006/A/1025, [2006] ISLR, SLR 149; *Despres v CCES*, CAS 2008/A/1489, para 7.19; see too *I v FA*, CAS 2010/A/2218 (reduction of code sanction for 12-year-old go-karter).

[324] Kiener, *Consequences of Doping in Collective Sports* [2011] ISLR 67.

[325] CAS 2011/O/2422, following the success of the American athlete LaShawn Merritt in earlier proceedings.

[326] See, for an earlier unsuccessful challenge, *Chambers v BOA* [2008] EWHC 2020, [2008] ISLR 2008, SLR 115.

[327] Michael Beloff had so advised WADA. See *BOA v WADA*, CAS 2011/A/2658. Blackshaw, *Opinion: BOA v WADA Lifetime Olympic Ban CAS Ruling: The Future* (2012) WLR.

[328] See paras 8.33–8.40.

8

Remedies: The Resolution
of Legal Disputes in Sport

Introduction

8.1 Our task in this final chapter is to provide a brief account of the law governing the availability of particular remedies sought by parties to legal disputes arising in the sporting field. We do not deal here with the operation of domestic disciplinary machinery within that field. We have already, in the previous chapter, considered the functioning of bodies exercising disciplinary jurisdiction over sportsmen and women, and over clubs, including disciplinary panels that are independent of the sport association. The following account proceeds mainly on the basis that such remedies have been exhausted. We deal here with remedies available before the ordinary courts; and before arbitral bodies empowered under the relevant rules to adjudicate upon disputes between players, clubs and sports associations; and before the Court of Arbitration for Sport (CAS), either on appeal from disciplinary decisions or by way of an arbitration claim seeking specific relief.

8.2 The rules of many sporting associations provide for a right of recourse to an external body such as an independent panel of arbitrators, or the CAS. In *Korda v ITF*,[1] Lightman J held that the then rule of the International Tennis Federation's Anti-Doping Programme providing that 'any dispute arising out of any decision made by the Anti-Doping Appeals Committee shall be submitted exclusively to the Appeals Arbitration Division of the Court of Arbitration for Sport' did not entitle the Federation to appeal to the CAS against a sentence it considered too lenient. The Programme also provided that the Appeal Committee's decision shall be the 'full, final and complete disposition of the appeal and will be binding on all parties'. He held that the arbitration provision would have entitled the player, but not the ITF, to challenge the enforceability of the Committee's decision on the ground of error of law or procedural unfairness, but the Court of Appeal allowed the ITF's appeal against the decision.[2]

8.3 In commercial arbitration, the modern approach of the English courts is to construe arbitration clauses widely, starting from an assumption that parties to commercial arbitration normally intend that all disputes arising in connection with, as well as directly out of, their contract should be submitted to arbitration.[3] In the context of sport, arbitration clauses are often quite specific but the same general approach is likely to be applied,

---

[1] *The Times*, 4 February 1999, transcript 29 January 1999.
[2] [1999] All ER (D) 337, CA. The case duly went before the CAS (CAS 99/223).
[3] *Fiona Trust and Holding Corporation v Privalov* [1007] UKHL 40, [2008] 1 Lloyd's Rep 254.

giving effect to limiting words excluding certain disputes from the scope of arbitration only if the words are clear.[4] The rules of the Football Association make provision for disputes between members and clubs, or between clubs, to be referred to arbitration. Such referrals are not confined to cases in which a sportsman or woman, or a club, wishes to appeal against an adverse ruling. The International Association of Athletics Federations[5] now recognises the jurisdiction of the CAS to deal with appeals in doping cases, superseding earlier decisions of 'sport specific' IAAF arbitration panels in earlier cases such as *Re Dean Capobianco*.[6]

8.4 In England, as in most other countries, supervisory jurisdiction over decisions of sporting bodies is exercised ultimately by the ordinary courts of law. There is no statutory or other specialist judicial body exercising general jurisdiction in the field of sport. The existence of the courts' ultimate supervisory jurisdiction, even where the rules provide for arbitration, is assured by the constitutional principle that the courts' jurisdiction over matters of law cannot be ousted. However the English court is not, in the sporting field, a court of merits in cases where the function of finding the facts is entrusted to officials under domestic sporting rules. In such cases, a court will not entertain a challenge founded on the contention that the sporting body came to an erroneous conclusion in point of fact, unless such conclusion was based on no evidence at all or was otherwise irrational. The court will not otherwise substitute its own view of the facts for that of the designated fact finding person or body. As the jurisdiction is supervisory, not original, a claimant seeking to impugn a decision must show that it was wrong in point of law, or tainted by some other vitiating factor rendering it legally objectionable.

8.5 Thus, a distinction must be drawn between cases where the rules of a sporting body confer jurisdiction over disputes on a judicial body of some sort, and cases where that is not the position. In the latter category of case, where rules conferring powers of adjudication are not in play, the courts in England retain their traditional function of exercising original jurisdiction over sporting matters in the same way as they do over other legal matters coming before them. In such a case, a claimant will have to show, just as any other citizen would have to show, that his or her rights have been infringed in a manner amounting to a legal wrong under the ordinary law of the land. An example of the latter type of case would be a personal injury claim arising from participation in sport, of the type described in chapter five.[7] Sports bodies have not, historically, established their own rules for compensating sports related injuries; that is left to the ordinary law of negligence.

8.6 Our consideration of remedies in the law relating to sport does not, in this chapter, extend to a detailed account of the ordinary remedies available to a claimant in a case, such as a personal injury claim, where no supervisory jurisdiction is being exercised. The remedies available to such a claimant do not differ from those applicable to ordinary claims brought daily by claimants from all walks of life and comprising the standard fare of our courts. Thus, a libel action may be brought by one sportsman against another, as

---

[4] See eg para 57 of Vos J's judgment in *Fulham FC (1987) Ltd v Richards* [2011] Ch 208, referring to the approach of Lord Hoffmann set out at para 13 of his speech in *Fiona Trust and Holding Corporation v Primalov*.
[5] Formerly, the International Amateur Athletic Federation, whose Congress in 2001 voted unanimously to change the organisation's name to International Association of Athletics Federations.
[6] Arbitration award of 17 March 1997, discussed in chapter 7 at paras 7.95–7.96.
[7] See para 5.33 ff.

in a celebrated case in which Ian Botham sued Imran Khan (and lost).[8] With increasing and depressing frequency, sportsmen (rather than sportswomen, so far) have in recent years brought actions seeking to prevent press revelations of what they contend to be their private life, usually seeking to conceal sexually controversial behaviour.[9]

8.7 As is clear from chapter one of this book, our conception of sports law does not include cases where the parties merely happen to be involved in sport. We steer clear of an account of the law of privacy as applied to sporting celebrities. Fortunately, that law is not applied differently in sport and outside it; the law must obviously be the same for everyone and if its application is affected by the claimant's celebrity status, we are pleased to see that it does not seem to matter whether the celebrity arises from sporting achievement or for any other reason. Personal injury merits separate treatment in chapter five because discrete principles have to some extent developed to cater for the specific characteristics of sporting activity. The same cannot be said of privacy claims in respect of footballers' sex lives.

8.8 More prosaically, the proprietor of a football club may bring proceedings against a building contractor for failing to complete stadium refurbishment works on time or to the required standard. Such claims do not differ, as to the remedies available, from other such claims outside the sporting field, any more than they differ as to the rights being asserted. Consequently, the remedies available in litigation of this type do not merit separate treatment in the sporting field from that which they have received in a vast legal literature on the subject of remedies generally, to which reference can be made as necessary.

8.9 We concentrate here mainly on the supervisory jurisdiction of the English courts and on the remedies available before arbitral tribunals in the sporting field, other than the ordinary courts. The supervisory character of the jurisdiction arises from our law's insistence on autonomy of decision making by domestic and public bodies alike, provided they act within their rules and otherwise lawfully in accordance with the principles of fairness, legality and good faith expounded in the previous chapter, and provided they do not seek to become the final arbiter on questions of law and construction.[10]

8.10 We have already looked at the various ways in which disciplinary and other tribunals exercising original jurisdiction over questions of fact may also have to deal with submissions of law, or of mixed fact and law, such as whether a life ban for a first doping offence would be in unreasonable restraint of trade. Likewise, such bodies commonly have to deal with submissions as to the true meaning of the rules they are applying. Generally, further redress in a court of law or other tribunal is only available if the primary tribunal makes

---

[8] Libel actions connected to cricket have also featured recently in the work of the courts: see *Chris Lance Cairns v Lalit Modi* [2010] EWHC 2859, in which a cricketer successfully complained of a 'tweet' said to contain an untrue imputation of match fixing (aggravated damages of £90,000 awarded by Bean J, 26 March 2012).

[9] *A v B plc (Flitcroft v MGN Ltd)* [2003] QB 195; *Terry (previously 'LNS') v Persons Unknown* [2010] EMLR 16; *Ferdinand v MGN Ltd* [2011] EWHC 2454 (QB); *Giggs (previously 'CTB' v News Group Newspapers Ltd* [2012] EWHC 431 (QB).

[10] See *Dawkins v Antrobus* (1881) 17 Ch Div 615, CA; *Lee v The Showmen's Guild of Great Britain* [1952] 2 QB 329, CA, per Denning LJ at 324; *Faramus v Film Artistes Association* [1964] AC 925, 944–8 (per Lord Pearce); and in Scotland, *St Johnstone FC Ltd v The Scottish Football Association Ltd* 1965 SLT 171, in which Lord Kilbrandon predictably held that a rule requiring the consent of the Scottish FA Council to litigation against the Scottish FA would be void as contrary to public policy. Totman and O'Grady, *Challenging a Sanctioning Decision in the Courts* (2012) 4(12) WSLR.

a mistake other than in relation to a question of fact. However, some independent and external appellate tribunals, such as the CAS, may have jurisdiction expressly conferred upon them by relevant domestic rules over questions of fact as well as questions of law; and over questions as to the severity of the penalty properly to be imposed in disciplinary cases. Such an arbitral body differs conceptually from a court in that its jurisdiction arises not from the general law of the land, but from the content of the rules establishing its constitution and powers.

8.11 We consider below, separately, the types of remedy potentially available in, respectively, the courts and other bodies exercising judicial functions. Rights of redress before the institutions of the European Union (EU), ie the Commission, the Court of Justice[11] and the General Court, may be of prime importance in sporting disputes which have an international impact within the EU. We touched on these separately in chapters four and six and do not deal with them in this chapter except in passing.

Court Proceedings

Non-Availability of Judicial Review

8.12 In this section we consider the scope for obtaining public law remedies in litigation concerning decisions of sporting bodies. It is not our purpose here to provide a comprehensive account of the nature and purpose of applications for judicial review. Reference should be made to the several excellent specialist works on the subject.[12] We can begin by observing pragmatically that, in the current state of English law, public law remedies are for the most part unavailable. In the first edition of this work, we expressed the view that this state of affairs was unsatisfactory. Other common law jurisdictions recognise the public law nature of legal challenges to decisions of sporting bodies, taking the view that sport engages public as well as private law rights. The law has developed considerably since we first looked at the issue in an article in 1996.[13]

8.13 We start by explaining why the question need arise at all. The fact that English law regards most sporting litigation, and in particular challenges to the validity of decisions made by sporting associations, as a matter arising in private law and not public law, might be thought of little consequence since there are perfectly good remedies available to the aspiring claimant in private law. Why should a player, club or sporting body be concerned about whether the body's decision, if overturned by a court, is overturned by means of a quashing order, which used to be called more quaintly an order of *certiorari* (a public law remedy), or by a declaration that it is void and of no effect (a remedy common to both

---

[11] On a reference from a national court under Art 267 of the Treaty on the Functioning of the European Union (TFEU), formerly Art 234 of the Treaty of Rome and before that Art 177 of the Treaty of Rome.

[12] See, in particular, Woolf, Jowell and Le Sueur, *De Smith's Judicial Review*, 6th edn (Sweet & Maxwell, 2007); Wade and Forsyth, *Administrative Law*, 10th edn (Oxford University Press, 2009); Fordham, *Judicial Review Handbook*, 5th edn (Hart Publishing, 2008); Supperstone, Goudie and Walker, *Judicial Review*, 4th edn (LexisNexis, 2010); Craig, *Administrative Law*, 6th edn (Sweet & Maxwell, 2008).

[13] See Beloff and Kerr, *Why Aga Khan is Wrong* [1996] Judicial Review 30; and Morgan, *A Mare's Nest? The Jockey Club and Judicial Review of Sports Governing Bodies*, (2012) 12(2) LIM 102.

private and public law), or by an injunction restraining the body from acting upon it (again, a remedy common to both public and private law)? It may be said that the effect is the same in each case, namely that the decision does not stand and may be ignored. But the question remains of more than academic interest for a number of reasons.

8.14 First, public law remedies cannot be obtained unless proceedings are brought within a very short time of the decision challenged,[14] while private law remedies are, in principle, available for up to six years from the date of the alleged breach of contract or other wrong.[15] In practice, however, the urgency of sporting cases and the prejudice to a claimant's position if he delays in seeking an injunction make it imperative to begin the proceedings promptly. Six years is manifestly too long to keep a sporting body in suspense, not knowing whether a decision it has taken is valid or not. An injunction claim will usually fail unless the proceedings are brought promptly, as we shall see below at para 8.81. Judicial review proceedings must, normally, be brought promptly and in any event not more than three months from the date when grounds for the challenge first arose.[16] In an urgent case, with an expedited hearing on the basis of written evidence only, without oral evidence and cross-examination, the court is able to deliver a considered and final ruling within weeks or even days of the decision challenged.

8.15 Second, the nature of the remedy available can impact on the procedure which the challenger must adopt in order to achieve any remedy at all. Lawyers with practical experience of challenging sporting bodies' decisions are aware of the tactical differences between judicial review and private law claim procedure. Because judicial review is usually available more swiftly than a private law remedy, the court's determination in judicial review is, more frequently than in private law proceedings, made on a final basis without the need for any hearing for consideration of interim relief. In private law proceedings, by contrast, the court is more likely to give an interim determination based not on its final view of the merits of the claim, but on its perception of the balance of justice at the date of the initial hearing. Normally such an interim hearing will take place within a very short time of the decision under challenge even though the claimant has—in theory—six years in which to bring the claim, since urgency is inherent in most disputed sporting decisions: the matter cannot await a full trial, for the effect of the decision is usually immediate and serious, requiring the court to respond quickly.

8.16 Thus, a decision challenged by means of a private law action may be treated as not susceptible of final resolution on the basis of written evidence alone, while the same decision may be resolved finally and quickly if judicial review is available. The hallmark of a private law action has traditionally been oral evidence and cross-examination, which are only necessary if there are genuine and material disputes of fact. Often, in sporting disputes, there are not. In private law, the procedural starting point is the assumption that

---

[14] Senior Courts Act 1981, s 31(6); Civil Procedure Rules 1998 (CPR) rule 54.5.

[15] See Limitation Act 1980, s 5, where the action is founded on 'simple contract'. Where the action is for a *declaration simpliciter* in the absence of contract (see further below at para 8.38), the scheme of the Limitation Act 1980 does not appear to cover the case but declaratory relief is always discretionary and the court would be likely to withhold relief where there has been undue delay. On limitation periods generally in public and private law, see Beloff, *Time, Time, Time, Is On My Side, Yes It Is* in *Essays in Honour of Sir William Wade QC*, ed Christopher Forsyth (Oxford University Press, 1998). On time limits generally, see McGee, *Limitation Periods*, 6th edn (Sweet & Maxwell, 2010).

[16] CPR rule 54.5.

evidence will be heard orally and that any preliminary ruling on written evidence will be a temporary holding operation not based on a final view of the merits. This is so even in cases started under Part 8 of the Civil Procedure Rules, using the private law procedure designed for cases not expected to generate disputes of fact or a need for oral evidence.

8.17 Third, the characterisation of a juridical right as one arising in public law or, as it may be, in private law, can—perversely, some would say—actually influence the substantive content of the right asserted, and may thereby determine the result of the case. The tests for obtaining interim relief in private law proceedings are easier for a claimant to satisfy than the tests for obtaining final relief in substantive judicial review proceedings, or after a full trial in private law proceedings. There is some evidence of distortion in the development of sports law resulting from the application of principles developed in the private law jurisdiction to grant interlocutory injunctions, which, superficially, can make the law appear more favourable to the claimant than it actually is.[17] Conversely, defendant sporting bodies have fared better in cases disposed of by means of a full trial—usually a speedy trial owing to the urgency of the matter.[18] It is unsatisfactory that substantive developments in any field of law should be influenced by questions of forum and procedure.

8.18 With that introduction, we return to our observation that judicial review is, in English law, rarely if ever available as a remedy to challenge the decision of a sporting body. That is the practical effect of the decision of the Court of Appeal in *R v Disciplinary Committee of the Jockey Club, ex parte Aga Khan*.[19] It is often said, inaccurately, that a particular body is or is not amenable to judicial review. However, the availability or otherwise of judicial review depends in the final analysis not on the body whose decision is challenged,[20] nor on the nature of the decision under challenge (though both these elements are significant), but on the nature of the right allegedly infringed. Thus the actual decision in the *Aga Khan* case was that the rights which the Aga Khan sought to enforce against the disciplinary committee of the Jockey Club were private rights enforceable by a private action founded on the contract subsisting between him and the Jockey Club. In theory, the decision leaves open the possibility that other decisions of other sporting bodies, or even of the Jockey Club itself, could infringe rights arising in public law which would be challengeable by—indeed, exclusively by—judicial review. But in practice the Court of Appeal's decision is rightly perceived as throwing an insurmountable roadblock in the path of any player or club wishing to bring judicial review proceedings against a sporting body, unless and until the Supreme Court decides otherwise.

8.19 The Court of Appeal had previously held that a decision of the National Greyhound Racing Club stewards to suspend a trainer's licence could not be judicially reviewed as the matter was governed by a contract between the trainer and the club.[21] That decision has been treated by the judges, sometimes with considerable reluctance, as binding authority for the non-reviewability of decisions of sporting bodies even in the absence of

---

[17] See, eg, *Jones v Welsh Rugby Union*, Ebsworth J, 27 February 1997; CA, *The Times*, 6 January 1998.
[18] See, eg, *Stevenage Borough FC Ltd v The Football League Ltd*, Carnwath J, 23 July 1996; CA (1997) 9 Admin LR 109.
[19] [1993] 1 WLR 909, CA; followed in *R (on the application of Mullins) v Jockey Club Appeal Board (No 1)* [2005] EWHC 2197 (Admin), [2006] ISLR, SLR 31, Stanley Burnton J.
[20] See Pannick, *Who is Entitled to Judicial Review in Respect of What* [1992] Public Law 1.
[21] *Law v National Greyhound Racing Club Ltd* [1983] 1 WLR 1302, CA.

a remedy in contract. Before the *Aga Khan* case itself, the Divisional Court had applied the greyhound case to preclude judicial review of decisions of the Jockey Club to remove a man's name from the list of chairmen of panels of stewards;[22] and to refuse to allow a company to run race meetings at a new racecourse in Telford.[23]

8.20 There is a difference between exclusion of judicial review on the ground that the decision challenged does not affect public rights, and its exclusion in the exercise of the court's discretion on the narrower ground that a private law remedy in contract is available on the facts. In the case law, those two distinct grounds for excluding judicial review became confused. Whether a decision affects public rights should be determined by applying the criteria in the Court of Appeal decision in *R v Panel on Takeovers and Mergers, ex parte Datafin*,[24] in which the ambit of judicial review was recognised as extending beyond decisions of bodies whose powers had been conferred by statute or the royal prerogative. Emphasis was placed on the argument that the regulatory powers of the body concerned should not be conferred merely by consensual submission to jurisdiction, as under a contract.

8.21 However, the *Datafin* decision in 1987 did not persuade the courts in England to countenance judicial review of sporting bodies' decisions. A football club was similarly unsuccessful in obtaining judicial review of the Football Association of Wales' decision to refuse it permission to join a particular lower league.[25] And in the Football League's celebrated challenge to the Football Association's decision to set up the Premier League, Rose J held that the court had no power to review that decision, on the basis that the FA was not a public law body.[26] In the *Aga Khan* case itself, the decision to disqualify the horse whose urine was found to contain a prohibited substance was held to be outside the scope of judicial review. Sir Thomas Bingham MR accepted that the Jockey Club exercised de facto monopoly powers over horse racing in this country, and that government would be driven to intervene if the Club did not exercise those powers. Nevertheless submission to its jurisdiction was said to be consensual, presumably because horse racing enthusiasts could choose not to engage in the sport.

8.22 We still consider that reasoning unsound, as we did when we produced the first edition of this book; it applies to all forms of voluntary activity subject to a licensing regime.[27] Any applicant for a statutory licence could be said to submit 'voluntarily' to the jurisdiction of the licensing authority, in the sense that the applicant could choose

---

[22] *R v Disciplinary Committee of the Jockey Club, ex parte Massingberd-Mundy* [1993] 2 All ER 207.

[23] *R v Jockey Club, ex parte RAM Racecourses Ltd* [1993] 2 All ER 225. Powers exercised pursuant to contract are sometimes regarded as necessarily private functions, but the touchstone should be the nature of the function not its source. A contractual relationship is not inconsistent with judicial review; thus, local authorities have contracts with their tenants, who may nonetheless be able to challenge eviction decisions by judicial review; cf *R (Heather) v Leonard Cheshire Foundation* [2002] EWCA Civ 366 in which claimant licensees were not precluded by contract alone from asserting that the Foundation was a body exercising public functions; cf the Court of Appeal's majority decision (Rix LJ dissenting) that a housing trust's decision to terminate a tenancy was not a private act and raised human rights considerations: *R (Weaver) v London and Quadrant Housing Trust* [2010] 1 WLR 363, following the reasoning in *L v Birmingham City Council* [2007] UKHL 27, [2008] 1 AC 95.

[24] [1987] QB 815, CA.

[25] *R v Football Association of Wales, ex parte Flint Town United FC* [1991] COD 44, DC.

[26] [1993] 2 All ER 833.

[27] See Beloff, editorials at [2006] ISLR 1 and [2007] ISLR 31 (the latter concluding that '[p]rocedure should be the servant of substance, not its mistress').

not to engage in the regulated activity and would not then need to apply for a licence. Even if the public character of sport is not accepted a priori, the tests serving to identify a public law right derived from the *Datafin* case[28] ought to have led to the conclusion that the decision of the Jockey Club's disciplinary committee engaged a right arising in public law. The upshot of these unsatisfactory precedents is that judicial review is a non-starter for any player or club wishing to challenge the decision of the sporting body, unless and until the Supreme Court reconsiders the position.

8.23 In *R (on the application of Mullins) v Jockey Club Appeal Board (No 1)*[29] Stanley Burnton J decided that the Appeal Board of the Jockey Club, as distinct from its disciplinary committee which had made the decision the Aga Khan had sought to challenge, was not a body exercising a public function when it upheld a decision to disqualify the winning horse in the 2002 Hennessy Gold Cup on the ground that its urine contained a prohibited substance.[30] The Appeal Board had been created in 2001 since the *Aga Khan* decision, under the influence of the Human Rights Act 1998, but the judge reasoned that the Jockey Club remained a private body and thus could not create a public one or convert its functions or those exercised by its creation into public functions.

8.24 Stanley Burnton J was not impressed by academic criticism of the *Aga Khan* decision, nor by decisions from other common law jurisdictions (some mentioned below) according greater recognition to the public character of sport. He found the criticisms misplaced on the ground that private law remedies were adequate. Finally, he rejected the contention that the authority of *Aga Khan* had been undermined by the post-Human Rights Act 1998 classification of public authorities into 'core' and 'hybrid' authorities[31] and that the Jockey Club and its organs fell within the latter class; and he concluded that *Aga Khan* 'is authority for the proposition that the Jockey Club is not a public authority for the purposes of s.6 [of the Human Rights Act 1998]' and that the decisions of its Appeal Board were not decisions in the exercise of a public function within Part 54 of the Civil Procedure Rules 1998, dealing with the scope of judicial review.[32]

8.25 We argued in the 1990s that many decisions of sporting bodies are, on a correct analysis, ones which affect public and not merely private rights, and that English law took a wrong turn in the *Law* case in 1983, from which it has not yet recovered.[33] A number of senior judges, as well as practitioners, expressed agreement that sports bodies' decisions should be susceptible to judicial review. In the *Massingberd-Mundy* and *RAM Racecourses* cases Neill LJ, Roch LJ, Stuart-Smith LJ and Lord Brown (as they later became) would, if freed from the constraints of precedent, have allowed judicial review of the Jockey Club.[34]

---

[28] [1987] QB 815, CA.

[29] [2005] EWHC 2197 (Admin), [2006] ISLR, SLR 31, Stanley Burnton J.

[30] The judge accepted that the substance, morphine, was probably present in the horse because of horse feed contaminated with poppy seeds, and that the claimant trainer bore no blame.

[31] Discussed in detail in the speeches in *Aston Cantlow and Wilmcote with Billesley Parochial Church Council v Wallbank* [2004] 1 AC 546, HL.

[32] Para 44 of the judgment. The claim was allowed to proceed as a private law claim, but failed on the facts before the same judge: *Mullins v McFarlane* [2006] EWHC 986 (QB), [2006] ISLR, SLR 65.

[33] See Beloff and Kerr (n 13); see also to similar effect Pannick, *Judicial Review of Sports Bodies* [1997] Judicial Review 150.

[34] Simon Brown J (as he then was) in the *RAM Racecourses* case [1993] 2 All ER 225 said at p 245 that he 'disagree[d] with the conclusions of the court in *ex p Massingberd-Mundy*' insofar as the court's decision in that case rested on the broad ground that 'the Jockey Club can never be reviewable in regard to any of their decision-making functions'.

Others, notably Lord Hoffmann and Stanley Burnton LJ (as he now is), favour the status quo. The debate is part of a broader one about the nature of public law functions, not confined to the realm of sport. The practical proposition must be accepted that the twenty-first century jurisprudence, in which public functions are now viewed through the prism of the Human Rights Act 1998, has not altered the status of sporting bodies' decisions, which must be challenged using private law causes of action, whether or not contractual rights are there to be invoked.

8.26 In other common law jurisdictions some courts have shown themselves willing to entertain public law challenges to sporting bodies' decisions. In New Zealand, a string of cases saw judicial review used to resolve disputes in association football, rugby union, rugby league and racing.[35] In *Western Australian Turf Club v Federal Commissioner of Taxation* the High Court of Australia, by contrast, held that the Turf Club was not a 'public authority constituted under any Act or State Act' and consequently was not exempt from income tax.[36] The court noted that although certain public powers and functions had been conferred on the Turf Club by statute, its principal functions were the ordinary private ones involved in running a racing club. The Club derived its revenue from those activities, to which its non-income producing public law functions were merely incidental.

8.27 Yet the Supreme Court of Australia in *Justice v South Australian Trotting Control Board*[37] was prepared to entertain applications for the public law remedies of *certiorari* and *mandamus* in view of the Board's statutory function of regulating and controlling the sport of trotting in South Australia. And in *Jockey Club of South Africa v Forbes*[38] the Club, taking the opposite line from its English counterpart, argued that a challenge to its disciplinary decision should have been brought by the South African equivalent of judicial review procedure. The court was prepared to assume that the procedure 'extends to decisions of domestic tribunals and does not apply only to breaches by officials of duties imposed on them by public law'.[39] The court went on to hold that the use of a private law procedure was not fatal to the application, even on that assumption.[40]

8.28 Returning to the English courts, the adverse impact of the *Aga Khan* case was that a party unable to rely on contractual rights risked being denied any remedy to challenge a

---

[35] *Simpson v NZ Racing Conference* 24 June 1980, High Court, Wellington, at A531–79; *Johnson v Appeal Judges*, CA 117/96, 16 July 1996; *Lower Hutt City AFC v NZ Football Association* 13 March 1993, High Court, Auckland M335/93; *Loe v NZ RFU* 10 August 1993, High Court, Wellington CP209/93; *Otahuhu Rovers RLC v Auckland Rugby League Inc* 12 November 1993, High Court, Auckland M818/93; *La Roux v NZ RFU* 14 March 1995, High Court, Wellington CP346/94; noted in *Judicial Review in the Commercial Arena*, paper and lecture given on 15 November 1996 by Paul Walker (now Walker J) in Wellington, New Zealand; see also *Ferguson v Scottish FA* (1996) Outer House Cases, 1.2.96; *Moran, Lynch and Butterly v O'Sullivan*, 18.3.03, unreported, Carroll J (Ireland); *Barrieau v US Trotting Association* (1986) 78 NBR (2d) 128; *Justice v South Australian Trotting Control Board* (1989) 50 SASR 613; *Forbes v NSW Trotting Club* (1979) 13 CLR 242; *NZ Trotting Conference v Ryan* [1990] NZLR 143; and *Finnigan v NZ RFU* [1985] NZLR 159. See also the useful Commonwealth update in Kelly, *Judicial Review of Sports Bodies' Decisions: Comparable Common Law Perspectives* [2011] ISLR 71.
[36] (1978) 19 ALR 167. The High Court noted that the possession of some statutory duties or powers is not enough to attract the exemption unless, upon an examination of all its characteristics, the body can be seen in general to conform to the common understanding of a public authority.
[37] (1989) 50 FAR 613.
[38] (1993) (1) FA 649.
[39] Ibid, 659E per Kriegler AJA.
[40] For a further review of 20th century Commonwealth authority see Beloff and Kerr, *Judicial Control of Sporting Bodies: The Commonwealth Jurisprudence* (1995) 3(1) SLJ 5; see also Beloff, *The Impact of Public Law and Sports Law* [2003] Journal of the Commonwealth Lawyers Association 51.

sporting body's decision adversely affecting him. Difficulties were caused by the inflexible 'procedural exclusivity' rule whereby a decision must be characterised as arising in public or private law, and the corresponding procedure followed on pain of dismissal of the proceedings.[41] Increased procedural flexibility has mitigated the harshness of the rule, but it is still the law that a right to relief can arise in private law or public law, but not both simultaneously.[42] The courts responded by developing a private law cause of action for a simple declaration, in the absence of contract. As we shall see, the leading cases developing this right of action were sports related.[43]

8.29 Although the development of private law claims makes the issue less important now, *Stevenage Borough FC Ltd v The Football League Ltd* remains a source of strong support for the view that judicial review is the preferable vehicle for resolution of sports related disputes. The case took the form of a private law challenge to a decision of the Football League to deny admission to Stevenage after it had won the Vauxhall Conference. The case proceeded by way of speedy trial, with oral evidence and cross-examination, within three months of issue of the writ. The judge analysed the divide between public and private law and remarked:

> ... the procedural distinctions are not obviously justifiable. Rose J's concern that extension of judicial review to such bodies as the Football Association, would result in excessive pressure on judicial time, is not borne out by the evidence of the present case. In spite of the efforts of the parties, and the economy of presentation, the writ procedure, with pleadings, discovery and oral evidence, inevitably is more elaborate, time consuming and expensive than judicial review. Most of the facts in the present case were uncontentious, and little emerged in the process of oral evidence which could not have been adequately dealt with by affidavit and examination of documents. Under the judicial review procedure, if properly conducted, the case for each party can generally be set out in one main affidavit on each side, supported only by relevant documents; rather than, as in this case, in some 16 witness statements, 15 files of documents and transcripts of 5 days of oral evidence.[44]

He went on to observe that it was

> difficult to see any reason in principle why the tests applied to the exercise of discretion by such regulatory bodies [as the Football League], acting in good faith, should be materially different to those applied to bodies subject to judicial review.[45]

8.30 Earlier in the same judgment, Carnwath J commented that the dividing line between governmental and non-governmental functions in the case law is not only

---

[41] *O'Reilly v Mackman* [1983] 2 AC 237, HL.

[42] Although public and private law rights may be found in the same factual matrix: see eg *R v City of Sunderland, ex parte Baumber* [1996] COD 211, QBD, Dyson J, where a psychologist had both contractual and statutory rights to enforce against her employer arising from unlawful strictures imposed on her in breach of both the statutory scheme and her contract.

[43] Starting with *Stevenage Borough FC Ltd v The Football League Ltd*, 23 July 1996, also reported at [2006] ISLR, SLR 128 and CA (1997) 9 Admin LR 109. Stevenage's appeal was dismissed but on the ground of delay; see (1997) 9 Admin LR 109. Carnwath J drew on the useful point that restraint of trade claims were not confined to cases where the claimant could rely on a contractual right; cf the discussion of access to competition cases in chapter 3, para 3.55 ff.

[44] Transcript, pp 36–37.

[45] Ibid, p 38. See also Lord Woolf MR in *Wilander v Tobin* [1997] 2 Lloyd's Rep 293, CA, at 299–300: 'If the Appeals Committee does not act fairly or if it misdirects itself in law and fails to take into account relevant considerations or takes into account irrelevant considerations, the High Court can intervene. It can also intervene if there is no evidential basis for its decision.' See also Dawn Oliver, *Administrative Decision Making; Common Law; Natural Justice* [1997] Public Law 630.

difficult to draw, but difficult to justify. He referred to academic writing suggesting that the extension of judicial review to non-statutory bodies such as the Takeover Panel has a 'common law root' in cases dealing with the exercise of monopoly powers.[46] Thus examination of the substantive rights in play in this field throws doubt on the validity of an approach which proceeds from a sharp divide between decisions affecting private and public rights. If, as Carnwath J's analysis suggests, there is an organic link between decisions of public bodies and those of domestic tribunals, the justification for separate procedural treatment is undermined.

8.31 Subsequently in *Modahl v British Athletic Federation Ltd*,[47] where the plaintiff athlete claimed damages for breach of contract arising from a wrong finding that she was guilty of doping which was subsequently reversed in a domestic appeal, Lord Woolf MR commented that it was wrong to suggest that public law principles governing judicial review have no relevance in domestic disciplinary proceedings. He went on to observe that the test of fairness should be the same whether the claim lies in private or in public law. He pointed out that the procedural differences in the respective regimes ought not to impact on the scope of any substantive right to damages, which would not be obtainable in a public law claim but could be in a private law claim. In *Mullins v McFarlane*[48] Stanley Burnton J assumed, without deciding, that the court had discretion to intervene in cases where a decision is arbitrary or capricious or results from a misconstruction of the relevant rules. *Bradley v Jockey Club*[49] also supports the proposition that the test for intervention does not differ significantly from that applicable to a public law decision on judicial review.

8.32 Our brief survey of the divide between private and public law and its impact on sports related disputes shows a rigidly enforced (and in our view still regrettable) prohibition against the use of public law remedies in England, not mirrored in other common law jurisdictions where the law is more flexible and the distinction less sharp. From the perspective of a player or club wishing to mount a challenge, pursuit of a public law remedy remains unlikely to be advisable in this country[50] except by a claimant with a penchant for law reform, a deep pocket and a willingness to attempt an Everest-like ascent to the Supreme Court. But we venture to question whether sporting bodies are better protected from judicial intervention than they would be if treated as bodies with a public element whose decisions could be challenged by judicial review. It is now clear that the tests for intervention by the courts do not differ in substance. But the rules governing the grant of interlocutory injunctions in private law are more favourable to claimants, generally, than defendants.

8.33 The argument that sport is by nature more a public than a private activity proceeds from an a priori judgment about its nature. We regard sporting activity as more public than private. We recognise that our view is not current orthodoxy but we continue to

---

[46] Ibid, p 36, referring to Forsyth [1996] Cambridge Law Journal 122; *Alnutt v Inglis* (1810) 12 East 527, in which it was held that the London Dock Company which owned the only warehouses in which wine importers could bond their wine had a correlative duty to charge only reasonable hire.

[47] CA transcript, 28 July 1997.

[48] [2006] EWHC 986 (QB), [2006] ISLR, SLR 65; judgment paras 37–39.

[49] [2004] EWHC 2164 (Richards J, as he then was), upheld on appeal [2005] EWCA Civ 851, also discussed in chapter 3 at paras 3.64, 3.85–3.86.

[50] Hence in the *Mullins* litigation, discussed above at paras 8.23–8.24, the claimant had made an open offer, not accepted by the Jockey Club, to consent to the transfer of the case to the ordinary Queen's Bench Division provided the Club accepted the supervisory jurisdiction of the court to a standard not less exacting than judicial review.

hold it, and we do so as commercial lawyers as well as administrative lawyers. Sporting endeavour is—and should be—undertaken for more than commercial gain. Clubs and players should be seen to represent themselves, their clubs, or their country, more than they represent the commercial sponsor whose logo temporarily adorns their shirts. Clubs in team sports have geographical roots which can never be completely destroyed by an increasingly international trade in players' services, however developed that market becomes. The injection of copious private capital into sport should not detract from its public character, any more than the function of managing a prison should be regarded as a private function merely because it happens to be entrusted to a private company.

8.34 Finally we observe that the public law remedy of judicial review remains available in the normal way where the decision under challenge is taken not by a sports governing body (SGB) but by a statutory or other undertaking sufficiently invested with public functions. Thus, in May 2011 the London football clubs Tottenham Hotspur and Leyton Orient launched an application for permission to apply for judicial review of the decision (since rescinded and subject to consideration not yet concluded at the time of writing) to award the 2012 Olympic Stadium to West Ham. The application was brought against Olympic Park Legacy Company Limited, the Mayor of London, the Minister for Sport and the Olympics and the Secretary of State for Communities and Local Government. Decisions of these defendants, excepting only possibly the first, would be amenable to judicial review in the normal way. Conceptually, such a judicial review differs little from an ordinary public law dispute relating to, for example, planning permission to extend a stadium.[51]

Private Law Claims

Introduction

8.35 In English private law, the remedies available in a sporting dispute depend upon the nature of the right asserted by the claimant and on the circumstances in which it is asserted. The remedies available are those available generally to litigants in private law proceedings. English law remedies have developed historically, under the influence of the historic division of the courts between those exercising common law jurisdiction and those—presided over by the Lord Chancellor—exercising jurisdiction in equity. It is not proposed here to give an exhaustive account of all the remedies open to claimants at common law and in equity; only of those that are most important in the sporting field. The common law traditionally leans towards the primacy of damages as a remedy.

8.36 Yet, in the field of sport, with notable exceptions such as the litigation involving the athlete Diane Modahl,[52] monetary compensation is not usually the remedy uppermost in the mind of the claimant. Sporting disputes which develop into

---

[51] Davis J dismissed the permission application on the papers in June 2011. Collins J granted permission in August 2011 but the claim was withdrawn in October 2011 following an announcement that the proposed deal with West Ham would not proceed.

[52] There were several phases in the *Modahl* litigation, culminating in the Court of Appeal's upholding of the dismissal of the claim for damages in *Modahl v British Athletic Federation Ltd (No 2)* [2001] 1 WLR 1192.

litigation, more often than not, arise at short notice and in circumstances where the swiftness of the court's ruling is as important as the result itself. This is because legal disputes often concern forthcoming competitions for which the date has been set, or which recur annually. Most litigation, unless deliberately expedited with the parties' timetable in mind, takes more than a year from claim to judgment. Often the question is whether a sportsman or woman should be permitted to take part in a particular tournament.

8.37 Damages may occupy a place in the background thinking of the parties, usually as a remoter consequence of failure to achieve the right to participate in a competition. But the immediate priority, in most sporting litigation, is likely to be the obtaining of an injunction or something as effective as an injunction; for example, a declaration or securing an undertaking from the other party. The remedy of injunction is often coupled with a claim for a declaration regulating the respective rights of the parties for the future. We therefore consider the non-pecuniary remedies of declaration and injunction before moving on to damages.

Contract Based and Non-Contract Based Private Law Claims

8.38 In our discussion in chapter three regarding the assertion of rights to participate in sporting competitions, we explained that the basis of a claim asserting such a right may be contractual or non-contractual; and that in either case the claim may include, but does not always depend upon, invocation of the restraint of trade doctrine and competition law. The same is true in the case of private law remedies to resolve sporting disputes generally, including in disciplinary cases, as discussed in chapter seven (see paras 7.35, 7.39–7.41. And as explained above at paras 8.23–8.24, in rejecting the notion that sports bodies exercise public functions amenable to the public law remedy of judicial review, the courts have developed further than ever before the private law remedy of granting a declaration in such cases, to protect against the injustice that would arise if a sporting litigant were left without a remedy through inability to assert a right of action founded on a contract. It is arguable that the remedy which we refer to below as a *declaration simpliciter* has a character specific to sports law, since it has been developed by the courts mainly in sports related cases.[53] It is strange for the development of sports law to be led by remedies rather than rights, but we find that is what has happened.

Remedies under the Human Rights Act 1998

8.39 Since October 2000 the Human Rights Act 1998 has brought nearly all rights under the European Convention on Human Rights into domestic law. We already considered the impact of this in chapter two.[54] The expectation that the 1998 Act might lead English

[53] The term *declaration simpliciter* was first used in the previous edition of this work, published in 1999. However, the remedy was also available in non-sport related restraint of trade cases without contract: *Pharmaceutical Society of Great Britain v Dickson* [1970] AC 403, HL, per Lord Reid at 420, rejecting the contention that there was 'no justiciable issue'.

[54] See paras 2.95–2.106.

courts to relax or attenuate the rigid distinction between public and private rights has not been realised. But sportsmen and women and clubs, like others, can now invoke Convention rights directly in the English courts, instead of having to bring a claim against the United Kingdom before the Court of Human Rights at Strasbourg. When the Convention rights scheduled to the 1998 Act became part of the domestic law of the United Kingdom, no case from the world of sport had yet (so far as we are aware) reached the Strasbourg Court during the 47 or so years that the Convention had been in force.[55]

8.40 In the first edition of this book, written shortly before the entry into force of the 1998 Act, we ventured the view that the incorporation into domestic law of Article 6 of the Convention could impact on disciplinary proceedings in sport, on the basis that such proceedings could involve a determination of civil rights and obligations within the meaning of the first paragraph of that Article. Under the Act, however, the definition of a 'public authority' which must observe Convention rights expressly excludes, in relation to a particular act, a person who is performing a private act.[56]

8.41 Twelve years after the 1998 Act incorporated the Convention rights into English domestic law, their impact on dispute resolution in sport has not proved overwhelming.[57] In *Stretford v The Football Association Ltd*[58] the Court of Appeal rejected a submission that a football agent was entitled to a public hearing of disciplinary charges relating to his representation of the footballer Wayne Rooney and evidence he had given in certain criminal proceedings. The court pointed out that parties who enter into a valid arbitration agreement providing for private dispute resolution are taken to have waived their right to a public hearing which Article 6 would otherwise guarantee if their civil rights and obligations are being determined. Few sportsmen and women want publicity anyway, particularly in disciplinary proceedings.

Forum and Multiplicity of Proceedings

8.42 The interface between disciplinary proceedings of an SGB and criminal proceedings is a boundary beset by friction.[59] The state and the SGB each have their own interests to advance: the state to ensure the integrity of the trial process and the avoidance of anything which might prevent suspected criminals from being brought to book or given a viable ground of appeal, the SGB to retain control over its sport and to mete out swift and effective punishment to those who break its rules.

---

[55] The Convention was adopted in 1950 and entered into force on 1 September 1953. The United Kingdom adopted the right of individual petition to the Court of Human Rights in 1966.

[56] See s 6(5) of the 1998 Act.

[57] Cf the case of the male athletics coach disciplined for having sexual relations with a female athlete he was coaching, discussed above at paras 7.66–7.69 and in principle capable of engaging Art 8 of the Convention. See also the valuable account of David Pannick QC and Jane Mulcahy in chapter C1 of Lewis and Taylor, *Sport: Law and Practice*, 2nd edn (Tottel Publishing, 2008), where they make the point that many sports bodies have (perhaps unnecessarily in the light of *R (Mullins) v Appeal Board of the Jockey Club*, cited above at para 8.23) adapted their procedures to make them compliant with Art 6 of the Convention (right to a fair trial).

[58] [2007] EWCA Civ 238, [2007] ISLR, SLR 41.

[59] See generally Harris, *Disciplinary and Regulatory Proceedings*, 6th edn (Jordan, 2009) 109–11.

8.43 The interests are not coincident and were highlighted in the cases of Messrs Butt, Asif and Amir,[60] three Pakistani cricketers accused of spot fixing contrary to the International Cricket Council (ICC) Code of Conduct. The issue was raised at an interlocutory stage as to whether the disciplinary proceedings should be postponed to what were then still potential, not actual, criminal proceedings arising out of the same incidents. The ICC Tribunal continued with its own proceedings notwithstanding that on the eve of the last day of the hearing, the Attorney-General gave his necessary consent to the criminal proceedings which again raised the issue as to whether the ICC Tribunal should refrain from continuing to make an award, and, if it did, the extent to which such award should be published. The award was made[61] but until conclusion of the criminal trial the full reasons were only made available to persons outside the United Kingdom and on conditions to avoid any possible contamination of the jury.

8.44 English case law (and other case law adopting English principles) has pronounced directly or indirectly on the relationship between criminal, civil and disciplinary proceedings. In our view the following propositions can be derived from the authorities, so far as overlapping criminal and civil proceedings are concerned:

(1) There is no automatic right to have civil proceedings postponed until criminal charges arising out of the same factual matrix have been finally determined: *Jefferson v Bhetcha*.[62]

(2) Each case must turn on its own facts.[63] In the criminal context 'much will depend upon the severity of the offence, the precise issue before the other court, and the extent of overlap'.[64]

(3) On the one hand the sorts of circumstances that will justify intervention by way of stay where civil and criminal proceedings are simultaneously afoot are provided by Megaw LJ:
   (a) the fact that the civil action or some step in it is likely to obtain such publicity as might sensibly be expected to reach and to influence persons who might be jurors in criminal proceedings, or
   (b) where there is some real and not merely notional danger that disclosure of the defence in the civil action will or might lead to a potential miscarriage of justice in criminal proceedings by, for example,
      (i)   enabling prosecution witnesses to prepare a fabrication of evidence, or
      (ii) leading to interference with witnesses, or
      (iii) in some other way.[65]

(4) On the other hand Megaw LJ noted in respect of the right to silence that 'the protection which is at present given to one facing a criminal charge ... does not extend to give the defendant as a matter of right the same protection in contemporaneous civil proceedings'.[66]

---

[60] The substantive aspects of which were discussed in chapter 7, paras 7.22–7.24.
[61] Award of 5 February 2011: Doha Michael J Beloff QC (Chairman); Justice Albie Sachs; Sharad Rao.
[62] [1979] 1 WLR 898, CA.
[63] Ibid, 905.
[64] See Lewis and Taylor (n 57) para A2.95.
[65] Ibid.
[66] Ibid.

8.45 The same principles apply *mutatis mutandis*[67] to overlapping criminal and disciplinary proceedings. In *R v British Broadcasting Corporation, ex parte Lavelle*, which concerned precisely such a coincidence, Woolf J said:[68]

> ... it seems to me that while the court must have jurisdiction to intervene to prevent a serious injustice from occurring, it will only do so in very clear cases in which the applicant can show that there is a real danger and not merely a notional danger that there would be a miscarriage of justice in the criminal proceedings if the court did not intervene.

8.46 In *Archer v South West Thames Area Health Authority*[69] the High Court refused a civil servant facing criminal proceedings an injunction to stay a disciplinary inquiry. Steyn J held that there was no automatic right to have disciplinary proceedings stayed pending criminal proceedings and the applicant's wish to have the criminal proceedings heard first had to be weighed against the prejudice to the defendant. He noted that even if the standard of proof in the two proceedings was the same, the issues would not be. In *R v Solicitors Disciplinary Tribunal, ex parte Gallagher*[70] the Court of Appeal declined to grant judicial review of the refusal by the Solicitors Disciplinary Tribunal of an application by a solicitor for an adjournment of the disciplinary proceedings concerning an alleged fraud where he was simultaneously the subject of criminal charges of dishonesty arising out of a mortgage fraud. A factor which may be relevant when considering a potential risk or danger of injustice is the proximity (or otherwise) of the criminal proceedings. In *Gallagher* Parker LJ said:

> It is perfectly plain, in my view, that the Disciplinary Tribunal, if faced with a situation where for example they were about to make a finding and order a day or two before the criminal proceedings began, might well consider that to do so would muddy the waters.[71] They might then say that they would not reach a conclusion until after the criminal proceedings had been disposed of, or they might simply reserve judgment, which they are entitled to do under the rules, pending the hearing of the criminal proceedings.

In the absence of any extant criminal proceedings it will not be possible to identify a real risk of injustice. In *A v Tayside Fire Board*[72] Lord Bonomy said:

> In the absence of any proceedings it is not possible to identify a real risk of injustice. Any risk is entirely notional and speculative. If and when any criminal proceedings are instituted the petitioners, or such of them as are involved in these proceedings, will be able to turn to the court before whom the proceedings are taken for protection against miscarriage of justice. It will be for that court to ensure that the proceedings are fair.

---

[67] The countervailing interest in a contest between priority of civil and criminal proceedings is the 'plaintiff's ordinary rights of having his claim processed and heard and decided': *Jefferson v Bhetcha* (n 62) 905.

[68] [1983] ICR 99, 116.

[69] (1985) unreported, 1 January 1985, Steyn J: 'The fair enforcement of the criminal law being of paramount importance, if the risk or danger of injustice is established, a domestic tribunal ought, save exceptionally, to adjourn its proceedings.'

[70] (1991) unreported, 30 September, CA.

[71] A phrase borrowed from Lord Donaldson MR in *Lipman Bray v Hillhouse* (1987) 137 NLJ 171, CA.

[72] 2000 SLT 1307, per Lord Bonomy at 1310. The gap between the two sets of proceedings can be crucial. In *Fallon v Horseracing Regulatory Authority* [2006] EWHC 2030 (QB) (further mentioned below) the High Court refused to order a stay of a disciplinary suspension (ban on riding) when a criminal trial arising out of the same facts was 18 months away.

8.47 Factors which tell against a stay are as follows. Any jury will naturally be directed by the trial judge to ignore the outcome—if unfavourable to the sportsman—of proceedings before the tribunal. Judges have in a variety of contexts, notably contempt of court, reiterated the mantra that juries do indeed focus on the evidence before them. In *R v Ali (Ahmed)* Thomas LJ said:[73]

> In considering whether a jury can, in circumstances of great publicity about defendants, act as a fair and impartial tribunal, the court has to have regard to the trial process and its ability to deal with the publicity that had arisen. In *R. v Abu Hamza* [2007] 1 Cr. App. R. 27 (p.345); [2007] Q.B. 659, Lord Phillips of Worth Matravers C.J. had referred to and endorsed the views of Sir Igor Judge, President of the Queen's Bench Division, in *R. v B* [2006] EWCA Crim 2692; [2007] H.R.L.R. 1, which were as follows at [31]:

> There is a feature of our trial system which is sometimes overlooked or taken for granted. The collective experience of this constitution as well as the previous constitution of the court, both when we were in practice at the Bar and judicially, has demonstrated to us time and time again, that juries up and down the country have a passionate and profound belief in, and a commitment to, the right of a defendant to be given a fair trial. They know that it is integral to their responsibility. It is, when all is said and done, their birthright; it is shared by each one of them with the defendant. They guard it faithfully. The integrity of the jury is an essential feature of our trial process. Juries follow the directions which the judge will give them to focus exclusively on the evidence and to ignore anything they may have heard or read out of court. No doubt in this case Butterfield J will give appropriate directions, tailor-made to the individual facts in the light of any trial post the sentencing hearing, after hearing submissions from counsel for the defendants. We cannot too strongly emphasise that the jury will follow them, not only because they will loyally abide by the directions of law which they will be given by the judge, but also because the directions themselves will appeal directly to their own instinctive and fundamental belief in the need for the trial process to be fair.

8.48 In the sports context, the standard of proof may be different in the two fora; 'comfortable satisfaction', albeit sometimes on a sliding scale calibrated by reference to the gravity of the charge (as in the case of the ICC Code Article 3.1) before the tribunal; and 'beyond reasonable doubt' in any criminal trial. In *Archer* Steyn J identified this as material to the balancing exercise. Further, the charges before the two bodies, although arising out of the same events, may be different. The Crown Prosecution Service does not administer the SGB's code. The SGB is not a prosecuting authority for purposes of criminal law.

8.49 The fact that the witnesses who appear for the SGB may reappear for the CPS and will have the 'advantage' of knowing what cross-examination will be directed to them is, in our view, a point without substance. If such witnesses have committed themselves to one version of events before the SGB tribunal, they will be vulnerable if they seek to put forward different evidence in any criminal trial. This is, in principle, no less likely to benefit than to prejudice the defendant.

8.50 Sometimes a question arises in a sporting dispute as to which forum is appropriate for its resolution. In *Enderby Town FC Ltd v The Football Association Ltd* the FA appointed a commission which found gross negligence in the management of the plaintiff club. The

---

[73] [2011] EWCA Crim 1260, [2011] 2 Cr App R 22, para 89.

club appealed to the FA on certain points of law 'of much complexity and difficulty',[74] which were that the charge was not properly formulated, that it was heard by three men without jurisdiction to hear it, and that the relevant rule on its true construction did not apply to club companies which were not members of the FA. The Court of Appeal, applying a dictum of Romer LJ in *Lee v The Showmen's Guild of Great Britain*,[75] refused the club an injunction to stop the FA hearing the appeal unless it permitted the club to be legally represented. The court reasoned that the rules did not permit representation in every case, and the club had not sought to bring the points of law before the High Court in an action for a declaration.

8.51 The inference is that, had the club brought an action for a declaration, the High Court would have determined the points of law and, presumably, compelled the FA by injunction to refrain from hearing the appeal until the points of law had been determined. However, the current FA rules provide for legally qualified members to sit on FA appeals, as well as an arbitration clause. Now that the rules of many sporting bodies are more sophisticated than in the 1970s, the involvement of the courts during disciplinary proceedings is less likely and is more likely to occur in the context of provisional suspension,[76] as discussed in chapter seven at paras 7.175–7.176. Nonetheless the court's power to stop disciplinary proceedings in their tracks still exists and should not be forgotten.

8.52 The power was exercised in an application to the High Court by the boxer John Conteh, while a disciplinary complaint against him was pending, alleging breach of an obligation, said to be contractual, to train for a fight. Mr Conteh disputed the validity of the contract and thus the existence of the obligation. He asked for an injunction to restrain the British Boxing Board of Control from hearing the complaint on the basis that an action against him, his former manager and promoter was pending in the Queen's Bench Division of the High Court.[77] The Court of Appeal articulated a wider principle, more conducive to a grant of stay. It held that it has 'power to restrain the hearing of a complaint by a domestic tribunal if in special circumstances the interests of justice so demand'.[78] The court allowed the appeal and granted an injunction restraining the Board of Control from hearing the disciplinary case, reasoning that the misconduct charge pending against Mr Conteh raised exactly the same issue as that in the High Court proceedings, namely whether Mr Conteh at the relevant date was bound by the very contracts for breach of which he was sued in those proceedings. The court was unwilling to countenance duplication of proceedings where the disciplinary case would 'amount to a prehearing of the issue pending in the High Court action'[79] and accorded priority to the court over the domestic body as a preferred forum.

8.53 Sir John Pennycuick said:

> I think an obvious ground for the intervention of the court so as to restrain proceedings before a domestic tribunal is that there are pending in the High Court proceedings in which the same issue,

---

[74] [1971] Ch 591, CA, per Lord Denning MR at 604D–E.
[75] [1952] 2 QB 329, CA at 354: 'the proper tribunals for the determination of legal disputes in this country are the courts and they are the only tribunals which, by training and experience, and assisted by properly qualified advocates, are fitted for the task.'
[76] As in *Fallon v Horseracing Regulatory Authority* [2006] EWHC 2030 (QB), [2007] ISLR, SLR 1.
[77] *Conteh v Onslow-Fane*, The Times, 26 June 1975, transcript 25 June 1975, CA.
[78] Transcript, p 13G–H.
[79] Ibid, p 15D–E.

or substantially the same issue, is raised and which the association concerned is not in a position to stay. The court will not as a rule allow the prosecution of the same issue in concurrent proceedings before different tribunals. It follows that, although the parties to the domestic hearing and the parties to the High Court action are different, the two sets of proceedings turn upon an identical issue and that if the domestic hearing is allowed to continue there will be in substance a duplication of proceedings. Indeed, the [British Boxing Board of Control] recognises that the determination before its committee can only be provisional and must yield to the decision in the action when it ultimately comes to be made. Given this state of affairs, the court has a judicial discretion to restrain the hearing before the committee on the ground of duplication of proceedings.

This more ample ground for intervention may be explained on the basis that the issue of the validity and meaning of the contract was one of law—and thus particularly within the province of the court.

8.54 Whether or not an injunction or stay will be granted in cases where there are concurrent proceedings is a question of fact and discretion in each case. The *Conteh* case was a rare one in which there was (to use a phrase taken from a different context) not merely 'virtual total eclipse',[80] but total eclipse of the issues in the respective proceedings. Normally, such a stay will be difficult to obtain, for:

[the] power to intervene to prevent injustice where the continuation of one set of proceedings may prejudice the fairness of the trial of other proceedings ... is a power which has to be exercised with great care and only where there is a real risk of serious prejudice which may lead to injustice.[81]

8.55 If the court is satisfied that, absent a stay or injunction, there is a real risk of such prejudice, it has to balance that risk against the countervailing considerations, which may include a strong public interest in seeing that the disciplinary process is not impeded.[82] But unless the party seeking a stay can show a real risk of serious prejudice which may lead to injustice, a stay must be refused.[83] A real risk of real prejudice is a necessary but not sufficient criterion for a stay. Thus in *R v Executive Council of the Joint Disciplinary Scheme, ex parte Hipps*, Dyson J said:[84]

... before any question of balancing can arise, the court must be satisfied that there is a real risk of serious prejudice. If it is not so satisfied, no question of a stay arises, and there is nothing to put into the scales against the public interest in the disciplinary process being unimpeded and any other countervailing factors ... Those considerations will almost always include the strong public interest in seeing that the disciplinary process is not impeded. *Ex p Brindle* [1994] BCC 297, 310E–G, *ex parte Smith* [1995] BCC 1095, at 1100G, 1103B–D. ... [T]he basic assumption therefore, in my view, is that the disciplinary proceedings will continue.

He added:

(i) The court is not concerned with a *Wednesbury* review of [the Executive Counsel's] decision not to adjourn the proceedings. Rather I am required to exercise an original jurisdiction

---

[80] See *R v ICAEW, ex parte Brindle* [1994] BCC 297, CA; *R v Chance, ex parte Smith* [1995] BCC 1095, CA at 1103H; see also *Re Abermeadow Ltd (No 1); Secretary of State for Trade and Industry v Pollock* [1998] CLY 681 (Judge Hegarty QC).

[81] *R v Panel on Takeovers and Mergers, ex parte Fayed* [1992] BCC 524, per Neill LJ at 531E.

[82] Per Dyson J in *R v Executive Council of the Joint Disciplinary Scheme, ex parte Hipps*, transcript, 12 June 1996, at p 13B–C; see also Moses J's decision in *R (Ranson) v Institute of Actuaries* [2004] EWHC 3087 (Admin).

[83] *Ex parte Fayed* (n 80) 531; *ex parte Brindle* (n 80) 316G–H.

[84] [1996] CLY 5; see also *R (Ranson) v Institute of Actuaries* [2004] EWHC 3087 (Admin).

whether to grant a stay: see *R v Take-overs and Mergers Panel, ex parte Guinness*, and *R v Chance, ex parte Smith*.

(ii) The jurisdiction to stay one two concurrent sets of proceedings must be exercised sparingly and with great care: see *R v Panel on Take-overs and Mergers, ex parte Fayed & Ors* [1992] BCC 524, 531E and *R v ICAEW, ex parte Brindle* [1994] BCC 297, 310D–E.

(iii) Unless a party seeking a stay can show that if a stay is refused there is a real risk of serious prejudice which may lead to injustice in one or both of the proceedings, a stay must be refused: see *ex parte Fayed* at 531, *ex parte Brindle* at 316G–H.

(iv) If the court is satisfied that, absent a stay, there is a real risk of such prejudice then the court has to balance that risk against the countervailing considerations. Those considerations will almost always include the strong public interest in seeing that the disciplinary process is not impeded. *Ex parte Brindle* 310E–G, *ex parte Smith*, 1100G, 1103B–D.

(v) In a case where the balancing exercise is carried out, the court will give great weight to the view of the person or body responsible for the decision as to the factors militating against the stay and the weight to be given to them, but the court is the ultimate arbiter for what is fair: see *ex parte Smith*, 1101F–G, 1102H to 1103F and *ex parte Guinness*, 184D–E.

(vi) Each case turns on its own facts. Accordingly, only limited assistance can be derived when comparing the facts of a particular case with those of other cases where a stay was granted (as in *ex parte Brindle*) or where a stay was refused (as in *ex parte Smith*) …[85]

8.56 It may be that civil proceedings would take so long that any disciplinary proceedings at their conclusion might savour of abuse: the civil proceedings may reach no conclusion other than by way of settlement, whose terms may be confidential.[86] For these reasons an SGB should not lightly, if ever, postpone disciplinary action until after the conclusion of civil proceedings. They should always bear in mind the words of Stanley Burnton J in *Land v Executive Counsel of the Joint Disciplinary Scheme*:[87]

> Regulatory investigations and disciplinary proceedings perform important functions in our society. Furthermore, the days have gone when the High Court could fairly regard the proceedings of disciplinary tribunals as necessarily providing second class justice, as indeed [counsel] fully accepted.

The principle that sporting bodies should, where possible, be allowed, indeed encouraged, to regulate their sport would support the same conclusion.

Declarations

8.57 A declaration[88] is a highly effective weapon in the hands of a sporting litigant, enabling both parties to know their rights and obligations which the court declares at the end of the case. Two types of declaration concern us particularly in the context of sporting litigation.[89] The first is a declaration of contractual rights. Obviously there

---

[85] See also Houseman, *Staying Disciplinary Proceedings: Whatever Happened to* ex parte Brindle? [1999] Judicial Review 60; cf Kerr, *Staying Disciplinary Proceedings: A Reply* [1999] Judicial Review 188.

[86] See Harris (n 59) 112.

[87] [2002] EWHC 2086 (Admin), (2002) 152 NLJ 16, judgment para 25.

[88] See generally Woolf, *Zamir and Woolf: The Declaratory Judgment*, 4th edn (Sweet & Maxwell, 2011).

[89] The Court of Appeal formerly regarded the scope for granting declaratory relief as narrower in private law than in public law proceedings; see eg *Meadows Indemnity Co v Insurance Corporation of Ireland* [1989] 2 Lloyd's Rep 298; *Trustees of the Dennis Rye Pension Fund v Sheffield City Council* [1998] 1 WLR 840; *Link Organisation v North Derbyshire Tertiary College*, CA, transcript 14 August 1998. But '[t]here is no doubt that the circumstances in which the court will be prepared to grant declaratory relief are now considerably wider than they were thought to be after *Gouriet* [*Gouriet v Union of Post Office Workers* [1978] AC 435] and *Meadows*', per Aikens LJ at para

must be contractual relations between the parties in order for the court to declare what their contractual rights are. However, cases may arise in which one party asserts the existence of a contractual right, for example to compete in a particular competition, while the other party denies its existence. In such a case, the court's role is to declare whether the contractual right exists or not, and how far it extends if it does exist. Thus in *Watson v Prager*[90] a professional boxer successfully claimed a declaration that a particular clause in his contract with his manager, which was in a form prescribed by the British Boxing Board of Control, was in unreasonable restraint of trade and therefore unenforceable. The same success was achieved by a professional rugby league player as against his club in relation to the retention and transfer system then used in New South Wales.[91]

8.58 The second type of declaration is now well established in sports law. It is a declaration in the absence of contract, referred to in the first edition of this book as a *declaration simpliciter*. This remedy was already mentioned in chapter three,[92] where we observed that an aspiring entrant to a sporting competition may lack a contractual right to enter it even though he fulfils the organising body's criteria for entry. Judges have recognised that there may be circumstances in which it would be unjust to deny a claimant declaratory relief in the absence of a contractual right, if his private rights are affected by unlawful conduct of the defendant. The law recognises a right to a declaration as against a party with whom the claimant is not in a contractual or other recognised legal relationship, where that party's actions affect or may affect the claimant's private rights.

8.59 As already noted in chapter three,[93] this principle assisted George Eastham with his troublesome transfer from Newcastle United to Arsenal.[94] Examples of cases in which it has been conceded or held that a right to a declaration can exist as a freestanding cause of action, without a need for a contractual peg on which to hang it, are now quite numerous. Even in 1966 the Court of Appeal thought it arguable that a female trainer of horses had a right to a declaration where her only ground for relief, in the absence of a contract, was her assertion that rules which discriminated on the ground of her sex were void as contrary to public policy.[95] The existence of the jurisdiction to grant freestanding declaratory relief has been recognised many times in subsequent case law, particularly in the sporting field[96] but also—especially in restraint of trade cases—outside it.[97]

118 in *Rolls Royce plc v Unite the Union* [2009] EWCA Civ 387, [2010] 1 WLR 318; and see his statement of the applicable principles at para 120, applied in *Milebush Properties Ltd v Tameside MBC* [2011] EWCA Civ 270.

[90] [1991] 1 WLR 726, Scott J.
[91] *Buckley v Tutty* (1971) 125 CLR 353 (High Court of Australia).
[92] See para 3.76 ff.
[93] See paras 3.79–3.80.
[94] *Eastham v Newcastle United FC* [1964] Ch 413 at 443, per Wilberforce, J; *Greig v Insole* [1978] 1 WLR 302 (Slade J); cf in the Antipodean jurisdictions *Finnigan* [1985] 2 NZLR 1959; *Adamson* (1991) 103 ALR 319.
[95] *Nagle v Feilden* [1966] 2 QB 633, CA.
[96] See, in addition to the 21st century cases already discussed, *McInnes v Onslow-Fane* [1978] 1 WLR 1520; *Buckley v Tutty* (1971) 125 CLR 353; *Gasser v Stinson*, transcript, 15 June 1988 (Scott J) at pp 24–25; *Newport AFC Ltd v Football Association of Wales Ltd* [1995] 2 All ER 1987 (Jacob J); *Lennox Lewis v Frank Bruno and The World Boxing Council*, transcript, Rattee J, 3 November 1995 (claim dismissed on other grounds); and *Stevenage Borough FC Ltd v The Football League Ltd* (1997) 9 Admin LR 109, CA. Cf in Australia *Dixon v Esperance Bay Turf Club Inc* [2002] WASC 110, at 113.
[97] *Pharmaceutical Society of Great Britain v Dickson* [1970] AC 403, HL.

8.60 The court has a discretion whether to grant or refuse a declaration. It cannot be assumed that one will automatically be granted even if the claimant succeeds in establishing the primary case. But in the sporting context the courts have generally been willing to assist those with legitimate complaints against their regulatory bodies. It seems likely that the courts would also be prepared to assist a commercial body adversely affected by unlawful regulatory action, as was contended in *R v Jockey Club, ex parte RAM Racecourses Ltd*.[98] The applicant company wished to establish a new racecourse but was turned down by the Jockey Club. It sought to bring a claim by way of judicial review. The Divisional Court considered the case on its merits and the applicant company lost on the merits. The court would have been prepared to grant a declaration if the decision under challenge had been shown to be unlawful, and subject to the difficulty that the claim had been brought by application for judicial review.[99]

8.61 We should not leave the remedy of declaration without pointing out one substantial drawback: it has in the past only been available as a final order at the conclusion of proceedings. An interim declaration, unlike an interim injunction, could not be obtained. This has serious ramifications for the practical utility of the remedy, since speed is often of the essence, as already noted.[100] The suggestion that interim declarations could be available in cases where due to the sensitivity of the circumstances the courts cannot grant injunctive relief, is attractive but is contrary to the authority of *International General Electric Co of New York v Commissioners of Customs & Excise*.[101] However, in the Civil Procedure Rules 1998, rule 25.1(1)(b), an 'interim declaration' is listed among interim remedies available. It is questionable whether such a procedural rule is capable of affecting the scope of the availability of the remedy as a matter of substantive law.[102] Yet, Eder J granted such a declaration with apparent equanimity on 26 April 2012[103] and it is likely that the old contrary authority has been superseded by developments in procedural law provided for in the Civil Procedure Rules 1998.

Injunctions

8.62 Injunctions are probably the most useful remedy in sporting disputes. An injunction can compel an unwilling competition organiser to permit an eligible entrant to

---

[98] [1993] 2 All ER 225, DC.

[99] Stuart-Smith LJ noted at p 244e–g that the court had the power under the then RSC Order 53 rule 9(5) to order that the proceedings continue as if they had begun by writ.

[100] See para 8.14.

[101] [1962] Ch 784 per Upjohn LJ at 789–90; see also *R v IRC, ex parte Rossminster* [1980] AC 952 per Lord Diplock at 1014 E–F and Lord Scarman at 1027 C–E.

[102] Cf *St George's Healthcare NHS Trust v S* [1998] 3 All ER 673 at 700C–D; and see Neenan [1999] Judicial Review 6, at 7, noting that as the CPR are procedural in nature by virtue of the Civil Procedure Act 1997 (esp s 1 and Sched 1 para 2), Part 25.1(1)(b) of the CPR may be ultra vires. Yet in *Astro Exito Navegación SA v Southland Enterprise Co (The Messiniaki Tolmi) (No 2)* [1982] QB 1248, the Court of Appeal upheld a decision to grant an interim mandatory injunction to enforce a contractual obligation; per Ackner LJ (judgment of the court) at pp 1267–9, noting that in *Smith v Peters* (1875) LR 20 Eq 511, Sir George Jessel MR said at 512–13: 'there is no limit to the practice of the court with regard to interlocutory applications so far as they are necessary and reasonable applications ancillary to the due performance of its functions, namely, the administration of justice at the hearing of the cause. I know of no other limit. Whether they are or are not to be granted must of course depend upon the special circumstances of the case.'

[103] *Transport for London v Griffin* [2012] EWHC 1105 (QB), paras 26, 65 and 95.

compete in the competition, though it could not compel an unwilling competitor to compete.[104] Injunctions probably best represent the capacity of the law to aid the weak against the strong, and to give vivid expression to the concept of equality before the law, redressing the imbalance of power between modest individuals and mighty institutions (or, occasionally, the other way round).[105] Again, it is not our purpose to expound the historical development of the equitable remedy of injunction, nor to give a full account of its scope. Reference should be made to specialist works for that purpose.[106] We confine our account to injunctions as used in the sporting context.

8.63 The principal relevance of the remedy is at the interim stage of proceedings, ie usually near the beginning. In much sporting litigation played out in the courts, the objective of obtaining an injunction is the claimant's main and often only goal. An applicant for an interim injunction must include in the relief sought a claim for an final injunction, which the court would be asked to grant in the event that the matter went to a full trial, albeit that a full trial may never take place. Subject to the discretion of the court, a claimant who can establish a legal wrong is normally entitled to a final injunction to restrain repetition of the wrong and, sometimes, to require the defendant to put it right.[107] This is all well trodden ground for lawyers. What is less well known to sportsmen and women is that, other than in rare cases, a claimant who seeks an interlocutory injunction must be prepared to offer an undertaking in damages and, if necessary, prove that he or she (or it) is in a position to honour it by supplying evidence of sufficient financial substance.

8.64 Two simple examples will serve to illustrate the point. Suppose that a hockey club wishes to prevent one of its players from entering into a lucrative advertising contract to promote certain sportswear. The club alleges that to do so would be contrary to the player's obligations under his contract of employment with the club, which obliges the player not to promote any product save those endorsed by the club and its commercial sponsor. The player alleges that this term in his employment contract is void as an unreasonable restraint of trade. The club seeks an interim injunction to prevent the player appearing in a national television advertisement scheduled for screening in a week's time. The player counterclaims for a declaration that the restrictive term in his contract with the club is void. The club, in that example, must give an undertaking in damages to the player that in the event of the court later deciding the substantive case in favour of the player, the club must pay to the player such damages, if any, as the court shall decide it ought to pay to compensate him for the loss occasioned by the granting of an interim injunction against him. If any question arises as to the club's ability to honour the undertaking, it will have to produce its accounts or other financial evidence to show its worth. If the club takes the form of a small subsidiary of a large company, the latter may have to give the undertaking as it might otherwise be worthless.

---

[104] An injunction would surely not be granted to regulate the *manner* of competing, eg to restrain a footballer from deliberately scoring an own goal in breach of his employment contract, as William Gallas allegedly threatened to do in 2006 if selected to play for Chelsea when he wished to leave the club and join Arsenal.

[105] Lord Denning, *The Discipline of Law* (Butterworths, 1979) cites at p 140 the words of Thomas Fuller over 300 years ago: 'Be you never so high, the law is above you.'

[106] See, eg, Spry, *Equitable Remedies*, 8th edn (Sweet & Maxwell, 2010).

[107] At least if the defendant's covenant is a negative one, ie an agreement not to do something: *Doherty v Allman* (1877–8) LR 3 App Cas 709, per Lord Cairns LC at 719–20; cf *Araci v Fallon* [2011] EWCA Civ 668 (injunction granted to restrain jockey from riding the wrong horse in the Derby, in breach of contract).

8.65 In the second example, suppose the facts are the same but that instead of seeking an interim injunction against the player, the club reports him to the league of which the club is a member. The league serves notice on the player not to appear in the television advertisement or otherwise contract with the sportswear manufacturer, on pain of punitive action. The player, fearing that he might lose his lucrative television appearance the following week, urgently consults with lawyers who advise him to seek an injunction restraining the league from instituting disciplinary action against him on the basis of a restrictive obligation in his contract which he alleges is void. An urgent court hearing is hurriedly arranged, just before the scheduled television appearance. The player must give an undertaking in damages to the league and produce evidence of financial worth to support it. Continuing with the example, one may suppose that at the hearing the league's counsel produces a letter from another, rival, sportswear manufacturer threatening to pull out of a proposed lucrative sponsorship arrangement with the league, should the claimant player appear in the television advertisement the following week. The player's undertaking in damages may or may not be sufficiently backed by financial worth to persuade the court to grant him his injunction.[108]

8.66 The risk of a high financial price for an interim injunction is apparent from the two examples. They serve to emphasise the importance of an undertaking in damages and the peril of overlooking it. They also should encourage the parties to sporting disputes to settle their differences if they can. The claimant in both of the above examples faces a difficult decision to be taken under severe time pressure.

8.67 We look next at some of the main features of injunctions in sports law. The test which the courts in England apply is well known. Provided there is a serious issue to be tried, the court looks at the adequacy of damages as a remedy for either party, and the balance of convenience, or the balance of justice, in deciding whether to grant or refuse the injunction. Without an undertaking in damages, as explained above, the court is unlikely to grant one. In a case where a final trial is impracticable because the whole of the issue between the parties turns on an event, for example a cup final, scheduled imminently, the court will look beyond the question whether there is merely a serious issue to be tried, to a fuller appraisal of the merits. This may be difficult as hurriedly garnered written evidence, without cross-examination, is not the best factual basis on which to assess merit.

8.68 The application of these well-established principles in the sporting field was illustrated in *Jones v Welsh Rugby Union*.[109] A rugby union player obtained an interim order restraining the Welsh Rugby Union from implementing a four week ban on the basis of arguable procedural defects in the disciplinary procedure applied to him following an altercation on the field of play. Ebsworth J was 'concerned with whether or not the plaintiffs can establish a case for interim relief on the usual principles applicable'.[110] She commented that 'the practical reality requires the suspension to be lifted until the issue is determined between the parties', saying she hoped that interim relief was a 'just and

---

[108] Cf *Nike European Operations Netherlands BV v Tomas Rosicky* [2007] ISLR, SLR 136 (Patten J) in which the player was sued by the sponsor direct for proposing to wear Puma boots instead of Nike boots, and an interim injunction was granted to preserve the status quo pending consideration of the matter by a Dutch court, but giving the player the option of wearing unmarked boots.

[109] Transcript, 27 February 1997.

[110] Ibid, p 3, referring *sub silentio* to *American Cyanamid v Ethicon Ltd* [1975] AC 396, HL.

workable compromise ... that the suspension ... shall not be enforced until the trial of this matter or further order'.[111] The *Jones* case went to appeal, following a further interlocutory skirmish in which Potts J held that the defendant union was precluded by Ebsworth J's initial order from imposing a subsequent suspension pursuant to further disciplinary proceedings. The Court of Appeal held that the initial discretionary decision of Ebsworth J could not be faulted, even though the Union's arguments on the merits might well succeed at trial, but upheld the Union's contention that the judge's order had not precluded it from holding a second disciplinary hearing and imposing a penalty in consequence.[112]

8.69 As already noted, regulatory bodies in sport usually fare better at final trial than they do in interim injunction applications, because the low threshold that a claimant must reach, coupled with inadequacy of damages as a remedy for a sportsman or woman with a short career span and a vital need to create and maintain a reputation in a short time, make it difficult for the sporting association to show a balance of justice in its favour at the interim stage. The susceptibility of such associations to negative injunctions restraining the implementation of disciplinary penalties was for a time exploited by claimant players in an increasingly professional climate. Their professional associations, the equivalent of trade unions in industry, can assist in the matter of undertakings in damages, if their club is not supporting them and they are insufficiently wealthy on their own account.

8.70 In more recent attempts to obtain interim relief, however, claimants have not fared so well. As noted in chapter seven, the jockey Kieren Fallon failed to obtain interim relief to overturn his provisional ban imposed by an independent panel and upheld on appeal pending his trial on conspiracy to defraud, charges of which he was later acquitted.[113] And the sprinter Dwain Chambers failed in *Chambers v British Olympic Association*[114] to secure an injunction preventing his exclusion from the 2008 Beijing Olympics after being banned for doping, founded on a restraint of trade challenge to the validity of a rule making anyone found to have committed a doping offence ineligible for selection.[115]

8.71 The interim injunction is also a powerful weapon in the hands of a claimant seeking to prevent implementation of a rule alleged to be in unreasonable restraint of trade, according to principles discussed in previous chapters. An example was *Newport AFC Ltd v The Football Association of Wales Ltd*. Jacob J commented that if an interlocutory injunction were not granted to prevent the Welsh FA imposing sanctions on the plaintiff club, the latter might well simply cease to exist, rendering worthless its chances of success at trial.[116] More recently, two distinguished rugby union football clubs in Wales, Cardiff and

---

[111] Ibid, pp 28–29.

[112] *The Times*, 6 January 1998.

[113] *Fallon v Horseracing Regulatory Authority* [2006] EWHC 2030 (QB); see chapter 7, para 7.176. And in *Sankofa and Charlton Athletic Football Co Ltd v The Football Association Ltd* [2007] ISLR, SLR 55, Simon J refused an interim injunction to permit the claimant player to play for Charlton against Middlesbrough the next day, deciding that the player did not have any prospect of succeeding in his challenge to the FA's match ban imposed in consequence of a red card, and noting that it would be hard on Middlesbrough to allow the player to play.

[114] [2008] EWHC 2028 (QB), [2008] ISLR, SLR 115.

[115] Doubt is cast on the validity of the rule by the CAS's decision in *USOC v IOC*, CAS 2011/O/2422, 4 October 2011, and the matter is again before the CAS at the time of writing, in CAS 2011/A/2658, *BOA v WADA*.

[116] [1995] 2 All ER 87, 98e–f. The club eventually won at trial before Blackburne J (unreported, transcript 12 April 1995) and obtained a declaration that the resolution of the Welsh FA was void as an unreasonable restraint of trade.

Ebbw Vale, succeeded against the Welsh Rugby Union in obtaining an interim injunction preventing the Union from implementing a decision that all clubs which wished to be part of it had to commit themselves to membership for a 10 year period. The matter was too urgent for a full trial as the effect of the decision would have been to prevent the plaintiff clubs from playing in European competition the following season and from playing in the Premier League.

8.72 The judge's order granted the injunction for one playing season or a year, but not so as to extend to the 1998–9 season.[117] He did not accept that the very future of the clubs was imperilled, but granted a limited order on orthodox principles, holding that there was a triable issue as to whether the decision under challenge was an unreasonable restraint of trade, that damages would not be an adequate remedy for the plaintiffs in view of the incalculable effect of loss of exposure to high level competition, and that the defendant Union was adequately protected by the plaintiffs' undertaking in damages. He pointed out[118] that if the clubs were to join the Union for the 10 year period and then lose the case at full trial, they would be locked in against their will without the opportunity to withdraw after the four or five years which they would have accepted as reasonable.

8.73 In our brief survey of interim injunctions in sporting litigation, the next point that arises is the question of jurisdiction to grant an interim injunction in a claim for a *declaration simpliciter*. Some doubt has been expressed as to whether the jurisdiction exists. The point is of considerable importance in view of the absence of contract, generally speaking, between a player and the league of which his club is a member. In *Newport AFC Ltd v The Football Association of Wales Ltd*[119] the point arose directly. Newport Football Club had no contract with the defendant Association, having resigned from it and joined its English counterpart. The Association contended at the interlocutory stage that the court lacked jurisdiction to grant an interim injunction as a remedy ancillary to a *declaration simpliciter* on the basis that a bare right to a declaration does not entail any actionable wrong by the defendant, and injunctions can only be granted in cases where there is a potential actionable wrong. The judge rejected that argument,[120] commenting that a right to a declaration is a sufficient cause of action on which to found jurisdiction to grant an interlocutory injunction.[121]

8.74 We respectfully agree with the reasoning and conclusion, but unfortunately a passage throwing doubt on the existence of the jurisdiction appears not to have been cited to the court in the *Newport* case. In *R v Disciplinary Committee of the Jockey Club, ex parte Aga Khan*[122] Hoffmann LJ said:

> … in cases in which power is exercised unfairly against persons who have no contractual relationship with a private decision-making body, the court may not find it easy to fashion a cause of action to provide a remedy. In *Nagle v Feilden* [1966] 2 QB 633, for example, this court had to consider the Jockey Club's refusal on grounds of sex to grant a trainer's licence to a woman. She

---

[117] *Williams v Pugh*, transcript, 23 July 1997, Popplewell J.
[118] Ibid, pp 13–14.
[119] [1995] 2 All ER 87.
[120] See ibid, 91j–93b.
[121] He drew support from *Buckley v Tutty* (1971) 125 CLR 353, per Barwick CJ at 380, and Wilberforce J in *Eastham v Newcastle United FC Ltd* [1964] Ch 413, Wilberforce J.
[122] [1993] 1 WLR 909, CA; see at 933A–C.

had no contract with the Jockey Club or (at that time) any other recognised cause of action, but this court said that it was arguable that she could still obtain a declaration and injunction. There is an improvisatory air about this solution and the possibility of obtaining an injunction has probably not survived *Siskina v Distos Compania Naviera SA* [1979] AC 210.

Yet, had that passage been cited to Jacob J in *Newport*, we believe he would nevertheless have accepted jurisdiction to grant the interim injunction sought. Hoffmann LJ's observations were not necessary for the decision in the case before him, and the *Siskina* case, which arose in a very different context, does not compel the conclusion he drew from it. As Jacob J recognised, in the case before him, unless the plaintiff were protected at the interlocutory stage from the defendant's unlawful act, it could not be protected from it at all.

8.75 There are, however, areas in which the law will not assist a claimant by injunction. As already explained in chapter three, the court has not yet ever enforced by injunction a claim to membership of an association unwilling to accept the new member, as observed by Carnwath J in *Stevenage Borough FC Ltd v The Football League Ltd*.[123] Nor would a court in normal circumstances compel by injunction a player unwilling to play for his or her club to do so, even if the refusal to play is a plain breach of contract. The normal principle would apply, namely that the law does not—absent special circumstances unlikely to be relevant in sport—compel by injunction performance of an employee's obligation to serve under a contract of employment, nor indeed other contractual obligations to render personal service or bringing the parties into a personal relationship requiring close cooperation between them.[124]

8.76 English law recognises the distinction between mandatory and prohibitory injunctions. As a general proposition, it is easier to obtain a negative or prohibitory injunction than a positive, or mandatory, one. A negative injunction requires the defendant to refrain from doing something; a positive injunction requires him to do something. The distinction can have particular relevance to sporting disputes. Generally, the jurisdiction to grant a mandatory injunction is exercised sparingly, only where the claimant shows a very strong probability that it will suffer grave damage if it is not granted.[125] The claimant will have to meet a higher standard at the interim stage in relation to the strength of his case than in the case of a prohibitory injunction.[126] In *Jones v Welsh Rugby Union* Ebsworth J treated the application before her as 'for essentially a mandatory injunction'.[127] With respect, it is not clear what was mandatory about it. Mr Jones was asking the court to prevent the Welsh Rugby Union from implementing its four week ban on him playing matches. The Union

---

[123] [2006] ISLR, SLR 128, 23 July 1996; see chapter 3, para 3.15.

[124] See McGhee, *Snell's Equity*, 32nd edn (Sweet & Maxwell, 2010) paras 17-012–17-014; Spry (n 106) 119–25; cf in the education field *R v Incorporated Froebel Educational Institute, ex parte L* [1999] ELR 488, Tucker J (no injunction to compel private school to admit excluded pupil pending trial). For an invaluable digest of sports related breach of contract and similar claims including injunction claims refused on this principle, see *Actions of participants affecting other participants* in Lewis and Taylor (n 57), in the lengthy footnotes 1–9 to para A3.43. In *Treherne v Amateur Boxing Association of England Ltd* [2002] EWCA Civ 381 the court would (had the claimant not in any event failed to show a contractual right) have refused an injunction to require an association to receive another association into membership.

[125] *Morris v Redland Bricks Ltd* [1970] AC 655, HL, per Lord Upjohn at 665–6.

[126] *Leisure Data v Bell* [1988] FSR 367, per Dillon LJ at 371–3.

[127] See transcript at p 25.

did not have to do anything to comply with the order except sit back and let him play.[128] Perhaps that is why the judge observed that to do what was required of it under the order 'will not cost the defendants money or reputation'.[129] The observation about reputation, incidentally, did not sit easily with the subsequent media coverage of the case.

8.77 As that case shows, one must not read too much into the distinction between mandatory and prohibitory injunctions. On the facts, the practical relevance of the distinction may be attenuated to the point of rendering it merely semantic. An example drawn from experience serves to emphasise this. In the 1990s, certain clubs made attempts to charge transfer fees in respect of out-of-contract players, notwithstanding the *Bosman* decision, in relation to transfers between clubs within one Member State of the European Union. They sought to argue that the then relevant rules applicable permitted such fees to be charged and that the *Bosman* ruling does not apply to intra-state transfers not falling within Article 48 of the Treaty of Rome.[130] In one such case the transferee club wished to engage a player's services without paying a transfer fee, which the transferring club wished to charge. The relevant leagues, under their rules, had to agree to the registration of the transferred player as a player with the transferee club. Without such registration, he would be ineligible to play for his new club.

8.78 Assuming, in that example, that the relevant leagues were (as was not in fact the position) unwilling so to register the player, the transferee club would have an urgent need for an injunction against those leagues to remove obstacles to receiving the player's services. Or, to put it another way, they would need an injunction to compel the relevant league to take the necessary steps to register him. Such an injunction, if it had been needed, could be seen as prohibitory, in the same sense as we have argued above in relation to *Jones v Welsh Rugby Union*, in that the receiving league could be treated as prohibited from attempting to prevent the player from playing. Or, the injunction could be treated as a mandatory one requiring the receiving league to take the positive steps necessary to register him with the transferee club. In that example, the distinction theoretically turns on the point that the registration procedure requires an actual step, probably the signing of a document, to be taken by an official of the league.

8.79 The courts are not blind to the fineness of the distinction on particular facts. The closer the relief is to being prohibitory in substance, the less the court is inhibited against granting an injunction. In the example above, the 'mandatory' injunction, if granted, would not require onerous work on the part of the league, as it would in a case where a claimant seeks to compel construction of part of a building.[131] Also in relation to the above example, where there is an indication from the European Commission that it views a particular transaction as contrary to Community law, then such an indication, though not binding on a national court, is a factor to be taken into account in the

---

[128] In extreme cases the court will intervene, not merely to prevent implementation of a disciplinary penalty likely to have been unlawfully imposed, but even to restrain unlawful disciplinary proceedings before they are heard: *Esterman v NALGO* [1974] ICR 625, Templeman J; cf *Longley v NUJ* [1987] IRLR 109, CA, and the other cases cited in Perrins et al, *Harvey on Industrial Relations and Employment Law* (LexisNexis, 1996) at M[3263] ff.

[129] Transcript at p 28.

[130] The substance of this issue is discussed in chapter 4 at paras 4.18–4.32.

[131] As in *Shepherd Homes v Sandham* [1971] Ch 340.

exercise of the court's discretion whether to grant or withhold an injunction.[132] So wide is the discretion of the judge hearing the application for interim relief that, in practice, factors such as an indication from the Commission are likely to be of considerably greater weight than mainly semantic arguments about the distinction between mandatory and prohibitory injunctions—which in any event is not a rigid distinction.[133]

8.80 It is necessary at this point to mention the issue of delay. It cannot be stressed too often that delay is usually fatal to an application for an interim injunction in a sporting case. The seasonal nature of most sports makes it imperative that the players, clubs and organising bodies concerned know where they stand for the following season. Litigation can only with difficulty be collapsed into the period between two seasons, and only by adopting truncated timetables in a speedy trial case, or deciding the issue taking account of the merits where a speedy trial is impossible. The maxim that equity aids the vigilant and not the indolent is of respectable antiquity in English law. The court may, and often does, refuse an injunction in a case where the claimant has slept on its rights and is guilty of undue delay amounting to laches.[134]

8.81 Delay is the banana skin on which claimants are more likely to slip than any other. In *Stevenage Borough FC Ltd v The Football League Ltd* Carnwath J refused an injunction more on the ground of delay than on any other ground.[135] Stevenage had won the Vauxhall Conference and had thus fulfilled the sporting criterion for entry to the Football League. The judge found aspects of the League's other entry criteria open to objection on restraint of trade grounds. Nevertheless, he refused relief because Stevenage had waited until they had won the Conference before launching the proceedings, near the end of the season and only about three months before the start of the next. The judge said that this might seem fair to Stevenage but it was not fair to all the other clubs and people involved. The criteria it sought to challenge had been in place for over a year and Stevenage had not raised any objection at general meetings of the Conference.

8.82 The commercial risk of launching proceedings at substantial cost with the risk of losing was not a factor that impressed the judge. He attached particular importance to the position of Torquay United, which had come bottom of the League and which would be relegated if Stevenage were promoted. True, that club had benefited adventitiously from Stevenage's failure to comply with the criteria, but that did not alter the point that it had presumably organised its affairs on the assumption that it would not be relegated. The judge also took into account certain misleading comments made by Stevenage to Torquay United's management, to the effect that Stevenage would not be promoted if they won the Vauxhall Conference. The moral of this difficult case is that clubs must, despite the commercial risk of litigation, proceed at the earliest possible opportunity if they wish to challenge the rules governing entry to competitions. To wait until the club may itself benefit from such a challenge is to wait too long.

---

[132] See *Lancombe v Etos* [1980] ECR 2511, ECJ, para 11 (reference under (then) Art 177 of the Treaty of Rome (now Art 267 TFEU)); cf *Commission Notice on the cooperation between the Commission and the courts of the EU Member States in the application of Articles 81 and 82 EC*, OJ C101, 27.4.2004.

[133] See also *Locabail International Finance v Agroexport* [1986] 1 WLR 657; *Rover International v Cannon Film Sales* [1987] 1 WLR 670, Hoffmann J; *Nottingham Building Society v Eurodynamic Systems plc* [1993] FSR 468, citing *Leisure Data v Bell* [1988] FSR 376, CA.

[134] See Spry (n 106) 414 ff, and 431 ff.

[135] Transcript, 23 July 1996, also reported at [2006] ISLR, SLR 128 and CA (1997) 9 Admin LR 109.

8.83 The same reasoning would apply to relegation imposed as a disciplinary penalty or as a consequence of deduction of points, as occurred in cases involving Tottenham Hotspur Football Club and Middlesbrough Football Club. A club from whose tally points are deducted as a disciplinary measure mid-season must not wait until it knows whether the consequence will be relegation before launching proceedings to challenge the validity of the deduction of points. That is a quite separate concern from any question as to whether the club has grounds for challenging such a deduction at all. In the case of Middlesbrough, it transpired that deduction of points in the middle of the 1997–8 season did make the difference between relegation and non-relegation (to the benefit of Coventry FC which had a windfall reprieve).[136]

8.84 Yet in one case an inordinate two year delay by Newport Football Club was, with some hesitation, allowed by Jacob J not to block an injunction against the Welsh Football Association. There was no adequate explanation for the delay, which caused the judge 'the greatest concern'.[137] He commented that it was a wholly exceptional case in that the club's very existence was at risk. No prejudice to the defendant Association or third party clubs was adverted to by the judge, though the Association relied strongly on delay and consequent changes to the status quo during the period of the delay.

8.85 Interim injunctions also feature in disputes between sportsmen and women, and their employer clubs or managers. In ordinary employment law, an employer may wish to prevent its employee, or former employee, from joining another employer or establishing a competing business. This is achieved by two principal methods, the first being a restrictive covenant whereby the employee agrees not to engage in certain competitive activities during employment and for a time thereafter; and the second being a contractual provision, embodied in an express term or otherwise, giving the employer rights to retain a contractual relation with the employee even if the latter is not actively working, provided the employee is paid in full. Arrangements of the latter type are often described as 'garden leave' arrangements. Another variant is a case such as *Julian White v Bristol Rugby Ltd*,[138] where the employee is prevented from leaving the club in breach of contract on the basis that the club is willing and able to let him continue playing for it.

8.86 These types of arrangement between employer and employee are fully documented in specialist works on employment law, and we do not propose to explain their scope here.[139] They have drawbacks. Restrictive covenants offend against the restraint of trade doctrine if

---

[136] See also *Ray v Professional Golfers Association Ltd*, transcript, 15 April 1996, p 12B–E (golfer refused injunction to challenge PGA's eligibility criteria on ground of, inter alia, delay). In *Leeds United FC v Rotherham United FC*, FA arbitration tribunal award of 1 May 2008, delay in challenging a 15 point deduction for going into administration was fatal to the claim, particularly since promotions were to be determined by imminent play-offs.

[137] *Newport AFC Ltd v FA of Wales Ltd* [1995] 2 All ER 87, 99b–f.

[138] [2002] IRLR 204, HHJ Havelock-Allan QC; see para 58: 'The employer is entitled to keep the contract open for performance even though he cannot obtain an order for specific performance of it (see Megarry V-C in *Thomas Marshall Ltd v Guinle* [1979] Ch 227 at 243C). However, if the employer wishes to enforce the contract to the extent of obtaining an injunction to restrain the employee from committing breaches of his obligations under it, the Court may, in the exercise of its discretion, require him to provide the employee with all of his contractual benefits, which would include paying the employee's salary (see *Evening Standard Ltd v Henderson* [1987] ICR 558).'

[139] In the sporting context see Goudie and Devonshire, *Garden Leave Injunctions in the Sporting Arena: Reading FC and West Ham United* [2004] ISLR 15, referring to settled proceedings arising from Alan Pardew's attempt to move from Reading to West Ham; and see the references to other settled club-manager and similar litigation in Lewis and Taylor (n 57) para A3.43, fn 4.

they go further than is reasonably necessary to protect the employer's legitimate business interests. Both types of contract term are only enforceable subject to the discretion of the court in an interim injunction application, which may, moreover, take place too late to be of much practical benefit to the employer. As already noted above,[140] normally it is not possible for an employer to obtain specific performance of a contract of employment, for that would be tantamount to personal servitude; nor, conversely, may an employee normally specifically enforce his own employment contract by means of an interim injunction to restrain his dismissal.[141]

8.87 In the sporting field the position is no different, with the consequence that a manager may not normally restrain his clients from dispensing with his services, even though to do so may be in breach of a valid exclusive services agreement. That was the outcome in *Warren v Mendy*.[142] The boxing manager and promoter Frank Warren was unable to prevent the well-known boxer Nigel Benn from dispensing with Mr Warren's services and working for a new manager, Mr Mendy, during the currency of Benn's contract with Mr Warren, which still had some two and a half years to run. The high degree of mutual trust and confidence between the parties was a factor strongly militating against the grant of an injunction which, in practice, could have the effect of compelling performance of the contract. That did not affect the availability of damages as a remedy.

8.88 The same principles apply in cases where the contract requires performance of particular sporting obligations, rather than an exclusivity arrangement over a period of time. In *Clansmen Sporting Club Ltd v Robinson*[143] the plaintiff promoters of the 1993 World Boxing Organisation featherweight championship contracted with the defendant boxer to promote his next three bouts should he win the championship. He duly won, and allowed the plaintiff to promote his next two fights, but refused in the case of the third, alleging that his exclusivity obligations were void because they operated in breach of the rules of the World Boxing Organisation. The court held that those rules were not incorporated into the plaintiff's option agreement and accordingly held that the plaintiff had a right to restrain the defendant from fighting a third bout under other auspices. Generally, the courts will be more willing to intervene by injunction to restrain a one-off sporting obligation than to restrain general obligations lasting over a period.[144]

8.89 To complete our brief account of interim injunctions in the English law relating to sport, we should mention finally the important principle, which may help to shorten proceedings and save legal costs, that an appeal will not be entertained from an order which it was within the discretion of the judge to make, unless it can be shown that he exercised his discretion under a mistake of law or in disregard of principle, or that he took into account

---

[140] See para 8.75.

[141] See generally *Harvey on Industrial Relations and Employment Law* (n 128) AII[424] ff; *Page One Records Ltd v Britton* [1968] 1 WLR 157; *Warner Brothers Pictures Inc v Nelson* [1937] 1 KB 209 (the Bette Davis case); cf *Hill v Parsons and Co Ltd* [1972] Ch 305, CA; *Powell v London Borough of Brent* [1988] ICR 176, CA. For a useful comparative survey of the English and North American approaches including an account of US and Canadian authority, see *Negative Enforcement of Employment Contracts in the Sports Industries* (1997) 17(1) Legal Studies 65.

[142] [1989] ICR 525, CA.

[143] *The Times*, 22 May 1995.

[144] See also Oliver J's decision in *Nichols Advanced Vehicle Systems Inc v De Angelis* (1979) unreported, 21 December (Italian Formula 1 racing driver 'defected' mid-contract to Lotus team; injunction to prevent him driving for Lotus refused).

irrelevant matters or failed to exercise his discretion, or that the conclusion he reached was outside the generous ambit within which a reasonable disagreement is possible.[145]

8.90 Interim relief may also be available under other systems of law, and in sports law proceedings before international or other arbitral tribunals. The extent to which such relief is available depends on the procedural rules governing the proceedings under consideration. The most important international tribunal dealing with sports law disputes is the CAS. It has the power to order 'provisional and conservatory measures', and normally acts on similar principles to those governing interlocutory injunctions in English law, though the threshold of merit that a claimant must attain is rather higher than under *American Cyanamid v Ethicon Ltd*.[146] In Swiss law, which the CAS often applies, a 'prima facie showing' is sufficient, which means that 'reasonable chances of success' must be shown. If that initial hurdle is surmounted, the CAS takes into account three considerations: 'first, irreparable harm to the Claimants; second, likelihood of success on the merits; and third, a balance of interests'.[147]

8.91 Under the rules of procedure governing the ad hoc proceedings of the CAS during the Atlanta Olympics in 1996, the President of the Ad Hoc Division, or the panel if it had already been set up, was empowered to grant 'a stay of execution of the decision being challenged or other provisional relief ex parte'. The test applied by the panel was 'whether the relief is necessary to protect the applicant from irreparable harm, whether the applicant is likely to succeed on the merits, and whether the interests of the applicant outweigh those of the opponent or of other members of the Olympic community'.[148] The CAS has on several occasions been asked to order provisional and conservatory measures, but is astute to ensure that the 'irreparable harm' test is satisfied.[149]

Damages

8.92 It is well known to lawyers and non-lawyers alike that damages are available as a remedy for breach of contract and other forms of civil wrong such as torts. The principles on which damages are awarded could fill an entire book, and indeed do fill an entire book,

---

[145] See *Hadmor Productions v Hamilton* [1983] 1 AC 191, per Lord Diplock at p 220; *G v G* [1985] 1 WLR 647, HL, per Lord Fraser at pp 650–3.

[146] [1975] AC 397; cf CAS Procedural Rules, as amended (version effective from 1 January 2012), reg R37.

[147] *AEK Athens FC and Slavia Prague FC v UEFA*, CAS 98/200, Procedural Order on Application for Preliminary Relief, 17 July 1998, paras 29 and 40.

[148] Report of the President of the Ad Hoc Division in *Mealey's International Arbitration Report*, February 1997, p 20, at 23.

[149] As it was in *Canadian Olympic Association v International Skating Union*, CAS OG 02/004 (Salt Lake City) (order made ex parte requiring ISU to use best endeavours to keep its judges in Salt Lake City to give evidence on substantive hearing the following day). In *M & FC Wil 1900 v FIFA & Club PFC Naftex AC Bourgas*, CAS/2008/A 1568, the panel granted a provisional and conservatory order staying a decision of the FIFA Dispute Resolution Chamber imposing a four-month ban on a player and preventing a club registering new players. Provisional and conservatory measures were refused in *P v International Ice Hockey Federation*, CAS/2005/A/990; *Wawrzyniak v Hellenic Football Federation*, CAS/2009/A/1918; and (for want of jurisdiction, there being no challengeable decision) *Leveaux & Aurore Mongel v FINA*, CAS/2009/A/1917. On 13 September 2011 a tribunal cantonal in Switzerland left undecided but questioned the validity of the provision in the CAS procedural regulation R37 whereby parties who have started an appeal arbitration procedure before the CAS waive their right to seek provisional and conservatory measures before state courts (see the newsletter issued by the Swiss law firm Lenz & Stählin, January 2012, p 2).

much longer than this one.[150] In contract, the fundamental principle is that the measure of damages should be such as to put the innocent party in the financial position he or she would have been in had the breach not occurred. In tort, the principle is that the claimant should be put in the position, so far as money can do it, he would have been in had the tort not been committed. Although damages are nearly always claimed in civil proceedings arising in the field of sport, they are rarely awarded at the end of a trial, for the reason already noted above that an injunction or declaration is usually the remedy uppermost in the claimant's mind.

8.93 Damages are therefore a less important arrow in the quiver of the sporting claimant. More important is the spectre of having to honour an undertaking in damages, which is the normal price for an interim injunction as explained above. However, there are cases in which damages have figured prominently as a remedy. In *Modahl v British Athletic Federation Ltd*,[151] Ms Modahl brought an action claiming damages by way of out of pocket expenses of £250,000 and loss of earnings of some £230,000, plus interest. The sole remedy claimed was damages, because Ms Modahl had already been exonerated by an appeal panel of the Federation following a doping charge of which she had previously been found guilty by a disciplinary committee. Media reports of the proceedings stated that she wished to highlight the defects in the Federation's doping procedures.

8.94 Her claim survived a striking out application, as already noted in the previous chapter,[152] but her claim ultimately failed because damages are not available in a case where the internal disciplinary system has operated to correct a defect at first instance (apparent bias on the part of one of the panel members) through an acquittal on appeal leading to the conclusion that there had been a fair procedure and result overall. Ms Modahl was forced to rely on breaches of doping procedures prescribed in the disciplinary code and on an alleged implied term in her contract with the Federation that she would have a fair and impartial hearing at first instance as well as on appeal. The Court of Appeal was unwilling to hold that such a term exists rather than the generally accepted narrower term that a claimant must receive fair treatment overall in the operation of a disciplinary process, including its appellate stage.[153]

8.95 It would be a different matter if a sportsman or woman had received unfair treatment overall and been wrongly convicted through breaches of fair procedure, bad faith or other unlawful conduct. In such a case the right to damages could not seriously be in doubt. However, we are not aware of any case in which they have been awarded for wrongful disciplinary action in sport. George Eastham, the footballer, did not succeed in his claim for damages against the directors of Newcastle United Football Club. It was not a disciplinary case, but one in which the club had acted in restraint of trade. That is not a wrong for which damages can be obtained; the only consequence is that the claimant can avoid the restraint.[154] Contractual claims also failed in *Newport AFC Ltd v FA of Wales Ltd*,[155] where the judge refused to infer or imply a term into Newport's contract with the

---

[150] See *McGregor on Damages*, 18th edn (Sweet & Maxwell, 2011).
[151] [2002] 1 WLR 1192, CA.
[152] See paras 7.103–7.108.
[153] *Calvin v Carr* [1980] AC 575, PC; cf *Lloyd v McMahon* [1987] 1 AC 625, HL.
[154] *Eastham v Newcastle United FC Ltd* [1964] Ch 413.
[155] Transcript, 12 April 1995, Blackburne J, pp 55–57.

FA of Wales whereby the latter undertook not to act in restraint of trade. In any case, the losses had been suffered after Newport's resignation from the Welsh FA, so the losses would not have flowed from any breach in any case.

8.96 A rare and substantial award of damages in a 'club on club' case was made by a panel of arbitrators in the dispute between Sheffield United and West Ham over the Carlos Tevez affair.[156] Tevez was playing for West Ham in breach of Premier League rules in the 2006–7 season. His performances for West Ham were held on the balance of probabilities to have been worth at least the three points West Ham needed to escape relegation and without which it would have been relegated, instead of the hapless Sheffield United. West Ham was held liable in damages for breach of a contractual obligation owed to Sheffield United, to abide by the Premier League's rules. The arbitrators were not asked to quantify the damages; the claim was settled in March 2009 for a sum estimated in press reports as being in the region of £20 million, just before the arbitrators were due to reconvene.

8.97 In the employment context, damages are more commonplace, particularly in the familiar case where a football manager is dismissed before the end of his fixed term or minimum term contract. Employment in the top echelons of football in England is so precarious that managers frequently insist on fixed or minimum terms, with a 'payment in lieu of notice' or 'PILON' clause which avoids the obligation the manager would otherwise have to give credit for sums earned or that would have been earned by taking reasonable opportunities to mitigate loss suffered[157] by obtaining alternative employment. Jean Tigana, former manager of Fulham FC, was among managers wrongly accused in recent years of 'gross misconduct' or a repudiatory breach of their employment contracts by clubs not keen to pay out their contractual entitlement. Kevin Keegan was constructively dismissed by Newcastle by having a player forced upon him in breach of his contractual right to have 'the final say' in relation to any new player signings. Both established valuable contractual rights in litigation against their former clubs.[158]

8.98 As to damages for negligence, so far as we are aware there is no authority to support the proposition that a drug tester owes a sportsman or woman a duty of care to conduct the test carefully. However, there is often controversy over testing procedures and it may be that such a case will be brought. On ordinary principles of professional negligence it may be held that a duty is owed, since drug testers profess particular skills and that usually carries with it an obligation to use reasonable competence when performing the task in question; though the scope of any duty is another question. It could be argued that the drug tester's duty is primarily owed to his or her employer, the sports body, in the same way as a doctor engaged by an insurance company to examine a person for the purpose of an insurance

---

[156] *Sheffield United FC Ltd v West Ham United FC plc* [2009] ISLR, SLR 25, FA Arbitration under rule K, Lord Griffiths in the chair; discussed in chapter 3, paras 3.46–3.47.

[157] See *Abraham v Performing Rights Society* [1995] ICR 1028, CA; cf *Cerberus Software Ltd v Rowley* [2000] ICR 35, CA.

[158] *Fulham FC (1987) Ltd v Tigana* [2004] EWHC 2585 (Elias J); affirmed in the CA, [2005] EWCA Civ 895; *Keegan v Newcastle United Football Co Ltd* [2010] IRLR 94, FA Arbitration, Philip Havers QC chairing (damages of £2 million awarded); applied by the EAT (Lady Smith presiding) in *McBride v Falkirk Football and Athletic Club* [2012] IRLR 22. But Crystal Palace's former manager Iain Dowie was less successful; he was found to be liable in damages for having procured a 'compromise agreement' terminating his employment with Crystal Palace by means of false representations that he had no present intention to join Charlton Athletic: see *Crystal Palace FC (2000) Ltd v Dowie* [2007] EWHC 1392 (QB), [2007] ISLR, SLR 90, Tugendhat J.

quote is thought to owe only a limited duty to the person examined not to damage him physically.[159] We are in some doubt as to whether English law would impose a duty of care in respect of financial loss occasioned by a 'false positive' arising from a negligently conducted doping test. If the duty, and a breach of it, could be established in law and on the facts, damages would in principle be available but proof of causation and recoverable loss could be difficult, particularly in amateur sports where no significant financial value can easily be directly ascribed to loss of the opportunity to win a medal.[160]

8.99 In claims founded on economic torts, there is the potential for very large sums to be awarded as damages in proceedings between organisations (through representatives) battling in the commercial arena for the right to enjoy the services of players and clubs and to organise competitions. Commercial rivalry in sport is always likely to spawn litigation. In competition law claims, of the type discussed in chapters four and six above, we discussed the principles on which damages may be awarded. But in cases involving simple breach of contract and inducing breach of contract, or interference with the claimant's trade or business, loss is assessed on familiar principles. In the substantial litigation arising out of the attempt by a company controlled by Mr Rupert Murdoch to set up a superleague in Australian rugby league football, damages issues were remitted for determination.[161]

Company Law: Unfair Prejudice Petitions

8.100 A remedy well known to company lawyers but little used in the sporting field is the statutory one under section 994 of the Companies Act 2006, which enables a minority shareholder to petition the High Court for appropriate orders on the basis that the affairs of the company are being conducted in a manner unfairly prejudicial to him. In one Antipodean case the Western Suburbs District Rugby League Football Club, with commendable ingenuity but no success, attempted to rely on the New South Wales equivalent of the UK provision.[162] The club was aggrieved at the decision of the defendant League to reduce the number of clubs participating in the premiership competition from 13 to 12 in late 1984, after its entry for the 1985 competition had been refused. Its representative plaintiffs initially obtained an order from Hodgson J restraining the League from implementing

---

[159] See the discussion in *X v Bedfordshire County Council* [1995] 2 AC 633, HL (psychiatrists and social workers); and in *Phelps v London Borough of Hillingdon*, CA, transcript 4 November 1998 (educational psychologist; pending in HL); cf Walton, *Charlesworth and Percy on Negligence*, 12th edn (Sweet & Maxwell, 2011) para 8-18, and *Spring v Guardian Assurance* [1995] 2 AC 296, HL, per Lord Goff at 318, Lord Lowry at 325, Lord Woolf at 342. The authorities have developed further since those seminal 1990s cases were decided, but the bedrock of the threefold *Caparo* test remains, the most important part of the test being the third part: whether it is just and reasonable to impose a duty of care and the scope of any duty (*Caparo Industries plc v Dickman* [1990] 2 AC 605, HL, per Lord Bridge at p 618). In the context of a 'tripartite' relationship such as that of drug tester, player and governing body, the law leans against imposing a duty which would be a heavy obligation on the service provider to both of the other parties; see eg *Islington LBC v University College London Hospital NHS Trust* [2005] EWCA Civ 596, (2005) 8 CCL Rep 337.

[160] Cf *Chaplin v Hicks* [1911] 2 KB 786, CA; *Kitchen v RAF Association* [1958] 2 All ER 241, CA; *Mulvaine v Joseph* (1968) 112 SJ 927; cf *Allied Maples Group Ltd v Simmons & Simmons* [1995] 1 WLR 1602, CA.

[161] *News Ltd v Australian Rugby Football League Ltd* (1997) 139 ALR 193 (Federal Court of Australia).

[162] See s 320 of the New South Wales Companies Code; and *Wayde v New South Wales Rugby League Ltd* (1985) 61 ALR 225. The then English equivalent was s 459 of the Companies Act 1985.

the decisions on the ground that they were oppressive in the statutory sense. The League's appeal was successful, and a further appeal by the club was unsuccessful.

8.101   The point that emerges from the two very short judgments, and which would apply equally in English law, is that the court will not interfere with a decision well within the objects of the company which organises the competition in question, provided there is no bad faith, misdirection in law or taking into account of wrong considerations. The object of the League in the case in question included that of determining which clubs should enter which competitions. The court was astute to distinguish between adverse impact on the club, which the decision challenged undoubtedly had, and unfairness towards the club which was not made out.[163]

Jurisdiction, Choice of Law and Forum

8.102   Sports related disputes have come before the courts in England without the subject matter being exclusively English. Sport is, as we have demonstrated, an international phenomenon. We mention further below the institutions involved in deciding disputes going beyond national frontiers. Where such disputes are not susceptible of resolution by those international institutions, they have to be decided in national courts. But, as shown by the *Harding* and *Reynolds* litigation in the USA in the 1990s, the America's Cup litigation in 2007,[164] a series of decisions of the Swiss Supreme Court (mainly unsuccessful attempts to overturn CAS decisions)[165] and, in the UK, cases such as *Walker v UKA and IAAF*[166] and *Cowley v Heatley*,[167] national courts sometimes have to adjudicate on the question of their own jurisdiction and, if they accept jurisdiction, must decide which is the substantive system of applicable law. To do that, the national court must apply its country's rules of private international law. It may have to decide whether the case ought to be disposed of in another country's courts.

8.103   In *Reel v Holder*[168] the English Court of Appeal was prepared to hold that the IAAF had misinterpreted its rules permitting only one member association for each country, in that it had allowed athletes from China to compete to the exclusion of Taiwanese athletes. The Court held that a country is not necessarily a recognised state but a term of art. This

---

[163] In *Fulham FC (1987) Ltd v Richards* [2011] EWCA Civ 855 the CA held, overruling *Exeter City FC Ltd v Football Conference Ltd* [2004] 1 WLR 2910, that an unfair prejudice could be the subject of an arbitration clause under the rules of the Football Association and Premier League.

[164] Mentioned in chapter 2, para 2.4.

[165] *Valverde*, 3 January 2011, No 4A 386/2010; *A v WADA, FIFA and Cyprus Football Federation*, 18 April 2011, No 4A 640/2010; *A v Trabzonspor and Turkish Football Federation*, 29 April 2011, No 4A 404/2010; *X SA v A and Caisse de Chômage V*, 28 April 2011, No 4A 53/2011; *X v Jamaican Football Federation and FIFA*, 20 July 2011, No 4A 162/2011; *X v Club Y*, 22 August 2011, No 4A 222/2011; and see the helpful account of Viret, Rondi and Fischer in *Swiss Supreme Court Decisions* in the newsletter published by Swiss law firm Lenz & Stählin, January 2012, pp 14–16).

[166] (2000) unreported, 3 July, Toulson J and 25 July, Hallett J; subsequent aspects of the litigation are referred to at [2000] ISLR 41 (Beloff, editorial) and [2001] ISLR, SLR 264; also helpfully described in Lewis and Taylor (n 57) A3.10, fn 9.

[167] *The Times*, 24 July 1986.

[168] [1981] 1 WLR 1226, CA.

is consistent with the participation in the Olympic teams of athletes from places such as Hong Kong (before its restoration to China), Gibraltar, Puerto Rico and so on.

8.104 In *Cowley v Heatley* the then Vice-Chancellor doubted whether he had jurisdiction to review, by reference to rules of English law, a decision of the Commonwealth Games Federation concerning the interpretation of the term 'domicil' used to determine eligibility to represent a particular country in the Commonwealth Games. The report in *The Times* includes the view of Browne-Wilkinson V-C[169]

> that the constitution covered a large number of different nations in the Commonwealth with members upholding many different systems of law. In those circumstances it was the court's view that the articles of the constitution could not be governed by the law of one constituent member country.

In *Gasser v Stinson*[170] Scott V-C commented:

> It is not entirely clear under what proper law the Rules of the IAAF fall to be construed and to be given effect. Since, however, the IAAF head offices are and have been since 1946 in London and are required to be there under Rule 2, it has been accepted by counsel that English law should be regarded as the relevant proper law, or … as the law applicable to the issues in the case.

On that basis the judge entertained the attempt by Miss Gasser, a Swiss athlete, to have her ban overturned in a doping case.

8.105 In *A v Z*[171] the Swiss Supreme Court upheld a lifetime ban for a second doping offence by a middle distance runner and rejected an argument that the CAS was insufficiently empowered to remedy procedural failings in proceedings before a national anti-doping commission which lacked the necessary qualities of independence and impartiality.

8.106 The lengthy litigation in the USA involving Harry 'Butch' Reynolds followed a strange course. Reynolds was a top class United States 400 metre runner who had tested positive for nandrolone during a competition in Monaco. The US courts handed down a bewildering array of decisions going as far as the Supreme Court.[172] Briefly, after initially failing in court and arbitration proceedings to overturn the IAAF's two-year ban on him, Mr Reynolds sued the IAAF and the Athletics Congress alleging breach of contract, defamation, denial of due process and tortious interference with business relations. After procedural battles and negotiations also involving the US Olympic Committee, the IAAF barred him from competing in the 1992 Games. Thereafter, amazingly, he obtained a default judgment for over US $27 million including treble punitive damages, followed by garnishee proceedings against four creditors of the IAAF. The saga ended after nearly four years with the Sixth Circuit Court of Appeals ordering the action to be dismissed for lack of jurisdiction, which the IAAF had never ceased to contest. It would have been better if the jurisdictional issue had been decided at the start of the litigation, and not after 12 hearings before various courts and arbitration bodies.

---

[169] *The Times*, 24 July 1986.
[170] (1988) unreported, 16 June, Scott V-C.
[171] Swiss Supreme Court, 3 October 2011, No 4A 530/2011.
[172] *Reynolds v IAAF*, 23 F 3d 1110 (1994); 115 S Ct 423 (1994); 968 F 2d 1216 (1992); 112 S Ct 2512 (1992); No C-2-91-003, 1991 WL 179760 (1991); 935 F 2d 270 (1991); and other unreported court and arbitration proceedings.

8.107 The US courts did rather better in the litigation arising from an attack on an American figure skater, Nancy Kerrigan, shortly before the 1994 Winter Games. Her rival, Tonya Harding, was accused of complicity in the assault. The US Figure Skating Association (USFA) considered that there was reason to suspect a violation of the Olympic code of fair play and in consequence the US Committee proposed to convene a disciplinary hearing in Norway. Ms Harding, however, sought an injunction against the US Olympic Committee to prevent the hearing taking place. She achieved her immediate objective of being able to compete in the Winter Games after which the deferred hearing took place, resulting in her enforced resignation from the USFA, which later stripped her of her 1994 title and banned her for life. The role of the court appears to have been mainly to broker the settlement enabling the disciplinary hearing to be deferred until after the Games.[173]

8.108 These sometimes colourful examples show the complexity and diversity of the judicial role in cross-border sports disputes. It is not appropriate in a book such as this to attempt a full exposition of English rules of private international law relevant to sport. Still less could we do so in relation to any other jurisdiction. English conflict of laws rules do not, generally, apply to sporting disputes any differently than to other disputes with an international dimension. Private international law is a vast subject and is covered admirably and in depth in specialist works.[174] Our aim here is the more limited one of identifying the main issues that may arise under the rubric of private international law in the context of sport, mentioning by way of example some instances in which the courts have resolved them. We hope thereby to assist the practitioner presented with a dispute involving an international dimension to focus correctly on the private international law issues that may arise in addition to, but are logically prior to, issues as to the merits of the dispute.

8.109 It may be a useful discipline for an English lawyer to consider these issues in the following order:

(1)   Can the jurisdiction of the English court be established?
(2)   What is the proper law applicable to each cause of action?
(3)   Is England the proper forum for the dispute?

8.110 The question whether an action should be brought in England or elsewhere depends on a number of factors. The traditional approach was to ask oneself whether the case is one to which the Brussels Convention of 1968 and the Lugano Convention of 1988 (and now the Lugano Convention of 2007) apply. Very broadly, those Conventions enact, where they apply, an elaborate code of jurisdictional rules common to all contracting states parties to them. The objective is to restrict multiplicity of proceedings in different countries. From 1 March 2002 EC Regulation 44/2001 on jurisdiction and the recognition and enforcement of judgments in civil and commercial matters ('the Judgments Regulation') superseded (except as regards Denmark) the Brussels Convention and (except as regards Iceland, Norway and Switzerland) the Lugano Convention. As the Judgments Regulation is directly applicable in the United Kingdom, there is no need for national implementing legislation.

---

[173] *Harding v United States Olympic Committee* No CCV – 942151 (Clackamas County Cir Or, 13 February 1994).
[174] The best account is in Collins et al, *Dicey, Morris and Collins on The Conflict of Laws*, 14th edn (Sweet & Maxwell, 2006) and 4th Cumulative Supplement (2011).

8.111 A full account of this area of law lies beyond the scope of this work.[175] The broad scheme of the Conventions and the Judgments Regulation is that where they apply, the legal nature of the claim determines which contracting state should be the venue for the action, or whether, in certain circumstances, proceedings may be brought in more than one contracting state. The Conventions were made part of English domestic law by the Civil Jurisdiction and Judgments Act 1982, as amended by the 1991 Act of the same name. If a claim relates to a 'civil or commercial matter' within the meaning of either the Judgments Regulation or the Conventions, the court has jurisdiction to entertain a claim *in personam* solely in accordance with the provisions of the Judgments Regulation and the Conventions. This is a field of law that may seem complex and technical to non-lawyers involved in sport, but it is standard fare for practitioners of commercial and private international law.

8.112 Article 1 of the Judgments Regulation and of each Convention provides that it applies in civil and commercial matters whatever the nature of the court or tribunal and that it is not to extend to revenue, customs or administrative matters. A sports related dispute would normally fall within the meaning of a 'civil and commercial matter'.[176] Where the Judgments Regulation or the Conventions apply, the English courts will have jurisdiction if the defendant is 'domiciled' in England. An individual is domiciled in the United Kingdom, or a particular part thereof, if he is resident there and the nature and circumstances of his residence indicate that he has a substantial connection with the United Kingdom or that part of it.[177]

8.113 The place where the claimant is domiciled is not normally relevant for the purpose of applying the jurisdictional rules of the Judgments Regulation or the Conventions.[178] Where the Judgments Regulation or the Conventions confer jurisdiction on a United Kingdom court, that court is precluded from dismissing the proceedings on the basis that it is not the *forum conveniens* (most convenient forum). This is so whether the proposed non-United Kingdom forum is one of the contracting states for the purposes of the Judgments Regulations and Conventions or a non-contracting state.[179]

8.114 Where the Conventions or the Judgments Regulation apply, two practical consequences ensue: first, the proceedings must be brought in the contracting state identified as the correct forum under its terms; and second, the permission of the English court to effect service of process in that jurisdiction is not normally required.[180] If claimant and defendant disagree about whether the English court should entertain the claim, the English court will have to entertain the claim to the extent of deciding that issue, namely, whether it should

---

[175] For the background see *Dicey, Morris and Collins*, ibid, vol 1, paras 11-004–11-012.

[176] Although the expression 'civil' is used in a European not domestic law sense and is therefore not coterminous with the use of the term in English law: see generally the cases in *Dicey, Morris and Collins*, ibid, vol 1, paras 11-025–11-028. Case law decided under the Conventions established that the activities of public bodies acting in the exercise of public functions are not within the words 'civil and commercial'.

[177] See Civil Jurisdiction and Judgments Order 2001 (SI 2001/3929) Sched 1 para 9(2) and (3) (Judgments Regulation); 1982 Act, s 41(2), (3) (Brussels and Lugano Conventions); *Dicey, Morris and Collins* (n 174) vol 1, para 11R-072.

[178] Case C-412/98 *Universal General Insurance Co (UGIC) v Group Josi Reinsurance Co SA* [2000] ECR I-5925, [2001] 1 QB 68) (subject to exceptions noted in *Dicey, Morris and Collins* (n 174) vol 1, para 11-273 fn 77).

[179] Case C-281/02 *Owusu v Jackson* [2005] ECR I-1383, [2005] QB 801, ECJ.

[180] See the useful account in *Civil Procedure* (*The White Book*) (Sweet & Maxwell, 2012) vol 1; see CPR rule 6.30–6.40.

entertain the claim. If proceedings in England are appropriate, either on the basis that the Conventions and Judgments Regulation do not apply and England is the appropriate forum, or because they do apply and their provisions establish England as the appropriate forum, it is still necessary to effect proper service of the proceedings on the defendant. The rules relating to service, whether abroad (and if abroad with or without permission being required) or in England and Wales, are found in lengthy provisions set out in Part 6 of the Civil Procedure Rules 1998, and in the case of companies, section 1139 of the Companies Act 2006.

8.115 In *Lennox Lewis v World Boxing Council and Frank Bruno*,[181] the boxer Lennox Lewis brought an action against Frank Bruno, who lived in England and could be served in England, and against the World Boxing Council (WBC), whose headquarters were in Mexico. Mr Lewis wished to restrain the defendants from implementing arrangements which would result in Mr Bruno accepting a challenge from Mr Mike Tyson instead of Mr Lewis. The latter was able to obtain leave in an *ex parte* (without notice) application to serve the WBC in Mexico or Puerto Rico, where it also had a presence. Leave was obtained pursuant to the then Order 11 rule 1(1)(c) on the basis that the WBC was argu-ably a 'necessary and proper party' to the action against Mr Bruno in England.[182] In the event, Rattee J subsequently held that suit against Mr Bruno in England was merely a peg on which to hang the action against the WBC,[183] which was the essence of the plain-tiff's grievance. It therefore did not assist Mr Lewis that he was an Englishman suing an Englishman in England. Rattee J also held that the action against the WBC ought to proceed in Dallas, Texas, because of an exclusive jurisdiction clause in the rules of the WBC providing for compulsory mediation under its auspices in Dallas. The judge did not accept that such a process would be other than impartial and independent.[184]

8.116 Another context in which questions of jurisdiction may arise is in cases of inter-national transfers of players between clubs located in different states. Where the terms of such a transfer are in dispute, and the states in question are parties to the Conventions mentioned above and the Judgment Regulation, then those instruments will govern the question of jurisdiction and forum. However, transfers may also occur between clubs located within a single state subdivided into more than one jurisdiction. The most obvi-ous example is the United Kingdom itself, in which Scotland and Northern Ireland are treated as different jurisdictions from the common jurisdiction of England and Wales. Leave to serve process in Scotland is not needed under English procedural rules.[185] Intra-UK disputes fall outside the terms of the Brussels and Lugano Conventions but similar jurisdiction rules are enacted for the United Kingdom by the Civil Jurisdiction and Judgments Act 1982 (as amended).

8.117 In a particular matter involving two of this book's authors, a question arose as to whether the English or Scottish courts would have jurisdiction over a dispute concerning

---

[181] (1995) unreported, 3 November 1995.

[182] See *Seaconsar (Far East) Ltd v Bank Markazi Jonhouri Islami Iran (Service Outside Jurisdiction)* [1994] 1 AC 438, esp at 456F.

[183] See transcript at p 22D–F, applying *Multinational Gas and Petrochemical Co v Multinational Gas and Petrochemical Services Ltd* [1983] Ch 258, per Dillon LJ at 285C.

[184] In the event Mr Bruno may have regretted the result. With no injunction impeding his participation in the title bout, he was knocked out in the fifth round.

[185] CPR rule 6.32; provided the conditions there set out are met.

the transfer of a player between clubs in England and Scotland. Two points emerged from consideration of the position: first, and importantly, the English court has jurisdiction to grant interim relief where proceedings have been or are to be commenced in another part of the United Kingdom.[186] Second, there was a risk, on the particular facts, that both the Scottish and the English courts might hold that they, respectively, each had exclusive jurisdiction.[187] Fortunately, the potential clash of jurisdiction did not materialise as the matter was not litigated.

8.118 The above are no more than illustrations of jurisdiction issues that may arise. Others may arise in future cases, though the increasing provision for international arbitration in sport may help to keep such disputes out of national courts. The question of forum can arise independently of jurisdiction, and independently of foreign law clauses in relevant contractual documents such as the rules of governing bodies. Even a foreign jurisdiction clause can be overridden by the English court, which can assert jurisdiction itself notwith-standing such a clause; but the onus on a plaintiff to displace the clause and obtain trial in England is a heavy one.[188] In essence the claimant would have to show that there could not be a fair trial at the foreign venue corresponding to the jurisdiction clause. Where forum is in issue, the onus is on the claimant to show that England is the most just forum.[189] We should also note at this point, briefly, the converse position whereby a party in this country seeks to restrain proceedings abroad. The courts here are cautious in exercising the jurisdiction but will intervene to prevent foreign proceedings where the ends of justice require it, including but not limited to cases where the foreign proceedings are vexatious or oppressive.[190]

8.119 Finally, the logically separate but in practice closely linked question may arise as to the proper law of each actionable wrong relied upon in the proceedings. This again is a substantial topic in its own right. English courts and arbitrators can and do apply foreign law to disputes, or issues forming part of such disputes, over which they have jurisdiction and as to which England is the most appropriate forum. The content of foreign substantive law is a question of fact for expert evidence. The questions most likely to concern sports lawyers in litigation before the English courts concern, first, the rules for ascertaining the proper law of a contract, or putative contract; and secondly, the rules for ascertaining the proper law applicable to a tort committed abroad, and the conditions for it being action-able in this country.

8.120 As to the first question, in the absence of an express clause stating the govern-ing law of the contract, the test appears to be: what is the system of law with which the

---

[186] *Dicey, Morris and Collins* (n 174) vol 1 para 8-025; section 25(1) of the 1982 Act.
[187] See Civil Judgments and Jurisdiction Act 1982, Sched 4 Art 1(5); *Dicey, Morris and Collins* (n 174) vol 1, Rule 28(2), pp 349–61, and 1997 Cumulative Supplement pp 46–48; *Barclays Bank plc v Glasgow City Council* [1996] QB 678, CA; cf *Kleinwort Benson Ltd v Glasgow City Council* [1996] QB 57, ECJ; [1999] 1 AC 153, HL; cf *Strathard Farms Ltd v GA Chattaway and Co* 1993 SLT 36; *Ferguson Shipbuilders Ltd v Voith Hydro GmbH & Co AG* 2000 SLT 229.
[188] *Dicey, Morris and Collins* (n 174) vol 1 Rule 32(2), para 12R-086; *Donohue v Armco Inc* [2001] UKHL 64, [2002] 1 All ER 749.
[189] See *The Spiliada* [1987] AC 460.
[190] See *Société Nationale Industrielle Aérospatiale v Lee Kui Jak* [1987] AC 871, PC, per Lord Goff at 892–6, reviewing the authorities; cf *Donohue v Armco Inc* (n 188) and *Royal Bank of Canada v Cooperatieve Centrale Raiffeisen-Boerenleenbank BA* [2004] EWCA Civ 7, [2004] 2 All ER (Comm) 847.

transaction has the closest and most real connection?[191] As to the second question, it is necessary first to identify in which country the tort (or delict) in question has been committed. This is done by looking back over the series of events constituting the tort and asking where, in substance, the cause of action arises.[192] The normal rule is that the law applicable to a tort or delict is the law of the state where it was committed, unless it is substantially more appropriate for the applicable law to be that of another state, having regard to factors connecting the tort with, respectively, one country or the other.[193] It is no longer necessary to establish, in English proceedings concerning a tort committed abroad, that the defendant's act would have been tortious if committed in England.[194]

Stay of Proceedings for Mediation

8.121 Since we wrote the first edition of this book, mediation has come to the fore as a way of resolving disputes without the need for a costly and debilitating trial. No one doubts the virtue of mediation in those cases where it succeeds, when the more traditional method of direct settlement negotiations may not. Where mediation fails to produce a settlement, however, it can merely build in an extra layer of cost and delay. Concerns have also been expressed that pressure on a defendant to engage in mediation can encourage speculative and meritless claims, and can constitute an improper means of extracting concessions from a defendant with a good defence.

8.122 The development of mediation and the debate over its utility is familiar to lawyers in all fields, and has no particular relevance to sports related disputes over and above its relevance generally. Practitioners engaged in sports related disputes would do well to consider carefully any offer of mediation. A refusal to do so can encourage the court to depart from the usual order that the successful party's costs should be paid by the unsuccessful party; but the burden is on a party seeking a departure from that default position to show that a refusal to engage in mediation was unreasonable; and in particular, whether it is unreasonable for such a person to take the view that a mediation exercise would have little chance of success.[195] The authorities to date show that neither the courts nor the legislature are moving towards compulsion to engage in mediation, which would be difficult to establish in view of the right of access to a court guaranteed by Article 6 of the European Convention on Human Rights.

---

[191] *Compagnie Tunisienne de Navigation SA v Compagnie d'Armement Maritime SA* [1971] AC 572; *C v D* [2007] EWCA Civ 1282, per Longmore LJ at para 23; *Dicey, Morris and Collins* (n 174) vol 2, para 32-094.

[192] Applying Part III of the Private International Law (Miscellaneous Provisions) Act 1995.

[193] Ibid, s 12(1) and (2).

[194] Private International Law (Miscellaneous Provisions) Act 1995, s 10, reversing the effect of the so-called double-actionability rule derived from *Philips v Eyre* (1870) LR 6 QB 1 (held by the majority of the House of Lords in *Boys v Chaplin* [1971] AC 356 to be the normal rule); see *Morin v Bonhams & Brooks Ltd* [2003] EWCA Civ 1802, [2004] 1 Lloyd's Rep 702 at [16]–[18] and cases in *Dicey, Morris and Collins* (n 174) 4th Supp, para 35-088 including *Middle Eastern Oil LLC v National Bank of Abu Dhabi* [2009] EWHC 2895 (Comm).

[195] See the discussion in Dyson LJ's judgment in *Halsey v Milton Keynes General NHS Trust* [2004] 1 WLR 3002, CA. Since *Halsey*, cases in which costs have been refused in reliance on a refusal to engage in mediation have been few and far between.

Stay of Proceedings for Arbitration

8.123 Where the parties have entered into an arbitration agreement within the meaning of the Arbitration Act 1996,[196] that Act makes detailed provision for the purpose of ensuring that the dispute between the parties is kept out of the courts and resolved, in private and on a (normally but not always) confidential basis, by arbitration. A party who seeks to circumvent an arbitration agreement and attempts to bring proceedings in the ordinary court is likely to face an application to stay the proceedings. The court must grant the stay unless satisfied that 'the arbitration agreement is null and void, inoperative, or incapable of being performed'.[197]

8.124 Thus, attempts to resort to the courts without regard to an arbitration clause will normally generate a stay of proceedings by the court at the behest of the defendant. In *Colchester United FC Ltd v Burley*[198] the High Court stayed Colchester's claim because a web of complex rules (respectively of the Football League, the Premier League and the Football Association) had the effect, on their true construction, that the dispute between Colchester, its former manager and Ipswich Town Football Club fell within the relevant arbitration provisions. Colchester's attempt to claim damages in court proceedings therefore failed.

8.125 However, the Football League failed to obtain a stay of proceedings brought by Notts County Football Club against the League and Southend United Football Club[199] in which Notts County sought a determination under what was then Order 14A of the Rules of the Supreme Court that Southend United had no right of appeal under the relevant rules against the League's dismissal of Southend United's complaint that its manager had been approached by Notts County contrary to a League rule. The League commission had declared itself unsatisfied that a breach of the rule had been committed when the manager was approached, but went on to note that Southend had a right of appeal. Notts County asked the court to make a determination to the contrary effect, and the League asked the court to stay Notts County's action so that the question whether or not Southend really did have a right of appeal could be determined by arbitration under Rule 41(a) of the rules of the Football Association. This procedural entanglement was duly unravelled by Neuberger J, who held, having heard full argument on the point, that he was, exceptionally, prepared to decide it. He did so on the basis of then current authority to the effect that a point of law not requiring resolution of contested facts may be resolved on a summary judgment application before a court notwithstanding any arbitration clause.[200]

---

[196] Ie, 'an agreement to submit to arbitration present or future disputes' (whether they are contractual or not); s 6(1) Arbitration Act 1996.

[197] Ibid, s 9(4). A stay was successfully sought in *Stretford v The Football Association Ltd* [2007] EWCA Civ 238, [2007] ISLR, SLR 41 (at first instance and upheld on appeal).

[198] (1995) unreported, 30 October. *Quaere* whether the result would have been the same if the case had been decided under the Arbitration Act 1996, s 9 of which is more narrowly worded than its predecessors in the Acts of 1950 and 1979.

[199] *Notts Incorporated FC Ltd v The Football League Ltd and Southend United FC Ltd* (1996) unreported, 28 November 1996, Neuberger J.

[200] *SL Sethia Liners Ltd v State Trading Corporation of India Ltd* [1986] 2 All ER 395, per Kerr LJ at 396h–397b (a case decided under the Arbitration Act 1975).

8.126 The judge noted that the cost of further arbitration proceedings would be disproportionate, and felt that he might as well decide the point notwithstanding the League's powerful arguments for a stay, which included the point that the international governing body of football, FIFA, required under Article 58 of its rules all clubs of its member associations to refrain from litigating in court 'until all the possibilities of sports jurisdiction within, or under the responsibility of their national association have been exhausted'. Moreover, FIFA's then Article 58 also required national member associations, including the Football League, to 'ensure, as far as they can competently do so, that their clubs ... observed this obligation', on pain of 'being suspended from all international activity ... in addition to receiving a ban on all international matches'. So the Football League was clearly wise to do what it could to prevent the involvement of the court. The judge, having decided to entertain the matter, then construed the relevant rules as conferring a right of appeal on Southend, which meant that the action failed.

8.127 An arbitration clause is unlikely to displace the right of access to court in a case where the claim is for membership of a body, rather than a claim by an existing member against the body. This is because the non-member will not, *ex hypothesi*, be bound by an arbitration clause in the rules of the body of which it seeks to become a member. However, such a claim may nevertheless proceed by arbitration, either through an ad hoc agreement conferring jurisdiction on an arbitral tribunal under the 1996 Act, or pursuant to the rules of an 'umbrella' body of which both parties are members.[201] Thus in the case of *Stevenage Borough FC Ltd v The Football League Ltd*,[202] Stevenage claimed a right of membership of the Football League, but was already a member of the Football Association, which also exercised supervisory powers over various football bodies including the Football League. The Association's rules contained an arbitration clause but it did not, by its terms, cover the dispute.[203]

Arbitration in Sport

Introduction

8.128 Assuming, then, that a sports related dispute is kept away from the ordinary courts, we now look briefly at arbitration in sport generally. As noted at the beginning of this

---

[201] Or through the medium of an arbitration clause in the rules of an umbrella body of which both parties are members or by the rules of which they are bound—such as, in the case of football, the Football Association or, at international level, FIFA which has a Dispute Resolution Chamber to deal with player versus club disputes and compensation claims arising from transfers of players between clubs in different countries; see, eg the dispute between Adrian Mutu and Chelsea arising from the player's dismissal for consuming cocaine (*Mutu v Chelsea FC Ltd* [2009] ISLR, SLR 138 (before the CAS; the player's appeal against an award of substantial damages failed)). On breaking of players' contracts, see Dubey, *La Jurisprudence du TAS sur l'Article 17 RSTJ (Règle sur le Transfert des Joueurs)*, paper delivered at CAS conference, Montreux, November 2011, to be published in [2012] ISLR.

[202] (1997) 9 Admin LR 109, CA.

[203] In *Sheffield United FC Ltd v FA Premier League Ltd* [2007] ISLR, SLR 77, Sheffield United failed in an arbitration under the Premier League's 'Rule S' to establish that the Premier League Disciplinary Commission's decision not to deduct points from West Ham's tally for improperly using the services of Carlos Tevez had been so unreasonable and irrationally lenient as to be unlawful.

chapter, we assume in the following exposition that purely internal domestic remedies, not involving any external tribunal, have been exhausted.[204] In this section, we look at the functioning of machinery used to resolve disputes of fact and law by a body separate from and independent of the players, clubs and sports bodies involved in the dispute.

8.129 One does not need to dwell on the potential advantages of arbitration over court proceedings as an instrument of dispute resolution in sport. As in other fields where the advantages of arbitration are recognised, the benefits appreciated by users of arbitration services are those of specialist expertise, privacy, relative swiftness, and relatively modest cost. It should be said that not all those benefits are delivered to the full in every case that goes to arbitration. But in general they are sufficiently in evidence to have convinced these authors of the virtues of arbitral process over court proceedings, where the choice exists.

8.130 If the objective of arbitration is efficient resolution of civil disputes as painlessly as possible for both winner and loser, then the objective in sport is no different. Disputes submitted to arbitration in sport are many and varied. The main types are: disciplinary proceedings for alleged misconduct on and off the field, including doping offences; disputes over eligibility to compete and selection; and financial disputes between clubs and managers, clubs and other clubs, clubs and players, clubs and agents, or players and agents. Purely commercial disputes arising from contracts to sponsor or broadcast sporting events are not likely to be resolved by arbitration under the rules of the sport concerned. They are likely to be resolved in state civil courts or by voluntary commercial arbitration pursuant to an arbitration clause in the relevant contract. The latter type of dispute is not generally regarded as sport specific but as normal commercial dispute resolution where the commercial actors happen to be purveyors of sport.[205]

8.131 Arbitration in English law is governed by the Arbitration Act 1996, whose main purpose, as its preamble states, is to 'restate and improve the law relating to arbitration pursuant to an arbitration agreement'. A full account of the English law relating to domestic and international arbitrations lies beyond the compass of this short book; reference should be made to specialist works.[206]

8.132 Arbitration in sport arises in two ways.[207] First, an arbitration clause may be written into the rules of a sporting association, requiring that an aggrieved member of the association must proceed in accordance with the procedure established by the rule, and not by court proceedings, as a means of resolving the dispute in question between him and the association.[208] Such a rule is conceptually distinct from a rule creating a right

---

[204] See para 8.1.

[205] An exception was *Cricket Australia v ICC Development (International) Ltd* [2007] ISLR, SLR 61, a dispute about sponsorship contracts in the 2007 cricket World Cup, decided by the ICC Disputes Resolution Committee, an arbitral panel chaired by the senior author.

[206] See Mustill and Boyd, *The Law and Practice of Commercial Arbitration in England*, 2nd edn (Butterworths, 1989); Mustill and Boyd, *Commercial Arbitration: 2001, Companion Volume to the 2nd edition* (Butterworths, 2001); St John Sutton, Gill and Gearing, *Russell on Arbitration*, 23rd edn (Sweet & Maxwell, 2007); Merkin, *Arbitration Law*, 2 vols (Informa, looseleaf).

[207] See Perry, *Dispute Resolution in Sport: New Challenges, New Options* [2001] ISLR 92.

[208] In *Walkinshaw v Diniz* (2000) 2 All ER (Comm) 237, Thomas J decided (obiter) that a process operated by three lawyers comprising a 'Contracts Resolution Board' with the task of determining whether a driver's contract had been terminated, thus freeing him to drive for another team, was an arbitration process and not merely a procedure for determining the rules of the sport; though he went on to hold that the dispute fell outside the jurisdiction of the arbitrators, the issue being whether termination had occurred by breach or by notice.

of internal appeal against a decision of the association's lower organs, for the latter does not involve recourse to an external body, but the former does. An arbitration clause in a sporting body's rules presupposes a possible dispute between the member and the association, but a right of appeal merely provides for a second tier ruling emanating from within the association. Secondly, the parties may agree to arbitration by means of an ad hoc agreement. If the rules of the body in question do not contain an arbitration clause at all, or the clause does not apply to the dispute as in the *Stevenage* case, then arbitration may only be used to resolve the dispute if both parties consent.

8.133 For example, Enfield Town Football Club agreed to submit its dispute with the Vauxhall Conference to arbitration pursuant to an ad hoc agreement, after Enfield Town had come top in the league immediately below the level of the Conference. The Conference had refused to admit Enfield Town, asserting that it did not comply with the Conference's financial criteria. Enfield argued that those criteria were an unreasonable restraint of trade, but the arbitrators disagreed.[209] Similarly, in the case in which Tottenham Hotspur regained admission to the FA Cup and had six Premiership points restored to it, the matter proceeded by way of arbitration pursuant to an ad hoc agreement announced to the media before the arbitration took place.[210]

8.134 A final point to note in cases where disputes are submitted to arbitration by consent is that the scope of the arbitrators' jurisdiction is strictly limited by the content of the agreement. In one case in which two of the authors were involved, their opponents sought to argue that their clients were precluded by estoppel from advancing one of their arguments. The arbitrators held that they had no jurisdiction to entertain the estoppel argument, which fell outside the purview of the arbitration agreement.

8.135 What, then, are the principal features of sport related arbitration?[211] The first is that the parties often cannot choose whether to submit their dispute to arbitration. Agreement to do so is usually a condition of participation in the sport or competition concerned. To assert that sports arbitration is voluntary because one can avoid it by abstaining from taking part in the sport is to take intellectual purity to an absurd extreme. Major SGBs tend to have an absolute or near monopoly on governance of their sport, including the power to withdraw—subject to the rule of law—the right to take part in it.

8.136 Second, the parties cannot always nominate an arbitrator of their choice. Frequently, the rules provide that the arbitrator or arbitrators are selected from a standing panel of members appointed by the governing body, or (as in the case of the International Tennis Federation) on an ad hoc basis but again appointed by the governing body. However, some rules (such as, in England, those of the FA and Premier League in non-disciplinary cases only) permit the parties to select an arbitrator of their choice from a standing panel of arbitrators. In this country, many sports bodies now provide for arbitration to take

---

[209] *Enfield Town v Vauxhall Conference*, arbitration chaired by Sir Michael Kerr, referred to by Carnwath J in *Stevenage Borough FC Ltd v The Football League Ltd* at p 39 of the transcript of his first instance decision.

[210] Mentioned in chapter 7 at para 7.158.

[211] See eg Mishkin, *Sports Arbitration in the United States*; Kerr, *La procédure arbitrale en matière sportive est-elle originale?*, papers delivered to the International Chamber of Commerce conference Arbitration and Sport, Paris, September 2010.

place under the auspices of Sport Resolutions UK, a body providing expert panel adjudication in many sports in this country.[212]

8.137 The right of objection to a particular arbitrator is generally confined under the rules to objection for cause, ie a risk of bias arising from a conflict of interests or personal involvement in the issues. The CAS changed its procedural rules in October 2009 to prohibit any CAS arbitrator (there are over 260 of them from 80 countries) from appearing before the CAS as an advocate. The communiqué publicising the change explained that it was being introduced to reduce the number of requests for recusal.

8.138 Third, the tribunal may be required to apply principles of law derived not exclusively from any one national legal system, but from what may be called international sports jurisprudence; ie from the jurisprudence of international tribunals, principally the CAS, which[213] has led to Swiss domestic and international law, especially the Swiss law of associations, occupying a predominant position in international sports jurisprudence.

8.139 Fourth, the tribunal may be required to punish as well as to compensate. It may have limited or no discretion as to what penalty to impose. Or it may have varying degrees of discretion depending on its primary findings. Thus, the regime enacted in the World Anti-Doping Code is now widely applicable in doping cases and features strict liability tempered by a judicious measure of discretion where uniform defences are made out, the burden being on the defence. Punishments for doping offences are principally a period of ineligibility and forfeiture of prize money, medals and ranking points. Punishments for other offences such as fielding ineligible players, failing to prevent disorder among spectators, failing to make compulsory disclosures to the governing body, cancelling fixtures without good cause, allowing a club to become insolvent or simple misconduct on the field of play, may be punished by a ban from competition, a fine, deduction of points or a combination of these. Some rules give the arbitral tribunal apparently untrammelled discretion as to penalty, and then provide a non-exhaustive list of examples.

8.140 In non-disciplinary cases the arbitral tribunal must consider ordinary civil disputes which would go to the state courts if sport specific rules did not compel arbitration. Examples are straightforward employment cases where damages for wrongful dismissal are claimed on ordinary principles; and cases where players are lured from one club to another, with or without a breach of contract, and compensation is claimed under the relevant rules or in tort for inducing breach of contract.[214]

---

[212] See Procter, *Dispute Resolution in Sport: The Role of Sport Resolutions (UK)* [2010] ISLR 3. However, an attempt to secure a referral to the predecessor body, the Sports Dispute Resolution Panel, failed before Lightman J in *Badrick v British Judo Association* [2004] ISLR, SLR 45, on the ground that the Association had not consented in its rules to such a referral and that an adjudication of the claimant's claim to have a right to be selected for a particular competition was not practicable in the time available. 'London 2012 brought an unprecedented series of challenges for Team GB across sports from track and field, swimming, judo, fencing and diving, to taekwondo. See *Hutchinson v BFA* SDRP 29 May 2012; *GB Rhythmic Gymnastics Team v British Gymnastics* 2012 SLR 23; *Couch v British Diving* SDRP 28 June 2012.'

[213] As noted in chapter 1 at paras 1.43–1.48.

[214] For a useful post-*Bosman* analysis of justification for restrictions on free movement of players, see Case C-325/08 *Olympique Lyonnais v Olivier Bernard and Newcastle United FC*, judgment of 16 March 2010; cf in the sport specific jurisprudence *FC Shakhtar Donetsk v Matuzalem Francelino da Silva & Real Zaragoza SAD & FIFA*, CAS 2008/A/1519, judgment of 19 May 2009.

8.141 Fifth, the rules of procedure in sports related arbitrations are no different from procedural rules that normally govern civil disputes in courts and arbitral tribunals alike. The arbitral tribunal, or the chairman alone, is normally given jurisdiction to make preliminary rulings on procedural points such as pleadings, disclosure, written statements of evidence and argument, and the like. Interim relief is also commonly provided for under the rules, but not always.

8.142 Speed and urgency are frequently emphasised in rules governing sports related arbitration, perhaps to a greater extent than in regular commercial arbitration. SGBs' arbitration rules often include short deadlines (eg 60 days from the date the player requests a hearing under the International Tennis Federation's Anti-Doping Rules) within which, absent agreement or unusual circumstances, a hearing must take place, followed by a decision within (normally) 14 days thereafter. The reason is not difficult to discern, especially in doping cases: the player needs to know urgently whether he or she should play or not. Eligibility to compete cases tend also to be, by their nature, urgent: sport timetables are tight.

8.143 Sixth, oral hearings in sports arbitration before domestic tribunals are no different in character from those in commercial or other arbitrations. The panel is likely to comprise a lawyer chairman sitting with two non-lawyer arbitrators with expertise in the sport—for example, in doping cases, often a scientist with knowledge of drug testing and a sports administrator or doctor. Documents are read, witnesses questioned and submissions made, in the usual way. The onus of proof is on the party asserting a particular proposition, in the ordinary way. The standard of proof is as provided for by the relevant rules, frequently that of 'comfortable satisfaction' that an offence has been committed.[215]

8.144 Seventh, there is no uniform practice in sports related arbitration concerning awards of costs. Everything depends on the applicable rules. It is still quite common in domestic sports related arbitration for the rules to be silent on the question of costs. If the rules are silent it is common practice not to award them, but under the Arbitration Act 1996 the arbitral tribunal will have power to award costs recoverable and specify the amount recoverable in respect of the arbitrators' fees and as between the parties.[216] Some bodies' rules (such as those of the FA Premier League) enact a presumption that costs follow the event, or provide that costs should only be awarded where one party behaves unreasonably. The CAS normally orders the loser to pay a fixed amount as a contribution to the winner's costs but it is seldom adequate to cover all the winner's costs. Until recently, the International Tennis Federation's Anti-Doping Programme made no mention of any power to award costs, but an express power was inserted in the 2009 version. So far as we are aware, it has yet to be exercised.

8.145 Eighth, as regards publicity and confidentiality, in sports related arbitrations the hearings themselves in disciplinary and non-disciplinary cases alike are almost always held in private pursuant to the rules, and this position has not yet (so far as we are aware) been challenged by reference to Article 6(1) of the European Convention on Human Rights or otherwise. The decisions of domestic arbitration tribunals in sport related disciplinary cases are now normally published on the websites of the governing

---

[215] As mentioned in chapter 7, paras 7.89–7.90.
[216] See ss 4(2), 59 and 61–65.

bodies concerned. Sensitive factual material (eg gynaecological evidence in a doping case involving a female defendant) may be excised to protect privacy, but otherwise the trend is gradually towards making the full decision publicly available, rather than just a summary or press release.[217]

8.146 Arbitration tribunal decisions in non-disciplinary sports cases are likely to remain confidential to the parties unless the rules provide otherwise or both parties consent, as happened in a recent domestic football related arbitration.[218] In England, there is a strong presumption that the parties intend arbitration to be confidential and it is not weakened by the silence of the Arbitration Act 1996 on the point.[219]

8.147 Ninth, and finally, what about rights of challenge to the arbitrators' decision? In sports related arbitration, some governing bodies' rules enact a right of appeal to the CAS in disciplinary cases, but some (such as the FA Premier League) provide for a right of appeal to an appeal board selected from a panel of members, who may or may not be lawyers. Unlike in the CAS, where proceedings on appeal are held on a *de novo* basis, in regular arbitration proceedings it is generally thought that the grounds for interfering with an award should be narrow, and in England they are indeed narrow under section 68 of the Arbitration Act 1996. The aim is to avoid defeating the advantages of speed, efficiency and certainty which arbitration is considered to have by comparison with court proceedings.[220]

The Court of Arbitration for Sport

8.148 The Court of Arbitration for Sport (CAS) was founded in 1983 to provide a mechanism outside the ordinary courts 'to secure the settlement of sports related disputes'.[221] It has been accorded by the Swiss Federal Tribunal (SFT) the following encomium: 'There appears to be no viable alternative to this institution, which can resolve international sports-related disputes quickly and inexpensively, having gradually built up the trust of the sporting world, this institution which is now widely recognised and which will soon celebrate its twentieth birthday, remains one of the principal mainstays of organised

---

[217] But in *Christine Ohuruogu v British Olympic Association* [2008] ISLR, SLR 113 (in which two of the authors represented the athlete) the rules provided for only a discretionary and abbreviated account of the decision of the appellate decision of the Sports Dispute Resolution Panel (chaired by Nicholas Stewart QC), to the dissatisfaction of our senior author *qua* editor of the International Sports Law Review; see editorial at [2008] ISLR 15, querying why the full judgment should not be shared with an interested readership.

[218] *Keegan v Newcastle United Football Co Ltd* [2010] IRLR 94, FA Arbitration, Philip Havers QC chairing (damages of £2 million awarded).

[219] See the judgment of Mance LJ (passim) in *Department of Economics, Policy and Development of the City of Moscow v Bankers Trust Co* [2005] QB 207, CA, explaining however (reviewing Strasbourg as well as domestic case law, and Art 6(1) of the European Convention on Human Rights) that different considerations apply to a court hearing and judgment where the award is challenged in court.

[220] For a sport related example of the Court of Appeal setting aside permission to challenge an arbitration award in a dispute over the employment of a professional basketball player, see *Athletic Union of Constantinople v National Basketball Association (No 2)* [2002] 1 WLR 2863, CA.

[221] For a history of its first two decades see Blackshaw et al, *The Court of Arbitration for Sport 1984–2004* (TCM Asser Press, 2006). See generally Nafziger, *International Sports Law* (Transnational Publishing, 2004) 40–45, 48–61; Lewis and Taylor (n 57) A7; Cox, Schuster and Costello, *Sport and the Law* (First Law, 2004) 1.7.3.1 and 1.7.3.2; Reeb, *The Court of Arbitration for Sport* SLB 3(4); Holmes, *The CAS: A Case Study of an International Arbitration Institution* (2005) 27 Australian Bar Review 56; Beloff, *CAS 25 Years On*, Focus Sports Law, Blackstone Chambers, April 2010; Ravjani, *The CAS: A Suitable Form of International Delegation* (2010) 1 Cas Bull 14.

sport.'[222] An increasing number of SGBs, national and international, accept in their rules its authority as a final appellate body.[223] Its governing instrument is currently the Code of Sports-Related Arbitration and Mediation Rules, 2010 edition ('the Code').[224]

8.149 The International Council of Arbitration for Sport (ICAS), which looks after the administration and financing of the CAS, has a dual purpose: to facilitate the settlement of sports related disputes through arbitration or mediation, and to safeguard the independence of the CAS and the rights of the parties.[225] It is composed of 20 members being high level jurists. Its main functions are to adopt and amend the Code; to appoint the list of arbitrators; to exercise functions conferred upon it by the procedural rules ('the Rules'), including functions concerning the challenge and removal of arbitrators;[226] to set up devolved arbitration structures; and to appoint the CAS Secretary-General.[227]

8.150 CAS arbitrators and mediators are lawyers with recognised competence with regard to sports law and/or international arbitration, a good knowledge of sport in general, and a good command of at least one CAS working language.[228] There are now more than 260 arbitrators ensuring a fair representation of the continents and different juridical cultures. As a condition of appointment they sign declarations of independence and objectivity.[229] They cannot appear as counsel for a party before the CAS.[230]

8.151 The CAS has its seat (and main arbitration premises) at Château Béthusy in Lausanne. In consequence the arbitration laws of Switzerland apply.[231] This remains the position in the interests of uniformity even at its devolved centres in New York and Sydney, and, as occasionally occurs, when for convenience an ad hoc panel sits elsewhere.[232] The basis for CAS jurisdiction is contractual. It may arise out of an ad hoc agreement entered into before or after the dispute arises,[233] or, more usually where an appeal is involved, by reason of a provision for CAS arbitration in the rules of the body whose decision is the subject of an appeal.[234]

---

[222] *Danilova and Lazutina v IOC and FIS* [2003] 3 Digest of CAS Awards 649, SFT.

[223] Notably in the last decade FIFA (see FIFA Statutes, Arts 62–64) and IAAF (IAAF Constitution, November 2009). In 2011 354 cases were registered. The most recent amendments, at the time of writing, entered into force on 1 January 2012.

[224] The Code is subject to a continuing process of review. The CAS website should be checked for any updates. See Reeb, *The New Code* (2010) 1 Cas Bull 31.

[225] Its organic and economic ties to the IOC were criticised by the SFT in *Gundel v FEI* CAS 92A//63, and in *Danilova and Lazutina v IOC and FIS* (n 222) the SFT was satisfied that the CAS was no longer 'the vassal of the IOC' which inspired the creation of ICAS.

[226] See, eg, *N, J, Y and W v FINA*, CAS 98A//208, unsuccessful petition challenge concerning Mr Michael Beloff QC.

[227] Code of Sports-Related Arbitration and Mediation Rules 2010, S6.

[228] Ibid, S14, currently English or French.

[229] Ibid, S19

[230] Ibid, S18. Previously the inhibition was more flexible and was validated by the SFT in *Danilova* (n 222); see, for a discussion of issues, Anderson, *Modern Sports Law: A Textbook* (Hart Publishing, 2010) 85–87; Beloff, editorial [2003] ISLR 89; Blackshaw, *Challenging Independence of CAS Arbitrators*, WSLR 9/09, p 10.

[231] *Raguz v Sullivan* (2000) 50 NSWLR 236 (New South Wales Court of Appeal); *Raducan v IOC*, 4 December 2000, 427/2000, SFT.

[232] For example, the CAS sat in Shanghai on the eve of the 2011 World Swimming Championships to adjudicate on whether certain Brazilian swimmers should be permitted to compete.

[233] See Bell, *Dispute Resolution and Applicable Law Clauses in International Sports Arbitration* (2010) 84 Australian Law Journal 116. See for standard clauses www.tas-cas.org/clausetemplates.

[234] Code of Sports-Related Arbitration and Mediation Rules 2010, R27; *Korda v ITF Ltd* (1999) 2(4) SLB, where it was held that the rules of the then Tennis Anti-Doping Programme allowed appeals by ITF to the CAS (contrast

8.152 In either event the dispute must be 'sports-related';[235] the CAS has never hitherto declined jurisdiction on the basis of non-satisfaction of this criterion.[236] Parties to proceedings before the CAS will sign an order of procedure which further confirms CAS jurisdiction. Swiss law recognises the validity of an athlete opting out of the jurisdiction of the ordinary courts of law as long as the chosen arbitration system recognises due process.[237]

8.153 The scope of the arbitration agreement, whatever its source, will depend upon its wording. Under Swiss law as the *lex arbitralis* such wording is to be interpreted in the light of its language and factual matrix.

8.154 The CAS has two regular divisions—an ordinary arbitration division (OAD) and an appeals arbitration division (AAD).[238] Disputes arising out of an arbitration clause inserted in a contract or regulations or an ad hoc arbitration agreement will be assigned to the OAD; disputes involving an appeal against a decision rendered by a federation, association, or sports related body, where the statutes or regulations of such body or a specific arbitration agreement provides for an appeal to the CAS, will be assigned to the AAD.[239]

8.155 According to Article 187 of the Swiss Private International Law Statute of 18 December 1987 (PILS), an arbitral tribunal shall decide the dispute according to the law chosen by the parties or, in the absence of such choice, according to the law having the closest connection with the dispute. The Code has different provisions for determination of the applicable law in ordinary and appeal proceedings.[240] For ordinary proceedings it is the rules of law chosen by the parties or in the absence of such choice Swiss law; but the parties may also authorise the panel to decide *ex aequo et bono*.[241] For appeal proceedings the applicable law is the applicable regulations and the rules of law chosen by the parties, or in the absence of such choice, the law of the country in which the respondent federation, association or sports related body is domiciled.[242] The panel may also in the alternative apply the rules of law which it deems appropriate, but, if so, must give reasons

---

Ashley Cole v FAPL, CAS 2005/A/952 where the rules did not give the player a right of appeal). See too *FIFA and WADA v Dodo*, CAS 2007/A/1364 for an example of a case where the rules (of the Hellenic Football Federation) were held not to allow an appeal to the CAS; *Iraklis Thessaloniki v HFF and Greek Super League*, CAS 2011/A/2483; see too *Russian Boxing Federation v AIBA*, CAS 2007/A/1266. Internal remedies must always be exhausted: *Aris FC v FIFA*, CAS 2007/A/1251. See now *Anti-Doping Schweiz v Ullrich*, CAS 2010/A/2070: associations cannot transfer powers to enforce membership obligations (here discipline for doping without consent of athlete concerned).

[235] Code of Sports-Related Arbitration and Mediation Rules 2010, S12; Nafziger (n 221): 'Basically the CAS hears three kinds of disputes: disciplinary, eligibility-related and commercial' (p 42); *NISA v ISU*, CAS 2003/A/466, [2004] ISLR, SLR 48: 'The CAS cannot substitute its own judgment for that of sports bodies with regard to policy choices and cannot pass judgments on political matters' (at 6.23).

[236] See illustrations in Anderson (n 230) 88.

[237] *Cañas v ATP*, SFT, 22 March 2007, ATF 133 III 235. For an attempt to bypass CAS see Blackshaw, *FC Sion Case: A Denial of Justice*, WSLR 10/3, 4; Anderson, *Regulations: The FC Sion Case and its Effects. Part Two*, WSLR (2012).

[238] Code of Sports-Related Arbitration and Mediation Rules 2010, S20.

[239] Ibid, S20. The *FC Sion* saga shows a recent attempt to bypass CAS jurisdiction. Time limits are strict: see Haas, *The Time Limit for Appeal in Arbitration Proceedings before CAS*, CAS Bulletin 2/11, p 3, but the athlete must be made aware of the decision before time runs against him: *WADA v CISM and Turrini*, CAS 2008/A/1565. They cannot be artificially extended by attempts to obtain reconsideration: *Netball NZ v IFNA*, CAS 2010/A/2315. See de la Rochefoucault, *Standing to be Sued: A Procedural Issue before CAS* (2010) 1 Cas Bull 52.

[240] Three volumes of CAS jurisprudence have been published: *Digest of CAS Awards 1986–1998* (Stämpfli editions); *Digest of CAS Awards II (1998–2000)* (Kluwer); *Digest of CAS Awards III (2001–2003)* (Kluwer). For updates see too the CAS website: www.tas-cas.org

[241] Code of Sports-Related Arbitration and Mediation Rules 2010, R45.

[242] Given that many international federations are domiciled in Switzerland, eg FIFA, UEFA, FISA, FINA and the IOC, Swiss Law is frequently applied 'complementarily'.

for its decision.[243] Foreign law, if chosen, includes all provisions of that law applicable to the case[244] unless in conflict with Swiss public policy.[245] While it does not have a strict doctrine of precedent, panels will only unusually depart from interpretations of law by previous panels because of considerations of comity and mutual respect.[246]

8.156 The CAS as an international sports tribunal has increasingly detached itself from its roots in Swiss law, and made use of the alternative facility of applying in appeal procedures its own perception of the appropriate rules of law.[247]

8.157 Apart from the regulations of the particular sport or of national legal provisions the CAS also applies:

> general principles of law drawn from a comparative or common denominator reading of various domestic legal systems and, in particular, the prohibition of arbitrary or unreasonable rules and measures.[248]

Such general principles of law in the *lex sportiva* or *lex ludica* consist or have affinity with, but are not identical to, well established doctrines of national law and bridge common law and civil law concepts. They include: legal certainty;[249] the presumption against retroactivity;[250] the protection of acquired rights and legitimate expectations;[251] the prohibition of arbitrariness, discrimination and violation of fundamental rights;[252] proportionality;[253] estoppels;[254] substantive rules such as freedom of contract, *pacta sunt servanda*, *force majeure*, *rebus sic stantibus* and good faith;[255] and rules of construction: purposive (as opposed to literal),[256] *in dubio contra proferentem*,[257] good faith in application

---

[243] Code of Sports-Related Arbitration and Mediation Rules 2010, R58.

[244] PILS, Art 13.

[245] Ibid, Art 17.

[246] See generally Kaufmann-Kohler, *Arbitral Precedent: Dream Necessity or Excuse? An example of divergent views of an interpretation of complex FIFA regulations on the compensation payable by a footballer in breach of contract with a club*, Freshfields Lecture 2006. See *Webster v Heart of Midlothian*, CAS 2007/A/1300; *Shakhtar Donetsk (Ukraine) v Matuzalem and FIFA*, CAS 2008/A/1519–20, and for a critique of allegedly divergent approaches to doping infractions see Straubel, *Enhancing the Performance of the Doping Court: How the Court of Arbitration for Sport Could Do its Job Better* (2005) 36 Loyola University of Chicago Law Journal 1203. The author argues for a specialist Chamber of CAS for doping offences.

[247] Code of Sports-Related Arbitration and Mediation Rules 2010, R58. The CAS's decisions have influenced, inter alia, the awards of the FIFA Dispute Resolution Committee, a first instance body whose awards are frequently appealed to the CAS; see De Weyer, *The Jurisprudence of the FIFA Dispute Resolution Committee* (TCM Asser Press, 2008).

[248] *AEK Athens FC and Slavia Prague FC v UEFA*, CAS 98/2000, 20 August 1999, para 156. This concept of a *lex ludica* had its origins in the rules of the Ad Hoc Division first created for the Olympic Games in 1996; see *Comité Olympique Congolais, Kibunde v AIBA*, CAS JO 00/004 (Sydney); and see Fosler, *Lex Sportiva and Lex Ludica: The CAS's Jurisprudence*, ISSN 1748-944X.

[249] *AEK Athens and Slavia Prague v UEFA*, CAS 98/200; *Sullivan v Raguz*, CAS 2000/A/284.

[250] *Re ICU and Italian NOC*, CAS 94/C/128.

[251] *AEK Athens and Slavia Prague v UEFA*, CAS 98/200, para 159 and interim relief decision, paras 50–60. *COC and Beckie Scott v IOC*, CAS 2002/0/373, para 14.

[252] *Hellenic NOC and Kaklamanakis v ISAF*, CAS OG 04/009 (Athens), para 24; *Watts v ACF*, CAS 96/A/153; *Paul King v AIBA*, CAS 2011/A/2452, para 6.26 (ability of member to campaign for office is exercise of political free speech).

[253] *AEK Athens and Slavia Prague v UEFA*, CAS 98/200, 20 August 1999, para 156.

[254] De Piero, *Rules of Interpretation, Statutes and Application of the Doctrines of Venire Contra Factum Proprium and Estoppel in the Case Law of the CAS Tribunal* [2008] ISLR 84.

[255] *AEK Athens v UEFA*, CAS 98/200, paras 155–66.

[256] Ibid, para 156; *Perez v IOC*, CAS OG 00/005 (Sydney), 19 September 2000, paras 26–28.

[257] *Korda v ITF*, CAS 99/A/223, paras 25 and 48.

and interpretation;[258] *nulla crimen sine lege*: both offence and sanction have to be expressly provided for;[259] and *lex mitior*, ie if the law providing for sanctions has changed since the date of the offence in a way favourable to the athlete, the athlete must benefit from that change.[260]

8.158 Particularly significant are principles which can have application *only* in a sporting context:

(a)   the field of play doctrine, which seeks to limit interference with an official's decisions;[261]

(b)   the strict liability rule in relation to doping violations;[262]

(c)   the concept of comfortable satisfaction as the standard of proof for sporting disciplinary offences.[263]

8.159 In 1996 ICAS created an Ad Hoc Division of CAS to be present at the Olympic Games in Atlanta and to determine, generally within a 24-hour period, any dispute arising during the Games. The philosophy behind its creation was articulated by the Swiss Federal Tribunal: 'In competitive sport, particularly the Olympic Games, it is vital both for athletes and for the smooth running of events that disputes are resolved quickly, simply, flexibly and inexpensively by experts familiar with both legal and sports related issues.'[264] It has been replicated at all subsequent Summer Olympiads (Sydney 2000, Athens 2004, Beijing 2008[265]) and Winter Olympiads, (Nagano 1998, Salt Lake City 2003, Turin 2006, Vancouver 2010) as well as at the Commonwealth Games (Kuala Lumpur 1998, Manchester 2002, Melbourne 2006 and Delhi 2010). There are 12 arbitrators at the Summer Olympics,[266] nine arbitrators at the Winter Olympics[267] and six arbitrators at the Commonwealth Games, reflecting the respective size of the events. The CAS has also

---

[258]   *Cullwick v FINA*, CAS 96/A/149.

[259]   *Quigley v UIT*, CAS 94/A/129, para 34.

[260]   *UCI v CONI*, CAS 94/C/128; *VH v FINA*, CAS 2003/A/459, [2004] ISLR, SLR 25; *S v FINA*, CAS 2003/A/507, [2004] ISLR, SLR 35; *Foggo v NRL*, CAS A2/2011, para 44.

[261]   *Mendy v AIBA*, CAS OG 96/006 (Atlanta); *Segura v IOC*, CAS OG 00/013 (Sydney) (*CAS Digest II*, p 680); *Korean OC v ISW*, CAS OWG 07/007 (*CAS Digest III*, p 611); *De Lima v Brazilian OC v IAAF*, CAS 2004/A/727; *Yang v Hamm*, CAS 2004/A/704 (Athens), para 37; and see most recently *Saarinen v FIS*, CAS 2010/A/2090. The doctrine applies equally to challenges to the accuracy of technical equipment: *Neykova v IOC*, CAS OG 00/06 (Sydney) (*CAS Digest III*, p 674).

[262]   *Quigley v UIT*, CAS 94/A/129.

[263]   *Korneev & Gouleev v IOC*, CAS OG 96/003 (Atlanta), the *fons et origo* of the doctrine.

[264]   *Danilova and Lazutina v IOC* (n 222); Kaufmann-Kohler, *Arbitration and the Games (Atlanta)* [1997] Arbitration International, February.

[265]   It will be replicated at the London 2012 Games; see Anderson, *CAS Ad Hoc Division and London 2012*, WSLR 9/6, p 10.

[266]   See Beloff, *The CAS Ad Hoc Division at the Sydney Olympic Games* [2001] ISLR 105; Blackshaw, *Sporting Justice at the Olympics*, WSLR 4/6, p 6; McLaren, *Introducing the Court of Arbitration for Sport, the Ad Hoc Division at the Olympic Games* [2001] 12 Marquette Sports Law Review 515; McLaren, *The CAS Ad Hoc Division at the Athens Olympic Games* [2004] Marquette Sports Law Review 175; Beloff, *CAS at the Beijing Olympics* [2009] ISLR 3.

[267]   See Kaufmann-Kohler, *Nagano et l'arbitrage* in *Mealey's International Arbitration Report*, vol 13 issue 6; Leaver, *The CAS Ad Hoc Division at the Salt Lake City Winter Olympic Games* [2002] ISLR 44; McLaren and Clement, *CAS: The Ad Hoc Division at the Salt Lake City Olympics* [2004] ISLR 44; Rigozzi, *The Decisions Rendered by the CAS Ad Hoc Division at the Turin Winter Olympics* [2006] Journal of International Arbitration 453; Zagklis, *The CAS Ad Hoc Division at the XX Olympic Winter Games in Turin* (2006) 3(4) ISLJ 42; Holmes, *The Ad Hoc Division of CAS at the XX Olympic Games in Torino* [2006] ISLR 58.

had ad hoc divisions *in absentia* at the UEFA European Football Championships in 2000, 2004 and 2008, and the FIFA World Cups in 2006[268] and 2010.

8.160 The basis for the CAS Ad Hoc Division's jurisdiction is contractual. All participants—athletes, coaches and officials—sign, as a condition for their participation, a document conferring exclusive jurisdiction on the panel for disputes arising in connection with the Games[269]—usually incepting from 10 days before the opening ceremony and prohibiting resort to other courts. The scope of jurisdiction has been recognised as extending to international governing bodies of Olympic sports based on the Article of the Olympic Charter providing for the CAS's jurisdiction over such governing bodies.[270] The legal seat for proceedings before the Division remains in Lausanne, although the physical seat is at the respective sites of the Games, so ensuring uniformity of arbitral law and route of challenge to the courts, ie the Swiss Federal Tribunal, a position hitherto accepted in the host country.[271]

8.161 The Ad Hoc Division has its own set of rules devised by ICAS for the particular sports event concerned. The rules for each Games must be individually consulted.[272]

8.162 The Ad Hoc Division has to deal with issues relating to team selection, national eligibility, satisfaction of entry requirements, application of competition rules, advertising and athlete misconduct.[273]

8.163 The Panel may, at the request of a party, order preliminary measures including a stay. A triple test is consistently applied: the measures must be necessary to protect the applicant from irreparable harm; there must be a likelihood of success on the merits of the claim; and the interests of the appellant in the protected measures must outweigh those of the other party.[274]

8.164 On an appeal the CAS panel has full power to review the facts and the law.[275] The degree to which the CAS defers to the first instance body is debatable; the better view is that there is no principle requiring it to do so. As a result, issues of procedural fairness in an appeal are of no substantial significance: the entitlement of the appellant is to

---

[268] Blackshaw, *The CAS at the 2006 FIFA World Cup*, WLSR 4/7.

[269] The validity of such a provision has not hitherto been challenged, but might in principle be impugned as an excessive ouster under local law: see Blackshaw, *Olympic Athlete Consent to CAS Arbitration*, WSLR 7/11, p 6, suggesting that it is coerced and hence unlawful.

[270] *Baumann v IOC, NOC, Germany and IAAF*, CAS OG 00/006 (Sydney); *Raducan v IOC*, CAS OG 00/011 (Sydney).

[271] *Raguz v Sullivan* (2000) 50 NSWLR 236 (New South Wales Court of Appeal).

[272] See generally Kaufmann-Kohler, *Arbitration at the Olympics* (Kluwer, 2001).

[273] See *CAS Awards, Sydney 2000, CAS Awards, Salt Lake City 2002 and Athens 2004, CAS Awards, Turin and Melbourne 2006 and Beijing 2008* (all published by the CAS).

[274] *AEK Athens v SK Slavia Prague*, CAS 98/200, 20 August 1999 (*CAS Digest II*, p 38). But on occasion the CAS has been able to reach final conclusions within a week: eg *FINA v Cielo*, CAS 2011/A/2495.

[275] Code of Sports-Related Arbitration and Mediation Rules 2010, R58; see *French v Australian Sports Commission Cycling Australia*, CAS 2004/A/651, 11 July 2005 (construing the rule to permit a cross-appeal as long as within the ambit of the original dispute). The CAS has treated its own rules as overriding those of the body against whose decision an appeal is brought, hence ignoring purported limits on its power of review: *Edwards v IAAF*, CAS OG/04/003 para 49. See generally Mavromati and Pellaux, *The Healing Effect of the Appeal to CAS*, Conference, Montreux, November 2011, forthcoming in [2012] ISLR; *Kendrick v ITF*, CAS 2011/A/2518, para 10.1–10.6; *Bucci v FEI*, CAS 2010/A/2283, para 14.36.

an adjudication which is fair overall.[276] An appeal to the CAS can cure even a decision taken at first instance by a body which lacks independence and impartiality[277] but not a procedural error that, for example, flaws a drug testing procedure.[278] The panel can uphold or vacate a decision appealed against wholly or in part. It can increase or extinguish a sanction. It can issue a fresh decision or remit the case back for reconsideration by the original decision maker.[279]

8.165 CAS awards are recognised and enforced by the New York Convention on the Recognition and Enforcement of Foreign Arbitral Awards.[280]

8.166 Challenges to CAS awards in international arbitration proceedings which are regulated by Chapter 12 of PILS may only be brought in the Swiss Federal Tribunal, and the grounds are those set out in Article 190 paragraph 2 of PILS. An arbitration award in international proceedings may only be set aside on limited grounds. Procedural grounds include lack of jurisdiction of the panel, irregular composition of the panel, denial of justice, and violation of due process.[281] Substantive grounds are limited to incompatibility with Swiss public policy (*ordre publique*) embracing good faith, prohibition of abuse of rights or discrimination, expropriation without compensation, and *pacta sunt servanda*.[282]

The Future of Dispute Resolution in Sport

8.167 The long term trends are not difficult to discern. There will be an increasing involvement of law in sport as the last redouts of amateurism fall, media technology finds means of engaging public attention in even the most unpromising athletic activities, sportsmen and women are increasingly used for product promotion while suffering increasing invasion of their residual privacy, and the boundaries between sport and business erode.

---

[276] For a summary see *Penang Centre v WADA*, CAS 2010/A/2612, para 13.1. See too *Aston Villa FC v B93 Copenhagen*, CAS 2006/A/1177, para 7.3.2, 7.3.3.

[277] SFT, 2 October 2011.

[278] *Kaisa Varis v International Biathlon Union*, CAS 2008/A/1607; *Oceanic v UEFA*, CAS 2003/A/277, [2004] SLR 21.

[279] The Panel's reach is limited by the claims made: it cannot rule *extra* or *ultra petita* (ie it cannot give a ruling beyond what the petition requests), CAS 2005/A/866, CAS/2006/A/1009, CAS 2006/A/1174, CAS 2008/A/1644, CAS 2009/A/1838. A problem arises in a 'triangular' case when the body whose decision is appealed both orders compensation and imposes sanctions; the parties to the dispute over compensation then seek before the CAS on appeal to agree findings contrary to those made below, but the regulator (whose imposition of sanctions is upheld) does not agree such findings. The better view is that the CAS must make its own assessment because the issue of sporting sanctions is live. The two awards on this issue are confidential. The CAS has power to award costs: see Code of Sports-Related Arbitration and Mediation Rules 2010, R64 and R65 for a recent discussion of costs. See *C Maher v WTC*, CAS 2011/A/2538, para 7.1–7.14.

[280] Art 194. See *Gundel v FEI*, CAS 92/63.

[281] See Haas, *The Role and Application of Article 6 of the ECHR in CAS Procedures*, paper delivered at the CAS conference at Montreux, November 2011, forthcoming in [2012] ISLR.

[282] See Mavromati, *The Jurisdiction of the Swiss Federal Tribunal in Appeals against CAS Awards on Jurisdiction* [2011/12] ISLR 37; Rigozzi, *Challenging Awards of the Court of Arbitration for Sport* [2010] 1 Journal of International Dispute Resolution; Netzle, *Appeals against Arbitration Awards for CAS*, CAS Bulletin 2/11, p 19.

8.168 While engagement of the courts of law in dispute resolution in a sporting context will never be excluded—indeed in principle, save for inconceivable legislation, they cannot be excluded—legal regulation will increasingly migrate from courts to arbitral bodies,[283] and, in an endeavour to cut costs, there will be increasing use of summary abbreviated procedures such as are imaginatively used in the field of basketball.[284] Increasing use will also be made of mediation.[285]

8.169 Pivotal to these developments will be the future of the CAS. Its reputation as an adjudicative body has been endorsed by the SFT and consolidated by the increasing number of SGBs that subscribe to it and the increasing volume of cases that are assigned to it. There are few sports which guard their own autonomy—Formula One, which established its own international two-tier panel in 2011,[286] baseball and the Hellenic Football Federation[287] are examples; but it is possible, even probable, that they may recognise the virtues of utilising an expert and well established resource.

8.170 For the CAS to become an ultimate court of appeal for all sports, certain changes will be necessary, or at any rate desirable. The CAS must establish further regional bases in continents where presently there are none, namely Latin America (the source of many football related cases), Central and Southern Africa.[288] While it remains essential to have a single legal seat for reasons of coherence, to oblige parties and witnesses always to travel to Lausanne (or Sydney or New York) imposes evident financial burdens, and may act as a deterrent to the use of the CAS. Video or telephonic conferences provide at best a partial solution, making acquisition and—from the perspective of the common lawyer at any rate—assessment of oral evidence more difficult. Spanish should be added to French and English as a language in which arbitrations can be conducted, and the cohort of arbitrators adjusted to provide that facility.

8.171 Consideration needs to be given to whether within the CAS framework specialist chambers should be developed to deal with discrete areas such as doping, intellectual property and particular sports—within the CAS there are already certain arbitrators who carry a 'football' card in the same way as judges in England have 'murder' or 'rape' tickets.[289] Another idea that has been canvassed is whether there should be a two-tier CAS—like the European Court of Human Rights, a grand chamber to which cases involving major principle could be referred either after having been first decided in a *'petite chambre'* or at once, so encouraging a more certain and consistent jurisprudence.[290] A third is whether there should actually be a CAS composed of five permanent chambers, so avoiding the scheduling problems that inevitably afflict a part-time body

---

[283] Such as in the UK the Sports Dispute Resolution Panel (now the panels set up by Sport Resolution UK); Sidd, *Building a National Dispute Resolution Service*, WSLR 2/4, p 10; Procter, *Dispute Resolution in Sport: The Role of Sport Resolutions (UK)* [2010] ISLR 3; Mestre, *The Sports Tribunal of Asia*, WSLR 9/3, p 8. Anderson, *Rushing to Judgment: The Evolution of Sports Disciplinary and Arbitral Bodies in Ireland* [2006] 4(3) Entertainment and Sports Law Journal (online); Blackshaw, *The WIPO Centre as a Litigation Alternative*, WSLR 4/1, p 11 LT A6; Anderson (n 230) ch 3; Foster, *Global Administrative Law for Next Step for Global Sports Law* (2011) 19(1) SLJ 45.

[284] Martens, *Basketball Arbitral Tribunal* [2010] German Arbitration Journal 317.

[285] Walsh, *Mediation in Sports Dispute Resolution*, WSLR 3/11, p 5.

[286] Of which Michael Beloff is a founding member.

[287] *Iraklis Thessaloniki v HFF and Greek Super League*, CAS 2011/A/2483.

[288] In 2012 new outposts were established in Shanghai, Kuala Lumpur, Abu Dhabi and Cairo.

[289] Straubel (n 234).

[290] Ibid.

composed of practitioners, academics, judges and jurists with other significant commitments in circumstances where—far more often than not—the trio selected all come from different countries.[291] It has indeed been imaginatively suggested that 'as travel and television contract the globe to bring international sport into every living room the concept of an international Court of Arbitration for Sport need not be a fanciful one'.[292] The logistical and cost implications of any of such proposals are significant; and change in the CAS is likely to be incremental rather than explosive.[293]

---

[291] See generally the discussion in Anderson (n 230) 91–95.

[292] Grayson, *Sport and the Law*, 3rd edn (Butterworths, 2000) 360.

[293] For a recent evaluation see Yi, *Turning Medals into Metal: Evaluating the Court of Arbitration for Sport as an International Tribunal* (2006) Student Scholarship Papers, Paper 24, available (at the time of writing) on the Yale University website.

BIBLIOGRAPHY

Abbreviations of common sports publications:
Cas Bull   *Bulletin of the Court of Arbitration for Sport*
ISLJ   *International Sports Law Journal*
ISLR   *International Sports Law Review*
SLB   *Sports Law Bulletin*
SLJ   *Sport and the Law Journal*
SLR   *Sports Law Reports*
WSLR   *World Sports Law Report*

Abramson, L, *Whose Rights Are They Anyway?* (1996) 4(3) SLJ 100.

Adams, M, *Volenti non fit injuria or Contributory Negligence? A Comparative Review of Three Football Cases* (1994) 2(2) European Review of Public Law 329.

Adolphsen, J, *Challenges for CAS Decisions following the Adoption of the New WADA Code 2009* (2010) 1 Cas Bull 10.

Ahdar, R, *Professional Rugby, Competitive Balance and Competition Law* [2007] European Competition Law Review 36.

Allen, S, *Loss of Congenial Employment* [2009] Journal of Personal Injury Law 135.

American Bar Association, Forum Committee on the Entertainment and Sports Industries, *Entertainment and Sports Law Bibliography: A Comprehensive Bibliography of Law-Related Materials on Sports, Motion Pictures, Music and the Right of Publicity* (1986).

Anderson, J, *CAS Ad Hoc Division and London 2012*, WSLR 9/6, p 10.

——, *Sports Law in an Olympic Year: Citius, Altius, Fortius?* (2012) 12(2) Legal Information Management (Journal of the British and Irish Association of Law Librarians) 72.

——, *Playing by the Rules* (2011) 175(4) Criminal Law & Justice Weekly 40.

——, *Modern Sports Law: A Textbook* (Hart Publishing, 2010).

——, *The Legality of Boxing: A Punch Drunk Love* (Taylor and Francis, 2007).

——, *Rushing to Judgment: The Evolution of Sports Disciplinary and Arbitral Bodies in Ireland* [2006] 4(3) Entertainment and Sports Law Journal (online).

Ashton, D and PW Reid, *Ashton and Reid on Clubs and Associations*, 2nd edn (Jordans, 2011).

Ashworth, A, *Principles of Criminal Law*, 2nd edn (Clarendon Press, 1995).

Bailey, D, *Ticketing: Meeting the Challenges of a Cross-Border Ticketing Programme* [2010] Sports Law Administration & Practice 4.

——, *The Tie that Binds: Restraint of Trade in Sports*, conference paper presented at Chelsea FC, 25 November 1996.

Barak, D, *Illegal Betting: Match Fixing and CAS Case Law*, CAS Conference, Montreux, November 2011.

Barnes, J, *Sports and the Law in Canada*, 3rd edn (Butterworths, 1996).

Barnes, M, *Crime and Punishment on the Sports Field*, WSLR 3/9, pp 6–7.

——, *Doping: Liability for Ingesting Contaminated Products*, WSLR 3/12.

Barnes, S, *Changing Face of Cheating: A Handy Reminder*, The Times, 24 June 2011.

Batchelor, B and T Jenkins, *FA Premier League: The Broader Implications for Copyright Licensing* [2012] European Competition Law Review 157.

Beale, HG et al, *Chitty on Contracts*, 30th edn (Sweet & Maxwell, 2011).

Bell, A, *Dispute Resolution and Applicable Law Clauses in International Sports Arbitration* (2010) 84 Australian Law Journal 116.

Bellamy, C, *Who would be a Referee?* [2004] ISLR 9.

Bellamy, C and GD Child, *Common Market Law of Competition*, 6th edn (Sweet & Maxwell, 2008).

Beloff, MJ, editorial [2011] ISLR 65.

——, *CAS 25 Years On*, Focus Sports Law, Blackstone Chambers, April 2010.

——, *CAS at the Olympics* (1996) 4(3) SLJ 5.

——, *CAS at the Beijing Olympics* [2009] ISLR 3.

——, editorial [2007] ISLR 31.

——, editorial [2006] ISLR 1.

——, *Is there a Lex Sportiva?* [2005] ISLR 49.

——, editorial [2003] ISLR 89.

——, *The Impact of Public Law and Sports Law* [2003] Journal of the Commonwealth Lawyers Association 51.

——, *The CAS Ad Hoc Division at the Sydney Olympic Games* [2001] ISLR 105.

——, *Time, Time, Time, Is On My Side, Yes It Is* in *Essays in Honour of Sir William Wade QC*, ed Christopher Forsyth (Oxford University Press, 1998).

——, *Pitch, Pool, Rink … Court? Judicial Review in the Sporting World* [1989] Public Law 95.

Beloff, MJ and R Beloff, *Blood Sports—Blood Testing, The Common Law and Human Rights* [2000] 2 ISLR 43.

Beloff, MJ and T Kerr, *Why Aga Khan is Wrong* [1996] Judicial Review 30.

Beloff, MJ and T Kerr, *Judicial Control of Sporting Bodies: The Commonwealth Jurisprudence* (1995) 3(1) SLJ 5.

Beloff, R, *Fast Cars and Soccer Stars* [2000] ISLR 29.

Benedetti, A and J Bunting, *There's a New Sheriff in Town: A Review of the USADA* [2003] ISLR 17.

Bitel, N, *Disciplinary Procedures from the Point of View of the Individual* (1995) 3(3) SLJ 7.

Blackett (Judge), *2010 Obolensky Lecture* [2010] ISLR 38 (on 'Bloodgate').

Blackshaw, IS, *FC Sion Case: A Denial of Justice*, WSLR 10/3, 4.

——, *Challenging Independence of CAS Arbitrators*, WSLR 9/09, p 10.

——, *Olympic Athlete Consent to CAS Arbitration*, WSLR 7/11, p 6.

——, *WADA Should Ban Athletes Who Take Recreational Drugs*, WSLR 5/1, p 16.

——, *Why Strict Liability is Essential to Policing Doping*, WSLR 4/11, p 4.

——, *The CAS at the 2006 FIFA World Cup*, WLSR 4/7.

——, *Sporting Justice at the Olympics*, WSLR 4/6, p 6.

——, *The WIPO Centre as a Litigation Alternative*, WSLR 4/1, p 11.

——, *Sport, Mediation and Arbitration* (TMC Asser Press, 2009).

——, *Mediating Sports Disputes: National and International Perspectives* (TMC Asser Press, 2002).

Blackshaw, IS and RCR Siekmann, *Sports Image Rights in Europe* (TMC Asser Press, 2005).

Blackshaw, IS, RCR Siekmann and J Soek, *The Court of Arbitration for Sport, 1984–2004* (Cambridge University Press, 2006).

Blakeley, A-M, *Governance: Tackling Sports Cheats*, WSLR 4/7, p 12.

——, *A New Era for Equestrian Sports*, WSLR 815, p 12.

Blanpain, R (ed), *International Encyclopaedia of Laws: Sports Law* (Kluwer, 2004).

Bogusz, B, AJ Cygan and EM Szyszczak, *The Regulation of Sport in the European Union* (Edward Elgar, 2007).

Boocock, S, *Child Protection in Sport*, WSLR 1/3, p 3.

Boyes, S, *Sports Law: Its History and Growth and the Development of Key Sources* (2012) 12(2) Legal Information Management (Journal of the British and Irish Association of Law Librarians) 86.

——, *Regulating Sport after the Human Rights Act* (2001) 151 New Law Journal 444.

Boyes, S, *The Regulation of Sport and the Impact of the Human Rights Act 1998* (2000) 6(4) European Public Law 517.

Brightling, C, *The Impact of the Bribery Act 2010 on Corporate Hospitality*, WSLR 9/3, p 15.

Broun, KS, *McCormick on Evidence*, 6th edn (Thomson/West, 2006).

Brown, C, *Bookmakers' Afternoon Greyhound Services Ltd v Amalgamated Racing Ltd: Anti-Competitive Agreements – Sports Media Rights* [2009] European Competition Law Review N184.

Bucher, A, *L'attente légitime de parties* in *Rechtskollisionen, Festschrift für Anton Heini* (Schulthess Polygraphischer, 1995).

Burnett, R and A Smith, *Super Injunctions and Use of the Protection of Privacy*, WSLR 8/10, p 8.

Burrows, T, *Assessing the Reliability and Legality of Lie-Detector Tests*, WSLR 9/6, p 11.

Caiger, A and S Gardiner, *Professional Sport in the European Union: Regulation and Re-Regulation* (TMC Asser Press, 2000).

Cairns, W, *Corruption in Football: The Saga Continues* (2010) 18(2) SLJ 61.

Carpenter, K, *Match Fixing: The Biggest Threat to Sport in the Twenty First Century?* [2012] 2 ISLR 13.

Champion, WT, *Sports Law in a Nutshell*, 2nd edn (West Group, 2000).

Charlish, P, *Drugs in Sport* (2012) 12(2) Legal Information Management (Journal of the British and Irish Association of Law Librarians) 109.

——, *A Reckless Approach to Negligence* (2004) 4 Journal of Personal Injury Law 291.

——, *Football Association of Wales v UEFA: Only Dopes Don't Cheat* [2004] ISLR 73.

——, *Tennis: When Liability is Not So Strict* [2004] ISLR 64.

Cho, E, *Olympics and International Sports Law Research Guide* (2012) 12(2) Legal Information Management (Journal of the British and Irish Association of Law Librarians) 92.

Coccia, M, *The Athlete's Biological Passport*, paper presented by Professor Massimo Coccia at Montreux conference, 16–17 November 2011, forthcoming in [2012] ISLR.

Cogman, S, Hunt, R and Blake, N, *The Bribery Act 2010, Applications to Sport* (2010) 18(2) SLJ 23.

Collins, L et al, *Dicey, Morris and Collins on the Conflict of Laws*, 14th edn (Sweet & Maxwell, 2006).

Collins, V, *Recreation and the Law*, 2nd edn (Routledge, 1993).

Commission Staff Working Document, *Sport and Free Movement* SEC(2011) 66/2.

Connolly, C, *A Warning to Disciplinary Panels of Regulatory Bodies: The Impact of 'Bloodgate' Goes Beyond Sport* (2010) 18(2) SLJ 6.

Cordes, M, J Pugh-Smith, A Ruck Keene and G Caulfield, *Shackleton on the Law and Practice of Meetings*, 12th edn (Sweet & Maxwell, 2012).

Cottrell, S, *Freedom of Religion and Rules on Safety*, WLSR 8/2, p 12.

Cox, N, *Legalisation of Drug Use in Sport* [2002] ISLR 27.

Cox, N, A Schuster and C Costello, *Sport and the Law* (First Law, 2004).

Cozzillio, MJ and MS Levinstein, *Sports Law: Cases and Materials* (Carolina Academic Press, 1997).

Craig, PP, *Administrative Law*, 6th edn (Sweet & Maxwell, 2008).

Cutting, S, *Feigning of Blood Injuries and Rugby Union: Implications*, WSLR 8/2, p 14.

Dasser, F, *Internationale Schiedsgerichte und Lex Mercatoria* (Zurich, 1989).

David, P, *A Guide to the World Anti-Doping Code: A Fight for the Spirit of Sport* (Cambridge University Press, 2008).

Davies, C, *Salary Cap Scandals in Australian Professional Team Sports* [2011] ISLR 30.

——, *Expert Evidence before CAS: A Question of Weight*, ISLR 2/12, p 25.

Davies, PL, *Gower and Davies: The Principles of Modern Company Law*, 8th edn (Sweet & Maxwell, 2008).

Davies, S et al, *The Modern Law of Meetings*, 2nd edn (Jordans, 2009).

De Piero, *Rules of Interpretation, Statutes and Application of the Doctrines of Venire Contra Factum Proprium and Estoppel in the Case Law of the CAS Tribunal* [2008] ISLR 84.

De Weger, F, *The Jurisprudence of the FIFA Dispute Resolution Committee* (TCM Asser Press, 2008).

Deloitte Sports Business Group, *Annual Review of Football Finance*, 2011.

Denning (Lord), *The Discipline of Law* (Butterworths, 1979).

DFES, *The Protection of Children Act 1999: A Practical Guide to the Act for All Organisations Working with Children*, September 2005.

Dickerson, J, J Pheasant and G Shaw, *Equine Supplement: No Fault and No Negligence Finding* WSLR 810, p 5.

Donnellan, L, *Sport and the Law: A Concise Guide* (Blackhall, 2010).

Dubey, J-P, *La Jurisprudence du TAS sur l'Article 17 RSTJ (Règle sur le Transfert des Joueurs)*, paper delivered at CAS conference, Montreux, November 2011, to be published in [2012] ISLR.

——, *The Sanctions Imposed on the Player for Breach or Unilateral Termination of Contract* (2010) 1 Cas Bull 35.

Duff, A, *Reasonable Case v Reckless Disregard* (1997) 7(1) SLJ 44.

——, *Civil Actions and Sporting Injuries* (1994) 144 New Law Journal 639.

Dugdale, AM and M Jones, *Clerk and Lindsell on Torts*, 20th edn (Sweet & Maxwell, 2010).

Dunn, HA Colmore, *Fencing* (1931).

Eaton, J, *Gender Equity in Canadian Ice Hockey: The Legal Struggle* (2012) 12(2) Legal Information Management (Journal of the British and Irish Association of Law Librarians) 121.

Ebsworth, J, *Reputations for Rent: Product Endorsement* (1997) 5(2) SLJ 34.

Egger, A and C Stix-Hackl, *Sports and Competition Law: A Never-Ending Story?* [2002] European Competition Law Review 81.

Erichsen, HU and D Ehlers, *Allgemeines Verwaltungsrecht*, 10th edn (de Gruyter, 1995).

Faire, J et al, *Arbitration in the America's Cup: The XXXI America's Cup Arbitration Panel and its Decisions* (Kluwer, 2003).

Farrow, S, *Team Sports' Issues with WADA Code*, WSLR 7/6, p 4.

——, *Injury Compensation: Collett v Smith; Compensation for Future Earnings*, WSLR 6/9.

Felix, A, *The 'Fleetwood Assassin' Strikes a Blow for Female Boxers* (1998) 1(3) SLB 1.

Felstead, I, *Public Figures and Private Lives*, WSLR 3/5, p 6.

Felstead, I and H Kingsley-Miller, *Forms of Legal Action when On-Pitch Remedies Fail*, WSLR 6/12, pp 10–11.

Findlay, R, *Harmonising Punishment for Cheats*, WSLR 4/8, p 11.

Fleming, H, *Exclusive Rights to Broadcast Sporting Events in Europe* [1999] European Competition Law Review 143.

Fordham, M, *Judicial Review Handbook*, 5th edn (Hart Publishing, 2008).

Forsyth, *Of Figleaves and Fairytales. The Ultra Vires Doctrine, the Sovereignty of Parliament and Judicial Review* [1996] Cambridge Law Journal 122.

Fosler, K, *Lex Sportiva and Lex Ludica: The CAS's Jurisprudence*, (2009) 3(2) Entertainment and Sports Law Journal 1.

Fraser, D, *Cricket and the Law: The Man in White is Always Right* (Routledge, 2005).

Gardiner, S, *The Third Eye: Video Adjudication in Sport* (1999) 2(1) SLB.

——, *Match Fixing in Sport: Recent Developments* (2011) 18(2) SLJ 28.

——, *Liability for Sporting Injuries* [2008] Journal of Personal Injury Law 16.

——, *Birth of a Legal Area: Sport and the Law or Sports Law?* (1997) 5(2) SLJ 10.

——, *Touchlines and Guidelines: The Lord Advocate's Response to Sportsfield Violence* [1997] Criminal Law Review 41.

——, *The Law and the Sports Field* [1994] Criminal Law Review 513.

——, *Should Coaches Take Care?* (1993) 143 New Law Journal 1598.

Gardiner, S, A Felix, J O'Leary, M James and R Welch, *Sports Law* (Cavendish, 1997).

Gardiner, S and U Naidoo, *On the Front Foot Against Corruption* (2007) 15(2) SLJ 16.

Gardiner, S, J O'Leary, M Welch and S Boyes, *Sports Law*, 4th edn (Routledge, 2012).

Gardiner, S, R Parrish, and RCR Siekmann, *EU, Sport, Law and Policy: Regulation, Re-Regulation and Representation* (TMC Asser Press, 2009).

Geey, D, J Burns and M Akiyama, *Live Premier League Football Broadcasting Rights: The CJEU Judgment* [2012] Entertainment Law Review 17.

317

Giulianotti, R and D McArdle, *Sport, Civil Liberties and Human Rights* (Routledge, 2006).

Goldberg, M, *Football Contracts: Seeking the Best Deal for your Client* (1992) 1(3) SLJ 101.

Goldberg, M and S Pentol, *Football Bungs Preventing an Inherent Problem*, WSLR 4/10, p 8.

Goldman, B, *La lex mercatoria dans les contrats et l'arbitrage internationaux: réalité et perspectives* (1979) 106 Journal de Droit International 475.

Goodhart, A, *The Sportsman's Charter* (1962) 78 Law Quarterly Review 490.

Goudie, J and S Devonshire, *Garden Leave Injunctions in the Sporting Arena: Reading Football Club and West Ham United* [2004] ISLR 15.

Gray, A, *Swimming and Child Protection: The Story So Far* (1999) 2(2) SLB 8–9.

Grayson, E, *Sport and the Law*, 3rd edn (Butterworths, 2000).

——, *Revisiting the Field of Play* (1985) 135 New Law Journal 628.

Greenberg, MJ and JT Gray, *Sports Law Practice*, 2nd edn (Lexis, 1998).

Greenfield, S and G Osborn, *Law and Sport in Contemporary Society* (Frank Cass, 2000).

Griffith-Jones, D with A Barr-Smith (consulting editor), *Law and the Business of Sport* (Butterworths, 1997).

Griffiths and Drew, *Developing the European Dimension in Sport* (2011) 22(5) Entertainment Law Review 136.

Griffiths, J, *Procedural Fairness and Regulation of Sport: Lessons from the Common Law* [2009] ISLR 69.

Grove, S and J Parks, *Sanctioning Ex-Athletes for Autobiographical Revelations*, WSLR 8/2, p 4.

Haas, U, *The Role and Application of Article 6 of the ECHR in CAS Procedures*, paper delivered at the CAS conference at Montreux, November 2011, forthcoming in [2012] ISLR.

——, *The Time Limit for Appeal in Arbitration Proceedings before CAS*, CAS Bulletin 2/11, p 3.

Harris, B, *Salary Caps* (2002) 10(1) SLJ 120.

——, *Disciplinary and Regulatory Proceedings*, 6th edn (Jordan, 2009).

Harris, P, *Abusive Sports Governing Bodies: Hendry and others v World Professional Billiards and Snooker Association* [2002] Competition Law Journal 101.

Hedley-Dent, S and K Wilde, *Sporting Rules and the Human Rights Act: Current Position*, WSLR 5/6.

Heron, M and C Jiang, *The Gathering Storm: Organised Crime and Sports Corruption* (2010) 5(1) Australian and New Zealand Sports Law Journal (online).

Hesse, V, *The Status of an Athlete during a Period of Ineligibility*, WLSR 9/5, p 6.

Hislox, W, *Anti-Doping Policy after the Human Rights Act* (2004) 12(2) SLJ 12.

Holmes, M, *The Ad Hoc Division of CAS at the XX Olympic Games in Torino* [2006] ISLR 58.

——, *The CAS: A Case Study of an International Arbitration Institution* (2005) 27 Australian Bar Review 56.

Houseman, S, *Staying Disciplinary Proceedings: Whatever Happened to* ex parte Brindle? [1999] Judicial Review 60.

Hyland, M, *The Football Association Premier League Ruling: The* Bosman *of Exclusive Broadcasting Rights?* [2012] Communications Law 7.

Ibarrola, J, *Contador: Burden of Proof and Presumption of Culpability*, WSLR 4/12.

Ionnaides, G, *Legal Regulation of Doping in Sport and the Application of Criminal Law in Doping Infractions* [2006] ISLR 2.

Ionnaides, G and G Alderman, *Freedom of Expression and Public Criticism of Officials*, WSLR 9/4, p 11.

James, M, *Sports Law* (Palgrave Macmillan, 2010).

James, M and F Deeley, *The Standard of Care in Sports Negligence Cases* (2004) 1(1) Entertainment Law 104.

James, M and G Osborn, *The Sources and Interpretation of Olympic Law* (2012) 12(2) Legal Information Management (Journal of the British and Irish Association of Law Librarians) 80.

Jarvis RM and P Coleman, *Sports Law: Cases and Materials* (West Group, 1999).

Joshi, A, *Tribunal's Verdict in Spot Fixing Case*, WSLR 9/2, p 11.

Bibliography

Joshi, A, *Combating Spot Fixing in Cricket: The Role of the ICC*, WSLR 9/1, p 6.

Josling, JF and L Alexander, *The Law of Clubs*, 6th edn (Sweet & Maxwell, 1987).

Junor, *Suing a Club: Substance and Procedure* (2008) 80 Civil Practice Bulletin 2.

Kaufmann-Kohler, G, *Arbitral Precedent: Dream Necessity or Excuse? An example of divergent views of an interpretation of complex FIFA regulations on the compensation payable by a footballer in breach of contract with a club*, Freshfields Lecture 2006.

——, *Arbitration at the Olympics: Issues of Fast-Track Dispute Resolution and Sports Law* (Kluwer, 2001).

——, *Nagano et l'arbitrage*, in *Mealey's International Arbitration Report*, vol 13 issue 6.

Kelly, E, *Judicial Review of Sports Bodies' Decisions: Comparable Common Law Perspectives* [2011] ISLR 71.

Kemp, S, *Doping: Athlete Impact and Whereabouts Information*, WSLR 3/12.

Kerr, T, *Sanctioning of a Football Team*, ch 9 in Wild (ed), *CAS and Football: Landmark Cases* (TMC Asser Press, 2012).

——, *La procédure arbitrale en matière sportive est-elle originale?*, paper delivered to the International Chamber of Commerce conference Arbitration and Sport, Paris, September 2010.

——, *Disciplinary Regulation of Sport: A Different Strand of Public Law?* in Bogusz, Cygan and Szyszczak (eds), *The Regulation of Sport in the European Union* (Edward Elgar, 2007).

——, *Doped or Duped? The Nandrolone Jurisprudence* [2001] ISLR 97.

——, *Staying Disciplinary Proceedings: A Reply* [1999] Judicial Review 188.

Kevan, T, *Sports Personal Injury* [2005] ISLR 61.

——, *Sports Injury Cases: Footballers, Referees and Schools* [2001] Journal of Personal Injury Law 138.

Kevan, T, D Adamson and S Cottrell, *Sports Personal Injury: Law and Practice* (Sweet & Maxwell, 2002).

Khan and Wolfgarten, *Liability for Foul Play*, 29 Solicitors Journal 859.

Kiener, J-M, *Consequences of Doping in Collective Sports* (2011) 4(11) ISLR 67.

Kino, D, *The Incursion of the Law into the Rules of Governing Sports Bodies: A Commonwealth and EC Comparison*, doctoral thesis, 1999.

Kovats, *Sportsman's Charter Revoked*, 115 Solicitors Journal 824.

Kuper, S, *Football Against the Enemy* (Orion Books, 1994).

Lalive, P, *Transnational (or Truly International) Public Policy*, in *Comparative Arbitration Practice and Public Policy in Arbitration*, ICCA Congress Series No 3 (1987) 257–318, 301–4.

Leaver, P, *The CAS Ad Hoc Division at the Salt Lake City Winter Olympic Games* [2002] ISLR 44.

Lewis, A and J Taylor, *Sport: Law and Practice*, 2nd edn (Tottel Publishing, 2008).

Lines, K, *Six Degrees of Sports Participation: Are the Olympics the Common Denominator for All Sports?* [2008] ISLR 53.

——, *Thinking Outside the Box (-ing Ring): The Implications for Sports Governing Bodies following Watson* [2007] ISLR 4.

Lines, K and J Heshka, *Ski Jumping through Olympic Solid Hoops* [2009] ISLR 92.

Livings, B, *'Legitimate Sport' or Criminal Assault? What are the Roles of the Rules and the Rulemakers in Determining Criminal Liability for Violence on the Sports Field?* (2006) 70(6) Journal of Criminal Law 495.

Ljungqvist, A, *Doping's Nemesis* (Sports Books, 2011).

MacDonald, A, *The Rights of the Child: Law and Practice* (Family Law, 2011).

McArdle, D, *From Boot Money to Bosman: Football, Society and the Law* (Cavendish, 2000).

McCutcheon, JP, *Negative Enforcement of Employment Contracts in the Sports Industries* (1997) 17(1) Legal Studies 65.

McEwan, *Playing the Game: Negligence in Sport*, 130 Solicitors Journal 581.

McGee, A, *Limitation Periods*, 6th edn (Sweet & Maxwell, 2010).

McGhee, A, *Snell's Equity*, 32nd edn (Sweet & Maxwell, 2010).

McGregor, H, *McGregor on Damages*, 18th edn (Sweet & Maxwell, 2011).

McGregor-Lowndes, M, K Fletcher and S Sievers (eds), *Legal Issues for Non-Profit Associations* (Law Book Co, 1996).

McLaren, R, *A New Era in the Control of Performance Enhancing Drugs*, WSLR, 1/2, p 7.

——, *CAS Doping Jurisprudence: What Can We Learn?* [2006] ISLR 4.

——, *Exceptional Circumstances: Is it Strict?* [2005] ISLR 32.

——, *The CAS Ad Hoc Division at the Athens Olympic Games* [2004] Marquette Sports Law Review 175.

——, *Doping Sanctions: What Penalty* [2002] ISLR 23.

——, *Introducing the Court of Arbitration for Sport, the Ad Hoc Division at the Olympic Games* [2001] 12 Marquette Sports Law Review 515.

McLaren, R and P Clement, *CAS: The Ad Hoc Division at the Salt Lake City Olympics* [2004] ISLR 44.

McLaren, R and E Douglas, *Women Ski-Jumpers Allege Human Rights Breach*, WLSR 5/5.

McNamara, D, *A Legal Guide for Clubs and Associations* (Bloomsbury Professional, 2005).

McNamee, M and L Tarasti, *Juridical and Ethical Peculiarities in Doping Policy* (2010) 36 Journal of Medical Ethics 165.

Mackay (Lord), *Halsbury's Laws of England*, 5th edn (LexisNexis, 2009).

Malek, H, *Phipson on Evidence*, 17th edn (Sweet & Maxwell, 2010).

Marshall, J and AC Hale, *Unilateral Unappealable Doping Sanctions* [2007] ISLR 39.

Martens, D-R, *Basketball Arbitral Tribunal* [2010] German Arbitration Journal 317.

Mavromati, D, *The Jurisdiction of the Swiss Federal Tribunal in Appeals against CAS Awards on Jurisdiction* [2011/12] ISLR 37.

——, *Lifetime Ineligibility According to the WADA Code* (2010) 1 Cas Bull 42.

——, *The Athlete's Biological Passport Programme*, Cas Bull 2/11, p 35.

Mavromati, D and Pellaux, P, *The Healing Effect of the Appeal to CAS*, Conference, Montreux, November 2011, forthcoming in [2012] ISLR.

Mayer, P, *Le principe de bonne foi devant les arbitres internationaux* in *Etudes de droit international en l'honneur de Pierre Lalive* (Helbing & Lichtenhahn, 1993).

Merkin, R, *Arbitration Law*, 2 vols (Informa, looseleaf).

Mestre, A *The Sports Tribunal of Asia*, WSLR 9/3, p 8.

——, *Ten Reasons Against Boycotting the Beijing Olympics*, WSLR 6/4, p 8.

——, *The Legal Basis of the Olympic Charter*, WSLR 5/11, p 6.

——, *The Law of the Olympic Games* (TMC Asser Press, 2009).

Michalos, C, *Five Golden Rings: Development of the Protection of the Olympic Insignia* [2006] ISLR 64.

Miller, F, *Not Every Agent is a Bad Guy* (1996) 4(1) SLJ 36.

Miller, S, *Criminal Law and Sport in Scotland* (1996) 4(2) SLJ 40.

Miller, T, *London 2012: Meeting the Challenge of Brand Protection* [2008] ISLR 44.

Mishkin, JA, *Sports Arbitration in the United States.*

Mitten, MJ, *Sports Law in the United States* (Wolters Kluwer Law & Business, 2011).

Monckom, S, *Smith and Monckom: The Law of Gambling*, 3rd edn (Tottel Publishing, 2009).

Moor, P, *Droit administratif, vol I, Les fondements généraux* (Stämpfli, 1988).

Moore, C, *Sports Law and Litigation* (CLT Professional Publishing, 1997; 2nd edn 2000).

Morgan, M, *WADA's Prohibited List and Similar Substances*, WSLR 9/2, p 3; 9/3, p 6.

——, *Sample Collection: Failure to Submit to Doping Control*, WSLR 7/11, p 8.

Morgan, M and Shevill, S, *Integrity: Tackling Sporting Fraud* (Parts 1, 2 and 3)10 WSLR 2, 3 and 4.

Morse, G, *Palmer's Company Law* (Sweet & Maxwell, looseleaf).

Morton-Hooper, T, *Sporting Disciplinary Proceedings in Practice—the Participant's View*, Sports Forum 1996, conference paper, pp 15–17.

Bibliography

Murphy, M, *Pistorious Case: Implications of his Successful IAAF Challenge*, WLSR 6/9, p 6.

Mustill, MJ and SC Boyd, *Commercial Arbitration*, 3rd edn (Butterworths, 2008).

Mustill, MJ and SC Boyd, *Commercial Arbitration, Companion Volume to the 2nd edition* (Butterworths, 2001).

Mustill, MJ and SC Boyd, *The Law and Practice of Commercial Arbitration in England*, 2nd edn (Butterworths, 1989).

Nafziger, JAR, *Circumstantial Evidence of Doping: Balco and Beyond* (2005) 16(1) Marquette Sports Law Review 45.

——, *International Sports Law*, 2nd edn (Transnational, 2004).

——, *Lex Sportiva and CAS* [2004] ISLJ 3.

——, *International Sports Law as a Process for Resolving Disputes* (1996) 45 International and Comparative Law Quarterly 130.

Naidoo, U, *On the Front Foot against Corruption* [2004] ISLR 1.

Neenan, C, *Disputing the Adjudicative Body: Finding of Fact* [2000] Judicial Review 6.

Netzle, S, *Appeals against Arbitration Awards for CAS*, CAS Bulletin 2/11, p 19.

Nicholls, C, T Daniel, A Bacarese and J Hatchard, *Corruption and the Misuse of Public Office*, 2nd edn (Oxford University Press, 2011).

Norris, W, *The Duty of Care Owed by Instructors in a Sporting Context* [2010] Journal of Personal Injury Law 183.

——, *Duty of Care and Personal Responsibility: Occupiers, Owners, Organisers and Individuals* [2008] Journal of Personal Injury Law 187.

O'Leary, J, *Drugs and Doping in Sport: Socio-Legal Perspectives* (Cavendish, 2001).

Oliver, D, *Administrative Decision Making; Common Law; Natural Justice* [1997] Public Law 630.

Opie, H, *Negligence Liability of Rule-Making Bodies in Sport* [2002] ISLR 60.

——, *Sports Associations and their Legal Environment* in McGregor-Lowndes, Fletcher and Sievers (eds), *Legal Issues for Non-Profit Associations* (Law Book Co, 1996).

Ormerod, D, *Smith and Hogan: Criminal Law*, 13th edn (Oxford University Press, 2011).

Owen, D, *Chemically Enhanced*, FT Magazine, 11–12 February 2006.

Pannick, D, *Judicial Review of Sports Bodies* [1997] Judicial Review 150.

——, *Who is Entitled to Judicial Review in Respect of What* [1992] Public Law 1.

Papaloukas, M, *Competition Rules and Sports Broadcasting Rights in Europe* [2010] ISLJ 81.

Parker, R, *Disciplinary Proceedings from the Governing Bodies' Point of View* (1995) 3(3) SLJ 3.

Parpworth, N, *Vicarious Liability on the Rugby Union Field* (2008) 172(35) Justice of the Peace and Local Government Law 572–4.

——, *Sports Governing Bodies and the Principles of Natural Justice: An Australian Perspective* (1996) 4(2) SLJ 5.

Parrish, R and S Miettinen, *The Sporting Exception in European Union Law* (TMC Asser Press, 2008).

Parsons, S, *Contact Sports and Criminal Law* (2011) 175(4) Criminal Law & Justice Weekly 40.

Patel, S, *Women's Ski Jumping and Olympic Programme Inclusion*, WSLR 8/7, p 11.

Payne, SDW and E Grayson, *Medicine, Sport and the Law* (Blackwell Scientific, 1990).

Pendlebury, A and J McGarry, *Location, Location, Location: The Whereabouts Rule and the Right to Privacy* [2009] Cambrian Law Review 63.

Perrins, B et al, *Harvey on Industrial Relations and Employment Law* (LexisNexis, 1996).

Perry, G, *Dispute Resolution in Sport: New Challenges, New Options* [2001] ISLR 92.

Pijetlovic, K, *Another Classic of EU Sports Jurisprudence* [2010] European Law Review 857.

Polvino, A, *Arbitration as Preventative Medicine for Olympic Ailments: The Olympic Committee Court of Arbitration for Sport and the Future for the Settlement of International Sporting Disputes* [1994] 8 Emory International Law Review 349–52.

Pound, RW *The World Anti-Doping Agency: An Experiment in International Law* [2002] ISLR 52.

Pradel, J, *Droit pénal, Tome 1, Introduction générale, droit pénal général*, 10th edn (Dalloz, 1995).

Procter, E, *Dispute Resolution in Sport: The Role of Sport Resolutions (UK)* [2010] ISLR 3.

Quirk, CE, *Sports and the Law: Major Legal Cases* (Garland, 1996).

Ravjani, A, *The CAS: A Suitable Form of International Delegation* (2010) 1 Cas Bull 14.

Reeb, M (ed), *Digest of CAS Awards: 1986–1998* (Stämpfli, 1998).

——, (ed), *Digest of CAS Awards II: 1998–2000* (Stämpfli, 2002).

——, (ed), in collaboration with E de la Rochefoucauld, *Digest of CAS Awards III: 2001–2003* (Stämpfli, 2004).

——, *The Court of Arbitration for Sport* (2000) 3(4) SLB.

——, *The New Code* (2010) 1 Cas Bull 31.

Rigozzi, A, *Challenging Awards of the Court of Arbitration for Sport* [2010] 1 Journal of International Dispute Resolution.

——, *The Decisions Rendered by the CAS Ad Hoc Division at the Turin Winter Olympics* [2006] Journal of International Arbitration 453.

——, *L'arbitrage international en matière de sport* (doctoral thesis, Geneva University (nd)).

Rigozzi, A, G Kaufmann-Kohler and G Malinverni, *Doping and Fundamental Rights of Athletes* [2003] ISLR 61.

Rochefoucault, E de la, *Standing to be Sued: A Procedural Issue before CAS* (2010) 1 Cas Bull 52.

Room, S, *The Use of Personal Data when Investigating Corruption*, WSLR 3/5, p 7.

Ross, T, *Corruption in Cricket: Using the Law to Cull the Crooks from the Gentleman's Game* (2010) 18(3) SLJ 28.

——, *Corrupting Cricket*, SLJ 2(10) 28.

Russ, T and J Foster, *Law of Field Sports* (Wildy, Simmonds and Hill, 2010).

Savulescu, J, B Foddy and M Clayton, *Why We Should Allow Performance Enhancing Drugs in Sports* (2004) 38 BVJ Sports Law 666.

Scherrer, U, *Einstweiliger Rechtsschutz im internationalen Sport* [Preliminary Remedies in International Sports Law] (Schulthess, 1999).

Scott, K, *Referees Win Case against Mandatory Retirement Age*, WLSR 8/9, pp 8–9.

Siddak, J, *Building a National Dispute Resolution Service*, WSLR 2/4, p 10.

Siekmann, RCR and J Soek, *The Council of Europe and Sport: Basic Documents* (TMC Asser Press, 2007).

Siekmann, RCR and J Soek, *The European Union and Sport: Legal and Policy Documents* (TMC Asser Press, 2005).

Siekmann, RCR and J Soek, *Arbitral and Disciplinary Rules of International Sports Organisations* (TMC Asser Press, 2001).

Siekmann, RCR and J Soek (eds), *Basic Documents of International Sports Organisations* (Brill, 1998).

Singh, K, *Consent to Violence in Sport* (1994) 2(3) SLJ 7.

Sithamparanathan, A and M Himsworth, *Are Sporting Bodies Abusing Human Rights?* (2003) 11(3) SLJ 138.

Smith, I, *WADA Should Not Ban Athletes for Recreational Drug Use*, WSLR 4/9.

——, *Why WADA Should Not Ban Athletes for Recreational Drug Use* [2007] ISLJ 119.

Smith, S and A Maxwell, *Premier League Football Cases: Linguistic Tactics, Non-Naked Match Feeds and the Away Goals Rule* [2012] Computer and Telecommunications Law Review 33.

Soek, J, *The Strict Liability Principle and the Human Rights of Athletes in Doping Cases* (TMC Asser Press, 2006).

Speed, M, *Sticky Wicket: A Decade of Change in World Cricket* (HarperSports, 2011).

Spengler, JO, *Introduction to Sport Law* (Human Kinetics, 2009).

Spry, I, *Equitable Remedies*, 8th edn (Sweet & Maxwell, 2010).

St John Sutton, D, J Gill and M Gearing, *Russell on Arbitration*, 23rd edn (Sweet & Maxwell, 2007).

Steele, C, *Commercial Exploitation of Sport* (1998) 6(2) SLJ 59.

——, *Sponsorship Contracts; 'The Full Monty'* (1997) 5(3) SLJ 25.

Bibliography

Steele, C, *Personality Merchandising, Licensing Rights and the March of the Turtles* (1997) 5(2) SLJ 14.

Stewart, N, N Campbell and S Baughen, *The Law of Unincorporated Associations* (Oxford University Press, 2011).

Stewart, WJ, *Judicial Control of Sporting Bodies in Scotland* (1995) 3(3) SLJ 45.

Stoner, C, *Competition Matters: The Rules of Snooker under Scrutiny in English Courts* (2002) 9(3) Sports Law Administration and Practice.

Stout, H, (2007) 8(3) Education Law Journal 191.

——, *Bias* [2011] Judicial Review 458.

Straubel, M, *Enhancing the Performance of the Doping Court: How the Court of Arbitration for Sport Could Do its Job Better* (2005) 36 Loyola University of Chicago Law Journal 1203.

Subiotto, R, *How a Lack of Analytical Rigour has Resulted in an Overbroad Application of EC Competition Law in the Sports Sector* [2009] ISLR 21.

Sullivan, A, *The Role of Contract in Sports Law* (2010) 5(1) Australia and New Zealand Sports Law Journal 3.

Supperstone, M, Goudie, J and Walker, P, *Judicial Review*, 4th edn (LexisNexis, 2010).

Szyszczak, EM, *Is Sport Special?* in Bogusz, Cygan and Szyszczak (eds), *The Regulation of Sport in the European Union* (Edward Elgar, 2007).

Tarasti, L, *Some Juridical Questions in the Revised WADC* [2008] ISLR 17.

——, *Legal Solutions in International Doping Cases* (SEP Editrice, 2000).

——, *Strict Liability in Doping Cases in the Light of Decisions made by the Arbitration Panel of the IAAF* (conference paper, 1997).

Taylor, S and J Foley-Train, *Preventing Match Fixing: Player Education is Fundamental*, WSLR 9/6, p 6.

Thorpe, D, *Sports Law* (Oxford University Press, 2009).

Tolman, M and Rugbynok, M, *Disqualification for Doping: The Marion Jones Case*, WSLR 8/9, p 6.

Townley, S and E Grayson, *Sponsorship of Sport, Arts and Leisure: Law, Tax and Business Relationships* (Sweet & Maxwell, 1984).

Turner-Kerr, P and A Bell, *The Place of Sport within the Rules of Community Law: Clarification from the ECJ? The Deliège and Lehtonen Cases* [2002] European Competition Law Review 256.

UK Sport, *Human Rights Act—Implications for Sport*, 14 December 2000.

Veljanovski, CG, *Markets in Professional Sports: Hendry v WPSBA and the Importance of Functional Markets* [2002] European Competition Law Review 273.

Verow, R, C Lawrence and P McCormick, *Sports Business: Law, Practice and Precedents*, 2nd edn (Jordan, 2005).

Wade, W and C Forsyth, *Administrative Law*, 10th edn (Oxford University Press, 2009).

Walsh, S, *Mediation in Sports Dispute Resolution*, WSLR 3/11, p 5.

Walton, C, *Charlesworth and Percy on Negligence*, 12th edn (Sweet & Maxwell, 2011).

Wearmouth, HJ, *No Winners on the Greasy Pole: Ethical and Legal Frameworks for Evaluating Disciplinary Processes in Sport* (1995) 3(3) SLJ.

Weatherill, S, *Fairness, Openness and the Specific Nature of Sport: Does the Lisbon Treaty Change EU Sports Law?* (2010) 3/4 ISLJ 11.14.

——, *European Sports Law: Collected Papers* (TMC Asser Press, 2007).

——, *Do Sporting Associations Make 'Law' or are they Merely Subject to It?* [1998] European Business Law Review, July/August, 217.

Weger, F de, *The Jurisprudence of the FIFA Dispute Resolution Chamber* (TMC Asser Press, 2008).

Weiler, PC and G Roberts, *Sports and the Law*, 3rd edn (Gale Cengage, 2004).

Weistart, JC and CH Lowell, *The Law of Sports* (Bobbs-Merrill, 1979).

Winnie, D, *FIFA's Code of Ethics: Rules of Conduct and Sanctions*, WSLR 8/11, p 4.

Wise, AN, *A 'Property Right' in a Sports Event: Views of Different Jurisdictions* (1996) 4(3) SLJ 63.

Wise, AN and BS Meyer, *International Sports Law and Business* (Kluwer, 1997).

Wong, GM, *Essentials of Amateur Sports Law* (Auburn House, 1988).

Wood, R, *Sports Governing Bodies* (1998) 1(6) SLB 5.

——, *The CJEU's Ruling in the Premier League Pub TV Cases: The Final Whistle Beckons* [2012] European Intellectual Property Review 75.

Woodhouse, C, *Sport and Law in Conflict: Role of Sports Governing Bodies*, conference paper, Stamford Bridge, 25 November 1996.

Woolf, J, *Zamir and Woolf: The Declaratory Judgment*, 4th edn (Sweet & Maxwell, 2011).

Woolf, J, J Jowell and A Le Sueur, *De Smith's Judicial Review*, 6th edn (Sweet & Maxwell, 2007).

Worley, K, *An Alternative to the IOC's Gender Testing Policy*, WSLR 8/2, p 10.

Yasser, RL, *Torts and Sports: Legal Liability in Professional and Amateur Athletics* (Quorum, 1985).

Yi, D, *Turning Medals into Metal: Evaluating the Court of Arbitration for Sport as an International Tribunal* (2006) Student Scholarship Papers, Paper 24.

Zagklis, AK, *The CAS Ad Hoc Division at the XX Olympic Winter Games in Turin* (2006) 3(4) ISLJ 42.

INDEX